MOUS Essentials Access 97 Expert

Robert Ferrett

John Preston

Sally Preston

QUE E&T

An Imprint of Macmillan Computer Publishing

MOUS Essentials Access 97 Expert

Library of Congress Catalog No: 98-066773

ISBN: 1-58076-057-0

01 00 99 4 3 2 1

Interpretation of the printing code: the rightmost double-digit number is the year of the book's printing; the rightmost single-digit number, the number of the book's printing. For example, a printing code of 99-1 shows that the first printing of the book occurred in 1999.

Screens reproduced in this book were created using Collage Plus from Inner Media, Inc., Hollis, NH.

Composed in *Stone Serif* and *MCPdigital* by Que® Education and Training

This book was produced digitally by Macmillan Computer Publishing and manufactured using computer-to-plate technology (a film-less process) by GAC/Shepard Poorman, Indianapolis, Indiana.

Publisher:
Robert Linsky

Executive Editor:
Randy Haubner

Acquisitions Editor:
Jon Phillips

Director of Product Marketing:
Susan L. Kindel

Managing Editor:
Caroline Roop

Development Editor:
Nancy D. Warner

Project Editor:
Tim Tate

Copy Editor:
Susan Hobbs

Indexer:
Chris Barrick

Acquisitions Assistant:
Ken Schmidt

Technical Editor:
Asit J. Patel

Cover Designer:
Nathan Clement

Book Designer:
Louisa Klucznik

Production Team:
Jeanne Clark
Christy M. Lemasters

About the Authors

Robert Ferrett is the Director of the Center for Instructional Computing at Eastern Michigan University. His center provides computer training and support to faculty at the university. He has authored or co-authored books on Access 1.1, PowerPoint 4.0, Word 2.0 and Word 6.0, Access 2.0 and Access 7.0 for Windows 95, PowerPoint for Windows 95, and books on Word 97, PowerPoint 97, Excel 97, and Access 97. He has a BA in Psychology, an MS in Geography, and an MS in Interdisciplinary Technology from Eastern Michigan University. He is currently enrolled in a Ph.D. program in Instructional Technology at Wayne State University.

John Preston is an Associate Professor at Eastern Michigan University in the College of Technology where he teaches microcomputer application courses at the undergraduate and graduate levels. He has been teaching, writing, and designing computer-training courses since the advent of the personal computer, and has authored and co-authored over twenty books on Microsoft Word, Excel, Access, and PowerPoint. He has received grants from the Detroit Edison Institute and the Department of Energy to develop Web sites for energy education and alternative fuels, respectively. He has also developed one of the first Internet-based microcomputer applications courses at an accredited university. He has a BS from the University of Michigan with a major in Physics and minors in Mathematics and Education, and an MS from Eastern Michigan University in Physics Education. He is ABD in the Ph.D. program in Instructional Technology at Wayne State University.

Sally Preston is President of Preston & Associates, a computer software–training firm. She combines her extensive business experience as a bank vice president in charge of branch operations with her skills in training people on new computer systems. She provides corporate training through Preston & Associates and through the Institute for Workforce Development at Washtenaw Community College where she also teaches computer courses part-time. She has co-authored several books on Access, Excel, and PowerPoint. She has an MBA from Eastern Michigan University.

Trademark Acknowledgments

All terms mentioned in this book that are known to be trademarks or service marks have been appropriately capitalized. Que Education and Training cannot attest to the accuracy of this information. Use of a term in this book should not be regarded as affecting the validity of any trademark or service mark.

Preface

Que Education and Training is the educational publishing imprint of Macmillan Computer Publishing, the world's leading computer book publisher. Macmillan Computer Publishing books have taught more than 20 million people how to be productive with their computers.

This expertise in producing high-quality computer tutorial and reference books is evident in every Que Education and Training title we publish. The same tried-and-true writing and product-development process that makes Macmillan Computer Publishing books bestsellers is used to ensure that educational materials from Que Education and Training provide the most accurate and up-to-date information. Experienced and respected computer application instructors write and review every manuscript to provide class-tested pedagogy. Quality-assurance editors check every keystroke and command in Que Education and Training books to ensure that instructions are clear, accurate, and precise.

Above all, Macmillan Computer Publishing and, in turn, Que Education and Training have years of experience in meeting the learning demands of students across all disciplines.

The "MOUS Essentials" of Hands-On Learning

The *MOUS Essentials* are appropriate for use in both corporate training and college classroom settings. They can be used effectively as computer-lab applications modules to accompany any of Que Education and Training's computer concepts text or as stand-alone texts for an applications-only course. The *MOUS Essentials* workbooks enable users to become self-sufficient quickly; encourage self-learning after instruction; maximize learning through clear, complete explanations; and serve as future references.

The *MOUS Essentials* series uses the following elements to get the most out of the material:

Objectives list what students do and learn from the project.

Required Activities are the objectives as they relate to the Microsoft Office User Specialist exams.

Why Would I Do This? shows students why the material is essential.

Step-by-Step tutorials simplify the procedures with large screen shots, captions, and annotations.

If you have problems... anticipates common pitfalls and advises students accordingly.

Inside Stuff provides tips and shortcuts for more effective applications.

Key Terms are highlighted in the text and defined in the margin when they first appear, as well as in an end-of-book glossary.

Jargon Watch offers a layperson's view of "technobabble" in easily understandable terms.

Exam Notes provide information and insight on topics that are covered on the MOUS exam and that should be reviewed carefully.

Checking Your Skills provides true/false, multiple choice, matching, and completion exercises.

Applying Your Skills contains directed, hands-on Practice exercises to check comprehension and reinforce learning, as well as self-directed Challenge exercises requiring students to use critical thinking skills.

CD-ROM contains files for the text's step-by-step tutorials and end-of-project exercises.

Annotated Instructor's Edition

If you have adopted this text for use in a college classroom, you will receive, upon request, an *Annotated Instructor's Edition* at no additional charge. The manual contains suggested curriculum guides for courses of varying lengths, teaching tips, answers to exercises in "Checking Your Skills" and "Applying Your Skills" sections, test questions and answers, and data files and solutions for each tutorial and exercise. Please contact your local representative or write to us on school or business letterhead at Macmillan Computer Publishing, 201 West 103rd Street, Indianapolis, IN 46290-1097, Attention: Education Channel Sales Support.

Microsoft Office User Specialist Exams

In order to validate your skills using Office, Microsoft has created the Microsoft Office User Specialist program. The Specialist Program is available for many Office 95 and Office 97 applications at both Proficient and Expert User levels.

The Specialist designation distinguishes you from your peers as knowledgeable in using Office products, which can also make you more competitive in the job market.

The *Microsoft Office User Specialist* exams are for anyone who:

- Wants to expand their skills.
- Is seeking certification in a particular software.
- Wants to learn or reference tasks in short, concise lessons.
- Is an instructor or trainer preparing groups of people for the Microsoft Exams.

Que Education & Training Certification Resource Center

To keep up to date on the Microsoft Office User Specialist program exams, check the following Web sites:

`www.queet.com/certification`

`www.mous.net`

`www.microsoft.com/office/train_cert`

MOUS PinPoint® Training and Testing Software

MOUS PinPoint training and testing software is designed to supplement the projects in this book. It aids you in your preparation for taking and passing the *Microsoft Office User Specialist* exams. The MOUS PinPoint software consists of:

- Trainers
- Evaluations

Each **trainer** asks you to perform specific tasks that were covered in a particular project of this book. If you don't know how to perform a particular task, you can watch a demonstration (**SHOW ME**) of the task. Immediate feedback (concerning the correctness of performance) is given after each task in each trainer. Each **evaluation** consists of the same questions that were given in the trainer. However, with an evaluation, you may not view demonstrations and you do not receive feedback after trying each task. After performing a **trainer** or **evaluation**, you can view a report of your overall performance.

Preparing to Install the MOUS PinPoint Training and Testing Software

To install the MOUS PinPoint training and testing software, we recommend following these steps:

1. Check to see if your computer meets the minimum requirements (see Table I.1).
2. Perform a full installation of Office 97 on your computer, if you have not already done so (see the section "Installing Office 97").
3. Install the MOUS PinPoint testing and training software (see the section "Installing the MOUS PinPoint Training and Testing Software").

Using the MOUS PinPoint Training and Testing Software

To use the MOUS PinPoint training and testing software, we recommend following these steps.

Study the projects in this book. After reading each project:

1. Run the **trainer** for the project (see the section "Running the MOUS PinPoint Software"). Then view a report on your performance (see the section "Viewing Reports").
2. Run the **evaluation** for the project (see the section "Running the MOUS PinPoint Software"). Then view a report on your performance (see the section "Viewing Reports"). Note: Some projects may not have a corresponding MOUS PinPoint trainer and evaluation.

After you have finished reading this book, take the MOUS PinPoint Final Exam:

1. Run the **evaluation** for the Final Exam Part 1. Final Exam Part 1 covers material included in the first half of this book.
2. Run the **trainer** for the Final Exam Part 1. Only the items missed in the trainer will be set to run.
3. Run the **evaluation** for the Final Exam Part 1 (again) as a final check.
4. Repeat the steps 1–3 given for Final Exam Part 2. Final Exam Part 2 covers material from roughly the second half of this book.
5. When you are finished using the MOUS PinPoint software, you can remove it from your computer (see the section "Removing the MOUS PinPoint Training and Testing Software").

Running MOUS PinPoint Testing and Training Software Requirements

The system components in Table I.1 are required to run the MOUS PinPoint Testing and Training Software.

Table I.1 System Component Requirements

Component	Minimum	Recommended
CPU	Pentium 90	Higher than Pentium 90
Operating System	Windows 95 or NT 4.0 Note: You must have an Administrator's or Power User's login if you are working on a Windows NT workstation.	N/A
Installed Apps	Office 97 (full installation)	N/A
RAM	16 MB	32 MB or higher

continues

Table I.1 Continued		
Component	Minimum	Recommended
Hard Drive	Adequate space for Office 97 and for MOUS PinPoint training and testing software	N/A
CD-ROM Drive	2X speed	4X speed or faster
Pointing Device	Windows-compatible mouse or pointing device	N/A
Video	Color VGA video display	N/A

Installing Office 97

Important: It is necessary to do a complete installation of Office 97. This means installing *all* components.

To perform a full installation of Office 97, complete the following steps:

1. Start Windows 95 or Windows NT 4.0 and close any applications that are running (other than Windows).
2. Insert the Office 97 CD and run **setup.exe**.
3. Click on the **Add/Remove** button, as shown in Figure I.1 (if a previous installation of Office 97 is already on your computer). If you do not have a previous installation of Office 97 on your computer, select **Custom** installation from a different screen.

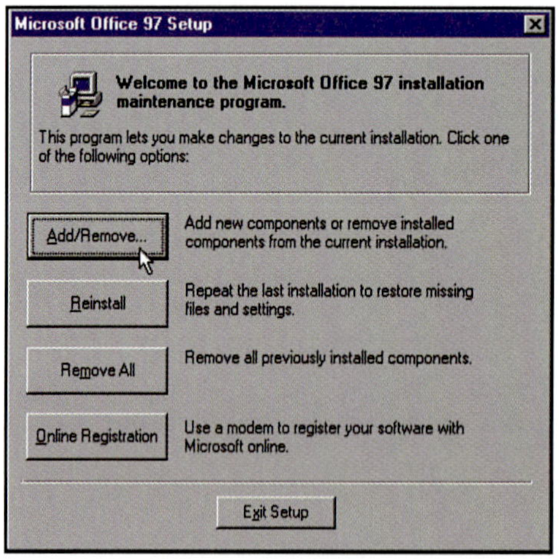

Figure I.1
The Microsoft Office 97 Setup dialog box.

4. Click on the **Select All** button (see Figure I.2).
5. Click on the **Continue** button.
6. Continue with the installation until it is finished.

Figure I.2
Choosing the Select All button will install *all* Office 97 components to the system.

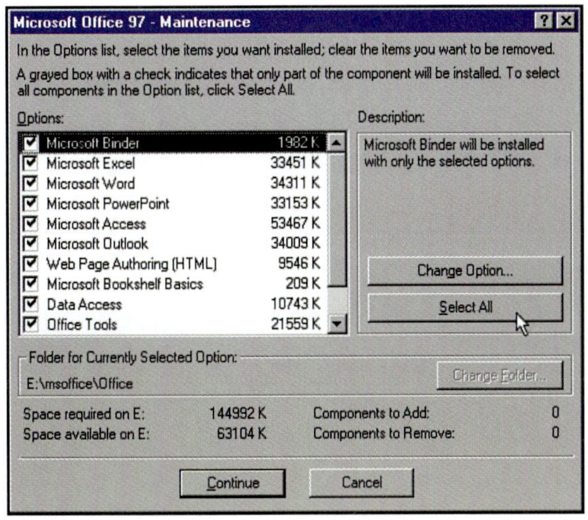

Installing the MOUS PinPoint Training and Testing Software

To install and run MOUS PinPoint trainers and evaluations on a single-user computer, you must first install the MOUS PinPoint **Launcher** by running a setup program from the MOUS PinPoint CD.

Installing the MOUS PinPoint Launcher

To run the setup program for the MOUS PinPoint Launcher:

1. Start Windows 95 or Windows NT 4.0 and insert the MOUS PinPoint CD into the CD-ROM drive.
2. Select **Start/Run** from the Windows desktop.
3. Enter (or browse to) **[Drive Letter]:\SETUP.EXE** (where **[Drive Letter]** is the assigned drive letter of the CD-ROM (see Figure I.3).

Figure I.3
Indicating the location of the setup.exe executable.

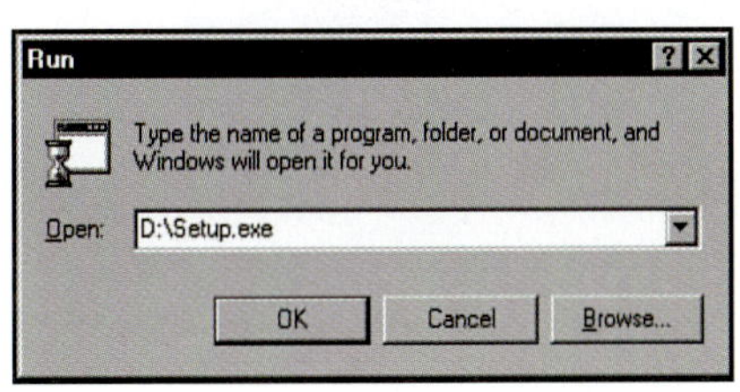

4. Click on **OK**. The setup program runs.
5. Answer the questions that appear during the installation.
6. When the dialog box in Figure I.4 displays, choose **Normal Single-User Installation**.
7. Click **Yes** when you are asked if you want to install MOUS PinPoint modules to your hard disk. The dialog box in Figure I.5 appears. The installation program is getting ready to install the **Launcher** to your computer. It needs to know the directory where you would like it installed.

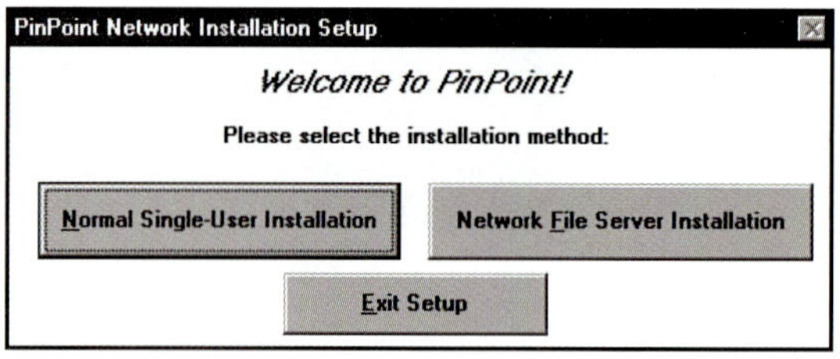

Figure I.4
The MOUS PinPoint Network Installation Setup dialog box.

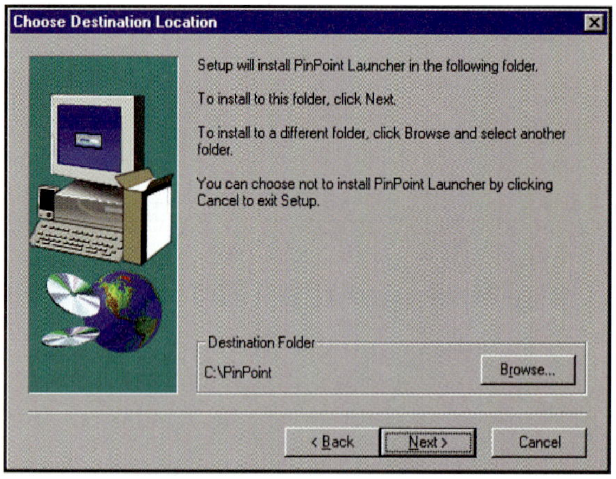

Figure I.5
The default location destination folder is shown.

8. To install the **Launcher** to the default location, click on the **Next** button. Otherwise, enter a new path for the **Launcher** and then click on the **Next** button.

9. Confirm the installation location by clicking on **Yes** in the dialog box in Figure I.6.

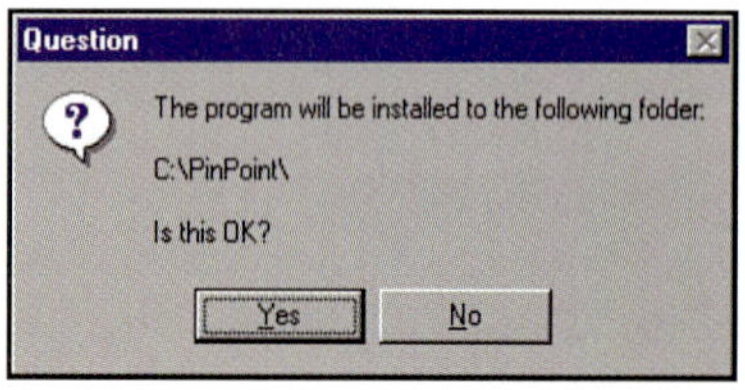

Figure I.6
The destination folder requires confirmation.

10. When Figure I.7 appears, click on **Next**.

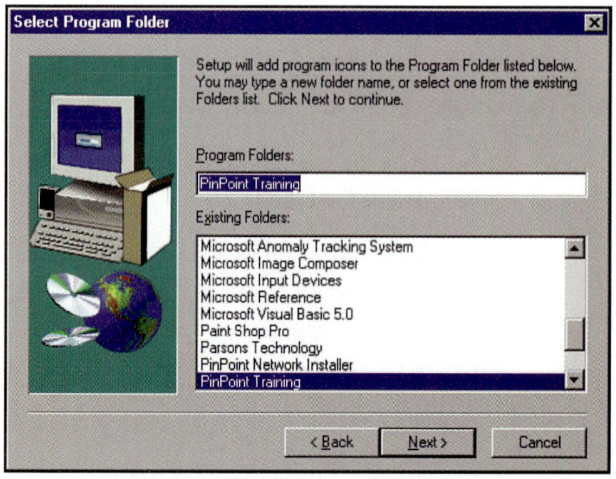

Figure I.7
Creation of the Program Folder.

A **PinPoint Training** group window is created (see Figure I.8). You can close this window. It is not necessary to use this window to start the PinPoint Launcher in the future since you can always select **Start/Programs/PinPoint Training/PinPoint Training** from your desktop.

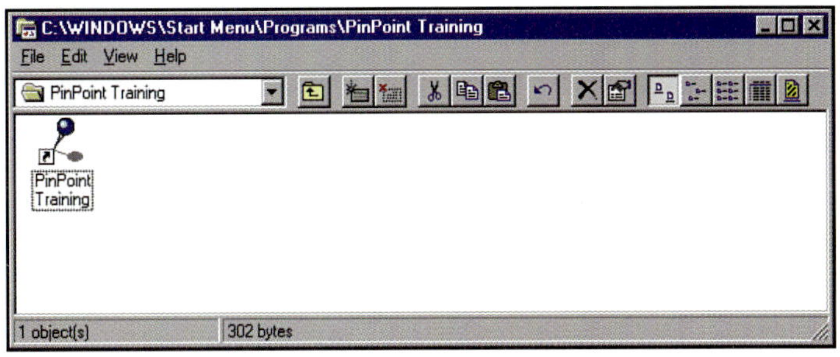

Figure I.8
The PinPoint Training group window that is created.

The PinPoint **Launcher** is used to:

- Logon with your **UserID** and **Password**.
- Install your MOUS PinPoint training and testing software for *an exam*.
- Run your MOUS PinPoint training and testing software for *an exam*.
- View reports after you have run the MOUS PinPoint training and testing software.

To install the MOUS PinPoint training and testing software for *an exam*, continue with the next section.

Installing the MOUS PinPoint Software

To install the MOUS PinPoint training and testing software:

1. Start the Launcher by selecting **Start/Programs/PinPoint Training/ PinPoint Training** (see Figure I.9).

Figure I.9
The **Home** screen of the Launcher.

2. Click on the **Installer** button (see Figure I.10).

Figure I.10
The **Installer** screen.

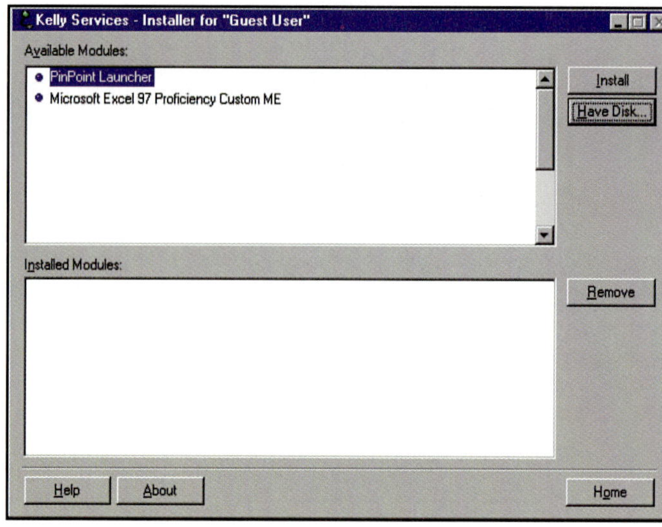

3. Install your MOUS PinPoint software by selecting the specific module (for example, **Microsoft Excel 97 Proficiency Custom ME**) from the **Available Modules** list box and clicking on the **Install** button. (Do not install the **Launcher**. It's already installed!)

4. Answer the questions that appear during installation. You are asked to verify the location where the MOUS PinPoint software will install to your hard drive (see Figure I.11)

Figure I.11
The default location destination folder is shown.

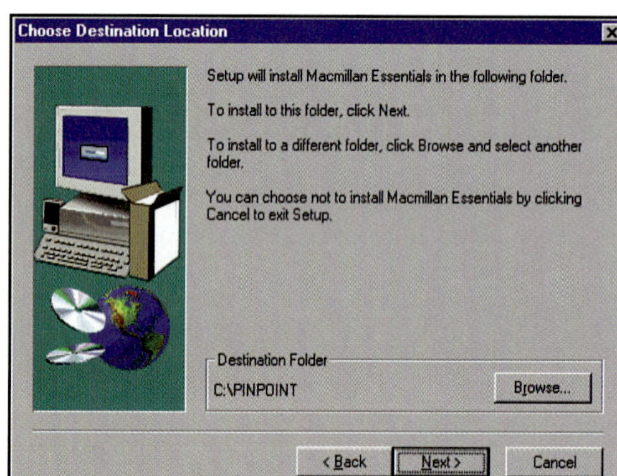

5. Make changes as necessary by clicking on **Browse** and selecting a different destination folder. Important: The MOUS PinPoint software for *the specific exam* and the PinPoint **Launcher** must be installed under the same main directory (for example, **C:\PinPoint**) in order to work properly.

6. Click on **Next**.

7. Accept the subdirectory (for example, **xl8prome**) where the MOUS PinPoint software will be placed. You do not have a choice concerning the name of this subdirectory.

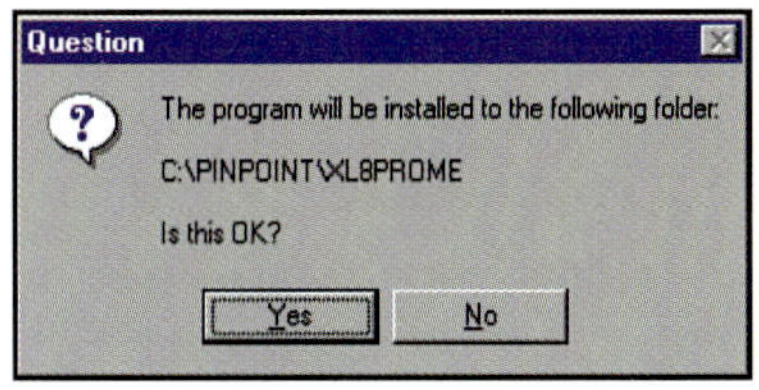

Figure I.12
The destination folder requires confirmation.

8. Click on **Yes.**
9. If you would like to view a README file concerning MOUS PinPoint software, click on **Yes** in the dialog box in Figure I.13. Otherwise, click on **No**.

Figure I.13
Specify whether you want to review the README.txt file.

A PinPoint Training group window is created (see Figure I.14).

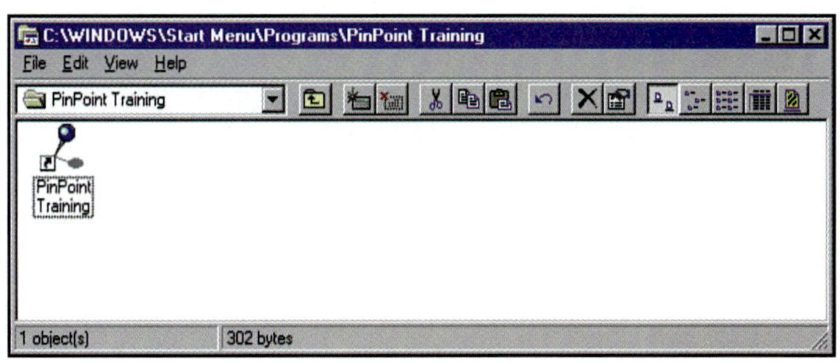

Figure I.14
The PinPoint Training group window that is created.

Close this window. It is not necessary to use this window to start the PinPoint **Launcher** in the future since you can always select **Start/Programs/PinPoint Training/PinPoint Training** from your desktop.

If you want to run the MOUS PinPoint software that you just installed, don't exit from the **Launcher**. Continue on with step 3 in the next section.

To exit from the **Launcher** to Windows, click on the **Exit** button.

Running the MOUS PinPoint Software

To run the MOUS PinPoint software, it is necessary to start the PinPoint **Launcher**. Important: Shut down all applications.

To run the MOUS PinPoint software:

1. Shut down all applications (except Windows and the Launcher) that are running, including any shortcut bars (such as Microsoft Office shortcut bar). If the Office 97 exam application is running, shut it down.

2. Start the Launcher by selecting **Start/Programs/PinPoint Training/PinPoint Training** from the Windows desktop.

3. Click on the **User Logon** button (see Figure I.15). Logging on under your name allows the **Launcher** to keep track of your personal progress. This enables the **Launcher** to reconfigure a module the next time you take it. It also enables the **Launcher** to create a report containing information about your training or evaluation sessions.

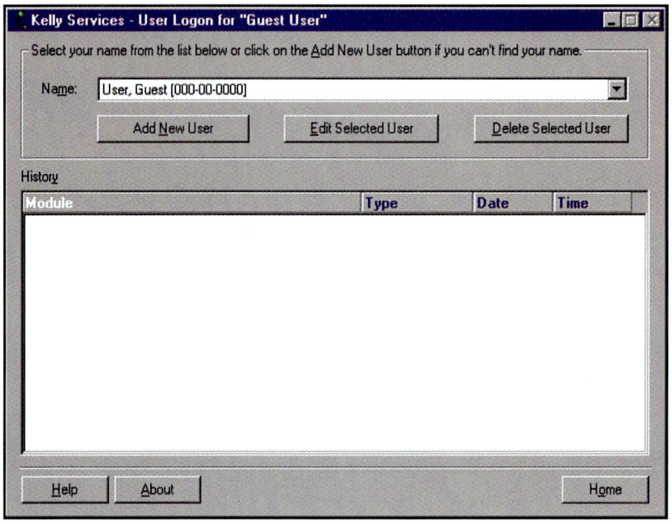

Figure I.15
The **User Logon** screen.

4. Select your name from the drop-down list in the **Name** combo box in Figure I.16:

   - You may need to use the scroll bar to find your name.
   - If your name is not in the list, go to step 5.
   - If you found your name, skip to step 8.

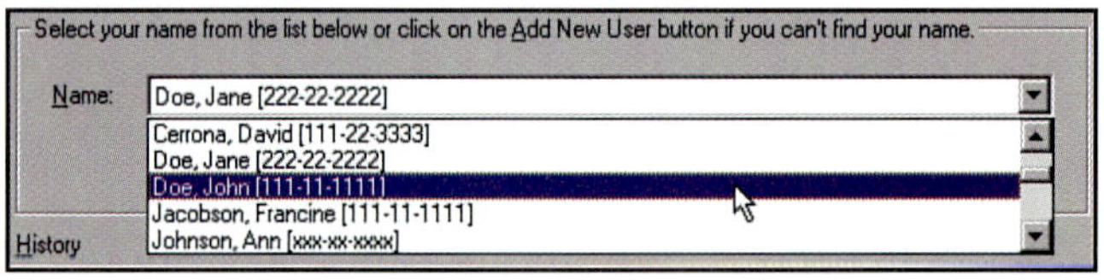

Figure I.16
Specify your logon name.

5. If this is your first time running MOUS PinPoint software, your name will not be in the list. If that is the case, create a user account for yourself by clicking on the **Add New User** button.

6. Enter your personal data, tabbing between fields in Figure I.17:

   - Enter all five data items. If one or more of the data items are missing, the **OK** button will remain grayed out (disabled).
   - Your **User ID** and **Password** may both consist of up to fourteen characters and are both case sensitive.

- After entering your **password** in the **Password** field, you must confirm this **password** by entering the identical **password** again in the **Confirm Password** field.

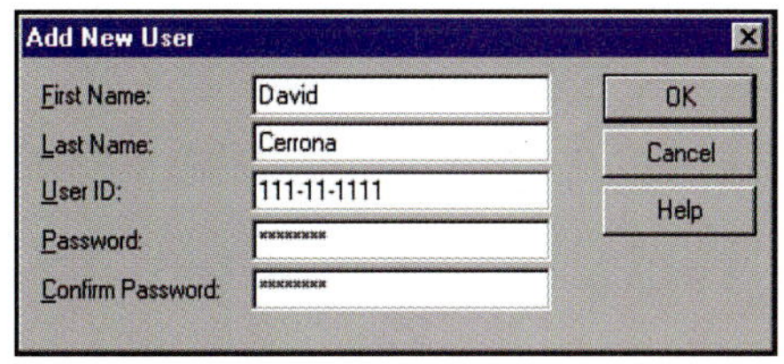

Figure I.17
The Add New User dialog box.

7. Click on **OK**. Your account is created and you are logged on. You are ready to move to the **Training & Testing** screen.
8. Click on the **Home** button to move to the **Home** screen.
9. Click on the **Training & Testing** button (see Figure I.18).

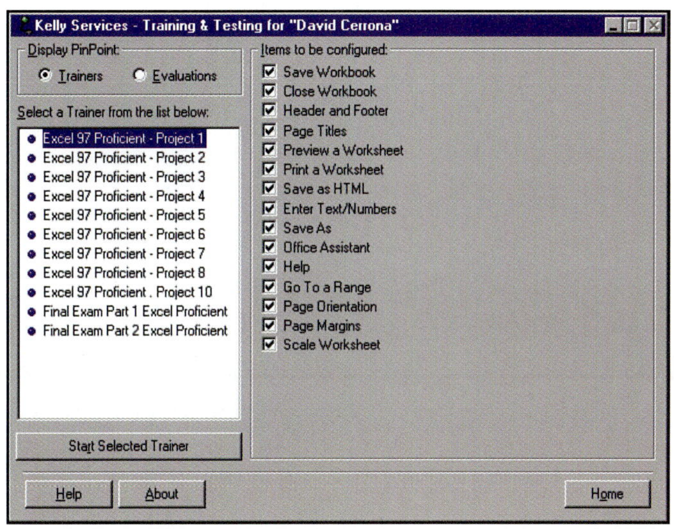

Figure I.18
The **Training & Testing** screen.

10. Select **Trainers** or **Evaluations**, depending on which you would like to run (see Figure I.19). A list of trainers or evaluations displays.

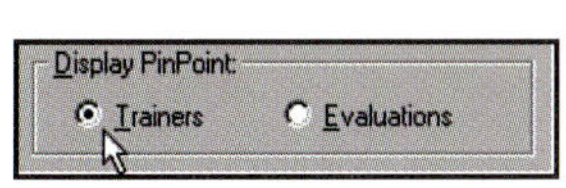

Figure I.19
Selecting trainers or evaluations.

11. Select the particular trainer or evaluation that you would like to run. Each trainer and evaluation is named by the project that it covers. Trainers may be configured. That means you can select the tasks that you would like to run. The first time you run a trainer, all tasks will automatically be selected. (Note: Evaluations may not be configured.)
12. If you are running a trainer, configure it by selecting or deselecting tasks in the **Items to be configured** section:
    - A check indicates that the task will run.
    - No check indicates that the task will not run.

You are now ready to start (launch) the trainer or evaluation for the project.

Figure I.20
Select the tasks you want to configure.

13. Click on the **Start Selected Trainer** button if you are starting a trainer or the **Start Selected Evaluation** button if you are starting an evaluation. Before the trainer or evaluation runs, you are asked to confirm (see Figure I.21).

Figure I.21
Confirm the running of the trainer or evaluation.

14. Click on **Yes** to confirm. While running the trainer or evaluation, you may use the controls in Figure I.22.

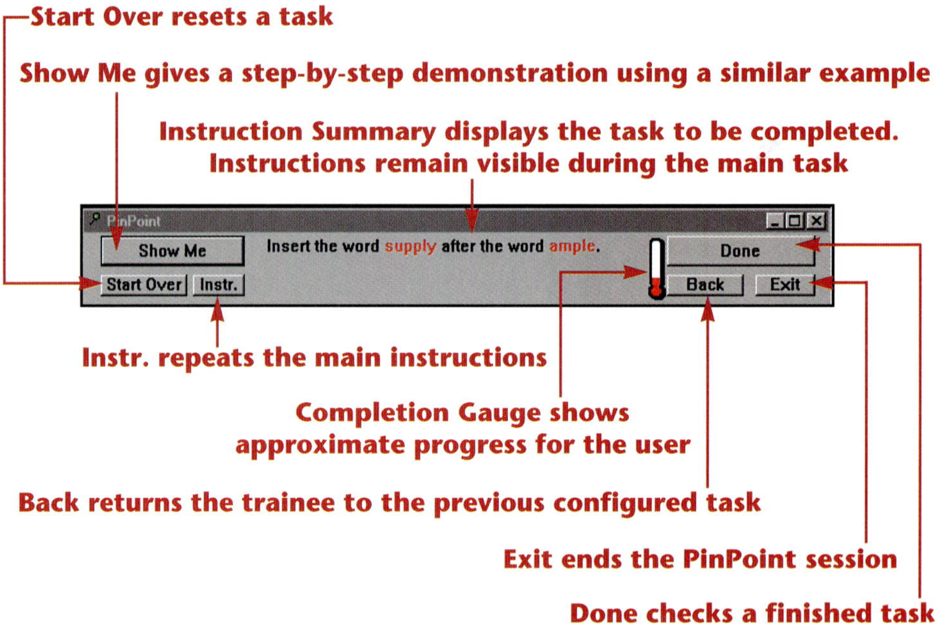

Figure I.22
Controls available while running the trainer or evaluation.

After running a trainer or evaluation, the **Training and Testing** screen reappears. You can continue to run other trainers or evaluations for other projects. When you are finished studying the whole book, you can also run the trainers and evaluations for the final exams.

To view reports for each trainer or evaluation that you ran, click on the **Reports** button (see the section "Running the MOUS PinPoint Software").

To exit from the **Launcher**, first move to the **Home** screen by clicking on the **Home** button. Then click on the **Exit** button.

Viewing Reports

In the **Launcher,** you can view two kinds of reports after running a MOUS PinPoint trainer or evaluation:

To display reports in the Launcher:

1. Start the **Launcher** and log on.
2. Click on the **Reports** button (see Figure I.23). This report displays a line (record) of data for each instance that you have run a MOUS PinPoint trainer or evaluation:
   - **Accuracy** is the number of tasks you performed correctly.
   - **Maximum** is the total number of tasks that were configured to run.
   - **Time** is the total elapsed time in minutes (from the moment you started running the trainer or evaluation to the moment that you exited the trainer or evaluation).

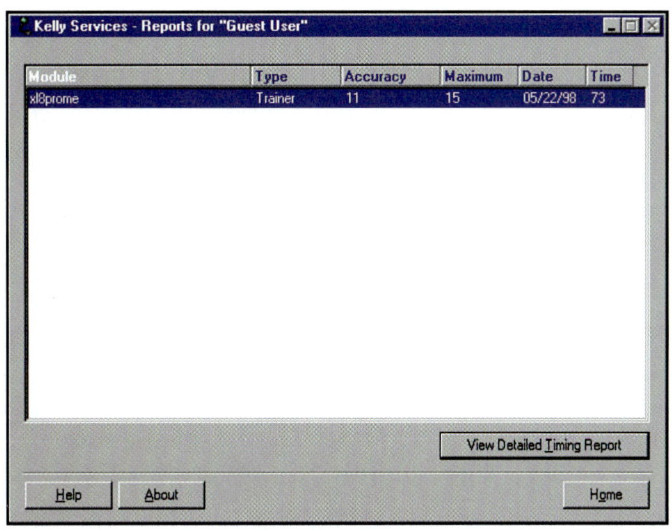

Figure I.23
The Reports screen appears, displaying the first kind of report.

3. The second kind of report is the **Detailed Timing Report** (see Figure I.24). If you wish to view this report, select the record for which you would like the timing report and click on the **View Detailed Timing Report** button.

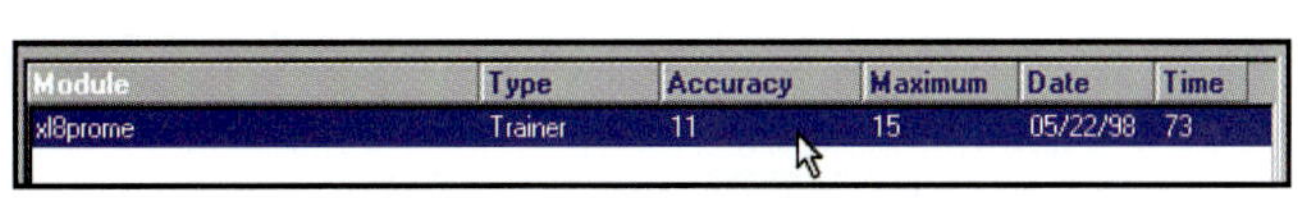

Figure I.24
Select the specific record.

4. To print the **Detailed Timing Report**, click on the **Print** button:
   - **Actual** is the time, in seconds, you used to complete the task. This time is considered the "involved time," the time that was taken from the moment that you clicked with the mouse (or entered something on the keyboard) to the moment that you clicked on the **Done** button. It does not count the "thinking time," before you first moved the mouse (or used the keyboard) and it does not count the time used to run and view a SHOW ME demonstration.

Figure I.25
The **Detailed Timing Report**.

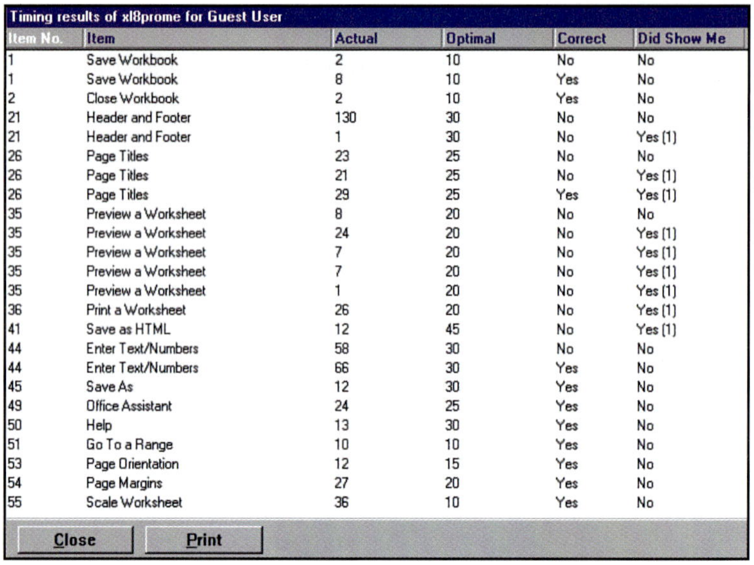
Timing results of xl8prome for Guest User

Item No.	Item	Actual	Optimal	Correct	Did Show Me
1	Save Workbook	2	10	No	No
1	Save Workbook	8	10	Yes	No
2	Close Workbook	2	10	Yes	No
21	Header and Footer	130	30	No	No
21	Header and Footer	1	30	No	Yes (1)
26	Page Titles	23	25	No	No
26	Page Titles	21	25	No	Yes (1)
26	Page Titles	29	25	Yes	Yes (1)
35	Preview a Worksheet	8	20	No	No
35	Preview a Worksheet	24	20	No	Yes (1)
35	Preview a Worksheet	7	20	No	Yes (1)
35	Preview a Worksheet	7	20	No	Yes (1)
35	Preview a Worksheet	1	20	No	Yes (1)
36	Print a Worksheet	26	20	No	Yes (1)
41	Save as HTML	12	45	No	Yes (1)
44	Enter Text/Numbers	58	30	No	No
44	Enter Text/Numbers	66	30	Yes	No
45	Save As	12	30	Yes	No
49	Office Assistant	24	25	Yes	No
50	Help	13	30	Yes	No
51	Go To a Range	10	10	Yes	No
53	Page Orientation	12	15	Yes	No
54	Page Margins	27	20	Yes	No
55	Scale Worksheet	36	10	Yes	No

- **Optimal** is a reasonable amount of time, in seconds, required to perform a task by an efficient method.
- **Correct—Yes**, if the you performed the task correctly; **No** if you did not perform the task correctly.
- **Did Show Me—Yes**, if you viewed a SHOW ME demonstration for the task; **No**, if you did not view a SHOW ME demonstration for the task. The **Did Show Me** column appears only if the timing report contains data for a **trainer** and not for an **evaluation**. (Evaluations do not have SHOW MEs.)

5. Close the **Detailed Timing Report** window by clicking on the **Close** button. The **Reports** screen of the **Launcher** returns.

Removing the MOUS PinPoint Training and Testing Software

When you are finished using the MOUS PinPoint training and testing software, you can remove it. Be sure to follow the procedure below.

To remove your MOUS PinPoint training and testing software:

1. Start the **Launcher**.
2. Click on the **Installer** button.
3. Select the exam module from the **Installed Modules** list.

Figure I.26
Choose from the **Installed Modules** available.

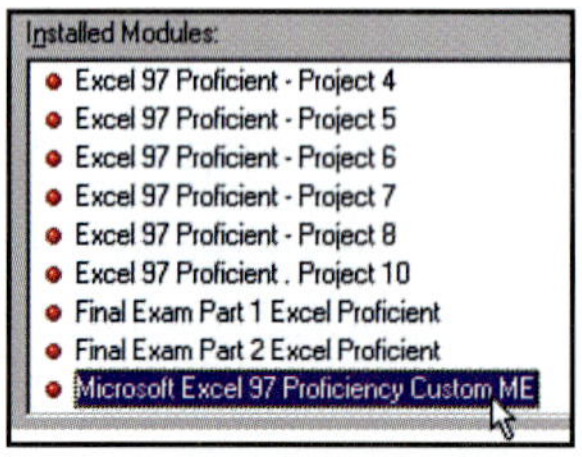

4. Click the **Remove** button.
5. When the **Confirmation** dialog box appears, click **Yes**.

6. When the **Remove** dialog box appears, click the **Yes** button.
7. An **"Uninstall complete"** message appears.
8. Find the MOUS PinPoint directory on your computer and delete it.

Troubleshooting

Table I.2 lists a few problems that can arise while running the MOUS PinPoint training and testing software. For each problem, a solution or explanation is given.

Table I.2 MOUS PinPoint Training and Testing Software Problems and Solutions

Problem	Explanation or Action
A task is grayed out and not selected on the Training and Testing screen in the Launcher program (see Figure I.27).	A particular component has not been installed. Exit the Launcher and perform a full installation of Office 97 (see the section "Installing Office 97").
Your computer crashes (locks up or exits ungracefully) while running the MOUS PinPoint training or testing.	Start your computer again and rerun the desired MOUS PinPoint training or testing. Exit the trainer or evaluation in the normal way. It is important to do this, even if you have no desire to run a trainer or evaluation. By running any trainer or evaluation, you will ensure that your computer's registry is reset to normal.
You see a message that says **"program was left in an unfinished state"** AND you have deleted the MOUS PinPoint directory (or one of its key components).	The problem is that your Windows registry was changed by running the registry and needs to be set back to the state it was in before you started the MOUS PinPoint training and testing. Do the following: 1. Go to the **Windows** directory and find the following files: **OFC97.PIN** **OFC971.PIN** **OFC972.PIN** **OFC973.PIN** **OFC974.PIN** 2. Delete the **OFC97.PIN** file. 3. Rename the other four **.PIN** files so that they have a **.REG** extension. 4. Double-click on each of the **.REG** files to run them. This will reset your registry.

Figure I.27
An example of a grayed out option.

Microsoft Access Expert Specialist User Skills

The skill areas covered in the exam and the required tasks for those skill areas are listed in Table I.3.

Table I.3 Expert User Skills

Skill Set	Required Activity	Project	Lesson
Create a database	Plan a database	1	7
		2	1
	Create a table	2	2
	Enter data into a table	3	1
		3	4
	Modify data in a table	3	3
	Enter data into a form	5	2
	Navigate through a table	3	2
		3	3
	Delete data from a table	3	4
Use forms	Create a simple form	5	1
		5	3
	Modify a form	5	6
	Create controls on a form	5	4
	Modify controls	5	6
	Add a record using a form	5	2
	Show related records on a form	12	8
		14	3
Modify a database	Open a database	1	2
	Modify field properties	7	1–3
		9	1–3
	Modify field layout	7	4
	Modify the presentation of a database	2	6
View information	Present information in a chart	14	5
	View information in a form	5	3–4
	View multiple records	5	4
	Switch between views	2	6
Organize information	Sort data on single fields	3	7
	Sort data on multiple fields	3	7
Locate information	Find a specific record	4	6
	Create a simple query	4	1
	Create a query with multiple criteria	4	6
	Add filters (selection and form)	16	3–4
	Remove filters	16	3
Refine results of a query	Add fields to a query	4	4
	Remove fields from a query	4	4
	Sort a query	4	5
	Join tables in a query	7	7
		11	3–4

Skill Set	Required Activity	Project	Lesson
	Remove joins in a query	7	7
	Save a query	4	3
Analyze data	Build summary queries	14	2
	Calculate fields	13	3
		13	5
		14	2
	Set crosstab queries	14	1–2
Create sub forms	Identify appropriate use	12	8
	for sub forms	14	3
	Add a record with a main form	12	8
	Add records with sub forms	12	8
	Merge two tables into a form	12	8
		14	3
Build a relational	Identify relationships	7	5
database		11	1
	Relate tables	7	6
		11	2
Integrate information	Import data	8	1–4
from other	Link data	8	5
applications	Add pictures to records	8	6
Utilize Web capability	Create hyperlinks	18	1–2
	Build order forms for Internet use	18	7
Maintain data	Identify criteria for data	9	1
integrity	integrity	9	7
	Validate text	9	4
	Set required properties	9	5
	Set validation rules	9	4
	Set lookup fields	9	7
	Use expressions in calculated	13	3
	controls	16	2
Build a form	Title a form	5	7
for other users	Modify form design	5	7
		10	6
		12	7
	Improve accuracy in forms	9	1–7
		10	4–6
		11	1
		11	3
		12	2–3
	Enhance design of a form	10	1–3
		11	1
		12	5–6

continues

Table I.3 Continued

Skill Set	Required Activity	Project	Lesson
Produce Reports	Create a report	6	2
		13	1-2
		13	4
	Modify a report	6	4
	Label a report	6	6
		13	5
	Customize headers and footers	13	5
	Make a calculation on a report	13	3
		13	5
	Group data in a report	13	4
	Sort data in a report	13	5
	Add custom pages	14	4
Print	Print a report	6	3
	Print a form	5	7
		12	9
	Print the result of a query	4	6

Table of Contents at a Glance

Table of Contents

Conventions Used in This Book

The *MOUS Essentials* series uses the following conventions to make it easier for you to understand the material:

- Text that you are to type or that appears onscreen appears in a `special font and color`.
- Underlined letters in menu names, menu commands, and dialog-box options are the shortcut keys. Examples are the File menu, the Open command, and the File name list box.
- Key terms appear in *italic* the first time they are discussed and are defined in the margin as soon as they are introduced.

Project One 1

Getting Started with Access 97

Learning the Basics

In this project you will learn the following objectives and their associated Microsoft Exam required activities.

Objectives	Required Activities
➤ Launch Access 97, Copy, and Rename a Database	
➤ Open and Close a Database	Open a database
➤ Open and Close a Database Table	
➤ Identify Access 97 Window Elements	
➤ Get Help in Access and on the Internet	
➤ Exit Access and Windows	
➤ Gather Data and Prepare to Plan the Database	Plan a Database

Why Would I Do This?

In order to make the best use of your time, there are numerous databases included with the book that you will open and modify rather than create from scratch. In this lesson, you launch Access, make a copy of a database file, and then give the copy a new name. In other Microsoft applications such as Word, Excel, or PowerPoint, you may have made copies of files by opening them in the application and then using the File and Save As menu options. The Access program uses files differently than most other programs and does not have a Save As menu option.

In this project, you learn how to launch Microsoft Access 97 for Windows 95 and copy a database. You also open a database and a database table in Access to get a taste of what databases do. Finally, you learn how to get help and exit Access.

Access

Desktop
The opening screen in Windows 95.

Taskbar
The area at the bottom of the screen that displays the Start button and buttons for applications that are open.

Folder
An icon that represents a group of files.

Icon
A pictorial representation of a program, a file, or other element.

Lesson 1: Launching Access

When you turn on a computer that has the Windows 95 operating system, the *desktop* and *taskbar* automatically display (unless you have activated the taskbar's Auto Hide property, in which case the taskbar is hidden until you move the pointer onto its location at the bottom of the screen).

Launching Access

In Windows, programs are stored together in *folders*, and folders are represented by a folder *icon*. Icons also represent the individual programs. The folders and program icons on your computer vary, depending on what programs are installed on it. You should have a folder, probably called Microsoft Office 97 or Microsoft Office, which contains the Access program icon. In most installations of Access, the Access program icon also shows on the menu under Programs and can be opened directly from the Programs list rather than opening the Office 97 folder.

To Launch Access

1. **Click the Start button at the lower-left corner of the Windows 95 screen.**

   This opens a menu similar to the one shown in Figure 1.1.

2. **Use your mouse to move the pointer to the Programs folder.**

   A submenu of the folders and individual programs is displayed.

Figure 1.1
The Windows 95 Start menu.

3 **If you installed Access 97 along with Microsoft Office 97, point to the folder for Microsoft Office 97 to reveal its contents (see Figure 1.2).**

The Access 97 icon may also be displayed on the Programs submenu and can be selected without opening the Office 97 folder. Note that the programs on your computer will differ from the example shown in Figure 1.2. If you installed Access but don't have Microsoft Office, you can start Access directly from the Programs submenu.

Figure 1.2
The Access program icon can be selected from the Microsoft Office 97 folder or directly from the Programs submenu.

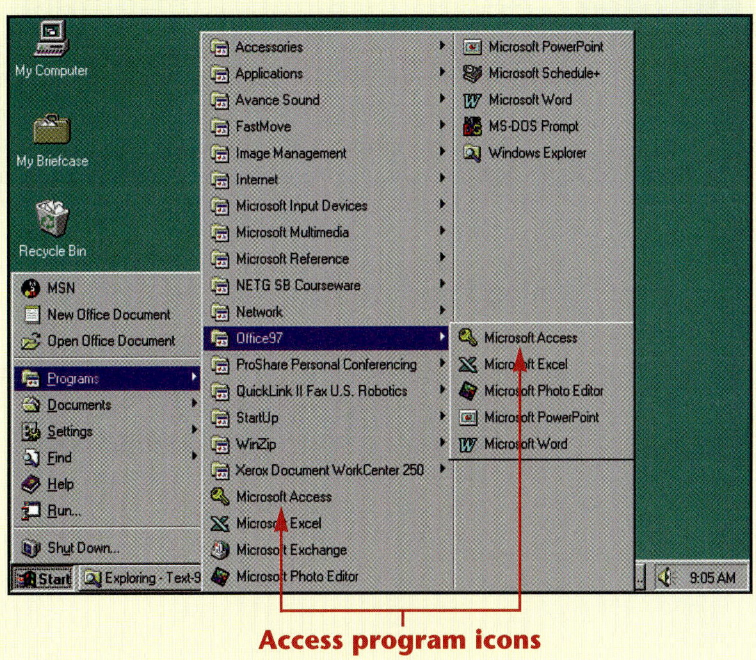

continues

To Launch Access (continued)

4 Click the Microsoft Access menu item.

The Microsoft Access screen appears with a dialog box, asking whether you want to create a new database (using either a blank database or a wizard) or open an existing database (see Figure 1.3).

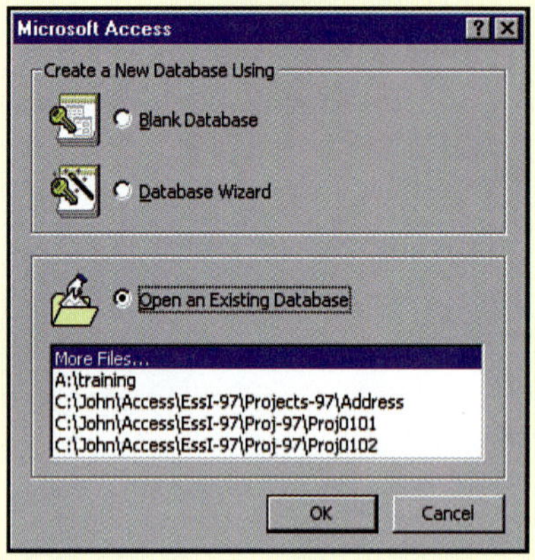

Figure 1.3
The Microsoft Access 97 screen with the opening dialog box.

5 Make sure the Open an Existing Database and More Files options are selected. Click OK to display the Open dialog box.

The Open dialog box is used to find and open existing databases.

Inside Stuff

Your menus may appear somewhat different from the examples shown in Figures 1.1 and 1.2. If the computer you are working on already had an older version of Windows on it when Windows 95 was installed, the old style program groups were converted to folders. In this example, the computer had a program group called Microsoft Office that contained the Access program. If you have a computer that came with Windows 95, you have a simpler structure of folders and all of the Office programs, like Access, are shown in the main folder.

Copying Project Files

A large number of database files are included on your student disk. Since you cannot open the databases on your CD and make changes, you will need to make copies of each file, place the files on another disk drive, and give each file a new name—one that describes the function of the database.

To Make a Copy of a Project File

1 Click the list arrow at the right end of the Look in box. Open the Project-01 folder on the CD that contains the database file, Proj0101.

The files supplied with the book may be on a CD that would be on drive D: or E:, or they may have been placed on a network drive if you are using this book in a classroom setting.

2 Move the pointer onto the name of the Proj0101 file. Click the right mouse button.

A shortcut menu displays (see Figure 1.4).

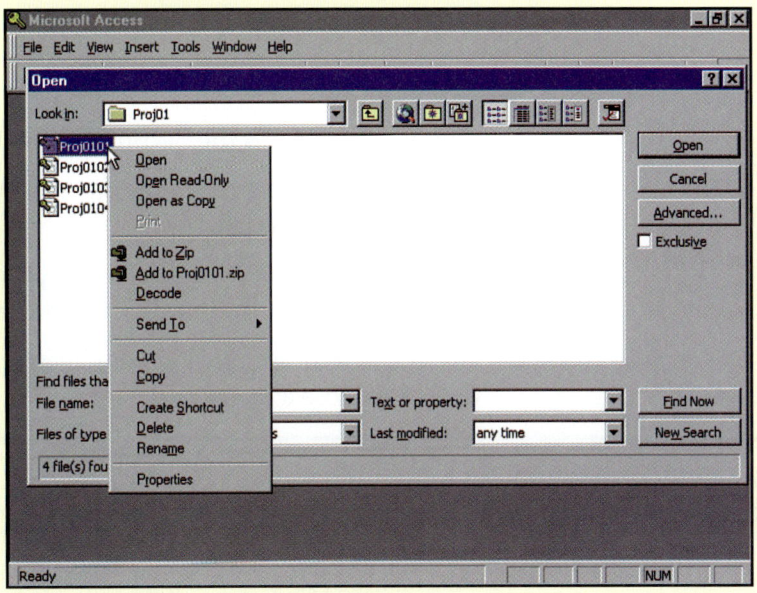

Figure 1.4
Clicking on the file name with the right mouse button displays a short menu of actions.

3 Click Copy.

A copy of the file is placed in the Clipboard.

4 Click the list arrow at the right of the Look in box and select a folder on your disk in which to store your working files.

If you are working on a computer that is shared with others and the sample files are on a CD or a network, save your files to a floppy disk. (You cannot save files to the CD or to protected network drives.)

5 Move the pointer to an empty area to the right of the list of files (if any) in the destination folder. Click the right mouse button.

The shortcut menu appears (see Figure 1.5).

continues

To Make a Copy of a Project File (continued)

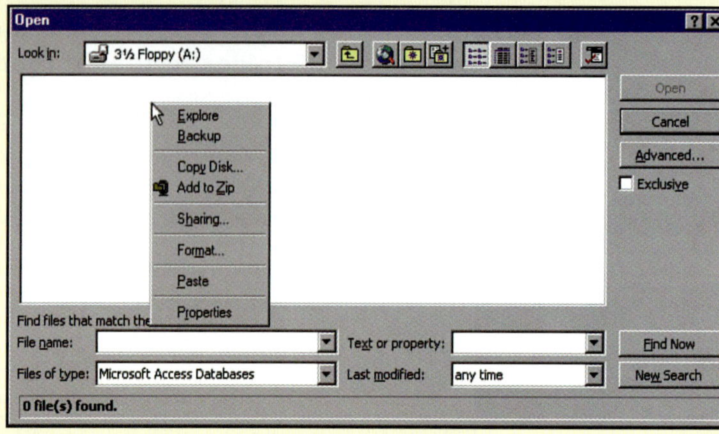

Figure 1.5
The shortcut menu can be used to paste the file into the current folder.

6. **Click Paste.**

   The file is copied to the destination folder.

7. **Right-click on the new copy of the Proj0101 file to display the shortcut menu again.**

8. **Choose the Rename command. Type `Address` and then press ↵Enter to change the name of the file.**

   Leave the dialog box open for use in the next lesson where you open and close a database.

Inside Stuff

The filenames for your practice files may show the database extension .mdb. This shows if the Hide MS-DOS file extensions option has not been turned on in the Windows Explorer View menu. If the extensions are showing, then the file extension (.mdb) must be included when renaming the file. In the previous example, the new file name would be Address.mdb. The rest of the procedure remains the same.

Lesson 2: Opening and Closing a Database

Typically, the first thing you do when you launch Access is open an existing database. You can open any database you have created, any database that is included as part of this course, or any database that was included with the Access program.

In this lesson, you open a sample database, called `Address`, that contains the same kind of information you would include in a personal address book. A database that lists contact information about family members, friends, and associates can be easily managed by Access.

To Open and Close a Database

1 If the Access program is not already running from the previous lesson, launch Access, click on OK, click the list arrow next to the Look in box, and find the folder that has the Address database.

If you left the program running at the end of the previous lesson, the Address database will already appear in the dialog box.

2 Click on `Address` to select it (see Figure 1.6).

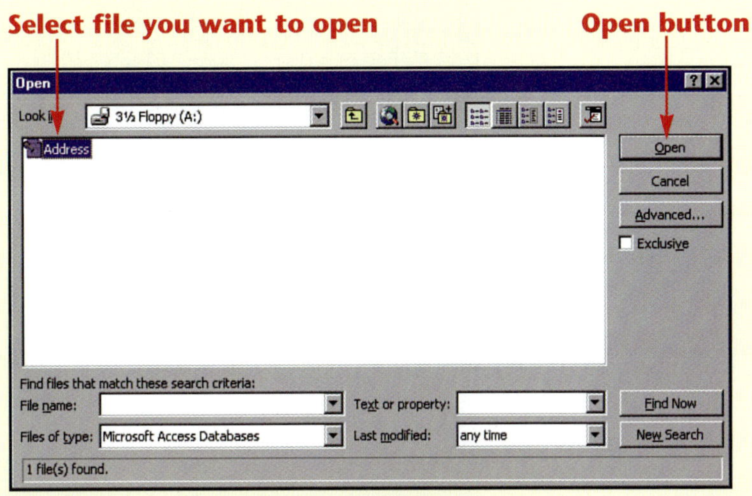

Figure 1.6
The Open dialog box with the Address file selected.

3 Click Open to open the database.

The sample Address **database** appears onscreen, as shown in Figure 1.7. This window (called the Database window) lists all the **tables** in the database. You can also display any **queries**, **forms**, **reports**, **macros**, and **modules** that are part of the database. In addition, you can create new tables, queries, and forms from this window. (See the Jargon Watch box at the end of this lesson to learn more about these database elements.)

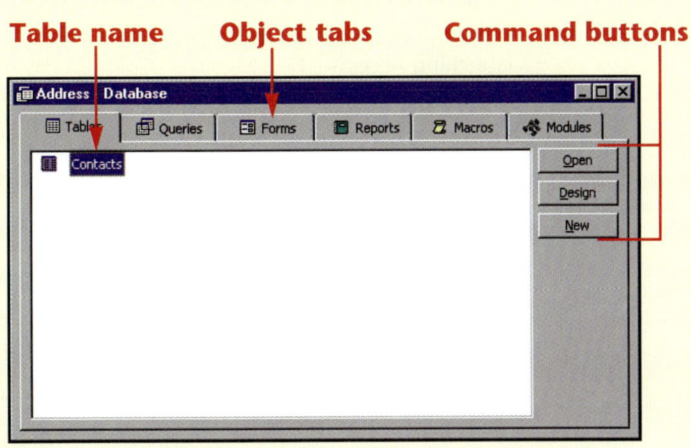

Figure 1.7
The Address database showing the table it contains.

continues

To Open and Close a Database (continued)

4 Click the Queries tab.

The Queries tab is displayed at the top of the window, along with the other object tabs. Clicking the tab displays the queries in this database, including a query named `Indiana` (see Figure 1.8).

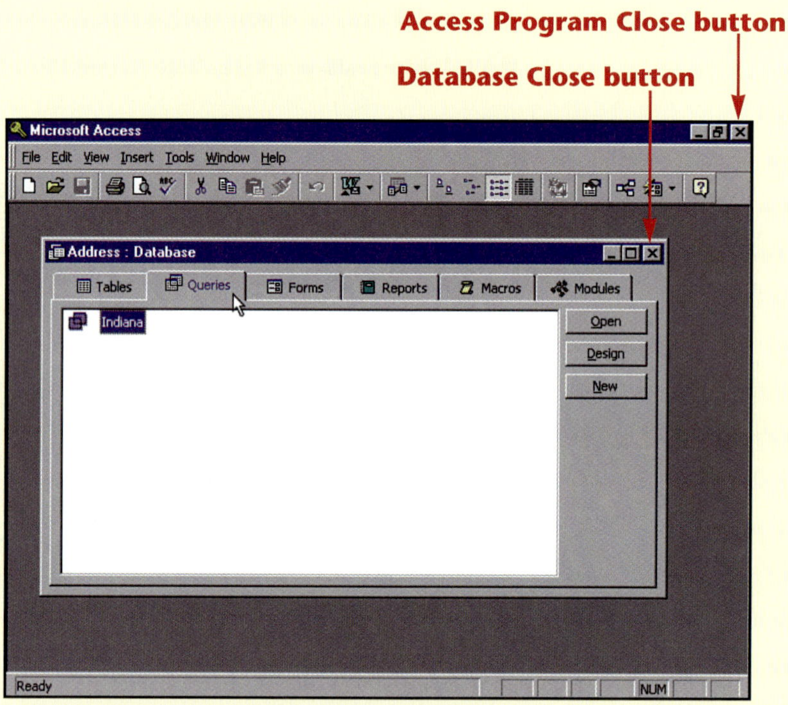

Figure 1.8
Clicking the Queries tab displays all queries contained in the database.

5 Close the database by clicking the Close button (the X icon) on the upper-right corner of the database window (not the Close button on the corner of the program title bar).

If you have problems...

If you accidentally close the whole Access program, just launch Access again. You will not lose any work by making this mistake. Refer to Lesson 1 if you need help launching Access.

Inside Stuff

You can open a database with the commands used in the preceding steps, but two shortcut methods are also available. You can open a new database by clicking the New Database button at the left end of the Database toolbar, or by pressing Ctrl+N (holding down Ctrl and pressing the letter N). You can open an existing database by clicking the Open Database button, second from the left end of the Database toolbar, or by pressing Ctrl+O (holding down Ctrl and pressing the letter O).

Access

Jargon Watch

In Lesson 2, you were confronted with many database terms. Don't be concerned. Some of these terms are database objects, and describe the various ways that data is displayed and handled in an Access database. With Access, you can create the following types of objects:

Database. A term used to refer to an application program, such as Access, or to a file created using that program. A database file can consist of related tables, queries, forms, reports, macros, and modules.

Tables. Used to store data.

Queries. Used to ask questions of the database. The answer is usually a group of records. For example, you might ask how many of your business associates work in Indiana.

Forms. Used to enter and display data in various formats.

Reports. Used to summarize and print data.

Macros. Used to automate commonly performed tasks.

Modules. Used by power users to write and customize Access programs in the Visual Basic programming language.

Lesson 3: Opening and Closing a Database Table

Tables are the primary workhorses of most databases. Access sets up tables as grids in which you can enter, edit, and view all the related information in your database. When you want to work with a table, you first open the database that contains the table, and then open the table.

In this lesson, you open a table in the Address database that you opened in Lesson 2.

To Open and Close a Database Table

1. **Open the File menu and choose the Open Database command.**

   Access displays the Open Database dialog box. If necessary, change to the drive or folder containing the database files for this book. Again, check with your instructor if you need help with this step.

2. **In the list of filenames, select `Address` by clicking it.**
3. **Click Open.**

   Access opens the Address database and displays the database window.

4. **Click the Tables tab.**
5. **Select the Contacts table by clicking it.**

continues

To Open and Close a Database Table (continued)

6 Click the Open button.

Access displays the Contacts table onscreen, as shown in Figure 1.9. Tables contain a grid of information made up of **records** and **fields**. Refer to the Jargon Watch box at the end of this lesson to find out more about records and fields.

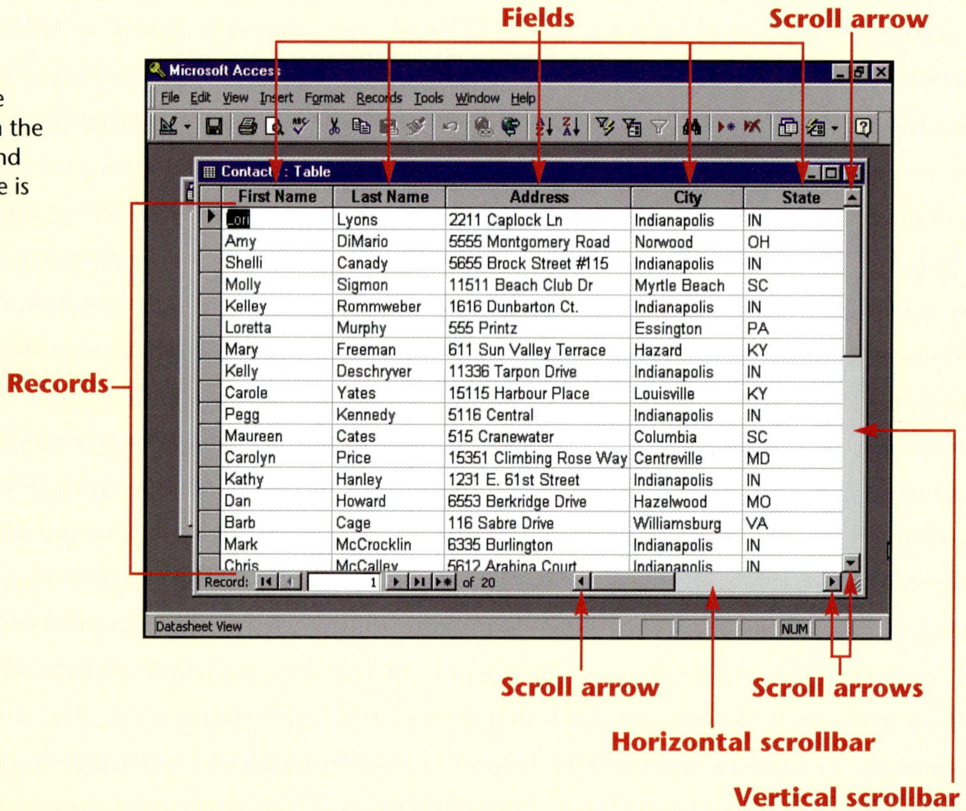

Figure 1.9
When you select the name of the table in the database window and click Open, the table is displayed.

Depending on the size of the table window, you may not be able to see all the information in the database table. To display other information, you can scroll the window.

7 Click the right scroll arrow on the horizontal scrollbar until you scroll to the last field.

Access displays the information in the ZIP and Phone fields that you may not have been able to see.

8 Click the left scroll arrow until you scroll back to the first field (First Name).

You learn more about scrolling through records, entering new records, and sorting records in Project 3. Now close the table.

Access

9 Click the Close box in the upper-right corner of the Contacts table.

The database window is still open. Keep the Address database open to use in the next lesson when you learn about the Access 97 window.

Jargon Watch

Each table in a database contains a group of related information, such as a list of your contacts' names, addresses, and phone numbers. Tables store the data in rows (records) and columns (fields). A **record** contains all of the related information about a single person, event, or transaction that is stored in a particular table. For example, the name, address, and phone number for Barb Cage is one record. Each separate piece, or category, of information stored in a table is called a **field**. First Name and Last Name are examples of fields.

Lesson 4: Learning About the Access 97 Window

The look of the Access 97 window changes, depending on what you are doing with the software. You may recognize many parts of the Access 97 screen as familiar parts of every Windows 95 program—elements such as the Minimize, Maximize/Restore, and Close buttons, as well as the scrollbars.

Other parts of the Access screen offer features that can help you complete your work quickly and efficiently. For example, the menu bar and toolbar are convenient features that you will use in most of the projects in this book.

When you first launch Access 97, you see only a few items on the menu bar, and most of the buttons on the toolbar are dim (or grayed), which means that they are unavailable. When you open a database, additional menu items appear on the menu bar, and most of the toolbar buttons become available.

As you open and work with individual objects within the database, you see that menu options and toolbar buttons change in relation to the type of object you selected. This lesson explains what you can expect to see in most Access 97 windows.

To Learn about the Access 97 Window

1 Look at the elements that appear in the Access 97 window when the Address database is open (see Figure 1.10).

The Address database window should be onscreen from the last lesson. Four key elements appear in the Access window: the title bar at the top of the window, the menu bar below the title bar, the toolbar under the menu bar, and the status bar at the bottom of the window. Each element displays commands and tools that relate to the current database object shown in the database window.

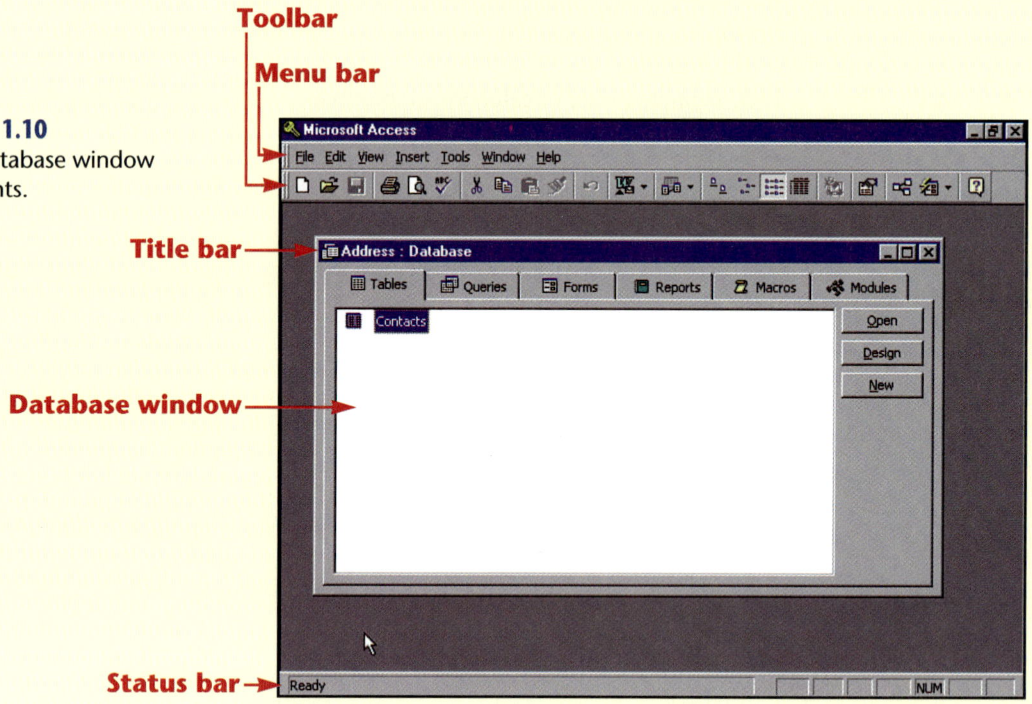

Figure 1.10
The database window elements.

2 Open the File menu.

Notice that the commands on this menu deal with opening, closing, and working with databases. You can use Access menus the same way you use menus in all other Windows applications. If you choose a menu command followed by an ellipsis (...), Access leads you to a dialog box with additional options. Also notice that shortcut keys are displayed to the right of some menu commands, such as Save.

3 Click on an unused part of the screen outside the File menu.

This step closes the menu. You can also close the menu by pressing Esc or clicking the File menu again.

ScreenTip
A pop-up box that appears when the pointer stays over a button and gives a short description of that button.

4 Move the mouse pointer over the button at the far left end of the toolbar.

Access displays a label called a *ScreenTip*, telling you the name of the button—in this case, New Database (see Figure 1.11).

Access

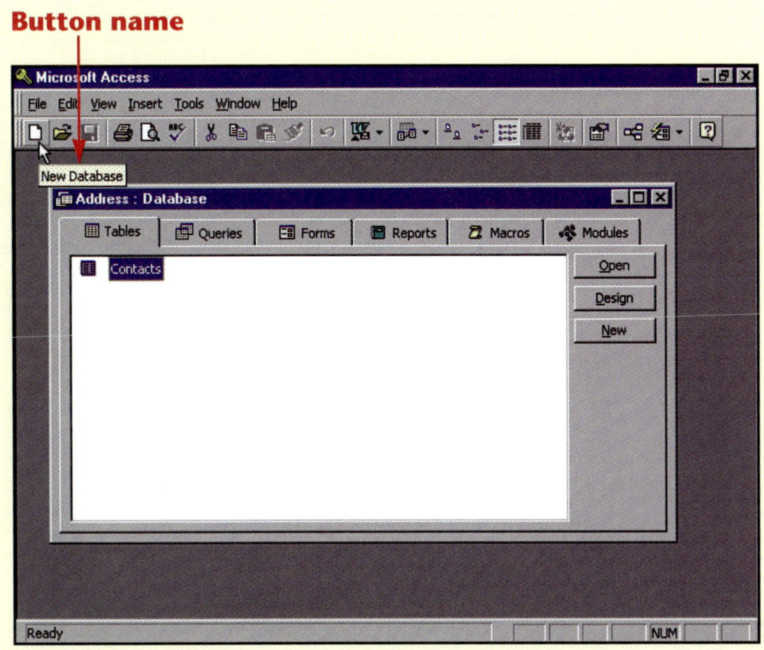

Figure 1.11
Use the mouse to determine the function of a particular toolbar button.

Now take a look at these elements when a table is open.

5 Click the Contacts table in the database window.

6 Click the Open button.

Access opens the table. You could also double-click the table name to open it. The menu bar, toolbar, and status bar change to reflect the tasks you can perform with tables (see Figure 1.12).

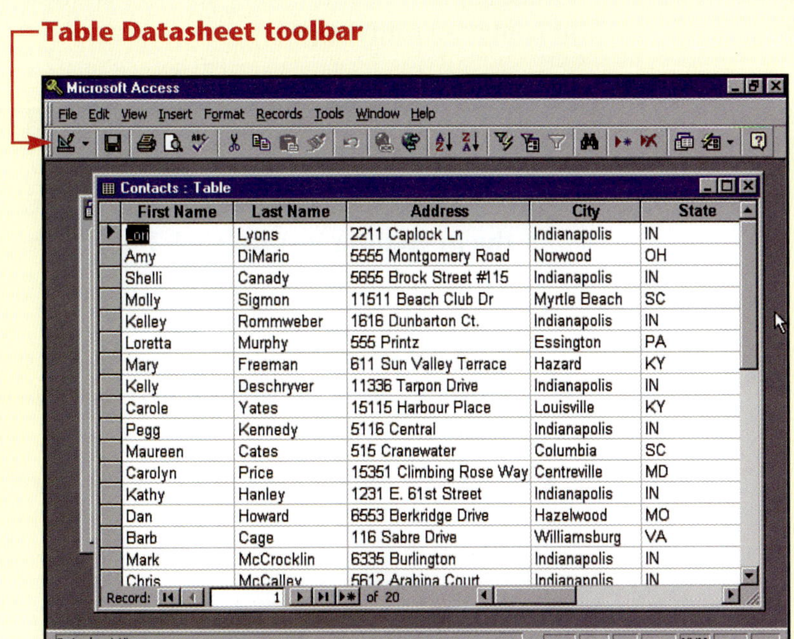

Figure 1.12
The table window elements change to reflect table-specific tasks.

continues

To Learn about the Access 97 Window (continued)

7 Move the mouse pointer over the View button at the far left of the toolbar.

The View button may be used to switch to another view of the table or to display a list of available views for the table.

8 Move the pointer over other buttons in the toolbar.

As you move the pointer over other buttons, read the name and description that Access provides so that you can get an idea of what each button does. Keep the Contacts table and the Address database open for now. At the end of this project, you learn how to close these files and exit Access. In the next lesson, you learn how to use the Access Help system.

Lesson 5: Getting Help

At some point, you may run into problems as you work with your computer and with software such as Access. If you need a quick solution to a problem with Access, you can use the program's Help feature. The Help system makes it easy to search for information on particular topics. In this lesson, you use the Office Assistant and the What's This feature.

Using the Office Assistant

The Office Assistant
An animated guide that helps you search for help.

The *Office Assistant* is a flexible help feature included with all Microsoft Office applications. It allows you to ask questions, search for terms, or look at context-sensitive tips.

To Get Help Using the Office Assistant

1 With the Address database and Contacts table still open from the preceding lesson, click Help in the menu bar.

Access displays a drop-down menu of choices. Note that the first item in the Help menu uses the same icon as one of the buttons at the far right of the toolbar. Both of these options launch the Office Assistant. (You can also launch the Office Assistant by pressing F1 at any time.)

2 Click the Microsoft Access Help command.

Access 97 opens the Office Assistant, as shown in Figure 1.13.

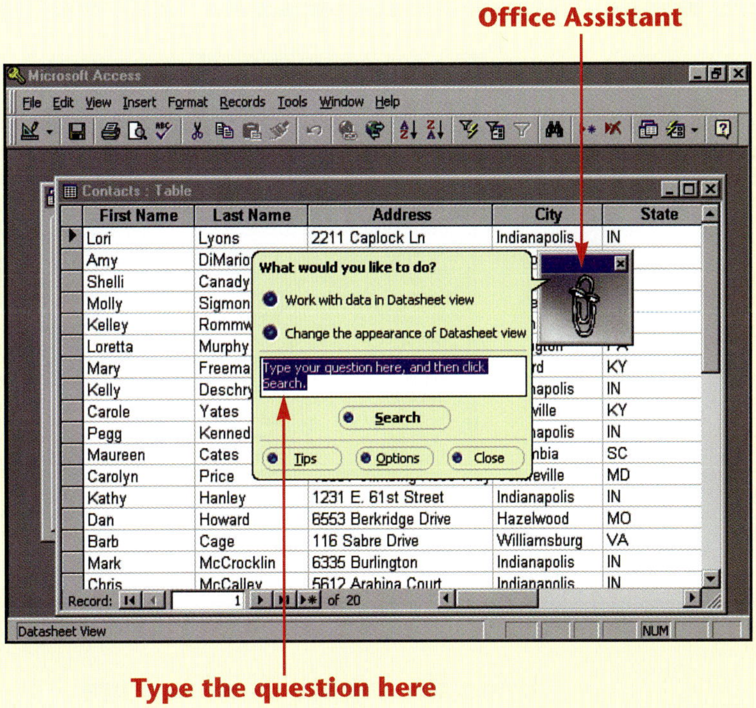

Figure 1.13
The Office Assistant can search for help information that you type as a question.

3 Type `How can I get data from an Excel file?` in the text box.

4 Click the Search button.

The program searches through your sentence and looks for keywords. Topics related to your question are listed. If there are too many topics to fit in the window you may need to click the See more button.

5 Select the topic Data sources Microsoft Access can import or link.

Access displays the Help window pertaining to this subject (see Figure 1.14).

6 Click the Close button in the upper-right corner of the Help window when you are done reviewing the types of data sources that Access can link with or import data from.

The Office Assistant remains on the screen.

7 Click the Close button in the upper-right corner of the Office Assistant window to close the Office Assistant.

This closes the Office Assistant window.

continues

To Get Help Using the Office Assistant (continued)

Figure 1.14
Access displays the Help topic Data sources Microsoft Access can import or link.

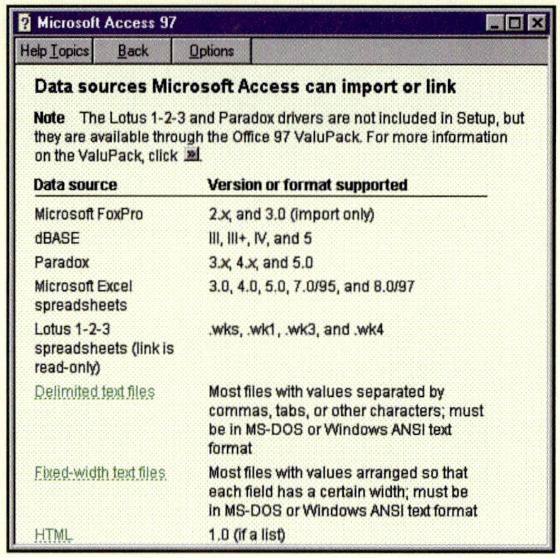

Data sources Microsoft Access can import or link

Note The Lotus 1-2-3 and Paradox drivers are not included in Setup, but they are available through the Office 97 ValuPack. For more information on the ValuPack, click

Data source	Version or format supported
Microsoft FoxPro	2.x, and 3.0 (import only)
dBASE	III, III+, IV, and 5
Paradox	3.x, 4.x, and 5.0
Microsoft Excel spreadsheets	3.0, 4.0, 5.0, 7.0/95, and 8.0/97
Lotus 1-2-3 spreadsheets (link is read-only)	.wks, .wk1, .wk3, and .wk4
Delimited text files	Most files with values separated by commas, tabs, or other characters; must be in MS-DOS or Windows ANSI text format
Fixed-width text files	Most files with values arranged so that each field has a certain width; must be in MS-DOS or Windows ANSI text format
HTML	1.0 (if a list)

Using the What's This? Feature

You can get helpful descriptions of different buttons, menu items, or screen objects by using the What's This? option. In the following section, you learn how to use this feature.

To Get Help Using the What's This? Feature

1. **Click Help in the menu bar.**
2. **Click the What's This? option.**

   The pointer changes to include a large question mark.

3. **Click the Find button on the toolbar.**

   A window opens that describes this feature in greater detail (see Figure 1.15).

Figure 1.15
The What's This? feature displays a description of the button or menu selection.

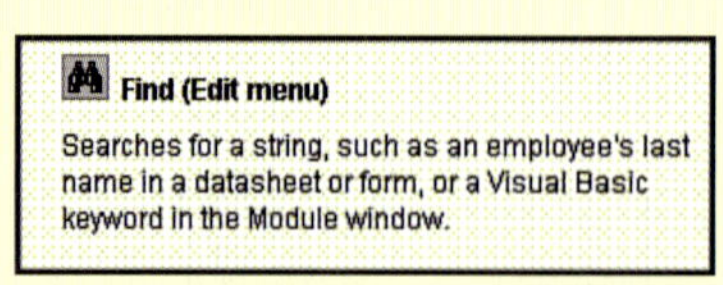

4. **Click anywhere else on the screen to close the Help window and disable the What's This? feature.**

There are several other options for getting help that are available from the Help menu. You can choose Contents and Index and search through the help topics alphabetically using the Index, or by topic using the list of topics in the Contents section. Most of your questions about the basic operation of Access can be answered using one of these methods. If you do not find what you need in the help topics supplied with the program, you can select Microsoft on the Web and Online Support to connect to Microsoft's support Web page on the Internet.

If you have problems...

To save space, some people delete help files or don't install them in the first place. If you get a message stating that the help file can't be found, use your original installation disks and add the help files.

Lesson 6: Exiting Access and Windows

When you have finished working with Access, you should close all open tables and databases, and exit the program. If you turn off your computer without closing Access (or if you lose power), you will probably be able to retrieve most of your data, but some of the recent changes you have made may be lost. You should get in the habit of saving formatting changes and closing the database before you close Access. You should also exit Windows 95 before you turn off your computer.

In this project, you close the Address database and then exit Access and Windows 95.

To Exit Access and Windows

1. **Click the Close button of the Contacts table window.**

   This closes the Contacts table.

2. **Click the Close button of the Address database window.**

   This closes the database window and leaves you with the main Access window open.

3. **Click the Close button for the Access program.**

   Access is closed, and you are returned to the Windows 95 desktop. Here you can launch another program or shut down Windows 95. If you want to work on the exercises at the end of the chapter at this time, do not close Access or exit Windows until you are done using the computer.

4. **To exit Windows 95 and shut down the computer, click the Start button.**

continues

To Exit Access and Windows (continued)

5 Click the Shut Down option.

6 Click Yes to confirm that you want to shut down.

Windows 95 checks your programs and files to be sure that they are closed and saved properly, and then shuts down.

7 When the message `It is now safe to turn off your computer` **appears onscreen, turn off the power to the computer and monitor.**

If you are finished with your session at the computer, continue with the sections "Checking Your Skills" and "Applying Your Skills" in this project.

Lesson 7: Gathering Data and Preparing to Plan the Database

The most logical place to start when learning a database management software is with the tables that store the data. When you do this, you must decide what types of data to store. There are two approaches to this problem that most people take. In this lesson we will look at those two methods so that you have a basis for making decisions about what should go into the tables that you will create in the next project.

Output
The data that is printed or displayed that represents the answer to a request or the results of an analysis or process.

Two Design Methods

The two methods commonly used are to include all the possible relevant data or focus on the data that is necessary to produce the desired *output*.

Include Everything

One method is to include all the types of data that you currently have on paper or are aware of. If you do not have a clear idea of what you want to do with the data at a later date, this method has its advantages. For example, if you were testing a rocket launch you would not know ahead of time what might fail and what you would need to analyze. It that case, you would measure everything that seemed likely to be important and store as much data as possible. This type of approach is used most often in science and engineering. The drawback to this method is that it takes up a lot of resources and you end up entering and storing data that never gets used. The advantage is that you can answer some questions at a later date that you did not know enough to ask when the data was gathered.

Consider Likely Outputs

If you know that you want to produce certain reports or be able to look up certain types of information, you already have a good guide as to what type of data must be gathered. Consider the following general ideas:

- If the data is going to be included in the output, it must be recorded in one of the tables.
- If a report will be sorted by date, name, department or some other type of data, that data should be in a field of its own. For example, if you want to produce a list of addresses that are sorted by the name of the street, you will have to enter the street name and the street number separately.
- If you want to limit the output to those items that meet certain criteria, the data that is used in the criteria should be entered separately. For example, if you want to produce a list of all the people who have been with the company more than thirty years, you would have to enter the date they were hired.
- You do not have to store data that is derived from other data. For example, if you intend to store the date someone was hired and the date they left, you do not have to store the number of years they were with the company. That value can be calculated whenever it is needed in a report or a form.

This is the approach that is most often used in business or personal applications and is the one used in this book.

Words of Advice and Encouragement

Designing a database is more complicated than designing a document, a spreadsheet, or a presentation. The database has several parts that work together and depend upon each other. You will start with designing tables, but the fields that go in them depend on the reports and forms that will use them. You must start somewhere so you will start by learning how to create tables and proceed to forms and reports. If you feel that you do not know enough yet to make all the decisions necessary for designing tables, you are right! Be patient; we will provide the necessary guidance in the early parts of the process.

Mistakes to Avoid

A common mistake that many people make when they create a database is to create the table(s) and then enter all the data. This gives them a sense of progress. It leads to frustration when they discover that they have to do most of it over again when their design cannot produce the desired output. Once the tables have been created, choose some data that is typical of the type of data that you will enter. Enter enough records of sufficient variety so that you can test the sorting and limiting criteria that will be used later. Once all the parts of the database are working correctly, then it is safe to enter the rest of the data.

Another common mistake is to gather the data before the database is designed. Many people design survey forms and questionnaires without consideration for how the data will be entered, validated, sorted, looked up, summarized, or reported. Whenever possible, design the data gathering forms after (or at the same time that) you design the database.

Encouragement

In the early chapters of this book you will be dealing with the structure of the database. In later chapters, we will supply you with tables that have already had additional data entered into them so you will not have to spend time typing.

If you design the tables with some idea of the desired output, and keep in mind the few points listed above, you will do well.

Project Summary

To	Do This
Launch Access	Turn on the computer and click Start in the Windows 95 taskbar. Then choose Programs, Microsoft Access.
Open and close a database	Open the File menu, choose Open Database, select the file from the list, and click the Open button. To close the database, click the Close button in the database window.
Open and close a table	Open the database, click the Tables tab, select the table, and click the Open button. To close the database table, click the Close button.
Learn about Access	Access window elements include the window menu bar, toolbar, and status bar. These offer specific tasks available in each window. Button names appear when you point to a toolbar button.
Get help with the Office Assistant	Choose Help from the menu bar, select Microsoft Access Help, type a question, and click the Search button.
Use the What's This? feature	Choose Help from the menu bar, choose What's This, then point and click any part of the screen.
Get help on the Internet	Choose Help from the menu bar, select Microsoft on the Web, click the type of help or support you want, enter your ID and password (if prompted), and click the Connect button.
Exit Access and Windows	Click the Close boxes for the table, the database, and the Access program. Click the Start button on the taskbar and choose the Shut Down option. Confirm and wait for the message `It is now safe to turn off your computer`.

To	Do This
Gather data and prepare to plan the database	Determine what data is already available. Think about the types of reports you want to produce or the types of information that you want to look up on the screen. Consider how you want to sort the reports or how you want to limit their content. Enter sample data into your tables and hold off on gathering data until you know what data you will need.

Checking Your Skills

True/False

For each of the following, check *T* or *F* to indicate whether the statement is true or false.

__T __F **1.** In Windows 95, one way to launch a program is to click the Start button and then search for the program in the Programs folder.

__T __F **2.** The toolbar and menu bar always remain the same in Access 97, no matter what window you are working in.

__T __F **3.** Once Access is open, you can open a database by using commands found on the menu bar.

__T __F **4.** Access includes a feature that can answer questions written in the form of sentences.

__T __F **5.** It's okay to turn off the computer when Access and Windows are still running.

__T __F **6.** You can make copies of Access database files while using the Open dialog box by using shortcut menus.

__T __F **7.** To close an Access database but leave the Access program running, click the Close button at the upper-right corner of the Access window.

__T __F **8.** The Office Assistant is an animated guide that helps you search for help.

__T __F **9.** You should gather and enter all the data you have into a table before you try to design the rest of the database.

__T __F **10.** A record in Access is a category of information that is stored in a column in a table.

Multiple Choice

Circle the letter of the correct answer for each of the following questions.

1. If your computer has Access 97 installed on it, how do you launch it?
   a. Type `Access97` at the DOS prompt.
   b. Click the Start button, click Run, and type `Access 97`.
   c. Click the Start button, click Programs, find Access on one of the menus of programs, and click it.
   d. Just wait, and it will come up by itself.

2. Which of the following is not a type of object that you can display by clicking a tab in the database window?
   a. macro
   b. table
   c. module
   d. spreadsheet

3. Which of the following is not a way to open a database?
   a. Open the File menu and choose the Open Database command.
   b. Click the Open Database button.
   c. Type `Open File`.
   d. Press Ctrl+O.

4. How do you display the name of a toolbar button?
   a. Place the mouse pointer on the button.
   b. Click the toolbar button.
   c. Point to the toolbar button and click the right mouse button.
   d. Hold down Ctrl and click the toolbar button.

5. Which of the following is not one of the ways you can open the Help program?
   a. Open the Help menu on the menu bar.
   b. Press F1.
   c. Click the Office Assistant button on the toolbar.
   d. Press Ctrl+F1.

6. Which of the following is loaded when you select Help, Microsoft Access Help from the menu?
   a. the Index of Help Topics
   b. a table of contents of Help subjects
   c. the Office Assistant Help utility
   d. a Find window that lets you search through the entire help file for a single word

7. To make a duplicate of a file, you first copy the file and then choose which of the following?
   a. Duplicate from the Tools menu
   b. Clone the file from the File menu
   c. Add Copy from the Edit menu
   d. Paste

Access

8. Which of the following is not a good idea when getting started on a database?

   a. Examine the data that already exists.

   b. Consider how you want the data sorted.

   c. Consider what type of data may be used to limit the output.

   d. Enter as much data as possible before designing the forms and reports that will provide the output.

9. What does it mean when the mouse pointer has a question mark attached to it?

   a. Access has detected an error and is helping you find it.

   b. You have activated the What's This? feature.

   c. The database you've loaded is missing a major component.

   d. You have activated a query or a module.

10. How do you access the Microsoft World Wide Web site?

   a. From the File menu, choose Link.

   b. From the Edit menu, choose URL Link Data.

   c. Click the Web Link button on the toolbar.

   d. From the Help menu, choose Microsoft on the Web.

Completion

In the blank provided, write the correct answer for each of the following statements.

1. The opening screen in Windows 95 is called the ____________.

2. The area at the bottom of the screen that displays the Start button and buttons for the applications that are open is called the ____________.

3. A pictorial representation of a program, a file, or other element is called a(n) ____________.

4. The action that brings up a shortcut menu is a(n) ____________ click.

5. An icon that represents a group of files is called a(n) ____________.

6. The data that is printed or displayed that represents the answer to a request or the results of an analysis or process is called the ____________.

7. Help topics that are organized alphabetically are found by searching the help ____________.

8. A(n) ____________ stores a group of related data that is displayed in rows and columns.

9. The menu bar, _______________, and status bar change when you open different windows in Access.

10. To change the name of a selected file in the Open dialog box, you would choose the _______________ command from the shortcut menu.

Matching

In the blank next to each of the following terms or phrases, write the letter of the corresponding term or phrase. (Note that some letters may be used more than once.)

a. Open
b. ScreenTip
c. icon
d. table
e. field
f. folder
g. output
h. query
i. Close
j. right

_______ 1. A column in a table

_______ 2. A menu item under File

_______ 3. An icon representing a group of files

_______ 4. Used to ask questions of a database

_______ 5. A report is a type of

_______ 6. A button that looks like an X

_______ 7. A momentary label for a button

_______ 8. A picture representing a file or program

_______ 9. The button on the mouse that is used to bring up a shortcut menu

_______ 10. Used to store data in a database

Applying Your Skills

Practice

The following exercises enable you to practice the skills you have learned in this project. Take a few minutes to work through these exercises now.

Finding Out What's New in This Version of Access 97

If you have used earlier versions of Access, the following exercise will give you an idea of the improvements to this new version. If you have not used Access, you will get an idea of some of the skills you will pick up in this book.

To find out what's new in Access 97, complete the following steps:

1. Choose Help from the menu bar.
2. Click Contents and Index.
3. Explore the contents of the Help Topics window.
4. Close Help.

Reading the Help Directions for Creating a Database

The Help features in Access can answer specific questions, or can guide you database processes and procedures.

To read the Help directions for creating a database, complete the following steps:

1. Click the Office Assistant button at the right end of the toolbar. (If you are not sure which one it is, point to any of the toolbar buttons and wait a moment. A ScreenTip appears that tells you what the button does.)
2. Type the question `How do I create a database?` and click Search.
3. Explore some of the related topics that appear.
4. Close the Office Assistant.

Composing a Mailing List

Assume that you are the owner and hands-on business manager of Sound Byte Music, a new music store located in a small midwestern town.

One of your first goals in launching Sound Byte Music is to let people know that the store is in business. To do this, you have started an advertising campaign using various types of advertising, including direct mail. To send your advertising message to potential customers through direct mail, you have purchased a database containing names of potential customers.

Open this database and review the customer information it contains. Think about how you would use this information to target customers for Sound Byte Music. What other categories of information would you like to have in this database?

To review the mailing list database, complete the following steps:

1. If necessary, start your computer and Windows 95. Then launch Access.
2. Make a copy of the Proj0102 database in the Project-01 folder of the CD accompanying the book. Paste the database in your work area and rename the new file `Mailing List`.
3. Open the `Mailing List` database, then open the `Prospects` table.
4. Using the information in the Prospects table, write a list of three ways to target the most likely customers of Sound Byte Music. (Scroll across the table to see all of the fields.) Which category of information is most important to use?
5. Write a list of other types of information you would like to have to help you find potential music store customers in the Prospects table. You can do this with pencil and paper, or you can switch to a word processor and write the list there.
6. Close the database.

Planning a Database to Track Personal Computer Hardware

Your company has many personal computers that were purchased at different times and that differ greatly in their capabilities. You have been assigned the task of keeping an inventory of these computers. This inventory is crucial to the success of any project to upgrade software or the operating system. Identify the types of information that you need to track according to the guidelines that follow.

To plan the database, do the following planning without opening Access:

1. List PC information. Here are some of the fields that you may want to keep track of: type of processor, amount of RAM, size of hard drive, presence of 3 1/2" floppy disk drive, presence of high-capacity disk or tape drive, type of monitor, speed of CD-ROM drive, type of network card, presence of sound card, name of vendor, inventory code number, and date of purchase. List any additional information that you think would be important.

2. List vendor information (that is, who supplied the equipment). This information is important when you need technical advice or repairs. Some of the information that you will need includes: name of vendor, street address, city, state, zip code, and phone number. List any additional information that you think would be important.

Getting a Helping Hand

Because software is constantly changing, you need a way of learning the changes and where to get help. This exercise takes you to the appropriate help topics for the material covered in this project.

To get help on topics in this project, complete the following steps:

1. Close all databases but leave Access open.
2. Press F1. The Office Assistant is displayed, offering four selections.
3. Select the third item, `Get Started With Microsoft Access 97`. The Help program displays a topic with the same name as your selection.
4. Select the third button with the double greater-than symbol beside the text `Using a database for the first time`. The Help system displays the topic `Ways to get started if you're using a database for the first time`.
5. Review each of the eight selections under `What do you want to read about?` to familiarize yourself with how Access views databases.
6. Close the Help file.

Challenge

The following challenges enable you to use your problem-solving skills. Take time to work through these exercises now.

Exploring the World of Alaska

You have always been interested in a number of places and have wanted to visit them. One place that you've found interesting is Alaska. Over the years, you've gathered data on the state, such as pictures, geographic sites, and area attractions. You have finally decided to organize this data by using a database you were given that contains some geographic information.

To examine a database of information on Alaska, complete the following steps:

1. Within Access, choose File, Open Database. The Open Database dialog box is displayed. If you do not see the files for Project 1, move to Proj0103 in the Project-01 folder of the CD accompanying the book.
2. Copy Proj0103 and paste it in the same location that you have been using for the other databases in this project.
3. Rename Proj0103 as `Alaska`.
4. Open the `Alaska` database and select the Tables tab.
5. Double-click the table named `Geography`. The Geography table opens. Study the table design and the data included.
6. Close the table and exit Access.

Doing Customer Research

You were recently hired to work in the marketing department of a cable television company. Your boss hands you a questionnaire and tells you that 2,000 of these questionnaires were sent randomly to customers throughout your service area. She tells you that your job is to fix a database started by a previous employee. The database holds the responses and is used to provide responses to questions from the managers. Study the following questionnaire. You set up a database to hold the responses to this questionnaire in later projects.

The questionnaire has the following questions:

1. How many adults are in your household?
2. How many children or teenagers (17 or under) are in your household?
3. How many hours each day is your television turned on?
4. Of the following five channels, which channel do you watch most often?

   [All News] [All Movies] [Science Fiction] [Science] [Children]

5. Of the following five channels, which channel do you watch the second most often?

   [All News] [All Movies] [Science Fiction] [Science] [Children]

6. Of the following five channels, which channel do you watch the third most often?

   [All News] [All Movies] [Science Fiction] [Science] [Children]

7. How are we doing with the service we provide? (circle one)

   [Great] [Good] [Okay] [Marginal] [Bad]

8. What can we do to make the service better?

Do the following:

1. Copy the file Proj0104 in the Project-01 folder of the CD accompanying the book and rename the copy `Customer Research`. Open `Customer Research` and view the `Questionnaire` table.
2. Compare the Questionnaire table to the questions asked on the survey to determine if additional fields are needed.
3. Close the table and close the database.

Owning a Vending Company

You have purchased a small vending company. When you took possession of the small storage building that served as the office and maintenance facility, the previous owner handed you a set of loose-leaf binders that contained all the information he used to run the company. The binders are labeled Suppliers, Locations, and Machines.

List on paper the information that you think should be included in each of the three categories represented by the loose-leaf binders.

In Project 2, you create a new database containing this information.

Managing a Video Store

You have been hired to be the manager of a local video store. Currently the owners are keeping track of the videos on a large spreadsheet. The spreadsheet lists title, source, purchase date, purchase price, video number, and number of rentals.

List on paper the information that you would include in a database to control the inventory.

In Project 2, you create a database containing this information.

Taking a Home Inventory

As you review your personal insurance, you realize that you don't have a good idea of what you have bought over the years or what you should insure and for how much. Think about what categories would be included in a home inventory database and sketch out a table identifying each of the fields you would use.

In Project 2, you create a database containing this information.

PinPoint Assessment

PinPoint Training

You have completed the project and the associated lessons, as well as the "Checking Your Skills" and "Applying Your Skills" sections. Now use the PinPoint software Evaluation mode to assess your comprehension of the specific exam tasks you have just learned. You can also use the PinPoint Trainer mode and the SHOW ME tutorials to practice these specific exam tasks.

Project 2

Two

Creating a Database

Working with a Database

In this project you will learn the following objectives and their associated Microsoft Exam required activities.

Objectives	Required Activities
➤ Plan the Database Tables	Plan a database
➤ Create a New Database Using a Wizard	
➤ Create a New Database	
➤ Create a New Table	Create a Table
➤ Save a Table Design and Create a Primary Key	
➤ Add Fields	
➤ Edit Fields	
➤ Change Views and Move Fields	Modify the Presentation of a Database Switch Between Views
➤ Delete Fields	

Why Would I Do This?

With Access, you can set up databases for a wide variety of purposes. For example, you may want a database (like the one you create in this project) to keep track of staff training for your company. You can set up various databases to store different sets of related information, and you can create as many databases as you need.

Object
A database element, such as a table, form, or report. An object can also refer to images, spreadsheets, graphs, or other items imported from other applications.

Think of the database as the shell that holds together all the other related *objects*. Within the shell, you can create other objects. The fundamental type of object in an Access database is a table. You use tables to store data and organize the information into a usable structure. You can also create other objects, such as forms and queries. You learn about these other database objects later in this book.

In this project, you learn how to create a database and table from scratch. You also learn how to edit the structure of the table.

Exam Notes

Once you have a general idea of which fields should be included in your database, you must decide how to divide them up into tables.

There are six rules for designing tables that were originally proposed by Dr. E. F. Codd in his 1970 paper entitled 'A Relational Model of Data for Large Shared Data Banks'. This paper and his following work provided the impetus for widespread research into numerous related areas, including database languages, query subsystems, database semantics, locking and recovery, and inferential subsystems.

Normalize
Apply design rules to the tables in a database.

When you apply these rules to your tables you are *normalizing* them. The rules are simplified and paraphrased as follows:

- Rule 1: Fields should be atomic; that is, each piece of data should be broken down as much as possible. For example, rather than creating a field called Name, you would create two fields: one for the first name and the other for the last name.

Primary key
A field that contains a unique value for each record.

- Rules 2 and 3: Each record should contain a unique identifier so that you have a way of safely identifying the record. A Social Security Number is ideal, because no two people have the same one. The unique identifier is called a *primary key*. You may select one of the fields in the table as the primary key if that field would never contain duplicate values for different records. An example of a good choice would be the social security number field. If none of the fields are suitable, the program can add a counter field that will automatically assign a unique number to each record as it is entered.
- Rule 4: The primary key should be short, stable, and simple. Addresses and even last names may change several times during a person's life. This is why governments and companies assign permanent identification numbers.

- Rule 5: Every other field in the record should supply additional information about the person or thing that is uniquely identified by the primary key. For example, a table that contains data about employees may include a field that indicates the employee's supervisor. It would be inappropriate to include a field that holds the supervisor's phone number. Consider what would happen if the supervisor changed phone number. Instead of changing it in one place, you would have to change it for each employee who reported to him/her.

- Rule 6: Information in the table should not appear in more than one place. For example, if you tried to create a table of the different committees in an organization and had fields with names like Chairperson, Member1, Member2, and Member3, the same person could be the chair of one committee and Member1 in another. If that person changed his name, you would have to change it in more than one place. Avoid numbered field names like those shown in this example.

Relational database
A database that has two or more tables that are linked together.

In order to conform to these rules, you may need to create more than one table in a database and connect them together. This is called a *relational database* and is demonstrated throughout this project.

Fortunately, you do not need to understand all of this in order to get started, and the application of these rules will become evident as you use the example tables.

Lesson 1: Creating a New Database

Remember that the table is the object in which you actually store and define the structure for your data and the database is the shell that houses all of the related tables and other objects. In your Address database in Project 1, "Getting Started with Access 97," you had a table for contacts. You might also include another table for equipment, and yet another table for employees.

Creating a New Database with the Database Wizard

In this exercise, you create a database using an Access wizard and then create another database on your own. The wizard has templates for common types of databases and is a good place to start to create a quick database. You can also get an idea of how a full-featured database will look. But like most templates, they seldom have everything that you need so it is still necessary to understand how to create your own database objects.

To Use the Database Wizard

1 Start Access and select the Database Wizard option (see Figure 2.1).

continues

To Use the Database Wizard (continued)

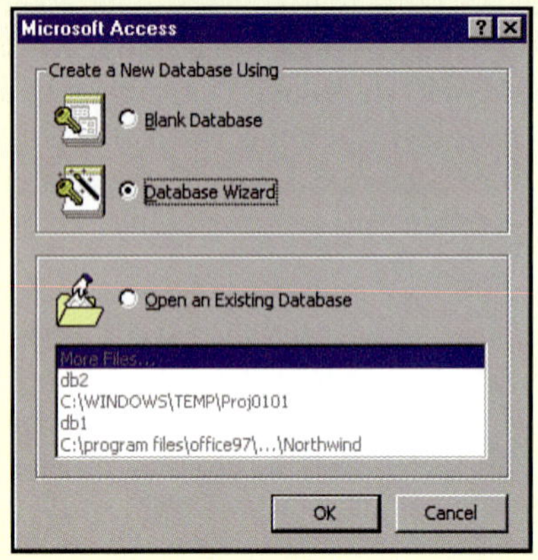

Figure 2.1
Using a Database Wizard is a quick way to get up and running with a new database.

2 Click OK, then click the Databases tab in the New database window to view available templates for databases. All the templates shown have a wand and key displayed across a table. The wand and key indicate that the template is a wizard template (see Figure 2.2).

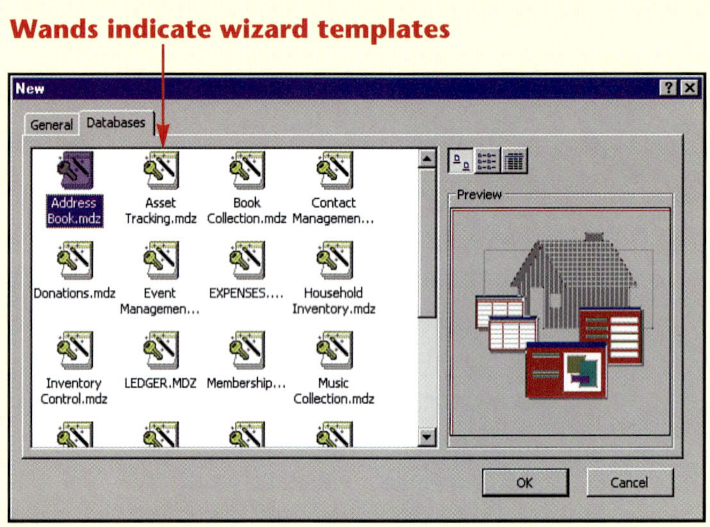

Figure 2.2
Select a Database Wizard type that best suits your new database needs.

3 Select the Music Collection Wizard and click OK.

The File New Database dialog box opens.

4 Select your disk or folder in the Save in box and click Create.

The next wizard dialog box appears and explains what the wizard does.

5 Click Next.

The wizard then displays a list of tables in the database, along with their fields. Optional fields are shown in italics (see Figure 2.3).

Access

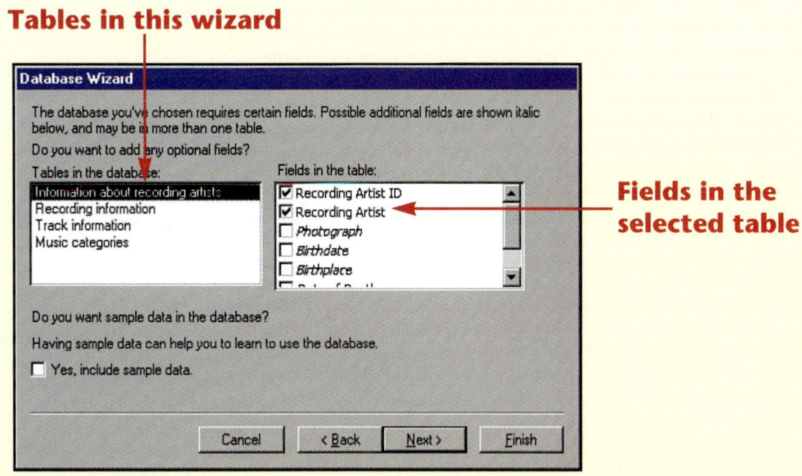

Figure 2.3
You can add optional fields to your tables, but you cannot deselect fields from the tables while using the wizard.

6. **Click the check box `Yes, include sample data` and then click Next.**

7. **Select the `Colorful2` style for your database and click Next.**

8. **Select the Bold report style for your database and click Next.**

9. **Type `My Music Collection` in the title box.**

   It is possible to include a picture in your database by clicking the check box and the Picture button. You learn more about pictures and other objects in Project 8, "Managing Data and Files."

10. **Click Next, then click Finish.**

    The program creates a database and includes sample data.

11. **The Main Switchboard appears for your newly created database (see Figure 2.4). The switchboard acts as a menu to your database. Switchboards are a great interface for end users.**

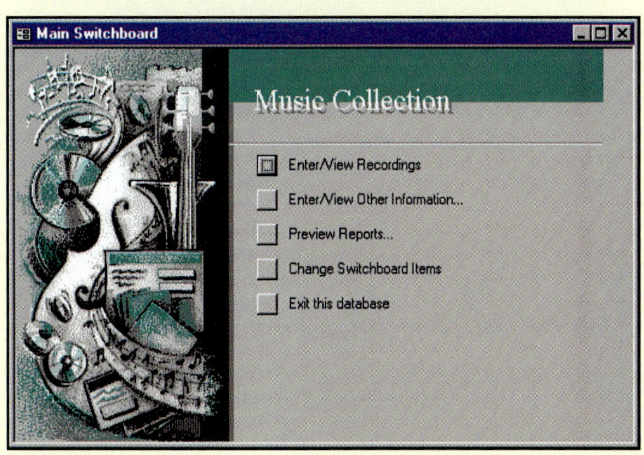

Figure 2.4
The switchboard makes it easy for users to navigate a database.

12. **Click on the some of the buttons on the switchboard, then click on the button labeled Return to Main Switchboard.**

continues

To Use the Database Wizard (continued)

⓭ **Click the button labeled Exit this database.**

The database closes, but Access remains open.

⓮ **Close Access.**

When you create databases using wizards, you can see various uses of tables, forms, queries, and reports. It's a good idea to explore these databases as they can help you when you are planning and designing databases for use by others.

It's tempting to create one big database that includes many tables to meet many different needs, but it's a better idea to create smaller databases, each of which is dedicated to a particular function. Doing so makes managing and using each database much easier. You can relate these smaller databases to one another later, if necessary.

Creating a New Database from a Blank Database

In this exercise, you create a new database to keep track of the personal computer software training received by your staff. You will start with a blank database, which will probably take more time than using a wizard, but which gives you much more control over the database design.

To Create a New Database

❶ **Launch Access.**

The Microsoft Access dialog box is displayed (see Figure 2.5).

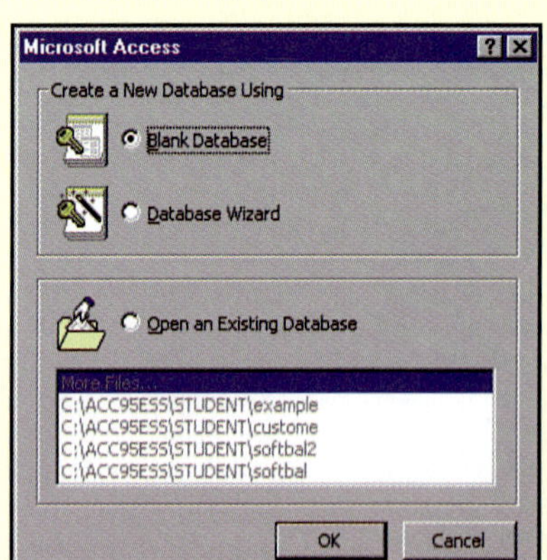

Figure 2.5
The Microsoft Access dialog box enables you to open an existing database or create a new one.

2 Click the Blank Database option, and then click OK.

Access displays the File New Database dialog box. Access suggests a default name (db1) for the new database; however, you can assign a more descriptive name here, and you can also tell Access where you want to store the database.

3 In the File name text box, type `Training`.

This is the name you want to use for the new database (see Figure 2.6). After you name the database the first time, you won't have to do it again. As you add or edit records, Access updates the database automatically. As you add new objects, however, you have to save each of them. When you add a table, for example, you have to save it. Access then updates the database to incorporate this new table name.

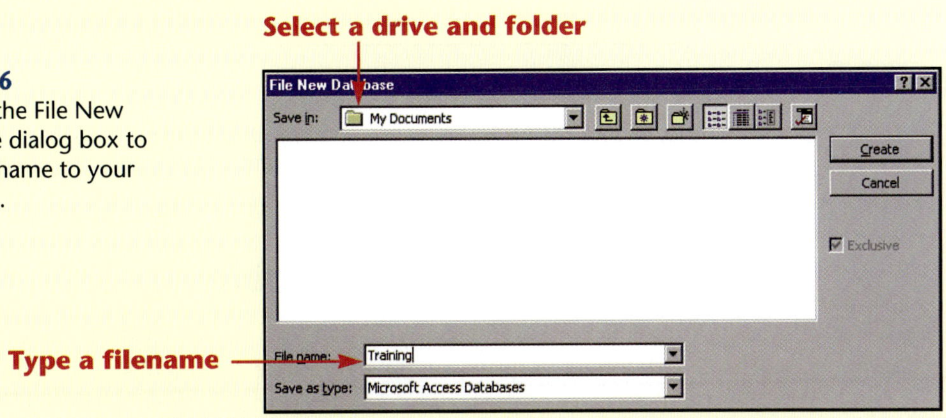

Figure 2.6
You use the File New Database dialog box to assign a name to your database.

4 Click the list arrow next to the Save in box and select your drive or folder.

Access suggests a default drive and folder for saving the new database. Your instructor may want you to store the database on another drive or folder; check with your instructor for specific instructions.

5 Click the Create button.

Access displays the database window for your new database. The name of the database is displayed in the title bar of the database window, as shown in Figure 2.7. Notice that the window is blank because you have not created any database objects (tables, queries, and so on). Keep the Training database open to use in the next lesson. In that lesson, you learn how to add a new table to the database.

continues

To Create a New Database (continued)

Figure 2.7
The name you assign to your database is displayed in the title bar of the database window.

Database name

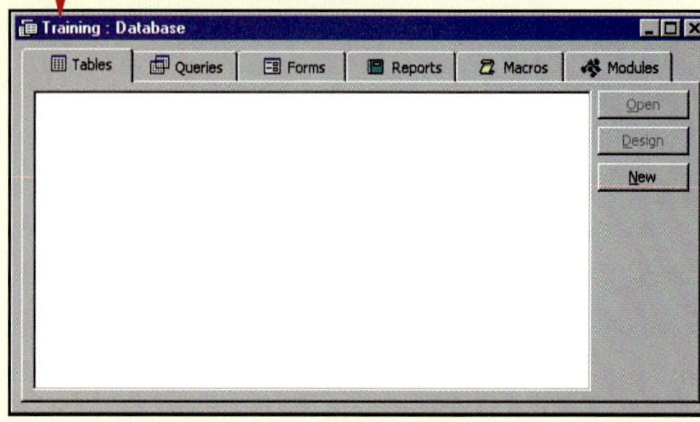

Inside Stuff

There is usually more than one way to perform each function in Access. For example, to create a new database, you can press Ctrl+N, select New Database from the File menu, or click the New Database button on the toolbar.

Access

Lesson 2: Creating a New Table

After you create your database, you can add tables to it to store your information. A database is built on one or more tables, each of which holds a distinct set of information. The table defines the structure of the data—what pieces of data you enter and in what order. You should spend some time planning the structure of your database. How many fields do you need? What are their data types? If necessary, you can add fields later if you need them, but it is very important to map out the fundamental structure of the table before you get started.

Building a database without a plan is like building a house without a blueprint. The more work you invest in the initial design, the less time you spend in patchwork repairs later. Design your table structures first so that you can immediately put the database to work with confidence.

When you create a new table, you can add any fields you want. Remember that the table consists of records (one set of information—such as the name, address, and phone number for one person) and fields. Fields are the individual pieces of information that together make up a record; for example, an address is a field. To add a field, you type a field name and then select a data type. Table 2.1 explains the various data types you can use. You can also type a description for the field and set field properties. You learn how to set field properties in Project 7, "Customizing Fields and Tables."

Table 2.1 Data Types and What They Mean

Data Type	Explanation
Text	The default data type. You can enter up to 255 numbers or letters.
Memo	This type of field is useful when you want to include sentences or paragraphs in the field—for example, a long product description. This type of field is not limited by size.
Number	You can enter only numbers.
Date/Time	You can enter only dates or times.
Currency	You can enter numbers. Access formats the entry as currency. If you type 12.5, for example, Access displays it as $12.50.
Counter	Access enters a value that is incremented automatically with each new record added to a table.
Yes/No	A Yes/No field type limits your data to one of two conditions. You can enter only Yes or No, True or False, or On or Off. For example, you may have a Sent Christmas Card field in your address database that would work best as a Yes/No field.
OLE Object	You can insert *OLE* objects, graphics, or other data.

Object Linking and Embedding (OLE)
A set of standards that enables you to insert objects, such as pictures or spreadsheets, from one document created with one application into documents created with another application.

In this lesson, you create a table containing fields for first names, last names, and department names.

To Create a New Table

1 Click the Tables tab in the Training database window.

2 Click the New button.

Access displays the New Table dialog box (see Figure 2.8). You can choose between two views of a blank database, or you can launch one of three wizards to create a new table.

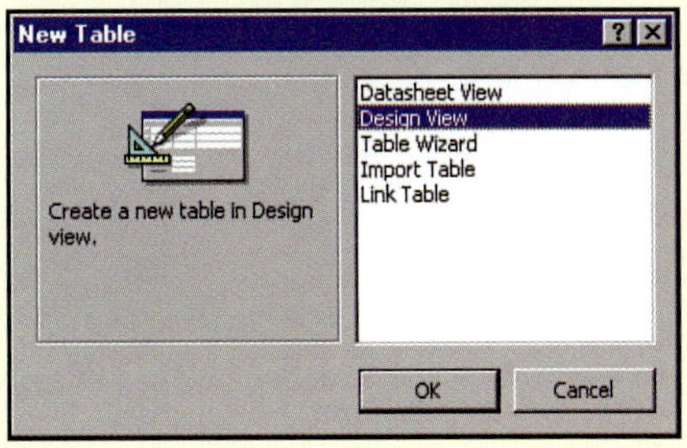

Figure 2.8
The New Table dialog box offers five choices for creating a database.

Design view
The view of the table you use when you are creating or changing fields. You see columns for the field name, data type, and description.

3 Select `Design View` and click OK.

You see the table in *Design view* with the default name of Table1 (see Figure 2.9). The new table, as you can see, contains no fields. To add fields to the table, you must first enter the field names, data types,

continues

To Create a New Table (continued)

and descriptions. The blinking insertion point is displayed in the first row of the Field Name column. Here you type the first field name.

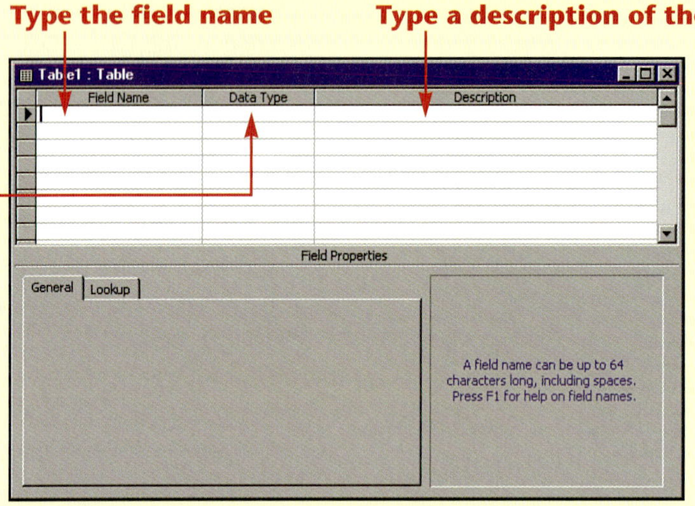

Figure 2.9
The blank table in Design view.

4 Type `First Name` and press Enter.

Access enters the field name for the first field. In the lower half of the window, Access displays the field properties you can set. Access moves the insertion point to the Data Type column so that you can choose the type of data you want the field to contain. The most common data type is Text, which is the default. You can click the down arrow (which is displayed when you move to the Data Type column) to display a drop-down list of data types. For First Name, leave the data type as the default, which is Text.

5 Press Enter.

Text is accepted as the data type, and Access moves the insertion point to the Description column.

6 Type `First name of staff member` and press Enter.

Access enters the field description and moves the insertion point to the next row (see Figure 2.10). The description column comes in handy when you are in *Datasheet view* and enter a value in the First Name field. The field description will be displayed in the status bar. You are now ready to enter the next field name.

Datasheet view
The view of the table you use when you enter or edit records. The field names you enter appear in the first row, followed by any records you have entered in the table.

7 Type `Last Name` and press Enter twice.

This enters the name for the field, accepts the default Text as the field type, and moves the insertion point to the Description column.

Access

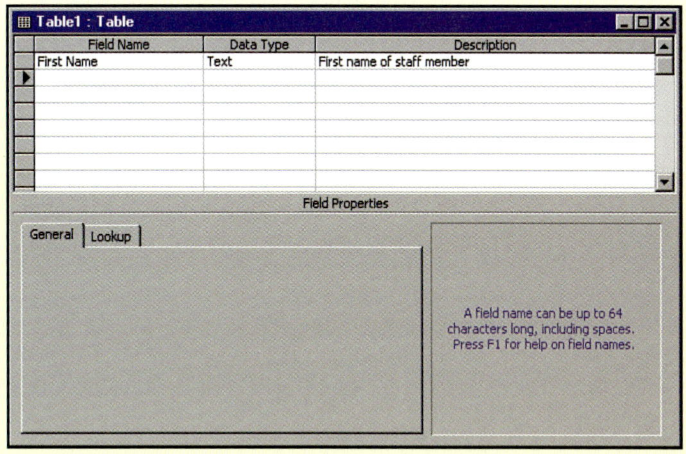

Figure 2.10
The first field of the Table1 table.

8 Type `Last name of staff member` and press Enter.

As before, Access enters the field description for this second field and moves the insertion point to the next row so that you can add another field. Adding a field description is optional. If you do include a description, however, it is displayed in the status bar whenever you are in Datasheet view or Form view and place the insertion point in that field. The information in the status bar provides the user with a more complete description of the purpose of the field.

9 Type `Department` and press Enter twice.

Again, this step enters the field name, accepts Text as the data type, and moves the insertion point to the Description column.

10 Type `Staff member's department` and press Enter.

This is the description for the third field of your table, as shown in Figure 2.11. By adding these fields to the database table, you have taken the first steps toward creating a database to track staff training. Keep both this table and the Training database open. You learn how to save the table in the next lesson.

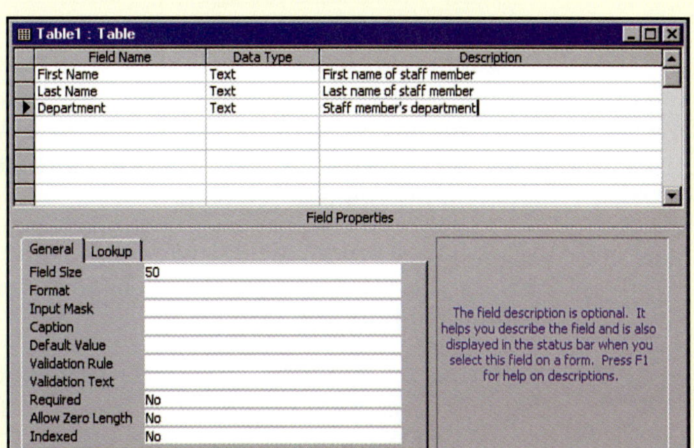

Figure 2.11
The Design view of a database table containing three fields.

Exam Notes

You can create a field name using up to 64 characters. Try to use names that are short but meaningful (long names make the system work harder). You can use any combination of letters, numbers, spaces, and characters, with a few exceptions: periods (.), exclamation points (!), single quotation marks ('), and brackets ([ ]) cannot appear anywhere in the name. Spaces are allowed but not as the first character of the field name.

You can also use the Tab key in place of the Enter key when adding fields, choosing field types, and entering descriptions in the table Design view.

Lesson 3: Saving a Table Design and Creating a Primary Key

The first time you save the table's design, you are prompted to assign a name. After you save and name the table the first time, it takes only a moment to save changes whenever necessary. If you make changes to the design, such as adding new fields, you must save the changes to the design.

If you have problems...

If you try to close the table without saving it, Access reminds you to save your work. Click the Yes button to save. Click the Cancel button to return to the table in Design view without saving.

In addition to saving new tables, you should assign or create a primary key field for each table in your database. Each record's primary key field contains a value that uniquely identifies it; no two records can have the same value in their primary key field. Examples of good primary key fields are things like Social Security numbers, student ID numbers, or automobile part numbers. You can use this feature to your advantage when you need to establish a **relationship** between one table and another.

Jargon Watch

The connection between the two tables is called a **relationship**. This relationship connects a field in one table to a field in a second table. Relationships allow you to draw information from more than one table at a time for forms or reports. This topic will be discussed in much more detail in Project 7.

Index
A location guide built by Access for all primary key fields that helps speed up searching and sorting for that field. Indexes can also be created for other fields, as long as they are not OLE or Memo fields.

Assigning a primary key also ensures that you won't enter the same information for the primary key field more than once in a table (because it won't accept a duplicate entry). Because Access automatically builds an *index* for primary keys, it can easily search for information and sort tables based on the primary key field.

If you have a unique field, such as an ID number in your table, you can use that as the primary key field. Or you can have Access create a simple counter field.

In this lesson, you have Access create a counter field to use as the primary key field because you cannot ensure that fields such as First Name, Last Name, and Department will contain unique information.

To Save a Table Design and Create a Primary Key

1 In the Training database, with Table1 open, click the Save button on the toolbar.

You could also open the File menu and choose the Save command. You see the Save As dialog box, which prompts you to type a name for the table (see Figure 2.12). As you can see, the default name that Access provides doesn't tell you much, so you want to provide a more descriptive name.

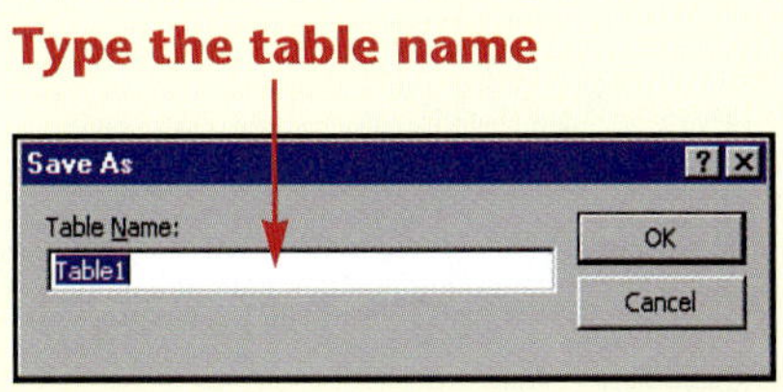

Figure 2.12
You must give the table a name the first time you save it.

2 Type `P C Software` and click OK.

This is the name you want to assign to the table for this example. The next time you see the list of tables in the database window, this name will be displayed. The size of a table name isn't limited to eight characters. You can use up to 64 characters, including spaces.

Access displays a reminder that no primary key has been defined (see Figure 2.13). You are not required to use a primary key, but it is a good idea to include one. An easy way to create a primary key field is to have Access create a counter field that automatically assigns a different number to each record in your table.

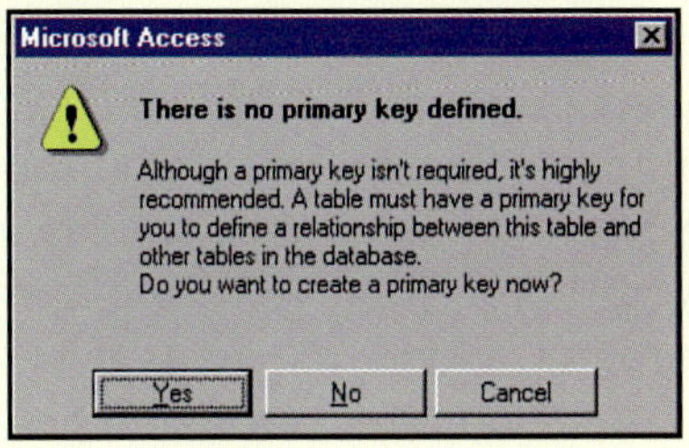

Figure 2.13
A dialog box warns you that you haven't defined a primary key.

3 Click the Yes button.

Access saves the table and adds a counter field named ID with an AutoNumber data type. This is now the primary key field. Access automatically places sequential numbers in this field as you add new records. Your table should look like the one shown in Figure 2.14. Notice the key symbol in the *row selector* for the ID field. The key indicates that the ID field is the primary key field for this table.

Row selector
The gray area to the left of a field in Design view. Clicking a box in this area selects the entire row.

Keep the P C Software table of the Training database open. In the next lesson, you learn how to add new fields to the table.

continues

To Save a Table Design and Create a Primary Key (continued)

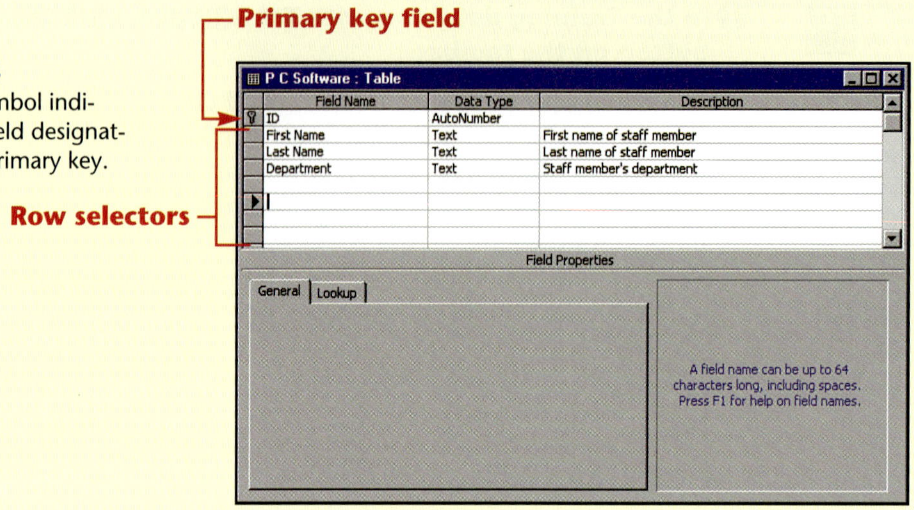

Figure 2.14
The key symbol indicates the field designated as the primary key.

Inside Stuff

To make another field in the database the primary key, click the row selector for the field you want. Then click the Primary Key button on the toolbar. You can also open the Edit menu and choose the Primary Key command. The primary key field is indicated by the key symbol in the row selector.

To save a table quickly, press Ctrl+S.

Lesson 4: Adding Fields

What happens if you decide you want to track more information than you included in your original P C Software table? You can add new fields to track this additional data. Keep in mind, however, that if you already have added records to the table, any new fields in those existing records will be empty until you type information into them. Other database objects such as queries, forms, or reports that are based on the table will not be automatically updated to include the new fields. Since you have not yet created any other database objects that use this table, this is a good time to make changes.

In this lesson, you add seven new fields to your P C Software table—one for training expense, one for employee number, one for employee's supervisor, and one each for four of the Microsoft Office software applications. Try adding these fields now.

To Add Fields

1. **With the P C Software table of the Training database still displayed in Design view, position the insertion point in the next blank row of the P C Software table.**

This is the row in which you want to enter the new field name. The black arrow should be displayed next to this row, as shown in Figure 2.15.

Figure 2.15
The black arrow indicates the current row.

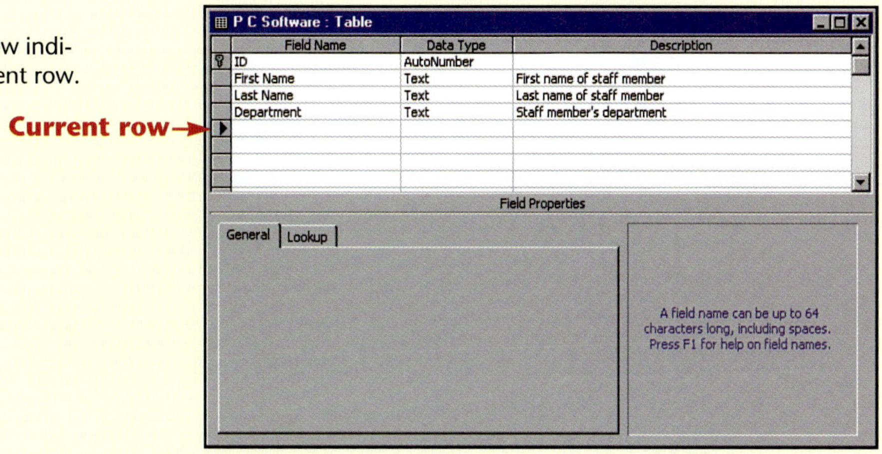

2 Type `Cost` and press ↵Enter twice.

This enters the name of the field, accepts Text as the data type (it will be changed later), and moves to the Description column.

3 Type `Cost of training` and press ↵Enter.

This is the description for the new field. When you press ↵Enter, Access moves the insertion point to the next row.

4 Type `Employee Number` and press ↵Enter three times.

By pressing ↵Enter three times you enter a name for this field, accept Text as the data type, and skip the Description column. Again, the insertion point is in position to add a new field to the table.

5 Type `Supervisor` and press ↵Enter three times.

Once again, you have added another new field to the table, accepting Text as the data type, skipping the description, and moving to the next row.

6 Type `Word` and press ↵Enter three times.

7 Type `Excel` and press ↵Enter three times.

8 Type `PowerPoint` and press ↵Enter three times.

9 Type `Access` and press ↵Enter three times.

You have now added seven additional fields to the table. Your table should look similar to the one in Figure 2.16, although you may have to scroll up or down to see all of the fields.

continues

To Add Fields (continued)

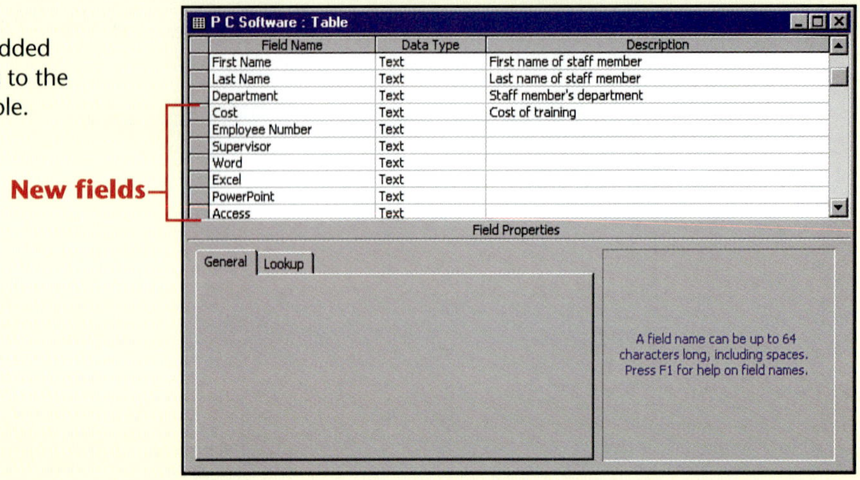

Figure 2.16
You have now added seven new fields to the P C Software table.

⑩ **Save your work and leave both the P C Software table and the Training database open.**

In the next lesson, you learn another way to alter the structure of your P C Software table.

Lesson 5: Editing Fields

As you create your database, you may want to modify the structure. For example, you may want to change field names, choose a different data type, or edit the description. You make these changes in Design view.

Changing the field name or description does not have any effect on the data you already have entered in the table. Changing the field name may have an unintended effect, however; if any forms, queries, or reports refer to the field name, you must manually change the reference to reflect the new name. Otherwise, these database objects will no longer work as they did before.

Changing the field type may have an effect on the data in your table. For example, if you type text into a field and then change that field to a Yes/No field, you may encounter problems. Access prompts you to let you know when changes in the field type are made and when they might result in a loss of data. Be sure that you want to make the change before you confirm it.

In this lesson, you edit the name of a field, add a description, and change the field type.

To Edit Fields

❶ In the Design view of the P C Software, position the pointer on the word Cost (the fourth field name) and double-click the mouse.

This selects the word you want to change as shown in Figure 2.17.

Figure 2.17
To change a field name, you first select it.

Selected text

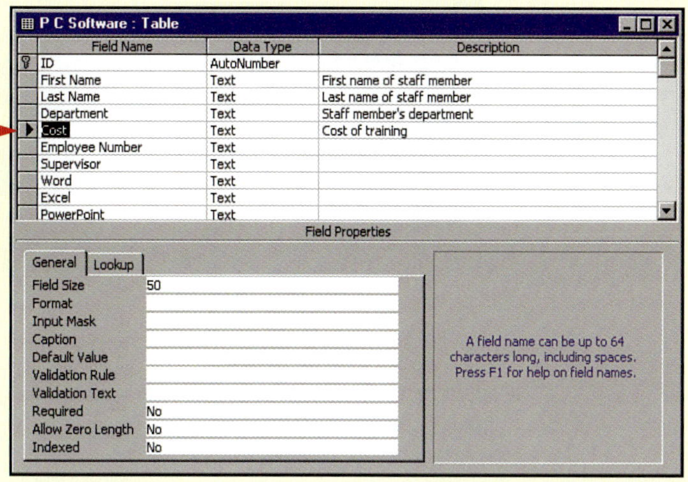

❷ Type `Training Expense`.

The existing highlighted text is replaced with the new text.

❸ Click in the Description column for the Supervisor field.

After moving the insertion point to this field, you can add a description.

❹ Type `Reporting Supervisor`.

The description that you enter provides information about what is stored in this field. Now try changing the data type for one of the fields in the table.

❺ Click in the Data Type column for the Training Expense field.

This is the field you want to change. Notice that a list arrow is displayed, which indicates a list of data type options is available.

❻ Click the list arrow.

You see a list of choices, as shown in Figure 2.18.

❼ From the list, click `Currency`.

You have changed the data type to a type that is more appropriate for the information in this field. All data in this field is now displayed with a dollar sign, commas (if needed), and two decimal places.

continues

To Edit Fields (continued)

Figure 2.18
When you click the down arrow in the Data Type column, a list of data types is displayed.

List of data types

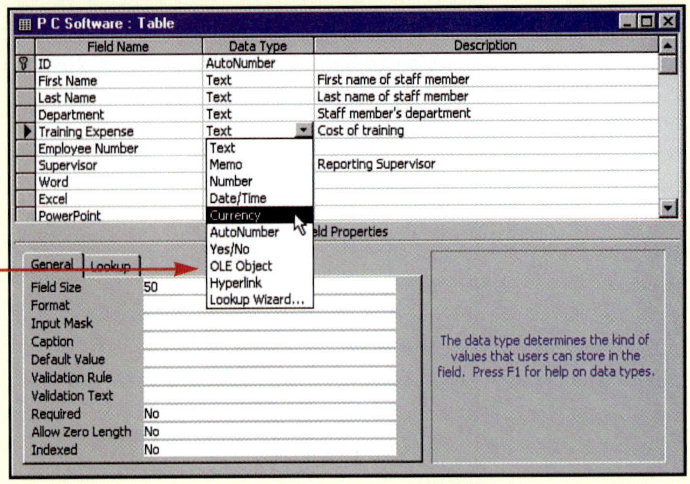

8 Click the Save button on the toolbar to save your work.

Leave both the P C Software table and the Training database open. In the next lesson, you learn how to move fields from one part of the table to another.

Access

Inside Stuff

If you know the name of the data type you want to enter in the Data Type column, you don't have to use the mouse to open the drop-down list. Instead, if the Data Type field is highlighted, you can type the first letter or two of the data type you want. Access fills in the rest of the characters for you. When you type the letters `Cu`, for example, Access fills in `Currency`.

Lesson 6: Changing Views and Moving Fields

In addition to changing the name and data type, you can change the order in which fields are displayed in your database. When you enter records, you may want the fields in a different order. In the P C Software table, for example, you may find it easier to enter the employee's number after you enter the employee's name. You may also want to move the ID or counter field to the end because you never have to enter anything in this field.

In this lesson, you first look at the table in Datasheet view—the view you use to enter records. You then change back to Design view to rearrange the fields.

To Change Views and Move Fields

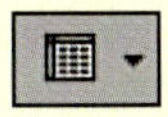

1 Click the View button on the toolbar to change from the current Design view to the Datasheet view.

Notice that the View button looks different in the Datasheet view than it did in the Design view. The icon on the View button indicates the view that would be displayed if you click it.

If you have problems...

If the Table Design toolbar is not showing, choose View, Toolbars, Table Design from the menu.

This changes your view of the database to Datasheet view (see Figure 2.19). Datasheet view is the view you use to enter, sort, and edit the records in the database.

The datasheet you see is blank, except for the field names, because the table doesn't contain records yet. You learn how to work with records in Project 3, "Entering and Editing Data." In Datasheet view, you cannot make any changes to the structure of the table.

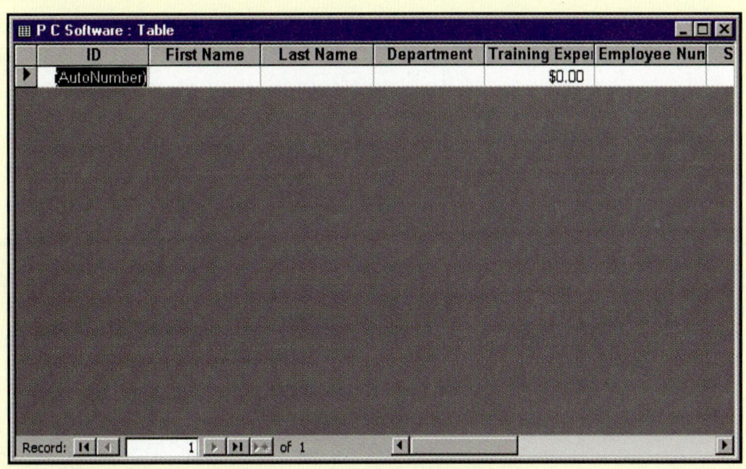

Figure 2.19 Viewing the P C Software table in Datasheet view.

2 Click the View button on the toolbar.

This step returns you to Design view so that you can make changes.

3 Click the row selector for the Employee Number field.

This step selects the field you want to move. Notice that the entire row is highlighted (see Figure 2.20). You move this field so that it immediately follows the Last Name field.

continues

To Change Views and Move Fields (continued)

Figure 2.20
You click the row selector to select the row you want to move.

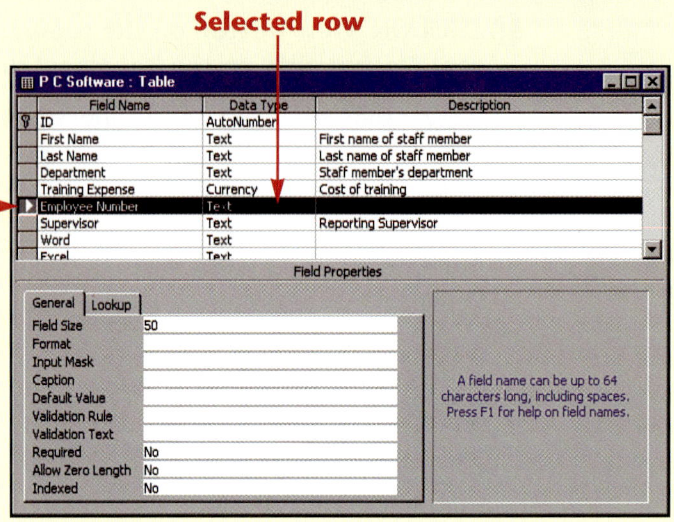

4 Click the mouse button and hold it down. Drag the row to its new position under Last Name and release the mouse button.

As you drag, a small gray box is displayed under the mouse pointer, along with a horizontal line showing where the row will be placed. When you release the mouse button, Access places the row in its new spot (see Figure 2.21).

Figure 2.21
The Employee Number field in its new location.

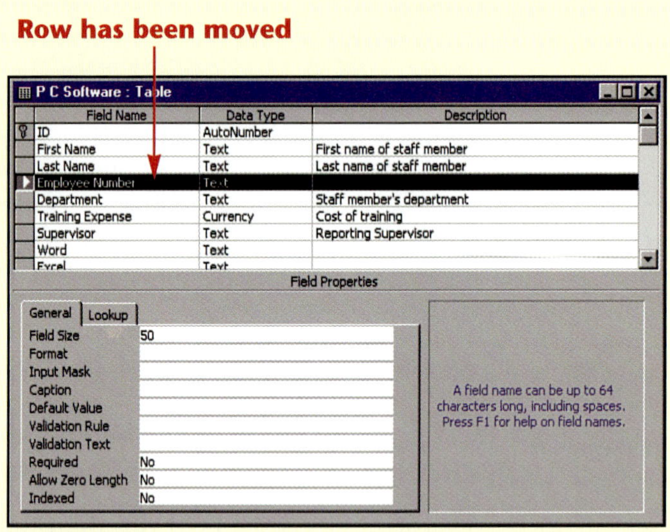

If you have problems...

If the field that you move is displayed in the wrong place after you drag and drop it, don't worry. Just move the field again.

If you see a double-headed arrow as you try to position the mouse, the mouse pointer isn't in the correct spot. If the double-headed arrow is displayed, Access thinks that you want to resize the row height or the design window.

If, when you drag, you accidentally resize rather than move your row, click the Undo button (or open the Edit menu and choose the Undo command). The Undo command reverses your most recent action, such as moving a row. Only the most recent change can be undone.

If your window is too small to see all of the rows, maximize the window by clicking on the Maximize button in the upper-right corner of the table window.

5. **Select the ID row and drag it down to the first empty row of the table.**

   This step moves the ID or counter field to the last position in the table. Next, try undoing the move.

6. **Click the Undo button.**

   With Access, you can undo some of the changes you make to the database. In this example, however, you decide that you really do want the ID field at the end of the table.

7. **Select the ID row again and drag it back to the end of the table.**

   This moves the ID field back to the end of the table.

8. **Click the Save button to save your work. Keep both the P C Software table and the Training database open in the Design view.**

   In the next lesson, you learn how to delete fields from your table structure.

Lesson 7: Deleting Fields

Another significant change that you can make to the structure of your P C Software table is to remove fields you no longer need. Suppose that you decide you don't really need a field for the supervisor. Instead of having it take up space in the table design, you can delete the field.

Keep in mind that deleting a field from your table also deletes all the data in that field. Because this may not be what you intended, Access displays a warning that asks you to confirm the change. Read the warning carefully and be sure that you want to delete all the data before you delete the field. If you had already created other database objects such as forms or reports that use this field, they would have to be revised individually.

To Delete a Field

1 In the P C Software table of the Training database, click the row selector for the Supervisor field.

Access highlights the entire Supervisor row, showing that the Supervisor field is selected. This is the field you want to delete.

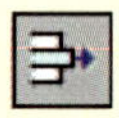

2 Click the Delete Rows button to delete the row from your table.

Access removes the field from the database table and deletes any data that was in that field. If you had entered any data into this field in the Datasheet view, Access would warn you that the data would be lost.

3 Click the Save button to save your changes.

4 Close the P C Software table by clicking the Close button in the upper-right corner of the table window.

5 Close the Training database by clicking the Close button in the upper-right corner of the database window.

If you are finished with your session at the computer, click the Close button in the upper-right corner of the Access window. Otherwise, continue with the sections "Checking Your Skills" and "Applying Your Skills" in this project.

Project Summary

To	Do This
Create a new database using a wizard	Launch Access and click Database Wizard. Follow the directions.
Create a new database	Launch Access and click Blank Database, then click OK. Type a filename and select the drive or folder location for the file. Click the Create button.
Create a new table	In the database window, select the Tables tab. Click the New button, choose Design View, and click OK. Enter the field name, choose the data type, and enter a description for the field.
Save a table	Click the Save button. Type a name for the table (on the first save only). Click OK.
Create a primary key	Use the counter field by clicking Yes when prompted by the save sequence; or use the row selector to select a field and then click the Primary Key button.

To	Do This
Add fields	Work in Design view. Go to the next blank row and insert the new field name, data type, and description for each field to be added.
Edit fields	Work in Design view. Go to the field name, data type, or description you want to edit. Select the information you want to change, and type the new information. Use the drop-down box in the Data Type column to change the type of data allowed for that field.
Move fields	Work in Design view. Use the row selector to select the row you want to move. Click and drag the row to a new location and then release the mouse button.
Delete fields	Work in Design view. Use the row selector to select the row you want to delete. Click the Delete Row button.

Checking Your Skills

True/False

For each of the following, check *T* or *F* to indicate whether the statement is true or false.

__T __F **1.** You can include only eight characters in a database name in Access 97.

__T __F **2.** You can include only eight characters in a table name.

__T __F **3.** The most common data type is Text, the default.

__T __F **4.** You must have a primary key field.

__T __F **5.** You can enter only numbers in a Number field.

__T __F **6.** After you save your table structure, you cannot edit or change it.

__T __F **7.** A Yes/No field type limits your data to one of two conditions.

__T __F **8.** When planning a database you should gather information from the people who will use the database to make sure you understand their needs.

__T __F **9.** It is best to build one large database with everything in one table.

__T __F **10.** If you add a new field to a database that already has data in other fields, the new field will be empty until you enter the information.

Multiple Choice

Circle the letter of the correct answer for each of the following questions.

1. Which of the following is not one of the ways you can create a new database?
   a. Click the Open menu and choose the New Database command.
   b. Open the File menu and choose the New Database command.
   c. Click the New Database button on the toolbar.
   d. Press Ctrl+N.

2. Which of the following is not a valid data type?
   a. Currency
   b. Yes/No
   c. Text
   d. Text & Numbers

3. How do you select a row in Design view of a table?
   a. Drag across the entire row.
   b. Click the row selector next to the row.
   c. Click the Select Row button on the toolbar.
   d. Press Ctrl+R.

4. If you let the program create a primary key for you, what field name does it use?
   a. Counter
   b. ID
   c. MDB
   d. Primary

5. In table Design view, how do you select a data type?
   a. Open the Edit menu and choose the type you want.
   b. Click the Data Type button on the toolbar.
   c. Press Ctrl+D.
   d. Select the data type from the list.

6. In table Design view, a black arrow appears on the row selector of which of the following?
   a. a row that has an error in the data
   b. the primary key
   c. a duplicate field definition
   d. the row you are editing

7. In Design view, how can you tell that a field is the primary key?
   a. The status bar displays text when you have the field selected.
   b. There is no way to tell in Design view.
   c. The field name is underlined.
   d. The key symbol appears on the row selector button.

8. Why is the Description entry in table Design view handy?
   a. It appears in the status bar when you enter data in the field in Datasheet view.
   b. It appears as a pop-up label when you place the mouse pointer on the field in Datasheet view.
   c. Access uses it to automatically test the data you enter into the field.

Access

d. It serves no purpose at all.

9. To change the order of fields in a table in Design view, you select the field and then do which of the following?

a. Press Ctrl+O, entering the destination in the dialog box that appears.

b. Drag the field to the new location.

c. Press Alt as you select the new location.

d. Press Ctrl as you select the new location and then select Swap from the shortcut menu.

10. Field names are limited to how many characters?

a. 255

b. 50

c. 64

d. 8

Completion

In the blank provided, write the correct answer for each of the following statements.

1. A(n) _____________ is a field that contains a unique value for each record in the table.
2. A(n) _____________ data type field is useful when you want to include sentences or paragraphs in the field.
3. Use _____________ view to enter records in a table.
4. Use _____________ view to change the table structure.
5. To select a row in Design view, click the _____________.
6. Table names are limited to _____________ characters.
7. To add a field in table Design view, type the field name in the _____________ box and press ↵Enter.
8. Changing a field name or description has no effect on the _____________.
9. To save an object quickly in Access, press the keyboard shortcut _____________.
10. The _____________ data type can hold up to 255 digits or characters.

Matching

In the blank next to each of the following terms or phrases, write the letter of the corresponding term or phrase. (Note that some letters may be used more than once.)

a. View button	______	1. A set of standards for inserting objects
b. Design	______	2. Appears on the status bar in Datasheet view
c. counter	______	3. A field that doesn't contain duplicate values

d. OLE

e. square brackets ([])

f. Text

g. row selector

h. field description

i. primary key

j. Undo button

_____ 4. Button at the left end of the toolbar that changes depending on the current view

_____ 5. Highlights the entire row

_____ 6. Used to reverse the last action some of the time

_____ 7. An automatically incremented field

_____ 8. View used to change the structure of a table

_____ 9. The default data type

_____ 10. Characters that cannot be used in field names

Applying Your Skills

Practice

The following exercises enable you to practice the skills you have learned in this project. Take a few minutes to work through these exercises now. If you are saving your files on a floppy disk, you may need to start with an empty disk to assure that you have enough room for all the files.

Keeping Track of Your Books

Suppose you want to set up a database to keep track of your books. Build a database and table for your personal library that enable you to keep track of the author, title, type of book (reference, mystery, biography, and so on), and track the publication date of each book.

To create a books database, complete the following steps:

1. Create a new database named `Library`.
2. Create a database table. Include fields for the author's last name, author's first name, book title, type of book, and year of publication. (Use a text field for the publication year; you usually don't have the day and month necessary for a date field.)
3. Set the book title field as the primary key field.
4. Save the database table and name it `Books`.
5. Close the database.

Creating a Music Store Database

As the owner and business manager of Sound Byte Music, one of your most important tasks in setting up the business is building a comprehensive database for your store. Create a new database for your business in which you can store all the tables, queries, and forms that you need for managing Sound Byte Music. Start building the database by creating a table to keep track of the record companies you deal with, including company names, addresses, phone numbers, and contacts.

To create the music store database, complete the following steps:

1. Create a new database and name it `SBMusic`.
2. Create a new table and add the following fields. All the fields can be text fields:

    `Record Company`

    `Contact Name`

    `Address`

    `City`

    `State`

    `ZIP Code`

    `Phone`

3. Set the Record Company field as the primary key field.
4. Save the table and name it `Suppliers`.
5. Close the database.

Creating a Database to Inventory Personal Computers

Whenever a company wants to upgrade its software, it must determine whether its computers are capable of running and storing the new, more demanding version. Having a list of equipment is useful in helping you determine which machines may need to be upgraded as well.

To create the personal computer inventory database, complete the following steps:

1. Create a new database named `PC`.
2. Create a table and include the fields that you identified in Project 1.
3. Choose a key field, such as inventory code number.
4. Save the table and name it `PC Hardware`.
5. Create a table named `Vendor` and include the fields that you identified in Project 1.
6. Choose a key field, such as the vendor's name.
7. Close the database.

Getting a Helping Hand

Because software is constantly changing, you need a way to learn new software programs and where to get help. This exercise takes you to the appropriate help topics for the material covered in this project.

Exploring the World of Alaska

Now that you have an idea of how to add fields to a database, you decide to add two fields to the Alaska database. These fields are to help you keep track of photographs that you've received or scanned into your computer. In order to assure that you are starting with a correctly functioning database, you copy and rename a new file for each project. That way, a simple mistake in one of the early projects will not affect your later work.

To add fields to the Alaska database, complete the following steps:

1. Copy the database named Proj0201 from the Project-02 folder on the CD to your work area and rename it `Alaska2`.
2. Open the `Geography` table in Design view.
3. Select the ID field and move it to the bottom of the list of fields.
4. Place the insertion point in the ID field name box.
5. Click the Insert Row button on the toolbar. If you do not have the Insert Row button on your toolbar, you can choose Insert, Rows from the menu. A blank row appears before the ID field.
6. Enter the field name `Picture` in the field name box and press Tab twice.
7. Enter the field description `File name of picture` in the field description box and press Tab.
8. Add a new row below the Picture field.
9. In the new field location, enter the field name `Source` and the description `Where the picture came from or who took it.`
10. Exit the table and save your changes.

Challenge

The following challenges enable you to use your problem-solving skills. Take time to work through these exercises now.

Creating a List of Club Members

Create a database to track information about members of an organization or club. Pick a name for the database that describes it. Create a table that includes fields such as `Name`, `Social Security Number`, `Street`, `City`, `State`, `ZIP`, and `Phone`. Do not enter club member information at this time. Save the database and its table, using meaningful names. You use this database in similar exercises in Projects 3–8.

Access

Doing Customer Research

You have viewed the database started by the previous employee and noticed that two of the questions are not reflected in the table. You noticed also that two of the data types should be changed.

To add fields and change data types, complete the following steps:

1. Copy the Proj0202 database from the Project-02 folder on the CD to your work area and rename the copy as `Customer Research2`.
2. Open the `Questionnaire` table in Design view.
3. Select the Data Type box for the Adults field.
4. Using the down arrow that appears in the box, change the data type to Number.
5. Change the data type in the Children field to `Number`.
6. Move the ID field to the end of the list.
7. Add fields, with descriptions, for the two missing questions on the questionnaire.
8. Close the table, saving your changes.

Owning a Vending Company

You have listed the information that you think should be included in each of the three categories, and you decide that you need three tables—one table for each category.

Create a new database called `Vending`, using the information you gathered in Project 1. In that database, create three tables named `Suppliers`, `Locations`, and `Machines`.

In the Suppliers table, add fields for `Name` (primary key field), `Address`, and `Phone`.

In the Locations table, add fields for `Site` (primary key field), `Owner`, and `Machine Type`.

In the Machines table, add fields for `Machine Type`, `Supplier`, and `Cost` (let program add a primary key field).

Managing a Video Store

Now that you have had a chance to work in the store for a few days, you begin to see the complexity of the database you need. Create a database for your store, using the information you gathered in Project 1. Give it a descriptive name. Create a table in the database that includes the video name and any other information you feel is necessary. Be sure that the database includes not only the information that the owners have in their spreadsheet, but also whether the video is currently rented (a Yes/No data type might work well here) and who the current renter is.

Taking a Home Inventory

Create the database for your home inventory, using the information you gathered in Project 1. Add a table that includes the name of the item, the cost, the purchase date, and the insurance carrier with which you have the item insured. Include other fields that you think are essential to tracking your possessions. Be sure to consider major items, such as a car or boat, which are not in the home.

PinPoint Assessment

PinPoint Training

You have completed the project and the associated lessons, as well as the "Checking Your Skills" and "Applying Your Skills" sections. Now use the PinPoint software Evaluation mode to assess your comprehension of the specific exam tasks you have just learned. You can also use the PinPoint Trainer mode and the SHOW ME tutorials to practice these specific exam tasks.

Project 3

Three

Entering and Editing Data

Working with Data

In this project you will learn the following objectives and their associated Microsoft Exam required activities.

Objectives	Required Activities
➤ Add Records	Enter Data in a Table
➤ Move Among Records	Navigate Through a Table
➤ Edit Records	Navigate Through a Table Modify Data in a Table
➤ Insert and Delete Records	Delete Data from a Table Enter Data in a Table
➤ Adjust Column Widths and Hide Columns	
➤ Find a Record	
➤ Sort Records	Sort Data on a Single Field Sort Data on Multiple Fields

Why Would I Do This?

After you create a database and table, you want to be able to put them to work. For your database to be useful, you must enter data into the table. For example, you can keep track of your business contacts by entering their names, addresses, and phone numbers into the Contacts table of the Address database you worked with in Project 1, "Getting Started with Access 97." You can use the Training database you created in Project 2, "Creating a Database," to keep track of training that your staff receives by entering information about the employees and the training they have received into the P C Software table. As you learned in Project 1, the set of information you enter for each row in a table is called a record.

One reason databases are so useful is that you can work with and modify the records after you enter them. With a paper filing system, you have to cross out, erase, or redo a record when the information changes. With database software, however, you can easily change a record in the table to correct a mistake or to update the information. You can delete records you no longer need, search for a particular record, and sort the records—all quickly and with little effort on your part.

In this project, you learn how to add records to your table, move around in the records within the table, and edit and delete records. You also learn how to search for a particular record and sort your records according to a system that you determine.

Lesson 1: Adding Records

As you recall from Project 2, you worked in Design view when you set up your table structure. In Design view, you can make changes to the fields in the table—change a field name, add a field, change the data type, and so on. Then, when you want to work with the data in the table, you switch to Datasheet view. In this view, you can add records or edit them.

In this lesson, you open a database, Training2, which matches your database and your P C Software table from Project 2. You switch to Datasheet view, then add records to the database.

To Add Records

1. **Make a copy of Proj0301 from the Project-03 folder on the CD and name the copy `Training2`.**

   Return to Access and open the Training2 database.

2. **Click the Open button to open the P C Software table in Datasheet view.**

   In this project, you use the Training database you created in Project 2. (Training2 is a completed version of your work from Project 2.

You may use this file or open the Training database that you created.) You should see the P C Software table onscreen in Datasheet view. Each of the field names appears along the top of the window. At this point, the table consists of only one row, and it is blank. The insertion point is in the first field, and you see a small, black arrow next to the first field. This arrow indicates the current record (see Figure 3.1).

Figure 3.1
A blank database table in Datasheet view.

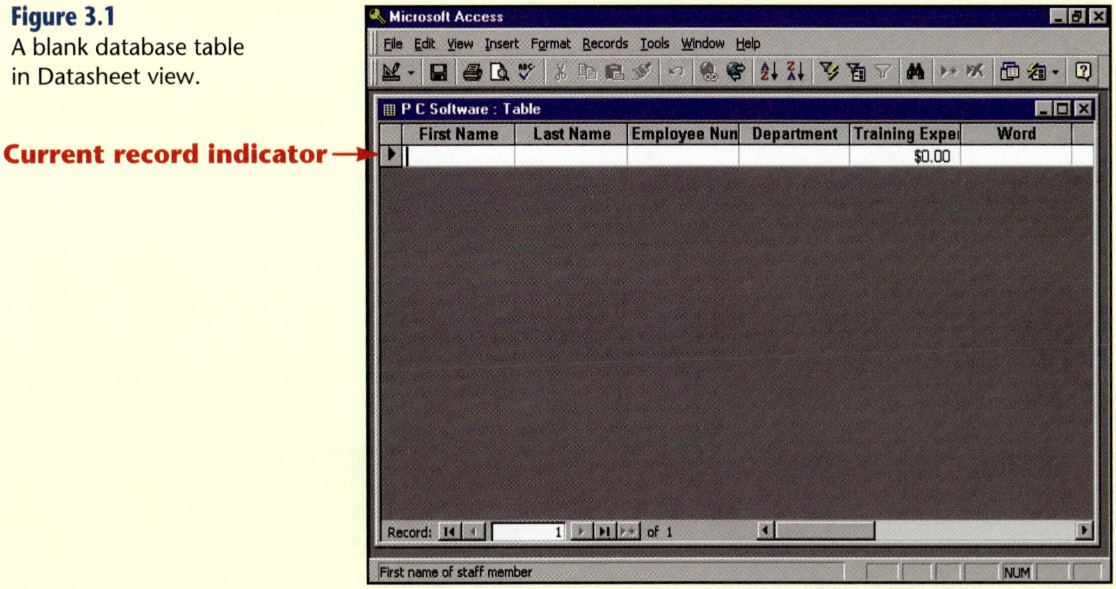

Record selector
The gray area to the left of a record in Datasheet view. Clicking in this area selects the entire record.

3 Type `Chantele` and press Enter.

As you type, Access displays a pencil icon in the *record selector*. You can also use the Tab key in place of the Enter key when adding data to the table.

4 Type `Auterman` and press Enter.

The staff member's name is entered, and you move to the Employee Number field.

5 Type `77171` and press Enter.

The employee number is entered, and you move to the Department field.

6 Type `Accounting` and press Enter.

The department is entered, and you move to the Training Expense field.

7 Type `300.00` and press Enter.

The expense for training this employee is entered, and you move to the four fields for specific software training. Notice that Access formats the Training Expense entry as Currency because in Project 2

continues

To Add Records (continued)

you set the data type to Currency after you created this field. Do not enter the dollar sign ($) into a currency field. If the dollar amount is a whole number, the program also adds the .00 automatically, even if you don't type it.

8 Type `3` and press ↵Enter, `1` and press ↵Enter, `0` and press ↵Enter, and finally `1` and press ↵Enter.

The level of classes taken are recorded in the four application fields. When you press ↵Enter the last time, Access moves to the counter field, which has a value that was automatically entered when you started entering data in the first field.

9 Press ↵Enter.

Access saves the record and moves to the next row so that you can add another record (see Figure 3.2). Whenever you move the insertion point off of the record you are editing, Access immediately saves the record or any changes you have made to the record.

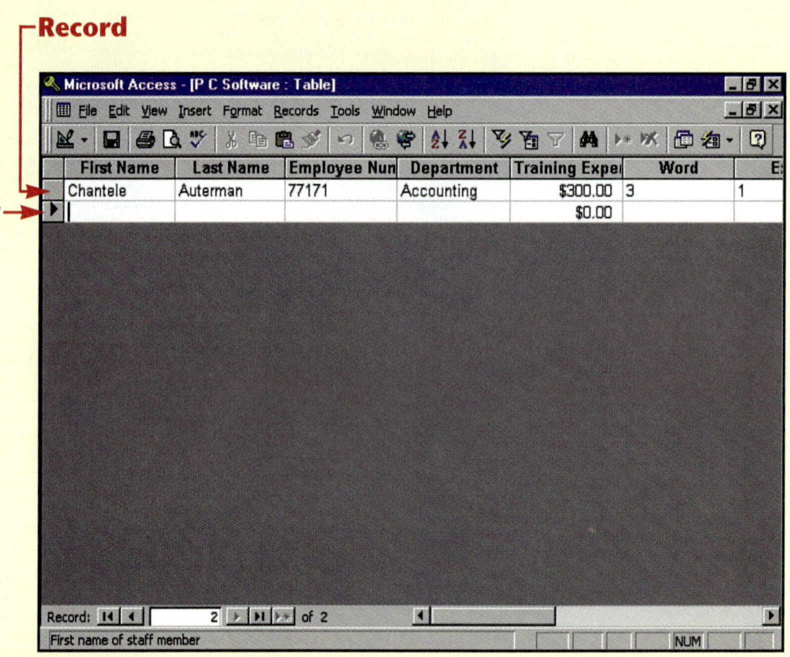

Figure 3.2
Access moves to the next row so that you can add another record.

10 Use the following list of data to add more records to the database table. (Because of the number of fields in each record, the items are separated by commas. Do not type in the commas.)

```
Chang,Sun,66242,Human Resources,0,0,0,0,0
Jane,Boxer,66264,Purchasing,450,1,2,1,3
Robert,Bauer,66395,Purchasing,0,0,0,0,0
Peter,Bullard,66556,Marketing,250,1,1,3,0
James,Baird,66567,Accounting,300,0,3,1,1
```

Access

```
Wayne,Wheaton,66564,Human Resources,150,1,0,2,0
Chris,Hart,77909,Marketing,250,1,0,3,1
```

Access adds these records to the database table. You don't have to worry about saving the records because Access does that each time you press ↵Enter and move to the next row to add a new record.

Keep the P C Software table and the Training2 database open. In the next lesson, you learn how to move among the records in your table.

Inside Stuff

In the beginning of this lesson, you were asked to make a copy of a file (Proj0301) and rename it. In Windows 95, the right mouse button can be used to open a short list of helpful menu options. For example, you can copy, paste, and rename files within the Access program without using the Explorer. To do this, you start with the File, Open Database command and locate the source file. If you point to the name of the source file (in this case, Proj0301) and click the right mouse button, a menu of options appears. Choose Copy, then click the right mouse button on an open area and choose Paste. The new file will be called Copy of Proj0301. Click on this new file with the right mouse button, choose Rename, and rename the file.

Lesson 2: Moving Among Records

Earlier, you noticed that Access displays an arrow next to the current row. When you want to do something with a record, such as edit a field to change or update its information, you first must move to the row containing the record that you want to change. You can tell what row you have moved to because the current record indicator is displayed next to the current row.

You can move among the records by using one of several methods. If you can see the record you want on the screen, you can simply click it to select it. If you have numerous records in your table, however, you may have to scroll through the records until you can get to the one you want.

To move to a particular record, you can use the vertical scrollbar, the navigation buttons displayed along the bottom of the window, or the arrow keys on the keyboard. Table 3.1 explains how these navigation buttons and keys work.

Table 3.1 Moving Among Records with the Navigation Buttons and Keys

To Move To	Button	Keyboard
First record in table		Ctrl+Home
Previous record in table		↑
Next record in table		↓
Last record in table		Ctrl+End
New record at end of table		Ctrl++

In this lesson, you move among the records in your table by using each of these navigational methods.

To Move Among Records

1 With the P C Software table of the Training2 database open, move the mouse pointer to the record selector at the left of the Wayne Wheaton record and click.

This selects the record.

2 Press Ctrl+Home. Access moves you to the first record in the database table. Notice the current record indicator arrow next to the active record (see Figure 3.3).

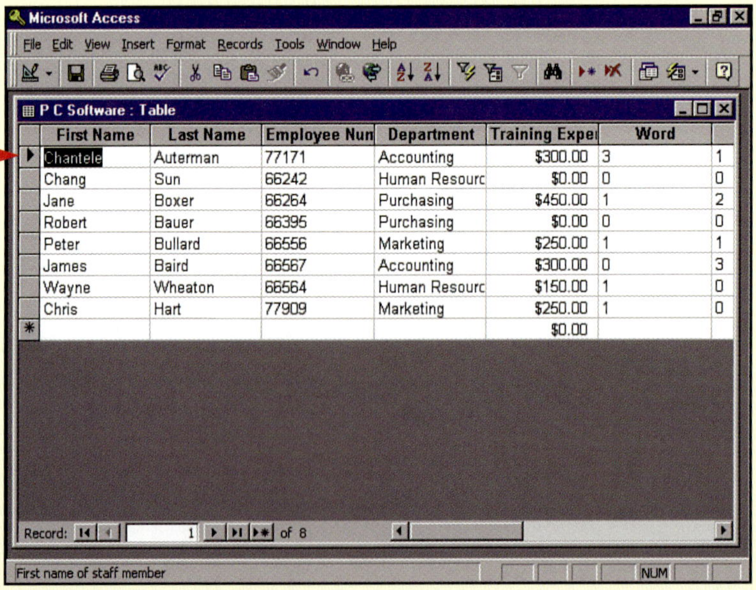

Figure 3.3
Pressing Ctrl+Home moves you to the first record.

Current record indicator

3 Press ↓.

Access moves you to the next record in the table.

4 Click the Last Record button.

Access moves you to the last record in the table.

5 Click the Previous Record button.

Access moves you to the previous record in the table.

6 Click the New Record button.

The pointer moves to the next empty record.

Now that you know how to move among the records in your table, the next lesson shows you how to make changes to the records. Keep Training2 database and the P C Software table open as you continue with Lesson 3.

If you have problems...

If you click on a particular field in the table and enter the editing mode, the Ctrl+Home and Ctrl+End commands only move to the beginning and end of the current field. These commands move to the beginning and end of the table if a field or record is selected.

Lesson 3: Editing Records

As you work with the data in the database table, you find that you need to make changes from time to time. In your P C Software table, for example, you might want to correct a typing mistake or change other information. You can update or correct any of the records in your table.

The first step in making any change is to move to the record that you want to change. Next, you have to move to the field that you want to edit. To move among fields using the mouse, click in the field to which you want to move. When you click, Access places the insertion point in the field and does not select the entire text in that field.

You can also use the keys listed in Table 3.2 to move among fields. When you use these keys, Access moves to the specified field and selects all the text in that field.

Table 3.2 Moving Among Fields with the Keyboard

To Move To	Press
Next field	Tab or →
Previous field	Shift+Tab or ←
First field in record	Home
Last field in record	End

After you are in a field, you can add to the current entry, edit the current entry, or delete the current entry. Try moving among the fields and making changes now.

To Edit Records

1 With the P C Software table of the Training2 database open, move to the record for Peter Bullard.

You can click in that record, use the arrow keys, or use the navigation buttons to move to this record. You should see the current record indicator to the left of the first field in this record.

2 In the record for Peter Bullard, click after the word `Marketing` in the Department column.

The insertion point is placed where you are going to add new text in the field.

3 Type a comma (,), press Spacebar, and type `Corporate`.

As you start typing, notice that Access displays a pencil icon in the record selector next to the record. This icon reminds you that you are editing the record and that the change has not yet been saved (see Figure 3.4).

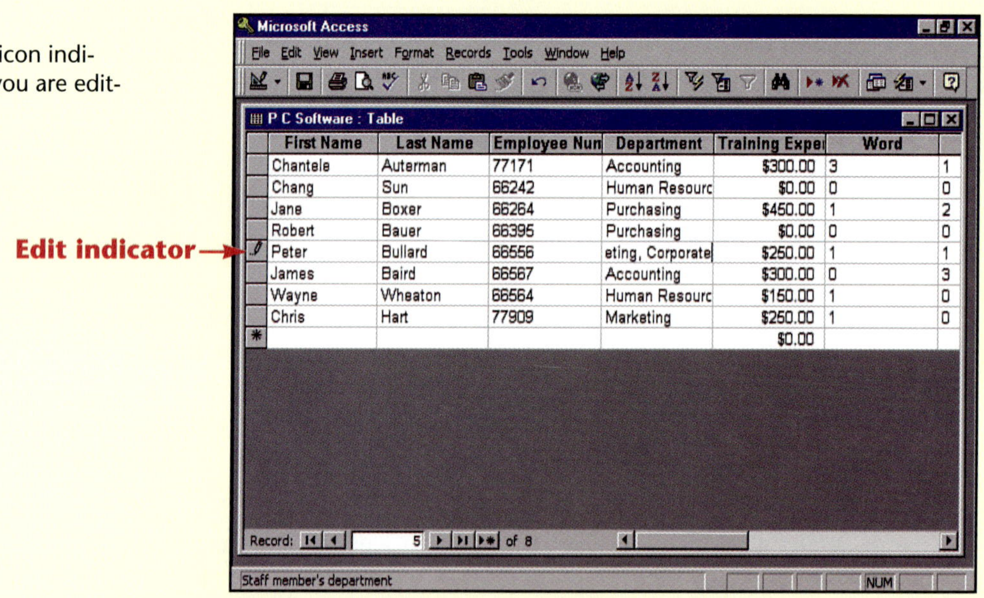

Figure 3.4
The pencil icon indicates that you are editing a field.

4 Press ↑ twice.

This moves you to the Department field in the record for Jane Boxer. When you move to another record, Access updates the record you just changed.

The text in that field is selected, as shown in Figure 3.5. Anything you type replaces the selected text.

Access

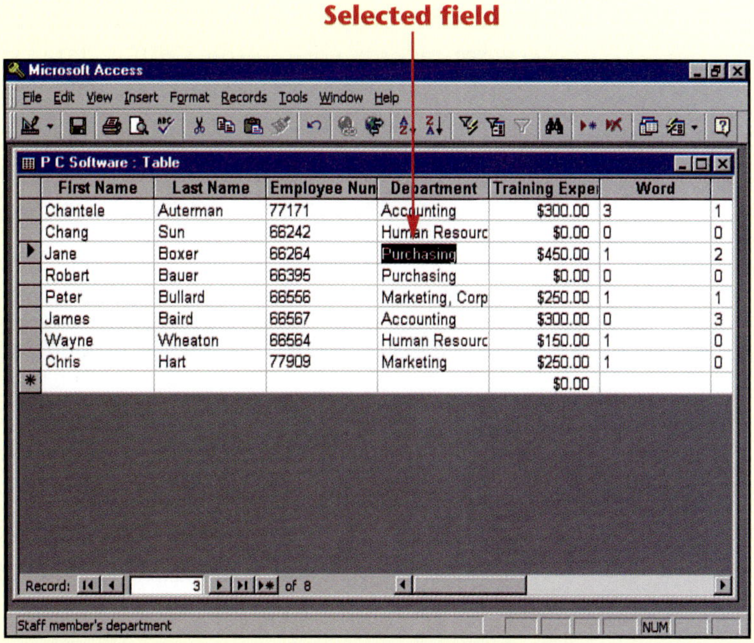

Figure 3.5
Typing replaces the selected text.

5 Type `Accounting`**.**

This employee is transferred to a new department.

6 Press ↓**.**

Access updates the record you just edited and moves to the next record.

Keep the P C Software table and the Training2 database open. In Lesson 4, you learn how to insert new records and delete records you no longer need.

If you have problems...

If you make a change by mistake, you can undo it by immediately clicking the Undo button, or by opening the Edit menu and choosing the Undo command.

Inside Stuff

When you move the insertion point off the record you are editing, Access saves the change to that record immediately. You can also save the change you make by pressing Shift+Enter while still on the record you are editing. To save a record using the menu, choose Records, Save Record command.

Lesson 4: Inserting and Deleting Records

When you first create your database table, you can't always predict exactly what information you want to include in it. As you use your database, you most likely will want to insert new records or delete outdated records.

With Access, you don't have to add all your records at one time. You can add a new record to the end of the table at any time. If you want to enter several records containing similar data, you can enter the data for one record, copy that record, paste the new record into your table, and then edit the data in that second record.

You can delete a record by removing the row from the database table. In this lesson, you learn how to insert new records and delete a record you no longer need.

Access

To Insert and Delete Records

1 With the P C Software table of the Training2 database open, click in the First Name field of the row marked by an asterisk (see Figure 3.6).

The insertion point is placed in the First Name field of the new record where the new record will be added. The asterisk is replaced by the record selector arrow.

Figure 3.6
Insert new records at the bottom of the table.

Record selector

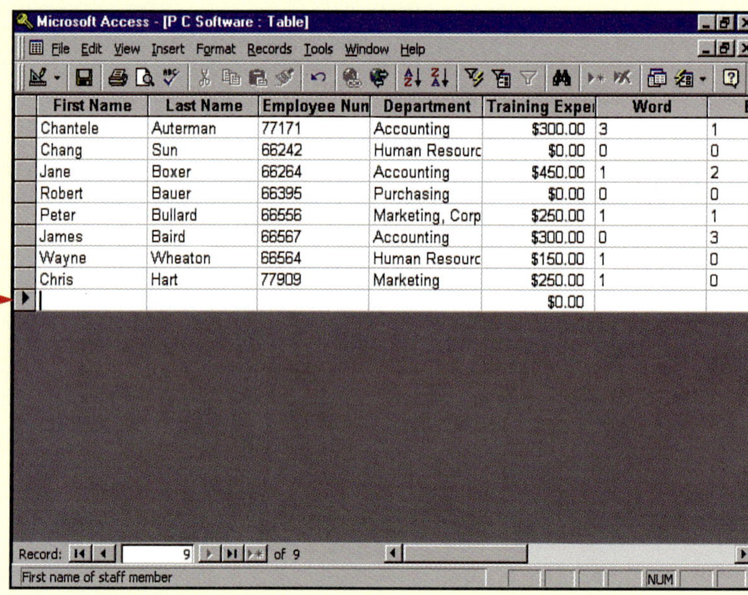

2 Type the following data for your new record, pressing Enter after each entry. After the last entry, press Enter twice.

```
William
Evich
77517
Accounting
300
0
3
```

0

2

Access adds the new employee record to the end of your table. You can also copy a record and add the copy so that you have two versions of the same record. You may want to do this if you have two or more similar records. This might be appropriate for an inventory database of computer hardware. To practice this skill, you can copy the record you just added.

3 To copy this record, click in the record selector to select the entire row.

Access highlights the entire row.

4 Click the Copy button.

Clipboard
A temporary storage area in Windows that stores copied data and from which you can paste that data.

Onscreen, you won't notice anything different after you copy the record. At this point, you have just placed a copy of the selected record onto the *Clipboard*. Next, you paste the copy of the record into your table.

5 Click the record selector to highlight the empty record at the end of the table, then click the Paste button.

Access adds, or appends, the record to the end of the table. Now that you have the basic data in place, you can make any changes necessary for this particular record. Rather than edit this duplicate record just now, you are going to use it to practice deleting a record.

6 Click in the record selector next to the new record you just inserted.

The record you just pasted is selected. You can also select the record by opening the Edit menu and choosing Select Record when the insertion point is anywhere in the record.

7 Click the Delete Record button.

Access wants to be sure that you intended to delete the record, so you are prompted to confirm the deletion (see Figure 3.7). You cannot undo record deletions, so be absolutely sure that you want to delete the record before you confirm the deletion.

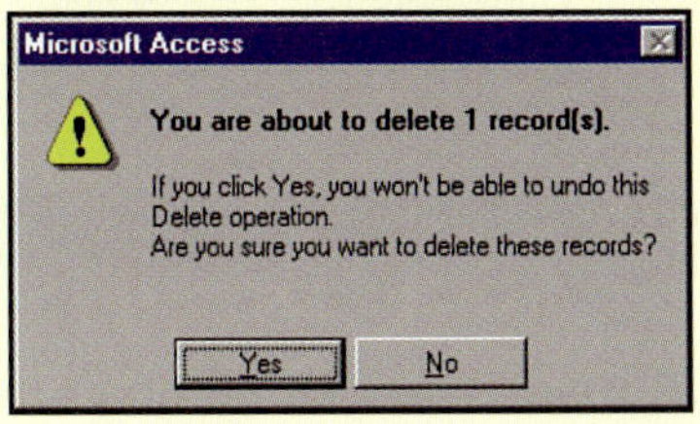

Figure 3.7
Access prompts you to confirm the deletion.

continues

To Insert and Delete Records (continued)

8 Click the Yes button.

Access deletes the record and saves the database table.

Keep the P C Software table open. In Lesson 5, you learn how to change the width of the columns in your table and how to hide and unhide columns.

Exam Notes

In addition to copying entire records, you can also copy an entry from one field to another. If you want to enter another record for someone from the Marketing Department, for example, you can copy `Marketing` from the Department column to the new record.

To copy an entry, move to the appropriate field and select the text you want to copy by dragging across it. Then click the Copy button. Move to the location where you want to place the copied text and click the Paste button. Access pastes the selected text.

You can also use shortcut keys: Ctrl+C for Copy and Ctrl+V for Paste.

To delete a record, you can select the record and press Del, or place the insertion point anywhere in the record and choose Delete Record from the Edit menu.

To add a new record you can click the New Record button on the toolbar.

Lesson 5: Adjusting Column Widths and Hiding Columns

By default, Access displays all the columns in your table with the same width. You can change the column width, making some columns wider so that you can see the entire entry, and making other columns narrower so that they don't take up as much space. The easiest way to adjust the column width is to use the mouse.

In addition to changing the column width, you can also hide columns that you don't want displayed, such as the autonumber field, which is never used for data entry. Adjusting the column width does not change the field size. You learn how to change the field size in Project 7, "Customizing Fields and Tables."

To Adjust Column Widths and Hide Columns

1 With the P C Software table of the Training2 database open, place the mouse pointer between the First Name and Last Name column headings.

The mouse pointer changes to a thick vertical bar with arrows on either side, as shown in Figure 3.8. This pointer indicates that you can now move the column borders.

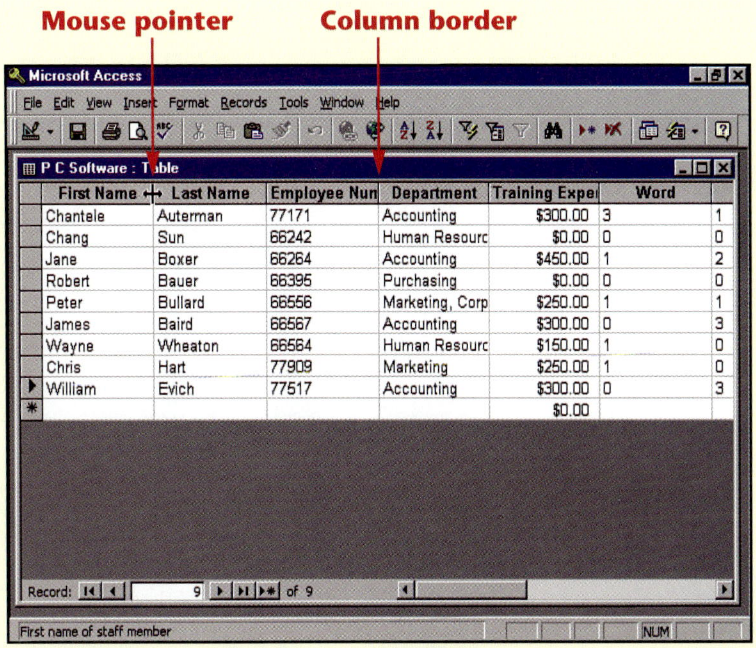

Figure 3.8
The appearance of the mouse pointer changes when you are preparing to resize a column.

2 Press and hold down the mouse button and drag to the left until you think the column is narrow enough and you can still see all the entries in the column. Release the mouse button.

The new width is set. As you drag to the left, you make the column narrower. Notice that you can see the border of the column move as you drag. You can shrink the size of the column far enough to cover up part of the field name.

If you have problems...

If you don't see the thick bar with the arrows, you don't have the pointer in the correct spot. Be sure that you are within the gray area of the column headings and that your pointer is sitting directly on the border separating the two columns.

3 Move the mouse pointer to the border between the Department and Training Expense columns and then double-click the mouse button.

Double-clicking is a shortcut method that automatically adjusts the column to fit the longest entry currently displayed onscreen in that column. This often creates a problem when you use long field names, because double-clicking widens the column to show the whole field name if it is the longest entry in the column.

4 Drag across the column headings for the Training Expense, Word, Excel, PowerPoint, Access, and ID fields. Use the horizontal scrollbar to view the selected columns.

When you drag across the headings, you select all six columns (see Figure 3.9). You can then adjust the width of the six columns at one time.

continues

To Adjust Column Widths and Hide Columns (continued)

Figure 3.9
You can select several columns and resize them together.

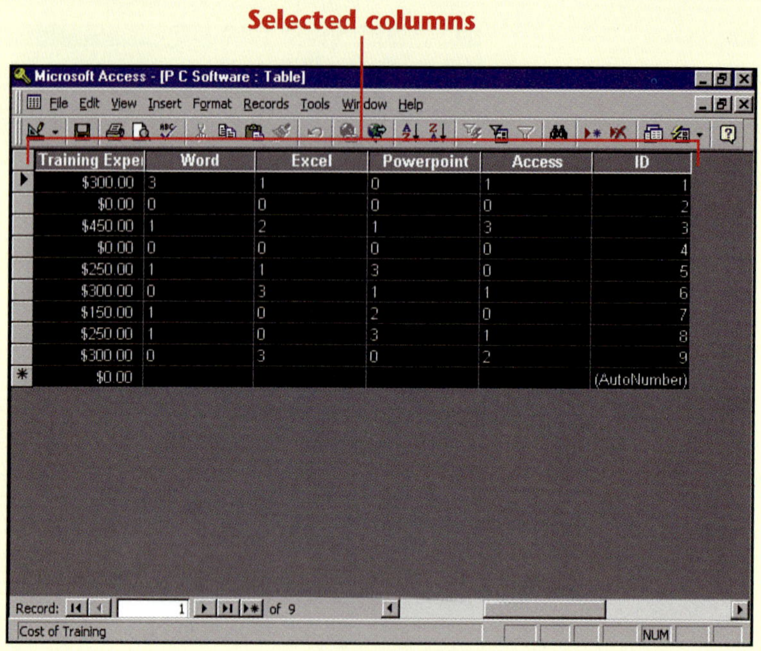

5 **Drag a border from one of the six columns so that the columns are just big enough to hold the longest entry.**

Dragging one of the borders resizes all six columns.

6 **Click anywhere in the table to deselect the columns.**

7 **Click in the column heading of the Employee Number field.**

Now that you have selected this column, you can practice hiding it.

8 **Open the Format menu and choose the Hide Columns command.**

Access hides the column you had selected.

9 **Open the Format menu and choose the Unhide Columns command to unhide the column.**

Access displays the Unhide Columns dialog box, as shown in Figure 3.10. If the column has a check mark next to its name, the column is displayed. If there is no check mark, the column is hidden.

10 **Click the Employee Number check box.**

11 **Click the Close button.**

Access closes the Unhide Columns dialog box. The Employee Number column reappears on the screen.

Save your work and keep the P C Software table open. In Lesson 6, you learn how to search for particular records in your database.

Figure 3.10
Use the Unhide Columns dialog box to unhide a column.

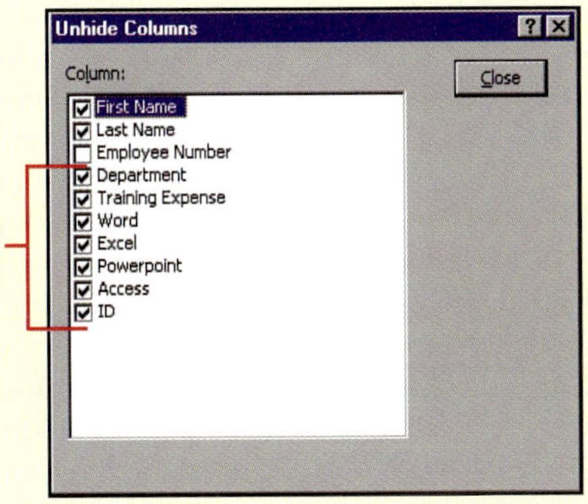

Inside Stuff

You can also use the menus to adjust the column width. Move the insertion point to the column you want to adjust. Then open the Format menu and choose the Column Width command. Type a new value (the width of the column in points) and click the OK button.

You can also hide multiple columns by first selecting them and then selecting the Hide Columns command from the Format menu. In addition, you can use the Unhide Columns dialog box to hide columns. In the list displayed in the dialog box, click on the check box next to a column to deselect it. This hides the column.

Lesson 6: Finding Records

In a table with many records and many fields, it may be time-consuming to scroll through the records and fields to find a particular record. Instead, you can search for a specific field entry in order to find and move quickly to a record.

For example, if you want to find the Wayne Wheaton record, you can search for *Wheaton*. It is usually faster to select the column you want to use for your search and then search just that column, but you can also search for text in any column in the table. In this lesson, you find a record by first searching a single column and then by searching all columns.

To Find a Record

1 With the P C Software table of the Training2 database open, click in the Last Name field.

It doesn't matter what row you click in. Clicking anywhere in the field tells Access that you want to search for a particular record using the Last Name field only.

continues

To Find a Record (continued)

2 Click the Find button.

Access displays the Find dialog box (see Figure 3.11). Here you tell Access what you want to find and where you want to look.

Type text you want to find

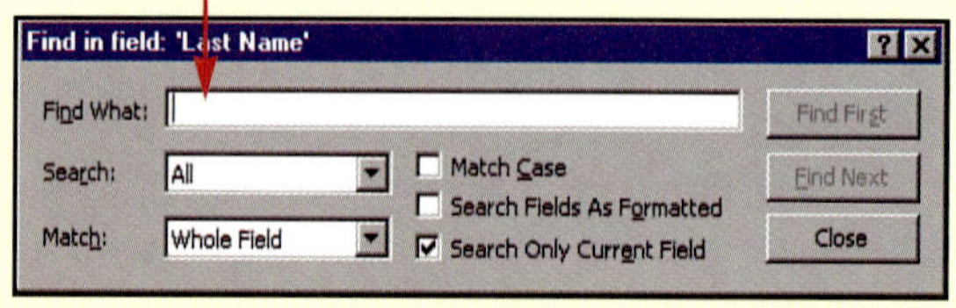

Figure 3.11
You use the Find dialog box to prepare for your search.

3 Type `Wheaton`.

This is the entry you want to find.

4 Click the Find First button.

Access moves to the first match, and the dialog box remains open. You can continue to search by clicking the Find Next button until you find the record you want.

If you can't see the match because the dialog box is in the way, move the dialog box by dragging its title bar.

5 Drag across the text in the Find What text box to select it; then type `Resources`.

This is the next entry you want to find.

6 Deselect the Search Only Current Field option.

Instead of restricting the search to just the current column, you are now telling Access to look in all columns.

7 Click the drop-down list button next to the Match box.

The drop-down list box gives you three choices (see Figure 3.12).

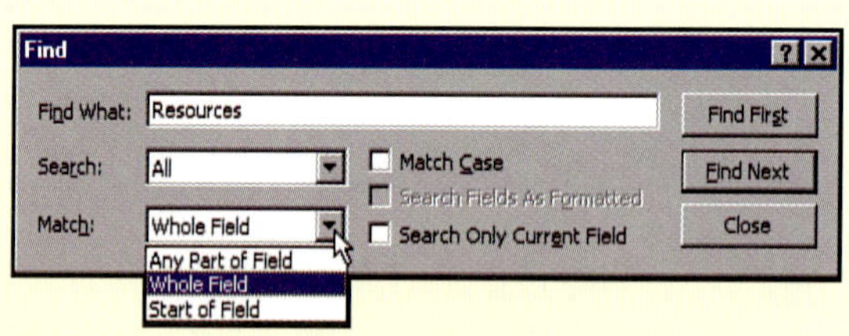

Figure 3.12
There are three choices in the Match drop-down box.

8 Select Any Part of Field.

The text you want to find (*Resources*) won't be the entire entry; it is only part of the field. For this reason, you have to tell Access to match any part of the field. Figure 3.13 shows the options you have requested for this search.

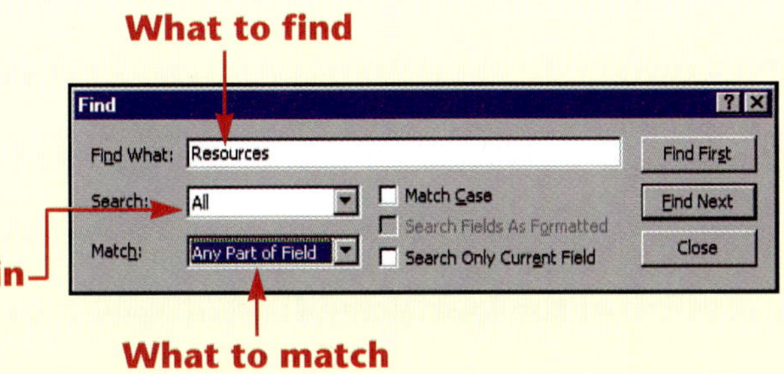

Figure 3.13
You can change your search options in the Find dialog box.

9 Click the Find First button.

Access moves to the first occurrence and highlights `Resources` in the Department column in the record for Chang Sun.

10 Click the Find Next button.

Access moves to the next occurrence and highlights Resources in the Department column in the record for Wayne Wheaton.

11 Click the Close button.

This step closes the Find dialog box.

Save your work and keep the P C Software table open. In Lesson 7, you learn how to sort the records in your table.

If you have problems...

If you see a message telling you that Access has reached the end of the records and asking whether you want to start searching from the beginning, click the Yes button. By default, Access searches from the current record down through the database. The record you want may be located before the current one.

If you see another message telling you that Access reached the end of the records, Access did not find a match. Try the search again. Be sure that you typed the entry correctly. You may need to change some of the options.

Lesson 7: Sorting Records

Access displays the records in your table in an order determined by the primary key. You learned how to create a primary key in Project 2. If your table has no primary key, Access displays the records in the order in which they were entered.

If you use a primary key, Access sorts the entries alphabetically or numerically based on the entries in that field. (If a counter field is your primary key, your records will be displayed in the order in which they were entered.) Fortunately, however, you aren't restricted to displaying your data only in the order determined by your primary key. With Access, you can sort the display by using any of the fields in the database table. You can also sort the display by multiple, adjacent fields.

In this lesson, you first sort your data on the Last Name field. You will then use the toolbar to sort on the Employee Number field.

To Sort Records

1 With the P C Software table of the Training2 database open, click in the Last Name field.

Clicking in this field tells Access that you want to base your sort on the Last Name field.

2 Click the Sort Ascending button.

Access sorts the records in ascending alphabetical order (a to z) based on the entries in the Last Name field (see Figure 3.14).

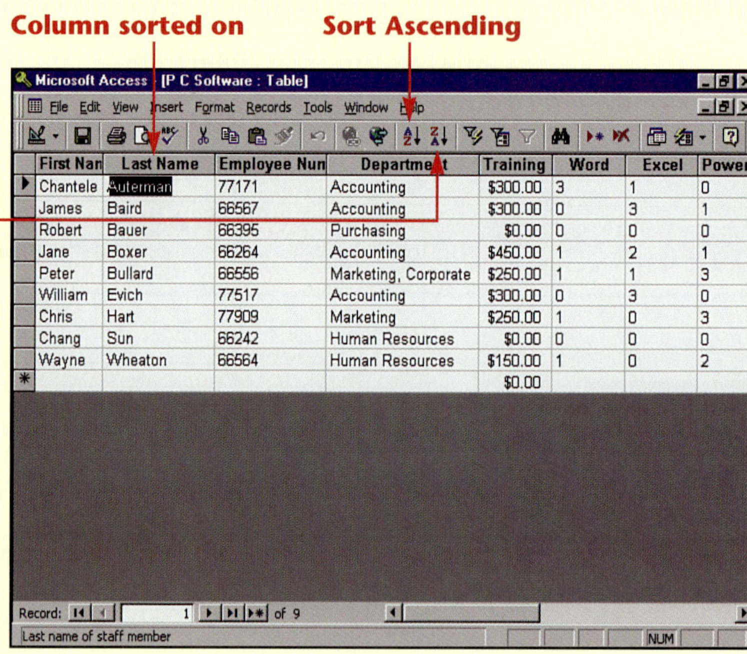

Figure 3.14
The result of an ascending sort based on the Last Name field.

3 Click in the Employee Number field.

Clicking in this field tells Access that you now want to base your sort on the Employee Number field.

4 Click the Sort Ascending button on the toolbar.

Access sorts the table by using the entries in the Employee Number field. Keep in mind that the sort order displayed onscreen does not affect the order in which the records are actually stored.

Close the P C Software table and save the changes. Close the Training2 database. In Project 4, "Querying Your Database," you use your P C Software table to learn about queries.

If you have completed your session on the computer, exit Access and Windows before turning off the computer. (Refer to Project 1 if you need help exiting Access or Windows.) Otherwise, continue with the "Checking Your Skills" and "Applying Your Skills" sections in this project.

Inside Stuff

You can also use the Record, Sort command from the menu and select the Sort Ascending or Sort Descending option. As with the buttons, you must first have the insertion point in the field you want to sort.

Exam Notes

To sort by multiple, adjacent fields (for example, last name then first name), select the field name for the first sort, hold down the Shift key, and select the second field to sort (the second field must be adjacent and to the right of the first field). You can also click in the first field name and drag to the right to select the second field. Click the Sort Ascending or Sort Descending button to perform the sort.

When you have completed a sort, if you wish to return records to their original order, choose Records from the menu and click Remove Filter/Sort.

If the fields you wish to sort upon are not in the proper order (for example, your database Training2 displays the first name column followed by the last name column), you can move the columns prior to the sort. By moving the column so that the last name column appears first in your table, with the first name field as the next field immediately to the right, you can then sort the table by last name, then by first name. To move a column, simply select the column, then click on the field name and drag the field to the desired location.

Project Summary

To	Do This
Add records	Open the table in Datasheet view. Type the appropriate information in each field. Move from field to field with Enter. At the end of the information for one record, press Enter. This moves you to the next row and saves the record just entered.
Go to first record in table	Click the First Record button.
Go to previous record	Click the Previous Record button.
Go to next record	Click the Next Record button.
Go to last record in table	Click the Last Record button.
Insert a record	Click the New Record button.
Edit records	Move to the record and field you want to edit. Click in the field and add, delete, or change the entry as needed. Press Enter to complete the entry.

continues

To	Do This
Delete a record	Click the record selector of the row to be deleted. Click the Delete Record button, then click Yes to confirm.
Adjust column widths	Place the mouse pointer between columns until it changes to a thick vertical bar with arrows on either side. Click and drag the line between the columns to the right or left to adjust the column width. Select several columns at once and double-click one of the bars between the selected columns for automatic adjustment of all selected columns.
Hide or unhide columns	Click in the column heading. Open the Format menu and choose the Hide Columns command. In the Format menu, use Unhide Columns to display the column again.
Find a record	Click the Find button. In the dialog box, type what you want to find. You can search in the current field or all fields. You can also search in Any Part of Field. Click the Find First button to begin the search.
Sort records	Click the field you want to sort on. Click either the Sort Ascending or Sort Descending button.
Move a column (reorder fields)	Select the column then click on the field name and drag it to its new position.

Checking Your Skills

True/False

For each of the following, check *T* or *F* to indicate whether the statement is true or false.

__T __F 1. You can edit records in Design view.

__T __F 2. When the pencil icon appears in the record selector, it reminds you that the record is being edited and the change has not been saved.

__T __F 3. When you change the column width, you also change the field size.

__T __F 4. When you add a new record, it is added to the end of a table.

__T __F 5. You can undo record deletions.

__T __F 6. The only way to delete a record is to use the Delete Record button.

__T __F 7. You can hide a column so that it does not appear on the screen.

__T __F 8. When using the Find dialog box, the default choice is to search in the field where the insertion point is located.

__T __F 9. You can hide only one column at a time.

__T __F 10. Multiple sorts can be created by choosing non-adjacent fields.

Multiple Choice

Circle the letter of the correct answer for each of the following questions.

1. Which of the following takes you quickly to the first record in a table?
   a. Ctrl+End
   b. Home
   c. Alt+Home
   d. the First Record button

2. Which command do you use to paste an entire record?
   a. Paste Record
   b. Paste All
   c. Paste
   d. None of the above

3. Which of the following is not a way to adjust the column width?
   a. Double-click the column border.
   b. Drag the column border.
   c. Open the View menu and choose the Column Size command.
   d. Open the Format menu and choose the Column Width command.

4. If you want Access to search all fields in the table, which option do you select in the Find dialog box?
   a. Current Field
   b. Match Case
   c. Search Fields As Formatted
   d. None of the above

5. Which of the following is not a way to sort the records in a table?
   a. Click the Sort Descending button.
   b. Click the Sort Ascending button.
   c. Open the Records menu and choose the Sort command.
   d. Open the Tools menu and choose the Quick Sort command.

6. Which of the following is not a way to delete a record?
   a. Highlight the record and press Del.
   b. Place the insertion point anywhere in the record and press Ctrl+D.
   c. Place the insertion point anywhere in the record and click the Delete Record button.
   d. Place the insertion point anywhere in the record and choose Delete Record from the Edit menu.

7. Access automatically saves the data you enter to disk when you do which of the following?

   a. Press Shift + Enter.

   b. Leave the field in which you entered the data.

   c. Choose Save Record from the Record menu.

   d. All of the above.

8. To hide a column, you should do which of the following?

   a. Select the column and press Alt+H.

   b. Select the column and double-click the right column separator on the border.

   c. Place the insertion point in the column and select Hide Columns from the Format menu.

   d. Place the insertion point in the column and select AutoHide from the Format menu.

9. Access identifies the record you are editing by which of the following?

   a. the arrow on the record selector

   b. the asterisk on the record selector

   c. the key symbol on the record selector

   d. the pencil icon on the record selector

10. What does the New Record button look like?

   a. an arrow pointing to an asterisk

   b. a folder with an arrow on it

   c. a folder with a star on it

   d. an arrow pointing to a line

Completion

In the blank provided, write the correct answer for each of the following statements.

1. To add a new record, click the ______________ button.
2. The ______________ field determines the sort order of the records.
3. To hide a column, open the Format menu and choose the ______________ command.
4. Press ______________ to move to the first field in the record.
5. Press ______________ to move to the last field in the record.
6. The ______________ is the gray box to the left of a record in Datasheet view.
7. To locate a record based on a specific entry, use the ______________ button on the toolbar.
8. When you enter a number in a(n) ______________ field, Access automatically adds the dollar sign and decimals to it.

9. You can change the arrangement of the records in Datasheet view by using the ______________ button.

10. You can ______________ to resize a column when you move the mouse pointer to the border between columns and it becomes a thick line with arrows on either side.

Matching

In the blank next to each of the following terms or phrases, write the letter of the corresponding term or phrase. (Note that some letters may be used more than once.)

a. Sort Ascending
b. Hidden Column
c. Clipboard
d. New Record location
e. Home
f. navigation buttons
g. Find button
h. Shift+Tab
i. Sort Descending
j. pencil icon

_______ 1. Used to move among records
_______ 2. Moves you to the first field in a record
_______ 3. Indicates the record you are editing
_______ 4. Where pasted information comes from
_______ 5. Arranges records by the chosen field starting with the letter closest to A
_______ 6. The same as ←
_______ 7. Arranges records in reverse alphabetical order
_______ 8. Holds a temporary copy of the item you copy
_______ 9. A field that is not visible
_______ 10. Last row of the datasheet

Applying Your Skills

Practice

The following exercises enable you to practice the skills you have learned in this project. Take a few minutes to work through these exercises now.

Cataloging Your Books

In "Applying Your Skills" in Project 2, you created a Library database with a table for your books. Now you can enter actual information about your book collection into this database table. Because you may not have access to your personal book collection while working through this project, some book information is provided for you.

To enter book information, complete the following steps:

1. Copy the Proj0302 database file from the Project-03 folder on the CD and name it `Library2`. Then open the `Books` table.

2. In Datasheet view, enter the author's last name, first name, book title, type of book, and year of publication for each book. Type the following information into the Books table:

Last Name	First Name	Title	Type of Book	Year of Publication
O'Rourke	P.J.	All the Trouble in the World	Nonfiction	1994
Gibbons	Kaye	Ellen Foster	Fiction	1990
Gibbons	George	Ellen Foster	Fiction	1990
Sandford	John	Silent Prey	Mystery	1992
Hiaasen	Carl	Skin Tight	Fiction	1989
Connelly	Michael	The Black Echo	Mystery	1992
Connelly	Amy	Birds in Flight	Reference	1998
Markoe	Merrill	What the Dogs Have Taught Me	Humor	1992

3. Adjust each column of the table so that you can see the longest entry in each field. If the column is much wider than the entry, make the column narrower.

4. Sort the records in ascending order by multiple fields—author's last name followed by the author's first name.

5. Save your work and close the table and database.

Access

Entering Record Company Information

In "Applying Your Skills" in Project 2, you created a database for your Sound Byte Music Store to help you keep track of data. You set up the database and also created a table for supplier information—that is, the names and addresses of the record companies you deal with. Now that you have the Suppliers table set up, you add records to it in this exercise.

To enter record company information, complete the following steps:

1. Copy the Proj0303 database files from the Project-03 folder on the CD and name it `SBMusic2`. Then open the `Suppliers` table.

2. Enter the following records in Datasheet view:

Record Company	Contact Name	Address	City	State	ZIP	Phone
MCA Records	Kelly Shannon	554 S. University	Xavier	CA	91608	(800)555-0122
Warner Bros. Records	Hurrle	3300 Warner	Burbank	CA	91505	(800)555-9022

Record Company	Contact Name	Address	City	State	ZIP	Phone
Atlantic Recording	Brendan O'Brien	75 Rockefeller Plaza	New York	NY	10019	(800)555-0917
Epic	Conner Denney	666 Fifth Avenue	New York	NY	10101	(800)555-7732

3. Adjust the column widths so that the column is just wide enough to display the longest entry in each field.
4. Save your work and close the database.

Creating a Database to Track Personal Computer Hardware

You may find it difficult to keep track of the many different combinations of computer hardware that may exist in an organization. A database can help.

To create the database, complete the following steps:

1. Copy Proj0304 from the Project-03 folder on the CD and rename it `PC2`. Open the database `PC2`.
2. Open the `PC Hardware` table and enter the following records. (Because of the number of fields in each record, the items are separated by commas.)

```
386,4,120,Yes,Yes,VGA,None,Yes,No,General Comp,1234,2/5/92
386,8,40,No,Yes,VGA,None,No,No,General Comp,1235,6/3/93
386,4,120,Yes,Yes,VGA,None,Yes,No,General Comp,1236,6/1/94
486,8,500,Yes,No,SVGA,2X,Yes,Yes,Acme Computer,1237,8/4/94
486,16,800,Yes,No,SVGA,2X,Yes,Yes,Acme Computer,1238,8/4/95
Pentium,32,1250,Yes,No,SVGA,4X,Yes,Yes,Wilson Electric,1239,
10/9/96
```

3. Open the `Vendors` table and enter the following vendor information:

Name of Vendor	Street Address	City	State	ZIP Code	Phone Number
General Comp	123 Main	Ann Arbor	MI	48105	313-665-2345
Acme Computer	234 Cross	Ypsilanti	MI	48197	313-482-3456
Wilson Electric	122 Sill	Ypsilanti	MI	48197	313-487-1161

4. Close both tables and the database.

Getting a Helping Hand

Many useful Help utilities are available. One of the easiest to use is the What's This? pointer. This feature can help you find out how to accomplish tasks and what certain parts of the window mean.

To get help on topics in this project, complete the following steps:

1. Open one of the databases that you have created. Open one of the tables in Datasheet view and choose the Help menu.
2. Select the What's This? menu item. The mouse pointer has a question mark appended to it.
3. Point to and click the record selector of any of the records. A window appears that explains the record selector and any of four conditions you will see.
4. Choose Help and What's This? again.
5. Point to and click any of the column headings. Notice that Access gives you hints on selecting and resizing the columns.
6. Choose Help and What's This? one last time.
7. Select the gray square at the intersection of the row and column selectors. Notice that you can use this button to select the entire datasheet.

Exploring the World of Alaska

You can use the sort buttons to answer questions in a database. Alaska has the northernmost, westernmost, and easternmost geographic points in the United States. You want to demonstrate this by using the limited Alaskan database.

To use sort in the Alaska database, complete the following steps:

1. Copy Proj0305 from the Project-03 folder on the CD and rename it `Alaska`. Open the database `Alaska`.
2. Open the `Geography` table in Datasheet view.
3. Maximize the window, if necessary.
4. Select the `Latitude` column. Latitude is the angle, in degrees, of a particular point from the equator. The north geographic pole is 90 degrees from the equator. As such, the northernmost geographic site in the database has the highest latitude.
5. Click the Sort Descending button on the toolbar. `Admiralty Bay` becomes the first record displayed, and it is the northernmost point listed in this database.

   The westernmost and easternmost points can be found in a similar way. Longitude starts at zero degrees in Greenwich, England, and is measured east and west from there. The opposite side of the earth, in the Pacific Ocean, is 180 degrees longitude.
6. Select the `Longitude` column.
7. Click the Sort Descending button on the toolbar. `Adak Strait` has the highest west longitude and is therefore the westernmost point listed in the database. `Aga Cove`, also in the Aleutian Island chain, has the largest east longitude and is therefore the easternmost point in the database—more east than Maine (geographically). Close the database.

Challenge

The following challenges enable you to use your problem-solving skills. Take time to work through these exercises now.

Creating a List of Club Members

Open the database that you created in "Challenge" exercise 1 in Project 2 to track information about members of an organization. Enter sample information for ten club members. Save the database and its table.

Doing Customer Research

You changed the database structure to reflect all the questions and have received a few responses. Three more responses have arrived.

To enter customer responses in the database, complete the following steps:

1. Copy file Proj0306 from the Project-03 folder on the CD and rename it `Customer Research3`.
2. Enter the following three responses:

Field	Adults	Children	Hours	No 1	No 2	No 3	Doing
Response1	2	4	1	DISNEY	TNT	DISCOVERY	Good
Response2	2	2	3	DISCOVERY	DISNEY	CNN	Okay
Response3	3	0	5	CNN			Okay

   As you begin to enter the first comment (provided in the next step), you notice that the comments do not fit in the space reserved. To get the data to fit, you must either increase the size of the text field or change the field type.

3. Change the type for the Improve field to `Memo` and continue to enter the data.

   Improvement comment for the first household: `You're doing all right, but we sure would like to see more channels for the children. More educational channels.`

   Comment for the second household: `Don't see anything.`

   The third household had no comments.

4. Save and close the database.

Owning a Vending Company

You have gathered more information from the binders and need to put it in the database you generated in the previous project. If you have not generated the database, you can use the file Proj0307 from the Project-03 folder on the CD.

To enter information in the tables, complete the following steps:

1. Open the file Proj0307 as a copy.
2. Enter the following data in the Locations table:

Site	Owner	Machine Type
National Airport	Biggy Jones, Inc	6 Head Candy
International Airport	Biggy Jones, Inc	6 Head Candy
Jakes Hardware	Paul Jakes	Rotary Sandwich
Carter's Gifts	Don Carter	Card Maker

3. Enter the following information in the Suppliers table:

Name	Address	Phone
Cardstock Vending	Grover's Mills	(619) 342-9823
Food Venders, Inc	Placid Lake	(722) 871-9943
Bulk Foodstuffs	Carrinton	(433) 762-1925

4. Enter the following information in the Machines table:

Machine Type	Supplier	Cost
6 Head Candy	Food Venders, Inc	1,500
Rotary Sandwich	Food Venders, Inc	2,200
Card Maker	Cardstock Vending	4,750

5. Adjust the column widths so that all data can be seen in each table.
6. Hide the Machine Cost field.
7. Save and close the database.

Managing a Video Store

Open your video store database you created in the previous project and open the primary table that contains the list of videos. Enter at least ten videos in the database, inventing the information.

Hide the current renter field so that prying eyes can't view the data.

Sort the primary table based on the title of the video.

Taking a Home Inventory

In the home inventory database you created in the previous project, open the table that includes the item field and add at least ten records with varying item costs. As you enter your data, be sure to include at least three different insurance companies; one for auto, one for home, and one for personal articles and furniture.

Sort the datasheet based on cost and then hide the cost field.

Sort the datasheet based on the insurance carrier to see the types of articles identified for each carrier.

PinPoint Assessment

You have completed the project and the associated lessons, as well as the "Checking Your Skills" and "Applying Your Skills" sections. Now use the PinPoint software Evaluation mode to assess your comprehension of the specific exam tasks you have just learned. You can also use the PinPoint Trainer mode and the SHOW ME tutorials to practice these specific exam tasks.

Project 4

Four

Querying Your Database

Working with Queries

In this project you will learn the following objectives and their associated Microsoft Exam required activities.

Objectives	Required Activities
➤ Create a New Query	Create a Simple Query
➤ Choose Fields for a Query	
➤ Save a Query	Save a Query
➤ Edit a Query	Add Fields to a Query Remove Fields from a Query
➤ Change Field Order and Sort a Query	Sort a Query
➤ Match Criteria	Find a Specific Record Create a Query with Multiple Criteria Print the Results of a Query
➤ Save a Query with a New Name and Open Multiple Queries	

Why Would I Do This?

Query
A question posed to the database that determines what information is retrieved.

Dynaset
A subset of records created as a result of a query.

The primary reason you spend time entering all of your data into a database is so you can easily find and work with the information. In your address database, for example, you may want to display all of your contacts in Florida. To do so, you would create a *query*. A query asks a question of the database, such as, "Which records have FL as the state?" and then pulls those records from the database into a subset of records. If the query simply selects or sorts data, the subset has the special name *dynaset*. You can then work with (or print) just those records selected by your query.

You can also create queries that display all of the records but only show selected fields. For example, you can display only the Last Name and Employee Number fields in the Training database. Or you can create a query that searches for values in one field, such as the Florida example just given, but displays only selected fields in the result. You can also create more complex queries. For example, you can query your Training database to display all staff members who have received training in either Microsoft Excel or PowerPoint. Queries are created and saved so they can be used over and over.

In this project, you learn how to create, save, and use a query.

Lesson 1: Creating a New Query

A table is the most common type of object you can include in a database, but as mentioned in Project 1, "Getting Started with Access 97," you can also create other types of objects. A query is one of the other objects you can create in a database.

You may remember that when you open the database, you see the database window that lists the tables contained in the database and also includes tabs for queries, forms, reports, and so on. If you want to add a query to the table, you can start from this window.

In this lesson, you work with the data in the P C Software table of your Training database. The P C Software table on disc that you copy and use in this project includes the records you entered in Project 3 as well as some additional records. The headings in the revised table have been modified slightly to adjust the size of each column, allowing more information to appear on the screen. You start by creating a query, and then you add the table you want to work with.

To Create a New Query

1. **Make a copy of the Proj0401 database file from the Project-04 folder on the CD and name the copy `Training3`. Then open the `Training3` database in Access.**

   In this project, you use the Training database you worked with in Projects 2, "Creating a Database," and 3, "Entering and Editing

Data," but additional records have been added to it and the headings have been modified to shrink the width of some of the columns. You should see the database window listing the P C Software table.

2 Click the Queries tab.

The Queries list is blank because you haven't created and saved any queries yet (see Figure 4.1).

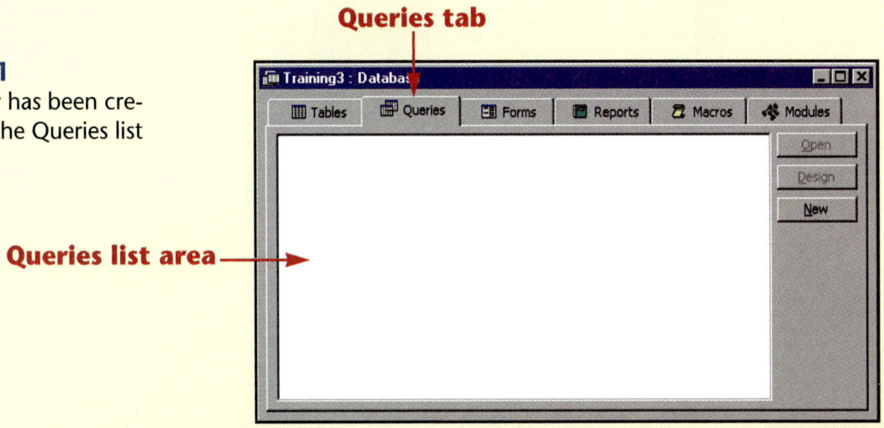

Figure 4.1
No query has been created, so the Queries list is blank.

3 Click the New button.

You see the New Query dialog box (see Figure 4.2). You can use one of the Query Wizards to create a query. This method works best for specific kinds of queries such as finding duplicate records. None of the wizards are appropriate for the query you want to create for this example, so use the more general method, Design view.

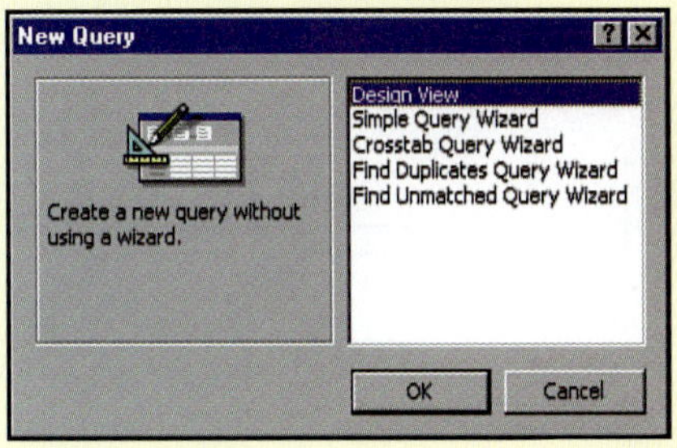

Figure 4.2
Choose the method you want to use to create a new query.

4 Click Design View and then click OK.

You see the Show Table dialog box (see Figure 4.3). Here you select the table(s) you want to use in your query. For complex queries, you can pull information from more than one table. (You learn how to work with multiple tables in a later Project.) For this example, you use just one table—the P C Software table.

continues

To Create a New Query (continued)

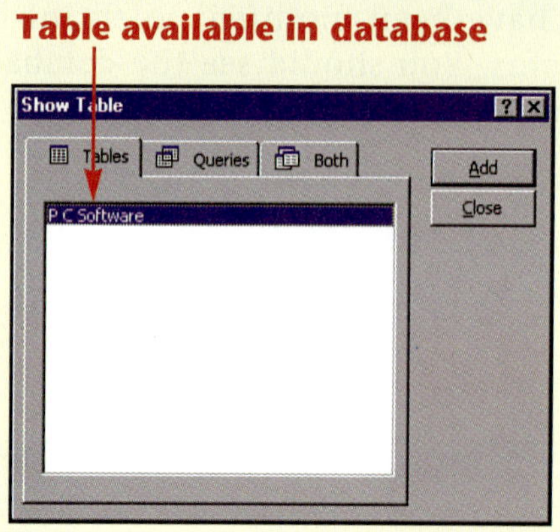

Figure 4.3
Select the table you want to use from the dialog box.

5 Click the P C Software table to select it, if necessary.

6 Click the Add button.

This step selects the table you want to use. The dialog box remains open so that you can add other tables if necessary.

7 Click the Close button.

Access closes the Show Table dialog box and displays the Select Query window (see Figure 4.4). You learn about Select Query in the next lesson. For now, leave the Select Query window open and continue with Lesson 2.

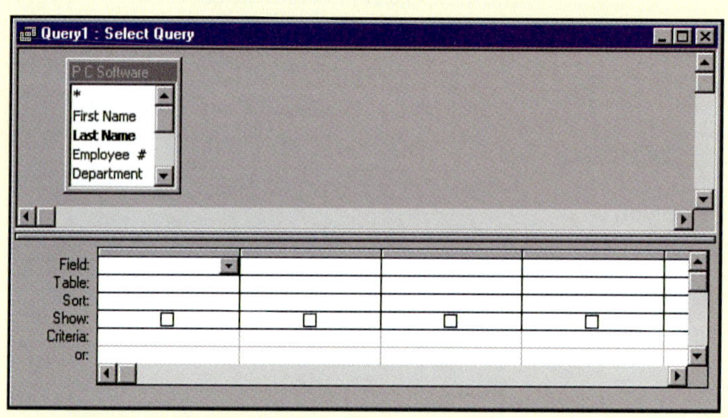

Figure 4.4
Use the query window to create a new query.

Lesson 2: Choosing Fields for a Query

After you open a new query and select a table, you see a window divided into two parts. The top half of the query window displays a scroll box containing a list of the fields from the table you selected. Notice that the primary key field appears in bold type. (In this version of the database, the Last Name field has been designated as the primary key.) You can use this field list to choose the fields you want to include in your query.

Design grid
The design grid is used to define the parameters of a query. You can specify fields, sort order, and criteria to be used to search your database.

Select query
A query that lists data that meets conditions set by the user.

In the lower half of the query window, you see the *design grid* with rows for Field, Table, Sort, Show, Criteria, and Or. All the columns are blank. The design grid controls which fields are included in your query. The simplest type of query, and the one you will probably use most often, is the *Select query*, which displays data that meets conditions that you set.

You can create a query that displays just the Last Name and Department fields from your P C Software table. You add the fields you want to include in the query to the Field row in the design grid. You can include as many fields as you want in the query, but you must include at least one field.

In this lesson, you create a query that contains only the Last Name and Department from your P C Software table. This list might be handy if you need to know who has received training in each department. You don't really need any other information from your P C Software table.

You can use one of several methods to add fields to your query. Try adding fields using these different methods now.

To Choose Fields for a Query

1 In the field list in the top half of the Select Query window, click the Last Name field.

The query window should still be open from the preceding lesson. This step selects the field you want to add to the design grid.

2 Drag the selected field from the field list to the first column in the Field row of the design grid.

As you drag, a little field box is displayed. When you release the mouse button, Access displays the field name in the Field row, and the table name in the Table row (see Figure 4.5). The Show row in this column then displays a check mark in the check box, indicating that this field will be displayed in the query. (There are occasions when you may want to use a field but not display its contents. In that case, you would click on the Show box to deselect it.) Next, you add a second field to the query.

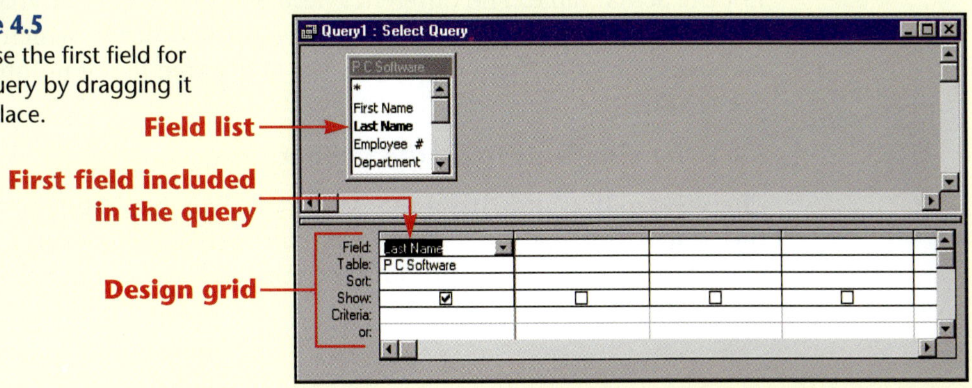

Figure 4.5
Choose the first field for the query by dragging it into place.

continues

To Choose Fields for a Query (continued)

3 Click in the second column of the Field row in the design grid.

You see a down arrow; clicking this arrow displays a drop-down list of fields from which you can choose the field you want to include in the query.

4 Click the down arrow.

Access displays the drop-down list of fields (see Figure 4.6).

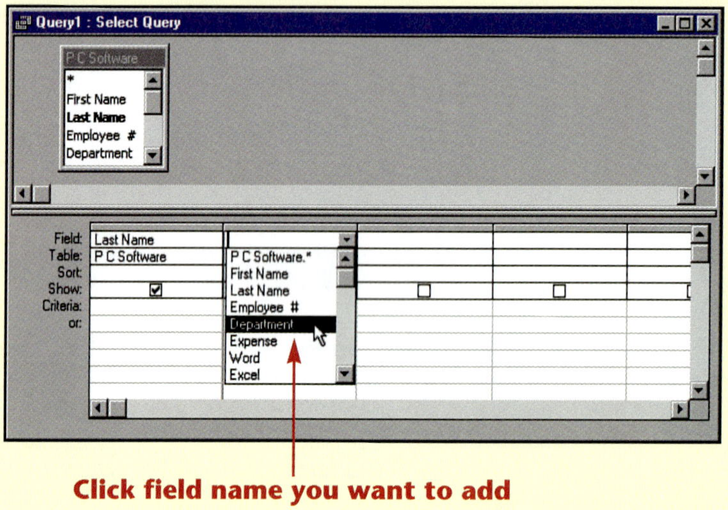

Figure 4.6
Use the drop-down list to select a field to add to the query.

5 Click Department in the list.

This selects the field to add to the query. This action has the same effect as dragging the field from the field list.

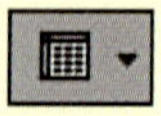

6 Click the View button on the toolbar.

This displays the records in Datasheet view, using the fields you selected in the query. Using this command, you can check to see how the query will look (see Figure 4.7). Notice that the title bar displays Select Query to remind you that you are viewing a dynaset, not the actual table. The difference between a table and a dynaset is that the table consists of all the records in the order in which they are stored on disk; the dynaset consists of a sorted list of pointers to the records, not the records themselves.

7 Click the View button on the toolbar.

The View button now has a different look. This step returns you to the Design view for the query. Keep the query window open in this view. You learn how to name and save the query in the next lesson.

Access

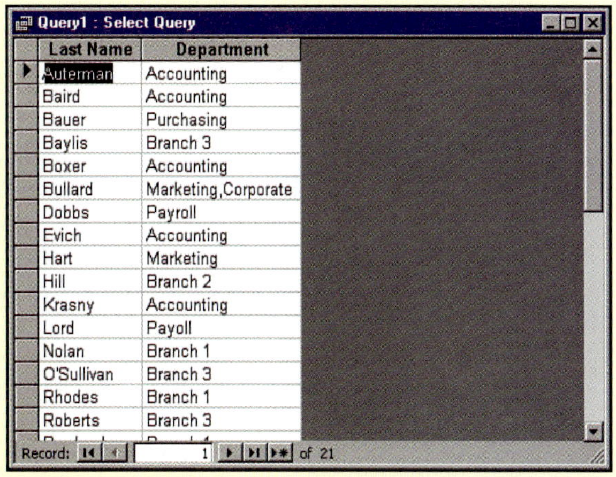

Figure 4.7
In Datasheet view, you can see that the query now includes two fields.

Inside Stuff

If you would rather use the menus, you can open the View menu and select the Datasheet View or the Design View command, instead of clicking the toolbar View buttons.

You can also add fields to the query by double-clicking the field name or by typing the field name in the Field row of the design grid.

You can select several fields and add them all at once from the field list. If the fields are listed next to each other, click the first field in the field list. Then hold down ⇧Shift and click the last field in the field list. Access selects the first and last fields and all fields in between. You can also select fields that aren't listed next to each other. Click the first field you want to select. Then hold down Ctrl and click the next field you want to select. Continue pressing Ctrl while you click each subsequent field. After you have selected all the fields you want, drag them to the design grid and place them in the first empty space in the Field row. This will add all of the selected fields to the query.

When you switch from Design view to Datasheet view, you are actually running your query. Instead of switching views, you can open the Query menu and select the Run command or click the Run button on the toolbar.

Lesson 3: Saving the Query

As with any object you add to a database, you must save and name the object if you want to keep it. If you want to keep the query you just created, for example, you have to save it. When you save a query, you save the structure of the query, not the dynaset. The dynaset is the result of running the query, which can be different each time it is run because it is based on the data in your table. If the records in the table have changed, the resulting dynaset will reflect those changes.

The first time you save a query, you are prompted to give it a name. After that, you can save changes to the query without retyping the name. You can open the File menu and choose the Save command, or you can click the Save button on the toolbar. You can also close the query window, at which point the program will ask if you want to save the query.

In this lesson, you save the query and name it.

To Save the Query

1 The query window based on the P C Software table should still be open from the preceding lesson. Open the File menu and choose the Save command.

You see the Save As dialog box, with the name Query1 displayed (see Figure 4.8). Access suggests Query1 as a default name, but as you can see, it isn't very descriptive. You can type a more descriptive name.

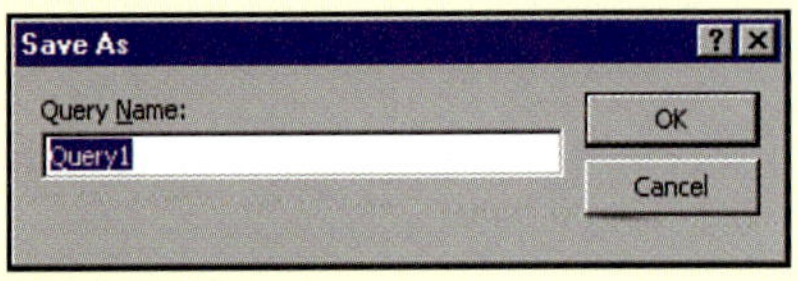

Figure 4.8
Replace the default name with a more descriptive name for the query.

2 Type `Department Training List`.

This is the name you want to assign the query. You can type up to 64 characters, including numbers, letters, spaces, and special characters except a period (.), an exclamation point (!), an accent (‘), and square brackets ([ ]). Also, you cannot include leading spaces in the query name.

3 Click the OK button.

Access saves the query and the database. The name of the query is displayed in the title bar of the query window and also in the list of queries in the database window.

4 Click the Close button in the upper-right corner of the query window.

Access closes the query window. You see the Department Training List query listed in the database window.

5 Click Department Training List on the Queries tab.

6 Click the Open button.

This step reopens the query. The query is now displayed in Datasheet view, instead of the Design view. Keep the Department Training List query open; you use it in the next lesson.

If you have problems...

If you don't like the name you used—for example, suppose that you accepted the default Query1 name—you can change the name. In Project 8, "Managing Data and Files," you learn how to rename objects such as tables and queries.

Inside Stuff

You don't have to save the query if you're sure you won't use it again. Just close the query window without saving. When Access prompts you to save, click the No button.

If you decide to save the query, you can do so by clicking the Save button on the toolbar or by pressing Ctrl+S.

When you are given choices in a dialog box, one of the buttons will have a dark border. This is the default choice and may be activated by pressing ↵Enter. If your fingers are already on the keyboard after typing data, it is faster to press ↵Enter than to reach for the mouse. Be sure to check the default choice before pressing ↵Enter to make certain it is the action you want to take.

Lesson 4: Editing the Query

Creating a query takes some practice and a little trial and error. You choose some fields, view the query, make some changes, view the query again, and so on, until you get the results you want.

You can edit the query to add or delete fields. In this project, you add three fields and then delete a field.

To Edit the Query

1. **With the Department Training List query window displayed, click the View button on the toolbar.**

   When you opened the query in the preceding lesson, it was displayed in Datasheet view. To make changes, you first have to change to Design view. Now you should see the query window with the field list box at the top and the design grid at the bottom.

2. **Click the Excel field in the field list (you may have to scroll down to find it) and drag this field to the third column of the design grid.**

   Access adds this field to the design grid. Now place the PowerPoint (labeled PP) field between the Department field and the Excel field.

3. **Click the PP field in the field list and drag this field to the third column of the design grid.**

   Access adds this field as the third column and moves the Excel field over one column to the right. You now have four fields in the query.

If you have problems...

If the PP field appears in the wrong location, drag across the PP name in the column where it appears, and press the Del key. Then repeat step 3. If it is necessary to fill an empty column, click in the Field row of the empty column, click on the drop-down arrow and select the appropriate field for that column from the pop-up field list.

continues

To Edit the Query (continued)

4 Double-click Access in the field list.

Access is added in the next field. You now have five fields in the query. In your window, you may not be able to see part, or even any of the fifth column, depending on the size of your computer monitor. Scroll the window to view the field you just added, if necessary.

Column selector
The area above a column in the design grid that enables you to select the entire column.

5 In the design grid, click the *column selector* (the thin gray bar just above the field names) over the PP column.

When you are in the column selector, you see a black downward arrow for the mouse pointer. When you click the mouse button, the entire column is selected (see Figure 4.9). After you select a column, you can move it or delete it. Try deleting this column.

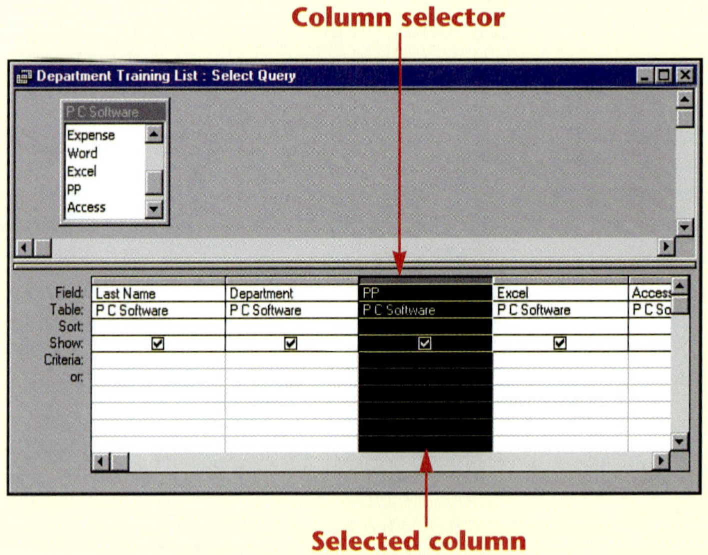

Figure 4.9
You can select a column by clicking the column selector.

6 Open the Edit menu and choose the Delete command.

Access removes the field from the design grid.

7 Click the Save button on the toolbar.

Access saves the query with the changes you made. Keep the Department Training List query open in Design view. In the next lesson, you learn how to rearrange the order of the columns in your query.

If you have problems...

You cannot use the Undo command to undo the deletion of a column. If you delete a column by mistake, simply add it again by dragging the name from the field list, double-clicking the field name in the field list, or using the drop-down list in the design grid.

Access

Inside Stuff

After you select a field to delete it, you can press Del instead of opening the Edit menu and choosing the Delete command.

Lesson 5: Changing Field Order and Sorting the Query

The way your table is arranged depends on two factors. First, the order in which the fields are displayed is determined by the order in which you add them to the Field row in the design table. If you don't like the order, you can rearrange the fields into a different order, as you learn in this lesson.

Second, the default order in which the records are displayed is determined by the primary key. You can change the query's sort order by using the Sort row in the design grid.

To Sort the Query

1 In the Department Training List query, click the column selector above the Department field.

The entire column is selected. After you select a column, you can move it or delete it.

2 Place the pointer on the column selector and drag Department until it is the first column in the design grid.

A dotted box is displayed as part of the pointer to signify that you are dragging the column (see Figure 4.10). A dark vertical line also is displayed to indicate the insertion point for the selected column. When you release the mouse button, Access rearranges the columns in the new order.

Figure 4.10
The pointer changes when you move a column in the design grid.

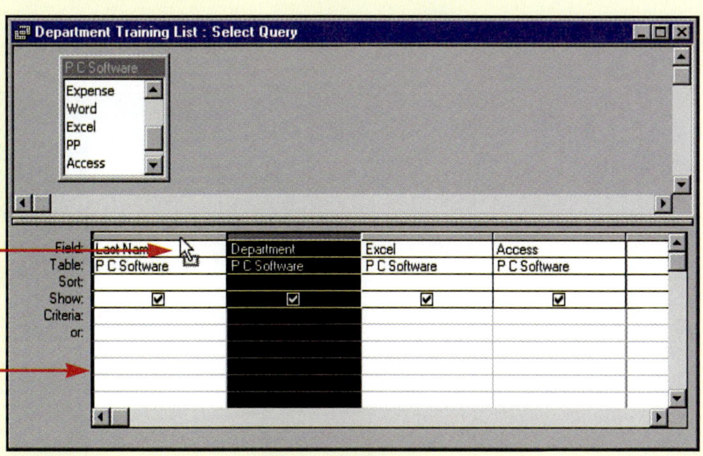

Column movement pointer

Dark line indicates where column will be inserted

continues

To Sort the Query (continued)

3 Click in the Sort row of the Department field.

In this example, you want to sort the query by Department. When you click in the field, Access displays a down arrow.

4 Click the down arrow.

Access displays a drop-down list of sort choices (see Figure 4.11).

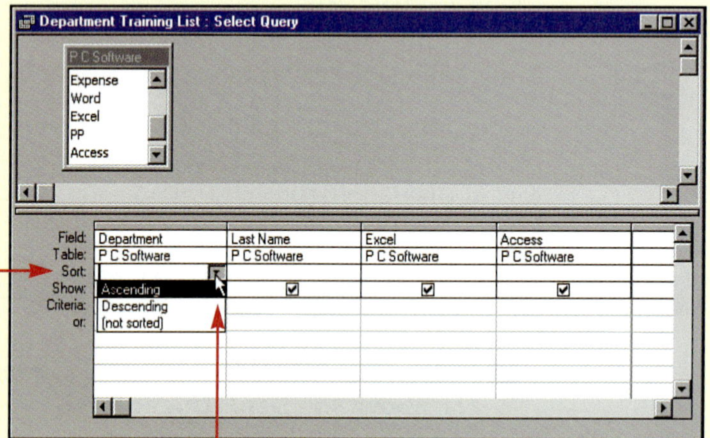

Figure 4.11
Choose a sort order for your query from the drop-down list.

5 Click Ascending.

This selects the sort order (*a* to *z*) you want to use. You can check the query by changing to Datasheet view.

6 Click the View button on the toolbar.

You can see the results of your query in the Datasheet view, as shown in Figure 4.12.

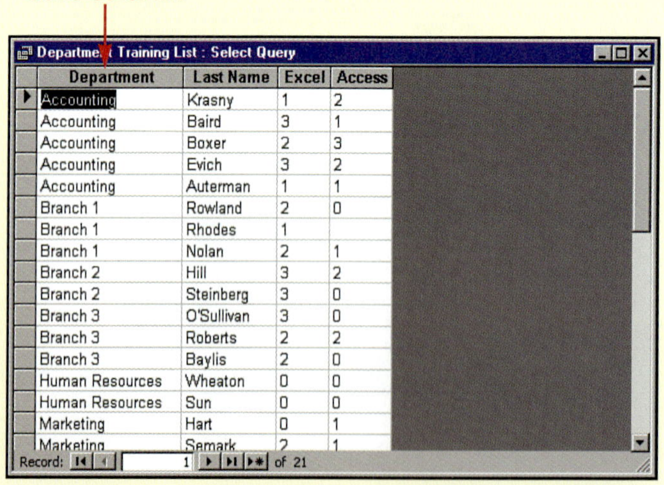

Figure 4.12
In Datasheet view, you can see that the query is now sorted by Department.

7 **Click the View button on the toolbar again.**

The query is once again displayed in Design view.

8 **Click the Save button on the toolbar.**

This saves the changes you made to the query. Keep the Department Training List query open in Design view as you continue with the next lesson.

Lesson 6: Matching Criteria

So far, the query you have created displays all of the records contained in the Training3 database, but only shows the fields you selected. You can also use a query to display only certain records—records that match certain *criteria*.

Criteria
A test or set of conditions that limits the records included in a query. A single condition is a criterion.

You can match a single criterion, such as the last names of staff members who have received training in Excel, or you can match multiple criteria, such as staff members in the Marketing or Human Resources departments who have received training in Access or Excel. In this lesson, you practice using the various types of criteria.

To Match Criteria

1 **In the Design view of the Department Training List query, click the Criteria box in the Department column.**

The insertion point is moved to this location of the design grid. Here you can type the value that you want to match.

2 **Type `Human Resources` and press Enter.**

Access automatically adds quotation marks around the criteria that has been entered (see Figure 4.13). However, in some cases, such as when entering values that contain any punctuation marks, you must type the quotation marks.

3 **Click the View button.**

You see the results of the query. Notice that Access now includes only the staff members in the Human Resources Department in the query (see Figure 4.14).

4 **Click the View button again.**

This returns you to the design grid so you can make a change to the query.

5 **Move to the box immediately below the Criteria box where you previously typed Human Resources. This is the or: row.**

continues

To Match Criteria (continued)

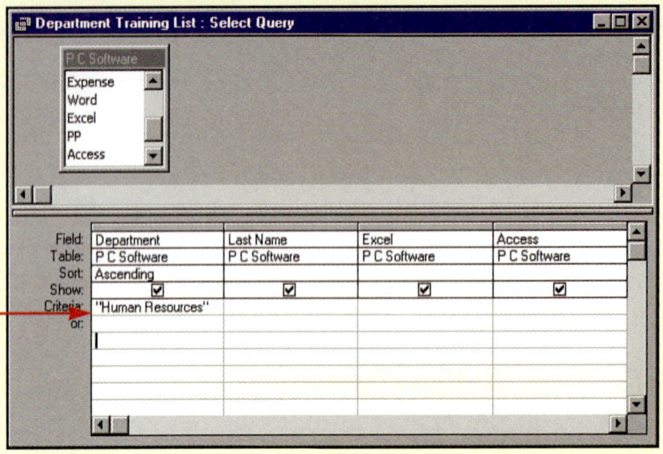

Criterion to match

Figure 4.13
Enter the criteria you want to match.

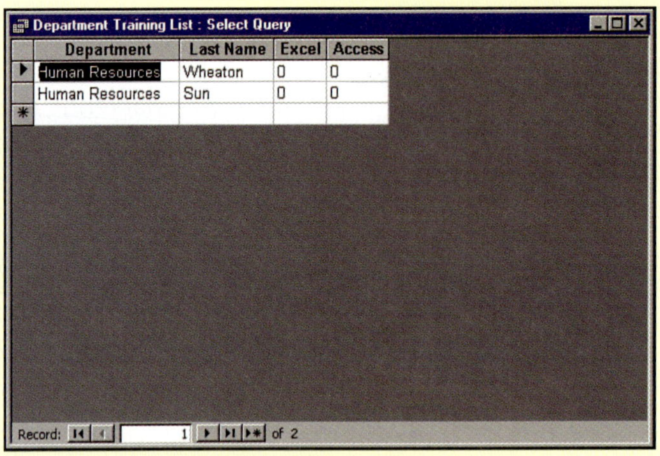

Figure 4.14
The query now lists all the people in Human Resources who are listed in our Training table.

6 Click this box.

If you have problems...

If the window for the dialog box is not large enough to display more than one line of criteria, the window may scroll the list automatically. This results in some of the criteria disappearing from view. Maximize this window before proceeding, if necessary.

If you want to match more than one value, you use this row to specify the second value. For this example, you might want to specify staff members in Human Resources or Accounting who have received training.

7 Type `Accounting`.

When the entry you want to match is one word and contains no punctuation, as in this example, you don't have to type quotation marks. Access adds them automatically.

8 Click the View button.

You see the results of the query. Notice that Access now includes trained staff members from Human Resources and Accounting.

9 Click the View button again.

You return to the Design view. Keep the Department Training List query open. In the next lesson, you learn how to save the query with a new name.

If you have problems...

If you see a blank dynaset when you switch to Datasheet view, it means that Access found no matching records. Be sure that you typed the value you are trying to match exactly as you entered it in the database table. For example, you can't type `"Human Resource"` to match `"Human Resources"`. Check your typing and try again.

If, when you are entering text into the Criteria rows to make a match, Access displays a syntax error message, it means that you did not type the entry in the correct format. Remember that if the text entry contains punctuation, you must supply quotation marks.

Inside Stuff

Access has many types of queries you can use. You can, for example, match a range of values, as you would if you asked Access to display all staff members who received training in Excel at a level 2 or above. You can also create other types of queries, such as a query to display all duplicate records in a table.

There are other types of criteria that may be used besides a direct match. You can use comparisons such as <, which means less than, or >, which means greater than. If you use < to make a comparison in a text field, it uses alphabetical order. For example, if your criterion was <Jones, you would get all the names that came before Jones in the alphabet. Similarly, if you use <1/1/95 in a date field, you would get all the dates before January 1, 1995. For more examples of different criteria, use the Access Help index to look up help for Criteria, then explore some of the different categories.

Exam Notes

To print the results of a query, click the Print button on the toolbar. Queries print from the Datasheet view and appear in the same format as printing a table. Printing the results of a query is part of the Microsoft Access Exam; however, reports are generally a better method for printing database information. You learn about creating and printing reports in Project 6.

Lesson 7: Saving the Query with a New Name and Opening Multiple Queries

In some cases, you may modify a query and then want to keep both versions of the query—the original and the modified query—for future use. In this lesson, you learn how to save a query with a new name.

You can also open a query from the database window, and you can have more than one query window open at a time. This lesson explains how to open multiple queries.

To Save the Query with a New Name and Open Multiple Queries

1. **In the Department Training List query, click the View button on the toolbar to go to the Datasheet view.**

2. **Open the File menu and choose the Save As/Export command.**

   You see the Save As dialog box, as shown in Figure 4.15, with the current name listed in the New Name text box.

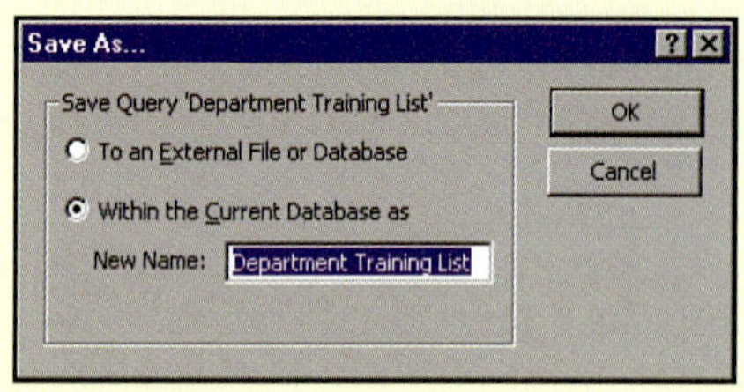

Figure 4.15
Prepare to save a query with a new name.

3. **Type `HR and Accounting`.**

   This is the name you want to use for the new query.

4. **Click the OK button.**

   Access saves the query with the new name, and the new name is displayed in the title bar. The original query remains unchanged on disc.

5. **Close the query window.**

   This step closes the query window and returns you to the database window. The Queries tab should be selected, and you should see the two queries displayed in the queries list (see Figure 4.16).

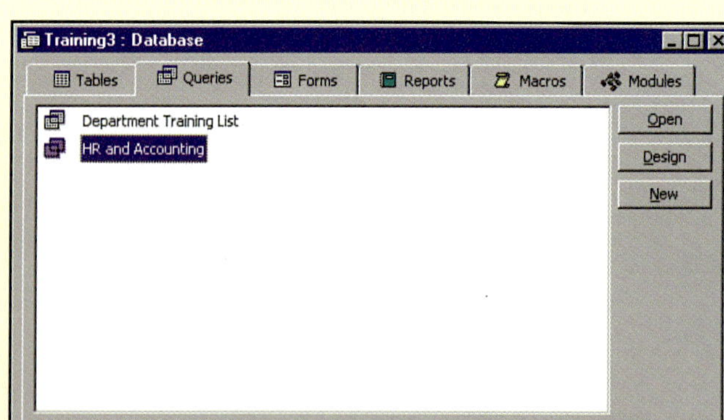

Figure 4.16
More than one query is displayed for the Training3 database.

6 Select and open the `Department Training List` query.

This step opens the query. Notice that the query displays all departments, not just the ones for Human Resources and Accounting.

7 Click the Database Window button on the toolbar.

8 Select and open the `HR and Accounting` query.

This opens your modified query. Now both queries are open onscreen, as well as the database window.

9 Open the Window menu and choose Cascade.

This step arranges the windows so that you can see which windows are currently open.

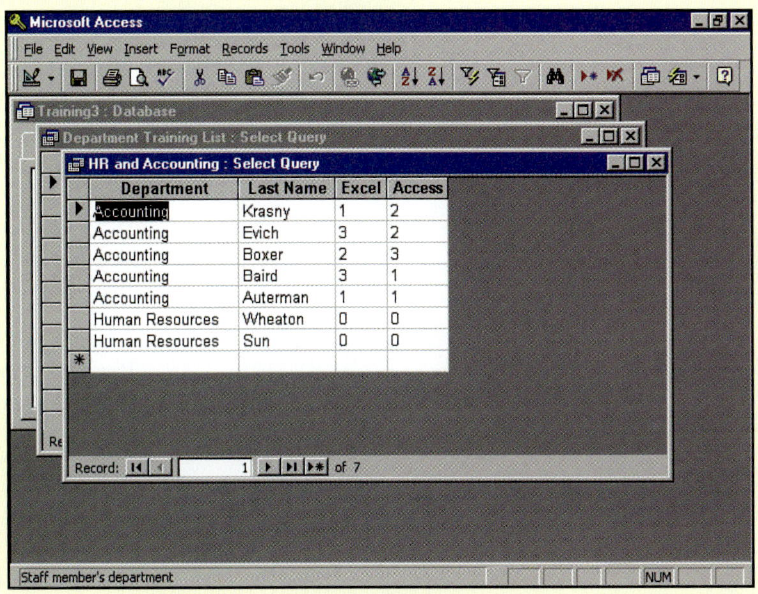

Figure 4.17
The open windows are placed on top of each other with the title bars displayed.

10 Close both query windows and the database.

If you have completed your session on the computer, exit Access. Otherwise, continue with the sections "Checking Your Skills" and "Applying Your Skills" in this project.

Inside Stuff

You can also make a copy of a query in the database window by selecting the query, clicking the Copy button, then clicking the Paste button. A Paste As dialog box opens so you can give the query copy a new name.

Once a query has been saved, you can open it in Design view instead of in Datasheet view. To open a query in Design view, click the query to select it, then click the Design button.

Project Summary

To	Do This
Create a new query	Open the database and click the Queries tab. Click the New button, Design view, and then OK. Select the table(s) you want to use, and click Add. Close the Show Table dialog box.
Choose fields for a query	Click and drag the field from the field list box to the design grid; or, in the design grid, click the drop-down arrow and choose the field you want; or double-click the field in the field list box.
Save a query	Open the File menu and choose the Save command. Type a descriptive name in the dialog box and click OK.
Edit a query	Work in Design view. Click and drag fields, or double-click a field to add it to the query. You can insert fields between existing fields in the design grid by clicking and dragging the field. Use the column selector to rearrange columns. You can delete selected columns by opening the Edit menu and selecting Delete.
Sort a query	Work in Design view. Click in the Sort row of the design grid of the field to be sorted. Select Ascending or Descending order.
Match criteria	Work in Design view. Click in the Criteria row of the field you want to match. Type the criterion you want to match. Add a second criterion by going to the or: row in the design grid. Use quotation marks if punctuation is included in the criteria.
Save a query with a new name	Open the File menu and choose Save As/Export command. Type a new name in the dialog box and click OK.
Open multiple queries	From the Database window, select and open first one query, then use the Database Window button to select a second query (or more). Open the Window menu and choose Cascade to view title bars for all queries.

Checking Your Skills

True/False

For each of the following, check *T* or *F* to indicate whether the statement is true or false.

__T __F **1.** You must include at least one field in a query.

__T __F **2.** You define the parameters of a query in the design grid.

__T __F **3.** A dynaset is stored on disk.

__T __F **4.** You cannot include spaces or punctuation in a query name.

__T __F **5.** If you see a blank dynaset when you run a query, Access found no matching records.

__T __F **6.** The first time you save a query, the Save As dialog box appears.

__T __F **7.** You must include all fields in a query, even though they may not be displayed.

__T __F **8.** If you accidentally delete a field from the query, you can click the Undo button to restore the field.

__T __F **9.** A query can use only one table.

__T __F **10.** As you drag a field name from the field list to the query, the mouse pointer becomes a little field box.

Multiple Choice

Circle the letter of the correct answer for each of the following questions.

1. Which of the following can you do to add a field to the query?

a. Double-click the field name in the field list.

b. Use the drop-down list in the Field row of the design grid.

c. Drag the field name from the field list to the design grid.

d. All of the above.

2. Which of the following is not a way to run a query when you are working in the query Design view?

a. Click the Run button.

b. Click the Go button.

c. Open the Query menu and choose the Run command.

d. Open the View menu and choose the Datasheet view command.

3. What is the lower half of the query window called?

a. field list

b. design grid

c. Criteria box

d. Query area

4. How should you enter criteria for text fields if the criterion contains punctuation?
   a. in all uppercase
   b. in all lowercase
   c. in bold
   d. within quotation marks

5. In what order are fields included in a query?
   a. the order in which you add them
   b. the order in which they appear in the table
   c. alphabetic order
   d. numeric order

6. What is the column selector?
   a. a dialog box listing all active columns
   b. a drop-down list that appears when you click the down arrow in a column field
   c. a shortcut list of columns activated by pressing the right mouse button
   d. a gray box on top of the column that enables you to highlight the entire column

7. How do you change the order of the fields in a query?
   a. Select one field, select a second field while pressing Ctrl, and choose Swap from the Edit menu.
   b. Select the field and then drag it to the new location.
   c. Drag the field from the field list to the new location. The other reference in the query will automatically be deleted.
   d. You can't change the order of the fields. They must appear in the same order as in the field list.

8. Queries can _______________.
   a. sort data, limit fields, and limit records
   b. be saved and used over and over again
   c. create a dynaset
   d. all of the above

9. Which of the following is not a way of creating another query?
   a. altering the current query and saving it with a new name
   b. selecting New on the Query tab and building a query from scratch
   c. selecting Duplicate from the Edit menu and saving the duplicate query with a new name
   d. copying the query in the database window and renaming the copy with a new name

10. How long can a query name be?
   a. 64 characters
   b. 255 characters
   c. 8 characters
   d. any length

Completion

In the blank provided, write the correct answer for each of the following statements.

1. A(n) ______________ is a subset of records displayed by a query.
2. A(n) ______________ is a question you ask of the database.
3. The set of conditions or limits you use to match entries in a field is called ______________.
4. To view a query, change to the ______________ view.
5. The top half of the query window contains the ______________, which you can use to choose fields.
6. To select multiple fields in a field list that aren't next to each other, use the ______________ key when you click the fields.
7. The ______________ button changes depending on which window is open.
8. You cannot change a query in ______________ view.
9. To display only the names that come before Matthews, you enter ______________ as the criterion for the name field.
10. From the Database window, you view the dynaset of data created by the query design by selecting the query and clicking the __________ button.

Matching

In the blank next to each of the following terms or phrases, write the letter of the corresponding term or phrase. (Note that some letters may be used more than once.)

a. Sort Ascending
b. dark-bordered button
c. Show box
d. field list
e. design view of query
f. design grid
g. dynaset
h. criterion
i. Run button
j. drop-down list

_____ 1. Answers to a question that has been asked
_____ 2. Contains field lists and locations for fields and settings for queries
_____ 3. Contains the scope, criteria, and order of the question asked of the database
_____ 4. Has an exclamation point on it
_____ 5. A shortcut group of entries available by selecting a down arrow
_____ 6. Arranges the records alphabetically in a dynaset
_____ 7. Can be activated by pressing ↵Enter
_____ 8. If checked, displays a field in a query
_____ 9. Shows fields that can be included in a query
_____ 10. A test or condition to limit a query

Applying Your Skills

Practice

The following exercises enable you to practice the skills you have learned in this project. Take a few minutes to work through these exercises now.

Querying Your Library Database

In the "Applying Your Skills" sections of Projects 2 and 3, you created a Library database with a Books table that listed the books in your library. You may be curious to see exactly what types of books you have. For instance, you may want to view a list of only book names and authors to see what your collection contains. Or, you may want to determine the most common type of book in your collection. You can create a query, for example, to display only mystery books.

To query your Library database, complete the following steps:

1. Copy the Proj0402 database file from the Project-04 folder on the CD and rename it `Library3`. Then open the `Library3` database in Access.
2. Create a query and add the fields for `Author Last Name` and `Book Title`. Sort the query by Author Last Name. Then view the results of this query in Datasheet view.
3. Change back to Design view. Save the query and name it `Book List`.
4. Add the `Type of Book` field to the query. In the Criteria row for this column, type `Mystery`.
5. View the results of the query in Datasheet view. Use the Print button on the toolbar to print a copy of this view.
6. Go back to Design view and save the query with a new name, such as `Mysteries`.

Querying Your Record Company Database

In a previous project, you set up and then entered records for a record company database. This database includes the names of the record labels that you stock in your Sound Byte Music Store. Suppose that you are planning a trip to New York and you want to contact your sales representatives for the companies in New York. You can use a query to create the list—all record companies in New York. In this list, you can include the record company name, contact name, and phone number.

To query your record company database, complete the following steps:

1. Copy the Proj0403 database file from the Project-04 folder on the CD and rename the copy `SBMusic3`. Then return to Access and open the `SBMusic3` database.
2. Create a query and add the fields for `Record Company`, `Contact Name`, and `Phone`.

3. View the results of this query in Datasheet view.
4. Change back to Design view and save the query with the name `NY Trip`.
5. Add the `State` field to the query. In the Criteria row for this column, type `NY`.
6. View the results of the query in Datasheet view. Save the query and name it `New York`.
7. Close both query windows and the database.

Querying a Database to Track Personal Computer Hardware

Your company is planning to install software that takes over 200 megabytes of hard drive space. You would like to know which machines have hard drives that may be too small to handle the new software.

To query the database, complete the following steps:

1. Copy the file Proj0404 from the Project-04 folder on the CD and rename the copy `PC3`. Open `PC3`.
2. Create a query, based on the PC Hardware table, which shows the PCs with hard drives of less than 500 megabytes of capacity. (The given ratings are in megabytes.) Include the following fields:

    `Processor`

    `RAM`

    `Hard Drive Size`

    `Vendor`

    `Inventory Code Number`

3. Sort the query by Processor.
4. Change to Datasheet view and click the Print button on the toolbar to print the query.
5. Save the query with the name `Hard Drives less than 500 meg`. Close the database.

Getting a Helping Hand

Queries can get complicated very quickly. It is important to understand how they are built and what they mean. The Help system provides an excellent review of queries.

To get help on topics in this project, complete the following steps:

1. With Access open, press F1. The Office Assistant opens and a dialog box in the form of a comment box opens beside it.
2. In the question area of the dialog box, type `Build a query` and press ↵Enter. The comment bubble changes, displaying a list of options that fit the statement.

3. Select the second entry, `Queries: What they are and how they work`. A Help window opens that provides a three-page overview of queries. Take a few minutes and read each page by selecting the numbers at the top left of the page.
4. Close the Help window. The Office Assistant remains open.
5. Click the Office Assistant once. The comment bubble reappears with your statement still in the question box.
6. Select Search. The same list of responses appears.
7. Select the first response, `Create a query`. The main Help window opens, displaying the central topic covering query creation.
8. Scroll toward the bottom of the window. You see a series of entries with buttons beside them ([>>]). The first entry, `Learn about the different types of queries I can create`, provides a good overview of the different queries. Farther down, you find the entry `Work on my own to create a Select query`. Selecting this entry shows you more about creating your own queries.
9. Take a few minutes and explore.

Exploring the World of Alaska

The project file Proj0405 (from the Project-04 folder on the CD) includes the partial Alaska database with some additional entries for pictures and sources. In Project 3, you considered how to answer questions by using sorting. Now you view the database by using queries.

To view the database by using queries, complete the following steps:

1. Copy Proj0405 and rename it `Alaska2`.
2. Select the Queries tab and click New.
3. Select Design View and click OK.
4. Select and add the `Geography` table.
5. Close the Show Table dialog box.
6. From the field list, add the `Object`, `Type`, `Picture`, and `Source` fields to the design grid.
7. Click the Run button. A dynaset appears, including only the four fields that were chosen.
8. Return to Design view and change the sort for the Type field to Ascending.
9. Run the query again. The dynaset is now sorted so that all the geographic features are grouped by type alphabetically.
10. Return to Design view and remove the sort setting for the Type field. Instead, add the criterion `island` to select only islands.
11. Run the query again. You should have 16 islands listed in the dynaset. Three of these islands have pictures.

12. Save the query as `Alaskan Islands`.

13. Return to Design view and try different settings and queries.

Challenge

The following challenges enable you to use your problem-solving skills. Take time to work through these exercises now.

Adding Club Member Names and Sorting

Open the database for tracking the members of a club or organization that you created in previous projects. Create a query named `Roster`. Include all the fields in the one table. Sort the query by last name. Use the Print button on the toolbar to print a copy for your records. If requested by your instructor, print an extra copy to hand in.

Doing Customer Research

Now that you have started to receive return questionnaires, your boss seems to come into your office every five minutes wanting to know which channels are being watched and what the other numbers are. You have received four more responses and decide to build a quick query to answer your boss's questions.

To build a quick query, complete the following steps:

1. Copy the database Proj0406 from the Project-04 folder on the CD and rename it as `Customer Research3`. Enter the following responses to the questionnaire:

Adults	Children	Hours	No 1	No 2	No 3	Doing
1	3	4	DISCOVERY	TNT	SCIFI	Great
2	2	1	DISNEY	TNT	CNN	Okay
2	1	6	SCIFI	CNN		Good
2	2	3	DISNEY	DISCOVERY		Marginal

   `Improvement comment for the first household: There are many times when we have to shut off the TV because of the graphic shows.`

   `Comment for the second household: You're doing all right, though it would be great to see some other channels.`

   `Comment for the third household: Need more action stuff.`

   `Comment for the fourth household: Please block out the violence and profanity. We understand you can do that.`

2. Build a query that lists the three cable channels. Try to build a query that would sort the records to show which channel is most watched.

   This is an example of a database that has a design flaw. Refer back to Rule 6 at the beginning of Project 2. Notice the warning to avoid designs that have numbered field names like Member1, Member2.... It is difficult to create a query that can answer this question conveniently, but give it a try.

3. Save the Query as Boss's Lament.

Owning a Vending Company

You have entered more records into your database, mostly in the Locations table. It is now time to see what some of the information can tell you.

To query the database, complete the following steps:

1. Copy Proj0407 from the Project-04 folder on the CD and save it as Vending2.
2. Create a query for the Locations table, including all fields, that sorts the records alphabetically based on the machine type.
3. Run the query. Look through the dynaset to see which machine type is used most often.
4. Save the query as Earner List.
5. Modify the query to list only that machine type.
6. Save the new query as Big Earner. You should have two different queries, each providing a different output.

Managing a Video Store

Open your video store database you created in previous projects and create a query that sorts the database by title. Save this query as Video List.

Then create a query that sorts all videos by age, listing the oldest video first. This query may help you decide which videos should be replaced. Save this new query as Replacement Candidates.

You should also have a field that lists the number of times the video has been rented. This field should be included in the Replacement Candidate query because it tells you the wear and tear on the video. Sort the table by both fields, age and number of rentals, to get more information from which to base your decision on what videos need updating.

Taking a Home Inventory

You should have a number of records in the main table of the inventory database you created in previous projects. Build a query that sorts the inventory table based on the cost of the item. If you have included your house and car in the inventory, you should see those items at the bottom of the list (provided the list is sorted in ascending order). Save the sort as By Dollar Listing.

Add additional records to the table to have at least 20 records. These records help you later in the book as you develop more complicated features for the database.

PinPoint Assessment

PinPoint Training

You have completed the project and the associated lessons, as well as the "Checking Your Skills" and "Applying Your Skills" sections. Now use the PinPoint software Evaluation mode to assess your comprehension of the specific exam tasks you have just learned. You can also use the PinPoint Trainer mode and the SHOW ME tutorials to practice these specific exam tasks.

Project 5

Five

Creating and Using Forms

Working with Forms

In this project you will learn the following objectives and their associated Microsoft Exam required activities.

Objectives	Required Activities
➤ Create an AutoForm	Create a Simple Form
➤ Enter and Edit Data Using a Form	Add a Record Using a Form Enter Data in a Form
➤ Save, Close, and Open a Form	
➤ Create a New Form from Scratch	Create a Simple Form Create Controls on a Form View Information in a Form
➤ Add Fields to Forms	View Information in a Form View Multiple Records
➤ Move and Resize Fields in Forms	Modify a Form Modify Controls
➤ Add a Form Header and Label	Print a Form Modify Form Design Title a Form

Why Would I Do This?

When you enter records in a table, each record is displayed in a row, and all records are displayed. If the table has many fields, you may not be able to see all of the fields in the table onscreen, and you may find it difficult to find the record you want with all the records displayed. A *form* is used to display one record at a time and you may place the fields anywhere on the screen. Even if a record has many fields, you may be able to see them all on one screen. You can move the fields around and add text to the form so that it resembles paper forms that are already in use. It is much easier for people to transfer data from paper forms to the form on the screen if they look the same.

Form
A type of object you can use to enter, edit, and view records. Think of a form as a fill-in-the-blanks screen.

Using a form offers the following advantages:

- You can select the fields you want to include in the form, and you can arrange them in the order you want.
- You can choose to display only one record at a time, which makes it easier to concentrate on that record.
- You can make the form more graphically appealing.

AutoForm
A form that is created automatically by Access that includes all the fields in a table.

Access provides an *AutoForm* that you can create quickly without a great deal of work. If this form isn't what you need, you can also create a form from scratch. In this project, you learn about both methods for creating forms.

Access

Lesson 1: Creating an AutoForm

If you want a simple form that lists each field in a single column and displays one record at a time, you can use one of the Access Form Wizards to create an AutoForm. The Form Wizards look at the structure of your database table and then create a form automatically. You simply choose the commands to start the wizards.

To Create an Autoform

1 Copy the Proj0501 database file from the Project-05 folder on the CD and rename it `Address2`. Then return to Access and open the `Address2` database.

In this project, you use a version of the Address database you worked with in Project 1, "Getting Started with Access 97." You should see the database window, listing the Contacts table.

2 Click the Forms tab.

The Forms list is blank because you haven't yet created and saved any forms (see Figure 5.1).

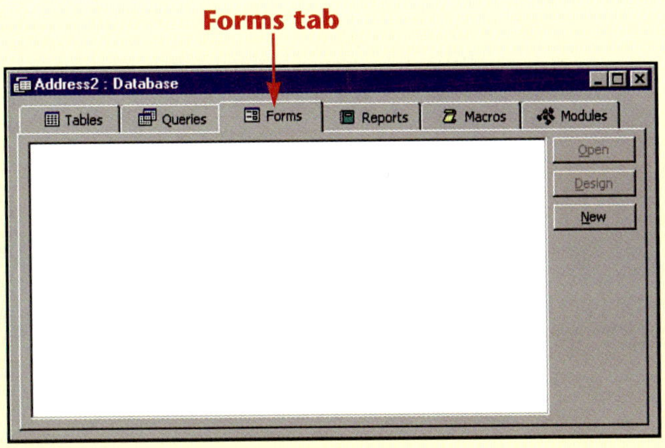

Figure 5.1
No forms are listed because you have not yet created any.

3 Click the New button.

You see the New Form dialog box. First, you have to select a table to use with the form. Then you must decide whether you want to use the Form Wizards or start with a blank form. In this lesson, you use the Form Wizards.

4 Click the down arrow in the box labeled `Choose the table or query where the object's data comes from`.

You see a list of the tables and queries available in the database (see Figure 5.2). You can base a form on either a query or a table. In this lesson, use the Contacts table.

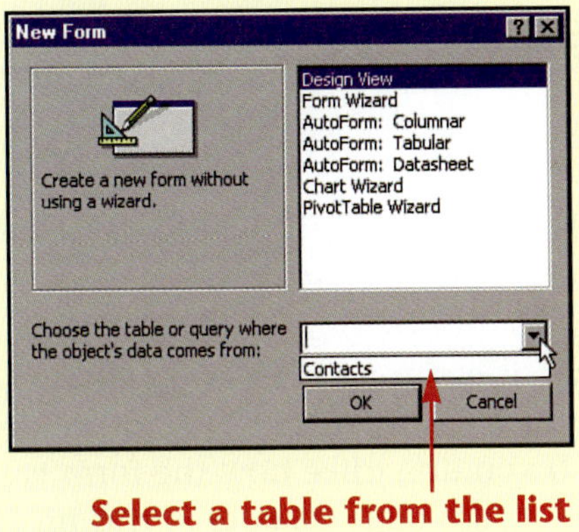

Figure 5.2
From the drop-down list, choose the table on which you want to base the form.

5 Click Contacts.

This step selects the table you want to use.

6 Click the AutoForm: Columnar option, and then click OK.

The Form Wizard creates the form; this step may take several seconds. The status bar displays the progress so that you can see that Access is working. After the AutoForm is built, Access displays the table's first record. Notice that the fields are displayed in columns in the form. Your screen may not have the same background settings.

continues

To Create an Autoform (continued)

The navigation buttons are displayed at the bottom of the form to enable you to move through the records (see Figure 5.3). Keep this form onscreen as you continue to the next lesson, where you learn more about the navigation buttons.

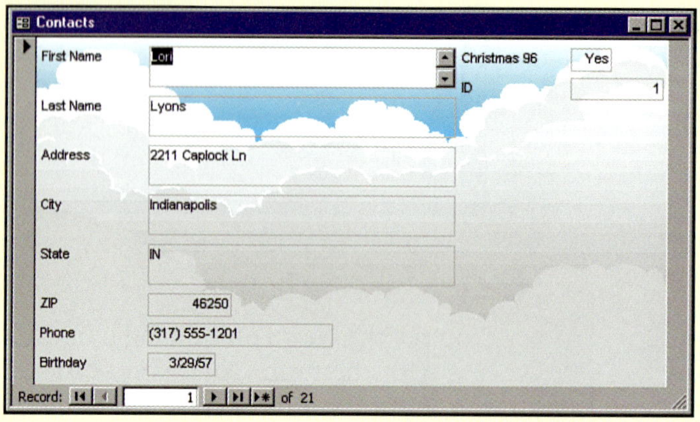

Figure 5.3
An AutoForm containing all fields displayed in a single column.

Inside Stuff

You can also create a new form by clicking the drop-down arrow to the right of the New Object button on the toolbar in the database window. When your table is in Datasheet view, you can click the New Object list button and select either the New Form button or the AutoForm button to create a new form.

Other wizard forms can be used to generate forms in different layouts, such as tabular, or to only include selected fields.

Lesson 2: Entering and Editing Data Using a Form

Forms make it easier to enter and edit data. Before you save the form, you may want to try some data entry to be sure that you like the structure of the form. If you don't like how the form is set up, you can change it or create a new one, as you learn later in this project.

You can use the same tools to enter, find, sort, and display records in a form that you use in a table. This lesson explains how to add and edit a record using a form.

To Enter and Edit Data Using a Form

1. **The AutoForm based on the Contacts table should still be on your screen from the previous lesson. Click the New Record button located both on the toolbar and with the navigation buttons on the bottom of the window.**

This step adds a new record, and a blank form is displayed (see Figure 5.4). The insertion point appears in the first field of the form.

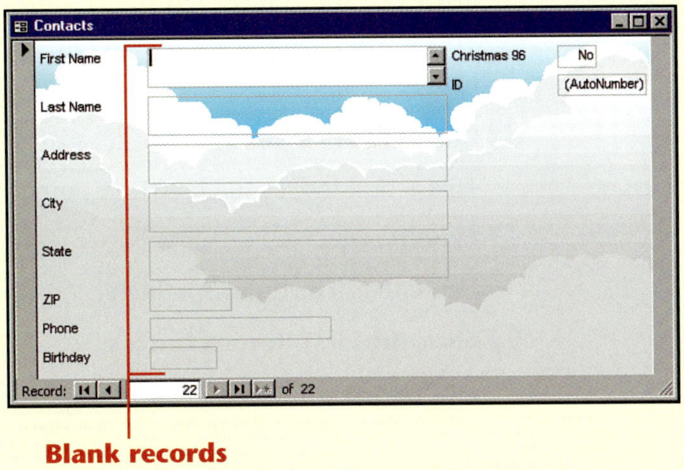

Figure 5.4
The new form is ready to have information added.

❷ Type the following data, pressing Tab after each entry (not Enter) to move to the next field:

```
Janet
Eisenhut
455 Sheridan
Indianapolis
IN
46204
(317) 555-6588
3/29/60
Yes
```

Notice that when you type the phone number, Access automatically provides parentheses around the area code, moves you over so that you can type the exchange, and provides a hyphen after the exchange.

You may have to scroll down to see all the fields in the form. When you reach the last field—the ID field—you do not have to enter a value because it is a counter field. Also, remember that when you move to another record, Access automatically saves the record you just entered. Keep in mind that the record is saved in the underlying Contacts table. You don't have to worry about updating the table separately.

❸ Click the First Record button.

This moves you to the first record in the table.

continues

To Enter and Edit Data Using a Form (continued)

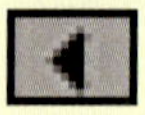

4 Click the Next Record button to scroll through the records until you see the record for Shelli Canady.

This is the record you want to edit. Notice that the Birthday field is blank.

5 Click in the Birthday field.

This action moves the insertion point to the field you want to edit.

6 Type 11/4/65.

This enters a birthday for Shelli.

7 Click the First Record button.

This moves you back to the first record and saves the change to the record you just edited. Keep the form open on your screen as you continue to the next lesson.

If you have problems...

If you can't find the record that you want to edit by scrolling, you can open the Edit menu and use the Find command. (Refer to Project 3, "Entering and Editing Data," for more information on searching records.)

If you press Enter your cursor will not move to the next box. Simply press Tab instead.

If you make an editing change and want to undo it, open the Edit menu and choose the Undo command or press the Undo button. This will undo your last change.

Inside Stuff

Besides using the navigation buttons, you can use the keyboard to move among records and fields. Press Tab or ↓ or → to move to the next field; Shift+Tab or ↑ or ← to move to the previous field; PgUp to scroll to the previous record; and PgDn to scroll to the next record. Ctrl+Home will move the insertion point to the first field in the first record and Ctrl+End will move the insertion point to the last field in the last record.

Lesson 3: Saving, Closing, and Opening a Form

If you use the form and like how it is organized, you can save the form so that you can use it again later. If you try to close the form without saving, Access reminds you to save. You don't have to save the form; you should save only if you intend to use it again.

If you have problems...

If you accidentally close the form without saving it, you can simply recreate it (follow the steps in Lesson 1 of this project).

As with the other objects you have created, you are prompted to type a name the first time you save the form. You can type up to 64 characters, including spaces. After you have saved the form, you can close it and open it again when you want to use the form.

To Save, Close, and Open a Form

1 The AutoForm that uses the Contacts table should still be open on your screen. Open the File menu and choose the Save command.

You see the Save As dialog box (see Figure 5.5). Here you type the form name, which can include as many as 64 characters and spaces.

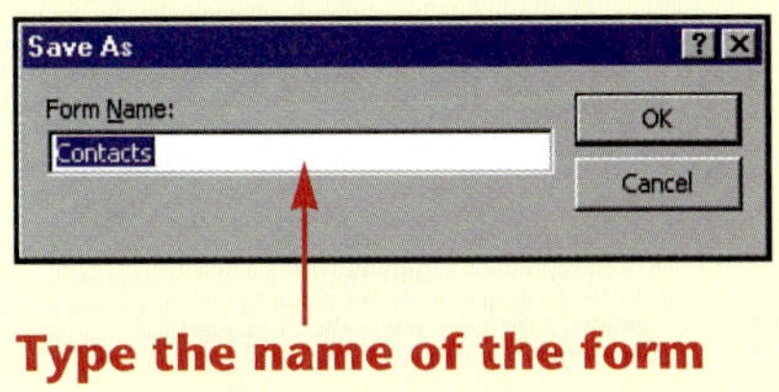

Figure 5.5
Give the form a name before you save it.

2 Type `AutoForm`.

This is the name you want to assign to the form.

3 Click the OK button.

Access saves the form.

4 Click the Close button in the upper-right corner of the form window to close the form.

The form window closes, and you see the database window again. Notice that your new form is now included in the Forms list when you click the Forms tab (see Figure 5.6).

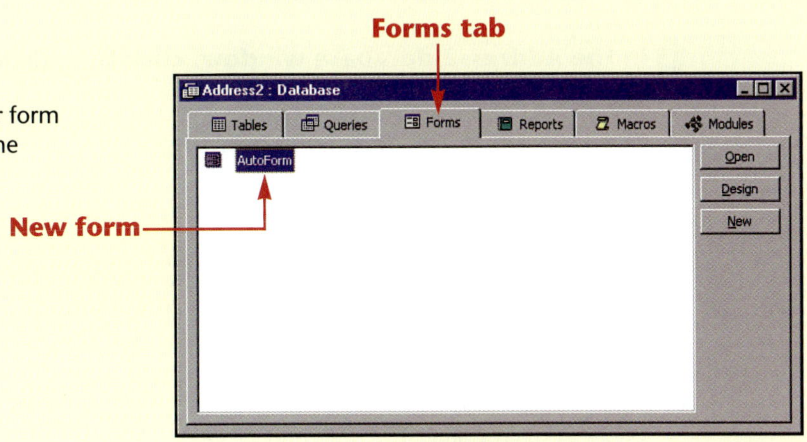

Figure 5.6
The name of your form now appears in the Forms list.

continues

To Save, Close, and Open a Form (continued)

5 Double-click AutoForm to open it.

Access displays the first record in the table using the form you created. You can add, modify, or delete records. When you are finished working in the form, close it again. As you move from field to field, Access automatically saves any changes you make.

6 Click the Close button to close the form.

Access closes the form. Keep the Address2 database open and continue to the next lesson.

Inside Stuff

You can press Ctrl+S to save the form instead of using File, Save.

Lesson 4: Creating a New Form from Scratch

Sometimes the Form Wizards do not create exactly the form you want. When that happens, you can start from a blank form and create the form you want. The form can include any text, fields, and other *controls* you want to incorporate.

Control
A control is any graphical object selected from the toolbox, such as a text box, check box, or option button that you add to a form or report.

The rest of this project covers some of the simple, common features you can use when you create a form from scratch. Keep in mind, however, that Access offers many form features, such as drop-down lists, groups of option buttons, graphic objects, and much more.

In this lesson, you create a new, blank form.

To Create a New Form from Scratch

1 In the Address2 database window, click the Forms tab (if necessary).

You should see the AutoForm form listed. Next, you are going to add an additional form.

2 Click the New button.

You see the New Form dialog box. Before you choose whether you want to use the Form Wizard or start with a blank form, you should select the table you want to use for the form.

3 Click the down arrow in the drop-down list labeled `Choose the table or query where the object's data comes from`.

A list is displayed showing the tables and queries contained in the database. You can base the form on either a query or a table. In this lesson, use the Contacts table.

4 Click Contacts.

This tells Access to use the Contacts table with the form you are creating.

5 Select the Design View option from the top of the list and click OK.

You see the form in Design view. To work on a blank form, it is useful to have the rulers turn on and the Field List and Toolbox windows open. If they were used the last time the program was in the Form Design view, they will be displayed. Examine your screen and compare it to Figure 5.7. Perform the following steps as needed.

6 If the list of fields does not appear on the screen, click the Field List button on the Form Design toolbar.

7 If the toolbox does not appear on the screen, click the Toolbox button.

8 If the rulers do not appear on the screen, choose View and Ruler from the menu bar.

The Design view should now include the rulers, toolbox, and field list.

9 Drag the two windows to the right of the Form Design window.

The blank form is displayed with the rulers, field list, and toolbox (see Figure 5.7). Keep this blank form open on your screen. In the next lesson, you learn how to add fields to a form.

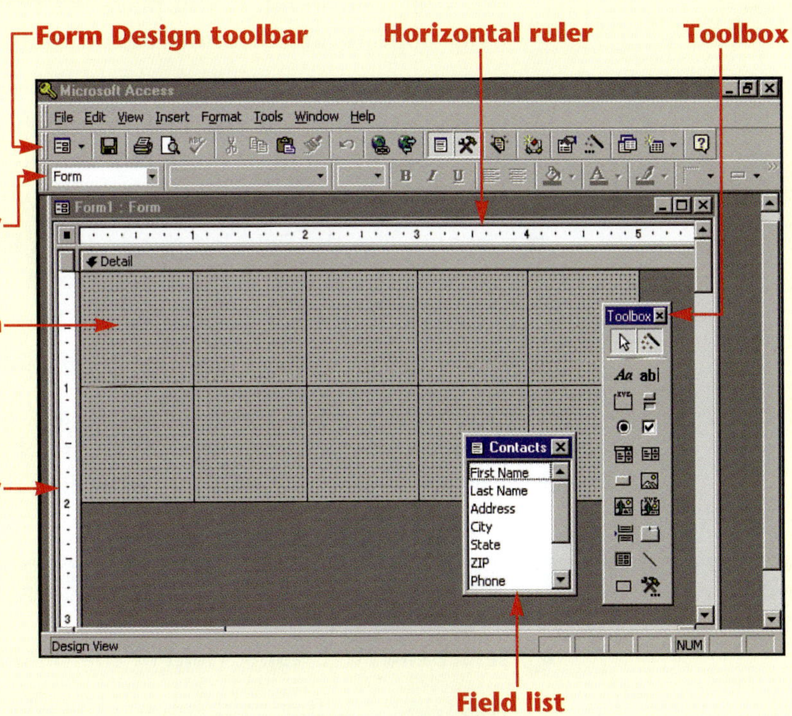

Figure 5.7
The blank form should display the field list and the toolbox.

Jargon Watch

A **form** consists of many different elements. Each part of the form is called a **section**. The main section is called the Detail section. This is the area in which records are displayed. You can also add **form headers** (top of form) or **form footers** (bottom of form). Anything you include in the section will be displayed onscreen in Form view when you use the form. You can also add page headers and page footers, which are not visible onscreen in Form view but will appear if you print the form.

Some controls are bound to the fields in the table. If you create a text box for a field and enter data in the field in the form, for example, the field in the table is updated. Other controls are not tied to the table but, instead, are saved with the form. For example, you may want to add a descriptive title to the form. This type of text is called a **label** and is not bound to the table.

Lesson 5: Adding Fields to Forms

You decided it would be a good idea to send birthday greetings to your customers to help maintain good relations. You added a birthday field to your Contacts table, but you have entered only the birthdays of contacts who are your customers. To make sure that birthday greetings are sent to your customers, you want to create a simple form that lists just the person's name and his or her birthday. This form will include three fields—last name, first name, and birthday—and will also include a label in the form's header.

When you want to set up or change the structure of a form, you use Design view. Access includes the following items to help you design the form:

- *Toolbar*. Use the toolbar to access some form design commands. You can click the Save button to save the form, the View button to view the form, and so on. If you place the pointer on a button, the button name appears directly under the button.
- *Toolbox*. Use the toolbox to add items, such as labels, to the form. As with the toolbar, you can place the mouse pointer over a toolbox button to see its name. The toolbox may not be displayed when you create a new form. If it is not, click the Toolbox button to display it.
- *Field list*. Use the field list to add fields to the form. The field list box may not be displayed when you create a new form. If it is not, click the Field List button in the toolbar to display the field list.
- *Rulers*. Use the rulers to help position controls on the form.

In this lesson, you use the field list to add fields to the form. The new, blank form you are creating for the Contacts table should still be on your screen from the preceding lesson. Try adding fields to the form now.

To Add Fields to Forms

1 Select the First Name field in the field list.

This selects the first field you want to add to your form.

Field text box
Holds a place for the contents of each field in the database.

Field label
Displays the field name.

2 Drag the First Name field from the field list to the Detail section of the form.

As you drag, your pointer becomes a small, boxed field name. You can use this *field text box* to help place the field onscreen.

3 Release the mouse button and drop the field at approximately the 1-inch mark on the horizontal ruler, and down about 1/4 inch from the top of the detail area.

This places the field text box and *field label* on the form (see Figure 5.8). The label box will be placed to the left of the text box so you need to leave space for it.

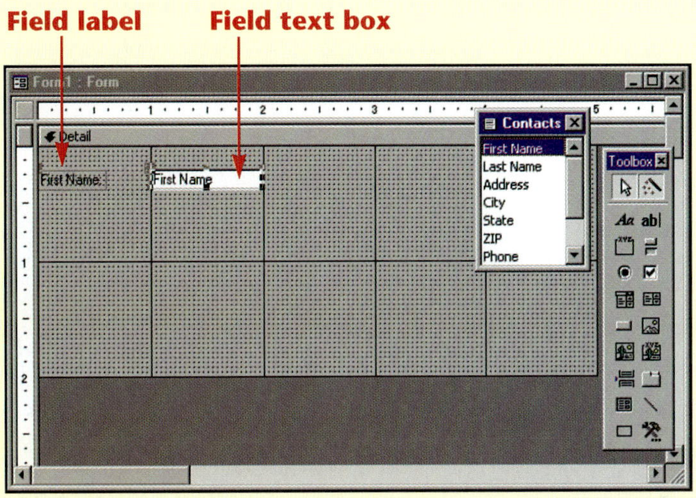

Figure 5.8
Adding a field to the form by dragging it from the field list.

4 Drag the Last Name field to the form; place this field below the First Name field, at the same horizontal location (the 1-inch mark) and about 1/4 inch below the First Name field.

This step adds a second field to the form. As you drag and drop the field, try to align the field with the field above it. Make sure that you leave enough room between the two fields—don't drop the fields on top of one another.

5 Drag the Birthday field to the form. Place this field below the Last Name field (also at the 1-inch horizontal mark).

Your form now includes three fields. You can save and name the form so that these changes won't be lost.

6 Open the File menu and choose the Save command.

You see the Save As dialog box, in which you can assign a name for this new form.

7 Type `Birthdays`.

You have now entered the name you want to give to the form.

continues

To Add Fields to Forms (continued)

8 Click OK.

Access saves the form and returns to Design view. You can continue building the form, or you can display the form.

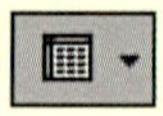

9 Click the View button on the toolbar.

The form is displayed as it will appear when you use it (see Figure 5.9). You can see whether you need to make any adjustments, such as adding a label or resizing the fields. Keep the Birthdays form open and continue with the next lesson.

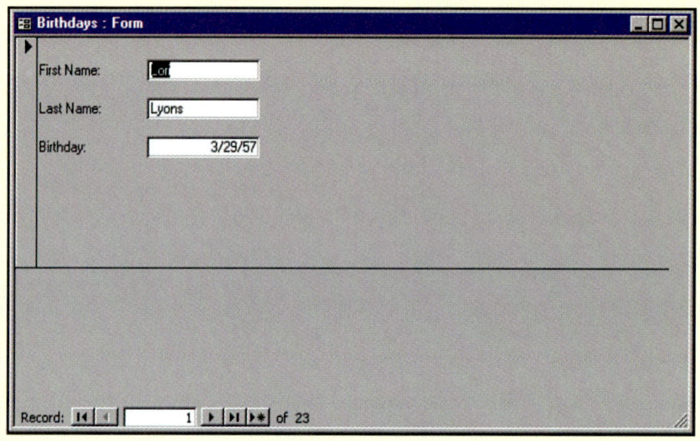

Figure 5.9
Your new form is displayed in Form view.

If you have problems...

If you see only one field box when you drag the field from the field list, you may have placed the field too far to the left (beyond the 1-inch horizontal mark, for example), or the field text box and field label may be on top of one another. You have to move or resize the field so that you can see both the field label and the field text box.

You can delete the field and start again if you run into problems. To delete a field, click it to select it and then press Del. This will remove the field from the form, but it will not delete the field or its contents from the table.

If you make changes to the form and then want to undo them, open the Edit menu and choose the Undo command.

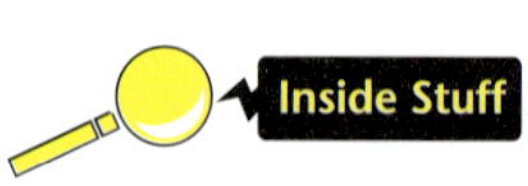

In addition to creating a blank form, you can use the Form Wizard to create other types of forms such as columnar, tabular, charts, and pivot tables.

To modify an existing form, click the name of the form in the database window and then click the Design command button. Alternatively, you can open the form and then change to Design view by clicking the View button.

Lesson 6: Moving and Resizing Fields in Forms

When you create your form, you may find that it is difficult to get the fields in the right place the first time. That's okay; you can move or resize the fields after you have added them to the form. You can drag and place them visually, using the rulers as guides. Or you can have Access align the fields with an underlying grid—making them an equal distance apart.

In this lesson, you move the Birthday field up next to the First Name field. Then, to make sure all the fields are aligned, you snap them to the vertical and horizontal grid.

To Move and Resize Fields in Forms

1 In the Birthdays form, click the View button.

To make changes to the form design, you must return to Design view. You cannot make changes in Form view.

2 If the Birthday field is not selected, click the field text box.

Selection handles
Small squares that appear at the corners and on the sides of boxes and that may be used to change the size of the box.

Selection handles appear around the borders (see Figure 5.10). Notice that both the field label and the field text box are selected because these two items are attached. However, handles appear all the way around only the object you clicked on. The other one (in this case the field label) has one large handle in the upper-left corner. Most of the time you want to keep the two together, such as when you want to move them.

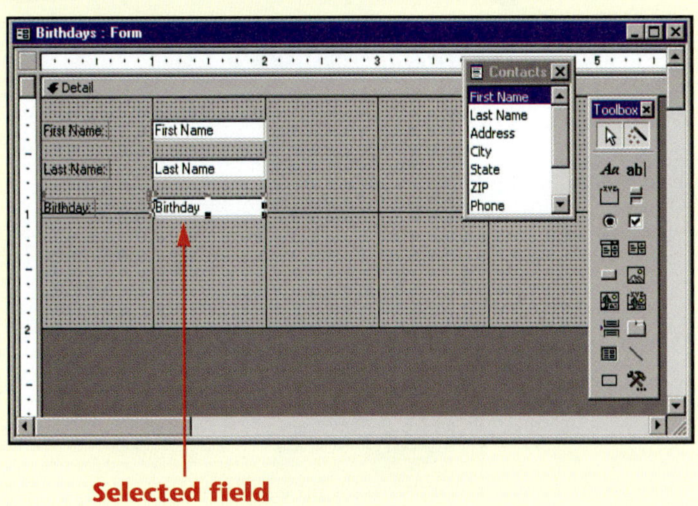

Figure 5.10
You must click a field to select it before you can move it.

3 Place the mouse pointer on one of the borders, but not on one of the handles.

When the pointer is in the correct spot, it should resemble a small hand (see Figure 5.11). If you see arrows rather than the hand, the pointer isn't in the correct spot. Move it around until you see the hand.

continues

To Move and Resize Fields in Forms (continued)

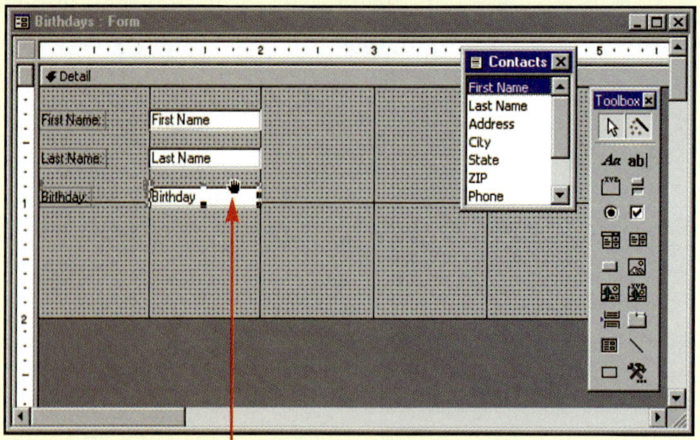

Figure 5.11
To move the field, the pointer must look like a hand.

Pointer appears as a hand

4 Drag the Birthday field up next to the First Name field and place it so that the left edge of the Birthday field label is at approximately the 2 1/2-inch mark on the horizontal ruler.

Notice as you drag that you can see the outline of both the field label and the field text box. When you release the mouse button, Access moves the field up next to the First Name field. (You may need to drag the field list box out of the way so that you can see where you are positioning the Birthday field.)

5 Move the pointer to the right side of the Birthday field and place it on the handle. The pointer turns into a two-headed arrow (see Figure 5.12).

The Birthday field is longer than necessary, so you are going to change the size of the birthday field so it is approximately 1/2 inch wide.

Pointer appears as a two-sided arrow

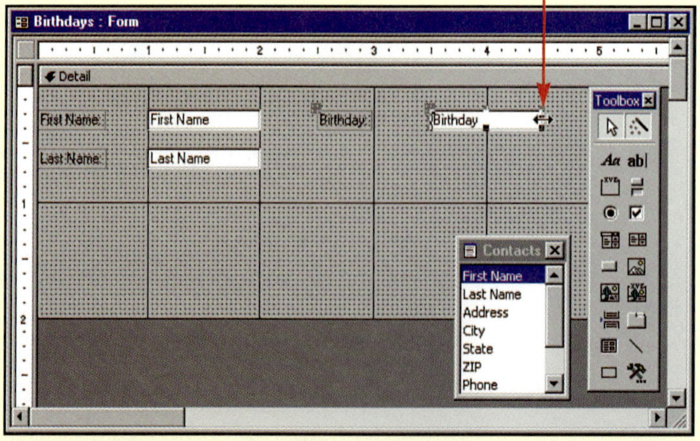

Figure 5.12
Preparing to resize a field.

Access

6 Make the field smaller by dragging the right side of the field to the left. Stop at the 4-inch mark on the horizontal ruler so that the field is about 1/2 inch wide.

The Birthday field is now about the right size to contain a date.

7 Click on the View button to see if the date will fit in the new box.

8 Click the Save button.

This step saves the form with the changes you just made. Keep your Birthdays form open. In the next lesson, you learn how to add a form header to the form.

If you have problems...

If you see arrows in the form and begin to drag, you will resize the field. You resize by putting the pointer on one of the selection handles. If you resize by accident, open the Edit menu and choose the Undo command to undo the change.

When you want to move a field, be sure to place the pointer on the edge of the field and wait until it changes to a hand; don't place the pointer on one of the selection handles.

If you want to move the label box separately from the text box, point to the larger square in the upper-left corner of the label box. When the pointer turns into a pointing finger, you can click and drag the label box to a new location. The text box can move independently from the label box by using the same technique. Point to the larger box in the upper-left corner of the text box until the pointer turns into a pointing finger, then click and drag the text box to the desired location.

Inside Stuff

When you enter data into a form, the insertion point jumps from one box to the next each time you press Tab. This is called the Tab Order. When you move fields around on a form, you may need to change the Tab Order. To do this, in the Design view, select View and Tab Order from the menu and a list of fields will be displayed. Click once on the field that you wish to move to select it, then click and drag it to the desired position on the list.

Lesson 7: Adding a Form Header and Label

The final step for this form is to add a form header that will appear at the top of the form and to include a label showing the name of the form.

In this lesson, you first add a new section to the form—the Form Header section—and then you add a label to the form. In addition to adding the label, you can change the font and font size of the text so that the form label stands out.

To Add a Form Header and Label

1 Click the View button to return to the Design view of the Birthdays form.

2 Open the View menu and choose the Form Header/Footer command.

Access adds two sections to the form, a Form Header and a Form Footer (see Figure 5.13). You want to include the form label in the header, but the section is too small. Therefore, you need to adjust the size of the section.

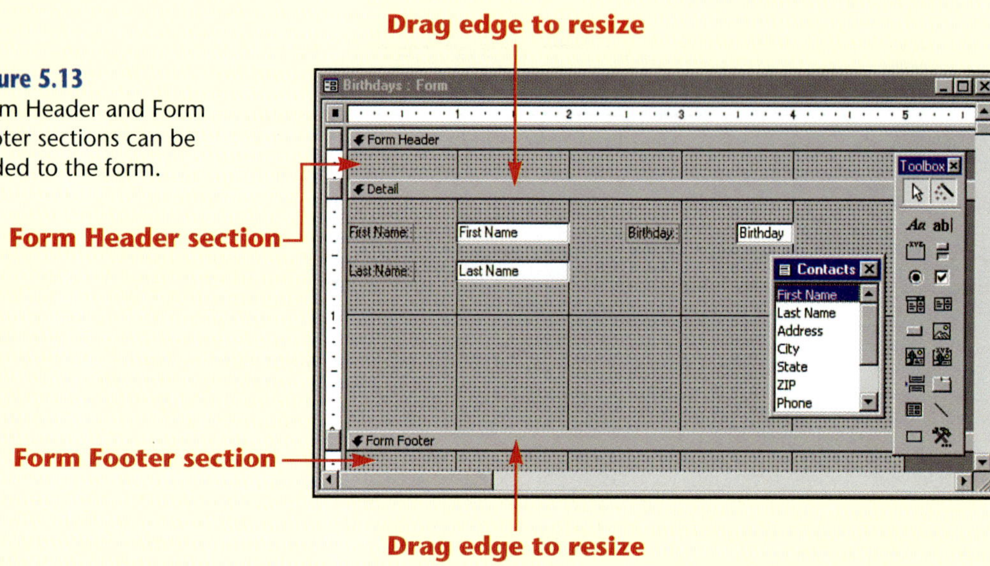

Figure 5.13
Form Header and Form Footer sections can be added to the form.

3 Place the mouse pointer on the bottom edge of the Form Header section (the top edge of the Detail section).

The pointer should change to display a thick horizontal bar with a two-headed arrow crossbar. This pointer shape indicates that you are about to resize this section.

4 Drag down until the Form Header is about an inch tall.

You can use the rulers along the left edge of the form's Design view to gauge the size of the section. Don't worry if the size isn't exact. Now that the header is a little bigger, you can add a label to the form.

5 Click the Label button in the toolbox.

The Label button has an uppercase and lowercase "A" on it. Remember that you can place your pointer on a button to see its name.

6 Position the crosshairs of the pointer in the upper-left corner of the Form Header section. Drag to the right and down to draw a box. Make the box approximately 2 inches wide and 1/2 inch tall.

The pointer should appear as a small crosshair with an A underneath while you are positioning it. When you release the mouse button, you see a label box with the insertion point inside.

7 Type `Birthdays!`.

This is the text you want to include as the label. As you can see, the text is fairly small, but you can change the text size.

8 Click outside the text area to end the text-editing mode.

9 Click inside the box to select it.

Notice that the formatting toolbar displays the font and font size in the Font Name and Font Size drop-down lists. You can use these lists to change the font and the font size (see Figure 5.14).

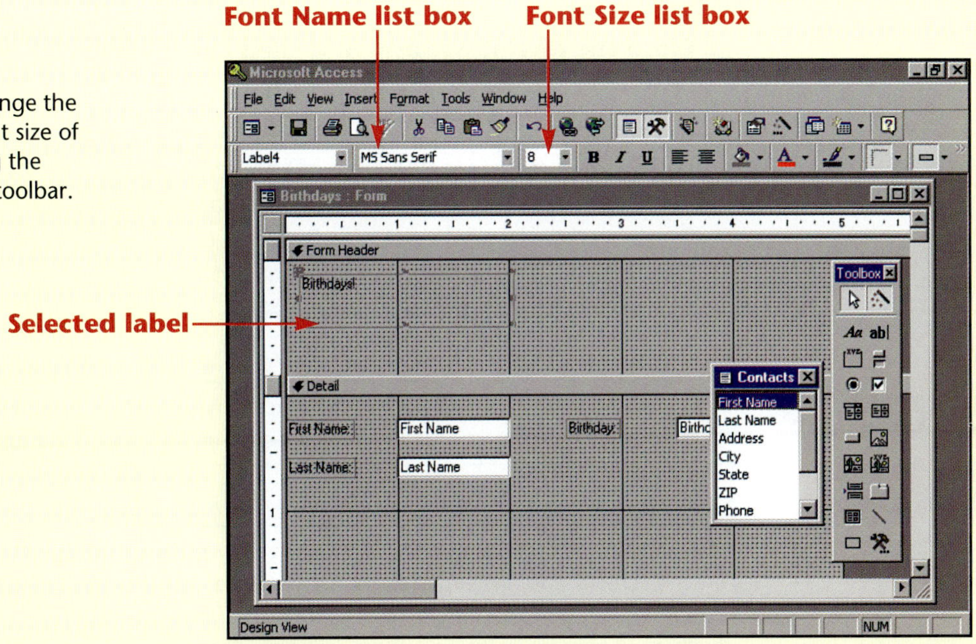

Figure 5.14
You can change the font and font size of a label using the Formatting toolbar.

10 Click the down arrow next to the Font Size box. Click 24 (or the next largest size available on your system).

This changes the font in the label box to 24-point type. You don't have to change the actual font, but you can make the text bold.

11 Click the Bold button on the toolbar.

Access makes the text bold.

12 Click the Save button on the toolbar.

The form is saved with the changes you have made.

13 Click the View button on the toolbar.

This switches you to Form view so that you can see the form you just created (see Figure 5.15).

continues

To Add a Form Header and Label (continued)

Figure 5.15
The Form view shows the results of your design changes.

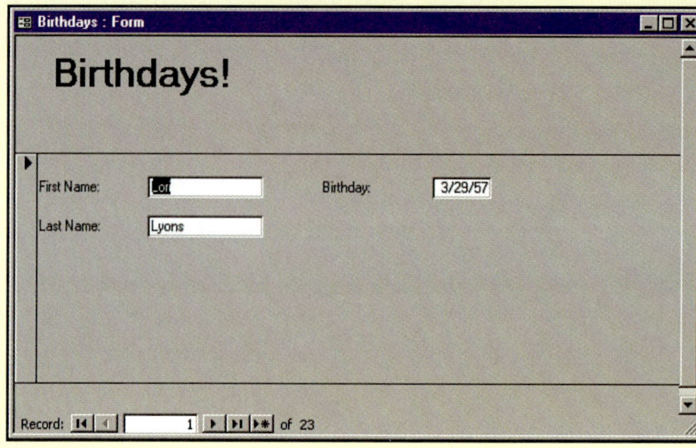

14 Close the Birthdays form and then close the Address2 database.

If you have completed your session on the computer, exit Access and Windows before you turn off the computer. Otherwise, continue with the "Checking Your Skills" and "Applying Your Skills" sections in this project. In Project 6, "Creating and Printing Reports," you use a different database to create a report.

Access

If you have problems...

If you make the label box too small, you can always resize it. Click the box to select it. Then place the pointer on one of the selection handles and drag to resize.

Exam Notes

The purpose of creating forms is to make it easy for users to input and read data on the screen. Should you need to print a form, you can view the form first by using Print Preview. If you choose the Print command from the menu or from the toolbar, all records in the database will be printed in a continuous form. If you want to print one record per page, click the Page Break button in the toolbox and drag the small Page Break symbol onto the form.

If you want to print selected records, select the Selected Record(s) option button on the Print menu (select File, Print to see the Print menu). Choosing this option, the record which currently contains your insertion point will print. To print multiple selected records, you should first create and run a query which results in the records you wish to print in the form, then from Form View, select Print.

Project Summary

To	Do This
Create an AutoForm	Click the Forms tab, click the New button, choose a table or a query to get the data from, and choose an AutoForm style.

To	Do This
Enter data using a form	Open the form in Datasheet view. Click the New Record button to add a new record.
Edit data using a form	Use the navigation buttons to move around the form. Click the field you want to edit and enter new data.
Save a form	Open the File menu and choose the Save command. Type a descriptive name in the Save As dialog box. Click OK.
Close a form	Click the Close button.
Open a form	From the database window, click the Forms tab and double-click the form you want to open.
Create a new form	Click the Forms tab, click the New button, and select the table or query you want to use. Choose the Design View option from the list and click OK.
Add fields	Drag fields from the selected field list box and place them on the grid until you have placed all the fields you need. Use the rulers to help align the fields. Save the form with a new name.
Move and resize fields	Work in Design view. Click in the field you want to move. When the pointer becomes a hand, you can click and drag the field to a new location. Click and drag the handles of a selected field text box or field label to resize it.
Add a form header and label	In Design view, use the View menu and choose Form Header/Footer. Adjust the size of the header area by dragging the edge. Use the Label tool to drag a label box within the header. Type the label text inside the label box. Click elsewhere to deselect the box. Click the box to select it again, then change the font, font size, or other characteristics.

Checking Your Skills

True/False

For each of the following, check *T* or *F* to indicate whether the statement is true or false.

__T __F **1.** AutoForm creates a form with all the fields in your table.

__T __F **2.** When you use a form to enter data, that data is saved in the form. You also have to update the table.

__T __F **3.** You must save a form if you want to use it again.

__T __F **4.** You can have only one section in a form.

__T __F **5.** To delete a field from a form in Form Design view, click once on the field to select it and then press Del.

__T __F **6.** By pressing Ctrl+Alt in Form view, you can use the mouse to make changes to the form while viewing the final product.

__T __F **7.** If you accidentally close a form without saving it, you can simply click the Undo button to restore the form.

__T __F **8.** In the toolbox of Form Design view, the Label button has both an uppercase and a lowercase "A" on it.

__T __F **9.** When a field text box is selected, its associated label will also have selection handles around it.

__T __F **10.** After you generate a form, you cannot change it. You must generate a new form in Design view.

Multiple Choice

Circle the letter of the correct answer for each of the following questions.

1. How do you create a new record using a form?

a. Scroll to the last record and then edit that record.

b. Edit the first record displayed.

c. Click the New Object button on the toolbar.

d. Click the New Record button on the Navigation bar and enter data into the empty form.

2. Which key(s) can you use to move from field to field in a form?

a. Tab

b. Shift+Tab

c. → or ←

d. all of the above

3. Which type of section includes the record information?

a. Detail

b. Page Header

c. Page Footer

d. Form Header

4. Which of the following is a way to select a field in Design view?

a. Choose File, Select Field.

b. Click it once.

c. Point to it.

d. Click the Select Field button on the toolbar.

5. What should the pointer look like to move a field?

a. a hand

b. a white cross

c. a two-headed arrow

d. a crosshair

6. Which of the following is not a part of a form?

a. Form Header

b. Page Footer

c. Detail Area

d. Format Area

Access

7. To save data to the table after you have entered several records using a form, you must do which of the following?
   a. Choose Save from the File menu.
   b. Choose Update from the File menu.
   c. Click the Save button on the toolbar.
   d. None of the above (because data is saved automatically).
8. Which of the following is a fast way to create a form based on the current table?
   a. Use the QuickForm.
   b. Use an AutoForm.
   c. Open a blank form and drag the fields onto it from the Field List window.
   d. Click NewForm on the toolbox.
9. You can generate all the following by using the Form Wizard except which?
   a. columnar forms
   b. charts
   c. pivot tables
   d. spreadsheets
10. How can you add the toolbox to the Design View window if the toolbox is not already present?
    a. Select Open Toolbox from the Tools menu.
    b. Choose Insert, Toolbox from the menu.
    c. Click the Toolbox button on the Form Design toolbar.
    d. Press ¶.

Completion

In the blank provided, write the correct answer for each of the following statements.

1. A type of object you can create to enter, edit, and view records is called a(n) ______________.
2. Any graphical object (text box, check box, option button, and so on) that you add to a form or report is called a(n) ______________.
3. An object that holds a place for the contents of each field in the database is called a(n) ______________.
4. An object that displays the field name is called a(n) ______________.
5. A bounded object is connected to the underlying ______________.
6. The order in which fields are addressed on a form is called the ______________ Order.
7. You can create a(n) ______________ quickly without a great deal of work, and it will include all fields from your table.
8. Deleting a text box from a form will not delete the ______________ in the underlying table.

9. Detail, Page Header, and Form Header are examples of form ____________.

10. The Form Header/Footer menu item can be found on the ____________ menu.

Matching

In the blank next to each of the following terms or phrases, write the letter of the corresponding term or phrase. (Note that some letters may be used more than once.)

a. toolbar	_____	**1.** A control on a form that isn't linked to anything else
b. rulers	_____	**2.** Used to add fields to a form
c. Ctrl+S	_____	**3.** The same as choosing Save from the File menu
d. page header	_____	**4.** Used to help position controls on a form
e. Find	_____	**5.** One of two parts of a text box control
f. selection handles	_____	**6.** Part of a form that shows up only when you are printing it
g. field text box	_____	**7.** Used to add items, such as labels, to a form
h. field list	_____	**8.** Used to access some form design commands
i. unbound	_____	**9.** A tool you can use on a form just as you would on a datasheet
j. toolbox	_____	**10.** Small squares that appear at the corners and on the sides of boxes that have been selected

Applying Your Skills

Practice

The following exercises enable you to practice the skills you have learned in this project. Take a few minutes to work through these exercises now.

Creating a Form for Your Library Database

In previous Practice exercises, you created a Library database and a Books table to keep track of the books in your personal collection. To make it easy to enter the books you have in your library, you may want to create and use a form. The form is similar to a card catalog and fits more with the purpose of the database. You can create an AutoForm that includes all the fields from the table and a special quick-entry form that includes just the author's last name, first name, and book title.

To create a form for your Library database, complete the following steps:

1. Make a copy of the database Proj0502 from the Project-05 folder on the CD and save it as `Library4`. Then return to Access and open the `Library4` database.

2. Create an AutoForm based on the Books table. Save the form as AutoForm.
3. Enter two new records into the form; then save and close the form.
4. Create a new form, based again on the Books table. Add fields for author last name, author first name, and book title to this form. Add a form header and include a label in this area that says `Books!`.
5. Save the new form with the name `Quick Entry`. Enter two more records using the Quick Entry form.
6. Choose File, Print, and select Selected Record(s) to print a copy of the form.

Creating a Customer Table and a Form for Customer Entry

In previous Practice exercises, you set up a database for the Sound Byte Music Store. So far, this database includes one table and one query. You can add additional tables to the database and, to make it easy to enter records into the new table, you can create an AutoForm.

In this exercise, you create a table for customers and then create a form based on the new table. Finally, you use the form to enter several records into the new table.

To create a customer table and form, complete the following steps:

1. Copy the Proj0503 database file from the Project-05 folder on the CD and rename it `SBMusic4`. Then return to Access and open the `SB4Music` database.
2. Create a new table and include the following text fields:

    `First Name`

    `Last Name`

    `Address`

    `City`

    `State`

    `ZIP Code`

    `Music Interest`

3. Save the table with the name `Customers`.
4. Create an AutoForm based on the new table. Save the form with the name `AutoForm`.
5. Choose File, Print, and select Selected Record(s) to print a copy of the form.
6. Using the AutoForm, enter five records for your customer table. When you are finished adding records, close the form and the database.

Creating Forms for the Database to Track Personal Computer Hardware

You can create forms that will help the user enter specific information about the computer hardware in the company.

To create forms for the personal computer hardware database, complete the following steps:

1. Copy the file Proj0504 from the Project-05 folder on the CD and rename the copy `PC4`. Open `PC4`.
2. Create a form based on the PC Hardware table that will make data entry more convenient. Add a title and save the form as `PC Hardware Form`.
3. Create a form based on the Vendors table. Use the AutoForm to create a simple columnar form. Name it `Vendors Form`.
4. Close the form and the database.

Getting a Helping Hand

The Access Help system provides a number of useful topics that cover forms and Form Wizards. All of these are interrelated, and you can view them by starting with a simple statement.

To get help on topics in this project, complete the following steps:

1. In Access, choose Help from the menu bar.
2. Choose Microsoft Access Help.
3. In the dialog box that appears, type the statement `create a form` and click Search. The Help system does not require a question but looks instead for key words. The simpler the interrogative, the more direct the response will be. You are then presented with a list of help topics or subject areas. The first item on the list should be `Create a Form`.
4. Select `Create a Form`. The Help program runs, and you see one of the basic topics on creating forms. This topic provides an overview with a series of selections at the bottom. Each of these selections details how to accomplish increasingly difficult tasks.
5. Take a few minutes and explore.
6. Use the same method to search for the phrase `add a control`. The first entry should be `Add a control to a form or report`. This topic is linked to the previous topic on creating forms but is easier to approach through the main dialog box.
7. Select `Add a control to a form or report`. This topic covers some detailed information about controls and will assist you in adding very complicated features to your forms and reports.
8. Take a few minutes to review the information provided.

Exploring the World of Alaska

Now that you have a database of information, you may find other information that you want besides the photographs and sources. Furthermore, referring to information by simply looking at a table can be confusing.

To create and view a simple form, complete the following steps:

1. Copy the database Proj0505 from the Project-05 folder on the CD and rename it `Alaska3`.
2. Select the Forms tab.
3. Click the New button.
4. Select the Autoform: Columnar form type.
5. Select the Geography table from the drop-down list. Notice that the Alaskan Islands query is listed. You can create a form from a query.
6. Click OK. Access generates a simple form based on the table and loads the first record in Form view. Look the form over. It is not necessary to see the primary key or ID field.
7. Click the View button to switch to Design view.
8. Maximize the window, if necessary. You should have a form header and footer already attached.
9. Drag the bottom of the form header down to increase the amount of working space.
10. Add the title `Alaskan Geographic Sites` to the header by using the Label tool.
11. Select the field text box for the ID field. Both the text box and the field label should be selected.
12. Press Del. Both boxes disappear.
13. Click the View button to switch to Form view to observe your work.
14. Close the form and save it with the name `Input and Viewing Form`.

Challenge

The following challenges enable you to use your problem-solving skills. Take time to work through these exercises now.

Creating a Form for Your Organization

In previous Challenge exercises, you set up a database to manage information about a club or organization. Create a form to make it easier to enter data for your organization or club. Include all the fields and arrange them so that they are not in a simple column format. Add a title to the form header. Choose File, Print, and select Selected Record(s) to print a copy of the form.

Doing Customer Research

You have been entering your data directly into the table, but you want an easier, cleaner way of entering information. It is time to build a form for inputting your data and viewing the information.

To build a basic survey input form, complete the following steps:

1. Copy the database Proj0506 from the Project-05 folder on the CD and rename it `Customer Research4`.
2. Select the Forms tab and create a new form using Design view and not one of the AutoForms. Remember to select the Questionnaire table.
3. Drag each of the fields to the new form and arrange them so that they fit in the form. Notice the size of the field as you drag each one. Not all the fields are the same size.
4. When you have completed adding and arranging your fields, add a form header and footer, and title the form `Basic Survey Input Form`.
5. Test the form in Form view by entering the following data:

Adults	Children	Hours	No 1	No 2	No 3	Doing
2	2	2	DISNEY	TNT	SCIFI	Good
4	1	4	DISNEY	DISCOVERY		Great
2	5	6	SCIFI	CNN		Okay
1	2	2	SCIFI	TNT	CNN	Okay

Improvement comment for the first household: `Need more fun programming that isn't violent or vulgar. Make it light.`

Comment for the second household: `We like what we watch, but there are days, even weeks, when we don't turn on the TV at all.`

Comment for the third household: `Less junk would be nice. How about some good old movies?`

Comment for the fourth household: `We don't really watch much though my children (both in their teens) love the SCIFI channel. I only watch CNN.`

6. Close the form and save it as `Basic Survey Input Form`.

Owning a Vending Company

You have three different tables that hold data for your vending business. To enter data, you will need to open each table. Instead of using the table directly, you can create an input form for each table.

To create input forms for tables, complete the following steps:

1. Copy the file Proj0507 from the Project-05 folder on the CD and rename it `Vending3`.

Access

2. Create a new form for the Locations table using the AutoForm: Columnar option.
3. Add a title, `Machine Locations`, to the form in the form header and save the form as `Machine Locations`.
4. Create a form for the Machines table using the AutoForm: Tabular option.
5. Add the title `Machine Descriptions` to the form header above the field names. When you go to Design view, notice the differences between this form design and the previous form.
6. Save the form with the name `Machine Descriptions`.
7. Create a form for the Supplier table using the Design View option. You will have to add and position the fields.
8. Add a title, `Product Suppliers`, for the form. You will have to add the header area for the form.
9. Save the form as `Product Suppliers`.
10. Close the database.

Managing a Video Store

You don't need to see an entire table in order to make use of the database. If you receive a new set of videos, you don't need to see the fields for renters when you are entering the videos in the database. Likewise, when you are renting out a video and have a customer there, you don't need to see the entire history of the video.

Create an input form that enables you to enter the data for new videos without seeing the information on whether the video is rented. Save this form with the name `New Video`.

Then create a form for entering the name of a renter for a specific video. Call this form `Video Rental`.

You will not want to type the name of the video in this form; instead, you will want to search through the database for the appropriate video and then enter the name of the current renter.

Taking a Home Inventory

The table in your database should have the item, purchase date, description, insurance company, cost, and so on. This is the main table, and it includes all the information you'll need for the insurance company.

Create a second table that lists the information on the insurance company, including the company name, address, phone, agent's name, policy number, and so on. Make the company name field the primary key. Create a form for the insurance companies. You may want to generate this form by using the tabular AutoForm so that you can see all the companies at one time. Name this form `Company Data`. Enter data for the insurance companies. Be sure that you spell the company name exactly the same way that it is used in the other table.

Create a form for each of these tables. The form for the inventory should include all the fields necessary to enter a new item or modify an existing item. Name this form `Add Inventory Item`.

PinPoint Assessment

PinPoint Training

You have completed the project and the associated lessons, as well as the "Checking Your Skills" and "Applying Your Skills" sections. Now use the PinPoint software Evaluation mode to assess your comprehension of the specific exam tasks you have just learned. You can also use the PinPoint Trainer mode and the SHOW ME tutorials to practice these specific exam tasks.

Project 6

Six

Creating and Printing Reports

Displaying Data

In this project you will learn the following objectives and their associated Microsoft Exam required activities.

Objectives	Required Activities
➤ Print the Data in a Table	
➤ Create a Report Using the Report Wizards	Create a Report
➤ Print and Rename a Report	Print a Report
➤ Modify a Report Design	Modify a Report
➤ Save a Report with a New Name	
➤ Add Labels to Reports	Label a Report

Why Would I Do This?

Report
A database object that is designed to be printed that displays selected fields from tables or queries.

There are several ways to display the information in your database. You can print a form or print copies of tables or queries. These printouts are limited in format and flexibility. In order to produce printouts of multiple records from tables or queries, you need to learn how to use *reports*. In this project, you learn the fundamental tasks involved in creating, modifying, saving, and printing a simple report.

Before you create a report, think about why you need the printed data. Do you want to check the entries to make sure they are correct? Do you need an address list or phone list? Do you need to pass the information along to someone else? If so, what information does that person need and in what order? If you spend a few moments determining the purpose of the report, you can design a report that truly meets your needs.

Access provides many tools for creating a report—you can create an AutoReport, use the Report Wizards to create other common report types (single-column report, mailing labels, and so on), or create a blank report that you add information to later. You can also change the layout of an existing report design and add report labels to help make the report more self-explanatory. This project shows you how to use the report tools included with Access.

Lesson 1: Printing the Table Data

If all you need is a printout of the entire table or query, it is faster to simply print the table without using a report. For example, you may want to print the data in a table so that you can check the accuracy of the records. In this case, you don't have to create a report; you can simply print the table.

To Print the Table Data

1. **Make a copy of the Proj0601 database file from the Project-06 folder on the CD and name the copy `Softball`. Open the `Softball` database.**

   The Softball database includes a table of team members and a table of game information. After you open the Softball database, you should see the two tables displayed in the Tables list. In this project, you work with the Team table.

2. **Click the Tables tab, if necessary, then double-click the Team table.**

   This step opens the database table in Datasheet view. You may want to scroll through the table to see how it is set up. The table includes fields for the first and last name of each player, along with his or her position, phone number, address, and dues. You can print this information; but before you print, preview the printout so that you have some idea of what the printed list will look like.

❸ Click the Print Preview button.

You see a preview of the printed list (see Figure 6.1). The structure of the printout is fairly simple; each record is displayed as a row in a grid. The navigation button that enables you to scroll to the next page is active. This indicates that there is more than one page. This means that all the table columns will not fit on one page width when the report is printed.

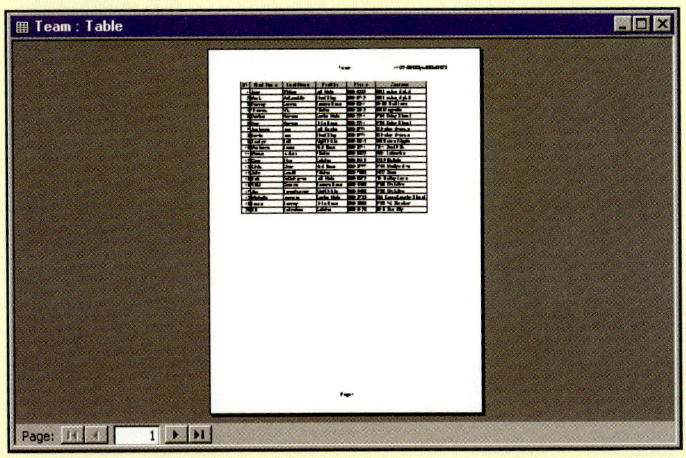

Figure 6.1
The table may be previewed before printing.

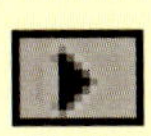

❹ Click the Next Page button.

This step displays the second page of the printout, which shows the remaining column. This is a problem with printing all the fields in the table. If the table is too wide by just a few columns, you can still get a usable printout by changing the orientation of the page so that Access prints across the long edge of the page, rather than down the page. Using this orientation, you can fit more columns across the page.

❺ From the File menu, choose Page Setup.

You see the Page Setup dialog box, which lists options for setting margins and page layouts.

❻ Click the Page tab to display the page orientation (see Figure 6.2).

❼ In the Orientation area, click the Landscape option button and then click OK.

This step changes the orientation of the page to landscape. Now when you print the report, all the columns fit on a single page.

❽ From the File menu, choose Print.

You see the Print dialog box (see Figure 6.3). Here you can control which pages are printed, how many copies are printed, and select other options. The default settings work fine for this lesson.

continues

To Print the Table Data (continued)

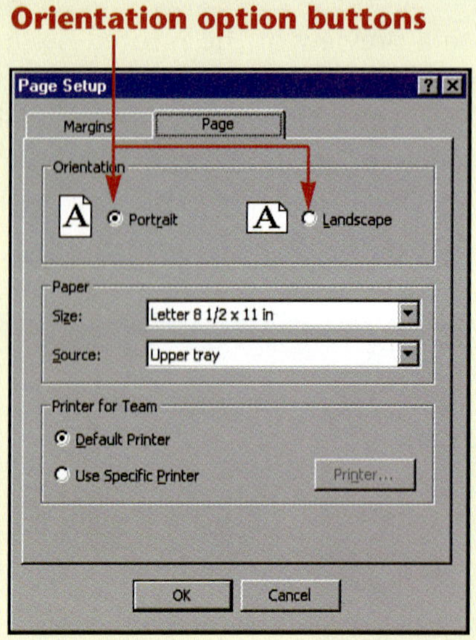

Figure 6.2
Use the Page Setup dialog box to change the page orientation.

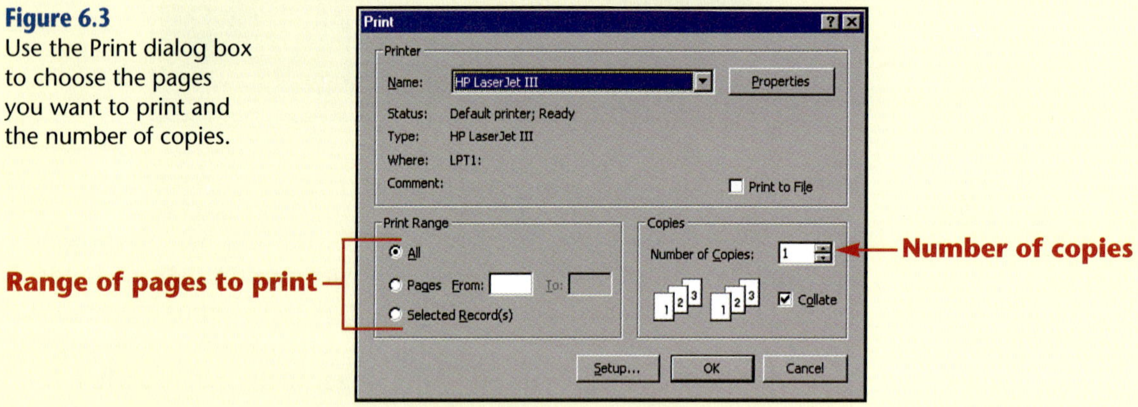

Figure 6.3
Use the Print dialog box to choose the pages you want to print and the number of copies.

9 Click OK.

Access prints the table data. If you don't have access to a printer, click Cancel.

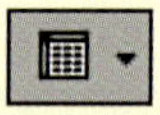

10 Click the View button.

This step closes the preview window and returns you to Datasheet view.

11 Click the Print Preview button again.

Notice that all of the output formatting that you did has been forgotten. This is another reason to create a report that can preserve such settings.

12 Click the Close button on the Print Preview.

Keep the Team table open on your screen and continue with the next lesson.

Inside Stuff

You don't have to preview the printout, but previewing is a good idea. You can print directly from Datasheet view. Simply click the Print button on the toolbar or open the File menu and choose the Print command. Access then prints the table.

The keyboard shortcut for the Print command is Ctrl+P.

To return to Datasheet view from the Print Preview window, you can also click the Close button on the toolbar.

Lesson 2: Creating a Report Using the Report Wizards

Simple table printouts are limited in what they can do. Access provides several reporting options to make it easy to create more sophisticated reports. Using the New Report feature, you can create the reports described in Table 6.1.

Table 6.1 Common Report Wizards

Type of New Report	Description
Design View	Opens a design window where you can add fields or text. This option does not use the wizards.
Report Wizard	Guides you through the process of creating a report. The Report Wizard has several options for layout and grouping of data.
AutoReport: Columnar	Places all the fields in a table in a single-column report.
AutoReport: Tabular	Places all the fields of the table in a row-and-column format similar to the layout of a spreadsheet.
Chart Wizard	Guides you through the process of selecting fields that you want to summarize in a graphical form. The Chart Wizard enables you to choose from several chart types, such as pie, line, and bar.
Label Wizard	Enables you to set up and print mailing labels in more than 100 different label styles.

A Report Wizard leads you step by step through the process of creating a report, asking you which fields to include in the report, which sort order to use, what title to print, and so on. After you make your selections, the wizard creates the report.

In this lesson, you create a columnar report for your Team table in the Softball database. This report works well as an address list.

To Create a Report Using the Report Wizards

1 Open the Team table of the Softball database (if necessary).

2 Click the down arrow next to the New Object button.

A list of objects is displayed (see Figure 6.4).

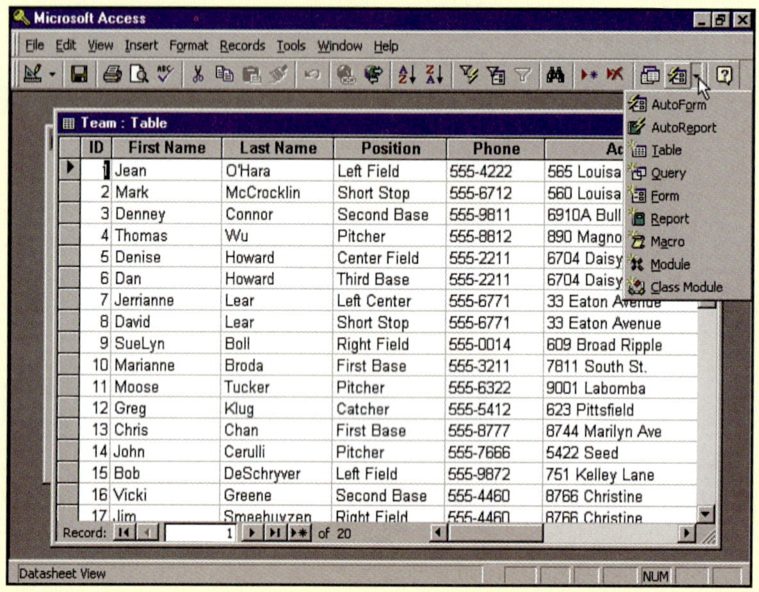

Figure 6.4
A list of available objects appears in a list.

3 Click on Report.

You see the New Report dialog box (see Figure 6.5). Notice that Access has already selected the table for you. You just have to tell Access whether you want to use a wizard, use an AutoReport, or start with a blank report and build it in Design view. In this lesson, you use the Report Wizard.

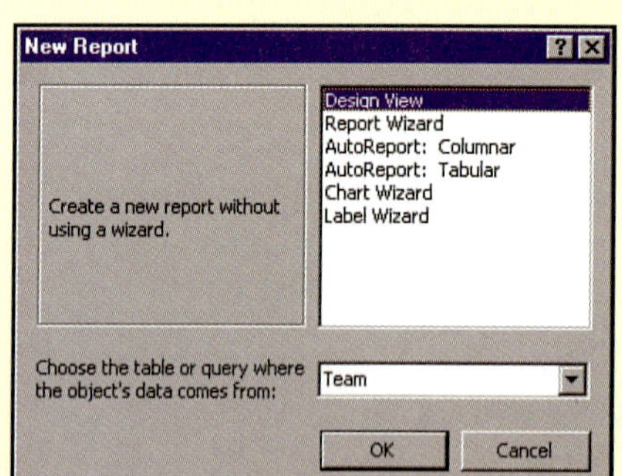

Figure 6.5
In the New Report dialog box, you choose the method you want to use to create a new report.

4 Select Report Wizard and click OK.

You see the Report Wizard dialog box, as shown in Figure 6.6.

Access

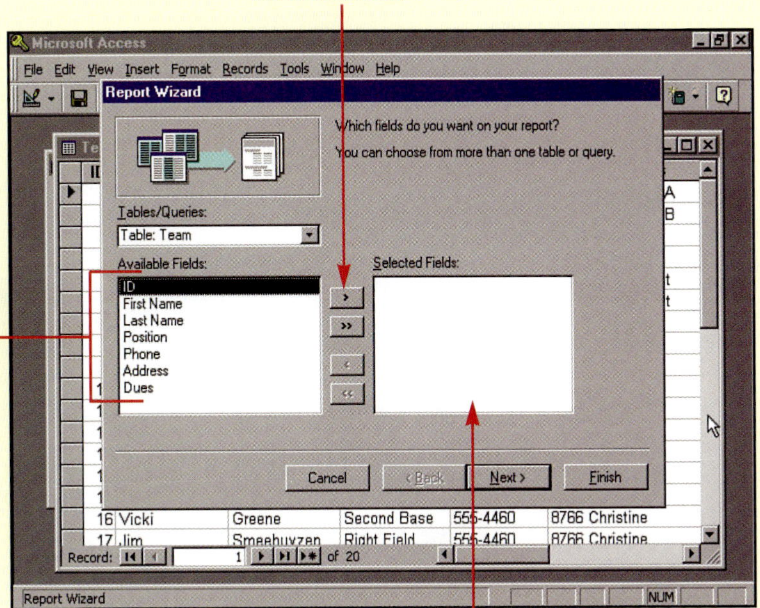

Figure 6.6
Choose which fields from the table you want to include in the report.

5 In the Available Fields list, click the First Name field. Then click the Add button (>).

The Wizard removes the field from the Available Fields list and places the field in the Selected Fields list. The fields will appear in the report in the order you select them. The First Name field, for example, will be the first field listed in the report.

6 Select the Last Name field and click the Add button.

The Last Name field is added to the report.

7 Select the Address field and click the Add button.

The Address field is added to the report.

8 Select the Phone field and click the Add button.

The Phone field is added to the report. Your report now includes four fields. That is all the fields you want to include for this lesson.

9 Click the Next button.

The Wizard displays a new screen for the second step. You could use this step to group similar records together, such as grouping the team by position played. In this example, we have not included any fields that need to be listed together as a group.

10 Click Next again.

The next Report Wizard dialog box allows you to sort the data on one or more fields.

continues

To Create a Report Using the Report Wizards (continued)

11 Click the down arrow next to the first sort selection to reveal the available fields. Select Last Name to sort on. Click Next.

The next Report Wizard dialog box allows you to select the layout, orientation, and fit (see Figure 6.7).

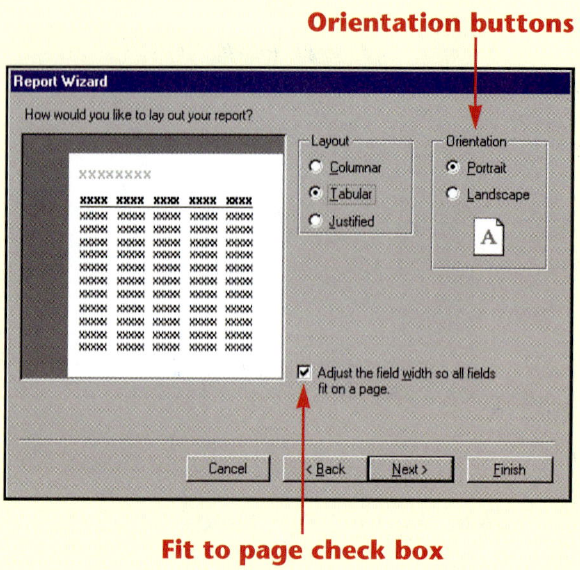

Figure 6.7
Select the layout, orientation, and fit options.

12 Select a Columnar layout, Portrait orientation, and fit to one page.

13 Click the Next button.

The Wizard displays the next step. In this screen, you select a report style. For this example, the Corporate selection works well.

14 Select the Corporate option and click the Next button.

You see the final step of the Report Wizard. In this screen, you enter the title for the report. By default, the Wizard uses the table name and prints the title on the first page. This format is okay, so you are finished with the Report Wizard.

15 Click the Finish button.

You see a preview of the report, as shown in Figure 6.8. You can print, zoom, and save the report, as you learn in the next lesson. Notice that the default label at the top of the report is also the name of the table the report was taken from. Keep the report open for the next lesson where you print and rename a report.

Figure 6.8
The columnar report may be reviewed onscreen.

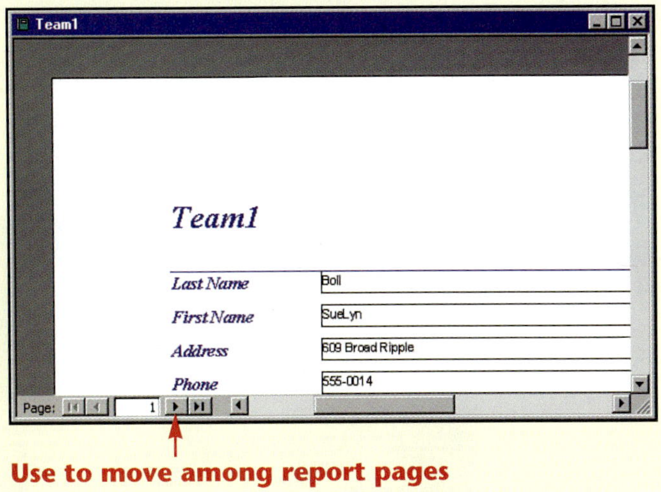

If you have problems...

If you make a mistake in the Wizard, you can back up by clicking the Back button in the Wizard dialog box.

Inside Stuff

In Project 5, "Creating and Using Forms," you used the Form Wizard to create an AutoForm. You can also create an AutoReport using the Report Wizards. An AutoReport includes all the fields from the table in the report. The report is in either a one-column or tabular format with as many records on the page as possible. The report also includes a header with the table name and current date, and a footer with the page number. To create this type of report, choose AutoReport from the list of new objects displayed in the New Objects list box.

Lesson 3: Printing and Renaming a Report

The next step is to print your report. However, before you print, it's always a good idea to preview the report. In the Print Preview mode, you can use the navigation buttons to check for unexpected additional pages, check the font, the font size, and the actual data in the report. Then, if you click the Zoom button on the toolbar, you can view the entire report to determine, generally, how the printed report will look on the page. If you do not like how the report is set up, you can make changes before you print it. This strategy can save you some time and paper.

You can also rename a report in the database window to ensure that it's not confused with other database objects with the same name.

To Print and Rename a Report

1 Click the Zoom button.

Access displays a full-page view of the report, as shown in Figure 6.9, so that you can see the entire page.

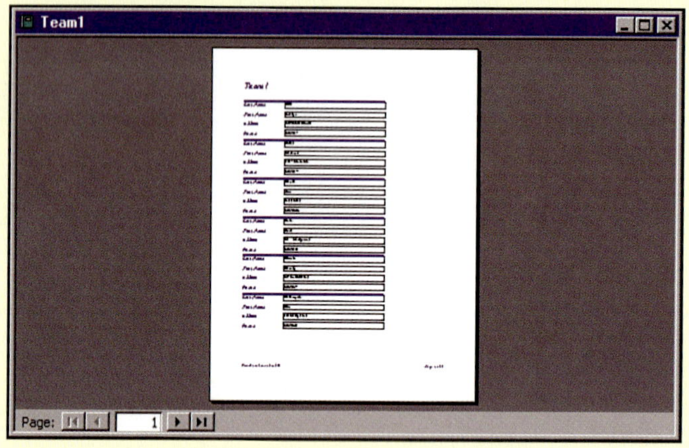

Figure 6.9
The full-page view may be used to preview the report.

2 Click the Zoom button again.

Access zooms in so that you can read the text of the report. Now you are ready to print.

3 Click the Print button on the toolbar.

Access prints the report. If you do not have access to a printer, skip this step.

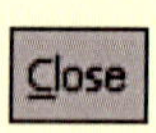

4 Click the Close button on the toolbar to close the report. Close the Team table as well.

The new report is shown in the database window under the Reports tab.

5 It may be confusing to use the same name for the report and the table. Click once on the name of the report to select it.

The name changes to edit mode, in which it can be changed (see Figure 6.10).

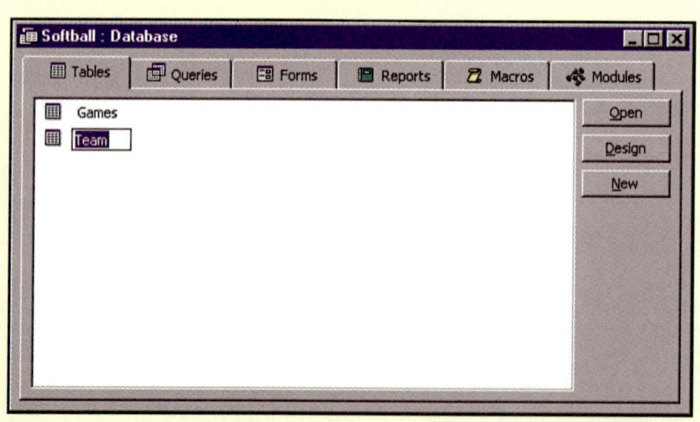

Figure 6.10
Select the report name so that it may be renamed.

6 Type the name `Roster`**.**

7 Press ↵Enter or click outside the name box to indicate that you are done.

The report name is now Roster. Keep the database open for the next lesson where you modify a report design.

Lesson 4: Modifying a Report Design

Once you have created a report, you may decide you want to modify it. The finished report may not be exactly what you intended. Rather than start over with a wizard or a blank form, you can modify the report design so that the report includes the information you want.

Suppose that you need a phone list in addition to the team roster. You can modify the Roster report to create this new report. Start by deleting the Address field, which you don't need in your phone list. Then add the position field so you have a list that includes the name, phone number, and position played by each member of the team.

To Modify a Report Design

1 Select the Roster report and click the Design button.

You see the report in Design view (see Figure 6.11). This view is similar to the Design view you used when you created a form. The same tools are available onscreen. You can use the ruler to place items on the report, the toolbox to add **controls**, and the field list to add fields.

2 Click the scroll arrows to scroll through the report and see how it is structured.

Expression
A predefined formula that performs some calculations. You can include an expression in a report and in other Access objects, such as macros.

Notice that the report includes a footer with the date and page number. The *expression* `=NOW()` inserts the current date. An expression is similar to a function in spreadsheet software. Access provides many expressions that you can include in your report.

The following expression prints the current page and the total number of pages:

```
="Page" & [Page] & "Of" & [Pages]
```

The Detail **section** includes four fields: First Name, Last Name, Address, and Phone.

3 Click the Address field text box.

The field **label** is on the left, and the field text box is on the right. If you click on the Address field text box, handles will appear at the

continues

To Modify a Report Design (continued)

sides and corners of the field text box and in the upper-left corner of the field label box.

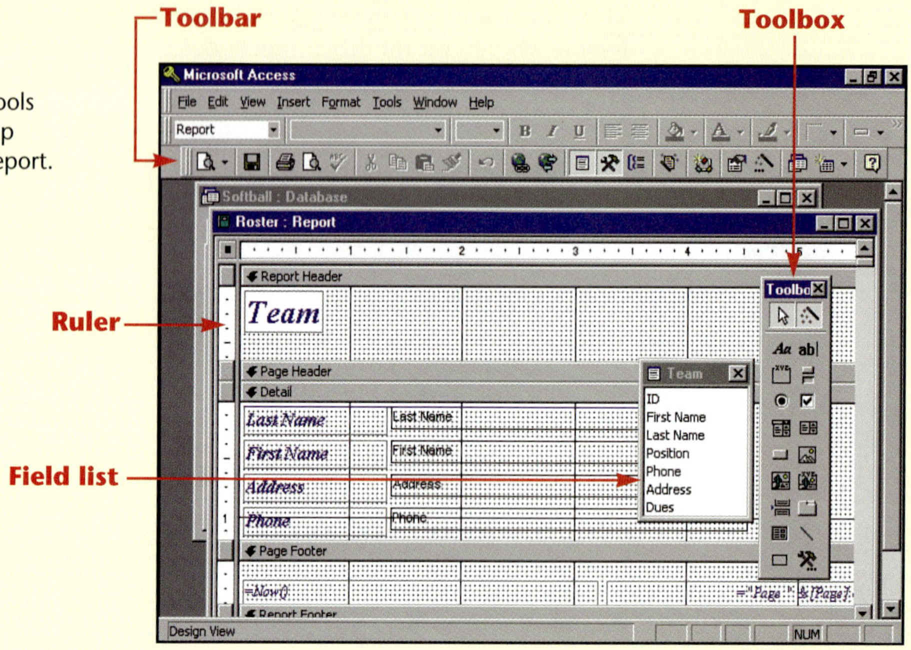

Figure 6.11
In Design mode, tools are available to help you modify your report.

4 Press Del.

Access removes the field and its label from the report. Now you have a gap between two of the fields. To fix this gap, you can move the Phone field up.

5 Click the Phone field to select it.

Position the pointer on the field so that it turns into an open hand.

6 Drag the Phone field so that it is directly under the First Name field.

The Phone field is now moved up closer to First Name. Now you will add the position field to the report.

7 In the field list box, click the Position field and drag it to the detail section of the report, directly below the Phone field text box, and release the mouse.

The pointer turns into a small field box when you are dragging the field onto the report. As soon as you release the mouse, the field text box is positioned under the Phone text box and the label for the new field is added to the left of the field (see Figure 6.12). Next, you need to format the new field to match the ones on the report.

Access

Figure 6.12
Fields may be added to a report using the field list.

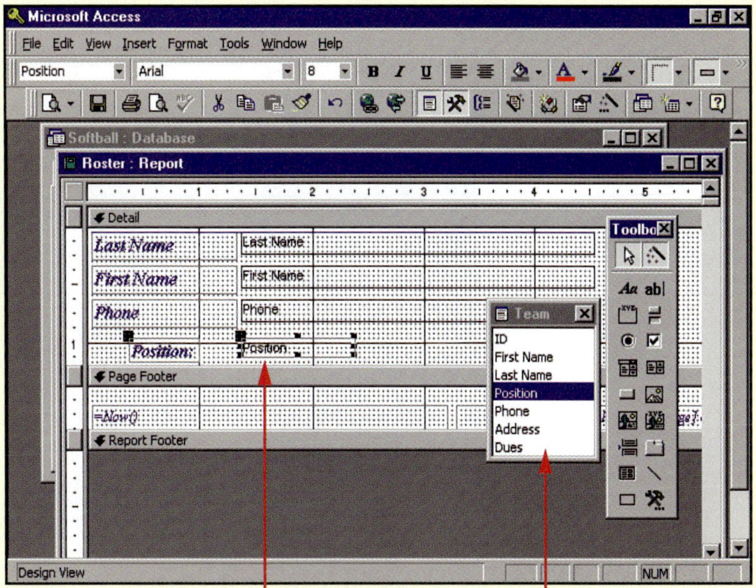

8 **Point to the Phone text box above the new Position text box. Hold down Shift and click. The Phone and Position boxes should both be selected.**

9 **Choose Format, Size, To Widest to match the length of the two boxes.**

10 **Choose Format, Size, To Tallest to match the height of the two boxes.**

11 **Choose Format, Align, Left to match the alignment of the two boxes.**

12 **Click in an unused space in the Detail area to deselect the boxes.**

13 **Select the label boxes for Position and Phone. Repeat steps 9 through 12 to get the Position label box to match the other labels in size and alignment.**

14 **Click the Print Preview button on the toolbar.**

The new field should now match the other boxes in size and alignment. However, the other text boxes have a dark border. Next you add the dark border to the Position text box.

15 **Click the View button to return to the Design view, then click the Position text box to select it.**

16 **Click the down arrow to the right of the Line/Border Color button (see Figure 6.13).**

continues

To Modify a Report Design (continued)

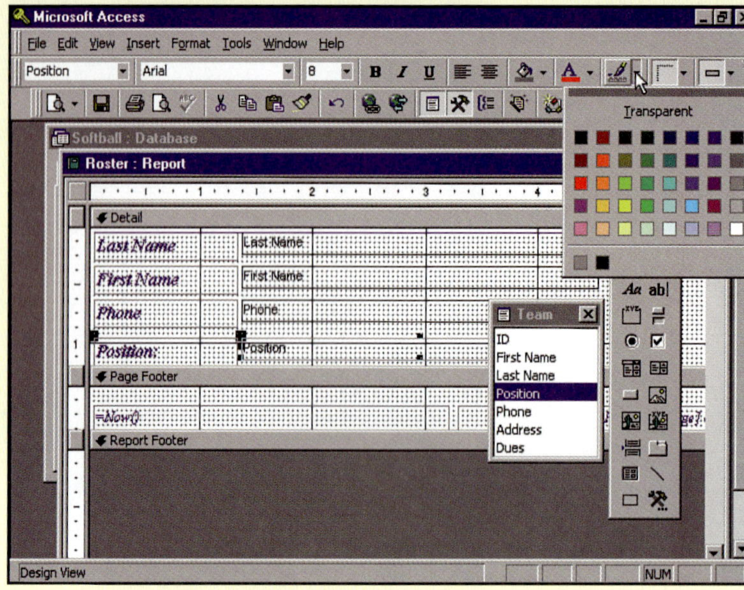

Figure 6.13
The Line/Border button is used to add a border or to change the color of a border to a selected control.

17. **Select black for the box border.**

18. **Save your changes and keep this report open for the next lesson where you save the report with a new name.**

Inside Stuff

Access often provides several ways for you to perform a task. To get to another view, for example, you can use the buttons on the toolbar. In addition, you can use the list of Report views to change views when you are in a form or table. You can use the View menu to change views when you are in a report.

Jargon Watch

Modifying a report design is similar to creating and modifying a form. Reports and forms include controls, labels, and sections. **Controls** are the interactive elements on a report or form, such as text boxes and check boxes. **Labels** have static, descriptive text you can add that is not tied to the underlying database. For example, you can include a label that provides the name of the report.

Sections are subdivisions of the form or report that control what is printed and where it is printed. Record information is printed in the Detail section, for example. Text and graphics included in the Page Header section are printed at the top of the page; information included in the Page Footer section is printed at the bottom of the page.

Exam Notes

The Report Wizards are used to give you all the necessary elements of a report, and to place these elements in their proper locations. The wizards will save you time, but will seldom provide finished reports. You will almost always need to modify field lengths, add or format labels, modify the spacing between fields, and change locations of some of the elements. If you are asked to create a report using a wizard, make sure you use the Print Preview feature to scan through the data and look for fields that may have been cut off and need to be modified.

Lesson 5: Saving the Report with a New Name

As you modify a report, you may decide that you want to keep the original report as well as your modified version. If this is the case, you can save the modified report with a new name. Doing so enables you to use both reports.

In addition to saving the report with a new name, you should change the Report Header so that it reflects the purpose of the new report.

To Save the Report with a New Name

1 With the Roster report still onscreen, open the File menu and choose the Save As/Export command.

You see the Save As dialog box, as shown in Figure 6.14, with the original name listed.

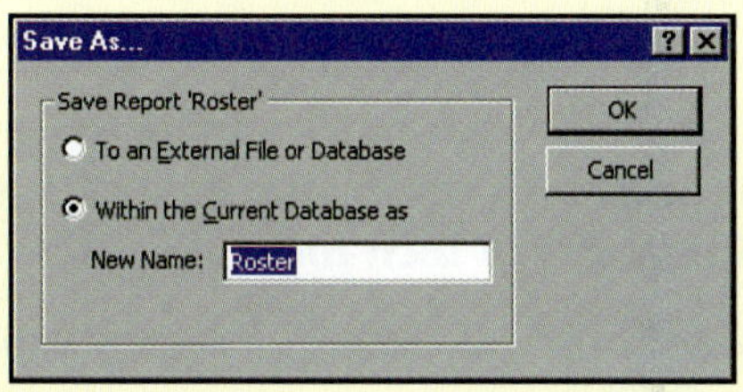

Figure 6.14
When you choose Save As/Export, Access displays the original name in the New Name box.

2 Type `Phone List` and click OK.

The report is saved with a new name.

3 Click in the label box in the Report Header section.

Here you want to replace the existing text, `Team`, with a more descriptive title.

4 Drag across the text to select it; then type `Phone List`.

The new text replaces the selected text.

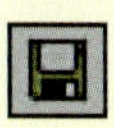

5 Click the Save button.

This step saves your changes to the Phone List report by writing over the report with that name. Keep the Phone List report open and continue to the next lesson where you learn to add labels to a report.

Inside Stuff

You can also create a duplicate report from the database window. With the Reports tab selected, right-click on the report name and select Copy from the shortcut menu. Right-click again in an open area of the window and select Paste from the shortcut menu. Give the duplicate report a new name when prompted.

Lesson 6: Adding Labels to the Report

When you create a report using a wizard, the labels tend to be short and non-descriptive. Once you have modified the report, as you did in Lesson 4, you will often find that additional labels are necessary to explain exactly what is in the report. Access gives you an easy way to add labels to either the Report Header or the Page Header. Labels added to the Report Header will show up on the first page of the report, while labels added to the Page Header area will appear on the top of every page.

In this lesson, you add the team name to the Report Header area.

To Add Labels

1 With the Phone List report open in the Design view, click the Label button in the toolbox.

When you move the pointer over an open area of the design window, the pointer turns into a large A with a crosshair attached.

2 Click at the 2-inch mark of the Report Header area and drag down and to the right until you have a text box about 2 inches wide and 1/4 inch high.

This label box will contain a second label for the Report Header (see Figure 6.15).

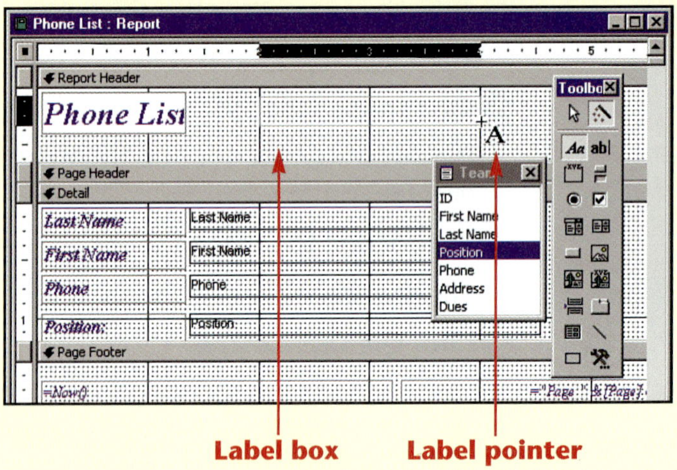

Figure 6.15
The Label button in the toolbox enables you to add new labels.

3 Type `The Oakville Tigers` in the label box.

If the text is too long for the box you created, you can select the box and resize it to fit.

4 Click in an open area of the Report Header.

This will turn off the text edit.

5 Click on the new label box and drag it under the original title.

If the label box is too big for the area under the original title, drag the Page Header bar down until it fits.

6 Click the Print Preview button.

The original title and the new title you just added are displayed at the top of the report (see Figure 6.16).

Figure 6.16
Labels can be added to the Report Header or the Page Header areas.

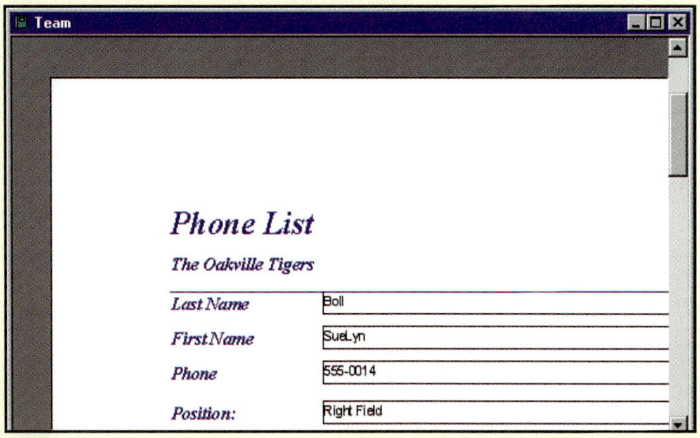

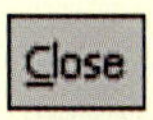

7 Click the Close button on the Print Preview toolbar.

8 Click the Save button.

9 Close the Report Design view and close the database.

If you have completed your session on the computer, exit Access and shut down Windows before you turn off the computer. Otherwise, continue with the "Checking Your Skills" and "Applying Your Skills" sections in this project.

Exam Notes

Remember, titles that are places in the Report Header area will only appear on the first page, and titles that are placed in the Report Footer area will only appear on the last page of the report. Text added to the Page Header and Page Footer areas will appear on every page of the report.

Project Summary

To	Do This
Print the data in a table	Open the database file in Table view. Open the File menu and choose Print Preview. Alter the layout by using the Page Setup command in the File menu, if necessary. When the page appears the way you want, open the File menu and choose Print.
Create a report using Report Wizards	Several wizard options are available (refer to Table 6.1). To open the wizard you want to use, click the down arrow next to the New Object button. Select Report, select Report Wizard, and click OK. Select the fields you want included in the report and click the Add button (>). Click Next. The wizard leads you through several more screens. Make your selections, click Next until you reach the final screen, and click Finish.
Print a report	When you click the Finish button using the wizard, you see a Print Preview of the report. If you are satisfied with the report, click the Print button.
Rename a report	Select the Reports tab in the database window. Click the report title you want to change. Pause and then click a second time. The box around the title will change, and you can edit the report title by typing over the existing name.
Modify a report design	Work in Design view. The same techniques used when designing a form apply here. You can start with an existing report. Click and drag the fields you want to move, add, or delete. The same tools are used in the toolbox or the Format menu to help align fields, add labels, modify fonts, or change headers and footers.
Save a report with a new name	Open the File menu and choose the Save As/Export command. Type a new name in the dialog box and click OK.
Add a label to a report	Click the Label button in the toolbox. Click and drag in the Report Header or Page Header area to create a text box. Type in the text for the new label, then format the text and move it to the desired location.
Add fields	Work in Design view. In the field box, click and drag the field you want to add to the report to the desired position. Click the Print Preview button to view the report. Adjust the fields until you are satisfied with the report design.

Access

Checking Your Skills

True/False

For each of the following, check *T* or *F* to indicate whether the statement is true or false.

__T __F **1.** To print table data, you have to use a Report Wizard. You can't just print directly from the table.

__T __F **2.** You can modify the report layout in Print Preview mode.

__T __F **3.** To rename a report in the database window, click once on the report name and type the new name.

__T __F **4.** You cannot add new fields to an existing report.

__T __F **5.** To add a label to a report, you use the Label tool on the toolbox.

__T __F **6.** When you drag a field name into a report, the mouse pointer turns into a small field box.

__T __F **7.** To save a report with a new name, select Save As/Export from the File menu.

__T __F **8.** If you delete a field text box, its label box will be deleted also.

__T __F **9.** The term [#Pages] on your report will insert the total number of pages of your report.

__T __F **10.** If the data in a report is too wide to fit in Landscape orientation, it may fit in Portrait orientation.

Multiple Choice

Circle the letter of the correct answer for each of the following questions.

1. Which of the following choices is not one of the selections when you select New from the Reports window?

a. Report Wizard

b. Double-column

c. AutoReport: Tabular

d. AutoReport: Single Column

2. To change the orientation of the report, which command do you use under the File menu?

a. Print Setup

b. Print Orientation

c. Page Setup

d. Printer Setup

3. If you make a mistake and want to go to the previous screen in a Wizard, which button do you use?

a. Next

b. Back

c. Previous

d. Go Back

4. Which report design tool helps you precisely position controls on the report?

a. toolbox

b. toolbar

c. field list

d. ruler

5. How do you delete a control from a report?

a. Click it and press Del.

b. Drag it off the report.

c. Double-click it and press Del.

d. Press ←Backspace.

6. If you have entered all the information you need on the Report Wizard, you can complete the process by selecting which button?

a. Finish

b. Complete

c. Done

d. OK

7. To make a group of text boxes the same dimension from top to bottom, select Format, Size, then _____.

a. Tallest

b. Highest

c. Height, Tallest

d. Largest

8. To display a full-page view of a report in Print Preview (if you are in a close-up view), which button should you click?

a. PageUp

b. Zoom

c. Magnify

d. Full Page

9. An AutoReport includes which of the following?

a. all non-automatic fields in the table

b. all fields in the database

c. the fields you designate in the third dialog box

d. all fields in the source table

10. Finished reports include all the following except which?

a. labels

b. find buttons

c. sections

d. controls

Access

Completion

In the blank provided, write the correct answer for each of the following statements.

1. ______________ orientation prints across the long side of the page.
2. To add controls to the report (such as check boxes, text boxes, and labels) use the ______________ in Design view.
3. Items that you add to a form or report are called ______________.
4. A(n) ______________ is a formula or function that performs a calculation.
5. To add a field to a report, drag the field from the ______________.
6. ______________ are subdivisions of a report or form.

7. You can use ______________ to see what a report will look like before you print it.

8. To have a selected group of controls line up on the report, you can select ______________ from the Format menu.

9. You can use ______________ to help you create several graphic representations of numeric data.

10. By default, a columnar report has ______________ column(s).

Matching

In the blank next to each of the following terms or phrases, write the letter of the corresponding term or phrase. (Note that some letters may be used more than once.)

a. Landscape

b. Print Preview

c. Ctrl+S

d. Format, Size, To Widest

e. AutoReport: Columnar

f. AutoReport: Tabular

g. Format, Size, To Length

h. Add button ([>])

i. Label Wizard

j. Border Color button

_______ 1. Used to save a report

_______ 2. Places all fields in a row-and-column format similar to a spreadsheet

_______ 3. Helps you set up more than 100 different label styles

_______ 4. Used to change the outline color of a box

_______ 5. Menu selections to make multiple selected items the same length

_______ 6. An electronic version of the final printed report

_______ 7. An orientation for the report

_______ 8. Places all of a table's fields in a single-column report

_______ 9. Not required, but a good choice before you print a report

_______ 10. Used to add fields from the Available Fields list in the Report Wizard

Applying Your Skills

Practice

The following exercises enable you to practice the skills you have learned in this project.

Creating a Book List

Printing a simple list of data in a database can be helpful in many ways. First, you usually use a database to track some item, as you have tracked your book collection by using the Library database you developed in earlier projects. You may want to have a complete list of all the entries you have made—that is, a printed copy of all the books in your collection. Second, when you want to share data in your database, you can print a report to give to someone else. For example, suppose that one of your friends wants to borrow some books to take on a trip. You can give her your book list and then let her select the titles that interest her.

To print data from your Books table, you can create a simple report. This report should include the fields for the author's last name, author's first name, and book title. You can sort the report by the author's last name.

To create a report for your Library database, complete the following steps:

1. Copy the Proj0602 database file from the Project-06 folder on the CD and rename it `Library5`. Then return to Access and open the `Library5` database and the `Books` table.
2. Create a report using the Report Wizard. Add the `Author Last Name`, `Author First Name`, and `Title` fields to the report. Choose Author Last Name as the sort field. Make it a columnar report.
3. Save the report with the title `Book List`.
4. Print a copy of the report. If requested by your instructor, print two copies.

Creating an Order Table and Printing an Order Report

In previous Practice exercises involving the Sound Byte Music store, you set up database tables for suppliers and for customers. In addition to tracking these two important sets of information, you may want to keep track of outstanding orders. This table can track which new products you have ordered, the number you ordered, and from whom you ordered the items. You can start by creating a new table with fields for `Order Date`, `Order Number`, `Supplier Name`, `Item Ordered`, and `Quantity`. Next, you can enter records for this new table. Then, to keep up-to-date on the orders, you can print a report that lists outstanding orders.

To create an order table and print an order report, complete the following steps:

1. Copy the Proj0603 database file from the Project-06 folder on the CD and change the name of the copy to `SBMusic5`. Return to Access, open the `SBMusic5` database, and create a new table that includes the following fields. All fields should have a data type of Text except for the Quantity field, which should be a Number field, and the Order Date, which should be a Date/Time field.

    `Order Date`

    `Order Number`

    `Supplier Name`

    `Item Ordered`

    `Quantity`

2. Make the Order Number field the primary key field.
3. Save the table with the name `Orders`.
4. Enter at least five records into the new table.
5. Create an AutoReport based on the new table. Save the report with the name `Outstanding Orders`.
6. Print the report. Close the report and the database.

Creating a Report Based on the Personal Computer Hardware Table

Create a report that shows the PC hardware owned by the company.

To create the PC Hardware report, complete the following steps:

1. Copy the file Proj0604 from the Project-06 folder on the CD and rename the copy `PC5`. Open `PC5`.
2. Create a report based on the PC Hardware table. Select all the fields in the table.
3. Use the tabular form in landscape orientation.
4. Go into Design view to adjust the size of the column headings so that they display the full text of each heading. (*Hint*: Increase the size of the Page Header and drag the line downward to make room for larger labels. Select all the label boxes in the Page Header, change the font to 8 points, and then drag the lower edge of the label boxes down to increase the vertical size.)
5. Save the report as `PC Hardware Report`.
6. Print the report.

Getting a Helping Hand

Often you have an idea of what something does, but you need to find just a little more information about it.

To get help on topics in this project, complete the following steps:

1. Open the `Softball` database you saved during your work earlier in this project.
2. Select the Reports tab.
3. Open the `Roster` report in Design view.
4. Maximize the window, if necessary. F1 opens the Office Assistant most of the time. However, if you have certain items selected, the Assistant will give you additional information about those items.
5. Select the title in the Report Header so that the control handles appear around the box.

6. With the title selected, press F1. You get a dialog box similar to What's This?, explaining what the label is. Notice at the bottom of the dialog box that you can elect to see more information.

   Now look at another example.

7. From the bottom left of the window, select the text box that contains the expression `=Now()`. The control handles should appear around the box.

8. Press F1. A new dialog box appears that discusses the text box. From the bottom of this dialog box, you can launch the appropriate Help topic by selecting `For more information, click [>>]`.

9. Select the small button with the double greater-than symbols. Access launches the appropriate Help topic. You can then get an overview or follow the links to more specific details on creating expressions.

Exploring the World of Alaska

Once you have a database of information, you may want to print the table so that you can check data or file the data as a hard-copy archive. First, you want to get an idea of how the report might look.

To view and print a table, complete the following steps:

1. Copy the database Proj0605 from the Project-06 folder on the CD and rename it `Alaska4`.
2. Open the `Geography` table in Datasheet view.
3. Click the Print Preview button on the toolbar. You see the first page of the report. If you click the Last Page navigation button at the bottom of the window, you should see that there are eight pages to the report. Depending on your hardware and software configuration, the total may be different.
4. Click the Multiple Pages button on the toolbar.
5. In the small window that appears, select the top-left box and drag down to the second row and across four boxes until you have a total of eight boxes selected. The complete report should appear. Notice that tables are split across pages.
6. Choose Page Setup from the File menu.
7. On the Page tab, change the orientation to Landscape.
8. Select the Margins tab.
9. Change the Left and Right margins to 0.5 inches.
10. Click OK. The view of the report in Print Preview displays only five pages. Each one will fill the page. You can zoom in on any page to see the detail of what the report will look like.
11. Choose Print from the toolbar and close the database.

Challenge

The following challenges enable you to use your problem-solving skills.

Creating a Report That Lists Your Club or Organization Roster

Use the AutoReport: Tabular option to create a report that lists the members of your club or organization. Name it `Membership List`. Open the report in design mode and change the title of the report so that it is different than the name of the table it is based upon. Print a copy of the report.

Doing Customer Research

Your boss has an important meeting on the survey and wants to study the comments people have made. Your job is to create a concise report that will enable your boss to review it quickly.

To create a report for quick review, complete the following steps:

1. Make a copy of the database Proj0606 from the Project-06 folder on the CD, or use the database you completed in the previous project.
2. Select the Tables tab. The Questionnaire table should be highlighted.
3. Select Report under the New Object button. The Questionnaire table should be the default table selected as the source for the report.
4. Using the Report Wizard format, create a report with the fields `Adults`, `Children`, `Hours`, and `Improve`. Don't group or sort the table, but use the Tabular format for the report. After selecting the Bold style, save the report as `Customers and their comments`.
5. View the report in Print Preview. The report you have created should be only one page and should provide a complete list of all the data your boss has requested. There is, however, a lot of wasted space for the first three fields.
6. Select Design view and shrink the width of the first three numeric fields. Be sure you move the heading as well.
7. View the revised report in Print Preview and then print a copy.

Owning a Vending Company

As you review your database, you realize that there are only two reports you will need. The first is a report from your Suppliers table that you can keep with you as a phone list. The second is a list of the locations that you can keep with you as you drive around town.

To generate two reports, complete the following steps:

1. Copy the file Proj0607 from the Project-06 folder on the CD and rename the copy `Vending4`.

2. Using the New Object button on the toolbar, select Report and Report Wizard to generate the new report based on the Suppliers table.

3. Add all the fields to your report without grouping the report by any of the fields. Then sort the report by the name field and use the columnar format.

4. Choose the Soft Gray style and name the report `Supplier Phone List`.

5. After you have generated the report and viewed it with Print Preview, print a copy of the report for your notebook. Notice that the Bulk Foodstuffs supplier should now be listed at the top of the report.

6. Close the report and return to the Reports tab of the database.

7. Select New and generate an AutoReport: Tabular using the Locations table. The ID field will be included because you have created an AutoReport.

8. The ID field doesn't concern you, so change to Design view and remove the ID field and its column label in the Page Header section of the report.

9. View the report once again in Print Preview and then print a copy, using the File menu.

10. Close the report, saving it with the name `Machine Locations`.

Managing a Video Store

After you have generated a fairly complete database of videos for your store, you will have to conduct an inventory. Several methods for conducting the inventory are available, some taking more time than others. One effective method is to create a list of the videos, separated by type, with each type alphabetized.

With this report format, you just have to assign a person to handle one or two types. All employees can be used to conduct the inventory simultaneously.

Open the video tape table in Design view and add a new field named `Type`. Switch to Datasheet view and enter a classification for each video that indicates whether it is comedy, drama, action, and so forth.

Generate a report by using the Report Wizard based on your table of video tapes. Include the video title, number, and type fields in your report. Group the report by type and sort by video title.

Save your new report as `Inventory Listing` and print a copy for your files.

Taking a Home Inventory

As you acquire more household items, you will see items that you need to add to your database. As you add more items, the list that the insurance company has will become out-of-date. It is important for the insurance company to have an accurate picture of what is in your household to ensure that you have set the proper level of insurance.

Create a tabular report by using your main item table and the Report Wizard, which lists specific information for the insurance company. Name the report `Periodic Update` and sort it by item name.

Then create a new report, with the same format used for the previous one, except sort the information by dollar amount, in descending order. Name this report `List by Value`. The new report will enable you to view the items that you want to ensure are covered.

PinPoint Assessment

PinPoint Training

You have completed the project and the associated lessons, as well as the "Checking Your Skills" and "Applying Your Skills" sections. Now use the PinPoint software Evaluation mode to assess your comprehension of the specific exam tasks you have just learned. You can also use the PinPoint Trainer mode and the SHOW ME tutorials to practice these specific exam tasks.

Project 7
Seven

Customizing Fields and Tables

Working with Tables

In this project you will learn the following objectives and their associated Microsoft Exam required activities.

Objectives	Required Activities
➤ Modify a Table Design	Modify Field Properties
➤ Enter a Default Value	Modify Field Properties
➤ Change a Field Type and Select a Format	Modify Field Properties
➤ Change a Field Size	Modify Field Layout
➤ Work with More Than One Table	Identify Relationships
➤ Create Table Relationships	Relate Tables
➤ Create a Multiple-Table Query	Join Tables in a Query Remove Joins in a Query

Why Would I Do This?

Access provides many features to help you customize your database table. You can select the field size, enter a default value, or select how data in that field is displayed.

Property
An attribute of a field that you can use to define characteristics of that field.

When you first create a database, you may not be sure which of these options you want to use. After you have entered several records, however, you may find that you need to make changes, and you can make them by modifying the table design. You can add fields to the table or delete fields. You can also change the field *properties* of the table entries. In this project, you learn how to modify a table design and change some of the field properties.

Another way you can customize tables is to connect two or more tables together. Access is a **relational database**, which means that data is stored separately in tables and then connected or related by common fields in each table. Connecting tables enables you to set up a sophisticated database system and makes managing the information easier.

An example of the advantage of using two tables is demonstrated by a database designed for a small company. The company sells supplies to 20 different retail outlets. Each month, the company sends several orders to each outlet. The company wants to record the mailing address of each of the outlets and the information about each order. If a single table were used with all the fields in it, the company would have to enter the address of the outlet every time an order was sent. If the database is designed with two tables, the mailing address information can be entered once for each outlet in one table, while the specific order information can be entered in a second table.

This project touches on some of the relational features of a database.

Jargon Watch

To understand the concepts of a relational database, you must be familiar with a few fundamental terms. A **relational database** is a database in which the data is stored in separate tables and the tables are related through a common field.

The connection between the two tables is called a **relationship**. The most common type of relationship is called a one-to-many. If two tables have a one-to-many relationship, it means that each record in the first table can be related to many records in the second table. Records in both tables must share a field that can be used to relate them. Other types of relationships are possible, such as a one-to-one relationship, in which one record from a table is related to one record in another table through a common field.

Lesson 1: Modifying a Table Design

It's a good idea to spend some time planning your database structure—thinking about which fields to include and in which order. If you had only one chance to get the database table right, you probably would get frustrated quickly because it is difficult to anticipate all the features you want to include in a table.

Fortunately, Access lets you make changes to a table design even after you have created the table. Consequently, you can add fields, delete fields, or modify field properties as the need arises.

If the field already contains data and you make a change to the field, the data will be affected. Sometimes the change doesn't cause any problems. For example, if you have already entered numbers in a field and then decide you want to format them as Currency, you won't lose any data.

However, if you enter a note in a field and then change that field type to a Yes/No field, you will lose most of the data in the field when Access reformats the field to the new type. Just be sure that you realize the changes you are making and understand how they will affect your data.

You begin this lesson by modifying the Team table of the Softball database by adding a few new fields.

To Modify a Table Design

1 Copy the Proj0701 database file from the Project-07 folder on the CD and rename it `Softball2`. Then return to Access and open the `Softball2` database.

In this project, you use a version of the Softball database you worked with in Project 6, "Creating and Printing Reports." The database includes a table of team members and a table of game information. You should see the Database window, listing the two tables. In this example, you work with the Team table.

2 Click the Team table and then click the Design button.

The Team table opens in Design view so that you can make changes (see Figure 7.1). When you first created the table, you didn't include the city, state, or ZIP code for the players because most of the players live in the same city; you didn't think you needed to track this information.

After using the database for some time, however, you have decided that you want to include the city, state, and ZIP code in the table so that you can have complete addresses for mailings. Now you want to add a city field and a state plus ZIP code field to the table, and you want to place these fields after the address field.

3 Click the field selector next to the Dues field and drag downward to select three rows.

This selects three rows. The new rows you want to insert will be placed above the row containing the Dues field.

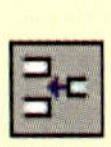

4 Click the Insert Rows button on the Table Design toolbar.

Access inserts three rows in which you can enter the City, State, and ZIP code fields. You can also insert a row by selecting the Insert menu and choosing the Rows command.

continues

To Modify a Table Design (continued)

Figure 7.1
Open the table in Design view so that you can modify its design.

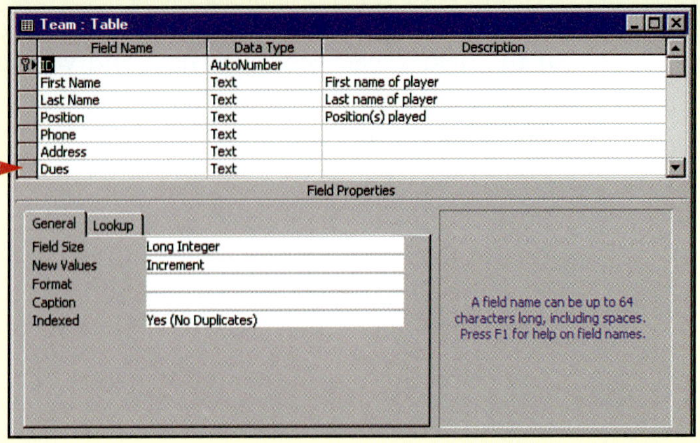

5 Click in the Field Name column and type `City`. Press Tab three times.

This enters the field name, accepts Text as the field type, skips the Description column, and moves you to the next row.

6 Repeat this step to enter the `State` and `ZIP Code` fields.

When you have finished, you will have inserted three new fields (see Figure 7.2).

Figure 7.2
You can add new fields to a table by inserting new rows.

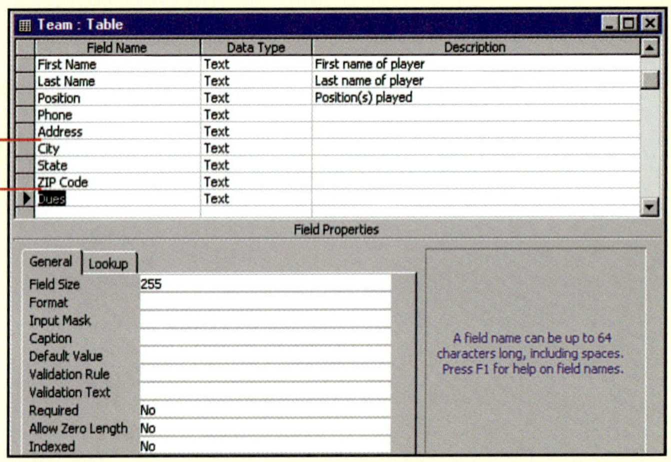

7 Click the Save button on the toolbar and then close the table. Leave the Softball2 database open.

The Team table is saved with the modifications you have made.

8 Click the Games table to select it and then click Design.

Notice that the table has a counter field that is used as the primary key. Since the team never plays more than one game on any given day, the Date field can serve as the primary key field.

9 Click the row selector for the Date field and then click the Primary Key button on the toolbar.

The primary key icon is now displayed on the row selector button next to the Date field.

10 Click the row selector button for the ID field and press the Del key.

A warning message will appear that tells you all data in this field will be lost.

11 Click Yes to confirm the deletion of the field. Close the table but keep the database open for use in the next lesson where you learn to enter a default value.

Inside Stuff

One of the rules of database design is to create fields that are of the smallest useable size. It is not always clear what that means until you have used the database for a while. In this table, the Address field contains the street number and the street name. This practice reduces the number of fields in the table but it also reduces your options for sorting the data. For example, if you wanted to sort the addresses by street name, it would be difficult because the street number comes first in the field.

Another example of this practice would be using a single field for a person's name. If you entered the names with last name followed by a comma and the first name (Preston, John), they would sort properly but you would have trouble when you wanted to print mailing labels.

In general, do not group two types of data into the same field unless you are confident that the need to use them separately is unlikely to occur. It is difficult to change this decision once the data has been entered.

Lesson 2: Entering a Default Value

At times, you may want a particular value to appear in a specific field for most of the records in your table. In the three new fields you entered in the preceding lesson, for example, you want to use the same city, state, and ZIP code for nearly all the records. You can type the entry over and over again for each record, or you can enter a default value.

When you enter a default value, Access automatically uses that field entry for all new records. (All records you entered previously, however, are not affected.)

To Enter a Default Value

1 Select the Team table and click Design. Click in the row selector next to the City field.

This step selects the field you want to modify. When a field is selected, you see the appropriate field properties for that field type in the lower half of the window. The available properties vary, depending on the data type. In this area, you can enter a default value (see Figure 7.3).

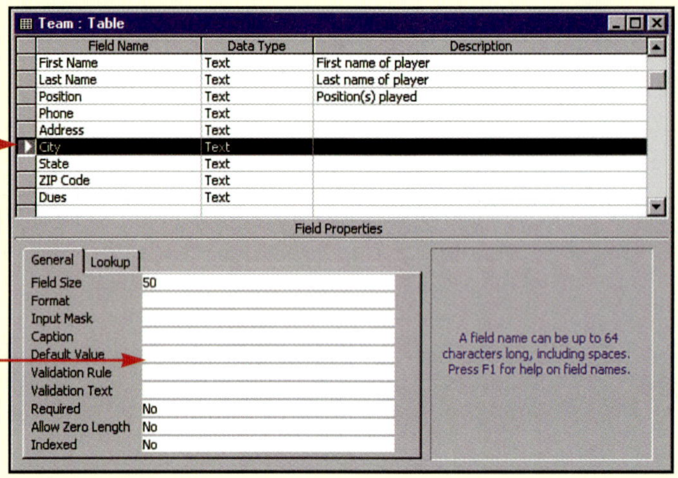

Figure 7.3
You can enter default values in the property boxes in the Field Properties area.

2 Click the Default Value property box in the Field Properties area.

Here is where you enter the value you want to use for all new records.

3 Type `Ann Arbor`.

All records you add to the table from here on will default to Ann Arbor in the City field. Typing in the city name can overwrite this field.

4 Click in the field selector next to the State field.

This selects the next field you want to modify.

5 Click the Default Value property box for this field and type `MI`.

Here is where you enter the value you want to use for all new records.

6 Click the field selector next to the ZIP Code field.

This selects the ZIP Code field and displays its properties.

7 Click the Default Value property box for this field and type `48103`.

8 Click the Save button.

This saves the changes you have made to the table design. Now try adding a new record.

9 Click the View button on the toolbar and then click the New Record button.

This switches you to Datasheet view and moves the insertion point to a new row so that you can enter a new record.

10 Press Tab to skip the Counter field; then type the following entries, pressing Tab after each one:

```
Steve
Rasche
First Base
555-8177
8409 Evanston
```

Notice that when you get to the City, State, and ZIP Code fields, the values have already been entered (see Figure 7.4).

Figure 7.4
Your default value is entered automatically.

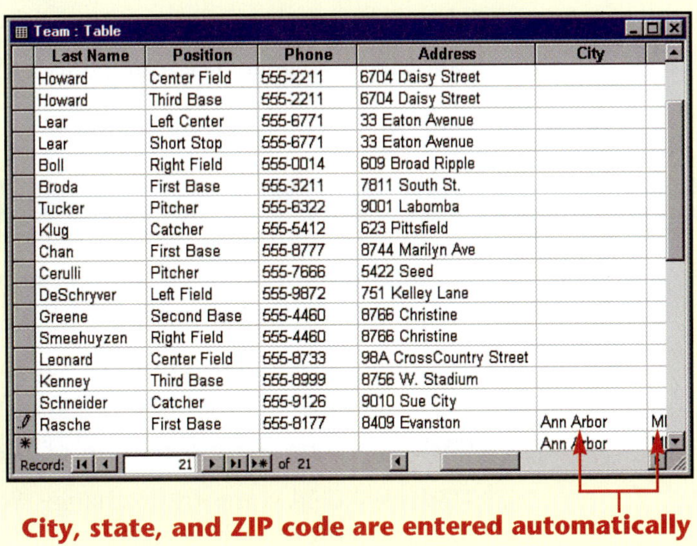

Last Name	Position	Phone	Address	City	
Howard	Center Field	555-2211	6704 Daisy Street		
Howard	Third Base	555-2211	6704 Daisy Street		
Lear	Left Center	555-6771	33 Eaton Avenue		
Lear	Short Stop	555-6771	33 Eaton Avenue		
Boll	Right Field	555-0014	609 Broad Ripple		
Broda	First Base	555-3211	7811 South St.		
Tucker	Pitcher	555-6322	9001 Labomba		
Klug	Catcher	555-5412	623 Pittsfield		
Chan	First Base	555-8777	8744 Marilyn Ave		
Cerulli	Pitcher	555-7666	5422 Seed		
DeSchryver	Left Field	555-9872	751 Kelley Lane		
Greene	Second Base	555-4460	8766 Christine		
Smeehuyzen	Right Field	555-4460	8766 Christine		
Leonard	Center Field	555-8733	98A CrossCountry Street		
Kenney	Third Base	555-8999	8756 W. Stadium		
Schneider	Catcher	555-9126	9010 Sue City		
Rasche	First Base	555-8177	8409 Evanston	Ann Arbor	MI
				Ann Arbor	MI

City, state, and ZIP code are entered automatically

11 Press Tab four times to move past the three fields that have default values and type `50` in the Dues field.

Keep the Team table open and continue with the next lesson.

If you have problems...

In some cases you must surround the default value in quotation marks, or Access may display an error message if the entry is mistaken for a command. For example, when you type only `IN` as the default value for the State field, Access thinks you are creating an expression (formula) rather than entering a default value for Indiana. Quotation marks indicate to Access that this is not an expression.

continues

Just because you inserted a default value doesn't mean that you have to use it for every record. You can always edit or delete the entry.

If you see a syntax error message, it means that you forgot to type the quotation marks around the default value in the table design. Click the OK button and then edit the entry in Design view to include the quotation marks.

If you try to switch to Datasheet view without first saving the table, you are reminded to save. Click the OK button to save the table.

Lesson 3: Changing a Field Type and Selecting a Format

In addition to adding fields to the database table, you can also modify existing fields. Suppose that when you first added fields to your table, you were unfamiliar with the other field types, so you used Text for all your fields. A Text field type is the most common type and works well in many cases.

Now you have a better understanding of the various field types, and you want to change a particular field type so that it more accurately reflects the format of the data being entered. In this case, you can modify the table design and change the field type.

In this lesson, you change the Dues field to a Number data type and then select a format to display the number as currency. The format controls how the data in that field is displayed and what kind of data can be entered.

To Change a Field Type and Select a Format

1. **With the Team table still open onscreen, click the View button to return to Design view.**

   Remember that you can't make changes to the structure of the table in Datasheet view; you must change back to Design view.

2. **Click in the Data Type column of the Dues field.**

   This is the field you want to change. You see a down arrow, and the field properties for this field are listed in the lower half of the window. Notice that this field currently has a Text field type, but you have entered numbers in this field. You can change it to a Number field.

3. **Click the down arrow.**

   A drop-down list appears, showing the available data types (see Figure 7.5).

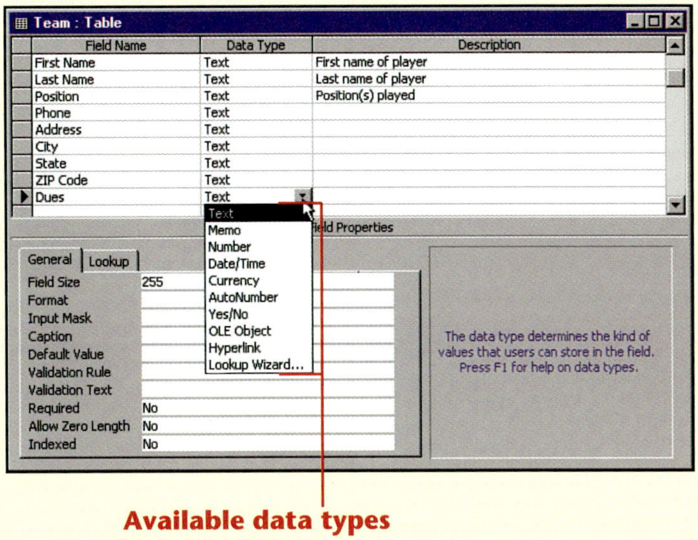

Figure 7.5
Choose a data type for the field from the drop-down list.

4 Click Number in the list.

This selects Number as the data type. You could have selected Currency from the list but this method will show you several other options for formatting numbers as well as currency.

5 Click the Format property box in the Field Properties area.

You see a down arrow in the text box.

6 Click the down arrow.

A drop-down list appears showing the available display formats (see Figure 7.6). The listed formats vary depending on the data type of the selected field.

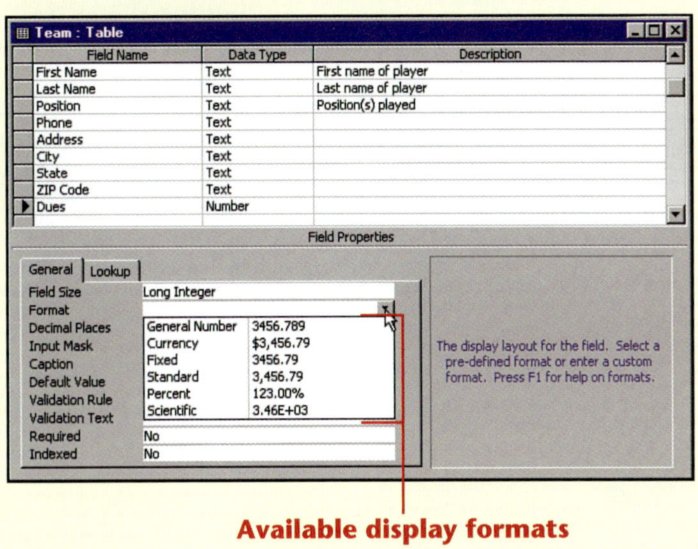

Figure 7.6
Choose a display format from the drop-down list.

continues

To Change a Field Type and Select a Format (continued)

7 Click Currency in the list.

This selects Currency as the display format for the selected field.

8 Click the Save button on the toolbar.

This saves the changes you have made to the table design. To take a look at how these changes affected your table, switch to Datasheet view.

9 Click the View button on the toolbar.

Scroll to the Dues column and notice how the data is now formatted (see Figure 7.7). Keep the Team table open and continue to the next lesson where you learn how to change a field size.

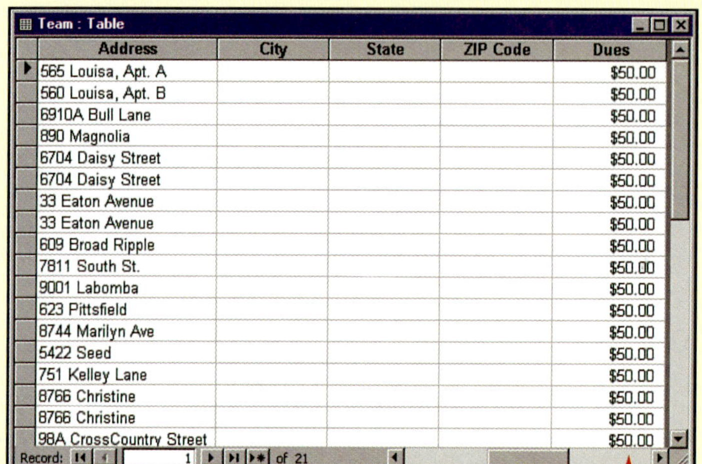

Team : Table

Address	City	State	ZIP Code	Dues
565 Louisa, Apt. A				$50.00
560 Louisa, Apt. B				$50.00
6910A Bull Lane				$50.00
890 Magnolia				$50.00
6704 Daisy Street				$50.00
6704 Daisy Street				$50.00
33 Eaton Avenue				$50.00
33 Eaton Avenue				$50.00
609 Broad Ripple				$50.00
7811 South St.				$50.00
9001 Labomba				$50.00
623 Pittsfield				$50.00
8744 Marilyn Ave				$50.00
5422 Seed				$50.00
751 Kelley Lane				$50.00
8766 Christine				$50.00
8766 Christine				$50.00
98A CrossCountry Street				$50.00

Record: 1 of 21

Figure 7.7
The Dues column is now displayed using the Currency display format.

Exam Notes

The Field Properties area is also the place to choose the number of decimal points to use for a number field. The default is Auto, which works well if you are using currency with two decimal places, but if you wanted a field displaying dollar signs and commas every third number, but with no cents, you would use the drop-down menu in the Decimal Places box and choose `0`.

Lesson 4: Changing a Field Size

Another property of your table that you may want to change is the field size. When a field is added to a form or report, the size of the field's text box is determined by the field size. Setting smaller field sizes in the table for fields like State that are only two characters long will reduce the modifications that you will have to do to forms and reports later. Be careful that you do not choose a field size that is too small; doing so limits what you can enter in that field. In the State field, for example, you want to type the two-letter state abbreviation. You can change the field size and then add a description to the field so that anyone who uses this table is aware of this restriction.

To Change a Field Size

1 With the Team table still open on your screen, click the View button.

This switches you to Design view, which is where you have to be to change to the table.

2 Click the Description column for the State field.

This is the field you want to change. The field properties for this field are listed in the lower half of the window.

3 Type `Enter two-letter abbreviation`.

This enters a description for this field.

4 Click the Field Size property box in the Field Properties area.

This moves the insertion point to the Field Size property box so that you can enter a new field size. The default for text fields is 50, which may be too long for some fields.

5 Drag across 50 and type `2`.

The new field size is large enough for a two-letter abbreviation for the state (see Figure 7.8).

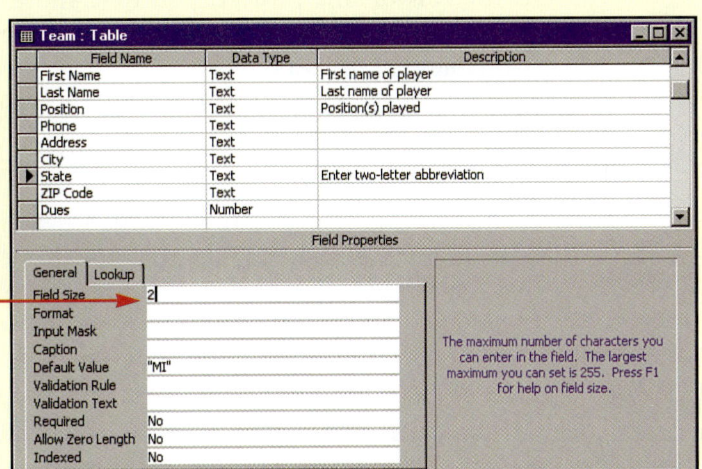

Figure 7.8
Use the Field Size property box to change the field size.

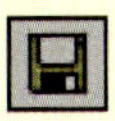

6 Click the Save button.

This saves the new table design. Access prompts you to indicate that you may lose some data by reducing the field size. In this case, none of the entries is longer than two characters, so it is safe to proceed.

continues

To Change a Field Size (continued)

7 When Access prompts you about saving the change, click Yes.

This confirms the change to the new field size. Now when you enter a state in the table, you will be able to type only two characters. Keep the Team table open and continue with the next lesson where you work with more than one table.

If you have problems...

Remember that changing the column width in Datasheet view has no effect on the field size. To change the field size, you must change the field property.

Lesson 5: Working with More Than One Table

Rather than lumping all the information you want to maintain in your Access database into one large table that may be difficult to manage, you can keep your data in more than one table. You can create separate tables and connect them by setting relationships.

In order to relate tables, the tables must share at least one common field. The data type for the common field must be the same for both tables. You cannot, for example, relate a Text field to a Date/Time field. Once the relationship is established, you can take advantage of it by creating queries that use data from several tables instead of only a single table.

In the rest of this project, you first add a common field you can use to relate two tables; then you enter the data, set the relationships, and use the two tables to create a query.

For this lesson, you want to relate the Games table to the Team table so you can see who is responsible for the equipment at each game. So that one person doesn't have to be responsible for the equipment all season, the job is rotated to a new player for each game. Start by adding a new field called Equipment Manager Date. This field shows the date on which a specific player acts as equipment manager. This date field will then be related to the Date field in the Games table.

To Work with More Than One Table

1 With the Team table still open on your screen, click in the field selector next to the Dues field.

This selects the row. The row you insert for the new field will be placed above this row.

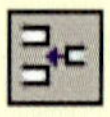

2 Click the Insert Rows button.

Access inserts a new row in which you can enter the new field information.

3 Click in the Field Name column and type `Equipment Manager Date`. Press Tab.

The field name is entered, and Access moves you to the Data Type column.

4 Click the down arrow.

A drop-down list appears, showing the available data types.

5 Click Date/Time in the list.

This selects a Date data type for the Equipment Manager Date field (see Figure 7.9).

Figure 7.9
Adding the field you will use to relate the tables.

New field

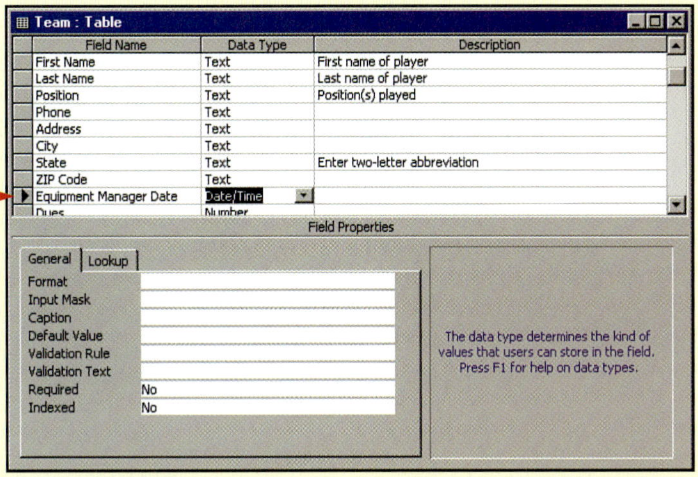

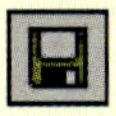

6 Click the Save button.

This saves the changes you have made to the table design. Next, you need to enter values in the field you just added.

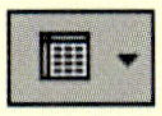

7 Click the View button.

Access displays the table in Datasheet view so that you can enter values into the new field.

There is a problem with entering the Equipment Manager Dates. The new field is several columns away from the column with the players' names.

8 Point to the column header for the first column. Click and drag across the first three columns (ID, First Name, and Last Name) to select them.

9 Select Format and Freeze Columns from the menu.

This will keep these columns onscreen while you scroll through the other columns.

continues

To Work with More Than One Table (continued)

10 Click anywhere in the table to deselect the columns and scroll the table columns until you can see the name columns and the Equipment Manager Date column at the same time (see Figure 7.10).

Figure 7.10
The table shows names and equipment fields next to each other to simplify the addition of the dates.

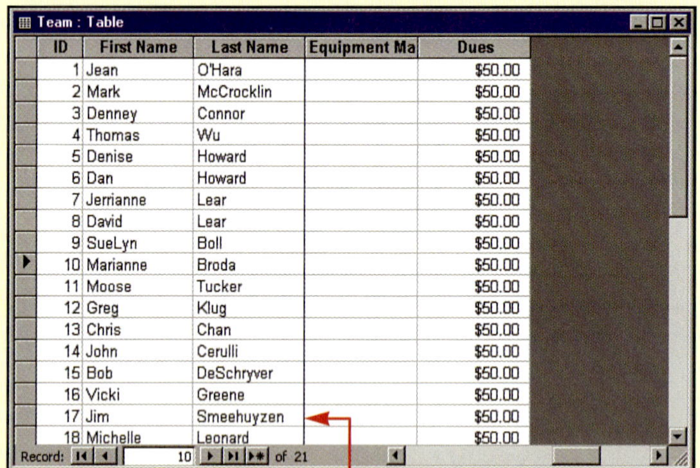
Team : Table

ID	First Name	Last Name	Equipment Ma	Dues
1	Jean	O'Hara		$50.00
2	Mark	McCrocklin		$50.00
3	Denney	Connor		$50.00
4	Thomas	Wu		$50.00
5	Denise	Howard		$50.00
6	Dan	Howard		$50.00
7	Jerrianne	Lear		$50.00
8	David	Lear		$50.00
9	SueLyn	Boll		$50.00
10	Marianne	Broda		$50.00
11	Moose	Tucker		$50.00
12	Greg	Klug		$50.00
13	Chris	Chan		$50.00
14	John	Cerulli		$50.00
15	Bob	DeSchryver		$50.00
16	Vicki	Greene		$50.00
17	Jim	Smeehuyzen		$50.00
18	Michelle	Leonard		$50.00

Record: 10 of 21

Heavier line indicates that columns are frozen

11 Enter the following dates for the appropriate team players:

Player	Equipment Manager Date
O'Hara	6/23/98
McCrocklin	6/30/98
Connor	7/6/98
Wu	7/13/98
Howard, (Denise)	7/20/98
Howard, (Dan)	7/20/98
Klug	7/27/98
Cerulli	8/3/98
DeSchryver	8/10/98
Greene	8/17/98
Smeehuyzen	8/24/98

These dates match the dates in the Date field of the Games table. Notice that Dan and Denise Howard are sharing the responsibility on July 20 since they ride to the game together. Access saves your entries automatically as you type an entry and move to the next row.

⓬ Close the table by clicking the Close button in the upper-right corner of the table window (not the Access window).

Confirm that you want to save your changes to the layout. This preserves the Freeze Columns feature.

The table closes, and you are returned to the Database window. From this window, you can set the relationship between the tables, which you learn to do in the next lesson. Keep the Database window open and continue with Lesson 6 where you learn how to create table relationships.

Inside Stuff

There is a case where the two fields that are used to relate the tables may be different. When the primary key in one table is a counter field and it is used as one of the related fields, it must be related to a number field stored as a long integer in the other table. Counter fields are actually stored as long integers, so this exception still conforms to the "same data type" rule, but it isn't obvious.

Setting up common fields among tables that you want to relate should be one of the ideas you consider when you are creating a new database. You can always edit the table to include a linking field, if necessary, and you can use an existing field if it is an appropriate data type.

Lesson 6: Creating Table Relationships

When you want to relate two tables, you choose a field in each table that contains the same values. For example, in the Team table, you now have a list of game dates in the Equipment Manager Date field. These are the same dates contained in the Date field of the Games table.

Often the fields have the same name, but that isn't a requirement for establishing a relationship between the two. The fields must, however, be the same data type.

You can create various types of relationships. In this lesson, you create a one-to-many relationship between the dates in the Games table to the dates in the Team table. A one-to-many relationship requires that the field in the table on the "one" side of the relationship does not contain any duplicate values. The Date field that is used as the primary key for the Games table has this property. The field that will be on the "many" side of the relationship may use the same date more than once. In this example, Dan and Denise Howard are both assigned to take care of the equipment on the same game date.

To Create Table Relationships

1 Click the Relationships button on the Database toolbar.

You can also select the Tools menu and choose the Relationships command. The Show Table dialog box is displayed (see Figure 7.11). The first step is to choose the tables you want to relate.

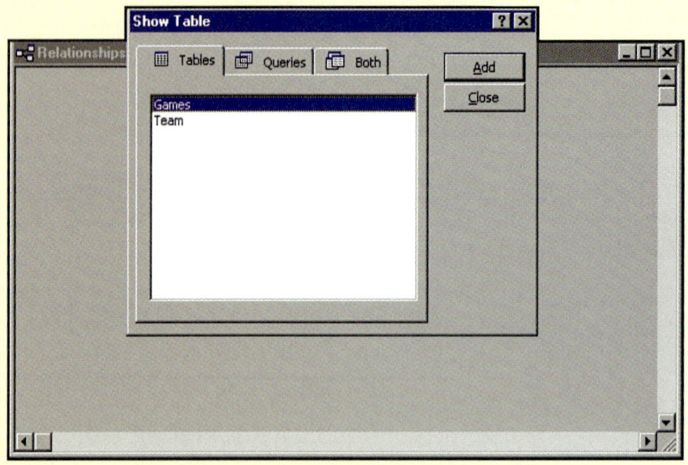

Figure 7.11
In the Show Table dialog box, you choose the tables you want to relate.

2 Click the Games table and then click the Add button.

Access adds the table to the Relationships window; the dialog box remains open.

3 Click Team and then click the Add button.

Access adds the Team table to the Relationships window. (The Team table may be hidden behind the Relationships window.)

4 Click the Close button in the Show Table dialog box.

This closes the dialog box and you see both tables listed in the Relationships window.

5 Place the pointer on the bottom border of the Team field list and drag until all the fields are visible (see Figure 7.12). Resize the Team field list, if necessary, so that you can see all of the fields in the table.

The primary key fields of each table are displayed in boldface type.

6 Click the Date field in the Games table and drag it to the Equipment Manager Date field in the Team table.

When you release the mouse button, you see the Relationships dialog box (see Figure 7.13). In this dialog box, you can confirm that the relationship is correct. You can also set other options, such as the type of relationship you want to set. For this lesson, the default settings are acceptable.

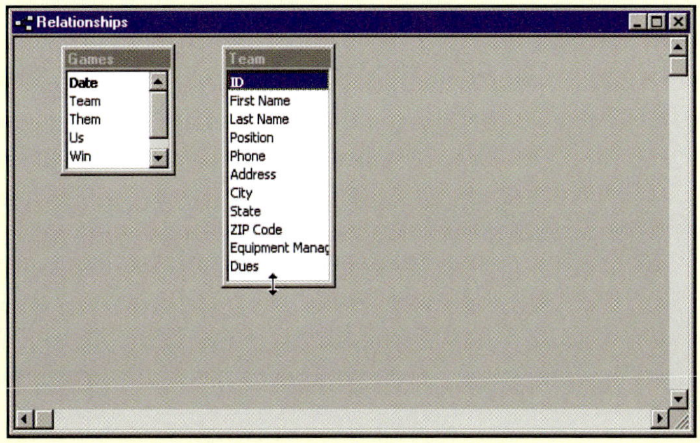

Figure 7.12
The Relationships window may be used to establish links between similar fields in two or more tables.

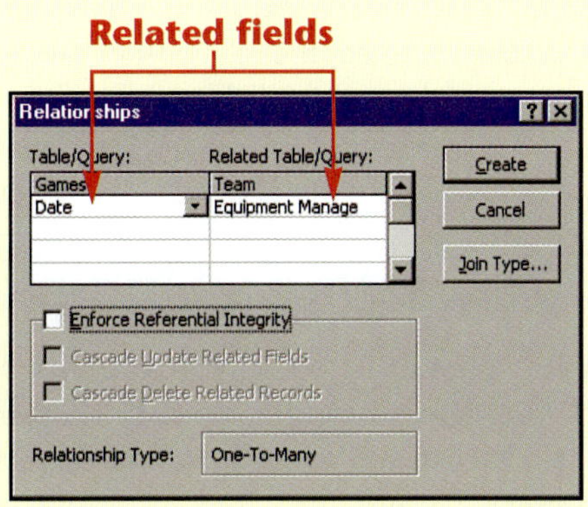

Figure 7.13
Use the Relationships dialog box to confirm whether you have selected the correct fields for the relationship.

7 Click the Create button.

Access creates the relationship. Onscreen, you see a line connecting the two fields (see Figure 7.14).

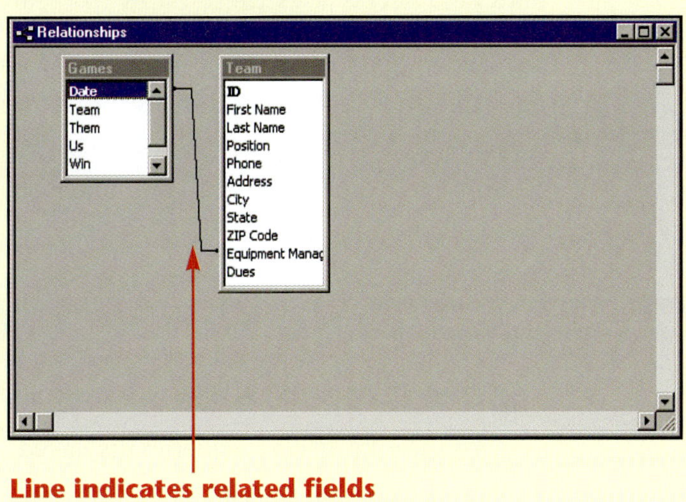

Figure 7.14
A line connects the fields you have chosen to relate.

continues

To Create Table Relationships (continued)

8 Click the Save button on the toolbar.

This saves the relationship you just created; the Relationships window remains open.

9 Close the Relationships window.

The Relationships window closes, and you are returned to the Database window. Keep the Softball2 database open as you continue to the next lesson where you create a multiple-table query.

If you have problems...

To delete a relationship, click the line connecting the two tables and press Del. Access prompts you to confirm the deletion. Click the OK button. Once the relationship has been deleted, the relationship can be re-created by dragging the field name from one table onto the field name in the second table.

Lesson 7: Creating a Multiple-Table Query

After you have established a relationship between tables, you can create forms and queries using data from both tables. When you have defined a relationship, Access automatically knows how to relate the data in the two tables and creates a *join*.

Join
The manner in which the common fields between two tables are associated.

When you create a query that involves two or more tables, Access gives you a choice of three types of joins. The most commonly used join includes only those records with matching values in the common field in both tables. For example, your Games table includes the dates for all the Softball matches. Access uses these dates to create the join and pulls only the records with matching date entries from the Equipment Manager Date field of the Team table. The other two types of joins include all the records from one table and just the matching records from the other table.

In this lesson, you create a query that lists three fields from the Games table—Date, Team, and Field—and one field, Equipment Manager, from the Team table.

To Create a Multiple-Table Query

1 Click the Queries tab in the Softball2 Database window.

You see the available queries displayed in the Queries list.

2 Click the New button.

The New Query dialog box is displayed, showing the different types of queries that are available.

3 Select Design View and click OK.

The Show Table dialog box is displayed with the Query window in the background.

4 Click the Games table and then click the Add button.

This adds the Games table to the Query window.

5 Click the Team table and then click the Add button.

This adds the Team table to the Query window.

6 Click the Close button.

The Show Table dialog box closes. Notice that the relationship between the two tables is displayed (see Figure 7.15). Also displayed are field lists for each table; you may need to scroll the list of Team fields to see all of them.

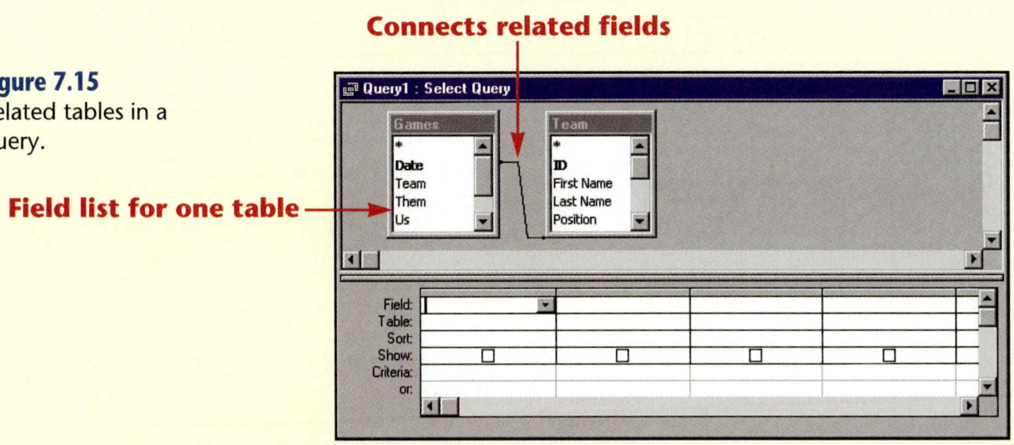

Figure 7.15 Related tables in a query.

7 From the Games field list, drag the Date field to the first column in the design grid. Then drag the Team field from the Games field list to the second column.

The Date and Team fields are added to the query.

8 Drag the Last Name field from the Team field list to the third column in the design grid.

The Last Name field is added to the query.

9 Drag the First Name field from the Team Field list to the fourth column in the design grid.

The First Name field is added to the query.

10 Drag Field from the Games field list to the fifth column of the design grid.

You now have added all the fields you want to include in the query. Check the results of the query.

continues

To Create a Multiple-Table Query (continued)

⑪ Click the View button on the toolbar.

You see the results of your query (see Figure 7.16). The query lists the game date, team played, equipment manager's name, and playing field location of the game. You can save this query.

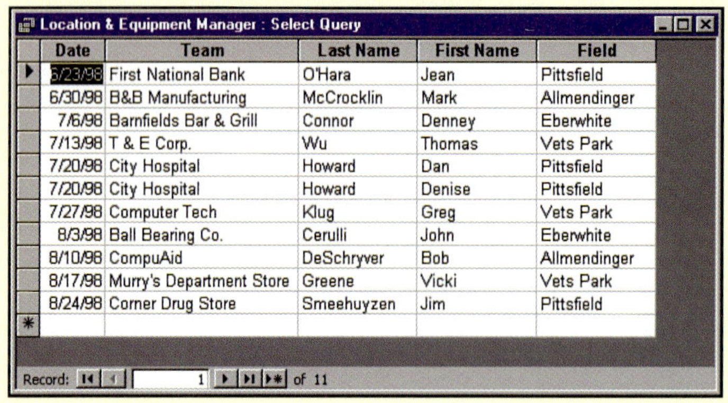

Location & Equipment Manager : Select Query

Date	Team	Last Name	First Name	Field
6/23/98	First National Bank	O'Hara	Jean	Pittsfield
6/30/98	B&B Manufacturing	McCrocklin	Mark	Allmendinger
7/6/98	Barnfields Bar & Grill	Connor	Denney	Eberwhite
7/13/98	T & E Corp.	Wu	Thomas	Vets Park
7/20/98	City Hospital	Howard	Dan	Pittsfield
7/20/98	City Hospital	Howard	Denise	Pittsfield
7/27/98	Computer Tech	Klug	Greg	Vets Park
8/3/98	Ball Bearing Co.	Cerulli	John	Eberwhite
8/10/98	CompuAid	DeSchryver	Bob	Allmendinger
8/17/98	Murry's Department Store	Greene	Vicki	Vets Park
8/24/98	Corner Drug Store	Smeehuyzen	Jim	Pittsfield

Record: 1 of 11

Figure 7.16
Your completed multiple-table query.

⑫ Click the Save button.

The Save As dialog box is displayed.

⑬ Type `Location & Equipment Manager` and click the OK button.

This step saves the query with the name `Location & Equipment Manager`.

⑭ Close the query so that you are back in the Softball Database window; then close the database.

In Project 8, "Managing Data and Files," you use a different database to practice working with database objects. You will also practice importing data from other sources into Access tables.

If you have completed your session on the computer, exit Access and close Windows before you turn off the computer. Otherwise, continue with the "Checking Your Skills" and "Applying Your Skills" sections in this project.

Exam Notes

You can also remove the joins between tables in a query. To do this, click on the line that joins the field lists. The line becomes much thicker, indicating that the relationship has been selected. Press Del. The line (and the relationship) is removed. This does not affect any relationships between the tables other than in this one query.

Access

Project Summary

To	Do This
Modify a table design	Once data has been entered, changes to the table design may affect the data. Open the database, click the Tables tab, and click Design. To insert a new field, click in the row below the position where you want to add a new field. Click the Insert Rows button. Enter the name of the field, type of data, and description in each column.
Enter a default value	Work in Design view. Click the field selector of the field you want to affect. In the Field Properties area, click the row titled Default Value. Type a default value on this line. Quotation marks may be required for certain words that may be used by Access in formulas.
Change a field type and select a format	Work in Design view. Click in the Data Type column of the field you want to affect. Click the down arrow and select the type of data you want. Click the Format property box in the Field Properties area and then click the down arrow. Select the type of format you want.
Change a field size	Work in Design view. Click in the column of the field you want to affect. Click in the Field Size property box of the Field Properties area. Drag across the number and type the size you want.
Prepare tables to be related	To relate tables, each table must contain at least one field with matching data. The data type for the common field must be the same. The name of the field in each table does not have to be the same, however. If needed, add a field to one of the tables before you try to create a relationship. To create a one-to-many relationship, one of the tables must have an indexed field that does not allow duplicates, such as a primary key field.

continues

To	Do This
Create table relationships	Click the Relationships button. Select the tables you want to include; click the Add button after each selection. Click the Close button. Resize the field lists as needed. Click the field name from one table and drag it to the field name in the second table where you want to join a relationship. In the dialog box that appears, click Create. Close the Relationships window.
Create a multiple-table query	Click the Queries tab in the Database window. Click New, New Query, and then click OK. Select the tables to be included and click Add after each selection. Close the dialog box. From each table field list box, drag the fields to be included in the query to the design grid. Place the fields in the order they are to appear in the query. Click the Table View button to view the results. Save your work!

Checking Your Skills

True/False

For each of the following, check *T* or *F* to indicate whether the statement is true or false.

__T __F **1.** To relate two fields, they must be the same data type.

__T __F **2.** The properties for a field are always the same, no matter what the data type.

__T __F **3.** You can change the field size by adjusting the column width in Datasheet view.

__T __F **4.** To create a relationship between two tables, the two tables must have at least two pairs of similar fields.

__T __F **5.** To create a relationship, the matching fields must have the same name.

__T __F **6.** You can't make changes to the structure of a table in Datasheet view.

__T __F **7.** Using the Freeze Columns menu selection, you can freeze columns onscreen so that they will always be visible.

__T __F **8.** A query displays only the data from related tables where the linked field matches if you use the default join type.

__T __F **9.** If you change the data type for a field that already contains data, you always lose the data you have already input.

__T __F **10.** When you enter a default value in a field for a table that already contains data, Access inserts the default value in all the existing records.

Multiple Choice

Circle the letter of the correct answer for each of the following questions.

1. Which button do you use to insert a new field into a table?

a. Insert Rows

b. Insert Fields

c. New Record

d. Field Design

2. What is the default field size for text fields?

a. 100

b. 50

c. 20

d. 25

3. How are related tables displayed in the relationship or query window?

a. Related fields are in boldface.

b. Related fields are underlined.

c. Related fields are connected by a line.

d. Related fields are aligned next to each other.

4. When you define a default value for a field, how or when is that value used?

a. for all existing records

b. only for new records

c. only for records that contain a blank field

d. only when you select a special command

5. In which view can you modify the structure of a table?

a. Any view

b. Datasheet view

c. Design view

d. Query view

6. Which of the following is the most commonly used relationship?

a. one-to-one

b. one-to-many

c. many-to-one

d. many-to-many

7. Why must you be careful about how you designate the information you use as default values?

a. You can't use default values.

b. The information must be used for every new record that follows.

c. Even though you designate the information, you must Paste it each time you are in that field.

d. Some words are reserved for Access commands and must be enclosed by quotation marks.

8. After you have defined a field in a table, which of the following can you change?
   a. the size
   b. the type
   c. the default value
   d. all of the above

9. Where are default values entered?
   a. in the dialog box that appears when you select the Properties button on the toolbar
   b. in the Default Value box in the Field Properties area of the table Design view window
   c. in the Default Value box next to the Data Type box in the field definition area of the Table Design view window
   d. in the dialog box that appears when you select Default Values from the Edit menu

10. The Currency data type ________.
    a. must always use two decimal places
    b. is the default data type for numbers
    c. displays a dollar sign and commas when necessary
    d. is a property of a text field

Completion

In the blank provided, write the correct answer for each of the following statements.

1. An attribute of a field that you can use to define characteristics of that field is called a(n) ______________.
2. The manner in which the common fields between two tables are associated is called a(n)______________.
3. To control how data is displayed, change the ______________ property.
4. A(n) ____________ relationship matches one record in one table to more than one record in another table.
5. When you relate tables, Access automatically creates a(n) ______________, which is an association between fields of the same type.
6. Access automatically uses a field size of ____________ for a text field.
7. Changing the column width in Datasheet view does not change the ______________ of the field.
8. Clicking the ______________ highlights the entire row in table Design view.
9. In order for you to relate two fields, they must have the same ______________.
10. The ______________ field type is the most common type and works well in many cases.

Matching

In the blank next to each of the following terms or phrases, write the letter of the corresponding term or phrase. (Note that some letters may be used more than once.)

a. Text
b. common field
c. join
d. Show Table dialog box
e. data type
f. Freeze Columns
g. Insert, Rows
h. Currency
i. relational database
j. field size

_____ 1. A special field data type

_____ 2. Data stored in separate tables and connected or related through common fields

_____ 3. Limits the number of characters that can be entered in a field

_____ 4. The menu and command you can use to add a field to a table

_____ 5. Required to join two tables

_____ 6. The connection between two tables

_____ 7. The most common data type

_____ 8. Used to keep fields on the screen

_____ 9. Used to identify tables for the Relationships window

_____ 10. A format that can be used for the Number data type

Applying Your Skills

Practice

The following exercises enable you to practice the skills you have learned in this project.

Lending Your Books

Suppose that you have a number of books you are keeping track of in the Library database you developed in earlier projects. You have so many books that people often come to you when they want something good to read. You don't mind lending your books, but you do like to keep track of who has borrowed what so that you know where all your books are. You also like to track what type of book each person borrows so that you have an idea of the kind of books each person enjoys. For example, you can see that one friend borrowed several mysteries over the past year. When his birthday comes around, you know what type of book to buy for a gift.

Instead of cluttering up your Books table with data about borrowers, you can create a new table and then relate the two tables.

To create a new table and relate it to the Books table, complete the following steps:

1. Copy the Proj0702 database file from the Project-07 folder on the CD and rename it `Library6`.

2. Create a new table and include the following fields:

Field Name	Data Type
Book Title	Text
Name	Text
Phone	Text
Date Loaned	Date/Time

3. Make the Book Title field the primary key field.
4. Save the table and name it `Borrow`.
5. Change to Datasheet view and enter at least five records in the new table. Be sure to use book titles that also appear in your Books table. (You can't lend books you don't have.)
6. Go back to the Database window and relate the Books table and the Borrow table by using the Book Title field.
7. Create a query and include the following fields:

Field	From Table
Book Title	Either
Type of Book	Books
Borrower Name	Borrow

8. Save the query as `Type of Book Borrowed`. Then view the query.

Relating Your Supplier and Order Tables

You created several tables in the Sound Byte Music database you set up in earlier projects. Now that the tables are established, you can relate tables that share common information. In this project, for example, you can relate the Supplier table to the Orders table. Both tables include a name field that you can use to relate the tables.

After you have created a relationship between the tables, you can create a query that displays all outstanding orders, the order date, supplier name, and phone number. You can then use this query to follow up on orders.

To relate the Supplier and Orders tables, complete the following steps:

1. Copy the Proj0703 database file from the Project-07 folder on the CD and rename it `SBMusic6`.
2. Relate the Orders table to the Suppliers table by using the Supplier Name field from the Orders table and the Record Company field from the Suppliers table.

3. Create a new query using both tables and include the following fields:

Field	From Table
Order Date	Orders
Item Ordered	Orders
Supplier Name	Orders
Phone	Suppliers

4. Save the query with the name `Orders with phone numbers`.
5. View the results of the query. Close the query and the database.

Creating a Database to Track Personal Computer Hardware

In this exercise, you modify the table design and create a query that will combine information from the Vendor and PC Hardware tables. Open the PC Hardware table in Design view and make the following changes.

To modify the table design and create a query, complete the following steps:

1. Copy the file Proj0704 from the Project-07 folder on the CD and rename the copy `PC6`. Open `PC6`.
2. Change the data type to Yes/No for the two floppy disk drive fields and the sound card field.
3. Use the default text `Ethernet` for the network card.
4. Add the description `386, 486, Pentium, PowerPC` to the Processor field.
5. Create a query, named `PCs by Vendor`, that uses fields from both tables and links the tables through the Vendor Name field. Include the following fields:

   `Name of Vendor`

   `Phone Number`

   `Inventory Code Number`

   `Date of Purchase`

   `Processor`

   `RAM`

   `Hard Drive Size`

   `CD-ROM Speed`
6. Sort the query by vendor.
7. Print the query in landscape orientation.
8. Save the query and close the database.

Getting a Helping Hand

Linking tables effectively can be confusing. The process is the heart of relational systems, however, and the power of Access. Take a look at where the answers are to a number of questions about relating tables.

To get help on topics in this project, complete the following steps:

1. Open the `Softball2` database you worked with earlier in this project.
2. From the Tools menu, choose Relationships. The Relationships window opens, and you see the joined tables you defined earlier.
3. Select the join line between the tables, where the line turns dark.
4. Select the Relationship menu and then choose Edit Relationship. The Relationships dialog box appears, showing you the fields that are joined.
5. Click the What's This? button in the upper-right corner of the dialog box.
6. Click the word `Intermediate` in the bottom center of the dialog box. An expanded tip appears, describing the types of relationships and the significance of the Intermediate relationship.
7. For more information, select the Go-to button (the double greater-than sign, [>>]) at the bottom of the dialog box. The Help topic that appears provides a good overview of the relationships, what they mean, and how to define them.
8. For a graphical explanation of join types, close the Help dialog box and click the Join Type button in the Relationships dialog box. The Join Properties dialog box appears. In this dialog box, the current type of join is selected. In this case, the current type is referred to as an inner join.
9. Click the What's This? button at the top right of the dialog box; then click the top radio button. The Help topic `Join types and how they affect query results` appears. This three-page Help topic provides a good explanation of how the join type can determine what your query will select.
10. Browse the pages of the Help topic.

Exploring the World of Alaska

You have looked at your printed list of information and noticed a lot of wasted space in the database. Each of the records has an entry for a picture and a source, causing the program to reserve space on the disk for that data. It would be better to have a separate file of pictures that you can update and expand.

To create a file of pictures, complete the following steps:

1. Open the file Proj0705 from the Project-07 folder on the CD and rename it `Alaska5`. In this file, the pictures are separated from the main table and placed in a new table called Pictures.

2. Select the Tables tab.
3. Open the `Pictures` table in Datasheet view. Notice that the table includes only the five pictures that were entered in an earlier exercise in this book. There is also a field called ID. The ID number is the same as the ID of the Object in the Geography table. Now change the name of the field so that it reflects more accurately the data it contains.
4. Select Design view. Notice that the name of the number field is still ID, and the type is AutoNumber. These attributes were from the original table you built earlier.
5. Select the field name ID.
6. Change the name to `ObjectID`.
7. Select the Data Type box for the ObjectID field.
8. From the drop-down box, select the Number type. The length should be Long Integer. Leave that selection as it is.
9. Close the table, saving your changes. Next, you want to generate a query that replicates the old table that included both the objects and the pictures.
10. Use the Relationships button and add both tables to the dialog box. Drag a relationship from the ID field in Geography to the ObjectID field in Pictures. Create the relationship and close the window.
11. Create a new query.
12. Add the field Object (from the Geography table) and the fields Picture and Source (from the Pictures table) to the design grid.
13. Run the query. You then see three fields listed in the dynaset. The query has selected all the records. If you move through the dynaset, you will notice that the pictures are where they were when you added them earlier in the book.
14. Close the query, saving it as `All objects including pictures`.

Challenge

The following challenges enable you to use your problem-solving skills.

Formatting the Fields in Your Organization Database

Open the organization database that you began in Challenge Exercise 1 in Project 2, "Creating a Database." Open the table(s) and check the format of the fields. Check for the proper format for currency, number, and date fields. Change the field that tracks donations to Currency. Print a copy of the table.

Doing Customer Research

In Project 6 it became apparent that the basic design of this database violated one of the basic design rules (no repeating fields). If this were a real life problem, you would probably have to scrap almost all of the data you had collected and start over. In this exercise you will open a new database that has been designed properly. It uses three tables: Households, Participants, and Viewing Data. The Households table contains mailing address information. The Participants table describes the individuals who are participating and which household they belong to. The Viewing Data table records each person's television watching activity.

To modify the tables, complete the following steps:

1. Copy the Proj0706 file from the Project-07 folder on the CD and rename the copy `Customer Research6`.
2. Select the `Households` table and open it in Design view. Select the State field and change the field size property to `2`. Select the ZIP Code field and change its field size to `10`. Close the table.
3. Select the `Participants` table and open it in Design view. Change the field size of the Sex field to `1`. Close the table.
4. Select the `Viewing Data` table and open it in Design view. Select the Date field and set the Format property to Short Date. Select the Beginning Time field and set the Format property to Medium Time. Do the same for the Ending Time field. Close the table.
5. Click the Relationships button and add all three tables to the window. Create a relationship between the Household ID field in the Households and Participants tables. Create a relationship between Person ID fields in the Participants table and the Viewing Data table. Close the Relationships window.
6. Create a query that uses all three tables. Include the following fields: `Last Name`, `First Name`, `Address`, `Date`, `Channel`, `Beginning Time`, and `Ending Time`. Save the query as `Viewing History`.
7. Close the database, saving your work.

Owning a Vending Company

You have been building three different tables and would like to have a way of seeing all the data at one time. To do this, you decide to build a query that provides a dynaset combining the different pieces.

To build a query that enables you to see all the data, complete the following steps:

1. Copy the database Proj0707 from the Project-07 folder on the CD and rename it `Vending5` (or open the database you completed in the previous project).
2. Check the Suppliers table. Make the Name field the primary key field and delete the Counter field if necessary.

Access

3. Open the `Machines` table in Design view. Change the Cost field to Currency and set the decimal places to `0`.

4. From the Tools menu, choose Relationships. In the Show Table dialog box that appears, select all three tables and add them to the Relationships window.

5. Link the Machine Type field from the Locations table to the Machines table, and the Supplier field from the Machines table to the Name field in the Suppliers table. You should accept the default values for each link. Close the Relationships window, saving the changes.

6. Select the Queries tab and create a new query using Design view. Add all three tables to the query. Notice that the join lines appear between the field lists in the top of the query design window. Add the following fields to your query:

Table	**Field**
Locations	Site
Locations	Owner
Locations	Machine Type
Machines	Supplier
Machines	Cost
Suppliers	Address
Suppliers	Phone

7. Run the query and observe the results. This query can be used as the basis of a form or a report to show you all the information for a particular site.

8. Close the query, saving it with the name `Full List`.

Managing a Video Store

After working in the store for some time, you realize that you should have two tables in your database, not just one. The first table is the one that you have been using to manage the inventory. This video table includes all the data pertinent to the video. But there is also a need for a table on customers and a table on rental activity. The Customer table should list the pertinent information on each customer, including addresses (so that you can send your customers promotional material). Complete the following steps:

1. Create the second table with fields for last name, first name, street, city, state, postal code, phone, and customer ID. The Customer ID field should be an AutoNumber data type.

2. Change the field size of the State field to `2`.

3. Enter five customer names.

4. Create the Rental Activity table. Add the following fields:

Field Name	Data Type	Formatting or Comments
Customer ID	Number	Must be compatible with the data type of the Customer ID field in the Customer table
Video ID	Text	Must match the data type in the Videos table
Date Rented	Date	
Date Returned	Date	Enter the Expression =Date() as the default value
Late Fee	Currency	
Rental Fee	Currency	Default value of 3

No primary key is needed.

5. Enter six or seven rental activities. Make sure that the customer and video numbers exist in the other tables.
6. Open the Relationships window and link the Customer table with the Rental Activity table using the Customer ID field. Link the Rental Activity table to the Videotapes table using the Video ID field.
7. Create a query that shows the last name, title, date rented, date returned, rental fee, and late fee. Name it `Rentals and Fees`.
8. Save both the new table and the query.

Taking a Home Inventory

You should have at least two tables in your home inventory database. The first lists all the items in your household, and the second lists the pertinent information for each of the insurance companies.

Open your database and, using the Relationships window, link the two tables with the insurance company name (or a similar field based on your structure) as the common field.

Create a query that will display in a dynaset the name and phone number of the insurance carrier along with the name of each insured item and its cost. Name the query `Claim List`.

PinPoint Assessment

PinPoint Training

You have completed the project and the associated lessons, as well as the "Checking Your Skills" and "Applying Your Skills" sections. Now use the PinPoint software Evaluation mode to assess your comprehension of the specific exam tasks you have just learned. You can also use the PinPoint Trainer mode and the SHOW ME tutorials to practice these specific exam tasks.

Project 8

Eight

Managing Data and Files

Getting Data from Other Sources

In this project you will learn the following objectives and their associated Microsoft Exam required activities.

Objectives	Required Activities
➤ Import Data from Other Databases	Import Data
➤ Import Data from Spreadsheets	Import Data
➤ Import Data from Word Processors or Files with Unknown Formats	Import Data
➤ Import Tables from Other Access Databases	Import Data
➤ Link Tables to Access from Other Databases	Link Data
➤ Add Pictures to Records	Add Pictures to Records

Why Would I Do This?

Although we learn computer applications one at a time, we use them simultaneously. In an office environment, you may be working on a spreadsheet to come up with the figures you need for the annual report that you are writing in a word processor. The phone rings, and you have to look up information in a database. Windows was designed for this type of workplace. Occasionally, you may need to transfer data from one application program into another.

Data comes in many forms. Some sets of data come from other database management programs or spreadsheets, and some come from word processors, mainframe computers, or unknown sources over the Internet. The name Access was chosen to indicate that the program provides powerful tools to enable the user to gain access to many forms of data. It is also possible to use Access as the user interface to large company databases that reside on a mainframe computer.

Lesson 1: Importing Data from Other Databases

Tables are often created in other database management programs. You can use the advanced, user-friendly tools in Access to work with this data. You have two options: You can import the data into a table in an Access database, or you can leave the table in its native form and link it to an Access database. In this lesson, you learn how to import data into an Access database.

Access has been available for only a few years, and there are many valuable tables of data available in other database formats. The most commonly used database management program for personal computers in the 1980s was dBASE. Consequently, most newer database programs have been designed to read dBASE files. These files are usually identified by the extension .dbf.

To Import a Table Created by Another Database Program (dBASE)

1. **Make a copy of the file Proj0801 from the Project-08 folder on the CD and name the copy `MichRetl.dbf`.**

   If you have opened Access and are using the Open dialog box, choose All Files in the Files of type box in order to see this file. Do not open this file at this time.

   Make sure that you include the .dbf extension in the name if it is displayed as part of the original filename. Most personal computers that use Windows or its predecessor, DOS, attach a three-letter extension to the filenames. Windows 95 normally does not display these letters when it lists files created by recent versions of Microsoft programs. All dBASE databases have the .dbf extension so Access will not identify this file as a dBASE file without the extension.

2. **Click Cancel to close the Open dialog box.**

   You are not required to create a new database; files can be imported as new tables into existing databases.

3. **Click the New Database button, select Blank Database, and click OK.**

4. **Select the drive and folder where you want to save this database.**

5. **Name it `Example` and click on the Create button.**

   A new database window appears. This database is called Example because a number of non-related sets of data are going to be imported into it.

6. **From the File menu, choose Get External Data. Move the pointer to the right and select Import.**

   The Import dialog box appears.

7. **Move to the Files of type box. Select dBASE III from the list of possible sources (see Figure 8.1).**

   Notice that Access can read several other types of files, including spreadsheets and text files.

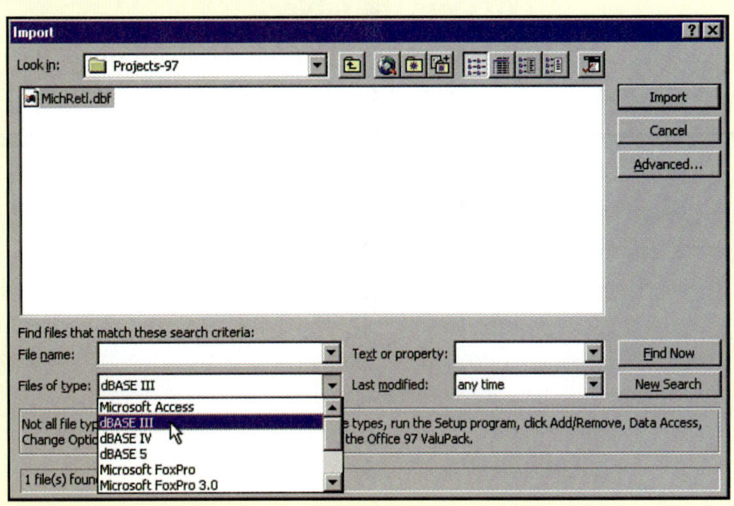

Figure 8.1
Several different types of files may be imported.

8. **Find the `MichRetl.dbf` file that you copied earlier, select it, and click the Import button.**

   Access notifies you when it has finished successfully importing the data.

9. **Click OK and then close the Import dialog box.**

continues

To Import a Table Created by Another Database Program (dBASE) (continued)

10 Open the new table.

This is a database of retail sales figures for each ZIP code area in Michigan for the year 1987 (see Figure 8.2). This type of data is available from the government on compact disk or over the Internet. In this example, the Sales and Payroll fields show numbers in the thousands. The first record is a summary for all the ZIP codes in the state.

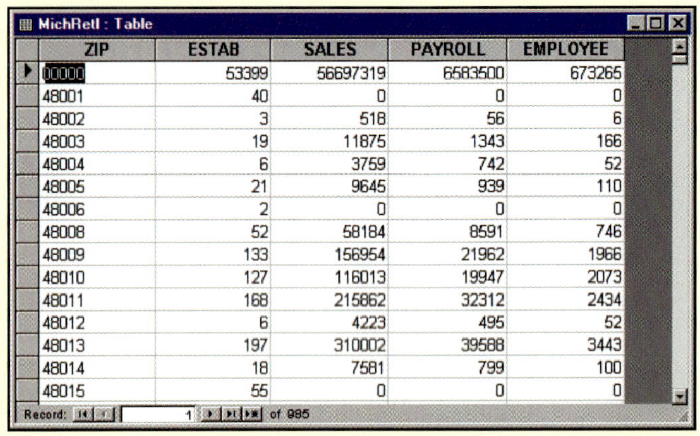
MichRetl : Table

ZIP	ESTAB	SALES	PAYROLL	EMPLOYEE
00000	53399	56697319	6583500	673265
48001	40	0	0	0
48002	3	518	56	6
48003	19	11875	1343	166
48004	6	3759	742	52
48005	21	9645	939	110
48006	2	0	0	0
48008	52	58184	8591	746
48009	133	156954	21962	1966
48010	127	116013	19947	2073
48011	168	215862	32312	2434
48012	6	4223	495	52
48013	197	310002	39588	3443
48014	18	7581	799	100
48015	55	0	0	0

Record: 1 of 985

Figure 8.2
The dBASE III file has been successfully imported.

11 Close the table.

Leave the Example database open for use in the next lesson where you import data from spreadsheets.

If you have problems...

It has been convenient to copy and rename new databases from within the Access Open window. In this Project you will be copying and renaming several files that are not Access databases and it may be inconvenient to work within Access. If you are familiar with copying and renaming files using Windows Explorer or My Computer, it may be easier to use either of these programs to copy and rename files while leaving the Example database open in Access.

Lesson 2: Importing Data from Spreadsheets

Next, you'll import a table from a spreadsheet. Spreadsheets are set up in rows and columns like a database table. However, in many cases, the data is interspersed with titles and formulas that do not correspond to a simple row-and-column format. If a spreadsheet is to be imported into Access as a table, the spreadsheet must have a structure that is very similar to a table.

If the first row of the spreadsheet contains labels, they can be converted into field names. The second row should contain the data for the first record in the table. If the spreadsheet that you want to import is not set up this way, copy the data from the spreadsheet and paste the data into a new spreadsheet in the simple row-and-column format, then save it.

Access

To Import a Table from a Spreadsheet Program (Microsoft Excel)

1. **Make a copy of the file Proj0802 from the Project-08 folder on the CD and name the copy `Expenses`.**
2. **Switch to Access and the Example database.**
3. **Choose File, Get External Data, Import from the menu.**
4. **Move to the Files of type box and select Microsoft Excel from the list of spreadsheets.**
5. **Find the Expenses file and click Import.**

   The Import Spreadsheet Wizard dialog box appears (see Figure 8.3).

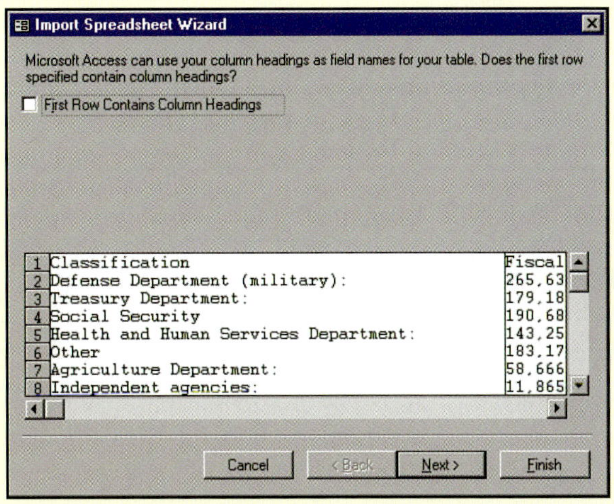

Figure 8.3
The Import Spreadsheet Wizard dialog box shows the structure of the data in the Excel spreadsheet.

6. **Click the First Row Contains Column Headings check box. Click Next.**
7. **Confirm that the data will be stored in a new table. Click Next.**
8. **Do not add indexes to any of the fields. Click Next again.**

   If this were a large table and you were going to do a lot of sorting, you would want to index the field you might sort on. To choose a field other than the first one, scroll to the right and click anywhere in the field.
9. **Select No Primary Key and click Next.**
10. **Name the table `Government Expenses` and click Finish.**

    A dialog box is displayed to indicate when the data has been imported.
11. **Click OK.**
12. **Open the `Government Expenses` table.**

    This is a table of the money spent by the U.S. government, in millions of dollars, from 1986 to 1989 (see Figure 8.4).

continues

To Import a Table from a Spreadsheet Program (Microsoft Excel) (continued)

Figure 8.4
The Excel spreadsheet has been successfully imported.

Government Expenses : Table

Classification	Fiscal 1986	Fiscal 1987	Fiscal 1988	Fiscal 1989
Defense Depart	265636	273938	281935	294876
Treasury Depart	179189	180345	201644	230573
Social Security	190684	202422	214178	227473
Health and Hum	143252	148893	158991	172301
Other	183175	176355	201372	212777
Agriculture Dep	58666	49593	44003	48414
Independent age	11865	14266	23446	32323
Office of Person	23955	26966	29191	29073
Transportation D	27365	25431	26404	26689
Defense Depart	20243	20659	22047	23427
Labor Departme	24141	23453	21870	22657
Education Depa	17673	16800	18246	21608
Housing and Url	14139	15464	18956	19772
Veterans Affairs	0	0	18528	18794
Energy Departm	11025	10688	11166	11387

Record: 1 of 35

13 Close the table but leave Access and the Example database open for use in the next lesson.

If you have problems...

If the data in the spreadsheet has been set up in a table format with one record of information per row, the data can be imported into the database. Most problems occur when the spreadsheet is not set up in a simple format. Check to see whether the column headings occupy one cell per column. Make sure that graphic characters, such as dashes or asterisks that may have been used to separate sections of the table, are deleted. Make sure that the data is arranged so that there is one record of information per row of the spreadsheet table.

Access

Lesson 3: Importing Data in Simple Text Form

Sometimes the data you have to work with is in simple text form. This type of table could come from a word processor, a mainframe computer, or some unknown source on the Internet.

Fixed-width fields
Fields that occupy a fixed position in the record, such as characters 5 through 12. No characters are used to separate the fields.

Delimiters
The characters that separate fields; set off text from numbers; and separate parts of dates, times, and currencies.

In some cases, databases records are stored as continuous strings of characters and numbers. When this method is used, the fields are always the same width. For example, the second field may be the 10th through the 20th characters in the record. These are called *fixed-width field* designs.

This fixed-width design can result in a lot of wasted storage space. In most designs, certain characters are used to mark the separation between fields. Special characters can also be used to designate the separation of the parts of a date, the dollars and cents of a currency field, or the minutes and seconds of a time field. These characters are called *delimiters*.

The fixed-width storage method is part of the Year 2000 problem. Many fixed-width files use only two character spaces to store the year rather than four spaces. If one tries to expand this field to four characters, all the references to fields that follow it would be off by 2. For example, if the year were stored as the 22nd and 23rd characters in the record and the Last Name were stored as the 24th through the 40th characters you would have a program that retrieves characters 24 through 40 and uses them as the last name. If we insert two more characters in the record for use as the year, we would have to reprogram any references to the last name as well as any references to the fields that follow it in the record.

Field separator
The delimiter that separates the fields in a row of data.

There are several ways to create separate columns of data in a table. In most word processing programs, the fields are separated by a tab character. In some database tables, a space is used. These are known as Space Delimited Fields (SDFs). Similarly, commas may be used in Comma Delimited Fields (CDFs). The type of delimiter that is used to separate the fields in a row of data is called the *field separator*.

In some database tables, the data in each field is assumed to be numeric, and text is enclosed by single or double quotation marks. These are called text delimiters.

The program must be told how to handle dates in the table. Many countries format dates in a Day/Month/Year sequence. For example, January 25, 1997 is written as 1/25/97 in the United States but would be written as 25.01.97 in France and 97-01-25 in Sweden. The program must also know whether zeros are used as leading characters for single-digit months and days. Access provides a dialog box where you can set these and other variables.

Identifying the Table Structure

In the following example, the table can be read as a text file. To analyze the structure of this table, use the steps that follow.

To Identify the Structure of a Table from an Unknown Source

1 Make a copy of the file Proj0803 from the Project-08 folder on the CD and name the copy `Parts`.

2 Open the Microsoft Word program.

If you have problems...

If you don't have Microsoft Word or any other word processing program available, skip to the second part of this lesson.

3 Click the Open button on the toolbar and change the Files of type box to All Files.

4 Open the `Parts` table.

5 Click the Show/Hide button on the toolbar to reveal the tabs (see Figure 8.5).

continues

To Identify the Structure of a Table from an Unknown Source (continued)

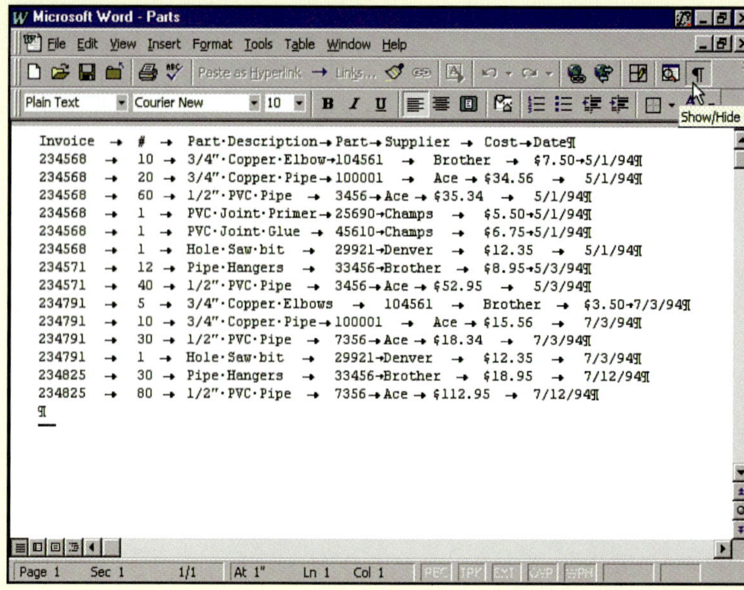


```
Invoice → # → Part·Description→Part→Supplier → Cost→Date¶
234568 → 10 → 3/4"·Copper·Elbow→104561 → Brother → $7.50→5/1/94¶
234568 → 20 → 3/4"·Copper·Pipe→100001 → Ace → $34.56 → 5/1/94¶
234568 → 60 → 1/2"·PVC·Pipe → 3456→Ace → $35.34 → 5/1/94¶
234568 → 1 → PVC·Joint·Primer→25690→Champs → $5.50→5/1/94¶
234568 → 1 → PVC·Joint·Glue → 45610→Champs → $6.75→5/1/94¶
234568 → 1 → Hole·Saw·bit → 29921→Denver → $12.35 → 5/1/94¶
234571 → 12 → Pipe·Hangers → 33456→Brother → $8.95→5/3/94¶
234571 → 40 → 1/2"·PVC·Pipe → 3456→Ace → $52.95 → 5/3/94¶
234791 → 5 → 3/4"·Copper·Elbows → 104561 → Brother → $3.50→7/3/94¶
234791 → 10 → 3/4"·Copper·Pipe→100001 → Ace → $15.56 → 7/3/94¶
234791 → 30 → 1/2"·PVC·Pipe → 7356→Ace → $18.34 → 7/3/94¶
234791 → 1 → Hole·Saw·bit → 29921→Denver → $12.35 → 7/3/94¶
234825 → 30 → Pipe·Hangers → 33456→Brother → $18.95 → 7/12/94¶
234825 → 80 → 1/2"·PVC·Pipe → 7356→Ace → $112.95 → 7/12/94¶
¶
```

Figure 8.5
The Parts table in Word, showing the table's structure.

You will be able to see where the spaces, paragraph marks, line breaks, and page breaks may be.

In this example, note the following features:

- The first row contains labels that can be used as field names.
- The fields are separated by tabs (indicated by the arrows).
- The text is not enclosed by quotation marks, but quotation marks are used to abbreviate inches.
- A currency field uses a decimal point to separate dollars and cents.
- None of the fields contains times with colons.
- A date field uses the Month/Day/Year method, slashes for separation, and no leading zeros.

6 Close the document and close Microsoft Word.

If you have problems...

Word processors insert special control characters whenever you press Spacebar or ↵Enter. They can also insert special characters to force a new page (page break) or a new line (line break). These additional characters can cause problems. If they do, make a backup copy of the file, then use the find and replace function of the word processor to remove them.

Importing the Table

After you have determined the structure of the table, you can tell the Access program what it needs to know to successfully import the table. To import a table that is in text form, use the following steps.

To Import the Table

1. **Switch to Access and the Example database that is still open from the preceding lesson.**

2. **Choose File, Get External Data, and Import.**

   The Import dialog box appears.

3. **Move to the Files of type box and select Text Files.**

   The Import dialog box shows the available text files.

4. **Select the Parts file and click Import.**

   The Import Text Wizard dialog box appears (see Figure 8.6).

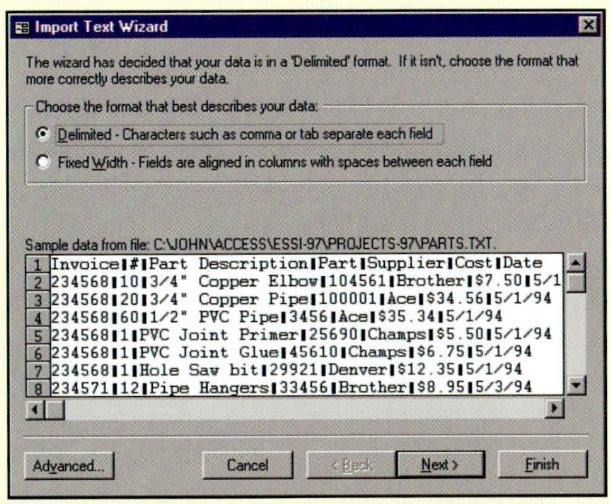

Figure 8.6
The Import Text Wizard dialog box shows delimiters between fields.

5. **Make sure that Delimited is selected.**

   Remember that when you looked at this file using Microsoft Word, the data was tab-delimited.

6. **Click Next.**

   A second wizard dialog box is displayed (see Figure 8.7).

7. **Set the following options as they are shown in Figure 8.8:**

   - Confirm that the Tab delimiter is used to separate fields.
   - Confirm that the Text Qualifier is set to {none}. The text fields did not have special delimiters to distinguish them from numeric fields.
   - Click the First Row Contains Field Names check box, and then click Next.

continues

To Import the Table (continued)

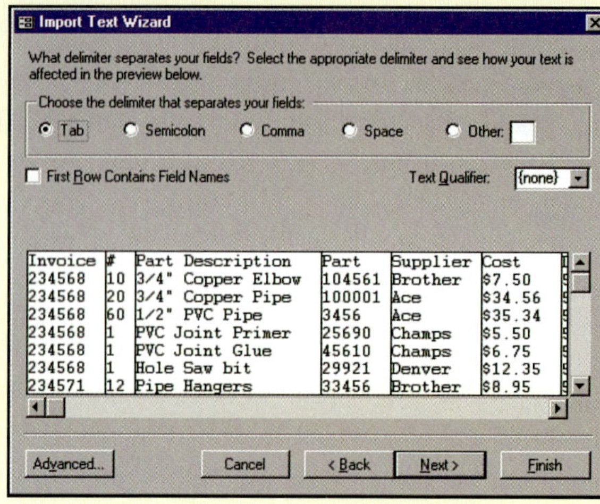

Figure 8.7
The second Import Text Wizard dialog box.

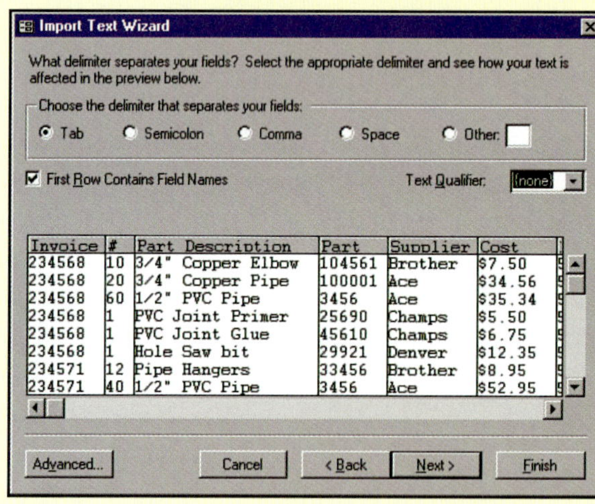

Figure 8.8
The Import Text Wizard dialog box displays the options for tab-delimited text with first row field names.

8. **Confirm the New Table option and then click Next.**

9. **Use the default settings to import all the fields; then click Next.**

10. **Select No Primary Key and click Next.**

11. **Accept the name `Parts` and click Finish to import the table.**

12. **Click OK after you have read the import statement.**

The Parts table is now a table in the Example database (see Figure 8.9).

If you have problems...

If Access does not successfully import the table, it will create a list of problems that it encountered. Because there are so many ways of storing data, the method described in this section is intended only as a guide to solving these problems, not as an exhaustive set of solutions. With these tools, you may be able to gain access (pun intended) to many other tables of data, but not necessarily all of them.

Access

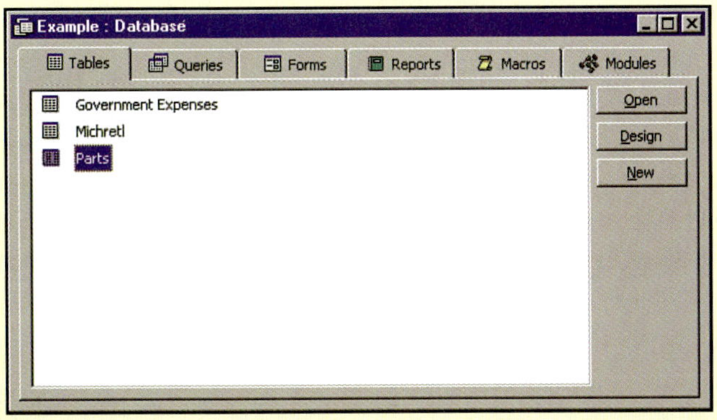

Figure 8.9
The Example database with the Parts table.

13 **Open the new `Parts` table in the Example database (see Figure 8.10).**

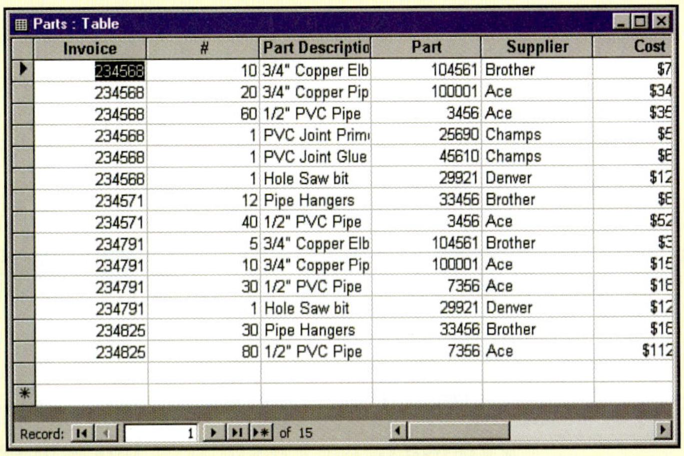

Parts : Table

Invoice	#	Part Descriptio	Part	Supplier	Cost
234568	10	3/4" Copper Elb	104561	Brother	$7
234568	20	3/4" Copper Pip	100001	Ace	$34
234568	60	1/2" PVC Pipe	3456	Ace	$35
234568	1	PVC Joint Prim	25690	Champs	$5
234568	1	PVC Joint Glue	45610	Champs	$8
234568	1	Hole Saw bit	29921	Denver	$12
234571	12	Pipe Hangers	33456	Brother	$8
234571	40	1/2" PVC Pipe	3456	Ace	$52
234791	5	3/4" Copper Elb	104561	Brother	$3
234791	10	3/4" Copper Pip	100001	Ace	$15
234791	30	1/2" PVC Pipe	7356	Ace	$16
234791	1	Hole Saw bit	29921	Denver	$12
234825	30	Pipe Hangers	33456	Brother	$16
234825	80	1/2" PVC Pipe	7356	Ace	$112

Record: 1 of 15

Figure 8.10
The text file has been successfully imported.

14 **Close the table, but leave the database open for use in the next lesson.**

Inside Stuff

If you ask someone from the computing division of your company for a copy of a database that you can use on your PC, request the data in one of the following formats:

- A dBASE III, dBASE IV, or dBASE 5 format
- An *ASCII* text file that uses tab delimiters as field separators

ASCII
A standard text format that all PCs can read.

If you need to import a table from a word processor or some unknown source, open the table in Microsoft Word and click the Show/Hide button. You can then see what type of delimiters are used. If the database is large, use the Find feature to search for quotation marks, slashes, hyphens, periods, or colons that may be used to delimit text, dates, times, and currency. Search for instances that may confuse the computer. For example, if the computer is using single quotation marks to distinguish text from numbers, the use of the same character as an apostrophe in words like John's or can't can cause problems.

Exam Notes

Data that comes from sources other than databases, such as spreadsheets and text files, may contain information that doesn't match the anticipated structure. For example, if the conversion process determines that a ZIP code file should be numeric but a few ZIP codes have the extra four digits and a dash, the program will not know what to do. Instead of trying to interpret the data, the conversion process will continue until completion. Access then provides you with a table of records that contain problems. You will need to examine the source data to find out what caused the problem.

Lesson 4: Importing Tables from Other Access Databases

There will be times when you want to use a table from another Access database in a new database. You can either link to the other table, or import the table into the new database. Importing the table is recommended when the table is small, and when there is a possibility that the file will be moved to a machine that does not have access to the linked database.

To import an Access table from one database to another, use the following steps.

To Import a Table from Another Access Database

1. **Choose File, Get External Data, and Import.**

   The Import dialog box appears.

2. **Move to the Files of type box and select Microsoft Access, if necessary.**

   The Import dialog box shows the available text files.

3. **Find the Softball2 database you worked on in Project 7, select it, and click the Import button.**

   The Import Objects dialog box is displayed, showing all of the tables in the Softball2 database (see Figure 8.11).

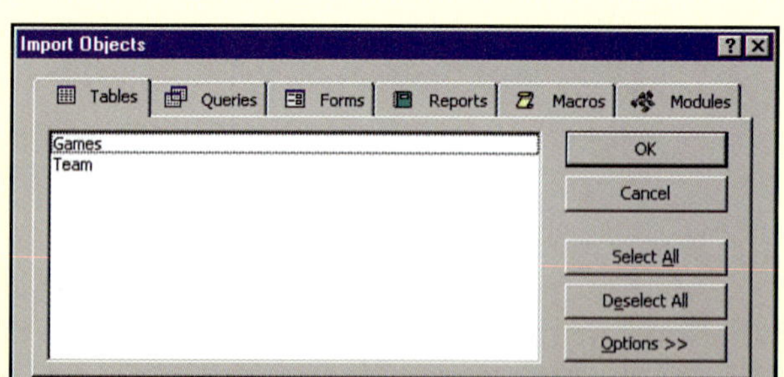

Figure 8.11
All of the tables of a second Access database are displayed.

4. **Select the Team table and click OK.**

   The Team table is copied from the Softball2 database and imported into the Example database.

5. **Select the Team table and click the Open button.**

   The Team table has been successfully imported (see Figure 8.12).

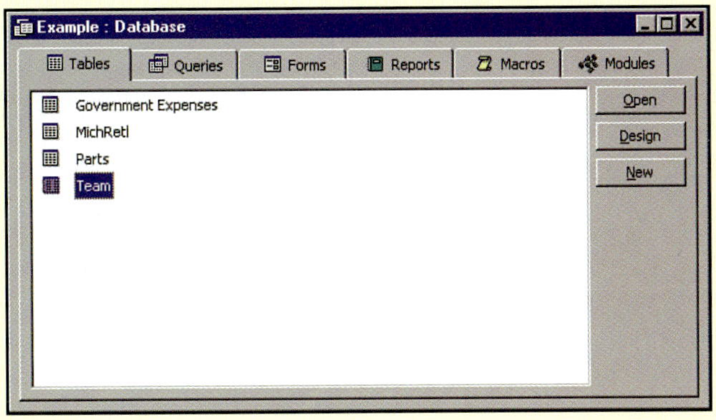

Figure 8.12
A table from one Access database has been imported into another Access database.

6. **Close the table but leave the Example database open for the next lesson.**

Lesson 5: Linking Tables to Access from Other Databases

Sometimes you may want to use data from another database and you do not need to make any changes to it. In this case, you can link a table from the other database to your database. This can even be done over a network and can work with mainframe databases. Now try linking a dBASE III database table to your Example database.

To Link a Table to Access from Another Database

1. **Make a copy of the file Proj0804 from the Project-08 folder on the CD and name the copy `MichServ.dbf`.**
2. **Switch to Access and the Example database.**
3. **Choose File, Get External Data, and Link Tables.**

   The Link dialog box appears (see Figure 8.13).

4. **Select dBASE III in the Files of type box.**
5. **Select the MichServ database that you just copied.**

continues

To Link a Table to Access from Another Database (continued)

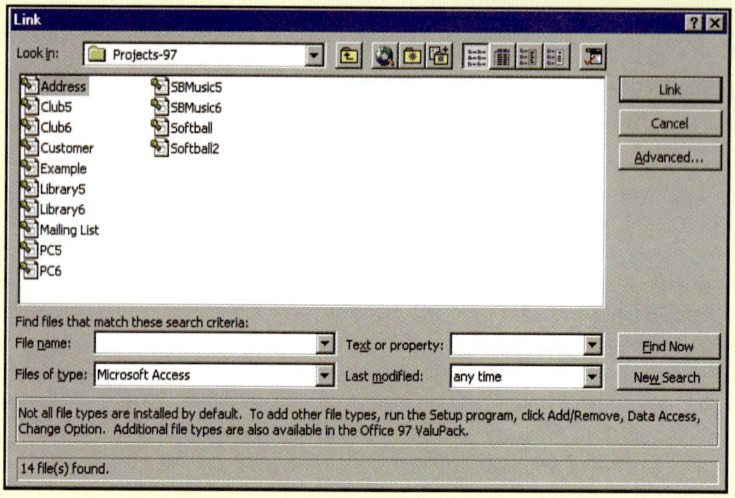

Figure 8.13
The Link dialog box enables you to specify file types and locations.

6 Click the Link button.

The Select Index Files dialog box appears.

7 Click Cancel.

The dBASE program stored its indexes as separate files. There are no index files in this example.

8 Click OK when the message appears that tells you the table has been successfully linked.

9 Close the Link dialog box.

The Example database window displays the linked table with a special icon to indicate that it is linked to a database (dB) file (see Figure 8.14).

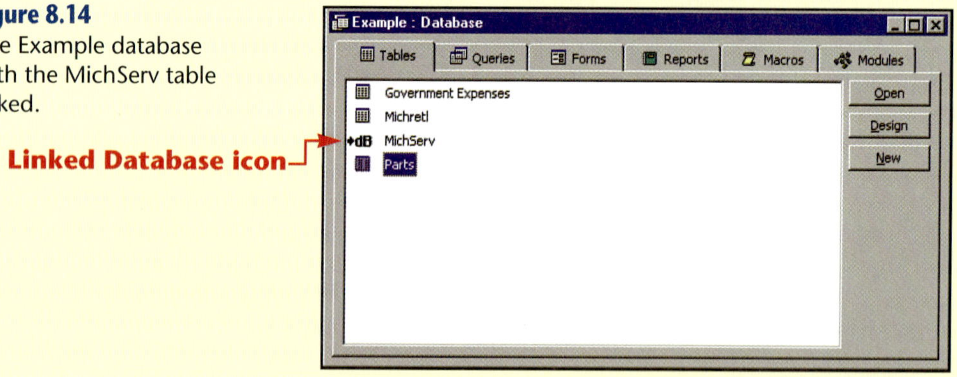

Figure 8.14
The Example database with the MichServ table linked.

10 Open the `MichServ` table and view the contents.

This table contains data from 1987 about the service companies in Michigan summarized for each ZIP code. The Receipts (RCPT) field and the Payroll field represent thousands of dollars. The record for ZIP code 00000 represents the totals for the whole state.

Close the table and the database. Leave Access open for the next lesson where you learn how to add pictures to records.

Lesson 6: Adding Pictures to Records

Graphics, such as scanned pictures and clip art images, can be added to an Access table through the use of an *OLE (object linking and embedding)* field type. As the name suggests, the graphic can be stored (embedded) right in the database file, or can simply be a reference to a link to another file. OLE fields are particularly helpful when you want to store company logos in a mailing list, pictures of personnel in a personnel file, pictures of parts in a parts inventory, or even your own batch of clip art images for newsletters.

OLE (object linking and embedding)
A type of Access field that enables the user to add pictures to databases. It is also the process of adding objects created outside the Access program.

Adding an OLE Field to a Database

In this lesson you will add an OLE field to a database, then add images of turn-of-the-century modes of transportation.

To Add an OLE Field and Pictures to Records in the Table View

1. **Make a copy of the file Proj0805 from the Project-08 folder on the CD and name the copy `Early Transportation`.**

   This database has a single table called Early Transportation Pictures. The table has a label field, but you will add an OLE field for your pictures.

2. **Open the `Early Transportation` database and click Design to open the `Early Transportation Pictures` table in the Design view.**

3. **Add a new field called `Pictures`, then select the data type, OLE Object.**

   Your table design window should look like Figure 8.15.

4. **Click the View button to move to the Datasheet view.**

   Save your changes when prompted. The data for the first field has been entered.

5. **Click on the Pictures field of the first record.**

   Notice that the box is selected, but no insertion point is displayed.

continues

To Add an OLE Field and Pictures to Records in the Table View (continued)

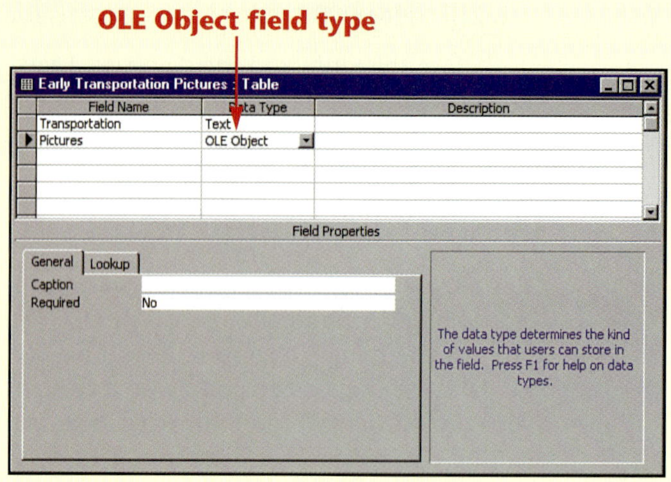

Figure 8.15
An OLE Object field has been added to the database.

6 Choose Insert, Object from the menu.

The Insert Object dialog box is displayed (see Figure 8.16).

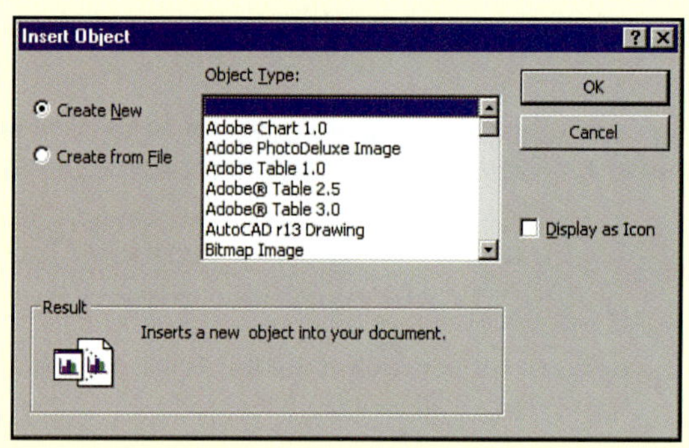

Figure 8.16
The Insert Object dialog box enables you to create a new object or search for an existing file.

7 Click the Create from File option button, then click the Browse button. Find the Automobile.bmp file in your student files.

8 Click Open, then click OK to close the dialog box. Widen the Pictures field until you can read the text in the field.

The name of the file type or the graphic editor associated with that file type will appear in the Pictures field (see Figure 8.17). If PC Paint is not associated with bitmap (.bmp) files on your computer, your screen will look different. The actual picture will appear when you create a form based on this table.

9 Double-click on the name that appears in the Pictures field for Automobile.

The graphic editor opens and displays the Automobile picture (see Figure 8.18).

Access

Figure 8.17
Either the name of the file type or the name of the graphic editor associated with that file type is displayed in the field.

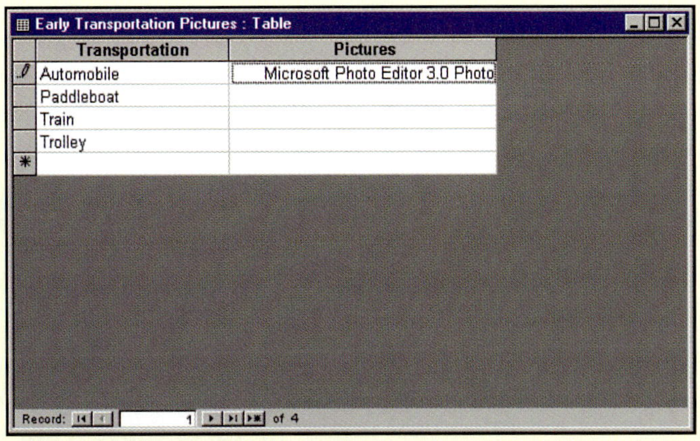

Figure 8.18
The graphic editor displays the picture.

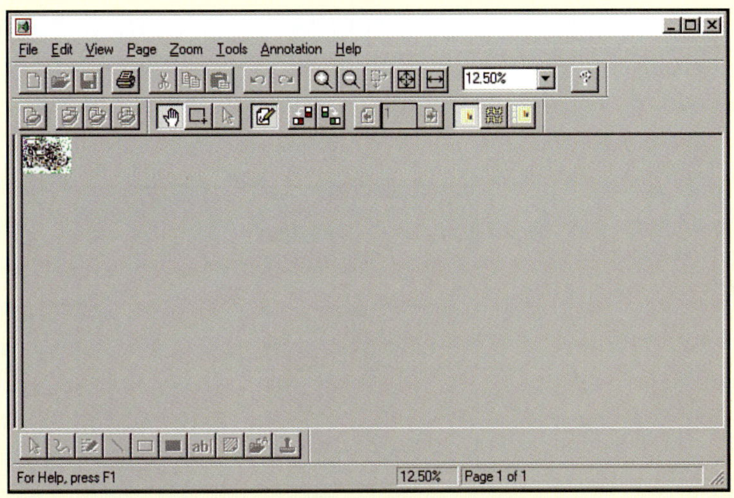

10 If the picture shown is full size (about 3 inches x 4 inches), close the window of your graphic editor and skip to step 11. If a small picture is shown, click the down arrow next to the Zoom button in the graphic editor toolbar and select `100%`.

The picture is displayed full-size.

11 Choose File, Update Early Transportation Pictures: Table from the menu. Close the graphic editor window.

The display size of the OLE object is adjusted

Inside Stuff

The command you use to save the altered picture may be slightly different, depending on the graphic editor that is activated.

12 Use the same procedure you used in steps 5–10 to add the pictures of the Paddleboat, Train, and Trolley to records 2–4.

To save time, you can right-click on the Pictures field and choose Insert Object from the shortcut menu.

13 Close the table and save your changes.

Adding Images

Once you have set up your table with an OLE field, you will want to see what the pictures look like. To do this you will need to set up either a form or a report. You will now set up a form so you can view your pictures.

To Create a Form to View Records with Pictures

1. **Click the Forms tab and click the New button.**

   The New Form dialog box is displayed.

2. **Select the AutoForm: Columnar wizard, choose the Early Transportation Pictures table from the drop-down list, and click OK.**

   The wizard creates a form with the Transportation field on top and the Pictures field below it (see Figure 8.19). The first record is shown, with the picture of the automobile cut off on the right side and bottom. You will need to adjust the size of OLE Object box.

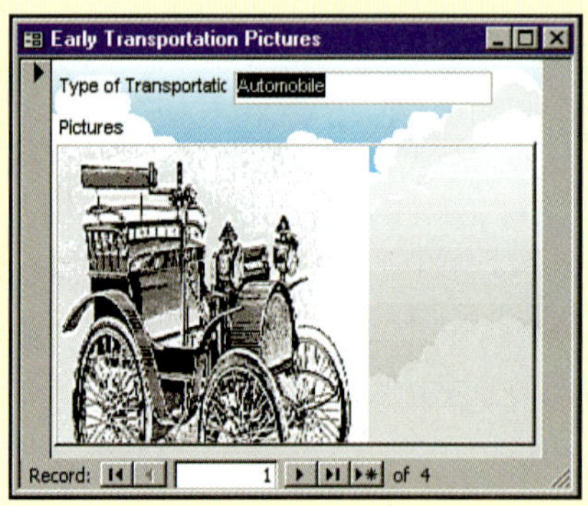

Figure 8.19
The picture does not fit the space allowed for it on the form.

Object Frame
A rectangular area in a form or report that is used to display an object such as a picture.

3. **Click the View button to go to the Design view.**

   The picture and its *Object Frame* need to be adjusted.

4. **Right-click on the object frame and click Properties on the shortcut menu.**

   The Bound Object Frame: Pictures property box is displayed (see Figure 8.20).

5. **Click the down arrow in the Size Mode box and click Zoom.**

   The picture will be adjusted to fit in the frame.

If you have problems...

If your picture is still very small, you will need to manually resize the picture. To do this, double-click on the OLE object. The associated graphic editor is opened and handles appear on the corners of the picture. Grab the handle on the bottom-right corner and drag down and to the right until the image size is about 3 inches high by 4 inches wide. Choose 100% from the Zoom drop-down menu, then close the graphic editor program.

Figure 8.20
The size of the picture can be adjusted using the properties box.

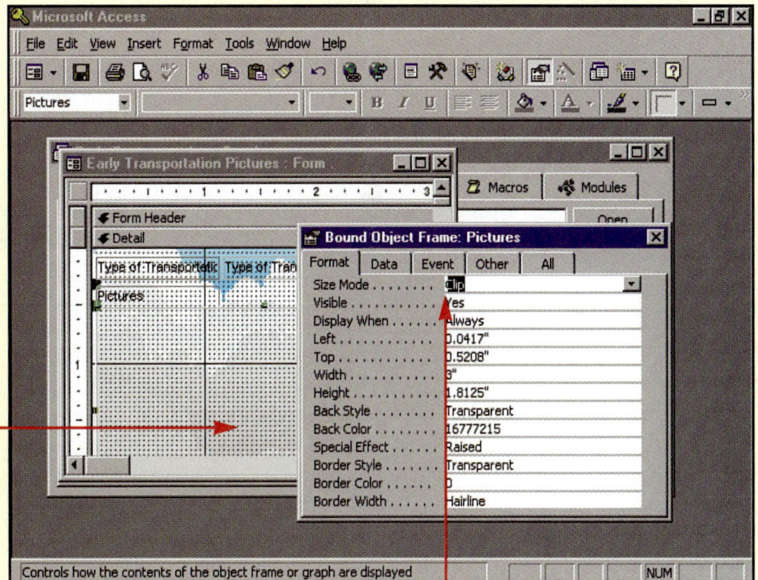

6 Click the View Button to return to Form view.

The picture now fits the frame (see Figure 8.21).

Figure 8.21
The OLE Object Frame and picture are properly coordinated.

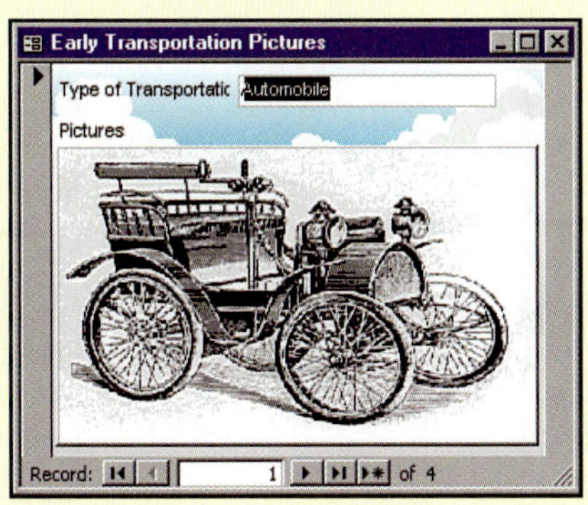

7 Use the navigation buttons at the bottom of the form window to view the four pictures.

8 Close the table and save your changes as `Early Transportation Pictures`.

If you have completed your session on the computer, exit Access and close Windows before you turn off the computer. Otherwise, continue with the "Checking Your Skills" and "Applying Your Skills" sections in this project.

Inside Stuff

There are many different graphic file formats, and some of them act differently in a database. This is complicated even further by file associations. For example, bitmap images are associated with PC Paint by default, but this association can be changed by a user, or may be automatically changed when you install a graphic editor program.

If you plan to use OLE Object fields on a regular basis, you will need to get a good graphic editor program, such as Microsoft Photo Editor, Imaging for Windows (Kodak), Multimedia Xplorer (Moon Software), or Adobe Photoshop. These (and many other) programs will allow you to take any graphic format and convert it to another format, often saving you a great deal of frustration and disk space.

Exam Notes

Embedding pictures into a table can greatly increase the size of the file. The table you just worked on had only four small pictures embedded, but the file size was over half a megabyte. If you have a lot of small pictures or a few large pictures and space is a problem, you might consider linking the pictures. This will keep the database small, but it will also require that the linked picture files be available. If you move the database, you must remember to move the linked files.

Project Summary

To	Do This
Import a table created by another database program	From the File menu, choose Get External Data, then choose Import. Choose the file type (such as dBASE III) from the Files of type box. Select the file and click the Import button.
Import a table created by a spreadsheet	From the File menu, choose Get External Data, then choose Import. Choose the file type (such as Excel) from the Files of type box. Select the file and click the Import button. Indicate whether the first row contains column headings, answer the wizard questions, then click Finish.
Import a table a word processor	Determine the file structure by loading the file into a word processor and turning on the feature that displays the hidden spaces, tabs, line breaks, and paragraph marks. Close the word processing file. From the File menu in Access, choose Get External Data, then choose Import. Choose the file type (such as Text) from the Files of type box. Select the file and click the Import button. Indicate how the data is delimited, answer the wizard questions, then click Finish.

To	Do This
Import a table from another Access database	From the File menu, choose Get External Data, then choose Import. Select the database file, then select the desired table from the Import Objects dialog box.
Link other database tables to Access	Open a database in Access. Choose File, Get External Data, Link Tables. Specify the type of table, select the table, and link it.
Add pictures to records	Create an OLE Object field in a table. Choose Insert, Object from the menu, then click the Create from File action button. Click the Browse button, find the file, then click OK.

Checking Your Skills

True/False

For each of the following, check *T* or *F* to indicate whether the statement is true or false.

__T __F **1.** Access is capable of importing tables from old standard formats like dBASE III.

__T __F **2.** Access can import tables of data from text documents.

__T __F **3.** If Access is importing a worksheet, the first row of cells must contain the field names and the second row must contain a row of dashes to separate the field names from the rest of the data.

__T __F **4.** If you are importing data from a text document, it is valuable to open the document first in Word and look at how the data is stored.

__T __F **5.** It is easier to import data into Access from another microcomputer database program such as dBASE than from an unknown file.

__T __F **6.** All word processors use the same characters to separate columns of data so that you can import data to programs such as Microsoft Access.

__T __F **7.** If you link a table to an Access database, you can use the data the same way that you would if it were imported including editing and deleting records.

__T __F **8.** If you embed pictures in an Access database, the field data type used is Graphic.

__T __F **9.** If you want a picture to fill up the maximum possible area within a Bound Object Frame without distorting the height or width of the picture, you set the frame's Size Mode property to Clip.

__T __F **10.** You can use any of the different picture file types as embedded OLE objects. Access treats them all the same.

Multiple Choice

Circle the letter of the correct answer for each of the following questions.

1. Which of the following is not recognized as a delimiter by Access when it imports text files?

a. commas

b. semicolon

c. tabs

d. capital letters

2. Which of the following statements is true about importing a table from Word into Access?

a. It's a good idea to open text documents in Word and determine what type of character is used as a field delimiter.

b. The process copies only the cell contents; you must type the labels for each column after the table has been transferred.

c. Access automatically recognizes which type of date format is used.

d. If the data contains possessive words or contractions that use single quotation marks as apostrophes, Access can determine that they are not text delimiters from context.

3. Which of the following statements is not true about importing an Excel spreadsheet into Access?

a. Any form of spreadsheet can be imported directly as a table.

b. The spreadsheet must be in a simple row-and-column format.

c. The spreadsheet may contain a row of labels that will serve as field names in the new table.

d. The copy-and-paste method does not work for importing spreadsheets into Access 2.0 tables.

4. Which of the following is the best reason to link a table rather than import it?

a. The table was created by another database management software.

Access

b. The table was created by (and will continue to be used by) someone else who has a different database management program.

c. The table is in a spreadsheet.

d. The table was created by a word processor.

5. Which of the following is not an extension indicating a common type of picture file?

a. .snip

b. .gif

c. .jpeg

d. .bmp

6. Which of the following Object Frame properties expands an embedded picture to fill the available space without distorting the ratio of height and width?

a. Clip

b. Zoom

c. Stretch

d. Proportional

7. Which of the following steps is not necessary when importing a text file to an Access table?

a. Determine the number of records to be imported.

b. Identify the file to import.

c. Determine whether the file is fixed-width or delimited.

d. Determine whether the data is to go into an existing table or a new table.

8. If you double-click on the name of a picture in a table (assuming the field type is OLE/Object) which of the following will happen:

a. The picture will be erased from the table.

b. A picture editor will launch and display the picture.

c. An Access AutoForm will be created that includes the picture.

d. All of the above.

9. Viewing pictures in Access without embedding them in the table is called?

a. connecting

b. corresponding

c. partnering

d. linking

10. If you import a table from an Excel workbook that has several worksheets, you must

a. pick one of the worksheets

b. click the Import All option

c. save the worksheet as a document first and import the text file instead

d. copy all the data from each worksheet onto one worksheet

Completion

In the blank provided, write the correct answer for each of the following statements.

1. Fields that occupy a fixed position in the record such as characters 5 through 12 are called ______________.
2. The characters that separate fields; set off text from numbers; and separate parts of dates, times, and currencies are called ______________.
3. The delimiter that separates the fields in a row of data is called a(n) ______________.
4. If you transform a database that was created in dBASE into a table in Access, you ______________ it.
5. If you link a table from another source to an Access database without turning the table into an Access table, you ______________ it.
6. A standard text format that all PCs can read is called ______________.
7. A type of Access field that enables the user to add pictures to databases is called ______________.
8. Excel uses the term ______________ to refer to a collection of spreadsheets.
9. A rectangular area in a form or report that is used to display an object such as a picture is called a(n) ______________.
10. The property that controls the way pictures fit within Object Frames is the ______________ property.

Matching

In the blank next to each of the following terms or phrases, write the letter of the corresponding term or phrase. (Note that some letters may be used more than once.)

a. import
b. first row
c. bmp
d. Text Import Wizard
e. field separator
f. OLE
g. tab
h. link
i. zoom
j. delimiter

______ 1. Stepwise process to assist in loading ASCII data into a table

______ 2. Term used to describe the fit of a picture inside an Object Frame

______ 3. The delimiter that separates the fields in a row of data

______ 4. To associate a table from another database without loading the database

______ 5. Character that is often used to separate fields in a text table

______ 6. General term for characters used to identify text or separate fields

______ 7. A type of picture file

______ 8. Stands for object linking and embedding

______ 9. Part of a spreadsheet or text document that can be converted into field names

______ 10. To load external data into Access

Applying Your Skills

Practice

The following exercises enable you to practice the skills you have learned in this project.

Changing the Tables Used to Track Your Loaned-Out Books

The Borrow table used in the previous project should be divided up into two tables: a table with contact information about the borrower and another table that tracks the individual books borrowed.

To copy table data from Access to Word, complete the following steps:

1. Make a copy of the file Proj0806 from the Project-08 folder on the CD and name the copy `Library7`. Then return to Access and open the `Library7` database.
2. Click the Relationships button and the Show Tables button. Add the two new tables.
3. Create a link between Borrowed Books table and the Borrower's Information table.
4. Close the window and the database.

Locating the Best Area in Michigan for a Uniform Store

Assume that you are employed by a company that sells uniforms. The company wants to locate an outlet in Michigan and wants to place the outlet where there is a concentration of retail establishments. You have obtained a table of data from the government that shows the number of retail establishments in Michigan, grouped by ZIP code. This table is named MichRetl.dbf, and it was created using the database program dBASE III.

Open a new database named `Uniform`. Import the MichRetl.dbf table that you have already copied and renamed, or copy and rename Proj0801 again.

Create a query that is based on this table and includes all of its fields. Sort it in descending order by the number of establishments (the ESTAB field). Limit the list to those records with more than 400 establishments (enter `>400` in the Criteria box). Do not show the summary record that has a ZIP code of 00000 (enter `>0` in the Criteria box of the ZIP code field). Switch to Datasheet view. You should get a list of about 12 records.

Copy this list of records and paste it into a Microsoft Word document. Add a few lines of text to the document to explain the list of figures. Print the document. (If requested by your instructor, print two copies.) Save the document as `Uniform`. Save and close the query and database.

Transferring Data to a Spreadsheet for Statistical Analysis

You want to study employee wages for those in service businesses in Michigan. You have obtained a table of data from the government that shows the number of employees in each ZIP code area of Michigan, and the total wages paid to those employees by ZIP code. This table was created by the dBASE III program. To do your study, you want to perform various mathematical and statistical analyses on the data using tools that are available in Microsoft Excel.

Use the copy of MichServ.dbf that you have already made, or copy and rename Proj0804 again. Open a new database in Access named `Wages` and import the MichServ table.

Create a query based on this table that contains all its fields. Eliminate the record that contains the totals for the state (ZIP code 00000) by entering `Not "00000"` as a criterion in the ZIP field. Include only the ZIP codes with 5,000 employees or more by entering `>5000` in the Criteria box for the EMPLOYEE field. Sort on the EMPLOYEE field in descending order. Save the query and name it `Areas With More Than 5000 Workers`.

Switch to Datasheet view and select all the records. Copy the records. Open a Microsoft Excel spreadsheet and paste the records into the spreadsheet. Then print it. (If requested by your instructor, print two copies.) Save the spreadsheet and name it `Wages`. Close the spreadsheet and close Excel. Close the database.

Getting a Helping Hand

Two of the common uses of Access are to store and manipulate data used in word processing or presentations. The Mail Merge feature was specifically designed to assist in the process. There are two ways to approach Mail Merge. One is from the word processor side (as with Microsoft Word, which you use in this text); the other is to view Mail Merge from the database side.

To get help on topics in this project, complete the following steps:

1. Start Microsoft Access.
2. Select Cancel in the opening dialog box.
3. Press F1. The Office Assistant opens, and the words `Type your question here, and then click Search` appear in the entry box.
4. Type `OLE` and press ↵Enter. A list of topics appears in the comment bubble.
5. Read about the different types of objects that can be linked or embedded.

Exploring the World of Alaska

As you search for information, you often find sources that may be similar to, but not exactly like, what you already have. In gathering data on Alaska, a friend has given you a text file that includes additional geographic features (including some errors), which you don't have.

To import a text file, complete the following steps:

1. Copy the file Proj0807 from the Project-08 folder on the CD and rename it `Alaska6`.
2. From the File menu, choose Get External Data and then choose Import.
3. In the Import dialog box, change the Files of type to Text Files.
4. If you are not in the folder where the student files are located, move to that folder.
5. Open the text file Proj0808 from the Project-08 folder on the CD. The first Import Text Wizard dialog box appears. Take a moment to study the data format.
6. Access should be able to identify the format. If it can't, select Delimited.
7. Select Next. In the dialog box that appears, ensure that the Comma delimiter is selected and that the Text Qualifier is set to a quotation mark. The first line does not contain the field names, so this box should not be checked.
8. Select Next. The third import dialog box gives you the option of importing the data into an existing table. Although you have a table that has generally the same information, it is not a good idea to merge the data until you are sure that it is correct.
9. Select Next. This dialog box gives you the option of naming each of the fields. Because you aren't sure what the fields contain, you can accept the defaults and change the names after you have imported the data.
10. Select Next. This dialog box helps Access determine whether you want a primary key. In this case, you should accept the system defaults even though a primary key is not required.
11. Select Next. The final dialog box appears, giving you the option of using the filename as the table name.
12. Change the name to `Additional Data` and click Finish. Access notifies you with an information item that it has finished the import process.
13. Open the new table and view the data. Compare the data with what you have.

For future study, see whether you can devise queries that will change the data you have imported into a form that can be merged with your base Geography table.

Challenge

The following challenges enable you to use your problem-solving skills.

Copying a List of Organization Members to a Word Document

Open the database that you created in earlier projects to track information about members of a club or organization. Open the table of member information in the Design view. Add a new field named Picture and choose the OLE Object data type. Switch to Datasheet view and insert the picture file, EmployeePic.bmp in one of the records. Close the table and create a new form using the AutoForm: Columnar option based on the members table. Go to the Design view of the form and change the property of the Bound Object Frame so that its Size Mode is Zoom. Close the form and save it as `Employees with Pictures`.

Doing Customer Research

Your boss liked the sheet you provided earlier and wants to include the comment data in a word processing report to provide to shareholders. The intent is to demonstrate how the company is concerned about the customers and how it is addressing their interests.

To place the comment data in a word processing report, complete the following steps:

1. Copy the file Proj0809 from the Project-08 folder on the CD and rename it `Customer Research7`.
2. Import the text file, Local Cable.txt, as a new table named `Local Cable`. Set CHANNEL NAME as the primary key.
3. Click the Relationships button and the Add Tables button. Add the Local Cable table and create a relationship between the Channel field in the Viewing Data table and the Channel Name field in the Local Cable table.
4. Open the query you created previously and add the Channel Number field from the Local Cable table.
5. Switch to the Datasheet view and see if the channel numbers are now shown for each channel. Save the changes.

Owning a Vending Company

Getting maintenance on your equipment has turned into a record keeping issue as well. Different repairmen know how to work on different machines. You have obtained a list of repair companies and the types of machines that they fix from an association of repair companies and would like to incorporate the list into your database.

To import a list of repair companies, complete the following steps:

1. Copy the file Proj0810 from the Project-08 folder on the CD and rename it `Vending6`.
2. Open the database and import the file Repairs. Repairs is an Excel file and the first row contains the field names. There is no primary key field.

3. Click the Relationships button and then click the Show Table button. Add the Repairs table.
4. Create a relationship between the Machine Type field in the Machines table and the Machine Type field in the Repairs table. Close the Relationships window and save the changes.
5. Open one of your queries in the Design view. Click the Show Table button and add the Repairs table. Drag a relationship between the Machine Type field of the Repairs table and the Machine Type field of the other table.
6. Add the Company Name, Phone Number, and City fields to the query. Save the changes and switch to Datasheet view. Check the results to see if the new fields are showing the correct data.
7. Close the query and the database.

Managing a Video Store

Open a blank database and create a new table that has the following fields: `Source`, `Street`, `City`, `State`, `Postal Code`, and `Phone`.

Make sure that the source names match those used in Your Video Store database and add address and phone information for each source. Close the database and name it `Sources`.

Open your `Video Store` database and import the table from the Sources database.

Taking a Home Inventory

It is a good thing you were prepared. You copied your inventory to your notebook computer and were away on a trip when a storm ripped through your town, damaging most of the houses. You were lucky. Lightning struck your workshop and destroyed many of your tools, but your children's toys and most of the household items remain intact.

Add a field named `Damaged` to your main table. This field should be a numeric byte. Select items from your inventory and assign a damage rating from 1 to 10 for each item (a 1 means minor damage and a 10 means destroyed).

Develop a query that lists only those items that have been damaged in the dynaset, sorting them in reverse numeric order. Print the query.

PinPoint Assessment

PinPoint Training

You have completed the project and the associated lessons, as well as the "Checking Your Skills" and "Applying Your Skills" sections. Now use the PinPoint software Evaluation mode to assess your comprehension of the specific exam tasks you have just learned. You can also use the PinPoint Trainer mode and the SHOW ME tutorials to practice these specific exam tasks.

Project 9 Nine

Making Data Entry Easier and More Accurate

Reducing Errors and Ensuring Accurate Data Entry

In this project you will learn the following objectives and their associated Microsoft Exam required activities.

Objectives	Required Activities
➤ Create Consistent Data Formats	Improve Accuracy in Forms Modify Field Properties Identify Criteria for Data Integrity
➤ Create Conditional Formats for Positive, Negative, and Null Values	Improve Accuracy in Forms Modify Field Properties
➤ Change the Data Input Structure Using Input Masks	Improve Accuracy in Forms Modify Field Properties
➤ Restrict Entry Using Validation Criteria	Improve Accuracy in Forms Validate Text Set Validation Rules
➤ Require Entry of Necessary Information	Improve Accuracy in Forms Set Required Properties
➤ Prevent Duplicate Entries Using Indexed Fields	Improve Accuracy in Forms
➤ Create a Lookup Column to Allow Selection from a List	Improve Accuracy in Forms Identify Criteria for Data Integrity Set Lookup Fields

Why Would I Do This?

It is important that your data is stored in a consistent format. If some phone numbers are entered as (XXX) XXX-XXXX and some as 1-XXX-XXX-XXXX, it may be difficult to sort or extract the data. If one person designs and enters all of the data, you may be able to get consistent input, but if that person is on vacation or out due to illness, your database could be filled with useless data by someone unfamiliar with your methods.

You may want your database to call attention to negative numbers or to suppress zeros in empty numeric fields. You learn how to use conditional formats to accomplish these goals.

You also want to avoid unnecessary typing if a field often contains the same data. For example, if you do most of your business in the same city, the program can enter the city, state, and ZIP code automatically. You can then change the information for the exceptions rather than type in the same text most of the time. Another feature you learn is how to create a list of possible entries. This allows you to pick an entry from a list rather than enter it from the keyboard.

It is also important to guard against common errors. You can check an entry against a set of rules to see if the entry is within allowable limits or matches a list of possible values. You may want to require that all records contain certain fields and to guard against duplicate entries.

Format
The way data is displayed.

Default value
A word, number, or date that is automatically entered in a field.

In this project, you learn how to control the *format* of your data, provide commonly used data as *default values*, check entries against a set of rules, and prevent duplicate entries. The database that you are modifying is designed to track the training employees have received on computer software packages.

Access

Lesson 1: Creating Consistent Data Formats

The first thing you need to do is to make a copy of a database file that has been included with this book. Once you have copied and renamed the file, you are ready to complete the first lesson.

To Open the PC Training Database

1 Make a copy of the student data file Proj0901 from the Project-09 folder on the CD and name the copy `PC Training`.

If you have problems...

The file may appear as `Proj0901.mdb`. This depends on whether the file extensions have been turned on in Windows. When renaming the file, make sure you add the `.mdb` extension if your original file shows it. Do not add it if the original file does not show it.

2 Launch Access.

❸ **Open the PC Training database.**

The Database window should now be open to the Tables tab (see Figure 9.1).

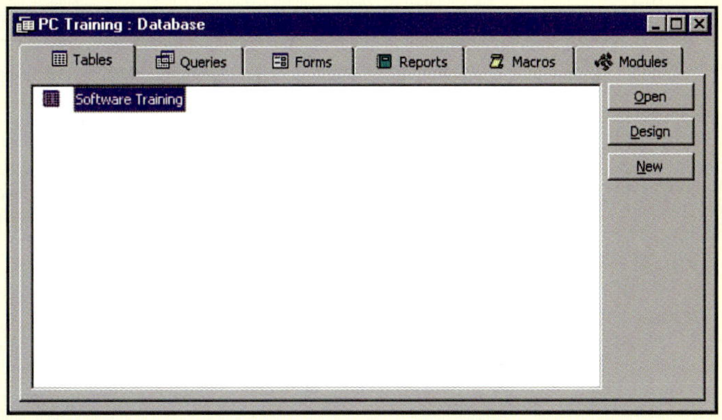

Figure 9.1
The Database window displays the Tables area of the PC Training database.

There are many occasions when you want your data to be displayed in a specific format. For example, you might want to have text displayed in uppercase letters, or you might want dates to appear in a consistent format. Some of these formats can be activated by using a drop-down menu, while others require that you enter a symbol in a special format box.

In the following procedure you learn how to change the appearance of two of the fields in the Software Training table. You change the format of the Last Name field to display all of the names in uppercase letters, and modify the date format in the Date Hired field.

To Use the Format Field Property to Control the Appearance of the Data

❶ **Click the Tables tab, if necessary.**

❷ **Click the Open button to view the data in the Software Training table.**

Notice that the data contained in the Last Name field is a mix of upper- and lowercase letters, and the Date Hired field is displayed in the mm/dd/yy format.

❸ **Click the View button on the toolbar to switch to the Design view.**

The Table Design view is displayed (see Figure 9.2).

❹ **Click the Last Name field to select it.**

The Field Properties section in the bottom half of the window changes to display the properties of the Last Name field.

continues

To Use the Format Field Property to Control the Appearance of the Data (continued)

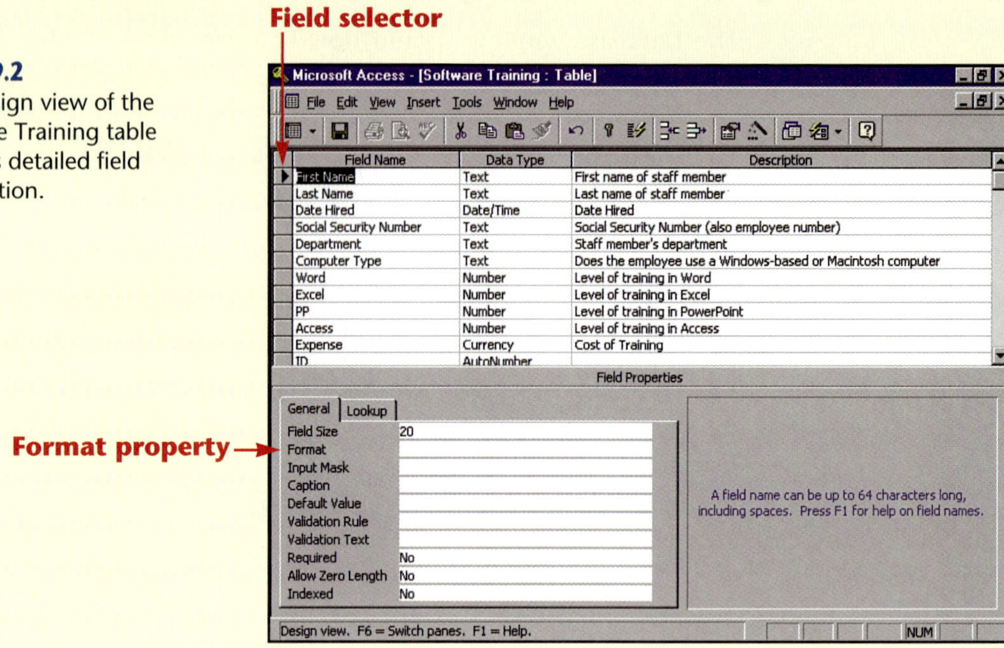

Figure 9.2
The Design view of the Software Training table includes detailed field information.

5 Click in the Format property box in the Field Properties section.

6 Type the "greater than" symbol, >, as the Format property.

The "greater than" symbol tells the program to display all text in the field as uppercase. The "less than" symbol displays all of the text in a field in lowercase. When no entry is made in the Format property box, text is displayed as entered.

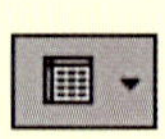

7 Click the View button on the toolbar to switch to the Datasheet view.

Whenever you make changes in field structures, the program asks you if you want to save your changes. Click Yes whenever this message appears.

Notice that all of the last names in the Last Name field are now displayed in capital letters. The Format property does not change the contents of the table, just how the data is presented. The last names are still saved on your disk as you originally typed them.

8 Click the View button to return to the Design view, then select the Date Hired field.

9 Select the Format property box, then click the drop-down arrow.

The date format drop-down list appears (see Figure 9.3). Notice that a format can be selected for dates and times, or the General Date can be used to display both date and time.

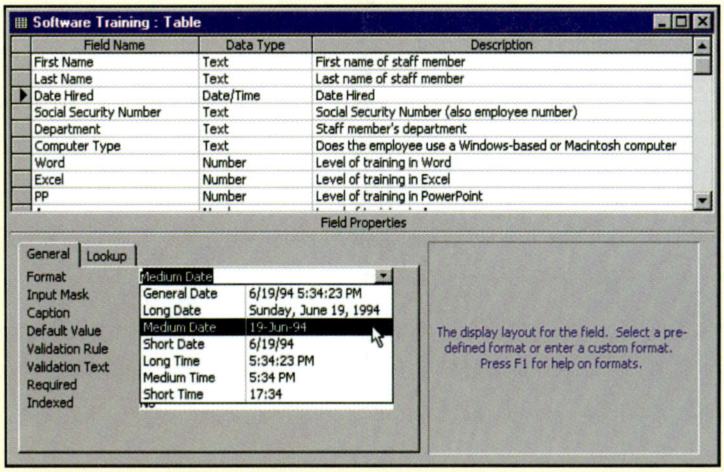

Figure 9.3 The date format drop-down list includes several unique date and time formats.

10 Select the `Medium Date` format.

Each format refers to the relative length of the date entries as they appear in the database.

11 Click the View button to return to the Datasheet view.

Once again, you have changed the structure of the table, and are asked if you want to save your changes.

12 Click Yes to save the change.

The Date Hired field now appears in the dd-mmm-yy format (see Figure 9.4).

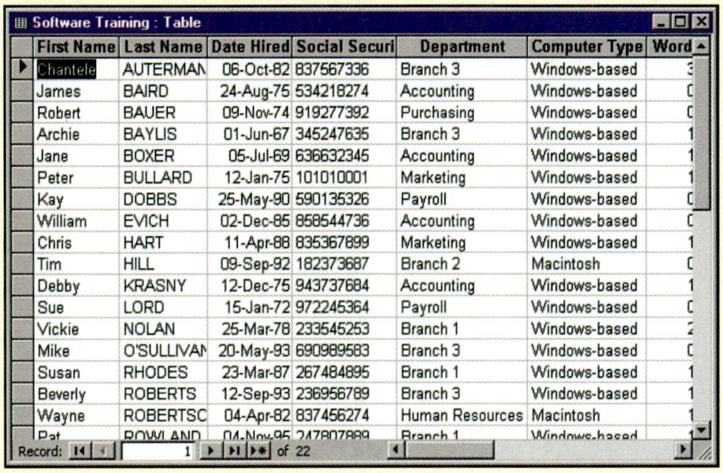
Software Training : Table

First Name	Last Name	Date Hired	Social Securi	Department	Computer Type	Word
Chantele	AUTERMAN	06-Oct-82	837567336	Branch 3	Windows-based	3
James	BAIRD	24-Aug-75	534218274	Accounting	Windows-based	C
Robert	BAUER	09-Nov-74	919277392	Purchasing	Windows-based	C
Archie	BAYLIS	01-Jun-67	345247635	Branch 3	Windows-based	1
Jane	BOXER	05-Jul-69	636632345	Accounting	Windows-based	1
Peter	BULLARD	12-Jan-75	101010001	Marketing	Windows-based	1
Kay	DOBBS	25-May-90	590135326	Payroll	Windows-based	C
William	EVICH	02-Dec-85	858544736	Accounting	Windows-based	C
Chris	HART	11-Apr-88	835367899	Marketing	Windows-based	1
Tim	HILL	09-Sep-92	182373687	Branch 2	Macintosh	C
Debby	KRASNY	12-Dec-75	943737684	Accounting	Windows-based	1
Sue	LORD	15-Jan-72	972245364	Payroll	Windows-based	C
Vickie	NOLAN	25-Mar-78	233545253	Branch 1	Windows-based	2
Mike	O'SULLIVAN	20-May-93	690989583	Branch 3	Windows-based	C
Susan	RHODES	23-Mar-87	267484895	Branch 1	Windows-based	1
Beverly	ROBERTS	12-Sep-93	236956789	Branch 3	Windows-based	1
Wayne	ROBERTSC	04-Apr-82	837456274	Human Resources	Macintosh	1
Pat	ROWLAND	04-Nov-95	247807889	Branch 1	Windows-based	

Record: 1 of 22

Figure 9.4 The Software Training table shows the changes in format.

Keep the database open for the next lesson.

There are many more options available for formatting fields. You can click in any of the Field Properties boxes, then click the Office Assistant button to get help on options for every data type.

Lesson 2: Creating Conditional Formats for Positive, Negative, and Null Values

There are more complex procedures available to format fields than those shown in Lesson 1. These require a succession of components containing instructions separated by semicolons. Each component represents a specific data format for a certain condition.

Null value
A field with no data entered into it. It is not the same as an entry of zero.

Conditional formats are particularly useful for dates and numbers. For example, you could set up a conditional format to display positive numbers with black text, negative numbers in red, and zeros or blanks when no data is entered in the field (a *null value*). In this lesson, you set up the expense field to leave cells blank when you choose not to enter a number.

To Create a Conditional Format

1 In the PC Training database, click the View button on the toolbar to switch to the Design view of the Software Training table.

2 Scroll down the list of field names, then click the Expense field to select it.

The Expense field is already formatted as Currency. Unfortunately, this displays fields with no entries as `$0`.

3 Click in the Format box in the Field Properties area.

4 Select the Currency format and delete it.

When formatting numeric fields (such as Number and Currency), the various components are separated by semicolons (;). The first component is always the format of a positive number, while the second is the format of a negative number. The third component tells the program how to display null values.

5 Enter the following in the Format property box, exactly as shown:

```
$#,##0.00;$#,##0.00[Red];#
```

The first component tells the program to display a dollar sign followed by the number for a positive number. The pound signs (#) to the right of the dollar sign tell the program to place a number there if one has been entered. If there is less than a thousand, a zero will not be forced in that location, and the comma will be dropped. If a number under $1 is entered, a zero is displayed in the first position to the left of the decimal.

Sometimes you want to force a leading zero to identify decimal numbers that may be less than one. There is less possibility of overlooking the decimal point or confusing it with a period if it follows a zero, 0.25, than if it does not, .25

The second component uses the same format but displays negative numbers in red. This is indicated by typing in the word `Red` surrounded by square brackets (not parentheses). The third component contains a pound sign (#), which tells the program to leave the field blank if no number is typed in.

The properties area should look like Figure 9.5.

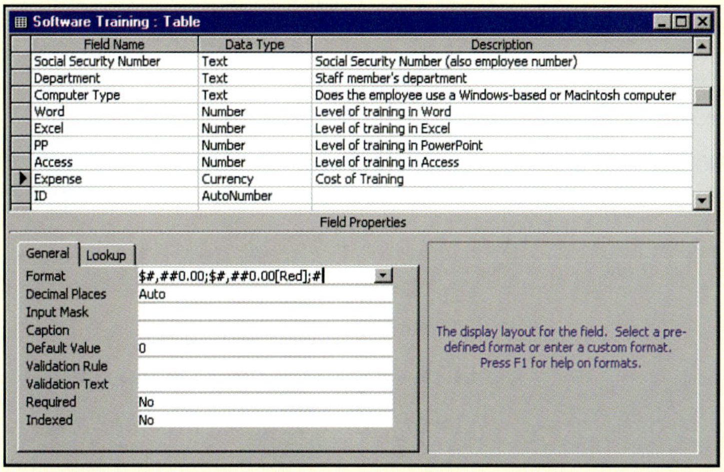

Figure 9.5
The property you entered for the Expenses field appears in the Format property box.

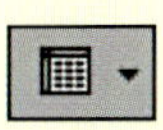

6 Click the View button on the toolbar to switch views to the Datasheet view.

Click Yes when prompted to save your changes to the table.

Scroll to the right and notice that the records that had no entries for the Expense field now display a blank instead of $0 (see Figure 9.6).

Keep the database open for the next lesson.

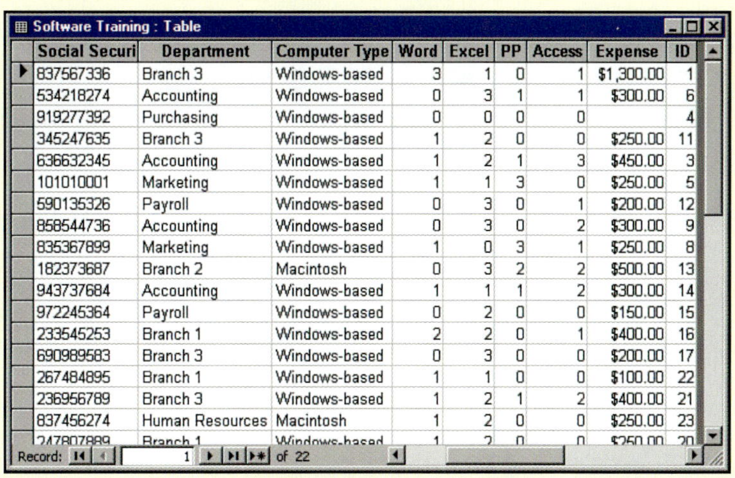

Figure 9.6
The Software Training table shows the change in the Currency format.

Lesson 3: Changing the Data Input Structure Using Input Masks

Input mask
A data entry structure that forces data entry into a selected format.

Input masks are data formats that make data entry more meaningful. They can be used to make certain types of data such as telephone numbers and Social Security numbers easy to enter. Input masks can be entered in the Input Mask properties box. They can also be added using the Input Mask Wizard. In this lesson, you add an input mask to the Social Security Number field to divide the number into the familiar XXX-XX-XXXX format. Input masks can control the format of the data as it is stored in the table.

To Create an Input Mask

1. **In the PC Training database, click the View button on the toolbar to switch to the Design view of the Software Training table.**

2. **Click the Social Security Number field to select it.**

   The Social Security numbers in this database have been entered as text. Since all Social Security numbers contain three blocks of numbers of 3, 2, and 4 digits, it would make data entry easier if the field was also set up in this format.

3. **Click the Input Mask box in the Field Properties area.**

   A Build button (the one with three dots) appears on the right-hand side of the Input Mask box (see Figure 9.7).

Figure 9.7
Use the Input Mask property box Build button to start the Input Mask Wizard.

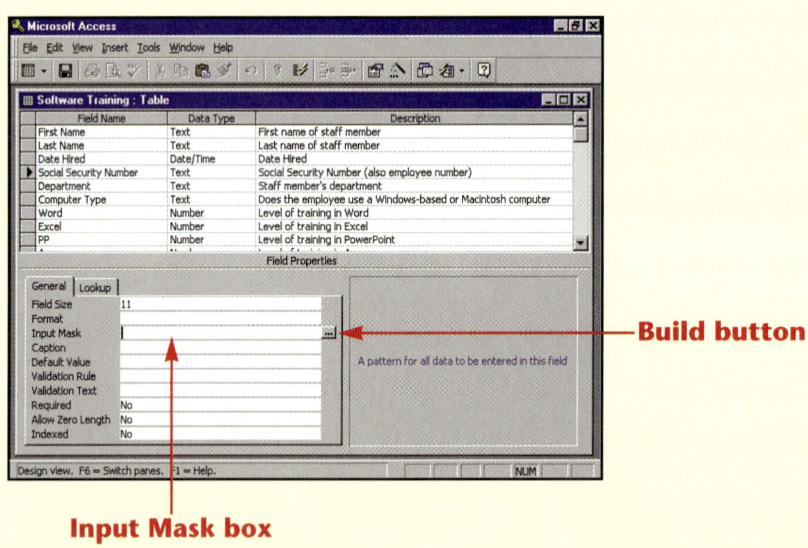

4. **Click the Build button.**

   Before the wizard opens, a dialog box appears telling you that you must first save the table. Click Yes to save the table. The first dialog box of the Input Mask Wizard appears, showing several of the preset masks (see Figure 9.8). The Input Mask Wizard is used to control the formatting for Text and Date fields. You can also set an input mask manually for Number or Currency fields.

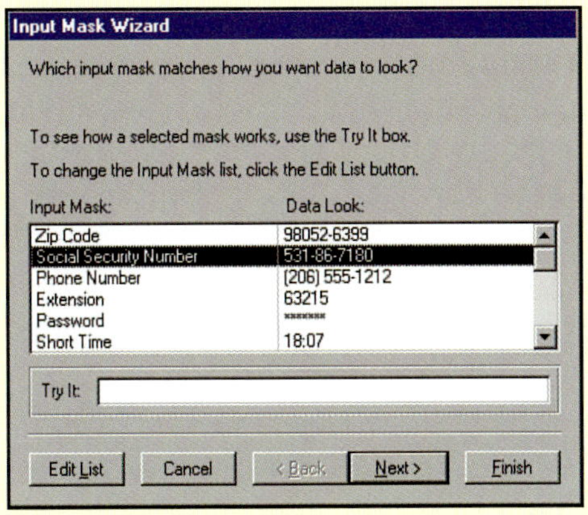

Figure 9.8
The first Input Mask Wizard dialog box asks how you want your data to look.

If you have problems...

The Input Mask Wizard will not be launched unless the Advanced Wizards are installed. If your installation of Access does not support the Input Mask Wizard, you can run Microsoft Office Setup and install the Advanced Wizard Tools. However, it is not absolutely necessary to use the Input Mask Wizard. If you know the expression you want to use, you can type it directly into the Input Mask property box. Look at the examples of the input masks in the following section and enter the expression directly into the Input Mask property box.

5 Select the Social Security Number option, then click in the Try It area to see the format that appears in the field.

6 Click the Next button.

The second Input Mask Wizard dialog box appears (see Figure 9.9). The basic format is shown. You are asked if you are satisfied with the format and the *placeholders* used to reserve spaces for the data. In this example, you accept the default settings.

Placeholder
A character used to reserve a spot for a character in an input mask.

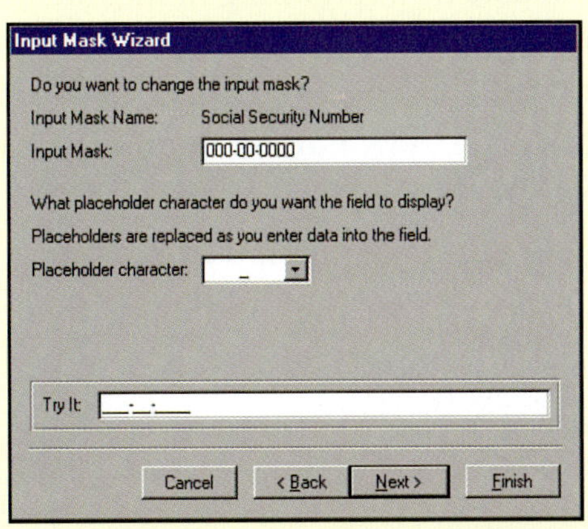

Figure 9.9
The second Input Mask Wizard dialog box enables you to modify the selected input mask.

continues

To Create an Input Mask (continued)

7 Click the Next button.

The third Input Mask Wizard dialog box appears (see Figure 9.10). This dialog box asks whether the program should save the characters, in this case dashes, used to separate the three parts of the Social Security number. The dashes will be displayed in forms and reports that use this field but they will not be part of the actual data stored in each field. If you export the data to another program, the dashes will not be there. The default choice is to not save the extra characters.

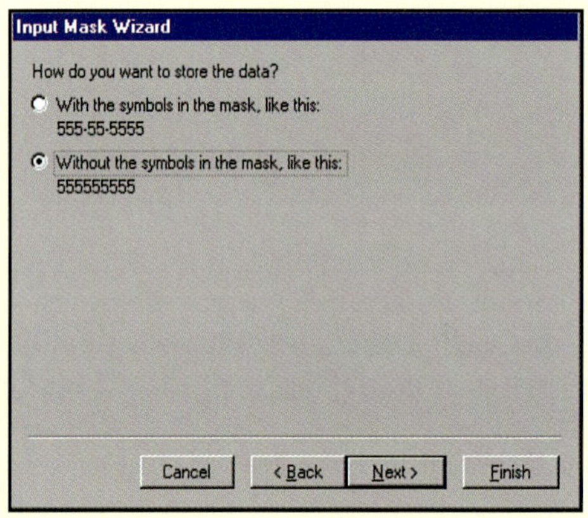

Figure 9.10
The third Input Mask Wizard dialog box asks you how you want to store the data.

8 Click the Next button to accept the default.

The fourth Input Mask Wizard dialog box appears. This dialog box tells you that you have completed the wizard.

9 Click the Finish button to complete the Input Mask Wizard.

The Input Mask property box contains the following:

```
000-00-0000;;_
```

The input mask contains three components, which are separated by semicolons. The first component shows the input format. The next component has nothing in it, which indicates that there is no special format for an empty field. The third component has an underscore to indicate that the placeholder for the field is an underscore.

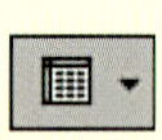

10 Click the View button on the toolbar to switch to the Datasheet view.

Click Yes when prompted to save your changes to the table. Notice that the Social Security numbers are now in the familiar format (see Figure 9.11).

Figure 9.11
The input mask for the Social Security Number field has been added.

Software Training : Table

First Name	Last Name	Date Hired	Social Securi	Department	Computer Type	Word
Chantele	AUTERMAN	06-Oct-82	837-56-7336	Branch 3	Windows-based	3
James	BAIRD	24-Aug-75	534-21-8274	Accounting	Windows-based	0
Robert	BAUER	09-Nov-74	919-27-7392	Purchasing	Windows-based	0
Archie	BAYLIS	01-Jun-67	345-24-7635	Branch 3	Windows-based	1
Jane	BOXER	05-Jul-69	636-63-2345	Accounting	Windows-based	1
Peter	BULLARD	12-Jan-75	101-01-0001	Marketing	Windows-based	1
Kay	DOBBS	25-May-90	590-13-5326	Payroll	Windows-based	0
William	EVICH	02-Dec-85	858-54-4736	Accounting	Windows-based	0
Chris	HART	11-Apr-88	835-36-7899	Marketing	Windows-based	1
Tim	HILL	09-Sep-92	182-37-3687	Branch 2	Macintosh	0
Debby	KRASNY	12-Dec-75	943-73-7684	Accounting	Windows-based	1
Sue	LORD	15-Jan-72	972-24-5364	Payroll	Windows-based	0
Vickie	NOLAN	25-Mar-78	233-54-5253	Branch 1	Windows-based	2
Mike	O'SULLIVAN	20-May-93	690-98-9583	Branch 3	Windows-based	0
Susan	RHODES	23-Mar-87	267-48-4895	Branch 1	Windows-based	1
Beverly	ROBERTS	12-Sep-93	236-95-6789	Branch 3	Windows-based	1
Wayne	ROBERTSC	04-Apr-82	837-45-6274	Human Resources	Macintosh	1
Pat	ROWLAND	04-Nov-95	247-80-7889	Branch 1	Windows-based	1

Record: 1 of 22

▶* **11 Click the Add New Record button near the bottom of the screen and add another record to see how the data is entered into the field.**

Do not use a Social Security number that is a duplicate of a number in the table. You learn how to automatically guard against this type of error in Lesson 6.

Keep the database open for the next lesson.

Inside Stuff

Adding an input mask puts certain limitations on data entry. If you have placeholders for nine characters, you need to enter all nine. If you enter eight or fewer characters, you get an error message, and you are not able to move out of the field until you correct the problem. If you do not have all of the characters to enter, don't put any of them in, but press Esc to leave the field blank for now.

APPROVED COURSEWARE Microsoft OFFICE USER SPECIALIST

Lesson 4: Restricting Entries to Those That Meet Validation Criteria

Validation Rule
An expression that Access uses to check the data entered into a field.

Validation Text
The text that appears when data that doesn't match a Validation Rule is entered into a field.

The data entered in some fields in a database need to be restricted in some way. For example, a field set up for coded data might only use 0s and 1s, while a text field might be used to enter only two possible values. Several fields in the PC Training table fit this category. The Computer Type field has only two possible answers: Windows-based or Macintosh. The four software fields, Word, Excel, PP, and Access, use only four numbers (0, 1, 2, and 3).

Access gives you the option of restricting the information that will be accepted into a field. This is done by constructing a *Validation Rule*, which is an expression that the program checks to see if the data that has been entered into a field is acceptable. If the data is not acceptable, *Validation Text* can be displayed to explain the reason the data is not acceptable.

Expression Builder
A program that helps the user create formulas for many Access uses.

Validation Rules are used for two purposes: to make sure the user does not enter incorrect data, and to help avoid typographical errors. In this lesson you use the *Expression Builder* to build a Validation Rule for the four software fields. You also create Validation Text to be used as an error message for incorrect data entry.

To Create Validation Rules and Validation Text Using the Expression Builder

1 In the PC Training database, click the View button on the toolbar to switch to the Design view of the Software Training table.

2 Click the Word field to select it.

3 Click the Validation Rule box in the Field Properties area.

Notice that a Build button (containing three dots) appears to the right of the Validation Rule property box.

4 Click the Build button on the right side of the Validation Rule box in the Field Properties.

The Expression Builder dialog box appears (see Figure 9.12). You now build a function, which is the default.

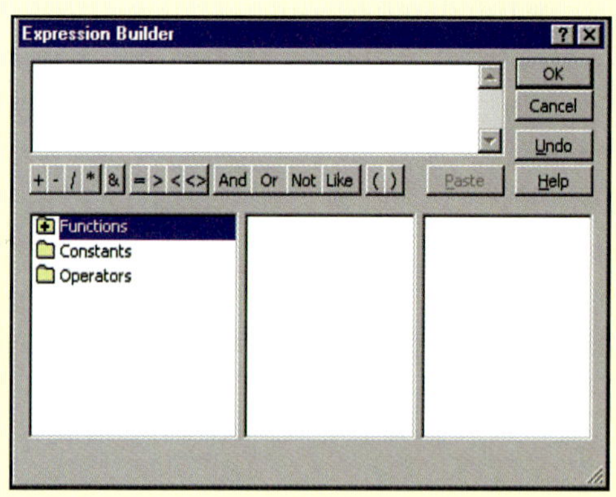

Figure 9.12
Use the Expression Builder dialog box to build a function in a Validation Rule.

5 Click the button with the = (equal sign) to begin building the expression.

The equal sign appears in the upper-left corner of the Expression Builder window.

6 Type in the number `0` (zero).

7 Click the Or button.

8 Follow this procedure until your expression says:

```
= 0 Or 1 Or 2 Or 3
```

The Expression Builder window should look like Figure 9.13.

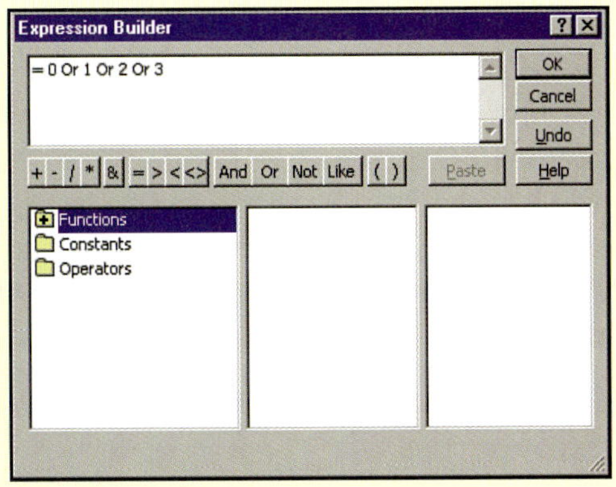

Figure 9.13
The Expression Builder window now contains a Validation Rule.

9 **Click OK, then place the cursor in the Validation Text box of the Field Properties area.**

10 **Type the following in the Validation Text property box:** `That is not a valid option. Please enter the number 0, 1, 2, or 3.`

You should now have entries in both the Validation Rule box and the Validation Text box (see Figure 9.14).

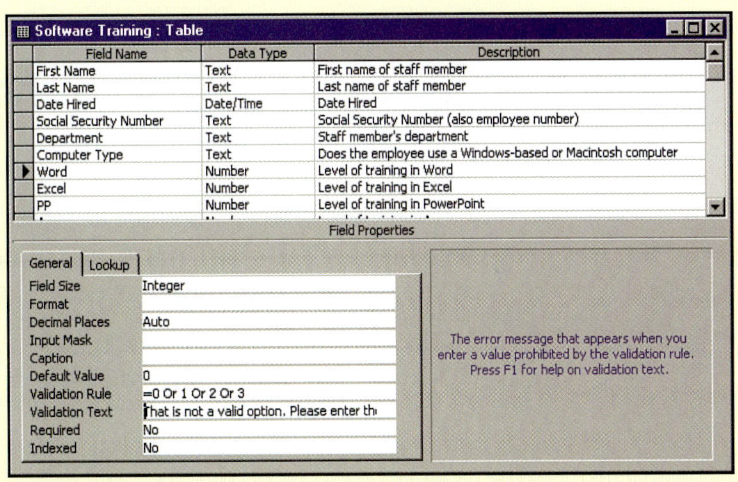

Figure 9.14
The Field Properties area should now contain both a Validation Rule and Validation Text.

11 **Repeat steps 2 through 10 for the other three software fields (Excel, PP, and Access).**

To save time and effort, you can use the Copy and Paste commands with Field Properties. Highlight the Validation Rule text in the Word property box, and click the Copy button. Then select the Excel field, click the Validation Rule property box, and click the Paste button. Do this to the other two fields (PP and Access), then go back and repeat the procedure with the Validation Text property boxes.

12 **Click the View button on the toolbar to switch to the Datasheet view.**

Click Yes when prompted to save your changes to the table.

continues

To Create Validation Rules and Validation Text Using the Expression Builder (continued)

As usual when you change the structure of the table, you will be prompted to save your changes. This time, however, an additional dialog box appears (see Figure 9.15). This dialog box warns you that, Data integrity rules have been changed. Existing data may not be valid for the new rules. Whenever a Validation Rule is added or modified, this warning is displayed. It is important that you are familiar with the content of your data so you can assess whether, in fact, the data in the table violates the new rule(s) that has just been added. In this case, the data will cause no problem.

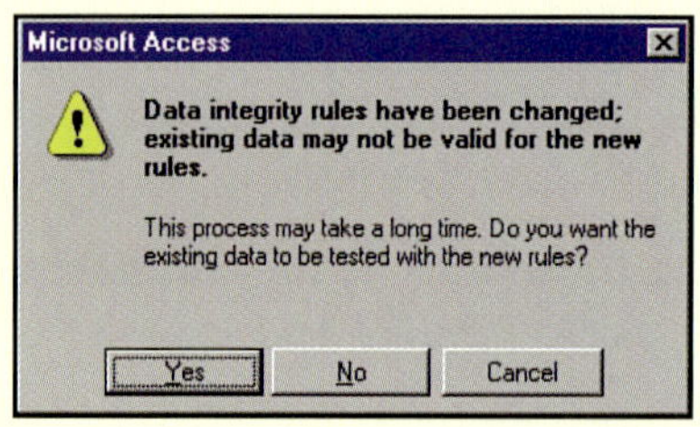

Figure 9.15
The Data Integrity warning dialog box notifies you that data integrity rules have been changed.

13. **Click Yes. The program tests your fields to find any conflicting data.**

If data integrity is violated, you receive an additional warning box telling you that data has been detected that violates the rules, but the program does not specifically identify the data. You then need to create a query to search for the data that was outside of the rules and change that data, if appropriate.

14. **Attempt to enter the number 5 in one of the software fields and press ↵Enter to move to the next field.**

Notice how the message you typed in the Validation Text property box appears in the error message window (see Figure 9.16).

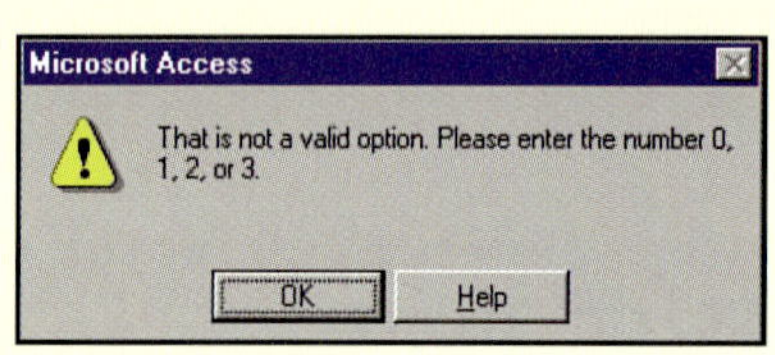

Figure 9.16
The Validation Rule text appears when an incorrect number is entered.

15. **Click OK in the error message box, then press Esc to return the field to its original number.**

Keep the database open for the next lesson.

Inside Stuff

It is a good idea to test your changes on a backup file before you make major changes to your table structure. If you change the structure of a table on the only file you have, and choose yes when it checks for data integrity, it is always possible that some data could be lost. By testing the structure change on a backup file, you can thoroughly test the change without having to worry that you are going to incorrectly change the "real" data.

Lesson 5: Requiring Entry of Necessary Information

There are times when you want to force the user to fill in a field. Access enables you to require a data entry in a field. Required responses can be added to all field types except the AutoNumber fields, which are used when sequential numbering is required.

In this lesson, you require that data be entered into the Last Name field.

To Require Entry of Necessary Information

1. **In the PC Training database, click the View button on the toolbar to switch to the Design view.**
2. **Click the Last Name field to select it.**
3. **Click the Required box in the Field Properties area.**
4. **Click the drop-down box to reveal the choices.**

   The screen should look like Figure 9.17.

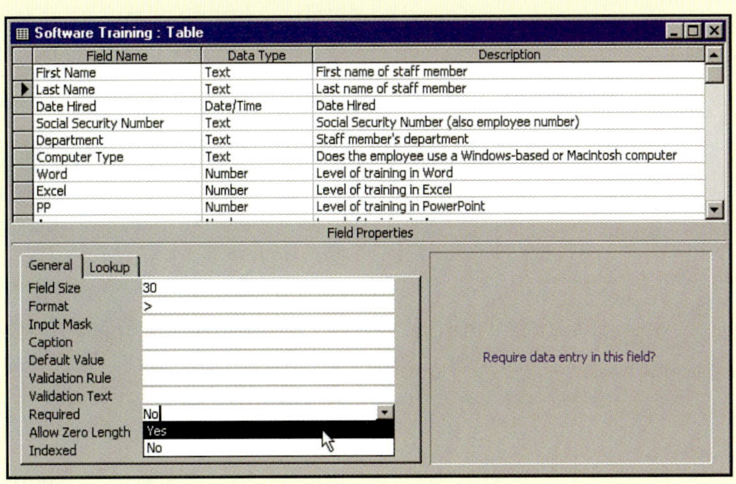

Figure 9.17
The Required property box now displays "Yes."

5. **Click** Yes **to make an entry into this field required.**
6. **Click the View button on the toolbar to switch to the Datasheet view.**

continues

To Require Entry of Necessary Information (continued)

Click Yes when prompted to save your changes to the table. You are warned about data integrity rule changes as you were when you changed the Validation Rule in Lesson 5. Click Yes to move to the datasheet.

If you have problems...

If you entered any records without a last name, you get another warning box that tells you `Existing data violates the new setting for the 'Required' property for the field 'Last Name'`. Choose Yes to continue testing with the new setting.

7. **Scroll down to the bottom of the table and enter a new record, but leave the Last Name field blank.**

The program enables you to continue entering data to the end of the record. However, when you press Enter after the last field, another dialog box appears (see Figure 9.18), warning you that the Last Name field cannot contain a null value.

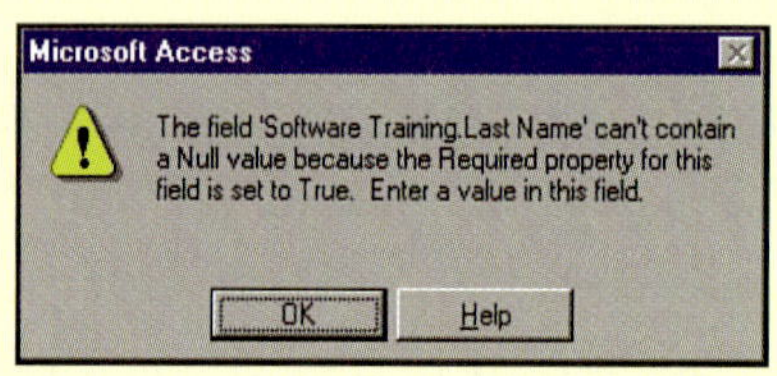

Figure 9.18
The null value warning dialog box appears if you try to skip the Last Name field.

8. **Click OK in the warning box.**
9. **Press Esc to back out of the entry.**

Keep the database open for the next lesson.

Lesson 6: Preventing Duplicate Entries Using Indexed Fields

It is possible in Access to build an *index* for a field. This acts like an index in a book; it speeds up searching and sorting for that field. Indexes can be created for all but Memo and OLE fields. Indexed fields can also be set up to prevent duplicate entries in a field. If a field has been designated as the *primary key field*, it is automatically indexed, with no duplicate entries allowed. Other fields can also be indexed and set to disallow duplicate entries.

Indexed field
A field for which Access builds a location guide; an index speeds up sorting or searching on a field.

Primary key field
A field that contains a unique value for each record in the table.

In this lesson, you index the Social Security Number field and prevent duplicate entries, since all Social Security numbers should be unique.

To Prevent Duplicate Entries Using Indexed Fields

1 In the PC Training database, click the View button on the toolbar to switch views to the Design view of the Software Training table.

2 Click the Social Security Number field to select it.

3 Click the Indexed property box.

A drop-down arrow appears at the right-hand side of the property box.

4 Click the drop-down arrow and select `Yes (No Duplicates)` from the drop-down menu.

The Social Security Number properties area should look like Figure 9.19.

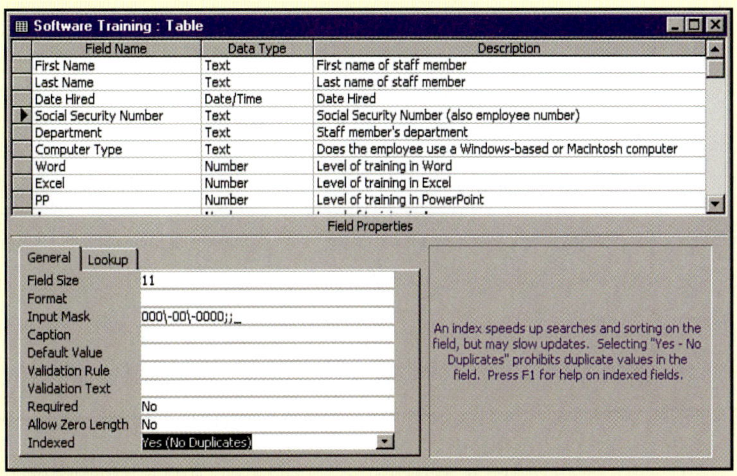

Figure 9.19
The Social Security Number Field Properties area now shows "Yes (No Duplicates)" in the Indexed property box.

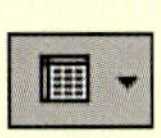

5 Click the View button on the toolbar to switch to the Datasheet view.

Click Yes when prompted to save your changes to the table and when warned about data integrity.

6 Scroll down to the bottom of the table.

7 Add a new record, but this time enter a Social Security number from a previous record.

When you try to complete the record, an error message appears (see Figure 9.20). Notice that the error message tells you that you have entered a duplicate value in an index, primary key, or relationship, but does not tell you in which field the error occurred. This can be a big problem in a database with a lot of indexed fields.

continues

To Prevent Duplicate Entries Using Indexed Fields (continued)

Figure 9.20
The Duplicate Value error message appears when you enter a Social Security number that is already used in the database.

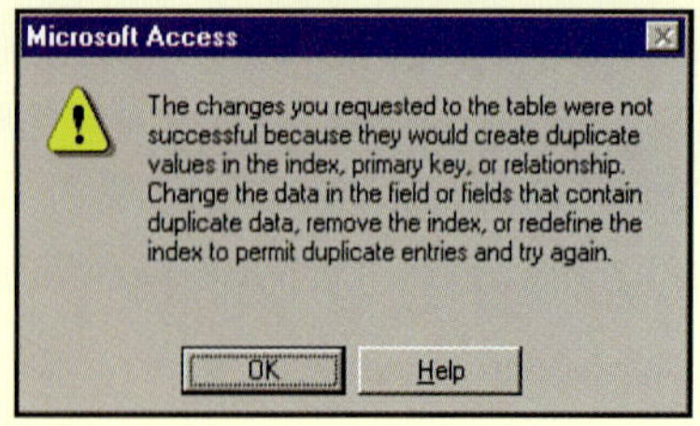

8 Click OK in the warning box.

9 Press Esc to back out of the entry.

Keep the database open for the next lesson.

Inside Stuff

One way to search for a duplicate entry is to use the Find button on the toolbar. Enter the number or word that caused a problem and search for each occurrence of it. Since the error message does not identify which field contains the duplicate entry, you may need to look at the design of the table to determine which fields are indexed or which field is the primary key. Search for duplicate values in these fields.

Access

Lesson 7: Creating a Lookup Column to Allow Selection from a List

There are times when you will have a field that has several common entries. This is particularly true of fields designed for such things as city or state names, job titles, and military ranks.

Access contains a Lookup Wizard in the Data Type column in the Table Design view. This enables you to either enter the common items, or have the program make up a list from a field in another table. Having pre-typed choices available makes data entry far easier, and also prevents the user from making typographical errors. When entering data, if the value you need is not on the list, you can type it in the field.

In this lesson, you add a Lookup list for the Department field. The Lookup Wizard walks you through the steps of creating the data list, and you end up with a drop-down box containing all of the department names in the database.

To Create a Lookup Column Using the Lookup Wizard

1 In the PC Training database, click the View button on the toolbar to switch views to the Design view of the Software Training table.

2 Select the Department field and click on the Data Type box.

A drop-down arrow appears on the right-hand side of the box.

3 Click the arrow in the Department Data Type box.

A drop-down menu appears (see Figure 9.21). The various data types are shown in this box. At the bottom of the box is the Lookup Wizard choice.

Figure 9.21
The Lookup Wizard option appears at the bottom of the drop-down list.

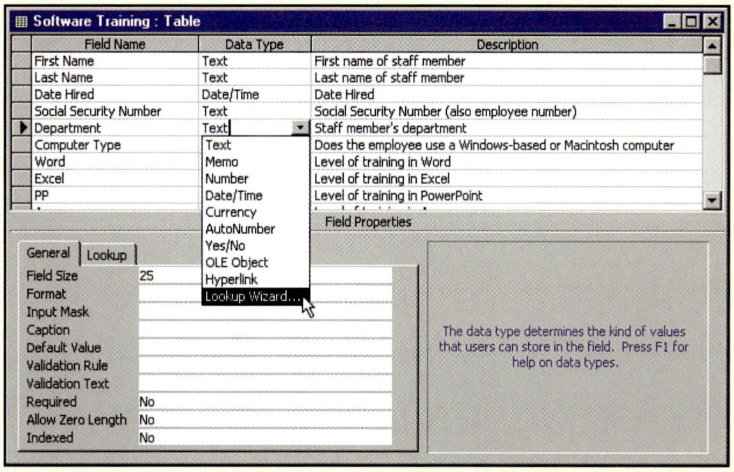

4 Select Lookup Wizard from the drop-down box.

The first Lookup Wizard dialog box appears (see Figure 9.22).

Figure 9.22
The first Lookup Wizard dialog box asks how you want your lookup column to get its values.

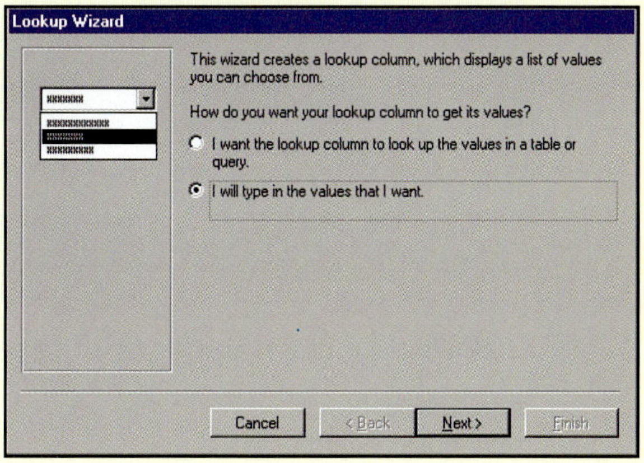

5 Choose the second option to type in the values you want, then click Next.

The second Lookup Wizard dialog box appears.

continues

To Create a Lookup Column Using the Lookup Wizard (continued)

6 Accept the default number of columns, then type in the departments listed below in the box labeled Col1:

Do not press Enter after each entry. This takes you to the next dialog box. Use the ↓ or Tab key to move down. If you accidentally move to the next dialog box before you finish entering the department names, click Back to return to the data entry area.

```
Accounting
Branch 1
Branch 2
Branch 3
Human Resources
Marketing
Payroll
```

As you enter the seven department names, the first one scrolls off the screen (see Figure 9.23). If you need to move up to edit an entry that has scrolled off the screen, use the ↑ key.

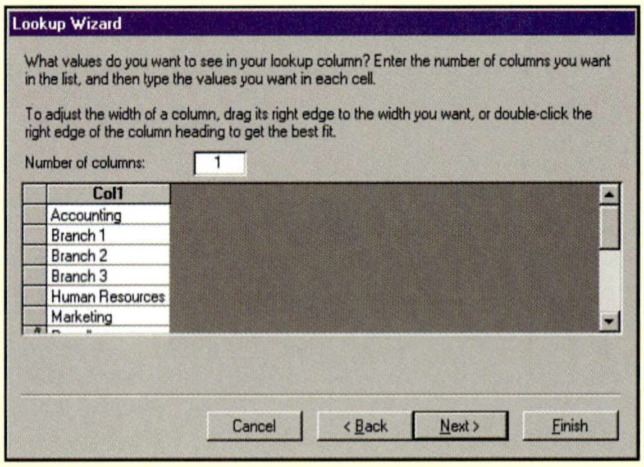

Figure 9.23
Use the second Lookup Wizard dialog box to enter the lookup column values.

7 Click Next to move to the third Lookup Wizard dialog box.

This dialog box asks what you want to name your lookup column (see Figure 9.24).

8 Accept the default, `Department`, as the lookup column name, then click Finish.

9 Click the View button on the toolbar to switch views to the Datasheet view.

Click Yes when prompted to save your changes to the table.

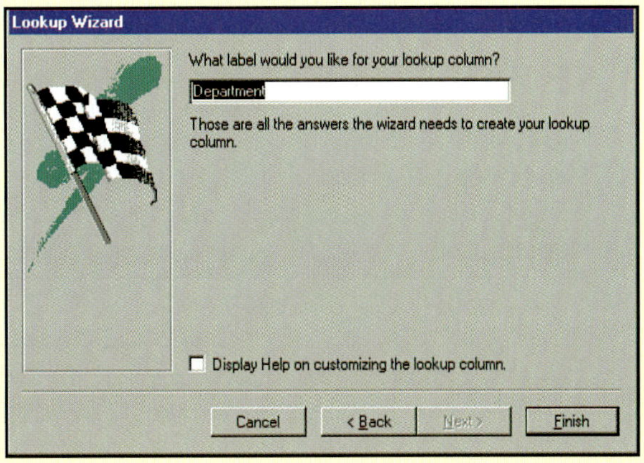

Figure 9.24
The final Lookup Wizard dialog box enables you to name the lookup column.

⑩ **Scroll down to the bottom of the table and enter a new record.**

When you get to the Department field, notice that a drop-down arrow appears.

⑪ **Click the arrow to display the drop-down box you just created, then select one of the departments.**

You have now created a time-saving feature for your table (see Figure 9.25).

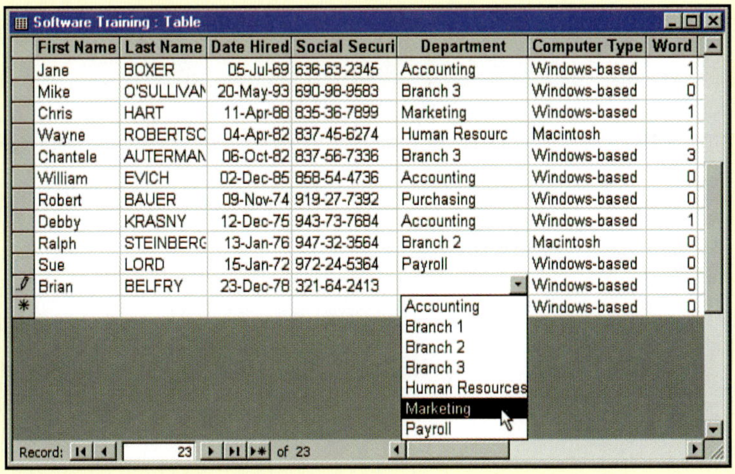

Figure 9.25
The Lookup Wizard created a drop-down box for the Department field.

⑫ **Close your table and Exit Access.**

If you have completed your session on the computer, shut down Windows before you turn off the computer. Otherwise, continue with the "Checking Your Skills" and "Applying Your Skills" sections in this project.

Inside Stuff

The changes made to the text and number formatting in table design, carry over to new forms and reports that are based on this table. Some of the changes, such as required fields, Validation Rules, and default values, also show in existing forms. It is always best to have the table structure complete before creating other objects to ensure that all of the formatting characteristics flow from the table to the objects based on that table. If you make changes to the table structure after other objects have been created, you can add those same formatting characteristics directly to the design of the form, reports, or queries.

Exam Notes

All of the topics in this project were performed and tested in the Table Design view. By changing the text and number formatting in table design, the formatting carries over to new forms and reports. One of the skills identified on the Microsoft list is to improve accuracy in forms. All of the following features help improve accuracy in forms (and also tables and reports):

- Consistent data formats
- Conditional formats
- Input masks
- Validation criteria
- Required fields
- Prevention of duplication

Project Summary

To	Do This
Create consistent data formats	In the Table Design view, select the field you want to format, click in the Format property box in the Field Properties area, then enter the character(s) needed to format the data.
Create conditional data formats	In the Table Design view, select the field you want to format, click in the Format property box in the Field Properties area, then enter the character(s) needed for each component of the series of commands. Separate the components with a semicolon (;).
Change the data input structure using input masks	In the Table Design view, select the field you want to format, click in the Input Mask property box in the Field Properties area, then click the button on the right side of the box to start the Input Mask Wizard.

To	Do This
Restrict entries to those that meet validation criteria	In the Table Design view, select the field you want to work on, click in the Validation Rule property box in the Field Properties area, then click the button on the right side of the box to activate the Expression Builder. Start the expression with the equal sign (=), then build your expression.
Require entry of necessary information	In the Table Design view, select the field you want to work on, click in the Required property box in the Field Properties area, then select Yes from the drop-down menu.
Prevent duplicate entries using indexed fields	In the Table Design view, select the field you want to work on, click in the Indexed property box in the Field Properties area. Choose Yes (No Duplicates) from the drop-down box.
Create a lookup column using the Lookup Wizard	In the Table Design view, select the field you want to work on, click in the Data Type property box in the Field Properties area, and choose Lookup Wizard from the drop-down menu. Choose to type in your own data, then enter the data.

Checking Your Skills

True/False

For each of the following statements, check *T* or *F* to indicate whether the statement is true or false.

__T __F **1.** When you change the format of a field in an existing table, the data already stored on your disk is changed also.

__T __F **2.** If you wanted to show negative numbers in red text, you would create a conditional format.

__T __F **3.** You must use the Input Mask Wizard to enter an input mask.

__T __F **4.** Text you enter into the Validation Text property box will appear in an error message dialog box if the Validation Rule is violated.

__T __F **5.** Data entry can be required in every type of field except AutoNumber.

__T __F **6.** If you want a text field displayed in all capitals, enter the > (greater than) symbol on the Format properties box for that field.

__T __F 7. When you add a format to a table after data has been entered, it does not change the way the existing data is displayed; you have to re-enter the data to have the new format take effect.

__T __F 8. Any formatting change you make to a table automatically flows to existing forms that are based on that table.

__T __F 9. When indexing a field, the Yes, no duplicates option can only be used for the primary key field.

__T __F 10. A null value is the same as a zero.

Multiple Choice

Circle the letter of the correct answer for each of the following questions.

1. In a conditional format, components are separated by _____.
   a. commas
   b. semicolons
   c. colons
   d. quotation marks

2. The Input Mask Wizard creates formats for _____.
   a. all types of fields
   b. all types of fields except OLE
   c. text fields only
   d. text and date fields only

3. A program that helps the user create formulas for Validation Rules is called a(n) _____.
   a. Expression Builder
   b. Validation Text
   c. Rule Wizard
   d. Restriction Builder

4. If you enter duplicate information in a field where duplicates are not allowed, how do you back out of that entry?
   a. Press Del key.
   b. You can't delete the record.
   c. Press Esc.
   d. Press Enter and go on.

5. One way to speed up searching and sorting on a field is to _____.
   a. prevent duplicate entries in the field
   b. make it a Required field
   c. index it
   d. make the data format consistent

6. Validation Text is used to _____.
   a. explain to the person entering data the reason why the data entered is not acceptable
   b. verify that only valid data is entered
   c. validate text fields only
   d. intimidate the user for making a mistake

7. Formats for dates can be set for _____.
   a. dates
   b. times
   c. date and time
   d. all of the above

8. Which of the following best describes a null value?
   a. zero in a Number field
   b. spaces in a Text field
   c. $0 in a Currency field
   d. no entry at all

9. A required property can be set for every type of field except _____.
   a. Memo
   b. OLE
   c. AutoNumber
   d. Yes/No

10. A Lookup list would be useful for a field that contained _____.
    a. Social Security numbers
    b. department names
    c. last names
    d. account numbers

Completion

In the blank provided, write the correct answer for each of the following statements.

1. The character that is used in a format to force all text to be capital letters is the ______________ character.
2. A(n) ______________ is used to reserve a spot for a character in an input mask.
3. A(n) ______________ is a data entry structure that forces data to be entered in a selected format.
4. A(n) ______________ Rule is an expression that Access uses to check the data entered into a field.
5. The Lookup ______________ helps you build a lookup column.
6. The ______________ symbol on the format properties line ensures that a text field is displayed in lower case letters.
7. A(n) ______________ value is a field with no data entered into it.
8. A ______________ text box appears when data that doesn't match a Validation Rule is entered into a field.
9. When you ______________ a field, Access builds a location guide for that field which speeds up sorting or searching on it.
10. The ______________ is a program that helps the user create formulas for many Access uses.

Matching

In the blank next to each of the following terms or phrases, write the letter of the corresponding term or phrase. (Note that some letters may be used more than once.)

a. null	_______	**1.** Used to help ensure that values entered are all spelled the same
b. Validation Text	_______	**2.** An example of a validation criteria that requires positive numbers in a number field
c. general	_______	**3.** A field that is empty
d. input mask	_______	**4.** May be violated when you make a field required
e. Lookup list	_______	**5.** Ensures that all letters are displayed in lower case
f. >0	_______	**6.** A message that explains what data is acceptable
g. Validation Rule	_______	**7.** Used to open the Input Mask Wizard
h. less than symbol	_______	**8.** Restricts entries to those that are allowed
i. Build button	_______	**9.** Used to set formatting for certain field types
j. data integrity	_______	**10.** Date format that is used to display both date and time

Applying Your Skills

Practice

The following exercises enable you to practice the skills you have learned in this project. Take a few minutes to work through these exercises now.

Keeping Track of Your Books

If you need to track your personal book collection, you may already have a database to record the basic information about it. In this section, you modify such a database to allow for faster entry of typical book categories and information about dates and phone numbers.

To add input masks and a lookup column for common book types, complete the following steps:

1. Copy the Proj0902 database from the Project-09 folder on the CD and name the new file `Library8`.
2. Open the database, then open the `Books` table in the Design view.
3. Select the Type of Book field and add a lookup column to it so that the user may select from typical choices such as: Fiction, Non-Fiction, Mystery, Classic, and Humor.
4. Switch to the Datasheet Table view and enter a new record to test the Lookup Column feature.
5. Close the table.
6. Open the `Borrow` table in the Design view.
7. Click the Borrower Phone field and add an input mask for phone numbers.
8. Click the Borrower Date field and add a format that uses the Medium Date form.

9. Change to the Datasheet view to look at your changes.
10. Close the table and the database.

Adding Data Entry Controls to a Small Business Database

Managing a small business requires good record keeping and advertising. A database can be invaluable for this purpose, but it also requires regular updating. To make this as easy and error-free as possible, add the following features to a database designed for a small company named Sound Byte Music.

To make it easier to enter data for Sound Byte Music Company, complete the following steps:

1. Copy the Proj0903 database from the Project-09 folder on the CD and name the new file `SBMusic7`.
2. Open the database and then open the `Customers` table in the Design view.
3. Add a lookup column to the Music Interest field that enables the user to select from a list of interest areas such as Rock, Country, Jazz, and Blues.

   Close the table and save the change.
4. Open the `Orders` table in Design view, and select the Order Date field.

   Apply an input mask that uses the short date mask.

   Save the change.
5. Click the Quantity field.

   Apply a Validation Rule that requires the quantity to be greater than zero. Type `>0` in the Validation Rule box.

   Enter a suitable Validation Text such as `The quantity must be greater than zero.`
6. Switch to the Datasheet view and save the change.
7. Test the rule by entering a negative or zero value for the quantity.

   Close the table.
8. Open the `Suppliers` table in Design view, and select the Phone field.

   Apply a phone number input mask.

   Close the table and save the change.

Adding Data Entry Controls to a Computer Inventory Database

If an organization has several computers, it becomes important to inventory them and their components. This enables you to plan for upgrades and to determine which machines can run any new software that is planned. In this practice exercise, you add some controls to the PC database.

To make it easier to enter data into the PC database, complete the following steps:

1. Copy the Proj0904 database from the Project-09 folder on the CD and name the new file `PC7`.
2. Open the database, then open the `PC Hardware` table in the Design view.
3. Add a lookup column to the Processor field that has choices such as 386, 486, Pentium, Power PC, and Other.
4. Add a lookup column to the Monitor field that has choices such as VGA, SVGA, and Other.

   Switch to the Datasheet view and enter a record to test the lookup columns.

   Close the table.
5. Open the `Vendors` table in Design view.
6. Add a phone number input mask to the Phone Number field. Save the mask symbols as part of the data.

   Save your changes, switch to Datasheet view and test your changes.
7. Add a lookup column to the Vendor field in the PC Hardware table that enables the user to pick from the following: Acme Computer, General Computer, and Wilson Electric. Instead of typing in a list, use the first option in the Lookup Wizard that looks up the values in a table or query. Include only the Name of Vendor field.

   Switch to the Datasheet view and test your changes by entering a new record.

   Close the table and the database.

Access

Adding Data Entry Controls to a Human Resources Database

Organizations that have numerous employees must be able to change their employee records regularly when employees change departments, phone numbers, or salary range. In this lesson, you add input masks and lookup lists to make it easier and more accurate to enter and edit these records.

To make it easier to enter data into the PC database, complete the following steps:

1. Copy the Proj0905 database from the Project-09 folder on the CD and name the new file `Human Resources`.
2. Open the database, then open the `Employee Information` table in the Design view.
3. Add a Lookup column to the Department field that has choices such as Marketing, Human Resources, Facility Management, and Other.
4. Add a Lookup column to the Specialty field that has choices such as Analysis, Secretary, Management, Personnel, Records, Real Estate, Maintenance Management, and Other.

5. Add an telephone number input mask to the Home Phone field.
6. Add a Social Security input mask to the Social Security Number field.
7. Add a Short Date input mask to the Date Hired field.

   Switch to the Datasheet view and test your changes by entering a new record.

   Close the table and the database.

Getting a Helping Hand

The following exercise gives you a chance to explore some of the formatting options available in Access. It also gives you a chance to explore what type of information is available in both the Office Assistant and the Help button.

To explore additional formatting options, complete the following steps:

1. Open the `PC Training` database and the `Software Training` table in the Table Design view.
2. Scroll down to the Expenses field, then click the Format box in the Field Properties area.
3. Press the F1 key. This will take you to the Format Property help section.
4. Click Number and Currency Data Types. This takes you to a help section on various options available to you.
5. Experiment with different ways of displaying the data, including the use of different colors.
6. Use this method to explore formatting options for Date/Time, Yes/No, and Text/Memo data types.

Challenge

The following challenges enable you to use your problem-solving skills. Take time to work through these exercises now.

Adding Data Entry Controls to a List of Club Members

You are responsible for maintaining a database of club members. You want to make sure that all members have a five-digit identification number and that data entry is as error-free as possible.

Open the `Club` database that you have been working on in previous projects. Add a field named `Title` to the members table. Add a Lookup list to the Title field and include the following titles: Mr., Mrs., Ms., Miss, or Dr.

Add an input mask to the Phone field properties, and save the symbols as part of the data. Review the other fields that you have used and add appropriate input masks and formatting. When you are done, save the changes and close the database.

Adding Validation Rules and Required Properties to Customer Research

Now that the design of the Customer Research database has been improved, you want to add more features to help ensure the accuracy of the data entered.

Make a copy of Proj0906 from the Project-09 folder on the CD and rename the copy `Customer Research8`, then open the file. In the Participants table, format the Last Name field to display in all capitals. Change the Sex to display in all capitals and add a Validation Rule to allow only *F* or *M* as the correct data. Make both the Sex and Birthdate fields required. Format the Birthdate field to short date. Test your changes by adding your name as a new participant. Skip the Birthdate and Sex fields to ensure the required warning box displays. In the Viewing Data table, add a lookup value to the Channel field that looks up the channel in the Local Cable table. Include both fields and elect to show the key column. Enter a new record in the Viewing Data table to test the lookup list.

Access

Using Lookup with the Vending Database

When you created this database, you had to be careful to enter the names of the machines and vendors exactly the same if they occurred in two different tables. In this exercise, you use the lookup feature to make this type of data entry easier.

Make a copy of the Proj0907 database from the Project-09 folder on the CD and rename the copy `Vending7`. Open the `Vending7` database and open the `Machines` table in Design view. Select the Machine Type field and choose the Lookup tab. Select `List Box` as the Display Control, `Table/Query` as the Row Source Type, and `Machines` as the Row Source. Use a similar procedure to link the Supplier field to the Supplier table. Switch to the Datasheet view and test the lookup lists.

Leave the database open for use in the next exercise.

Using Additional Options for Input Masks with the Vending Database

The Input Mask Wizard enables you to add special formatting for text and date fields. It is also possible to create your own format for a invoice numbering system or other special purpose identifying systems that a company may use. The Help system offers information about the codes used to create an input mask. Explore these options so you can understand how to manually write an input mask.

If you have not done the previous Challenge exercise that uses this table, make a copy of the Proj0907 database from the Project-09 folder on the CD and rename the copy `Vending7`. Open the `Vending7` database and open the `Suppliers` table in Design view. Click in the input mask property box for the Phone Number field. Click the Office Assistant and type the phrase `Input Mask examples`. Look at the options available and the definitions of the literal characters that are used to create a mask. Write an input mask using the literal code for the Phone Number field. Write the code to allow for an area code, but not require it. Be sure the phone number fills up the last seven digits if no area code is included. Test your design by adding a new record with a phone number without the area code. Compare your design to the one used by the Input Mask Wizard.

Using IN Validation Rule with the Video Store Database

Validation Rules can take several different formats. If you need to use a string of options, you can do this by using the IN operator and enclosing the choices in parentheses.

Make a copy of Proj0908 from the Project-09 folder on the CD and rename the copy `Video Store6`. Open the database and open the `Rental Activity` table in Design view. Add a Validation Rule to limit the rental rates to $1.50, $2.50, $3.00. Use the IN operator. Use information in Help on Validation Rules or on the IN operator, if needed, to create your Validation Rule. Be sure to add a Validation Text box to assist the user. Make this a required field, then test your results by adding a new record. When you are done, save the changes and close the database.

PinPoint Assessment

PinPoint Training

You have completed the project and the associated lessons, as well as the "Checking Your Skills" and "Applying Your Skills" sections. Now use the PinPoint software Evaluation mode to assess your comprehension of the specific exam tasks you have just learned. You can also use the PinPoint Trainer mode and the SHOW ME tutorials to practice these specific exam tasks.

Project 10

Ten

Making the User Input Form More User-Friendly

Adding Color and Customizing Controls Can Enhance a Form

In this project you will learn the following objectives and their associated Microsoft Exam required activities.

Objectives	Required Activities
➤ Change the Color of Text, Backgrounds, and Borders Using Buttons	Enhance Design of a Form
➤ Using the Format Painter to Copy Formats Between Individual Controls or Format Several Controls at Once	Enhance Design of a Form Copy Formats Between Individual Controls and Format Many Controls at Once
➤ Change Colors and Align Text Using Properties	Enhance Design of a Form
➤ Add Status Bar Instructions in the Form View	Improve Accuracy in Forms
➤ Add Customized ControlTips to Controls	Improve Accuracy in Forms
➤ Customize a Toolbar with Predefined Buttons	Improve Accuracy in Forms Modify Form Design

Why Would I Do This?

Customizing the appearance and functions of Access helps to personalize the database, while at the same time making it more interesting, informative, and easier to use. Effective use of colors, buttons, and help features can make the difference between a boring database and a professional-looking product.

Most data entry is done in the Form view. Changing the color of the text, background, and border colors can improve the look of the form and can also be used to provide important information to the user. You can use colors, for example, to warn the user of required fields.

Control
A general term for objects on a form or report such as text boxes, label boxes, buttons, and calculated fields.

Changing the format or adding new features to each *control* on a form can be time-consuming. Access has a rapid format feature that can save a great deal of time.

Access gives you the option of adding customized help for the user. You can place instructions on the status bar, and you can even add ControlTips to the controls on a form.

It is also possible to customize any of the toolbars. Predefined buttons that are included with Access can be added to any toolbar, and seldom-used buttons can be removed. The order of the buttons can be rearranged.

In this project, you learn how to change the appearance of various form controls to give the user more information and to make the database look professional.

Lesson 1: Changing the Color of Text, Backgrounds, and Borders Using Buttons

You can make the form easier to read through a restrained use of color. Try not to overdo the use of colors. Too many different colors on a screen can be very distracting, and bright colors with high contrast can be very hard on the eyes. You can also use colors as cues for the user.

In this lesson, you learn how to change the colors of the text (foreground), background, and control borders in a form using buttons on the Form Design toolbar.

To Change the Color of Text, Backgrounds, and Borders Using Buttons

1. **Make a copy of the Proj1001 database file from the Project-10 folder on the CD and name the copy `Federal Census`. Return to Access and open the `Federal Census` database.**

   The Database window should now be open to the Tables area (see Figure 10.1).

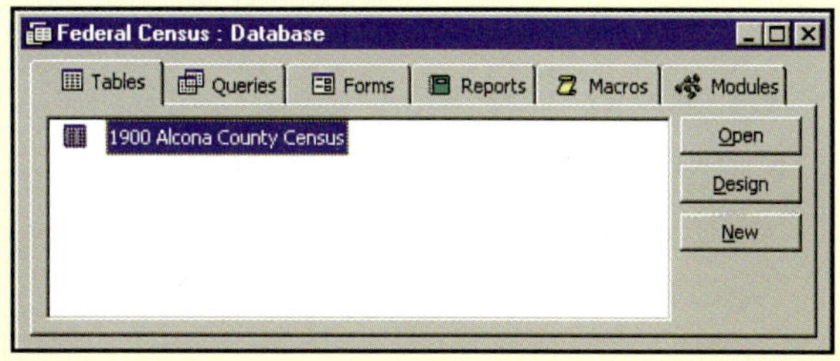

Figure 10.1
The Database window displays the Tables area of the Federal Census database.

❷ **Click the Forms tab.**

The 1900 Alcona County Census form should be highlighted.

❸ **Click the Design button. Maximize the Design window and the Access window, if necessary (see Figure 10.2).**

The 1900 Alcona County Census form is ready for design changes.

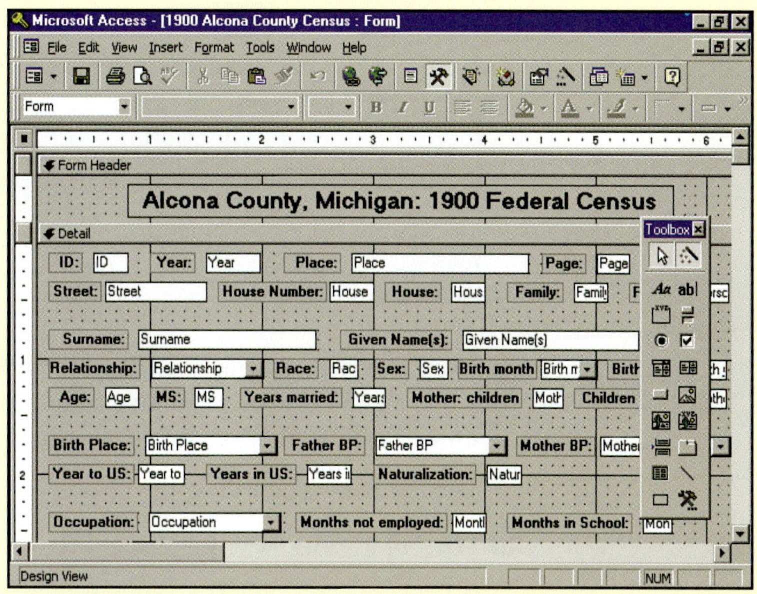

Figure 10.2
The Design window displays the design area of the 1900 Alcona County Census database.

❹ **Click the title** `Alcona County, Michigan: 1900 Federal Census` **to select it.**

Handles should appear around the title.

❺ **Click the down-arrow on the Font/Fore Color button on the Form Design toolbar.**

The Font/Fore Color drop-down box appears. The Font/Fore Color button could, in this case, be called the Text Color button, although it can change the color of any foreground. The left side of the button shows the current text color. The down-arrow button is used to display a menu of optional colors.

continues

To Change the Color of Text, Backgrounds, and Borders Using Buttons (continued)

6 Choose dark blue.

The dark blue color, which appears in the sixth box to the right in the second row, would be a good choice (see Figure 10.3).

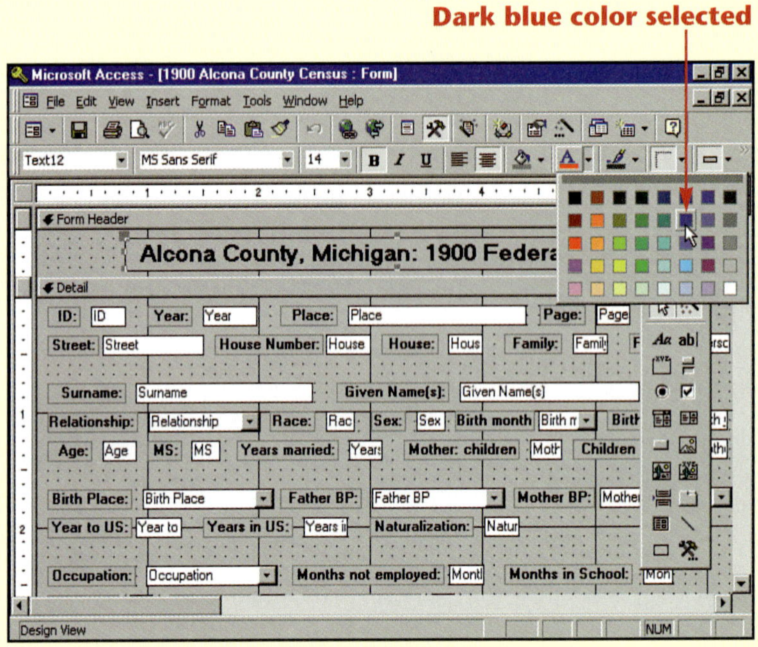

Figure 10.3
The Font/Fore Color drop-down menu offers a variety of colors for text.

7 Click the gray background area to the left of the title in the Form Header area. Click the down-arrow on the Fill/Back Color button on the Form Design toolbar.

The Fill/Back Color drop-down box appears.

8 Choose a light blue background.

A background color that goes well with dark blue text is the fifth box to the right in the fifth row (see Figure 10.4).

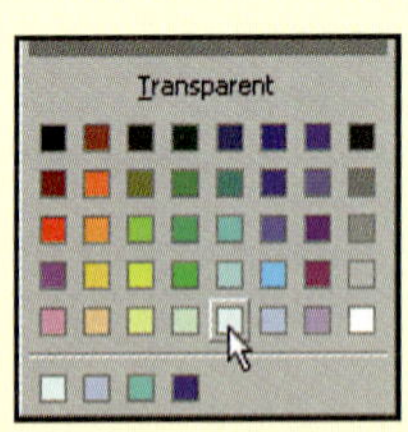

Figure 10.4
The Fill/Back Color drop-down menu offers a variety of colors for the background.

Notice that the background of the title is still gray.

9 Click anywhere on the title to select it.

The title should show a border with handles as it did when selected before.

10 Click the down-arrow on the Fill/Back Color button and click the Transparent choice.

When you want the background of a box to be the same as the background color of the area behind it, you can make the background of the box transparent.

11 Click the down-arrow on the Line/Border Color button.

A drop-down menu appears. This menu shows 40 colors, and is identical to the one found under the Fill/Back Color button.

12 Choose the same shade of dark blue you selected for the title text.

The menu of colors shows the most recently selected colors at the bottom of the menu. You can select the dark blue color from this area as well as its original location on the menu.

13 Click the View button.

You leave the Design view and open the Form view. Notice the color combination in the Form Header area.

14 Save the changes and close the form.

Keep the database open for the next lesson.

Inside Stuff

Once you choose a color for the foreground, background, or lines, it becomes the default choice for that button on the toolbar. The color of the button changes to indicate the current default and you can apply that color to a selected object by clicking the left side of the button.

Lesson 2: Using the Format Painter to Copy Formats Between Individual Controls or Format Several Controls at Once

You can easily copy the format from one control to another. The Format Painter button, on the Form Design toolbar, can be used in several ways to copy formats from one control to one or more other controls. You can also select many fields and format them all at once.

To Copy Formats Between Individual Controls and Format Many Controls at Once

1 In the Federal Census database, click the Forms tab and open the `1900 Alcona County Census` form, if necessary.

Look at the appearance of your form.

continues

To Copy Formats Between Individual Controls and Format Many Controls at Once (continued)

2 Click the View button.

This switches from the Form view to the Design view. Maximize the form, if necessary.

3 Click the label for the ID field (ID:).

Handles should appear around the Label control box, but not the Field Text control box.

4 Use the Font/Fore Color, Fill/Back Color, and Line/Border Color buttons to change the colors to those you used for the title in Lesson 1.

Just change the ID label box on the left, not the ID text control box on the right. Simply click the left side of each formatting button to apply the same colors you used in the previous lesson. If the default color for one of the buttons has been changed, use the drop-down arrow on the right of the button and choose the color the way you did in Lesson 1.

5 Click the Format Painter button in the Form Design toolbar.

The pointer changes shape, adding a paintbrush to the normal arrow (see Figure 10.5).

Mouse pointer for the Format Painter

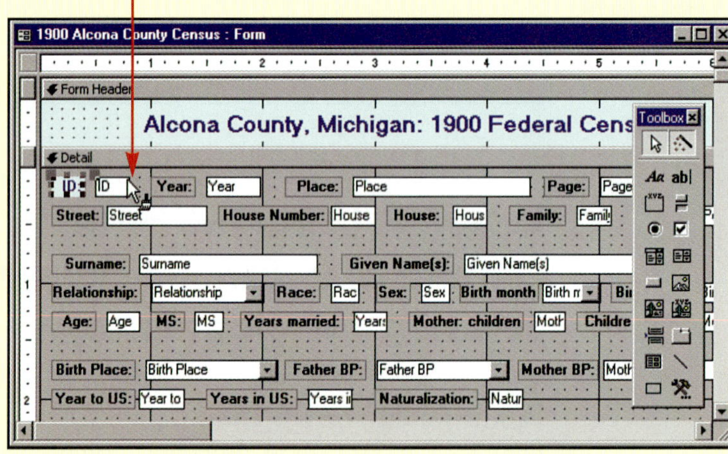

Figure 10.5
The Format Painter pointer has a paintbrush added to the arrow.

6 Click the label for the Year control box (Year:).

The Fore Color, Back Color, and Border Color now match the ID label. Notice that the pointer no longer has a paintbrush attached.

The Format Painter will also apply the settings for font style, point size, and alignment.

7 With the ID label still selected, double-click the Format Painter button.

Double-clicking locks the button on for repeated use.

8 Click the Label control box for the Place field.

The Fore Color, Back Color, and Border Color now match the ID field label. Notice that the pointer still has a paintbrush attached. You can continue to "paint" as many label and field text controls as you want.

9 Click two or three other labels.

Notice that the paintbrush remains with the mouse pointer.

10 Click the Format Painter button once to turn off the Format Painter.

There is an even faster way to change the format of several controls at once.

11 Move the pointer to the vertical ruler, immediately to the left of the ID field.

The pointer turns into an arrow pointing to the right.

12 Click and hold down the left mouse button.

A thin line appears through the first row of controls.

13 Drag the pointer down until it is to the left of the Age field.

A thin line should appear through the row of fields that begin with the Age field, and the ruler will be black between the two lines (see Figure 10.6).

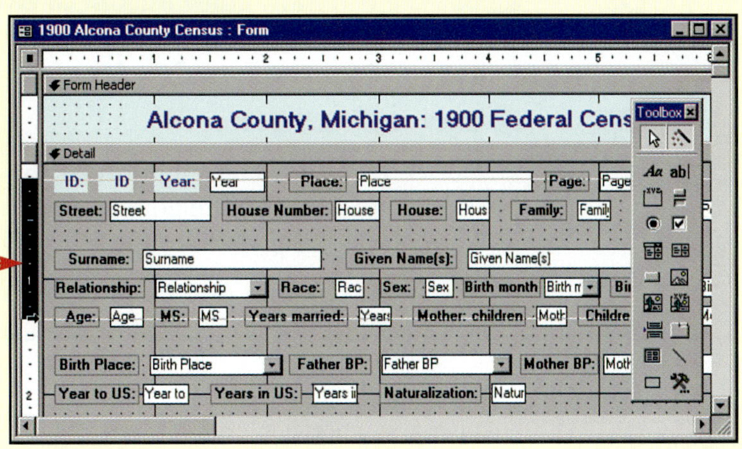

Figure 10.6
The vertical ruler turns black to show the selected area.

14 Release the left mouse button.

All of the labels and controls to the right of the dark area of the ruler are selected (see Figure 10.7).

continues

To Copy Formats Between Individual Controls and Format Many Controls at Once (continued)

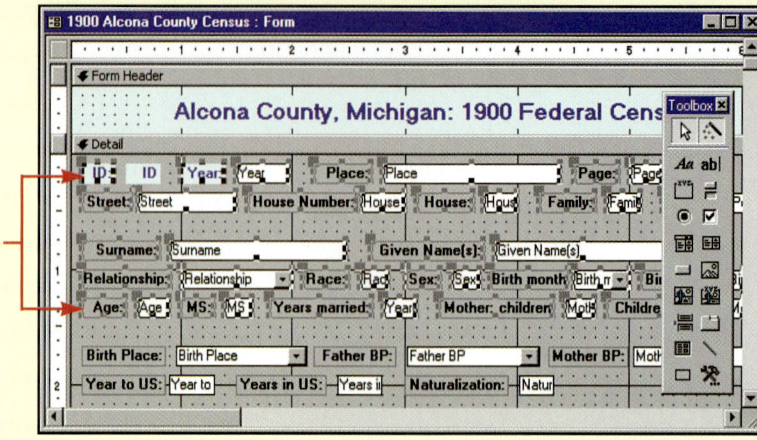

Figure 10.7
Many controls can be selected at once.

15 Use the Font/Fore Color, Fill/Back Color, and Line/Border Color buttons to change the colors to those you used in step 4 of this lesson.

The background, text, and border of the selected labels and controls should be changed. Notice that this method enables you to select the formats separately and does not change the font alignment.

16 Repeat steps 11–15 to change the colors of the rest of the controls in the Detail area of the form.

The background, text, and border of all of the labels and controls should now match the Form Header area.

17 Click in a blank area of the Detail section.

18 Use the Fill/Back Color button to change the background of the unused portion of the Detail area to the same light blue you used for the Form Header area.

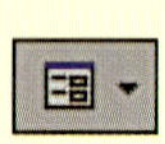

19 Click the View button.

Notice the color combination of the form. Also notice that the combo box buttons remain gray and black, as do the perimeter portions of the screen, such as the status bar and the scrollbars.

20 Save your changes and close the form.

Exam Notes

The previous procedure involves several steps to select all of the components of the Detail area. If you know that all of the objects on the form will be formatted the same, you can use the Select All option from the Edit menu. If you are going to format most of the objects the same way, you can use the Select All option, then hold the Shift key down and click the ones you don't want to format to deselect them. If you want to format only a few controls, you can hold down the Shift key and click to select the controls that you want to format the same.

Access

If you use the Format Painter to copy the format of a label onto a text box, you will not see any immediate problem. However, when you use the form, the text box shows a gray background instead of white when you tab to it to enter data.

Lesson 3: Changing Colors and Aligning Text Using Properties

In Lesson 2, you used the buttons on the Form Design toolbar to change the color of the background, text, and borders. Using the property sheet to change color gives you many more colors and shades from which to choose. This is especially important if, for example, you are attempting to make your form colors match your company's colors. There are other formatting options available in the property sheet.

In this lesson, you use the property sheet to change the color of the three required fields in this form. This warns users that these fields are "special" in some way. You also align the label text of one of the fields.

To Change Colors and Align Text Using Properties

1. **Highlight the `1900 Alcona County Census` form on the Forms tab, click the Design button, and maximize the form, if necessary.**
2. **Right-click the Surname label control box.**

   A shortcut menu appears.
3. **Choose Properties from the shortcut menu.**
4. **Click the Format tab, if necessary.**
5. **Scroll to the bottom of the Format area to display the Fore Color box.**

   The last format option to appear should be Text Align (see Figure 10.8).

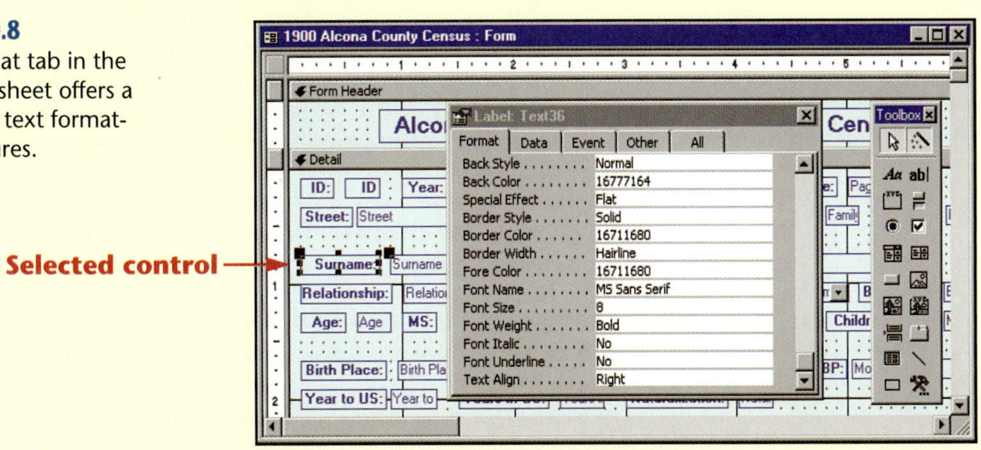

Figure 10.8
The Format tab in the property sheet offers a variety of text formatting features.

continues

To Change Colors and Align Text Using Properties (continued)

6 Click the Fore Color box.

A Build button appears on the right side of the Fore Color box.

7 Click the Build button.

The Color dialog box appears.

8 Click the Define Custom Colors button.

The Color dialog box expands to include a box showing a range of color options. The current color is indicated by an arrow on the right-hand slide and by crosshairs at the top edge of the multicolored box (see Figure 10.9).

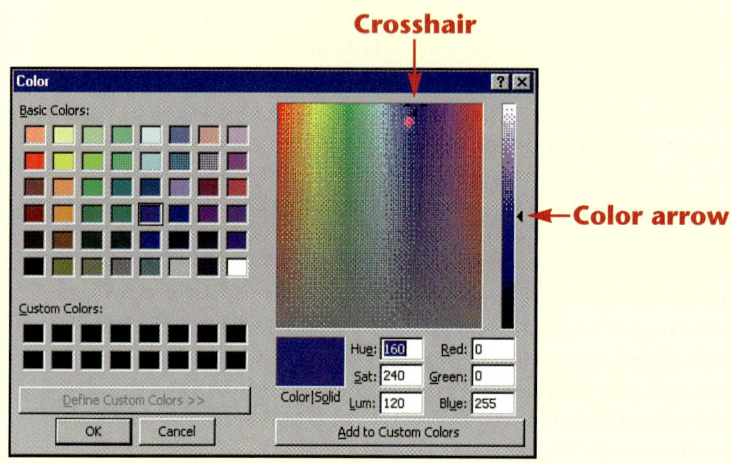

Figure 10.9
The Color dialog box has been expanded to show custom colors.

9 Click on a bright red area of the multicolor box and click OK.

10 Click in the Text Align box.

The Surname label changes to the new color when you move to another area of the property sheet. Notice that the Surname label is right-aligned and does not look correct.

11 Choose Left from the Text Align drop-down box.

12 Close the property sheet.

You have now warned the user that the Surname field is special in some way (you let them know exactly what is special about it in a later lesson). Now copy the format of the Surname label to the other two required fields.

13 With the Surname label control still selected, double-click the Format Painter.

14 Click the Given Name(s) and Relationship label controls to change the color of the text to match the color of the Surname label.

15 **Click the Format Painter button again to turn it off.**

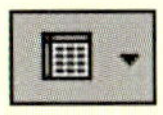

16 **Click the View button.**

Notice that the three required fields stand out on the screen.

17 **Save your changes and close the form.**

Exam Notes

You can also change the alignment of the text on any control by selecting the control and then clicking one of the alignment buttons on the Formatting toolbar in the Form Design view.

Lesson 4: Adding Status Bar Instructions in the Form View

In Lesson 3, you learned how to give the user a visual cue that there was something special about a field. If you want to make the form easy to use, you may also need to give the user help on what to put in the field, and provide information on any special characteristics of the field. There are several ways to help the user, ranging from printed instructions to status bar messages to custom ControlTips. In this lesson, you add help to the status bar. Lesson 5 shows you how to create custom ControlTips.

To Add Status Bar Instructions in the Form View

1 **Highlight the `1900 Alcona County Census` form on the Forms tab, click the Design button, and maximize the form, if necessary.**

2 **Right-click the Surname text control box (not the Label control box you worked on in Lesson 3).**

A shortcut menu appears.

3 **Choose Properties from the shortcut menu.**

4 **Click the Other tab.**

5 **Click the Status Bar Text box.**

If you have problems...

If you don't see the Status Bar Text box, you probably right-clicked the Surname label control box instead of the Surname text control box in step 2. Leave the property sheet open and click the Surname text control box. The property sheet displays the properties of the currently selected object.

continues

To Add Status Bar Instructions in the Form View (continued)

6 Type in the following text:

```
Enter the person's surname. If unreadable, type in ?; if
blank, type in "not given".
```

This is the text that appears in the status bar when the cursor is in the Surname field (see Figure 10.10). The property sheet in Figure 10.10 has been expanded to show the entire label in the Status Bar Text box.

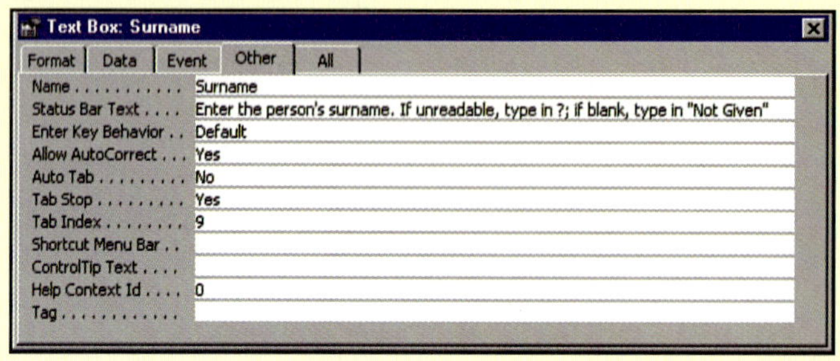

Figure 10.10
Whatever is typed into the Status Bar Text box appears in the status bar.

7 Click the Text box of the Given Name(s) field. Enter the following text in its Status Bar Text box:

```
Enter the given name(s). If unreadable, type in ?; if blank,
type in "not given".
```

This message is slightly altered from the text used for the Surname field. The word `person's` was removed because that made the text too long for the space allowed in the status bar. When creating a message for the status bar, you want to limit the length of the message so that the entire message is visible on the status bar when that field is selected.

If you have problems...

To see the Text box of the Given Name(s) field, you may need to drag the property sheet out of the way. Click the blue title bar of the property sheet and drag it to another part of your screen so you can select the new field. When you click the Given Name(s) Text box, the title on the property sheet changes to reflect the new field that has been selected. Make sure the title bar says Text box: Given Name(s).

8 Click the Relationship Text box and place the following text in the Status Bar Text box:

```
Enter the relationship. If unreadable, type in ?; if blank,
type in "not given".
```

9 Close the property sheet.

10 Click the View button, then click the Surname text box.

The message you typed should appear in the status bar (see Figure 10.11).

Figure 10.11
The status bar displays the text entered into the Status Bar Text option of the property sheet.

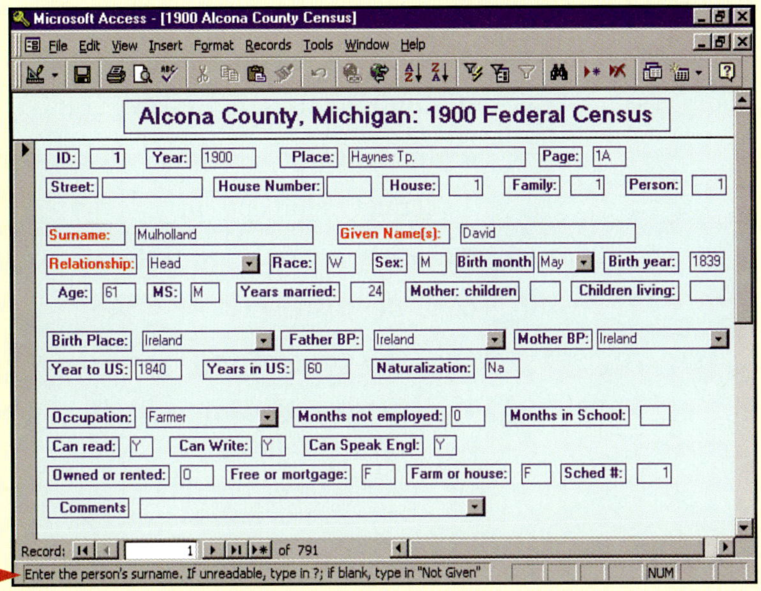

Status bar message

⑪ Save your changes and close the form.

Exam Notes

It might seem that the Format Painter could be used to copy status bar text. The Format Painter, however, works on those functions that change the appearance of an object. It does not work on any of the customized features that require that text be entered. If you are entering identical (or similar) text to the status bar for several fields, type the text into a field, highlight it, then use the Copy and Paste commands to place the text in the Status Bar Text areas of subsequent fields. (You have to use the keyboard shortcuts or the right mouse shortcut menu to copy and paste because the menu and toolbar versions of Copy and Paste apply to the selected object, not the boxes in the properties menu.)

Lesson 5: Adding Customized ControlTips to Controls

ControlTip
A pop-up tip that can be added to a control; similar to a ScreenTip.

In Windows 95, when you move the pointer over a button on a toolbar and leave it there for a short time, a ScreenTip appears telling you what the button does. You can add the same feature to the controls on your forms, which can help make the form easier to use. In a form, these ScreenTips are known as *ControlTips*.

In this lesson, you add ControlTips to augment the status bar messages you created in Lesson 4. You also use a ControlTip to tell the user how to change a default value.

To Add Customized ControlTips to Controls

1 Highlight the 1900 Alcona County Census form, click the Design button, and maximize the form, if necessary.

2 Right-click the Surname text control box.

A shortcut menu appears.

3 Choose Properties from the shortcut menu.

4 Click the Other tab.

5 Click the ControlTip Text box.

6 Type in the following text, adding a Shift+Enter after each of the first three lines:

```
Do not leave this blank.
Check the Status bar on
the bottom of the screen
for further instructions.
```

This is the text that appears in the ControlTip when the pointer is moved over the Surname field. If you don't add the Shift+Enter at the end of each line, the ControlTip is displayed as a single line, often disappearing off the edge of the screen. The property sheet has been widened to display the entire text of the status bar. Only the last line entered for the ControlTip is displayed (see Figure 10.12).

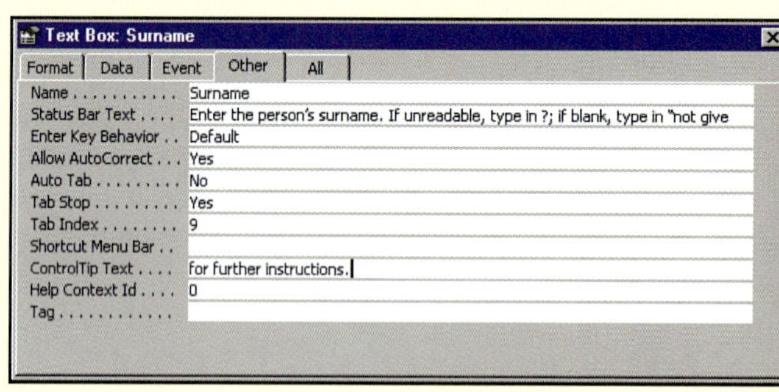

Figure 10.12
The ControlTip Text box will appear when the pointer is held over the field in Form view.

7 Click the Given Name(s) text box. Locate the ControlTip Text box in the property sheet and enter the same message.

8 Repeat step 7 to place the identical text in the ControlTip Text box of the Relationship text control box.

In each case, the ControlTip tells the user how to find more information. The same procedure can be used to give instructions for anticipated problems. In this database, for example, the Place field has a default value. As the user moves from township to township, this default value has to be changed.

9 Repeat step 7 for the Place field, but enter the following text in the ControlTip Text area. Remember to add a Shift+Enter after each of the first three lines:

```
To change the Place default value, close this form and move to the
Tables tab. Select the 1900 Alcona County Census table and click
```

```
the Design button. Select the Place field, then type the new
Default Value in the Field Properties area.
```

There is a limit of 255 characters for a ControlTip message. This message is close to the maximum size.

10 **Close the property sheet.**

11 **Click the View button. Click the Surname field and leave the pointer over the Surname field.**

Look at the ControlTip and the status bar (the cursor is in the Surname field). These types of messages can be very helpful, especially to a new user (see Figure 10.13).

Figure 10.13
Status bar and ControlTip messages can be of great help to the new user.

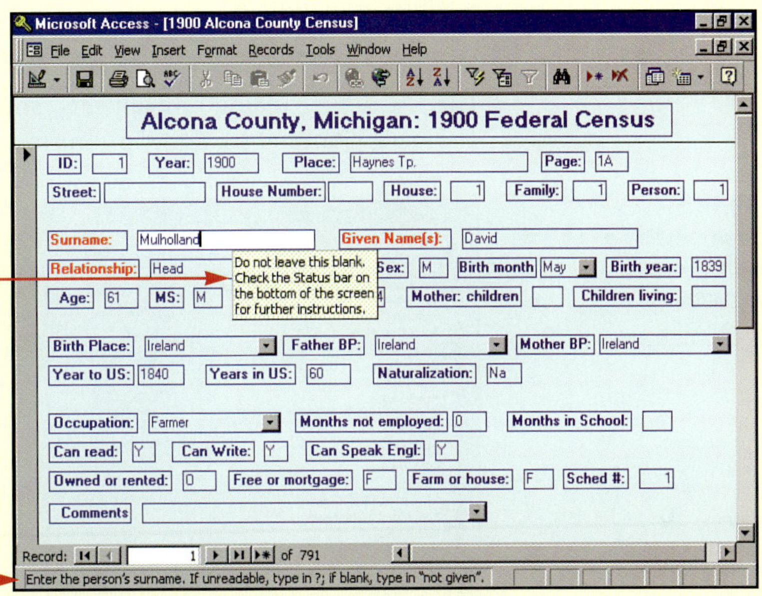

12 **Save your changes and close the form.**

Inside Stuff

The ControlTip is linked to the pointer while the status bar is linked to the cursor. If you have the cursor in one box and point at another, they will not refer to the same box.

Lesson 6: Customizing a Toolbar with Predefined Buttons

The toolbars associated with the various components of Access are helpful to both the database designer and the end user. While the end user seldom uses any of the buttons associated with the various design views, there are always tasks that can be performed using toolbars, such as sorting, filtering, and printing. There are more buttons available than are shown in the default toolbars. These buttons can be added to toolbars, and unused buttons can be removed.

Datasheet view
A Form view that is similar to the Table view. It displays data in a row and column format.

When entering information like that in the Federal Census database, the user must often look at several records at once to see previous entries. Changing the form's *Datasheet view* can do this. In this lesson, you remove unused buttons and add buttons to make it easy for the user to toggle between the Form view and the Datasheet view.

To Customize a Toolbar with Predefined Buttons

1. **Highlight the `1900 Alcona County Census` form, click the Open button, and maximize the form if necessary.**

2. **Right-click the Form View toolbar.**

   A shortcut menu appears.

3. **Choose Customize from the shortcut menu.**

   The Customize dialog box appears, showing tabs for three sections: Toolbars, Commands, and Options (see Figure 10.14).

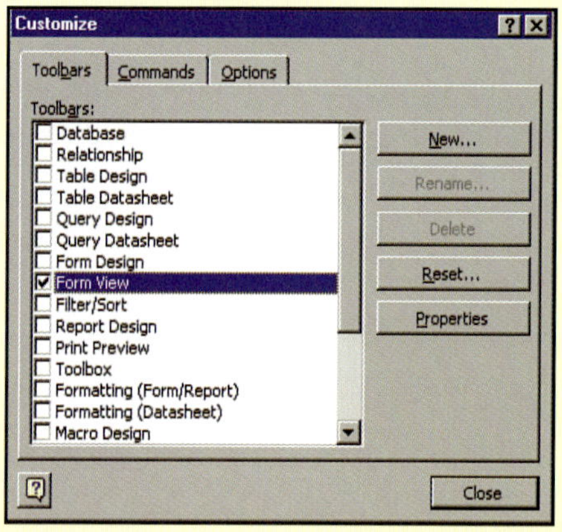

Figure 10.14
The Customize dialog box has three sections. The Toolbars section displays existing toolbars.

4. **Scroll down the list of toolbars and click the check box for the Utility 1 toolbar.**

   This toolbar is normally empty and can be used to create a customized toolbar. As soon as you check the box, an extra toolbar is added (see Figure 10.15).

5. **Click the Commands tab.**

   There are many buttons that can be added to the toolbar. They are grouped by the categories displayed on the left, with the individual buttons shown on the right.

6. **Click Records in the Categories section.**

   A list of commands that are useful for dealing with records is displayed.

Access

Figure 10.15
The Utility 1 toolbar is added as soon as its box is checked.

Utility 1 toolbar

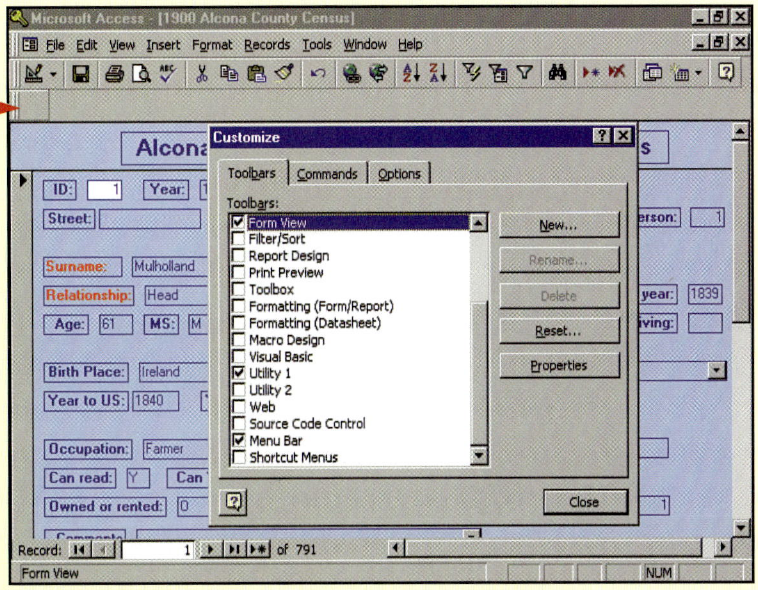

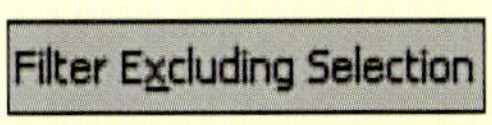

7 Click the Filter Excluding Selection command and drag it up to the new Utility 1 toolbar (see Figure 10.16).

Utility 1 toolbar

Figure 10.16
When adding a button to the toolbar, a small button appears to be attached to the pointer arrow.

Insert Command pointer

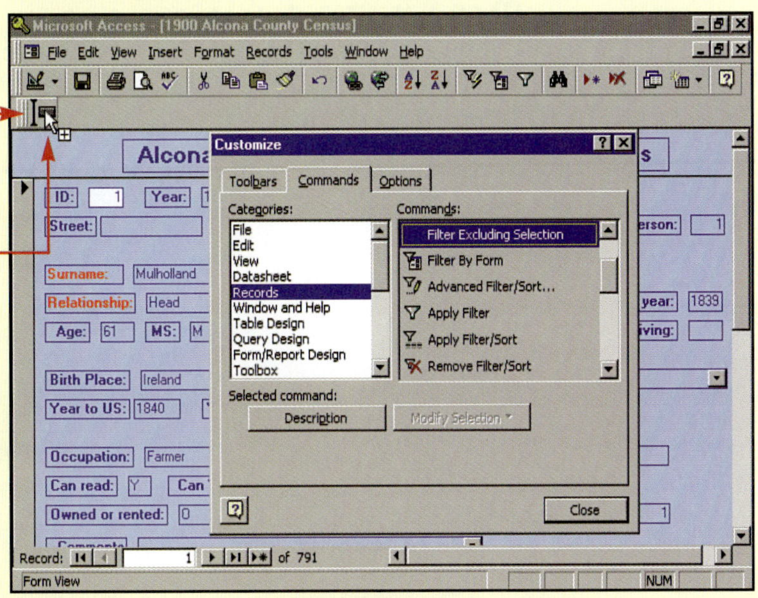

8 Release the mouse button.

The command is added to the toolbar.

continues

To Customize a Toolbar with Predefined Buttons (continued)

If you have problems...

To add a new button, you need to drag the button to the beginning of the toolbar at the far-left end where a small box marks the current size of the toolbar. When the button is successfully placed, a large, bold **I** displays to show the insertion point.

9 Scroll down the list of Records commands to the Delete Record command. Drag it onto the Utility 1 toolbar to the right of the first command.

You have now added two buttons to the Utility 1 toolbar. Next you add two more buttons and separate them from the first two on the toolbar.

10 Click the Form/Report Design category. Drag the Tab Order command to the toolbar and place it to the right of the Delete Record button.

You now have three buttons on the Utility 1 toolbar. In the next step, you create a separation mark on the toolbar that is useful for visually grouping similar buttons. In this case, the first two buttons are used to manage records while the next two can be used when designing forms.

11 Click the Tab Order button that you just placed on the toolbar and drag the pointer so that the small box attached to its end is about half off the button to the right. Release the mouse button.

This moves the button to the right and insert a vertical separating bar (see Figure 10.17).

Vertical separator

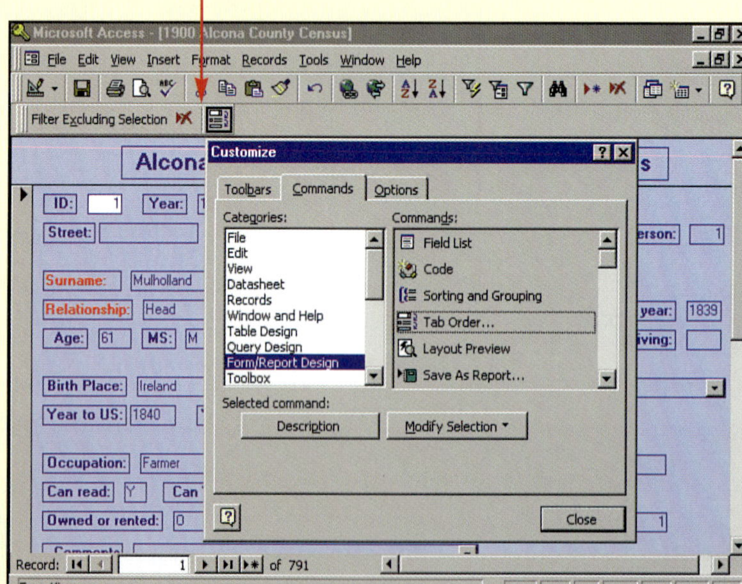

Figure 10.17
Dragging the button slightly to the right inserts a vertical bar on the toolbar that can be used to visually separate groups of buttons.

Access

12 **Drag and drop the Layout Preview and Ruler commands to the toolbar. Place them to the right of the Tab Order button you just added.**

Scroll down the list of commands to find the Ruler command. Your Utility 1 toolbar should look like Figure 10.18.

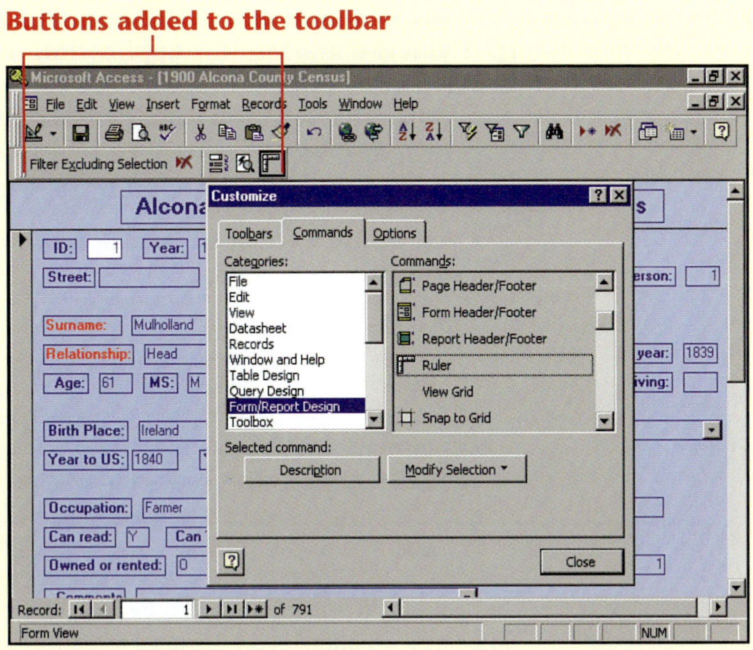

Figure 10.18
The Utility 1 toolbar has had five buttons added and separated into two groups.

You also need to know how to remove buttons from the toolbar. When the Customize dialog box is open, they can be removed by dragging them from the toolbar.

13 **Click and drag the Layout Preview button from the toolbar to any part of the screen below the toolbar.**

The button is removed from the toolbar but still exists in the list of commands and can be placed on the toolbar again using the previously described method above.

14 **Close the Customize dialog box.**

15 **Click the View button to switch to the Design view.**

16 **Click the new Ruler button on the Utility 1 toolbar to toggle the ruler on or off.**

The two buttons on the left of the toolbar that manage records are not active in the Design view. They can be used in the Form view.

continues

To Customize a Toolbar with Predefined Buttons (continued)

If you have problems...

The new Utility 1 toolbar you created may piggyback on one of your other toolbars and not all of the buttons may be visible. Point to the two vertical lines at the beginning of the toolbar and click and drag it down onto your screen, or anchor it in another location so you can see all four buttons that you added to the toolbar.

17. **If you are sharing this application with others and do not have permission to change the toolbars, you should reset this toolbar to its original condition. Right-click the toolbar, click Customize, select the Utility 1 toolbar and click the Reset button. Click OK when prompted to reset toolbar.**

18. **Click Utility 1, click the check box to deselect it. Close the Customize dialog box.**

19. **Close the form.**

If you have completed your session on the computer, exit Access and close Windows before you turn off the computer. Otherwise, continue with the "Checking Your Skills" and "Applying Your Skills" sections in this project.

Inside Stuff

You can create additional toolbars by opening the Customize dialog box and clicking the New button on the Toolbars section. You can also choose the name of the toolbar.

The toolbars are part of the Access interface, not one particular database. When you change the toolbars, it affects anyone else who is using the application. Do not change the standard toolbars unless you have the permission of other users or it is your personal machine.

Project Summary

To	Do This
Change the color of text, backgrounds, and borders using buttons	In the Form Design view, select the control or label you want to format. Use the Font/Fore Color button to change the foreground (usually text) color; the Fill/Back Color button to change the background color; or the Line/Border Color button to change the border color.

To	Do This
Copy formats between individual controls and format many controls at once	In the Form Design view, select the control or label that is formatted the way you want it. Click the Format Painter button, then click the control you want to copy the format to. Double-clicking the Format Painter button keeps it active until you click the Format Painter button again.
Change colors and align text using Properties	In the Form Design view, click the right mouse button on the control or label you want to format. Choose Properties, then go to the Format tab. In the Font/Fore Color, Fill/Back Color, or Line/Border Color area, click the Build button to choose a color. Choose alignment from the Text Align drop-down box.
Add status bar instructions in the Form view	In the Form Design view, click the right mouse button on the control and choose Properties from the shortcut menu. Click the Other tab, then type in the desired status bar text in the Status Bar Text box.
Add customized ControlTips to controls	In the Form Design view, click the right mouse button on the control and choose Properties from the shortcut menu. Click the Other tab, then type in the desired ControlTip text in the ControlTip Text box. If the ControlTip is long, create multiple lines by type Shift+Enter at desired break points.
Customize a toolbar with predefined buttons	Click the right mouse button on the toolbar, then choose Customize from the shortcut menu. Select the category containing the desired button(s). Drag the button to the toolbar and drop it. To remove a button, drag it off the toolbar and let go.

Checking Your Skills

True/False

For each of the following statements, check *T* or *F* to indicate whether the statement is true or false.

__T __F 1. Double-clicking the Format Painter button takes you to the Format Painter dialog box.

__T __F 2. One reason you might use the property sheet to change a color is that this method gives you more color options than the toolbar button does.

__T __F 3. If you customize a toolbar, the changes only appear when you use the database that was open when the toolbar was customized.

__T __F 4. To apply the same format to the entire form, you can use the Select Entire Form command under the Format menu.

__T __F 5. The number of characters you can put in a ControlTip is unlimited.

__T __F 6. To change the color of the background for a control or a group of controls, you must first select the control(s).

__T __F 7. The only way to change the alignment of the text on a control is to set the alignment in the Text Alignment box on the property sheet.

__T __F 8. A message that is entered on the Status Bar Text box should be limited so that the entire message shows on the status bar when that field is selected.

__T __F 9. The Format Painter can be used to copy a status bar message from one control to another.

__T __F 10. To change the property sheet from one control to the next, you must close the first property sheet before you can open the next property sheet.

Multiple Choice

Circle the letter of the correct answer for each of the following questions.

1. To change the color of text in a form, use the _____ button.
   a. Fill/Back Color
   b. Line/Border Color
   c. Font/Fore Color
   d. Special Effects

2. The Status Bar Text option is found in the _____ tab of the property sheet.
   a. Format
   b. Data
   c. Event
   d. Other

Access

3. To remove a button from a toolbar, go to the Customize dialog box, then _____.

   a. drag the button below the toolbar and let go

   b. select the button, then press the Del key

   c. select the button, then choose Cut from the Edit menu

   d. click the button with the right mouse button and select Remove from the shortcut menu

4. To select a group of controls at one time, hold down the _____ key(s) while clicking each control.

   a. Shift

   b. Ctrl

   c. Alt

   d. Shift+Ctrl

5. A ControlTip is activated when you _____.

   a. place the cursor in the appropriate control

   b. place the mouse pointer over the appropriate control for a short time

   c. click the field with the left mouse button

   d. click the field with the right mouse button

6. To aid a user who enters data on a form, you can add _____.

   a. colors to text to make them stand out as special

   b. ControlTips to a field to provide direction

   c. status bar messages to guide the user

   d. all of the above

7. To copy a message for the status bar from the property sheet for one field text box to another, _____.

   a. use the Copy and Paste commands from the Edit menu

   b. use the keyboard combinations to copy and paste the text

   c. use the Format Painter button

   d. either a or b

8. The Fore/Font Color and Text Alignment boxes are found on the _____ tab of the property sheet.

   a. Data

   b. Event

   c. Format

   d. Other

9. A ruler button added to a toolbar _____.

   a. only works in the Design view

   b. only works in the Form view

   c. turns just the horizontal ruler on and off

   d. turns just the vertical ruler on and off

10. To have a ControlTip break over several lines, press _____ to create breaks between the lines of text.

    a. Shift+F5

    b. Ctrl+Enter

    c. Shift+Enter

    d. Alt+Enter

Completion

In the blank provided, write the correct answer for each of the following statements.

1. Most data entry is done in the _______________ view.
2. An easy way to copy the format from one control to another is to use the _______________ button.
3. A(n) _______________ is a pop-up help feature that is similar to a ScreenTip.
4. To create a gap when customizing buttons, drag the button to the _______________ about 1/8 inch.
5. You can add helpful information to the _______________ at the bottom of the screen.
6. A(n) _______________ is a general term for objects such as text boxes, label boxes, buttons, and calculated fields on a form or report.
7. Choose the _______________ option to give your label and text boxes the same background color as your form.
8. A view of a form that displays data in a row and column format is known as the _______________ view.
9. The _______________ can be used to change format, data, event, and other options related to each control on a form.
10. The ControlTip is linked to the _______________ while the status bar message is linked to the _______________.

Matching

In the blank next to each of the following terms or phrases, write the letter of the corresponding term or phrase. (Note that some letters may be used more than once.)

a. Format Painter
b. status bar message
c. Line/Border
d. Edit, Select All
e. right-click
f. Fore/Font
g. ControlTip
h. vertical ruler
i. customized toolbar
j. property sheet

_______ 1. Can be used to change multiple characteristics of a field in a form
_______ 2. Activated when the mouse pointer is placed over a field
_______ 3. Can include buttons that work in either the Design view or Form view of a form
_______ 4. Shows at the bottom of the screen in Form view
_______ 5. Used to change the color of the edge around a control
_______ 6. When you do this, a shortcut menu is displayed
_______ 7. To change the text color of a control use this button
_______ 8. Used to copy the format from one control to another
_______ 9. Clicking here selects several controls at once
_______ 10. Highlights all of the controls on a form

Applying Your Skills

Practice

The following exercises enable you to practice the skills you have learned in this project.

Enhancing the Form Title in the Federal Census Database

In this exercise, you enhance the title of the 1900 Alcona County Census form.

To enhance the form title in the Federal Census database, complete the following steps:

1. Open the `Federal Census` database, and move to the Design view of the 1900 Alcona County Census form.
2. Change the color of the title to a bright red to match the required fields.
3. With the title still selected, go to the property sheet, click the Format tab, and change the Special Effect format to Shadowed.
4. Change the Special Effect for all of the controls in the Detail area to either Raised, Sunken, or Etched (choose your favorite).
5. Italicize the title.
6. Change the text color of the three required fields to match the other text (dark blue), then set them off by changing the background color of the label control boxes for those fields only. Try several colors to come up with a readable background/foreground combination.
7. Leave the database open for use in the next exercise.

Adding Status Bar Messages and ControlTips to the Federal Database

The database you are using in this project is one used to transcribe historical documents. Although many of the census takers were very bad spellers, historical transcriptions must always be taken exactly as written. It is always a temptation to correct an obvious misspelling in a primary source, particularly for something like a state or country name. This makes the Access status bar text options very useful for constantly reminding the transcriber *not* to make changes.

To add status bar messages to the Birthplace and Naturalization fields and a ControlTip to the Year to US field, complete the following steps:

1. The Federal Census database should be open from the previous exercise. Move to the Design view of the 1900 Alcona County Census form.

2. Go to the property sheet and add the following text to the status bar for the Birthplace field:

    `Type the birthplace exactly as written; include spelling errors.`

3. Go to the property sheet and add the following text to the status bar for the Naturalization field:

    `Na - Naturalized; Pa - Permanent Alien`

4. Add the following ControlTip to the Year to US field:

    `Year to US and Years in US sometimes don't match. If not, mention the discrepancy in the Comments area.`

5. Leave the database open for use in the next exercise.

Customize Toolbars in the Federal Database

The capability to customize toolbars means that you can make an Access database more user-friendly for the end user. There are many buttons that can be added to the various toolbars, all of which can be helpful in various situations.

To add the View Grid button to the Utility 1 toolbar, complete the following steps:

1. The Federal Census database should be open from the previous lesson. Move to the Design view of the 1900 Alcona County Census form.
2. Add the Tab Order button to the Utility 1 toolbar. Hint: It can be found in the Form/Report design category of the Customize dialog box.
3. Reset the Utility 1 toolbar you changed in this exercise if you do not have permission to change toolbars.
4. Close the database.

Add Status Bar Instructions to the Sound Byte Music Database

Some postal codes in the United States display four additional numbers. In this exercise, you add a status bar message to prompt the user to enter them when available.

To add the status bar message to the ZIP field, complete the following steps:

1. Copy Proj1002 from the Project-10 folder on the CD and rename the copy `SBMusic8`. Select the form named `AutoForm` and open it in Design view.
2. Right-click the text box for the ZIP field and select Properties from the shortcut menu.
3. Click the Other tab and locate the Status Bar Text box.

4. Type the following message into the Status Bar Text box:

   `Use Zip plus four when available.`

5. Switch to the Datasheet view and test the status bar by selecting the ZIP field. Leave the database open for use in the next exercise.

Add Status Bar Instructions to the Sound Byte Music Database

Some postal codes in the United States display four additional numbers. In this exercise, you add a status bar message to prompt the user to enter them when available.

To add the status bar message to the ZIP field, complete the following steps:

1. Select the form named `AutoForm` in the SBMusic8 database and open it in Design view.
2. Right-click the text box for the Music Interest field and select Properties from the shortcut menu.
3. Click the Other tab and locate the ControlTip Text box.
4. Type the following message into the ControlTip Text box:

   `Do not abbreviate.`

5. Switch to the Datasheet view and test the ControlTip.
6. Close the database.

Challenge

The following challenges enable you to use your problem-solving skills.

Enhancing the Form Design of Club Members Database

Open the `Club` database that you have worked on in previous projects. Open the form that is based on the membership. Select (or create) the title and change the color of its text and background.

Select all the controls in the detail section and change their special effect property to raised or shadowed.

Choose one field and change its label to a color that is different from the others. Add a status bar message to the corresponding text box.

Creating and Enhancing an AutoForm for the Customer Research Database

Use the AutoForm feature to quickly produce a columnar form that you can enhance with a title.

Locate the Customer Research8 database that you worked on in the previous project. Rename it `Customer Research9`, then open the file. Create a columnar AutoForm based on the Participants table. Switch to the Design view of the form. Use the View menu to add a Form Header/Footer. Click the Toolbox button and drag a label box in the Form Header to be used as a title. Type in an appropriate title. Change the size of the font to 14 points. Center the text in the box. Change the color of the font and the background of the title. Select all the controls in the detail section and change their Special Effect to Raised.

Select Birthdate text box and add the following status text to it: `Use the format mm/dd/yy`. Select the Household ID text box and add the following control tip text to it: `Each person must be assigned to a household.` Select the label for the control that has status bar text and change its color. Use the Format Painter to copy the new color to the control that has a control tip. Save your work and name the form `Survey Participants`.

Aligning Text and Adding ControlTips and Status Bar Messages in the Vending Database

Columnar forms display the data with the labels at the left. All the label boxes are the same size and the short labels end up fairly far from their text boxes. In this exercise, you change the alignment of the label boxes so the labels are right aligned and add a ControlTip to one field and a status bar message to another.

Locate the Vending7 database that you worked on in the previous project and rename it `Vending8`. Open the `Vending8` database and open the `Machine Locations` form in Design view. Select the label boxes and right-click to bring up the shortcut menu. Select Properties from the shortcut menu and find the Text Align property. Change it from General to Right. Switch to Datasheet view to confirm that the labels are now next to their respective text boxes.

Select Site text box and add the following status text to it: `Use the common name of the building`. Select the Machine Type text box and add the following ControlTip text to it: `Must be an existing Machine type.` Select the label for the control that has status bar text and change its color. Use the Format Painter to copy the new color to the control that has a ControlTip. Save your changes.

Adding an Enhanced Title and Raised Controls to a Form in the Video Store Database

You want the screens that the customer sees to look good. In this exercise, you add a title to the Video Rental form and enhance its appearance.

Locate the Video Store6 database and rename it `Video Store7`. Open the `Video Store7` database and open the `Video Rental` form in Design view. Use the View menu to add a Form Header/Footer (if necessary). Expand the width of the header to accommodate a title. Click the Toolbox button and drag a label box in the Form Header to be used as a title. Type in an appropriate title. Change the size of the font to 14 points. Center the text in the box. Change the color of the font and the background of the title. Select all the controls in the Detail section and change their Special Effect to Raised.

Select Current Renter text box and add the following status text to it: `Use Customer ID number.` Select the Video Number text box and add the following ControlTip text to it: `Must be current video ID number.` Select the label for the control that has status bar text and change its color. Use the Format Painter to copy the new color to the control that has a ControlTip.

Switch to the Datasheet view and test your messages. Save the changes.

Adding an Enhanced Title, ControlTips, and Status Bar Text to the Home Inventory Database

Good appearance and helpful tips are useful when working with a database, especially one that is likely to be used by people who have little training.

Locate the Home Inventory6 database that you used in the previous project and rename it `Home Inventory7`. Open the database and select one of your forms. Add a title to the form in the Form Header section. Change the color of the font and its background. Center the text in the label box. Select an appropriate text box and add status text to it. Select an appropriate text box and add a ControlTip text to it. Select the label for the control that has status bar text and change its color. Use the Format Painter to copy the new color to the control that has a ControlTip. Save your work.

PinPoint Assessment

PinPoint Training

You have completed the project and the associated lessons, as well as the "Checking Your Skills" and "Applying Your Skills" sections. Now use the PinPoint software Evaluation mode to assess your comprehension of the specific exam tasks you have just learned. You can also use the PinPoint Trainer mode and the SHOW ME tutorials to practice these specific exam tasks.

Project 11

Eleven

Managing Data Using Smaller, Related Tables

Using Relational Database to Save File Space and Reduce Data Redundancy

In this project you will learn the following objectives and their associated Microsoft Exam required activities.

Objectives	Required Activities
➤ Design Related Tables to Hold Repetitive Data	Identify Relationships Enhance Design of a Form
➤ Define the Relationship Between the Tables	Relate Tables Improve Accuracy in Forms
➤ Create Queries That Draw Data from Both Tables	Join Tables in a Query Improve Accuracy in Forms
➤ Automatically Fill In Data from One of the Joined Tables	Join Tables in a Query
➤ Update Tables by Entering or Deleting Data in the Query	
➤ Find Duplicate Records in an Existing Table	

Why Would I Do This?

To manage your data effectively, you need to be able to reduce the size of databases and limit repetitive data entry. Instead of using large tables with many fields that contain identical entries, you need to know how to create separate tables and join them when necessary.

Once you have separated your data into smaller, single-purpose tables, you can recombine the data as needed by creating queries that draw data from the tables.

If a form is based on a query that is, in turn, based on more than one table, it is possible to have the program automatically fill in some of the needed information. It is also possible to enter new data into the tables by entering it into the query.

In some cases, you may want to be sure that all the records in one table have a corresponding record in another table. For example, if you have a table of vendor names and a table of purchases, you might want to make sure that you have a vendor name for each purchase. You might also want to know if you have a vendor from whom you have made no purchases. In this case, the data about the vendor might be unnecessary and could be deleted.

Lesson 1: Designing Related Tables to Hold Repetitive Data

In this lesson, you see how two tables are designed to store related data and how to use them to minimize duplicate data entry.

To Examine the Structure of Related Tables

1 Make a copy of the Proj1101 database file from the Project-11 folder on the CD and name the copy `Hardware Inventory`. Return to Access and open the `Hardware Inventory` database.

The database window should now be open to the Tables area (see Figure 11.1).

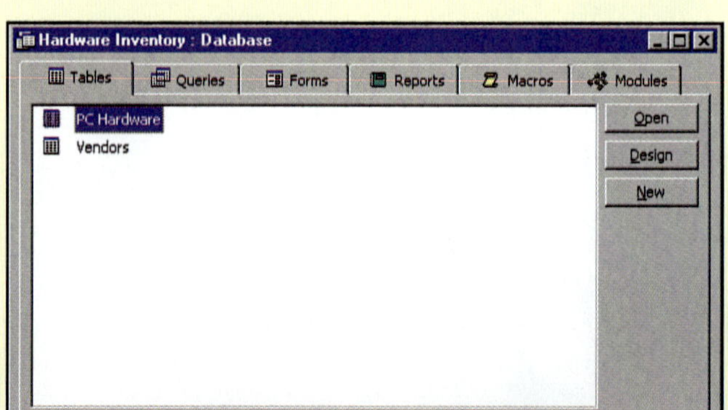

Figure 11.1
The Hardware Inventory database includes the PC Hardware and Vendors tables.

❷ Click the `Vendors` table to select it, and then click Open.

You could also double-click the Vendors table to open it. This table contains data that is necessary to contact the vendor by mail or by phone (see Figure 11.2).

Figure 11.2
The Vendors table is shown in the Datasheet view.

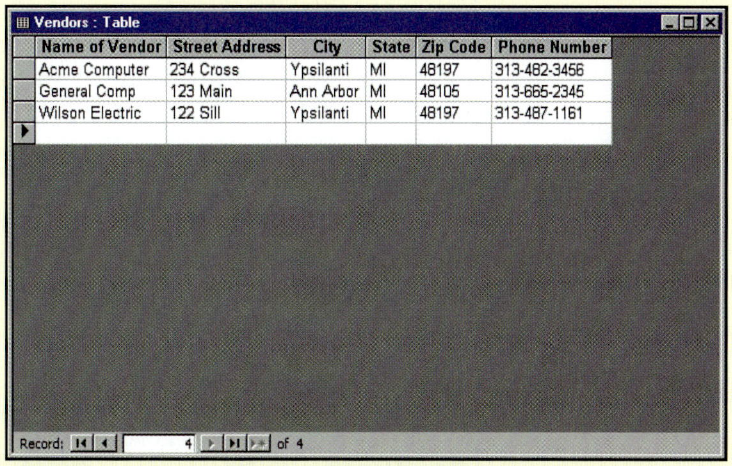

Notice that each vendor's name only appears one time.

❸ Click the View button to switch to Design view.

The Name of Vendor field is the primary key field in this table (see Figure 11.3).

Figure 11.3
The Vendors table shows a primary key field in Design view.

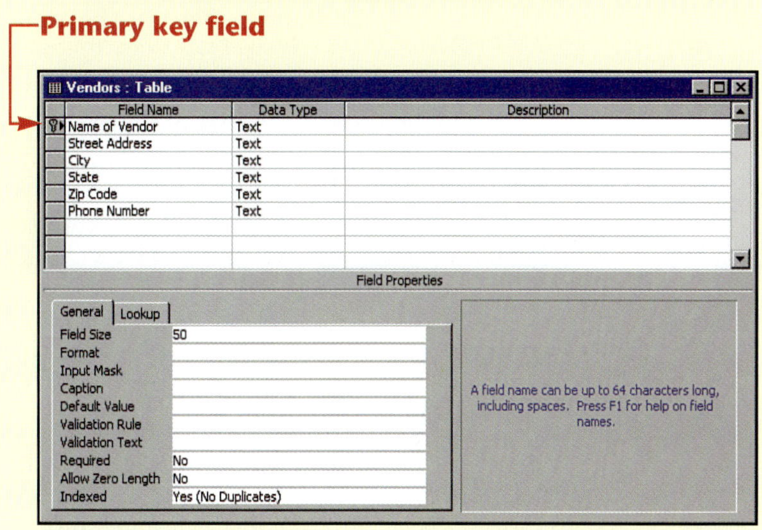

❹ Close the Vendors table so you can look at the PC Hardware table.

❺ Click the `PC Hardware` table to select it, and then click Open.

The PC Hardware table is now displayed in the Datasheet view.

continues

To Examine the Structure of Related Tables (continued)

6 Scroll the table to the right to display the Vendor field.

7 Click in the Vendor field, and then click the arrow on the right side of the Field box.

Notice that the Lookup Wizard has been used to attach a combo box to the Name of Vendor field (see Figure 11.4). This combo box uses the contents of the Name of Vendor field in the Vendors table to form its list. This makes it easy to enter the vendor's name so that there will be an exact match.

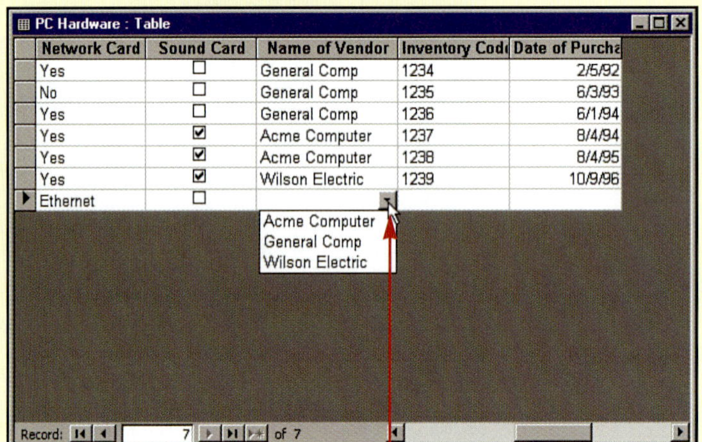

List box showing contents of the Name of Vendor field in the Vendors table

Figure 11.4
The Name of Vendor field of the PC Hardware table contains a combo box.

Notice that the same vendor's name can appear more than once in this table. It can occur many times.

8 Close the table.

Keep the database open for the next lesson.

Access

Lesson 2: Defining the Relationship Between the Tables

Whenever the same information is repeated in numerous records, it is more efficient to create two tables and join them with a single field. In this example, the name of the vendor is used to link the two tables. When the user enters the name of the vendor in a record in one table, all of the data for that vendor is available from the other table without entering it again.

Exam Notes

Linking a pair of similar fields, one from each of the two tables, joins those tables. The two fields do not have to have the same name, but they must be the same data type. If they are Number fields, they must also have the same Field Size property setting.

One-to-many
A relationship that links one record in a table to many records in a different table.

The most common type of database relationship is called a *one-to-many* relationship. In the following lesson, you learn how to join the Vendors table to the PC Hardware table using a one-to-many link between the Name of Vendor field in the Vendors table and the Name of Vendor field in the PC Hardware table. In the Vendors table, there is only one record for General Comp, while in the PC Hardware table there are three (many) records for General Comp.

To Join Two Tables with One-to-Many Relationship

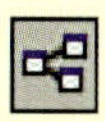

1 With the Hardware Inventory database open, click the Relationships button.

The Relationships dialog box is displayed (see Figure 11.5). The Relationships dialog box enables you to create and edit relationships between tables.

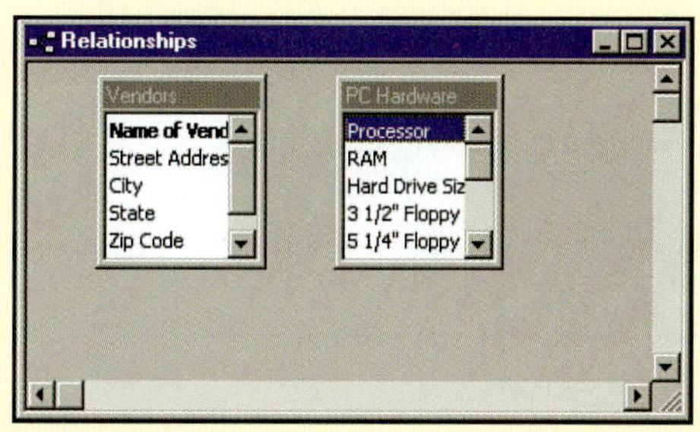

Figure 11.5
The Vendors and PC Hardware tables are displayed in the Relationships dialog box before the link is established.

2 Scroll down to the bottom of the list of fields in the PC Hardware list.

Foreign key
The corresponding field in another table that is linked to the primary key.

Notice that the Name of Vendor field in the Vendors table is indicated in boldface type. This is because it is the key field in the Vendors table. The corresponding field in the PC Hardware table, Name of Vendor, is not in boldface type because it is not the key field in the PC Hardware table. When the tables are linked, the non-key field is identified as the *foreign key*. It is important that you know which field from which table is identified in this manner (see Figure 11.6).

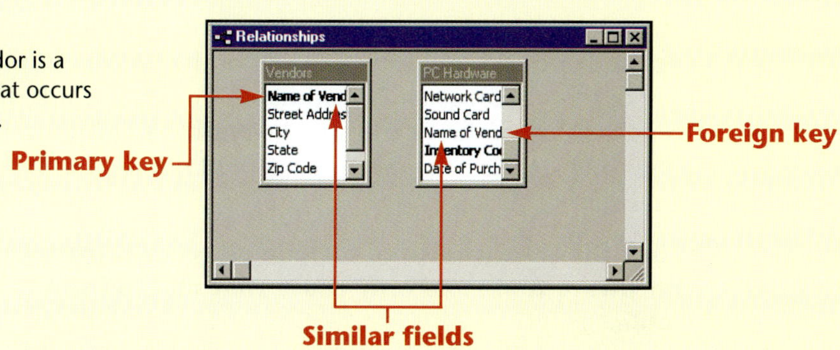

Figure 11.6
Name of Vendor is a similar field that occurs in both tables.

continues

To Join Two Tables with One-to-Many Relationship (continued)

3 Click the Name of Vendor field name in the Vendors list to select it.

4 Click and drag this field name to the corresponding field, Name of Vendor, in the PC Hardware field list, and then release the mouse.

This creates a relationship between the two tables. Once this relationship is created, you are able to create queries that draw from both tables.

A second Relationships dialog box appears showing that the Name of Vendor field from both tables has been linked (see Figure 11.7).

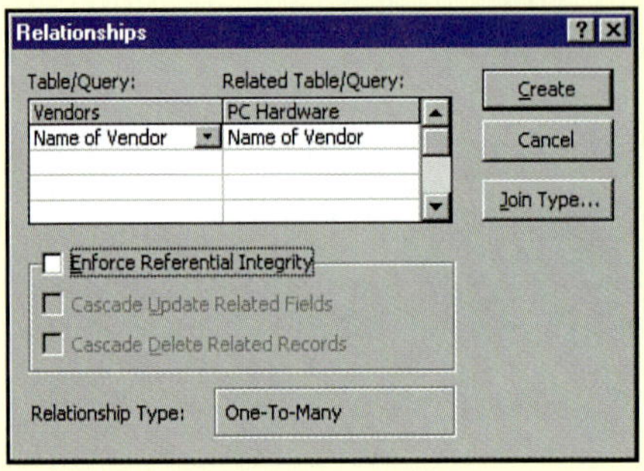

Figure 11.7
The second Relationships dialog box shows that the two tables have been linked on the Name of Vendor field.

5 Click the Join Type button to view the options.

The Join Properties dialog box appears (see Figure 11.8).

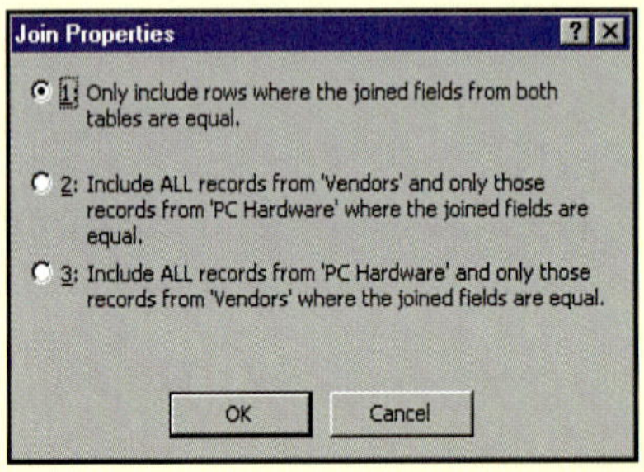

Figure 11.8
The Join Properties dialog box enables you to specify the type of join you want to use.

These join properties influence the query you create in a following lesson. For this example, you list all of the PC Hardware records and any of the vendor records that match. In other words, if you have a vendor listed in the Vendors table, but have not purchased any PCs from them, their name and address will not appear in the following query.

6 Click the third choice to include all records from the PC Hardware table and only those that match from the Vendors table.

7 Click OK to return to the second Relationships box.

Access

8 Select the Enforce Referential Integrity text box.

Checking this box prevents the user from entering a record in the PC Hardware table that does not have a corresponding entry in the Vendors table (see Figure 11.9). Likewise, you cannot delete a record in the Vendors table as long as it is related to records in the PC Hardware table. Enforcing referential integrity prevents having orphan records in the many table.

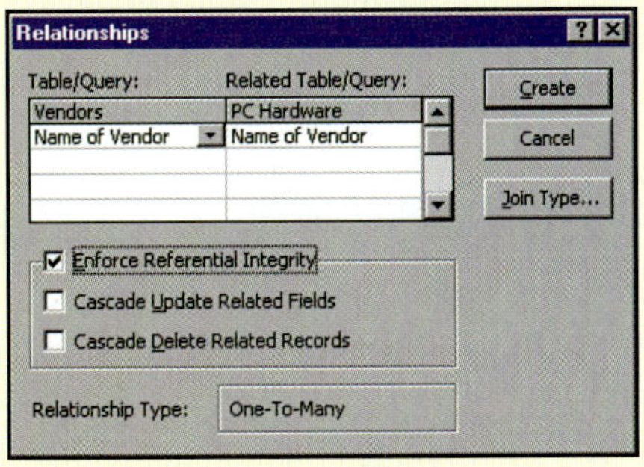

Figure 11.9 The second Relationships dialog box is shown after Enforce Referential Integrity has been selected.

When this box is checked you also have two other options. If you select Cascade Update Related Fields, changes in the Vendor table are automatically transferred to the PC Hardware table. For example, if the General Comp company changes its name to Allied Computers, all occurrences of its name would be changed in the PC Hardware table, as well. Similarly, if you select Cascade Delete Related Records, deleting a vendor name from the Vendors table would delete all related records from the PC Hardware table.

These two features should be used sparingly and only after careful consideration. Do not select either of them for this example.

9 Click Create to establish the relationship.

The Relationships box appears with a new line displaying the one-to-many relationship (see Figure 11.10).

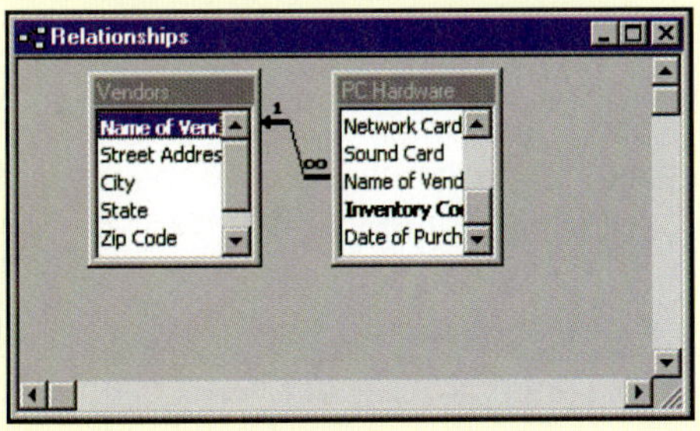

Figure 11.10 A one-to-many relationship has been created.

10 Close the Relationships box.

Access automatically saves the new relationship.

Keep the database open for the next lesson.

Lesson 3: Creating Queries That Draw Data from Both Tables

Queries can be used to look at subsets of data from a single table or to combine fields from more than one table. Since the queries draw from existing tables, they do not take up large amounts of space on your disk. This lets you create as many special-purpose queries as you desire. Queries can also be used as the basis for forms. If a form requires data from more than one table, it should be based on a query.

In this lesson, you learn how to create a query that includes data from the Vendors table and from the PC Hardware table.

To Create a Query Based on Two Tables

1. **With the Hardware Inventory database open, click the Queries tab.**

2. **Click the New button.**

   The New Query dialog box appears (see Figure 11.11).

   In this exercise, you design your own query. The other options that appear in the dialog box are query wizards that are used for specific purposes. You can click each option and read the explanation on the left side of the dialog box to get a brief description of what each wizard will do.

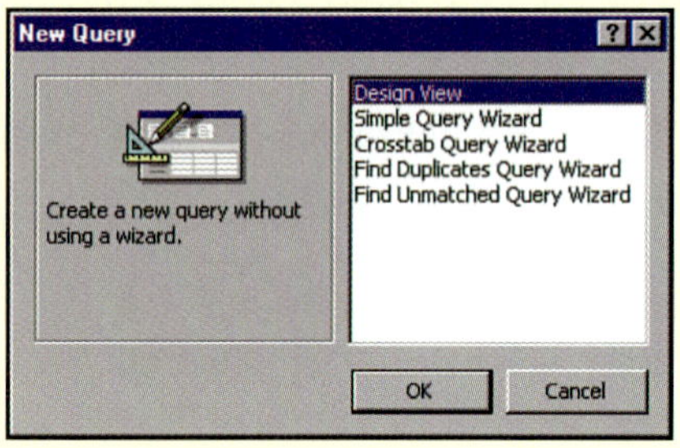

Figure 11.11 Use the New Query dialog box to start a query.

3. **Click Design View to select it, and then click OK.**

   The Select Query window opens with the Show Table dialog box in front of it (see Figure 11.12).

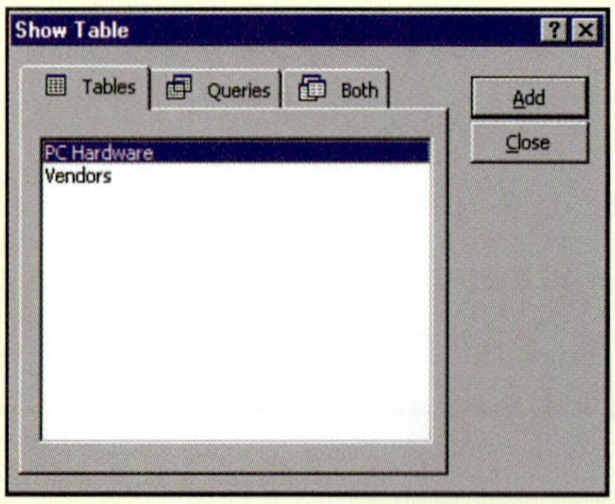

Figure 11.12 The Show Table dialog box opens in front of the Select Query window.

Access

4. **Click PC Hardware from the list to select it, and then click the Add button to add the PC Hardware table to the Select Query window in the background.**

5. **Click Vendors to select the table, and then click the Add button to add the Vendors table to the Select Query window.**

6. **Click the Close button to close the Show Table dialog box.**

   The Select Query window becomes active, showing that the Vendors table and the PC Hardware table have been selected for use in this query. The relationship between the tables is also shown, although the Name of Vendor field is hidden for the PC Hardware table.

7. **Click the maximize button in the upper-right corner of the Select Query window to maximize the window.**

8. **Point your mouse pointer at the thick line dividing the Select Query window into two parts. When the mouse pointer turns into a double-headed black arrow, click and drag the line down to expand the upper portion of the window (see Figure 11.13).**

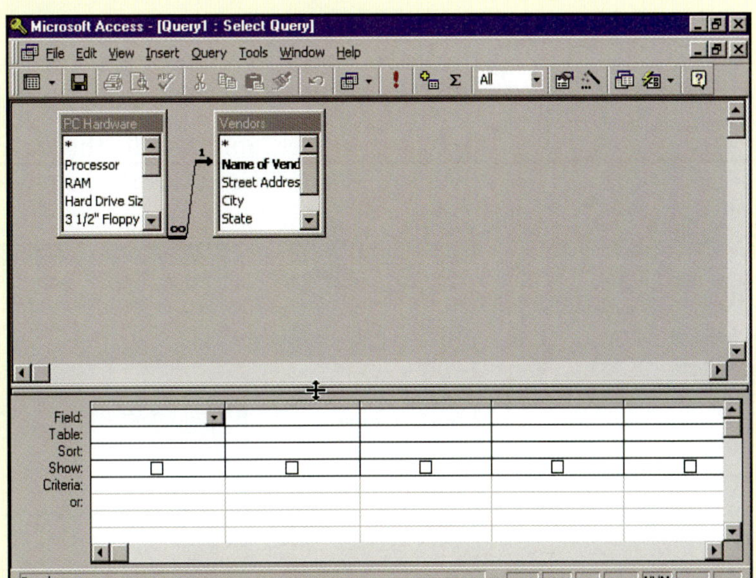

Figure 11.13
The upper portion of the Select Query window has been expanded.

9. **Point to the lower edge of the PC Hardware list box. When the mouse pointer turns into a double-headed black arrow, drag the lower edge of the box until you can see all of the field names. Do the same for the Vendors list box.**

   You can also drag the right border of each box (to the right) to adjust the size and position of the boxes so you can see the full length of the field names (see Figure 11.14).

continues

To Create a Query Based on Two Tables (continued)

Notice that the Name of Vendor field is the key field in the Vendors table, but it is not the key field in the PC Hardware table.

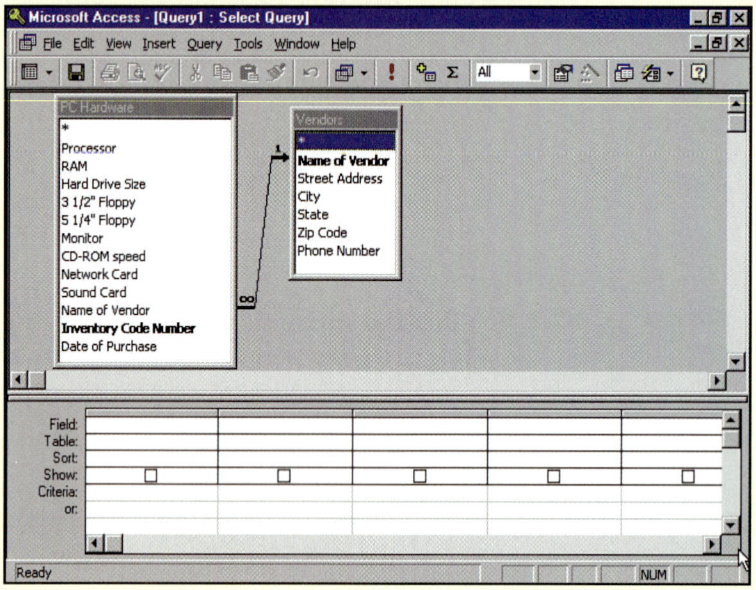

Figure 11.14
The Select Query window includes the two expanded table list boxes on which you want to base your query.

10 Drag the Name of Vendor field from the PC Hardware list to the first Field box in the query design area.

Notice that the Table box in the query design indicates that this field comes from the PC Hardware table (see Figure 11.15).

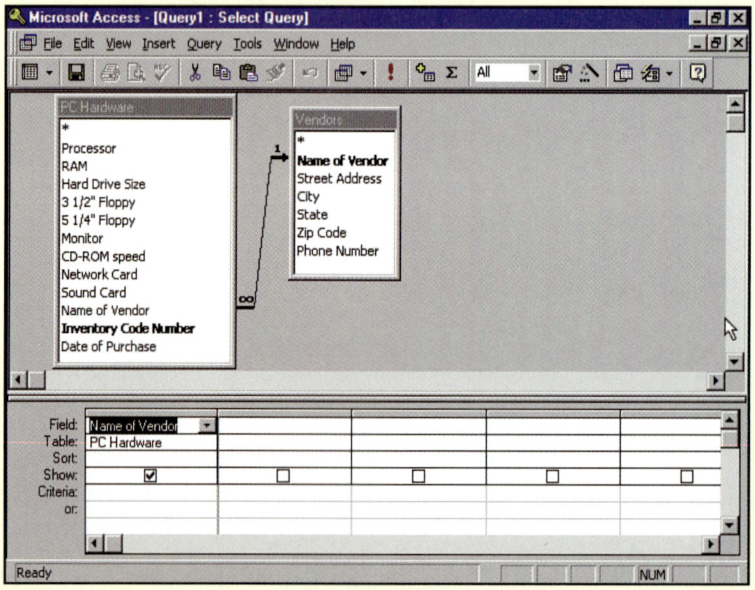

Figure 11.15
The foreign key field, Name of Vendor, is selected from the PC Hardware table.

The foreign key is used in this case to enable automatic updates. This feature is explained later in this project.

Access

In the next several steps, additional fields are moved to the query design. These fields are being selected so that a maintenance contact list can be created with pertinent information needed to call for repair or maintenance.

11. **Drag the Phone Number field from the Vendors table to the second Field box of the query design.**

12. **Drag the Processor field and then the Inventory Code Number field from the PC Hardware list to the next two fields of the query design.**

13. **Use the horizontal scrollbar to reveal the next available column, if necessary.**

14. **Drag the Date of Purchase field from the PC Hardware table to the next available Field box.**

The final query design should look like Figure 11.16.

Figure 11.16
The completed query design includes five fields.

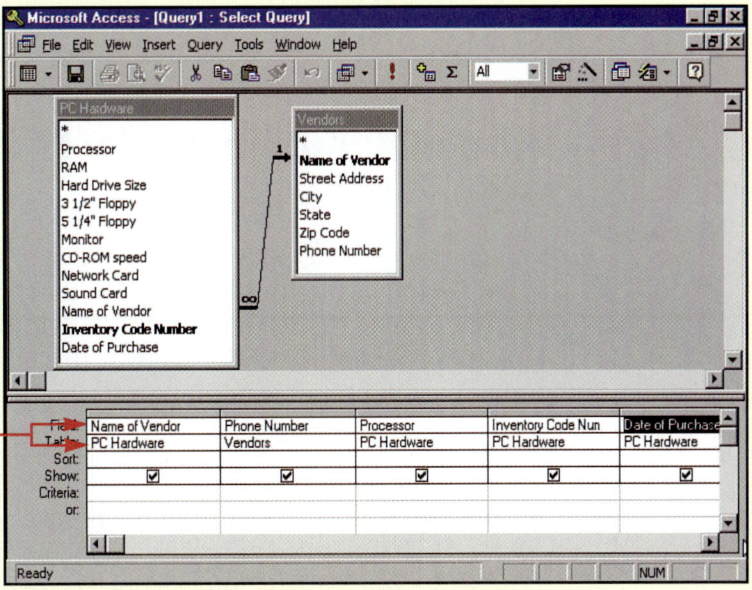

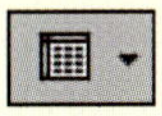

15. **Click the View button to switch to the Datasheet view.**

The query displays the *dynaset* of data from both tables (see Figure 11.17).

Dynaset
A temporary table of data that is assembled from other tables and is not stored as a separate table.

16. **Close the query, and click Yes to save the changes.**

17. **When prompted for a Query Name, type `Vendor Name and Phone Number for each PC`, and then click OK.**

Keep the database open for the next lesson.

continues

To Create a Query Based on Two Tables (continued)

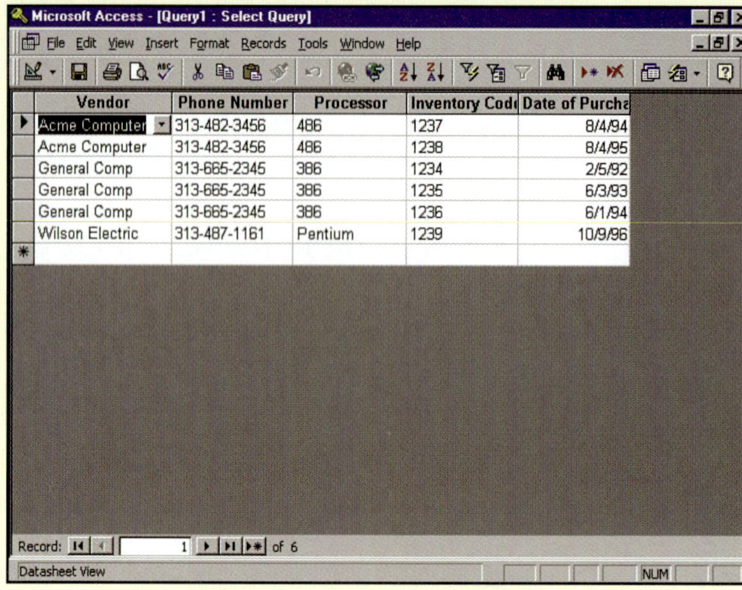

Figure 11.17
The query dynaset appears when you switch to the Datasheet view.

Lesson 4: Automatically Filling In Data from One of the Joined Tables

When you create a query that is based on joined tables, you need to be careful how you deal with the two fields that are used to join the tables. In the Vendors table, the Name of Vendor field was the primary key. The corresponding Name of Vendor field in the PC Hardware table that is used to join the tables is called the foreign key.

When you design a query that draws data from two or more tables, you can get it to fill in some of the fields automatically by selecting the foreign key of the linked fields rather than the primary key. In the example that will be used, the Name of Vendor field from the PC Hardware table will be used. This is the foreign key. Information relative to that vendor will be added to the query from the Vendors table. When new data is entered using this query, the fields that have been added from the Vendors table will be automatically filled in once the Name of Vendor (foreign key) has been entered. This saves time in entering repetitive data and helps to ensure that the information entered is correct.

To Automatically Fill In Fields from Joined Tables

1. **In the Hardware Inventory database, click the Queries tab, if necessary.**
2. **Click New to design a new query.**
3. **Select Design view and then click OK.**

4 Add both tables to the query design and close the Show Table dialog box.

5 Scroll down and drag the Name of Vendor field from the PC Hardware list of fields to the first Field box in the query design.

Notice that this field is at the many end of the join line, distinguished by the infinity symbol. It is the foreign key.

6 Add the Street Address, City, State, Zip Code, and Phone Number fields from the Vendors list to the next five Field boxes in the query design.

Your query design window should look like Figure 11.18.

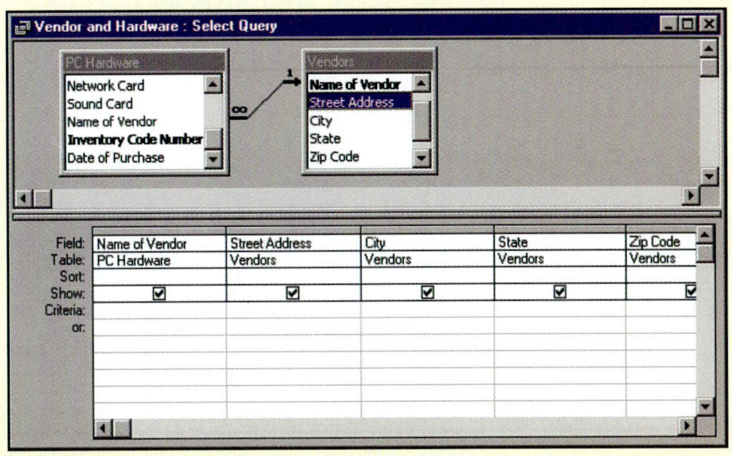

Figure 11.18
The query design window after the vendor information has been added.

7 Add the remaining fields from the PC Hardware list by selecting every field except the Name of Vendor field, and then click and drag the group of fields to the next open field in the query.

Access will spread out the fields, one to each of the next available query fields. Be sure you do not include the Name of Vendor a second time.

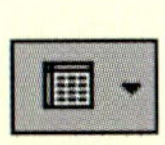

8 Click the View button to view the dynaset.

9 Go to the bottom of the list and click in the empty Vendors field.

Notice that the Lookup list included in the table design also works in the query.

10 Click the list button to reveal the list of vendors (see Figure 11.19).

continues

To Automatically Fill In Fields from Joined Tables (continued)

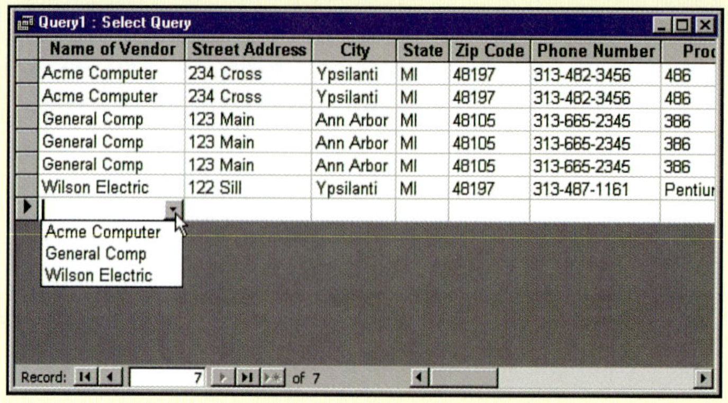

Figure 11.19
The list of vendors from the Vendors table appears in the query.

11 Click Acme Computer to select it.

Access automatically retrieves the data from the other fields in the Vendors table that have been included in the query (see Figure 11.20).

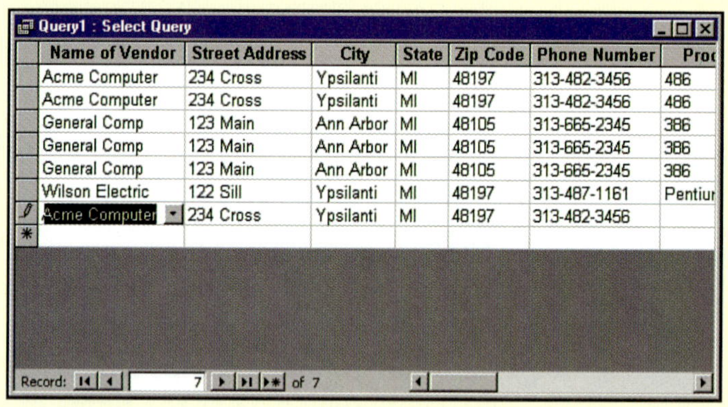

Figure 11.20
Data from the Vendors table is automatically filled in.

12 Do not enter a new record at this time. Press the Esc key to abort the input process.

13 Close the query, and click Yes to save the changes.

14 When prompted for a Query Name, type `Vendor and Hardware`, and then click OK.

Keep the database open for the next lesson.

Access

Exam Notes

There are several timesaving shortcuts available when you add fields in the query design window. You can double-click a field name to add it to the query design in the next available Field box. You can also click the down arrow in a Field box and select the field from the drop-down list. To select several fields at once, click the first name in the list and Shift+click a name farther down the list to select those two fields plus all of the field names between them. You can then drag the whole list over to the next available Field box. Finally, you can click one field to select it, and then select one or more nonadjacent fields by holding down Ctrl and clicking the other fields you want to select.

Lesson 5: Updating Tables by Entering or Deleting Data in the Query

Queries can be used to enter data into the tables they are based on. This must be done with care. In some cases, you will get error messages that are difficult to understand. In this lesson, you will learn some guidelines for successful data entry and how to interpret some of the error messages that you may receive.

To Enter New PC Hardware Data Using the Vendor and Hardware Query

1. **In the Hardware Inventory database, select the `Vendor and Hardware` query and click the Open button.**

2. **Go to the bottom of the list and click in the empty Vendors field.**

   Use the list button to reveal the list of vendor companies.

3. **Select `Acme Computer` from the drop-down list.**

   The remaining fields that are linked to the Vendors table are filled in automatically.

4. **Press Tab until you get to the Processor field.**

   Enter the following data in the remaining fields in this record. (Use the mouse to click the check box to indicate the presence of a floppy drive or sound card. You can also press the Spacebar to place the check mark in the box or Tab to skip over a box and leave it empty.)

   ```
   Power PC
   16
   800
   Check mark for the 3 1/2" Floppy
   No check mark for the 5 1/4" Floppy
   SVGA
   4X
   Yes
   Check mark for Sound Card
   1240
   6/6/97
   ```

5. **Close the query.**

6. **Click on the Tables tab and open the `PC Hardware` table in the Datasheet view.**

continues

To Enter New PC Hardware Data Using the Vendor and Hardware Query (continued)

Notice that the new PC has been entered in the table (see Figure 11.21).

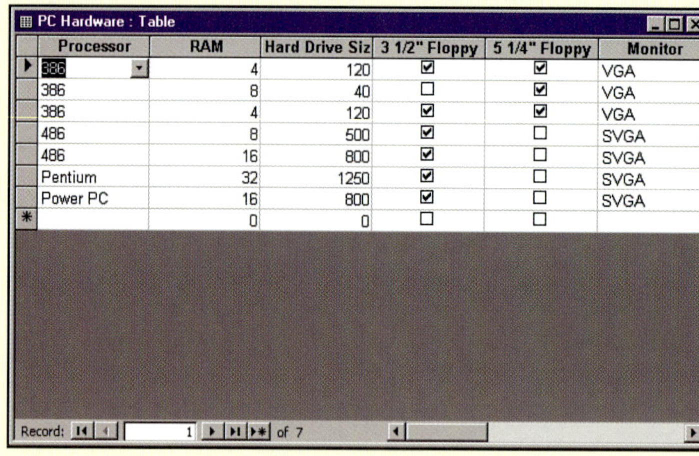

Processor	RAM	Hard Drive Siz	3 1/2" Floppy	5 1/4" Floppy	Monitor
386	4	120	☑	☑	VGA
386	8	40	☐	☑	VGA
386	4	120	☑	☑	VGA
486	8	500	☑	☐	SVGA
486	16	800	☑	☐	SVGA
Pentium	32	1250	☑	☐	SVGA
Power PC	16	800	☑	☐	SVGA
	0	0	☐	☐	

Figure 11.21
The PC Hardware table includes the new record for the Power PC.

7 **Close the PC Hardware table, click the Queries tab and open the `Vendor and Hardware` query in the Datasheet view.**

8 **Click the record selector button to select the record for the Power PC that you just entered.**

The record you just entered is not at the bottom of the record anymore (see Figure 11.22).

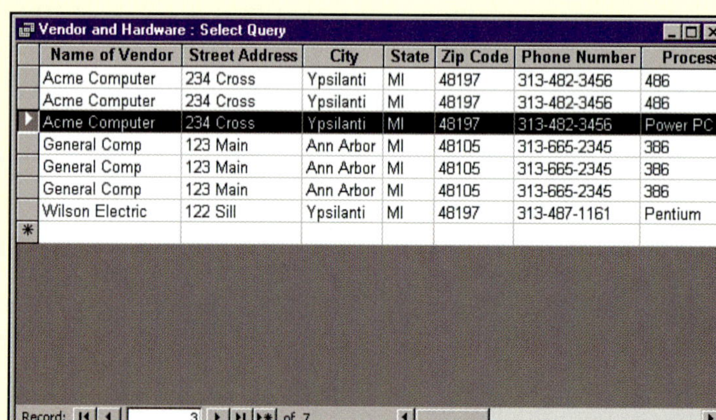

Name of Vendor	Street Address	City	State	Zip Code	Phone Number	Process
Acme Computer	234 Cross	Ypsilanti	MI	48197	313-482-3456	486
Acme Computer	234 Cross	Ypsilanti	MI	48197	313-482-3456	486
Acme Computer	234 Cross	Ypsilanti	MI	48197	313-482-3456	Power PC
General Comp	123 Main	Ann Arbor	MI	48105	313-665-2345	386
General Comp	123 Main	Ann Arbor	MI	48105	313-665-2345	386
General Comp	123 Main	Ann Arbor	MI	48105	313-665-2345	386
Wilson Electric	122 Sill	Ypsilanti	MI	48197	313-487-1161	Pentium

Figure 11.22
Because of automatic sorting, the record you just entered is no longer at the end of the table.

9 **Press the Del key on the keyboard to delete the record, and then click Yes to confirm that you want to delete the record.**

10 **Close the query.**

11 **Click the Tables tab and open the `PC Hardware` table in the Datasheet view.**

Confirm that the record has been deleted from the table.

12 **Close the table and close the database.**

Access

Inside Stuff

Fields that are formatted as Yes/No fields use a check box as the default format. If you prefer a different format, change the format in Design view.

You should not try to change the contents of the Name of Vendor field from this query. The Name of Vendor field in this query is the foreign key from the PC Hardware table, not the primary key field from the Vendors table. When we defined the join between these two tables, we specified that referential integrity should be enforced. This meant that there could not be a value in the Name of Vendor field in the PC Hardware table that did not already exist in the Vendors table. Use the list box to select an existing vendor.

This query also contains the primary key field from the PC Hardware table, Inventory Code Number. When you use this query to add new records to the PC Hardware table, you must enter a new inventory code number that is not the same as any other code number in the table. If you leave this field empty or enter a duplicate number, you get an error message. If you want to back out of this record and start over, press the Esc key.

Lesson 6: Finding Duplicate Records in an Existing Table

In some cases, you inherit a table of data from another source where the data entry was not carefully controlled. This table may contain duplicate entries that are difficult to find. Locating duplicates can be useful when you append two data tables together and are uncertain if there is a duplication of some records. It is also useful to look for duplicates when you want to establish a field as the primary key field but are uncertain if there are duplicates in that field.

Find Duplicates Query Wizard
Creates a query that finds records with duplicate field values in a single table or query.

Find Unmatched Query Wizard
Creates a query that finds records in one table that have no related records in another table.

Fortunately, Access provides a special query that can be used to locate duplicate records. The *Find Duplicates Query Wizard* creates a query that lists the duplicate values in a single table or query.

Another type of error may occur when two related tables have records in one table without corresponding records in the second table. This occurs when referential integrity has not been enforced. The *Find Unmatched Query Wizard* can be used to locate these types of errors. Both of these special purpose queries work in a similar manner. In this lesson, you use the Find Duplicates Query Wizard to locate duplicate entries in a database of economic data. (The database used in this lesson was compiled by the government and contains information about the number of service businesses in each ZIP code area in Michigan. Some duplicate records have been added for this exercise.) The database does not have a primary key, but the natural choice is the ZIP code. When we try to set a primary key, we get an error message that says there is a duplicate value in the primary key, indexed field, or relationship.

We could scroll through the records looking for the duplicate, but there are over 900 records and we do not know how many duplicates there are! This is an instance where we need the Find Duplicates Query Wizard.

To Find Duplicate Entries

1 Make a copy of the Proj1102 database file from the Project-11 folder on the CD and name the copy `Service Businesses in Michigan-1987`**. Return to Access and open the** `Service Businesses in Michigan-1987` **database.**

2 Click the Queries tab, and then click New.

The New Query dialog box is opened (see Figure 11.23).

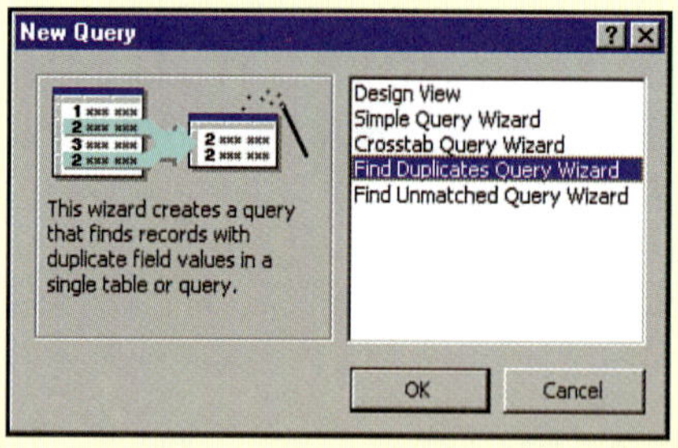

Figure 11.23
The New Query dialog box enables you to select the wizard you want to use.

3 Select the Find Duplicates Query Wizard, and then click OK.

The first Find Duplicates Query Wizard dialog box is displayed (see Figure 11.24).

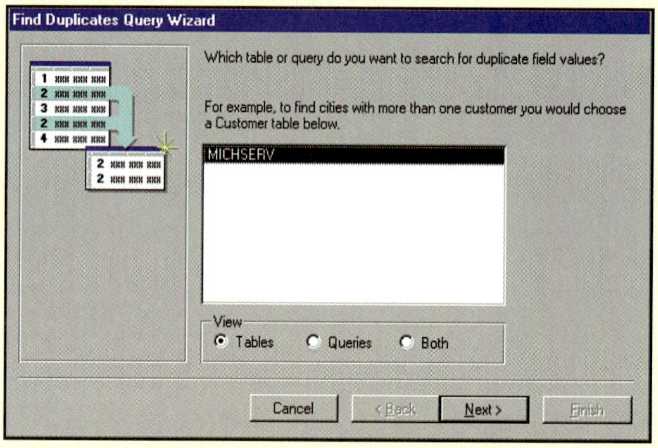

Figure 11.24
The first Find Duplicates Query Wizard dialog box asks which table or query you want to search for duplicates.

4 Click the Next button to accept the default selection of the MICHSERV table.

The second Find Duplicates Query Wizard dialog box is displayed (see Figure 11.25).

5 Click the ZIP field to select it.

6 Click the Select button to move the ZIP field into the Duplicate-value fields box, and then click Next to move to the next dialog box.

The third Find Duplicates Query Wizard dialog box is displayed (see Figure 11.26).

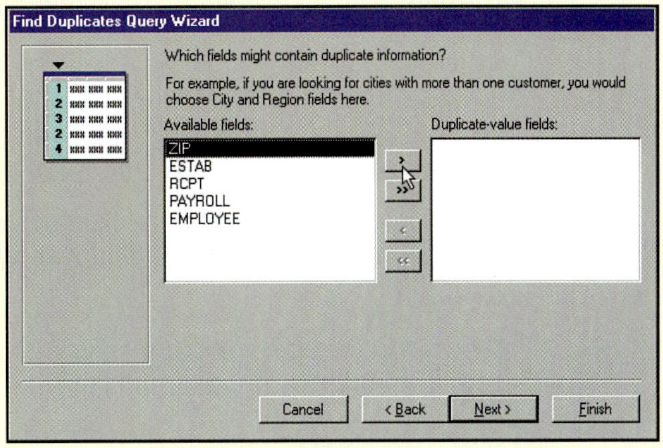

Figure 11.25
The second Find Duplicates Query Wizard dialog box asks which fields might contain the duplicate information.

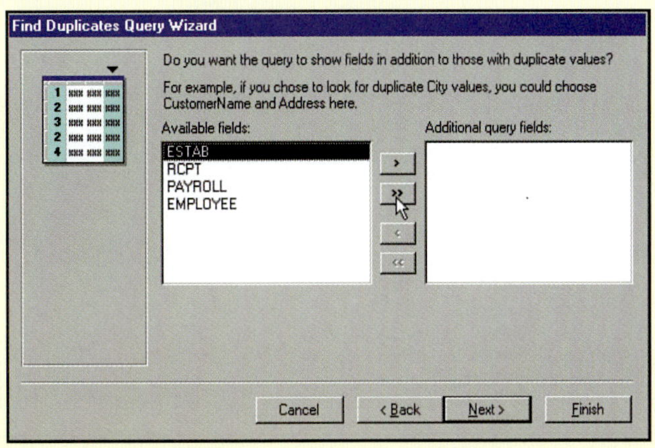

Figure 11.26
Use the third Find Duplicates Query Wizard dialog box to specify other fields you want to use in the Find.

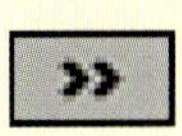

7 Click the Select All button, which selects and moves all of the remaining fields into the Additional query fields box.

These additional fields help you to determine how to deal with the duplicate records when you find them.

8 Click the Finish button.

This accepts the default name for the query and displays the final results of your query (see Figure 11.27). It shows each instance of a duplicate entry in the ZIP field, and also shows the contents of each of the other four fields.

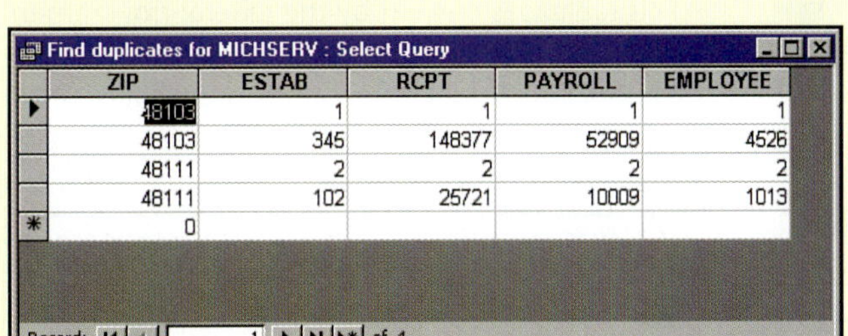
Find duplicates for MICHSERV : Select Query

ZIP	ESTAB	RCPT	PAYROLL	EMPLOYEE
48103	1	1	1	1
48103	345	148377	52909	4526
48111	2	2	2	2
48111	102	25721	10009	1013
0				

Record: 1 of 4

Figure 11.27
The Find duplicates for MICHSERV: Select Query found two sets of duplicate ZIP code entries.

continues

To Find Duplicate Entries (continued)

When you display the duplicate entries, you need to decide what to do with them. In this example, the two entries for each of the ZIP codes might need to be added together. Let's assume that you do a little research and find that the smaller duplicate entries are errors.

9. **Click the record selector to the left of the first record for ZIP code 48103 (the one that shows 1 in the ESTAB field) and delete it.**

10. **Delete the next erroneous record (the one that shows 2 in the ESTAB field) for ZIP code 48111.**

11. **Close the query.**

Access creates a query called `Find duplicates for MICHSERV` (see Figure 11.28).

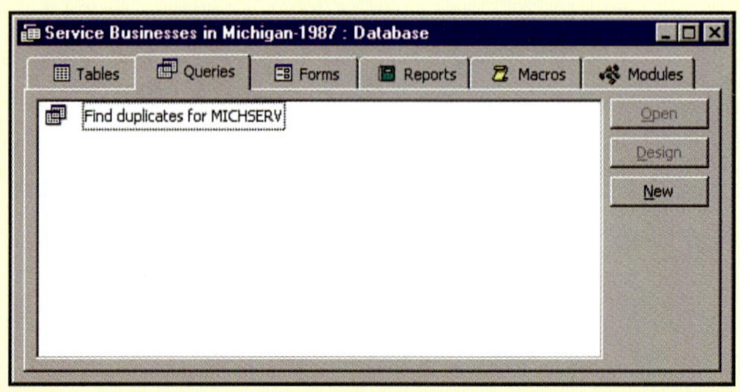

Figure 11.28
Access created the query and automatically named it Find duplicates for MICHSERV.

The MICHSERV table can now use the ZIP field as a primary key. (Do not perform that operation at this time.)

12. **Close the database and close Access, unless you want to continue working on the following exercises.**

If you have completed your session on the computer, exit Access and shut down Windows before you turn off the computer. Otherwise, continue with the "Checking Your Skills" and "Applying Your Skills" sections in this project.

Inside Stuff

This table was created by the federal government using a database program called dBASE III. Programs that use older operating systems that predate Windows 95 (not including Macintosh computers) were restricted to filenames of eight characters or less. Notice how much more descriptive your filename of `Service Businesses in Michigan-1987` is compared to `MICHSERV`.

Project Summary

To	Do This
Design related tables to hold repetitive data	Create separate tables to hold data that would otherwise have to be entered repeatedly. Make sure related tables contain fields of similar data types that can be joined.
Define the relationship between the tables	Use the Relationships option from the Tools menu to select the tables to be joined. Drag a connection between the two related fields. Identify the type of join, and then decide whether to enforce data integrity and whether to cascade deletes and updates.
Create queries that draw data from both tables	Add both tables to the query design. Drag fields from either table to the query.
Automatically fill in data from a joined table	Add both tables to the query design. Add the foreign key from one table, and the fields you want to automatically fill from the table with the corresponding primary key.
Update tables by entering or deleting data in the query	Open the query in Datasheet view. When you enter a value for the foreign key, the other fields from the corresponding table will be automatically filled in. Do not try to enter a new value in the foreign key field.
Find duplicate records in an existing table	Create a new query designed for that purpose using the Find Duplicates Query Wizard. Identify the field you want to check, and then add fields that help you identify what to do with duplicate records.

Checking Your Skills

True/False

For each of the following statements, check *T* or *F* to indicate whether the statement is true or false.

__T __F **1.** It is best to put as many fields as possible in the same table to keep the organization of the database as simple as possible.

__T __F **2.** If there is one record for Sally Jones in a table of employee records and her name occurs several times in a table of sales commissions, those two tables could be linked in a one-to-many relationship.

__T __F **3.** When you create a query that automatically fills in fields from table A, you drag the primary key from table A into the query design.

__T __F **4.** The contents of tables cannot be changed by entering new data into queries.

__T __F **5.** A special wizard exists to help you find unmatched records between two tables.

__T __F **6.** To create a query based on two tables, both tables must have a field with the same name and data type.

__T __F **7.** A lookup list can be created to look up values in a field from a different table.

__T __F **8.** When you create a Find Duplicates query, you need to include enough fields to enable you to decide what to do with the duplicate records.

__T __F **9.** The Find Duplicates query is used when referential integrity has not been enforced and you are looking for duplicate records between two tables.

__T __F **10.** To base a form on more than one table, you can first create a query that is based on those tables and then base your form on the query.

Multiple Choice

Circle the letter of the correct answer for each of the following questions.

1. One-to-many means _____.

a. one field can have many different entries

b. one record can relate to many records in a different table

c. one table can have many records

d. one database can have many tables

2. In a one-to-many relationship, _____.

a. the field in the many table is the foreign key

b. the field in the one table is the foreign key

c. the field in the many table is the primary key

d. neither field is indexed

3. To create a query that automatically fills in data from one of the joined tables, _____.

a. use the primary key and the other fields from the same table

b. use the foreign key from the second table and the other fields from the table that has the primary key

c. select a one-to-one join

d. select Automatic Fill from the Tools menu

4. The best way to find records that have the same entry in a given field is to _____.

a. use the Find Unmatched Query Wizard

b. use the Find Duplicates Query Wizard

c. scroll down the list and visually inspect the contents of the fields

d. sort the table using the sort button on the toolbar. If there are duplicates, a message appears asking if you want to delete them

5. If you have created a query that uses a foreign key and fills in fields automatically, _____.

   a. you should not try to enter a completely new value in the foreign key field

   b. you can change any field in either table

   c. you can only change values in the table that contains the primary key of the two joined fields

   d. you can only look at the contents of the table without making any changes

6. When you select enforce referential integrity in a relationship, it means _____.

   a. you cannot enter a record in the many table that does not have a corresponding entry in the one table

   b. you cannot delete a record in the one table that has an entry in the many table

   c. your data is protected from having orphan records

   d. all of the above

7. To create a query on your own, use the query _____.

   a. Design Wizard

   b. Datasheet view

   c. Design view

   d. template

8. To change the size of the field list box, point to the edge of the box and drag the edge of the box when the mouse pointer turns into a _____.

   a. a pointing finger

   b. an open hand

   c. double-headed black arrow

   d. a single-headed vertical arrow

9. To include a field in a query _____.

   a. click on the field and drag it to an open field box

   b. double-click on the field name

   c. click on the down arrow in the field box and select the field

   d. all of the above

10. To create a join between tables click the relationship button, and then _____.

   a. drag the primary key field from one table to the matching field in the second table and click the Create button in the second relationship window

   b. click the Join button to join the two tables, and then specify the fields that are to be joined

   c. make sure the field names and data types are the same

   d. click the Join button, match the fields, select enforce referential integrity, and save your changes

Completion

In the blank provided, write the correct answer for each of the following statements.

1. A relationship that links one record in a table to many records in a different table is called a ______________ relationship.
2. A temporary table of data that is assembled from other tables and is not stored as a separate table is called a(n) ______________.
3. The corresponding field in another table that is linked to the primary key is called a(n) ______________.
4. To find fields that contain the same entry, use the ______________ Wizard.
5. To find records in two tables that do not contain matching entries, use the ______________ Wizard.
6. In the Relationship dialog box, if you select ______________ Related Fields, changes in the primary key table are automatically transferred to the foreign key table.
7. To create a join between two tables, click the ______________ button.
8. To place a check mark in a Yes/No data field using the keyboard, press the ______________ key.
9. When entering a record, you can back out of the record if necessary by pressing the ______________ key.
10. A field name that appears in boldface type in a field list is the ______________.

Matching

In the blank next to each of the following terms or phrases, write the letter of the corresponding term or phrase. (Note that some letters may be used more than once.)

a. join line
b. infinity symbol
c. double-click
d. Create
e. Enforce Referential Integrity
f. primary
g. Find Duplicates
h. query
i. foreign
j. dynaset

_____ 1. In the Relationships dialog box, click this button to establish the relationship between two tables

_____ 2. A type of key field in the query that enables fields to be filled in automatically

_____ 3. Visually shows the relationship between two tables

_____ 4. Contained in one side of a relationship

_____ 5. The results of running a query

_____ 6. When creating a query, do this to a field to add it to the query design

_____ 7. Can be used to update records

_____ 8. Ensures that two related tables will not have unmatched records

_______ **9.** A special purpose query wizard

_______ **10.** Visually identifies the many sides of a relationship

Applying Your Skills

Practice

The following exercises enable you to practice the skills you have learned in this project.

Enforcing Referential Integrity in Your Library Database

In this exercise, you have a database that has a table of information about the books in your library and another table that tracks the books others have borrowed from you. When this database was created, referential integrity between the two tables was not enforced, so it is possible that a book was loaned out before it was recorded in the master list of books.

To check the referential integrity of an existing relationship, complete the following steps:

1. Copy the file Proj1103 from the Project-11 folder on the CD and rename the copy as `Library9`.
2. Open `Library9`.

   Notice that there are two tables, one that lists the books in the library and one that lists the books that have been borrowed. Every book that has been borrowed should be listed in the table of books in the library.
3. Select Tools, Relationships from the menu.
4. Double-click the line that joins the tables to display the Relationships dialog box.

   Notice that the Enforce Referential Integrity box was not selected when this relationship was established. There may be unmatched records in the Borrowed table.
5. Select the Enforce Referential Integrity box and click OK.

   An error message appears. There are unmatched records in the Borrowed table.
6. Click OK to acknowledge the message.

   Close the Relationships window. You work with this problem in the next section.

Finding an Unmatched Record

In Lesson 6, you learned how to use a query design wizard to find duplicate records. In this case, you can use a similar wizard to find unmatched records.

To find an unmatched record, complete the following steps:

1. Open the `Library9` database, if necessary.
2. Click the Queries tab.
3. Click New to start a new query.
4. Use the Find Unmatched Query Wizard to find the borrowed book that is not listed in the Books table.
5. When you have identified the book, enter a new record in the Books table for this book. The author is `Robert Heinlein`, and the name of the book, as you found out in the previous step, is `Notebooks of Lazarus Long`. It is a science fiction book that was originally published in 1978. (The type of book is not limited to those in the attached list. You may enter a new type, such as Science Fiction.)
6. Go back to the previous exercise and follow those steps to enforce referential integrity. It should work now that there are no unmatched records. (Make sure that the Title is an exact match in both tables. It is the joined field.)

   Leave the database open for use in the next exercise.

Creating a Query Based on Two Tables

In a previous lesson, you learned how to use a query design wizard to find duplicate records. In this case, you can use a similar wizard to find unmatched records.

To create a query based on two tables, complete the following steps:

1. Open the `Library9` database, if necessary.
2. Click the Queries tab.
3. Click New to start a new query and choose Design View.
4. Add both tables to the query design and close the Show Table window.

   Notice the relationship between the two tables is displayed as one-to-many.
5. Select the Book Title field from the Borrow table (not the Books table) as the first field in the query design.
6. Select the Author Last Name and Type of Book fields from the Books table.
7. Select the rest of the fields from the Borrow table.
8. Switch to Datasheet view. Click the New Record button on the navigation bar and enter the name of one of the books shown.

   When you press Enter, the information in the next two fields appears automatically.
9. Make up a name, phone number, and date and enter them in the following fields.
10. Close the query and name it `Books on Loan`.

11. Open the `Borrow` table. The new record should be in the table.
12. Close the table and the database.

Enforcing Referential Integrity for the Sound Byte Music Company

A database for a small music retail business keeps a table of music orders and a table of suppliers. Each order table has an entry for the supplier that should match an entry in the supplier table.

To check for unmatched records in the Orders and Suppliers Tables, complete the following steps:

1. Copy the database Proj1104 from the Project-11 folder on the CD and name the new file `Sound Byte Music9`.
2. Open the new database.
3. Choose Tools, Relationships to determine which fields are linked between the Orders and Suppliers tables.
4. Double-click the link between the two tables.

   The Relationship window opens. Notice that the Relationship Type is listed as Indeterminate. This relationship was created before the Record Company field was made the primary key of the Suppliers table. This needs to be changed to a one-to-many relationship if we are to enforce referential integrity.
5. Click Cancel to close the Relationships window.
6. Confirm that the relationship line between the two tables is still selected and press Del.
7. Drag a new relationship between the Record Company field and the Supplier Name field.

   The Relationships window opens again and indicates that the type of relationship is now a one-to-many.
8. Click the Enforce Referential Integrity option box, and then click Create.

   An error message appears that informs you that there are unmatched records.
9. Click the Queries tab, and then click New to create a new query.
10. Use the Find Unmatched Query Wizard to look for unmatched records in the Orders table that do not have a matching record in the Suppliers table.
11. Compare the name of the supplier in the unmatched order to the Record company name in the Suppliers table to determine why there is no match.

    Notice that one mismatch was caused by entering the name of the company incorrectly. Open the Orders table and correct that mistake. The second error results from a missing record company. Add that company to the Suppliers table. Make sure the name matches but make up an address.

12. Run the Unmatched Records query again. It should have no records this time.
13. Click the Relationships button and drag a relationship between the Record Company field and the Supplier Name field.
14. Select Enforce Referential Integrity, and then click OK.

    The relationship should display a one at one end and an infinity symbol at the other to indicate a successful one-to-many relationship.

15. Close the Relationships window and close the database.

Creating a Query Based on Two Tables in the Sound Byte Music Company

In a previous lesson, you enforced referential integrity and created a relationship that could be used in a query.

To create a query based on two tables in the Sound Byte Music Company, complete the following steps:

1. Open the `Sound Byte Music9` database, if necessary.
2. Click the Queries tab.
3. Click New to start a new query and choose Design view.
4. Add the Orders and Suppliers tables to the query design and close the Show Table window.

   Notice the relationship between the two tables is displayed as one-to-many.

5. Select the Supplier Name field (foreign key) from the Suppliers table as the first field in the query design.
6. Select the Contact Name and Phone fields from the Suppliers table.
7. Select the rest of the fields from the Orders table.
8. Switch to Datasheet view. Click the New Record button on the navigation bar and enter the name of one of the suppliers shown.

   When you press ↵Enter, the information in the next two fields appears automatically.

9. Make up values for the following fields.
10. Close the query and name it `Orders and Supplier Contact`.
11. Open the `Orders` table. The new record should be in the table.
12. Close the table and the database.

Challenge

The following challenges enable you to use your problem-solving skills.

Adding a Table, Relating to the Table, and Creating a Query Based on Both Tables

This database has been a single table design up to this point. If you want to track several donations or several months of dues payments, it needs a second table. Open the `Club` database that you have worked on in previous projects.

Open the `Membership` table in Design view and make sure that it has a Membership ID field that is used as the primary key field. If not, add such a field and use the Counter data type. Remember what the data type is for this field. Close the table.

Create a new table to track donations. Include a Member ID field, a donation field, and a date field. Make sure the Member ID field in this table is the same data type as in the other table.

Create a one-to-many relationship between the two tables using the Member ID field in each.

Create a query that uses the Member ID field from the Donations table (foreign key), two or three fields from the Members table, and the other fields from the Donations table. Save this query as `Names and Donations`.

Establishing Referential Integrity Among Tables

This database has four tables and three relationships. They were created without enforcing referential integrity so there could be orphan records.

Locate the Customer Research8 database that you worked on in the previous project and rename it `Customer Research10`, and then open the file. View the relationships.

Observe that each of the relationships is between the key field of one table to a non-key field of another table. All three of these relationships should be one-to-many. Double-click on one of the relationship lines and attempt to enforce referential integrity. This is easy to do in two of the three.

When you identify which relationship has a problem with unmatched records, close the Relationships window and run an unmatched records query to find the problem. (Warning: It makes a difference which table you pick first when looking for unmatched records. If your first try doesn't find the problem, run the query again but reverse the order of the two tables.) Fix it and then go back and enforce the referential integrity on that relationship, as well.

Create a query that uses two tables that are related directly to each other. Use the foreign key from one table and some additional fields from each table. Switch to the Datasheet view and test the query. Save it and name it `Two Table Query`. Do not use it to add a new record.

Enforcing Referential Integrity and Creating One-to-Many Relationships Among Tables

The tables in this database were created without concern for data integrity. In this exercise, you establish key fields where appropriate and create one-to-many relationships with referential integrity.

Locate the Vending8 database that you worked on in the previous project and rename it `Vending9`. Open the `Vending9` database and open the Relationships window. Notice that only one of these tables has a primary key (Locations). The Name of the Supplier should be a unique field in the Suppliers table and the Machine Type field should be the key field in the Machines table. Close the Relationships window and make those changes to the two tables.

Open the Relationships window again. Select and delete the old relationship lines and drag new ones. Enforce referential integrity.

Create a query that uses fields from the Locations and Machines tables. Name the query `Machines and Sites`.

Save your changes.

Revising Tables and Relationships in a Database

In this exercise, you remove three redundant fields from one of the tables, enforce referential integrity, and create a query based on three tables.

Locate the Video Store7 database and rename it `Video Store8`. Open the `Video Store8` database and click the Relationships button to view the relationships between the tables. Double-click one of the relationship lines to open the Relationships window. Click the check box to enforce referential integrity. Repeat this process for the other relationship. Close the Relationships window.

Study the fields in each of the three tables. The Video Tapes table has three fields that actually describe the rental activity. Open the `Video Tapes` table and delete the Currently Rented, Current Renter, and Number of Rentals fields.

Create a query that uses fields from all three tables. Do not include any of the fields that used to provide links between the tables. This tells you if it is necessary to include at least one link or not.

Switch to Datasheet view and test your messages. Save the query as `Three Tables`.

Changing a Relationship and Enforcing Referential Integrity

Database design becomes more important as the number of tables grows. In this exercise, you delete unnecessary fields and enforce referential integrity.

Locate the Home Inventory7 database that you used in the previous project and rename it `Home Inventory8`. Open the database and click the Relationships button. Change the relationship by adding referential integrity. Close the Relationships window.

Create a new query that includes the foreign key (Insurance Carrier in the Items table). Include all the other fields in the Insurance Companies table. Include the Name of the Item, Purchase Date, and Cost fields from the Items table. Switch to Datasheet view and check for errors.

Save your query as `Two Table Query`.

PinPoint Assessment

PinPoint Training

You have completed the project and the associated lessons, as well as the "Checking Your Skills" and "Applying Your Skills" sections. Now use the PinPoint software Evaluation mode to assess your comprehension of the specific exam tasks you have just learned. You can also use the PinPoint Trainer mode and the SHOW ME tutorials to practice these specific exam tasks.

Project 12 Twelve

Using Advanced Form Features

Features Can Be Added for Accuracy and Ease

In this project you will learn the following objectives and their associated Microsoft Exam required activities.

Objectives	Required Activities
➤ Add Formats in the Form Design View	
➤ Select Entries from a List	Improve Accuracy in Forms
➤ Look Up Valid Entries from a Table or Query	Improve Accuracy in Forms
➤ Use Information from Tables to Fill In Fields Automatically	
➤ Enter the Current Date in a Field Automatically	Enhance Design of a Form
➤ Add the Current Date and Time to a Form Automatically	Enhance Design of a Form
➤ Change the Tab Order	Modify Form Design
➤ Creating Subforms	Show Related Records on a Form Identify Appropriate Use for Subforms Add a Record with a Main Form Add Records with Subforms Merge Two Tables into a Form
➤ Print the Form for Filing Purposes	Print a Form

Why Would I Do This?

Consistent data input is one of the primary reasons for using a form. This is particularly true when several people are entering information into the same tables. In Project 9, "Making Data Entry Easier and More Accurate," you looked at ways of creating consistent data input structures, and you learned how to change the look of the data when it is displayed in the datasheet. You can also customize the fields in a similar manner in a form.

You also learned how to use a default value to avoid unnecessary typing if a field often contains the same data. A default value solves this problem if there is one piece of information that is used in a field the majority of the time. But what if there are five or six items, such as city names, that all occur frequently? The Lookup Wizard helped you build a list that appeared in a drop-down box in Table view. Forms have a similar feature that offers additional options.

Another way to avoid extra typing is to set up a form based on more than one table. You can set up the form to look up information from a table and automatically fill in several fields when you enter the information for only one field.

Frequently, you will be required to enter the current date (and even time) in a record. There are ways of automating that procedure so that the user does not have to enter anything.

When you enter data, the cursor jumps from one text box to the next when you press Tab. This is called the tab order. If you move the fields around in the form, the tab order may no longer make sense. You learn how to change this sequence to match the layout of the form.

Another useful type of a form is the main form/subform. This design places a form within a form and is very useful for displaying a one-to-many relationship between tables. In the main part of the form you see the one side of the relationship, and in the subform you see the many related records from the second table. This type of design could be used to display all of the inventory that was purchased from each vendor, or all of the employees that work in each department in a company.

In this project, you learn how to improve data entry speed and accuracy by adding lists and combo boxes, and you add dates that are needed in two different situations. You create a main form/subform and use it to enter new records. Finally, you learn how to print the Form view of a single record.

Lesson 1: Adding Formats in the Form Design View

The database used in this file is similar to the one you worked on in Project 9. An extra table and a query have been added for the lessons in this project, and a basic form has been created. A new text field, called City, has been added. You work on the form in all of the lessons in this project.

To Open the PC Training Data Entry Form

1 Make a copy of the Proj1201 database file from the Project-12 folder on the CD and name the copy `PC Training2`. Return to Access and open the `PC Training2` database.

The database window should now be open to the Tables area.

2 Click the Forms tab, if necessary.

Only one form should appear—the PC Training Data Entry form—and it should be highlighted (see Figure 12.1).

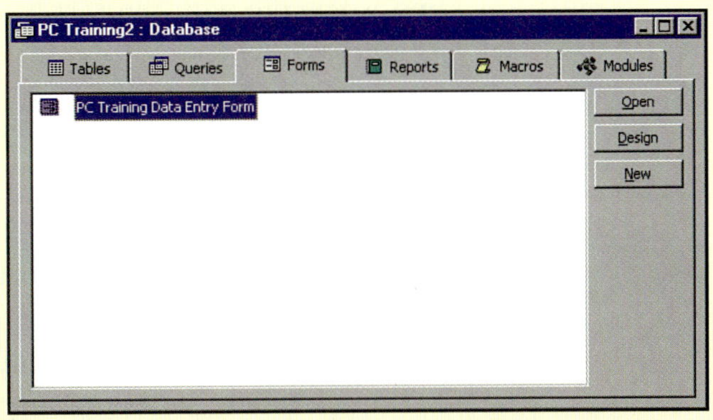

Figure 12.1
One form is listed in the Forms area of the PC Training database.

3 Click Open to open the form, and then click the Maximize button to open the Form window to its maximum size.

4 Maximize the Microsoft Access window, if necessary.

Your screen should resemble Figure 12.2.

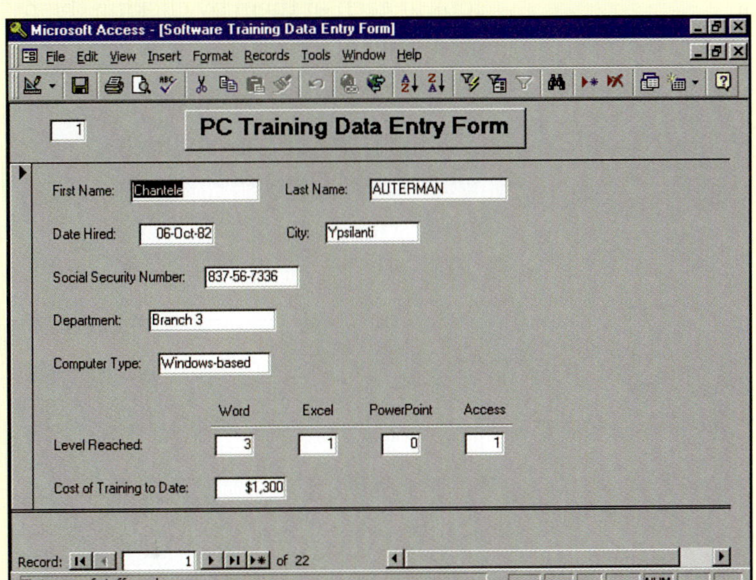

Figure 12.2
The maximized PC Training Data Entry Form displays the first table record.

Keep the database open for the next part of this lesson.

When you create a form, any input masks, data format expressions, validation rules, and required field properties are brought to the form from the underlying table. You can add additional properties to any field, although you cannot add or change the Required property option in the Form property box.

Inside Stuff

Changes that you make to the properties of a field in Form view are valid for Form view only, and will not affect the properties of the field in Table view.

In the following procedure, you use two formatting techniques to make your data look different. You make the Department name all capital letters, much the same as you did with the Last Name field in Project 9. You then use a standard formatting button to right-align the Social Security Number field.

Access

To Use Buttons and Properties to Control the Appearance of the Data

1 With the PC Training Data Entry form open, click the View button to switch to Design view.

2 Click the Department text box to select it.

Handles should appear around the text box, and a single large handle should appear in the upper-left corner of the label box. Make sure you have selected the Department text box and not the label box.

3 Click the Properties button on the Form Design toolbar.

The property sheet is divided into five sections. Take a moment to look at each of them by clicking the five tabs.

Another way to activate the property sheet is to click the right mouse button on the field and choose Properties from the shortcut menu.

4 Click the Format tab.

Once the Format tab is chosen, the property sheet for the Department field appears as in Figure 12.3.

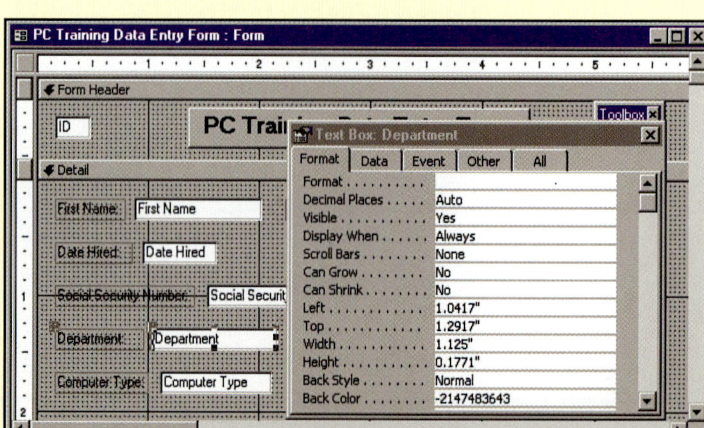

Figure 12.3
The property sheet showing the Format options.

5 Type the "greater than" symbol, >, in the Format box.

This is the same procedure you used in Table view in Project 9.

6 Click the Text Box Close button to close this property sheet.

7 Click the View button to return to Form view.

The Department name should now be capitalized, along with the Last Name, which you formatted in Project 9.

You can also control the alignment of the text within the box. To right-align the Social Security number:

8 Click the View button to move back to Design view.

9 Click the Social Security Number text box to select it.

10 Click the Align Right button on the Formatting toolbar.

If the Align Right button has not been added to your Formatting toolbar, you can go to the property box as you did in step 3, click on the Format tab, scroll to the bottom, and choose Right in the Text Align box.

You have now aligned the Social Security number to the right, the way users expect numbers to be displayed. The reason that this number was aligned left was that it was originally set up as a text field to take advantage of input masking.

You can use any of the formatting buttons on either the text box or its label. This means that you can display the data using boldface or italics, and you can even change the color of the text.

11 Click the View button to return to Form view.

Notice that the department in the Department field is now in capital letters, and the Social Security Number field is aligned right (see Figure 12.4).

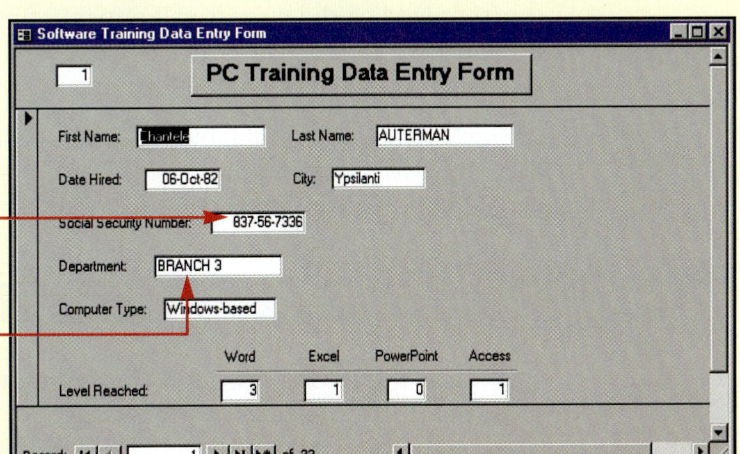

Figure 12.4 The PC Training Data Entry Form shows the changes made to the form.

Social Security number right-aligned

Department name capitalized

continues

To Use Buttons and Properties to Control the Appearance of the Data (continued)

12 Close the form.

A dialog box appears asking if you want to save your changes (see Figure 12.5).

Figure 12.5
A dialog box appears asking if you want to save changes to your form.

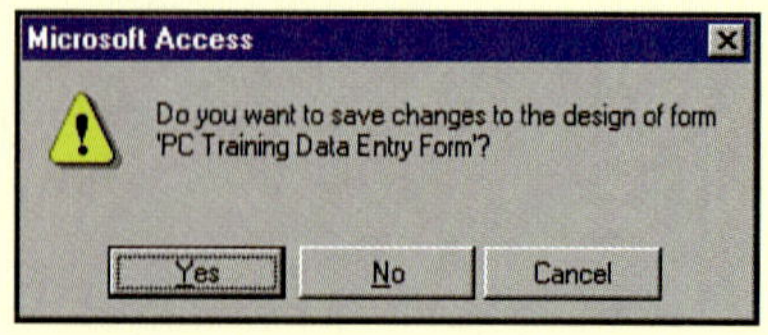

13 Click Yes to save your changes.

14 Click the Tables tab, and then open the `Software Training` table.

Notice that the Department field is not uppercase, and the Social Security number is still aligned left.

15 Close the table.

Exam Notes

It is important to remember that formatting changes you make go one way but not the other. The changes you make in a field's properties in Form view do not affect the formatting of the data in the underlying table. If you want to create formats that appear universally throughout the database, make those changes in Table Design view.

Lesson 2: Selecting Entries from a List

List box
A data entry list that looks up valid entries from a table, query, or source list, and does not allow the user to type in new data.

Sometimes, when the number of possible values that will go in a field is small, you can put the entire list of values on the screen. This way, the user can simply click the correct value for that record. The *list box* is easy to set up and easy to use. The user does not have the option of adding a value that is not on the list, which helps to ensure that correct data is entered.

In the Software Training table, there is a field called Computer Type. There are only two values for this field: Windows-based and Macintosh. In this lesson, you create a short list for this field.

To Create a List Box

1 Click the Forms tab, and then open `PC Training Data Entry Form`. Maximize the form, if necessary.

2 Click the View button to move to Design view.

3 Position the pointer on the Computer Type text box, and then click the right mouse button.

The shortcut menu appears. Make sure you have selected the Computer Type text box and not the label box.

4 Point to the Change To option from the shortcut menu.

The Change To menu appears to the right of the shortcut menu (see Figure 12.6).

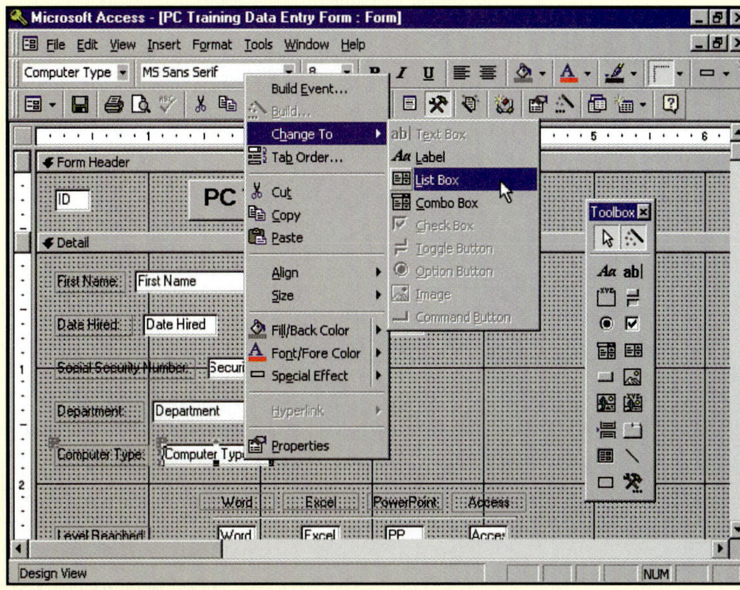

Figure 12.6
Use the shortcut Change To menu to change the field type to a list box.

5 Click the List Box option.

The text box for Computer Type appears larger on the screen (see Figure 12.7).

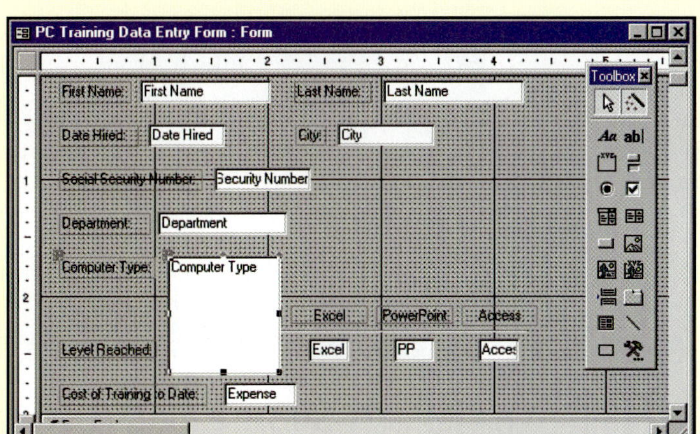

Figure 12.7
The list box field area appears on the form.

6 Click the right mouse button on the new text box, and then click Properties.

The List Box property sheet appears on the screen.

7 Click the Data tab.

continues

To Create a List Box (continued)

8 Click the Row Source Type option, and then click the drop-down arrow.

The Row Source Type drop-down menu appears (see Figure 12.8).

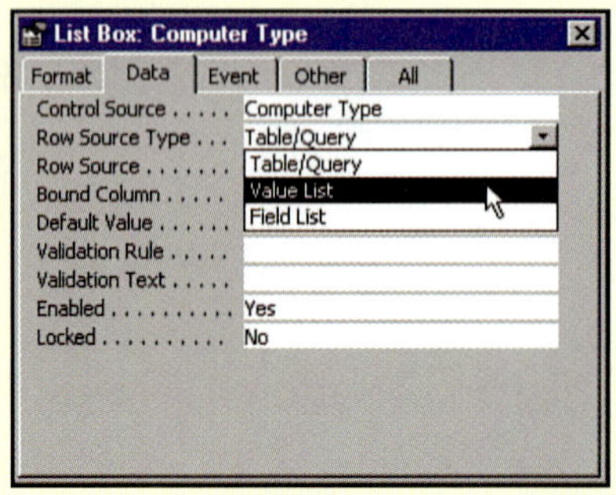

Figure 12.8
The Row Source Type drop-down menu lists three options.

9 Click Value List from the Row Source Type drop-down box.

This tells the program to look for the data for the list in the Row Source box, just below the Row Source Type box. You type the values into the Row Source box. All values must be separated by semicolons.

The table/query option could be used with a list box, but it is demonstrated in the next lesson on using combo Boxes.

10 In the Row Source box, type the following:

```
Windows-based;Macintosh
```

The Data tab in the List Box property sheet should look like Figure 12.9.

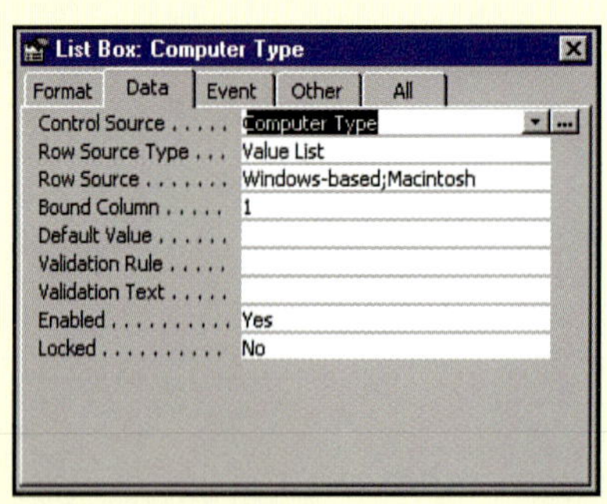

Figure 12.9
The Computer Type List Box Data window with the Row Source Type and the Row Source changed.

11 Close the List Box property sheet.

There will be times when you have made a spelling error or want to add another word to the list box. You can edit the list box in Design view by clicking the text box field with the right mouse button and choosing Properties.

⑫ Use one of the handles on the bottom of the Computer Type text box to decrease the height of the box to about the height of two lines of text.

You may have to use the vertical scrollbar to move down to the bottom of the text box (see Figure 12.10).

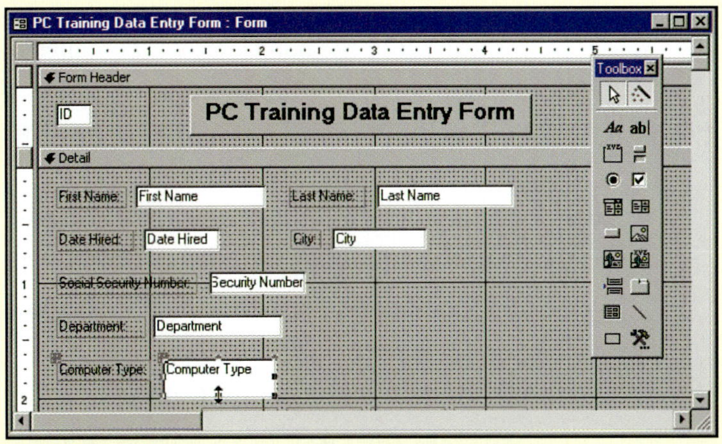

Figure 12.10
You can resize the Computer Type text box.

⑬ Click the View button to move to Form view.

⑭ Scroll through your records using the Next Record button.

Notice that when you come to a record that contains `Macintosh` for the Computer Type field, the word is highlighted in the list. Try adding a couple of records to see how this would work if you were entering data.

Keep the database open for the next lesson.

Inside Stuff

You can type the first letter of a selection in a list. The first word in the list beginning with that letter will be highlighted. When there is only one word beginning with that letter, as there is in this case, you can use this method to select the entry for the field. This is one of the advantages of a list box. A list box remains visible on your screen at all times and is generally best used when the list is short. For further information on how to set up a list box, use the F1 key or the Office Assistant for help.

Lesson 3: Looking Up Valid Entries from a Table or Query

Combo box
A data entry list that looks up valid entries from a table, query, or source list.

When the number of possible values that will go in a field is small, you can put the entire list of values in a list box, as you did in Lesson 2. If there are many possible entries, you want to use a combo box that can look up values in an existing field or query. With a combo box, you also have the option to prevent or allow the user to enter items that are not in the list.

Inside Stuff

In a list box, you can type in the first letter of a selection in a list. The first word in the list beginning with that letter is highlighted. Using a combo box, however, you can then type in the second letter of the word, and you can get the value you are looking for by typing in enough letters to make your desired value unique.

In this lesson, you create a combo box for the City field, then have the program look up the city names in the City and County Names query. The query was created so the records could be sorted on the City field. By doing this, the list in the combo box is alphabetized.

To Look Up Valid Entries from a Table or Query Using a Combo Box

1. **In the PC Training Data Entry Form, click the View button on the toolbar to switch to Design view, if necessary.**
2. **Position the pointer on the City text box, and then click the right mouse button.**

   The shortcut menu is displayed.
3. **From the Change To option in the shortcut menu, choose Combo Box.**

   The text box should now have a drop-down arrow on the right edge.
4. **With the City text box still selected, click it with the right mouse button, choose Properties, and go to the Data tab, if necessary.**

   The Data properties for the City field appear. The default for the Row Source Type should be Table/Query. If it is not, activate the drop-down box for the Row Source Type and change it.
5. **Click the Row Source option, and then click the drop-down box.**

   The Row Source drop-down box should show all of the tables and queries associated with this database (see Figure 12.11). Notice that there are two buttons available on the right side of the Row Source box: a Build button and a drop-down box arrow. Make sure you choose the drop-down box.

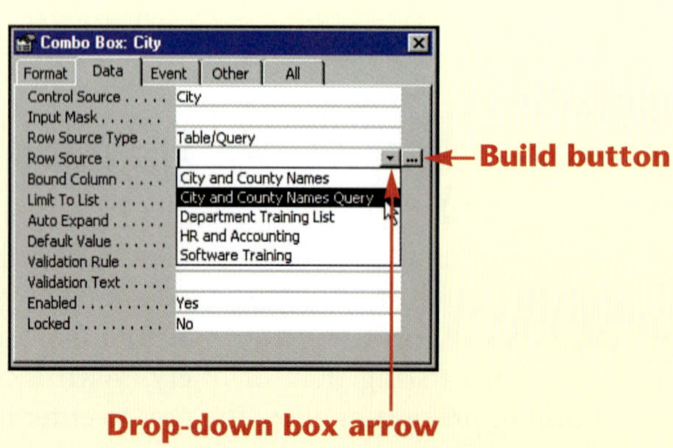

Figure 12.11
The Row Source drop-down list shows all available tables and queries.

6 Choose City and County Names Query from the list.

Notice that you have several other options available in this dialog box, such as adding input masks for text and date fields, setting default values, and validating data. You also have the ability to restrict the user to only those items on the list by changing the Limit To List box from No to Yes.

7 Close the Combo Box property sheet, and then click the View button on the toolbar to switch to Form view.

Notice that the City field now has a drop-down box attached to it.

8 Click the drop-down box of the City field.

A list should appear (see Figure 12.12). Notice that there is a vertical scrollbar on the list, indicating that there are more items than are shown on the screen. Scroll down to look at the rest of the items.

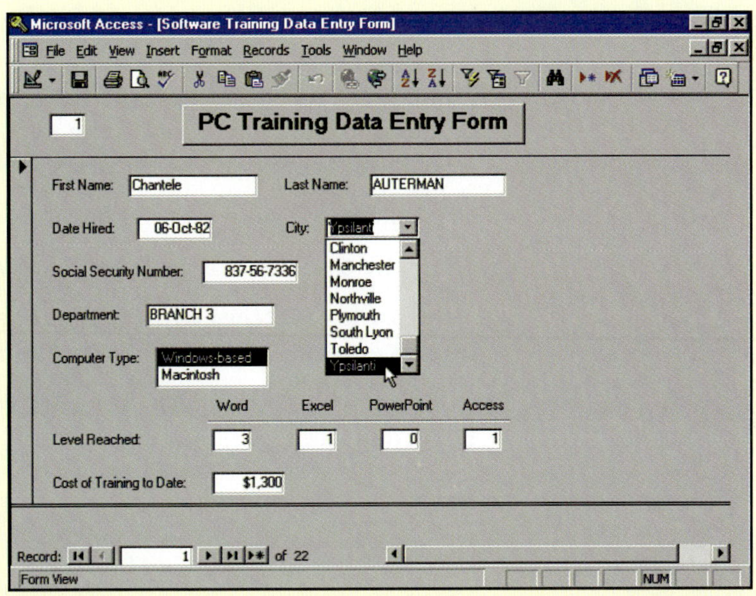

Figure 12.12
The combo box for the City field displays a list of cities.

9 Add one or two new records to try out your new combo box.

10 Save the changes to your form, close the form, and then close the PC Training2 database.

Inside Stuff

For further information about using list boxes and combo boxes and how to decide whether to use value lists or links to tables, use the Office Assistant or the F1 key.

Lesson 4: Using Information from a Query to Fill In Fields Automatically

In Project 11, "Managing Data Using Smaller, Related Tables," you worked on a database containing two tables: PC Hardware and Vendors. To save a lot of work entering all of the vendor information each time you entered a new record into the query, you used the foreign key field to automatically update the other fields in the Vendors table.

In this lesson, you use the query you created in Project 11. You then create a form based on the query.

Observing a Query Filling In Data Automatically

In this form, when you enter the vendor's name, all of the other fields from the Vendors table are filled in automatically.

To Observe How a Query Can Fill In Data Automatically

1. **Make a copy of the Proj1202 database file from the Project-12 folder on the CD and name the copy `Hardware Inventory2`. Return to Access and open the `Hardware Inventory2` database.**

   The Database window should now be open to the Tables area.

2. **Click the Queries tab and open the `Vendor and Hardware` query.**

3. **Move to the bottom of the datasheet and use the drop-down box to enter `Acme Computer` in the Vendor field.**

   Notice that the other fields from the Vendors table are automatically filled in (see Figure 12.13).

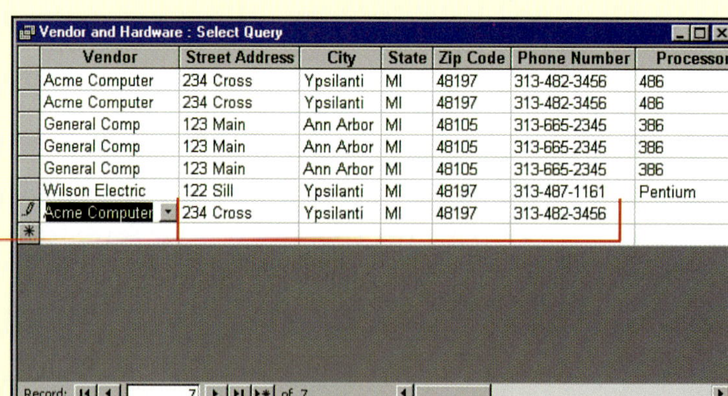

Vendor and Hardware : Select Query

Vendor	Street Address	City	State	Zip Code	Phone Number	Processor
Acme Computer	234 Cross	Ypsilanti	MI	48197	313-482-3456	486
Acme Computer	234 Cross	Ypsilanti	MI	48197	313-482-3456	486
General Comp	123 Main	Ann Arbor	MI	48105	313-665-2345	386
General Comp	123 Main	Ann Arbor	MI	48105	313-665-2345	386
General Comp	123 Main	Ann Arbor	MI	48105	313-665-2345	386
Wilson Electric	122 Sill	Ypsilanti	MI	48197	313-487-1161	Pentium
Acme Computer	234 Cross	Ypsilanti	MI	48197	313-482-3456	

Record: 7 of 7

Figure 12.13
The Query automatically fills in related fields when the vendor is selected.

Fields filled in automatically

4. **Press the Esc key to remove the new entry, and then close the Query.**

   If you create a form that is based on this query, it will have the same ability to fill in data.

Creating a Form to Fill In Data Automatically

Since most data is entered in Form view, it is helpful to automatically fill in repetitive data in the same manner you did using queries.

To Create a Form That Fills In Data Automatically

1 Click the Forms tab, then click New.

The New Form dialog box is displayed.

2 Select Form Wizard, and then choose Vendor and Hardware as the query or table to be used as a source for the form.

The New Form dialog box should look like Figure 12.14.

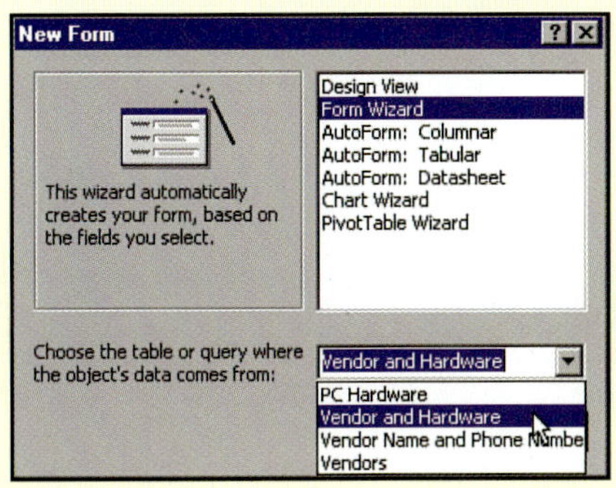

Figure 12.14
Use the New Form dialog box to start the Form Wizard.

3 Click OK.

The first Form Wizard dialog box appears. It may take several seconds for the Form Wizard dialog box to appear as the program builds the wizard. You may also experience similar delays between screens.

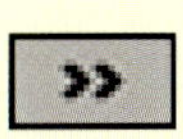

4 Click the Select All button to move all of the fields from the Available Fields window to the Selected Fields window.

The fields should all move to the right-hand window (see Figure 12.15).

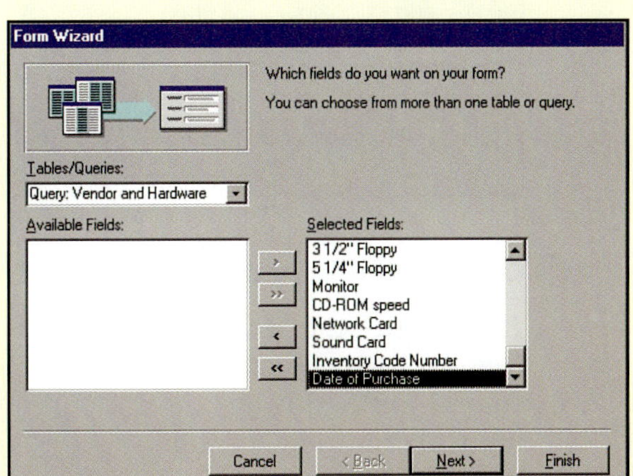

Figure 12.15
In the first Form Wizard dialog box, select which fields you want to include on your form.

continues

To Create a Form That Fills In Data Automatically (continued)

5 **Click Next.**

The second Form Wizard dialog box is displayed (see Figure 12.16). This dialog box gives you the option of four layouts for your form. Click each of them. A sample of the formats appears in a window on the left side of the dialog box.

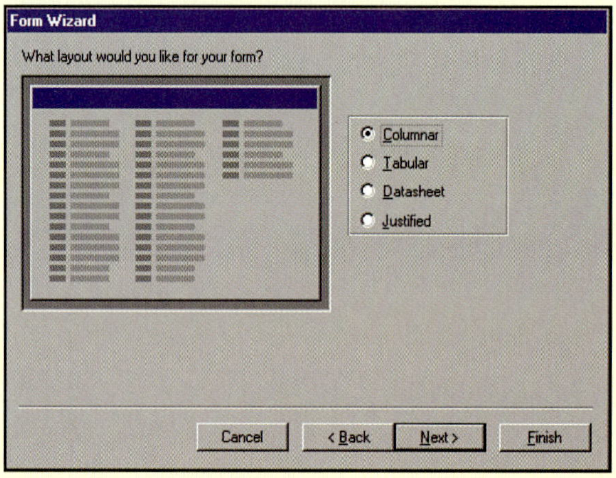

Figure 12.16
Choose a form layout in the second Form Wizard dialog box.

6 **Choose Columnar format, and then click Next.**

The third Form Wizard dialog box is displayed (see Figure 12.17). This dialog box gives you the various style options. Click a few of them to see what styles are available.

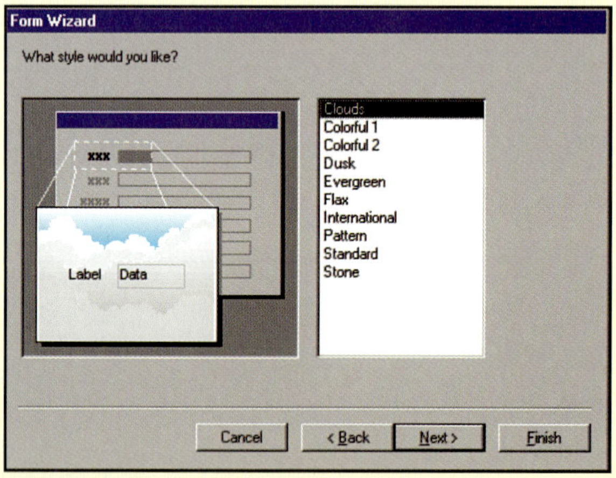

Figure 12.17
Choose a style for your form in the third Form Wizard dialog box.

7 **Choose Clouds, and then click Next.**

The fourth (and final) Form Wizard dialog box is displayed (see Figure 12.18). A default name of Vendor and Hardware has been entered in the title box. At this point, you have the choice of moving to Form view, or going to Design view to modify the form design. Accept the default name and move to Form view.

Access

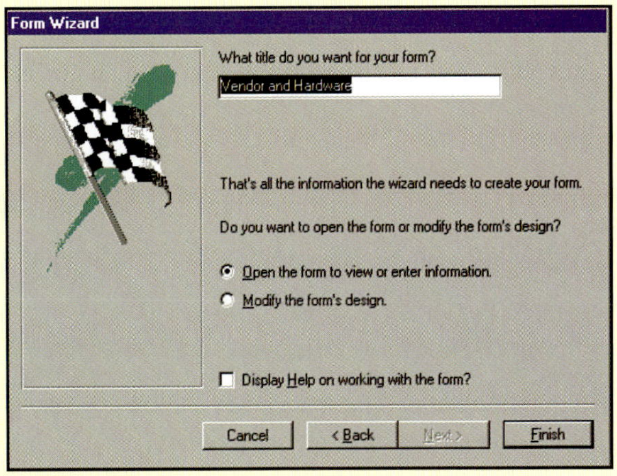

Figure 12.18
Enter a title for the form in the final Form Wizard dialog box.

8 Click Finish.

The Vendor and Hardware form is created (see Figure 12.19).

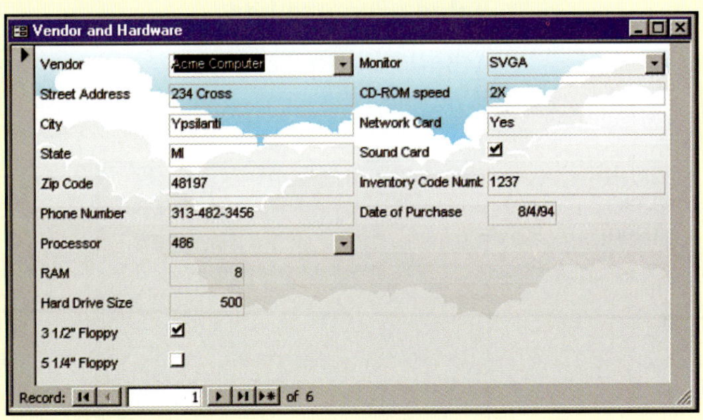

Figure 12.19
The form has been automatically created by the Form Wizard.

9 Click the New Record button and enter one of the company names from the drop-down list in the Vendor field.

Notice that the other fields from the Vendors table are entered automatically.

10 Finish filling in the information for the new record, and then close the database.

Lesson 5: Entering the Current Date in a Field Automatically

There are many occasions where a database calls for the current date. This is particularly true in the business world, where orders are dated as they are received and when they are sent out.

In the PC Training Data Entry Form of the PC Training2 database, where Date Hired is the only date field, let's assume that the vast majority of the personnel files are started on the day the employee is officially hired. On those occasions when the data is not entered on the date of hiring, the user has the option of typing in a new date.

In this lesson, you change the default for the Date Hired field to the current date.

To Enter the Current Date in a Field Automatically

1. **Open the `PC Training2` database.**
2. **Click the Forms tab.**
3. **Open `PC Training Data Entry Form` in Design view, and maximize the window, if necessary.**
4. **Position the pointer on the Date Hired field, then click the right mouse button. Choose Properties from the shortcut menu.**
5. **Click the Data tab, if necessary, and then click in the Default Value property box.**

   A Build button appears on the right side of the box (see Figure 12.20).

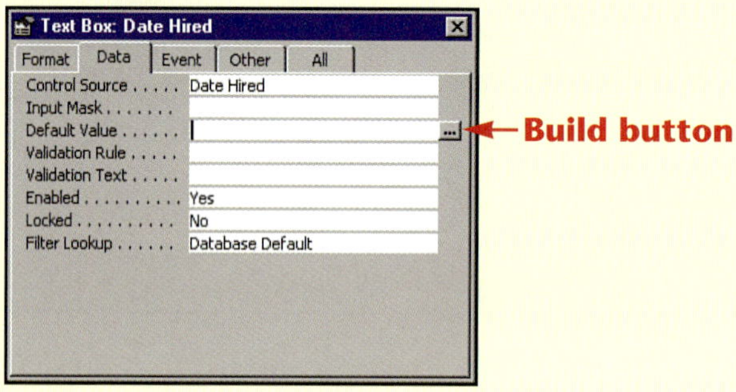

Figure 12.20 The Default Value box includes a Build button.

6. **Click the Build button.**

   An Expression Builder dialog box appears.
7. **Select Common Expressions from the left column.**

A list of common expressions appears in the middle column (see Figure 12.21).

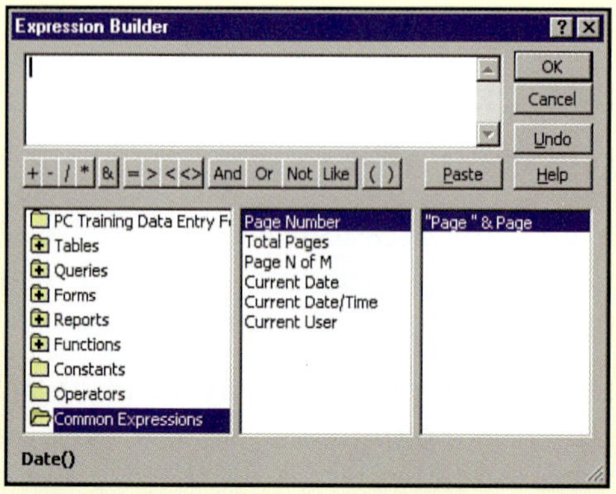

Figure 12.21 The Expression Builder is shown with Common Expressions selected.

8 Double-click the Current Date option.

Notice that the expression `Date()` appears in the third column and in the dialog box window (see Figure 12.22). This is the programming code you would use for this property if you were programming in Visual Basic.

Code for current date

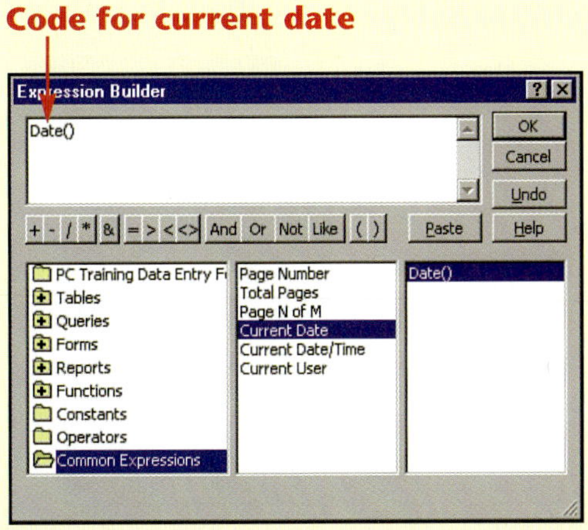

Figure 12.22
The Expression Builder is shown with the Date() expression selected.

9 Choose OK and close the property sheet.

10 Click the View button on the toolbar to switch to Form view.

11 Move to a new record by clicking the New Record button near the bottom of the screen.

12 Enter a new record.

Notice that the current date is automatically posted in the Date Hired field.

Keep the database open for the next lesson.

Lesson 6: Adding the Current Date and Time to a Form Automatically

There are times when you want to print out an individual form. It is possible to type in a date or time on the form using the Text tool, but Access gives you a way to add this information automatically. This information, called a date stamp or a time stamp, is usually placed in the form's Header or Footer area.

In this lesson, you add a date to the Header area of the PC Training Data Entry Form, then use the same procedure to add the time.

To Add the Current Date and Time to a Form Automatically

1 In the PC Training Data Entry Form, click the View button to switch to Design view.

2 From the Insert menu, choose Date and Time.

The Date and Time dialog box is displayed (see Figure 12.23). You see your current date and time on the dialog box.

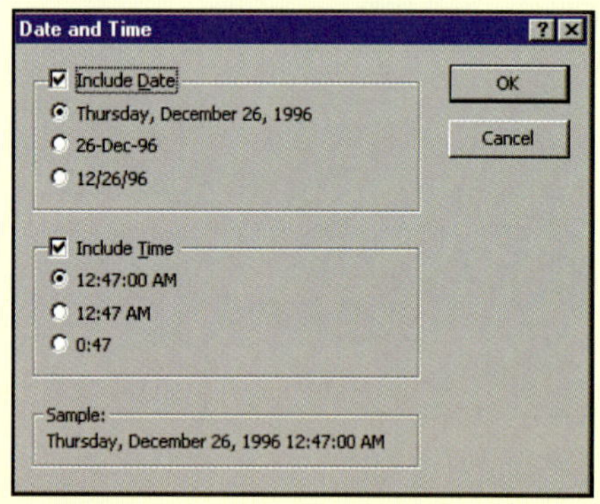

Figure 12.23
Use the Date and Time dialog box to add a date and/or time to a form.

3 Click the check box next to Include Time to deselect this option.

The Include Time area should now be off.

4 Click the middle option button in the Include Date area.

The date format is now the same one you used in the Date Hired field.

5 Click OK.

The date expression is automatically placed in the upper-left corner of the Form Design work area.

6 Drag the date to the upper-right corner of the work area.

Your date expression should be in the Form Header area.

7 Drag the middle handle on the left side of the date box to reduce the length of the date control box to about 1 1/4 inches.

The Form work area should now resemble Figure 12.24.

8 With the date expression still selected, use the Align Right button to align the date to the right.

If the Align Right button has not been added to your Formatting toolbar, you can click on the date text box with the right mouse button, choose Property Box, click on the Format tab, scroll to the bottom, and choose Right in the Text Align box.

9 Follow steps 2–8 to add a right-aligned time stamp just below the date stamp.

Figure 12.24
The Form window with a date added in the Form Header.

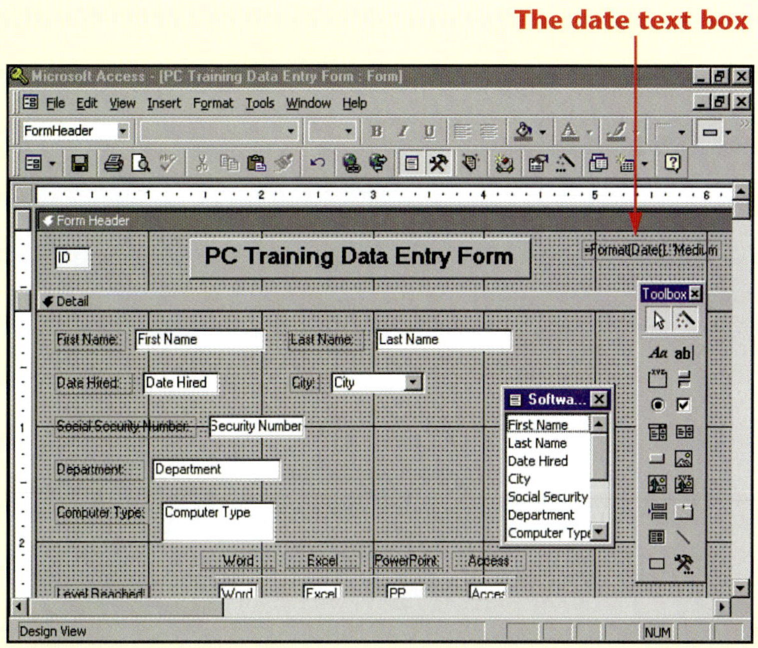

You may have to move the toolbox to place the time control properly. Use the middle format (2:17 PM). Make sure you deselect Include Date.

10 Click the View button on the toolbar to switch to the Form view.

Notice that the date and time are to the right of the title (see Figure 12.25). If necessary, move back to the Design view and adjust the location of the date and time.

Keep the database open for the next lesson.

Figure 12.25
The form displays the final location of the date and time stamps.

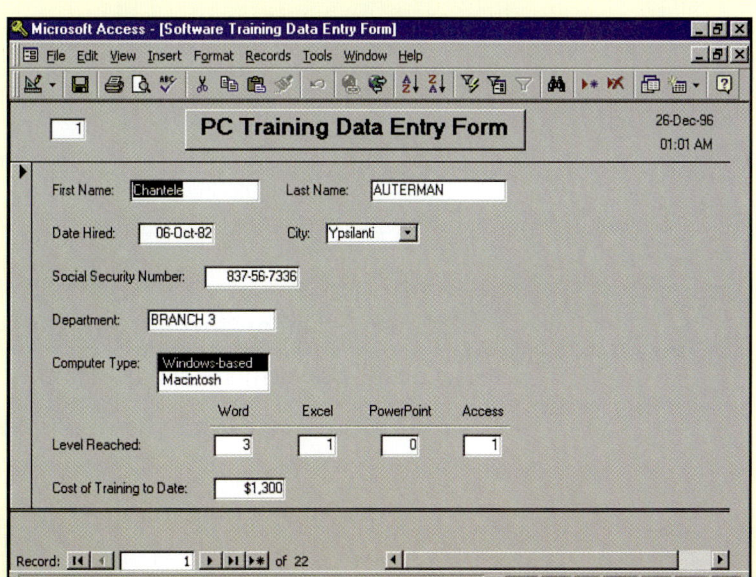

Lesson 7: Changing the Tab Order

When you enter data into the text boxes in a form, the cursor jumps from one text box to the next in a certain sequence. This sequence is called the tab order. In the case of an AutoForm, the tab order is initially determined by the order of fields in the underlying table or query. If you use the Form Wizard to create a form, the original order in which the fields are selected determines the tab order. When you move fields around in Design view, the tab order needs to be adjusted so the cursor moves from field to field in the order in which they are arranged. Fortunately, it is easy to change the tab order to read left-to-right, or in columns, depending on how the information flows in your form.

In this lesson, you learn how to change the tab order.

To Change the Tab Order

1. **In the Form view of the PC Training Data Entry Form, click on the First Name text box.**
2. **Press the Tab key repeatedly and watch how the cursor jumps from one text box to another.**

   Notice that it skips the City text box and does not return to it until after the Cost of Training to Date box.

3. **Click the View button to switch to Design view.**
4. **From the View menu, click on Tab Order.**

   The Tab Order dialog box is displayed (see Figure 12.26).

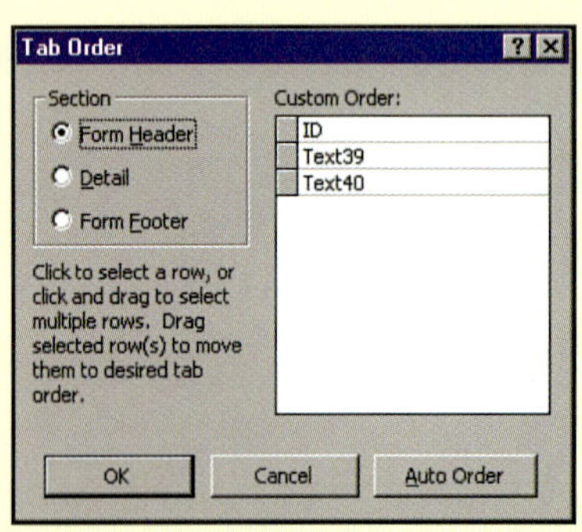

Figure 12.26 The Tab Order dialog box allows you to change the order of data entry on a form.

5. **Click the Detail option button, if necessary.**

   The dialog box displays the fields in the detail section of the form.
6. **Scroll to the bottom of the list of field names to show the City field.**

   The order of the field names in this dialog box represents the order in which they are selected when you tab through the form.

7 Click the Auto Order button.

This changes the tab order automatically so that the text boxes are selected from left to right and top to bottom, the way you would normally read a page of text.

Notice that the City field has been moved up in the list to follow Date Hired (see Figure 12.27).

Figure 12.27
The tab order is shown after it has been automatically rearranged.

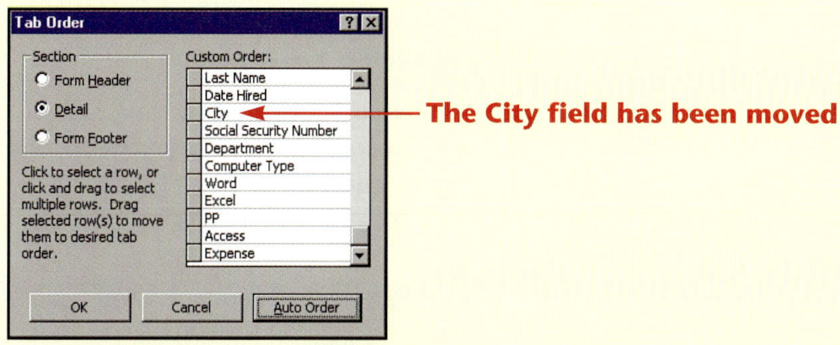

8 Click OK to save the change and close the Tab Order dialog box.

9 Click the View button to switch to Form view.

10 Press the Tab key repeatedly and observe how the cursor now jumps from the Date Hired text box to the City text box.

11 Save the changes to the form, close the form, and close the database.

Exam Notes

You can rearrange the fields to appear in any order you desire. With the Detail option button selected on the Tab Order dialog box, select a field by clicking on the select box to the left of the field name. Click on the same spot, hold the mouse button down, and drag the field up or down to a new location.

Lesson 8: Creating Subforms

At times, you might want a form that shows the one-to-many relationship between two tables. The main form/subform design is useful for displaying the one side of a relationship in the main part of a form and the related records in a subform. The subform is usually displayed in a datasheet layout. While these are technically two forms, they can be created together using the Form Wizard. With this design, you can display all of the employees who work in each department, the furniture and equipment that is assigned to each department, or the clients assigned to each sales representative. In order to create this type of form, a relationship needs to be established between the two tables. This was done in Project 11.

Creating a Subform

In this lesson, you create a main form/subform that shows all of the computers that were purchased from each vendor in the Hardware Inventory2 database.

To Create a Subform

1 Open the `Hardware Inventory2` database and click on the Forms tab. Click the New button to create a new form. The New Form dialog box opens.

2 In the New Form dialog box, select the Vendors table from the Choose Table or Query drop down list, select Form Wizard, then click OK. The first Form Wizard dialog box opens (see Figure 12.28).

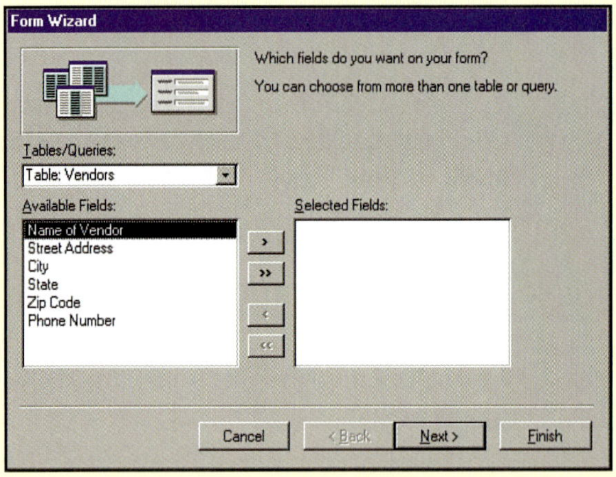

Figure 12.28
The first Form Wizard dialog box asks which fields you want to include in your form.

3 Click the Select All arrow to move all of the fields to the Selected Fields box.

All of the fields from the Vendors table are included in the main part of the form.

4 Click the down-arrow at the end of the Tables/Queries box and select Table: PC Hardware (see Figure 12.29).

Once you click on the new table name, the fields for that table are displayed in the Available Fields box.

5 Move all of the fields to the Selected Fields box except the vendor name field. You can use the Select All arrow to move all of the fields to the Selected Fields box, then highlight the Name of Vendor field from the PC Hardware table and use the single arrow pointing to the left to move this field back to the Available Fields box.

The selected fields from the PC Hardware table are the fields included in the subform (see Figure 12.30).

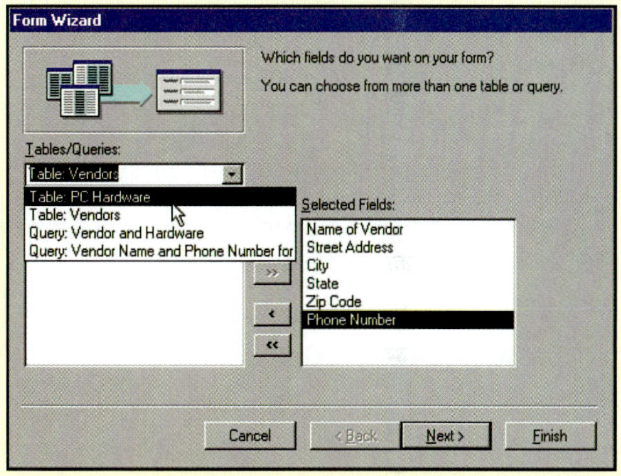

Figure 12.29
The table can be changed in the Form Wizard so you can select fields from more than one table or query for a form.

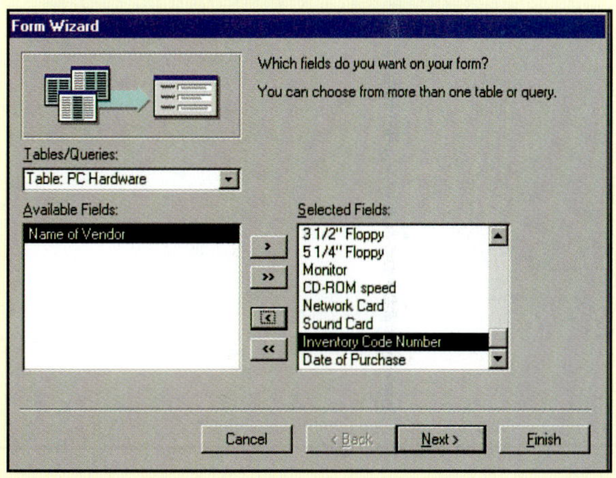

Figure 12.30
The fields for the subform are selected from a second table.

6 Click Next. The second dialog box asks how you want to view your data.

By default, the Vendor fields show at the top of the preview area, which is the way you want the data displayed. Notice the option button for Form with subform(s) is also selected by default (see Figure 12.31). Accept the default settings.

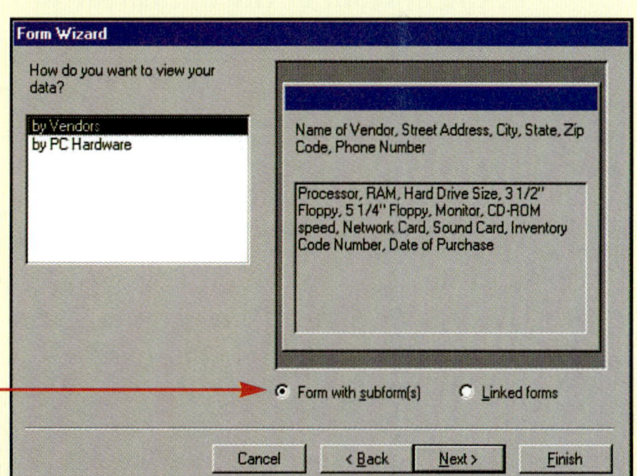

Subform option is selected

Figure 12.31
The main form shows the vendor information and the subform shows the related records.

continues

To Create a Subform (continued)

7 **Click Next. The next wizard dialog box asks which layout you want for the subform.**

Accept the default setting of Datasheet.

8 **Click Next. Choose the Colorful 2 style and then click Next to move to the final wizard dialog box.**

9 **The final dialog box suggests titles for the two parts of this form. Accept the suggested titles by clicking the Finish button.**

The form is created and displayed on your screen (Figure 12.32).

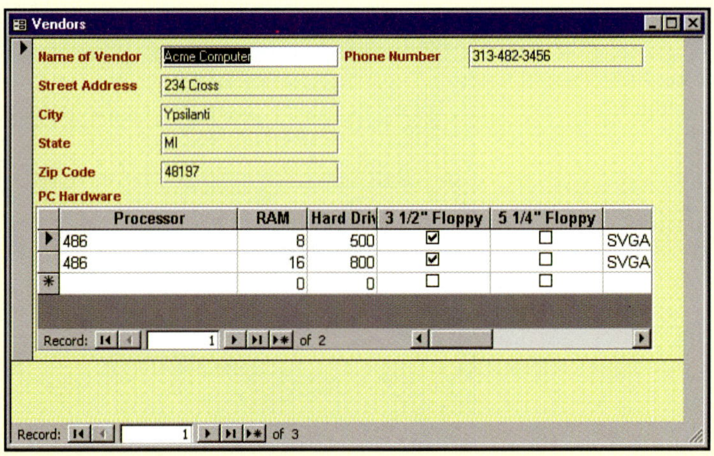

Figure 12.32
The finished main form/subform shows two sets of navigation buttons.

Notice that the form has two sets of navigation buttons. The navigation buttons at the bottom of the form scroll through the vendors. As the vendor changes, the related records in the datasheet (subform area) change. The navigation buttons in the subform scroll through the PC records that are displayed for each vendor.

10 **Use the navigation at the bottom of the form to scroll through the list of vendors. Then use the navigation buttons at the bottom of the datasheet to scroll through the PC hardware listed for the vendor.**

11 **Leave the form open for use in the next part of this lesson.**

Adding Records Using a Main Form/Subform

A main form/subform can also be used to edit or add new records to your two tables. You want to make sure that if you use this type of form for adding records, that all of the fields for each of the tables are included. Otherwise, you will end up with records with missing information. In order for this to work properly, the primary key from the one side of the relationship must be included. Next, you add a record to the main form and to the subform.

To Add Records Using a Main Form/Subform

1 With the Vendors form open, click on the New Record button to move to an empty record.

2 Enter the following vendor information:

`Computer Tyme, 1233 Second Street, Macon, MI 48134, (517) 555-2233`

You have added a new vendor to the list of available vendors. Now add a record of hardware purchased from Computer Tyme.

3 Press Tab to move to the first field for the hardware information and enter the following information.

`Pentium II, 64, 2500, Yes, No, SVGA, 16X, Yes, Yes, 1240, 8/27/97`

A record for the PC Hardware table has been added (see Figure 12.33.

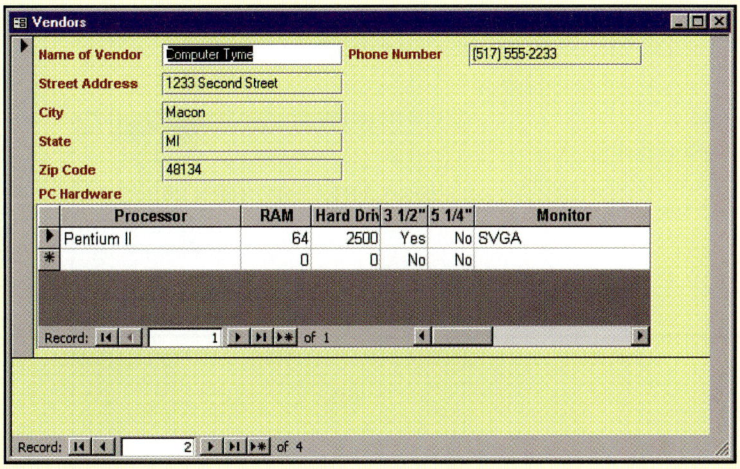

Figure 12.33
New records can be added using the main form and the subform.

4 Click the down arrow on the View button and select the Datasheet View.

The datasheet of the form shows the four vendors, including the new one you just added.

5 Close the form and save changes, if prompted.

Vendors and PC Hardware Subform have been added to the list of forms on the Forms tab.

6 Click on the Tables tab and open the `PC Hardware` table.

Observe the new record that you just added using the main form/subform.

7 Close the table, and then close the database.

Lesson 9: Printing the Form for Filing Purposes

You might want to print the form for an individual record for filing purposes, as a rough draft to check on a particular piece of data, or as a check on the layout when the form is longer than the screen. While most of the printing in Access is done in reports, some is also done in forms.

In this lesson, you print the information for one of the records. You then change the background color to try to make the printout more readable.

To Print the Form

1 Open the `PC Training2` database, and then open the PC Training Data Entry Form and maximize the window, if necessary.

2 From the File menu, choose Page Setup.

The Page Setup dialog box is displayed, with the Margins tab chosen (see Figure 12.34).

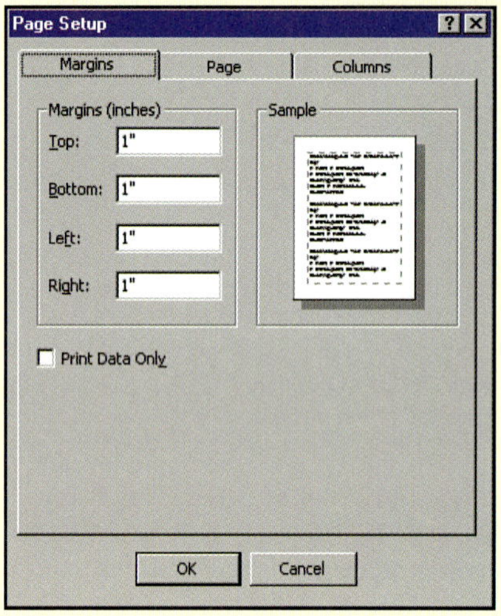

Figure 12.34
The Page Setup dialog box appears with the Margins tab selected.

3 Change the left and right margins to .75 inch.

To do this, highlight the old margins and type the new margins over them.

4 If the Print Data Only check box is checked, deselect it, and then choose OK.

The Print Data Only selection might be used if you have a slow printer and speed is more important, or if you only want to archive the data.

5 Click the Print Preview button.

The preview screen shows that the printout is continuous; two complete records are shown, along with most of a third (see Figure 12.35). You can use the pointer, which has changed into a magnifying glass, to zoom in or out on the preview page.

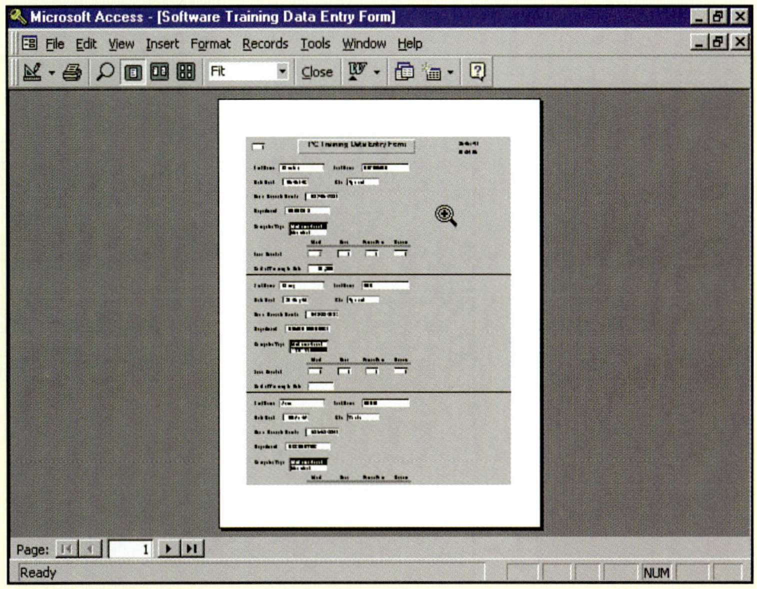

Figure 12.35
The Print Preview screen shows nearly three complete records.

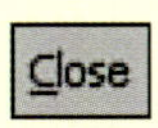

6 Click the Close button in the toolbar to close the Print Preview window.

Before you send this form to the printer, there are a few more steps you need to perform.

7 Click the View button on the toolbar to switch to Design view.

8 Click the right mouse button on the background of the Detail area.

Make sure you do not accidentally click on a text or label box.

9 Move the pointer to Fill/Back Color in the shortcut menu.

A color palette appears (see Figure 12.36).

10 Select white, which is located at the lower-right corner of the color palette.

The background color of the Detail section turns white, but the Header and Footer sections remain dark gray.

11 Repeat steps 8–10 for the Header section, and then scroll down and do the same for the Footer section.

All three backgrounds are now white. When you print the form, the printer will use less ink.

You are almost ready to print the form, but you need to make sure you only print one form per page.

continues

To Print the Form (continued)

Figure 12.36
Use the color palette to choose a background color.

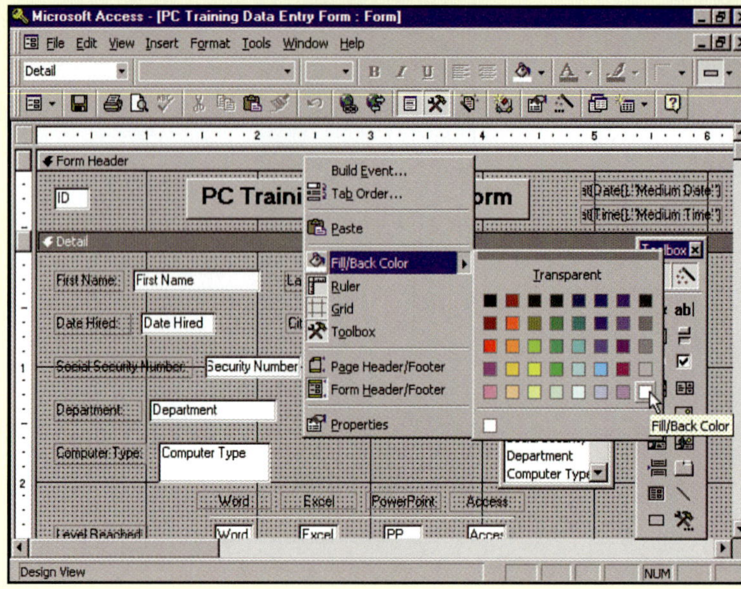

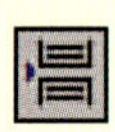

12 **Open the toolbox, if necessary. Scroll down so that you can see the Cost of Training to Date field, and then click the Page Break button in the toolbox.**

13 **Move the cursor just below the Cost of Training to Date field in the Detail area and click the left mouse button.**

A page break, which is displayed as a series of six dots, is now inserted in that spot (see Figure 12.37). If you want to see what your printout will look like, use the Print Preview as you did in step 5.

Figure 12.37
A page break can be inserted to print the forms one page at a time.

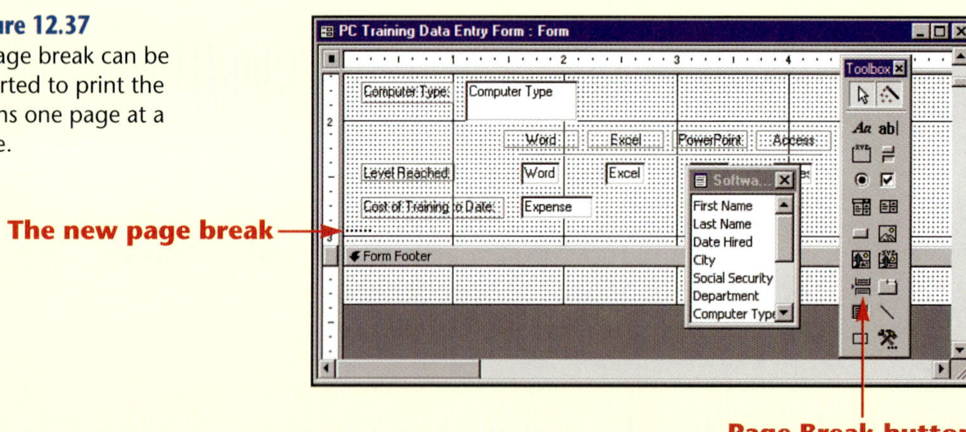

14 **Click the View button on the toolbar to switch to Form view, and then go to the File menu and choose Print.**

15 **Click the Selected Record(s) option button in the Print Range area (see Figure 12.38).**

Access

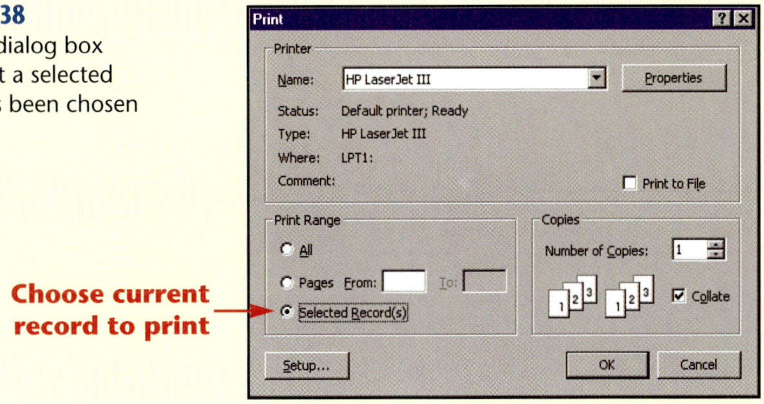

Figure 12.38
The Print dialog box shows that a selected record has been chosen to print.

16 Choose OK to print the current record.

This particular form does not have a lot of information on it, but you can see where the ability to print forms could be very helpful. Depending on the type of printer you have, the computer type may be completely hidden by the highlight, making it appear that the selected value was Macintosh, when it was, in fact, Windows-based. This is one of the drawbacks of using a list box in a form.

17 Close the PC Training Data Entry Form and save your changes when prompted. Close the database.

If you have completed your session on the computer, exit Access and shut down Windows before you turn off the computer. Otherwise, continue with the "Checking Your Skills" and "Applying Your Skills" sections in this project.

Project Summary

To	Do This
Add formats in the Form Design view	In Form Design view, select the field you want to format, click the Properties button, go to the Format tab, and enter your format in the Format box. You can also select a field and use the buttons on the Formatting toolbar to alter the format.
Select entries from a list	In Form Design view, select the field you want to add a list to, choose Change To and List Box from the shortcut menu. From the shortcut menu, choose Properties. In the Data tab, change the Row Source Type to Value List, and then type your list in the Row Source box, using semicolons between values.

continues

To	Do This
Look up valid entries from a table or query	In Form Design view, select the field you want to format, choose Change To and Combo Box from the shortcut menu. From the shortcut menu, choose Properties. In the Data tab, make Table/Query the Row Source Type. Using the drop-down menu from the Row Source, choose the table or query to use as a source.
Use information from a query to fill in fields automatically	Choose New from the Form tab, and then choose a query that has merged data from two tables. Using the Form Wizard, select the fields that you want to include, then select a format and a style.
Enter the current date automatically	In Form Design view, select the date field you want to work on, choose Properties from the shortcut menu, and then click in the Default Value property box. Click the Build button, and then choose Common Expressions, Current Date.
Date and time stamp the form automatically	In Form Design view, choose Date and Time from the Insert menu. Select date or time, or both, and choose the format you want. Move the date or time fields to the desired location, and format them using the Formatting toolbar.
Change the tab order	In Design view, select Tab Order from the View menu. Click the Detail button. Click Auto Order button to select a left-to-right, top-to-bottom order. Click OK.
Create a subform Print the form for filing purposes	In Form view, select Page Setup from the File menu. Change margins and other options as necessary. Choose Print Preview from the File menu to see what your printout will look like. Choose Print from the File menu, and then select which records to print.

Access

Checking Your Skills

True/False

For each of the following statements, check *T* or *F* to indicate whether the statement is true or false.

__T __F 1. When you create a form, any input masks you created in the underlying table appear on the form.

__T __F 2. The formatting changes you make in Form view will also appear in the underlying Table view.

__T __F 3. In a list box, you can type in the values in the Row Source box of the List Box property sheet.

__T __F 4. A date or time stamp is usually placed in the form Detail section.

__T __F 5. To make a field required in a form, you must specify it as a required field in the underlying table.

__T __F 6. In order to include fields from more than one table in a form, you must first create a query and then base your form on the query.

__T __F 7. You can set up the form to look up information from a table and automatically fill in several fields when you enter the information for only one field.

__T __F 8. If you format a field in a form to be in capital letters, it does not change the appearance in the form of the records that have been previously entered.

__T __F 9. A list box allows users to enter items that are not on the list.

__T __F 10. The Row Source Type property box tells the program where to look for the items in a list or combo box.

Multiple Choice

Circle the letter of the correct answer for each of the following questions.

1. You can use buttons from the _____ toolbar to change the appearance of the data in a form.
    a. Standard
    b. Formatting
    c. Form Design
    d. Database

2. In list and combo boxes, the _____ determines where the list values come from.
    a. Expression Builder
    b. Validation Rule
    c. Row Source
    d. Row Source Type

3. When you type in the values for a list box, each value must be separated by _____.
    a. quotation marks
    b. semicolons
    c. colons
    d. commas

4. Automatically adding the current date to a field is done using the _____ in the Default Value area.
    a. Validation Rule
    b. Expression Builder
    c. Row Source
    d. Input Mask

5. Use the _____ menu to change the background color of a form.

   a. View

   b. Format

   c. Shortcut

   d. Tools

6. When you want a form to show all of the records in one table that are related to one record in another table on one page, you can create a _____.

   a. main form/subform

   b. find matched records form

   c. form based on a query

   d. tabular form

7. A list box _____.

   a. remains visible on your screen at all times

   b. is best used when the list is short

   c. can be accessed by typing the first letter of a word on the list

   d. all of the above

8. A combo box _____.

   a. appears as a drop-down box

   b. can be overridden by typing in a field that is not available in the combo box

   c. can be set to only accept the fields showing in the combo box

   d. all of the above

9. To set a date field to the current date, you must select the _______ category in the Expression Builder.

   a. Common Expressions

   b. Date Formats

   c. Constants

   d. Operators

10. To change the Tab Order of a form, _____.

    a. choose Format, Tab Order from the menu

    b. open the detail section property sheet and select Tab Order from the Format tab

    c. choose View, Tab Order from the menu

    d. open the detail section property sheet and select Tab Order from the Data tab

Completion

In the blank provided, write the correct answer for each of the following statements.

1. A(n) _______________ box sets up a data list, but does not allow the user to input a value that does not appear on the list.

2. A(n) _______________ box is a list that uses a drop-down box and allows the user to enter information that does not appear on the list.

3. A form's print margins can be changed using the _______________ command from the File menu.

4. The button that opens the Expression Builder is called a(n) ______________ button.

5. You can tell what your form will look like when it is printed by clicking the ______________ button.

6. In a form, the sequence in which you move through fields is known as the ______________.

7. To be able to see all of the related records in a one to many relationship, you can create a ______________ form with a ______________.

8. In a date field, to have a date fill in automatically on a form, you set the ______________ property to current date using the expression builder.

9. To have text in a text box line up on the right, click the ______________ button.

10. A form can be based on a ______________ or a ______________.

Matching

In the blank next to each of the following terms or phrases, write the letter of the corresponding term or phrase. (Note that some letters may be used more than once.)

a. tab order
b. combo box
c. list box
d. subform
e. =Date()
f. background color
g. Common Expressions
h. page break button
i. main form
j. Insert, Date and Time

_______ 1. A form within a form

_______ 2. Use this to print one record to a page on a form

_______ 3. Shows as a drop-down box

_______ 4. Category used to set the current date on a field

_______ 5. Shows the one side of a one-to-many relationship

_______ 6. Change this to rearrange the sequence in which you move through fields on a form

_______ 7. Used to place the date on a form

_______ 8. Code for current date

_______ 9. Shows as a list

_______ 10. You might need to change this before printing a form so your printer does not use extra ink

Applying Your Skills

Practice

The following exercises enable you to practice the skills you have learned in this project.

Adding a Combo Box to a Form

In this exercise, you have a database that has a table of information about the books in your library and another table that tracks the books others have borrowed from you. The Type of Book field has a limited number of possible entries and is a perfect candidate for a combo box.

To add a combo box to a form, complete the following steps:

1. Copy the file Proj1203 from the Project-12 folder on the CD and rename the copy as `Library10`.
2. Open `Library10`.

   Notice that there are two forms; the AutoForm and the Quick Entry form.
3. Open the form called AutoForm.

   Notice that the fourth field is called Type of Book. Possible entries for this field are limited (mystery, science fiction, non-fiction, classics). It would be nice to have the most common entries available with a combo box.
4. Go to Form Design view and change the Type of Book field to a Combo Box.
5. Go to the property sheet for the Type of Book field.
6. Choose to get the values for the combo box from a Value List.
7. Enter the following into the Value List:

   `Mystery`

   `Science Fiction`

   `Non-Fiction`

   `Classics`
8. Enter a couple of new records and try out the combo box.
9. Save your changes and close the database.

Adding the Current Date to a Date Field and the Time to a Form

In this exercise, you have a database that has an Order Date. This date could be filled in automatically when a new record is added, but to do that you first have to change the field type. You then add the current date to the input form.

To add the current date to a date field and the time to a form, complete the following steps:

1. Copy the file Proj1204 from the Project-12 folder on the CD and rename the copy as `SBMusic10`.
2. Open `SBMusic10`.
3. Open the `Orders` table.

Access

Notice that the first field is called `Order Date`.

4. Go to Table Design view and confirm that the Order Date field is a Date/Time field type.
5. Go to the Default Value Expression Builder and set the default to the current date.

   Adding a default date in the table expression builder requires that you double-click the Functions folder, click once on the Built-in Functions folder, click once on the Date/Time option in the second column, and then double-click the Date function in the third column.
6. Save your changes, and then open the form called `AutoForm`.
7. In Form Design view, add the current time in the form header.
8. Rearrange the fields into two columns. Place `ID`, `Last Name`, `First Name`, and `Music Interest` in the first column and the mailing address fields in the second column.
9. Change the tab order so that the selection moves down the first column, and then down the second column when the Tab key is pressed repeatedly.
10. Save your changes.
11. Leave the database open for use in the next exercise.

Printing a Copy of a Form

In this exercise, you print out a copy of a single form from a database.

To print a copy of a form, complete the following steps:

1. Use the SBMusic10 file from the previous lesson or copy the file Proj1204 from the Project-12 folder on the CD and rename the copy as `SBMusic10`.
2. Open `SBMusic10`, if necessary.
3. Go to the AutoForm in Design view.
4. Put a page break after the last field in the form.
5. In Page Setup, change all four margins to 2 inches.
6. Change the background color of the Header and Detail sections to white.
7. Print page 3 only.
8. Save your changes and close the file.

Creating a Form with Two Combo Boxes and Today's Date in the Human Resources Database

In this exercise, you create a form that is used to update employee records. You add a combo box that will make it easy to select department names from a new table that lists department information and another combo box that will replace the list box on the Specialty field.

The Human Resources database that you used earlier has been modified for this project. A new table that lists information about the employee's department has been added. A one-to-many relationship between the two tables based on the Department field has been created and the Lookup feature has been removed from the Department and Specialty fields in the Employees table.

To add a combo box to a form, complete the following steps:

1. Copy the file Proj1205 from the Project-12 folder on the CD and rename the copy as `Human Resources2`.
2. Open `Human Resources2` and open the `Employee information with List box` form.

   Notice that the list box that was added to the field in the table design in the earlier project does not behave the same way in a form. The entire list is displayed rather than a drop-down list. For this reason, the list box lookup has been removed from the field in the table design.
3. Close the form and open the `Employee information` form. Click on the Analysis and Department fields to confirm that neither has a list or combo box attached.
4. Switch to Design view and right-click on the Specialty text box. Change this box to a combo box.
5. Right-click on the Specialty text box again and choose Properties from the shortcut menu.
6. Set the Row Source Type to Value List and enter the following list of specialties:

   ```
   "Analysis";"Secretary";"Management";"Personnel";"Records";
   "Real Estate";"Maintenance Management";"Other"
   ```
7. Set the Limit To List option to Yes.
8. Change the Department text box to a combo box.
9. Use the Properties sheet to set the Row Source Type to Table/Query. Set the Row Source to Departments, and Limit To List to Yes. Close the Properties sheet.
10. Insert a date in the Form Header.
11. Save your changes and switch to Datasheet view. Select each of the two text boxes and test the combo boxes to see if they display the list of specialties you typed in, and the list of departments from the Department table.
12. Close the form but leave the database open for use in the next exercise.

Using a Form with a Subform to Update Employee Records in the Human Resources Database

In some cases, you want to make it easy to update some of the fields in the table without displaying sensitive data in other fields. In this exercise, you design a form that could be used by a temporary worker to catch up on entering changes of address and phone number. The information is submitted by each department supervisor, so it would be convenient if the employee records were displayed by department. It is also important that some fields such as the salary field are not included in this form.

To create a Department form with an Employee Information subform, complete the following steps:

1. Use the Human Resources2 file that you worked on in the previous exercise, or copy the file Proj1205 from the Project-12 folder on the CD and rename the copy as `Human Resources2`.
2. Open `Human Resources2`, if necessary. Go to Forms and click New.
3. Use the Form Wizard to create a form with fields from both tables. First, select all the fields from the Department table.
4. Select the following fields from the Employee Information table:

   Name, Street, City, State, ZIP, Home Phone
5. Choose Spreadsheet layout and any color scheme you like. Finish the form and examine the results. Notice that all the fields do not fit in the subform.
6. Switch to Design view. Click the white rectangle that marks the subform and drag the right side to the right to the 6 1/2-inch mark on the ruler.
7. Switch back to Datasheet view. Move your cursor to one of the lines between the column headers in the subform until it becomes a double-headed arrow. Drag the boundary between the columns to improve the fit. Repeat this process until all of the columns can display their contents.
8. Use the navigation bars to scroll through both sets of records. Find the Marketing department in the main form, and then find the record for Mary Davis. Change the area code of her home phone from `513` to `429`.
9. Save your changes and close the form and the database.

Challenge

The following challenges enable you to use your problem-solving skills.

Adding a Combo Box to a Database

Sometimes you want to enter an ID number but it would be unreasonable to expect anyone to remember such a number for numerous records. A combo box can help you find one field by looking up a value in a different field of the same record. Open the `Club` database that you worked on in the previous project.

Create a new form that contains all of the fields in the Donations table.

Switch to Design view of the new form. Select the Member ID text box and convert it to a combo box. Use the following property settings to create a combo box:

Property	Setting	Effect
Row Source Type	Table/Query	Shows all of the tables and queries associated with the database
Row Source	Membership Information	Selects fields from this table
Bound Column	1	Column in the Membership table that will supply the value
Column Count	13	Number of columns in the Membership table
Column Heads	Yes	Displays field names
Column Widths	1";1";1";1"	Widths of columns displayed in inches separated by semicolons
List Rows	8	Number of records to display
List Width	4"	Sum of the column widths in inches
Limit To List	Yes	Similar to Validation Rule

Switch to Datasheet view and add a new record. Click on the list arrow in the Member ID field. You should see a list of the first four fields in the Membership table. Click on one of them. The contents of the first column (bound column) are placed in the Member ID field in the Donations table. Complete the record and close the form.

Create a new form that uses the fields that describe the member's name from the Membership table and the Donation and Date fields from the Donations table. Put the Donation and Date fields into a subform.

Add the date to the main form's Form Header. Test the form.

Adding a Date to a Form and Creating a New Form with Subform

This database has four tables and three relationships. They were created without enforcing referential integrity, so there could be orphan records.

Locate the Customer Research10 database that you worked on in the previous project and rename it `Customer Research11`, and then open the file.

Open the `Survey Participants` form and add a date to the Form Header.

Change the Households text box to a combo box. Set the following properties:

Property	Setting	Effect
Control Source	Households	Links the box to the Households table
Row Source	Households	Selects fields from this table
Bound Column	1	Column in the Households table that will supply the value
Column Count	5	Number of columns in the Households table
Column Heads	Yes	Displays field names
Column Widths	1";1";1"	Widths of first three columns displayed in inches separated by semicolons
List Rows	8	Number of records to display
List Width	3"	Sum of the column widths in inches
Limit To List	Yes	Similar to Validation Rule

Save the changes and switch to the Form view. Test the combo box, then close the form.

Create a new form that uses the First Name and Last Name from the Participants table, and the Date, Channel Name, Beginning Time, and Ending Time from the Viewing Data table. Use the Subform option.

Creating a Form with a Subform

A supplier might have several different types of machines available. In this exercise, you create a form that shows the supplier information and, within it, embed a subform that shows the different machines that they handle.

Locate the Vending9 database that you worked on in the previous project and rename it `Vending10`.

Create a new form that uses the Name, Address, and Phone fields from the Suppliers table and the Machine Type and Cost fields from the Machine table. Use the subform option to display the machine types.

Add the Date to the Form Header.

Test the form to see if it works, and then close the database.

Revising Tables and Relationships

In this exercise, you add combo boxes to the Rental Activity form to help look up the Customer ID and the Video ID.

Locate the Video Store8 database and rename it `Video Store9`.

Open the `Customer` table and determine which column contains the Customer ID number (count from the left in the Datasheet view). Close the table.

Open the `Rental Activity` form. Change the Customer ID text box into a combo box. Set the properties to display the first three columns of the Customer table but use the Customer ID (bound column=8, column count=8) as the source of the value that is placed in the text box. Set the other properties as necessary to display the three columns when the down arrow is used.

Add a date to the Form Header.

Switch to Form view and add a new record. Notice that when you use the combo box to choose a customer name, it displays the name in the box. Close the form and open the Rental Activity table. Notice that the value placed in the Customer ID field is the value that was in the bound column (8).

Repeat this process for the Video ID text box.

Add a new record using the combo boxes. Check the Rental Activity table to make sure that the new record contains the correct Customer and Video ID numbers.

Create a new form with a subform that includes fields from three of the tables:

`Last Name`, `First Name`, and `Street` from the Customers table

`Title` from the Video Tapes table

`Date Rented`, `Date Returned`, and `Late Fee` from the Rental Activity table

The last four fields go in the subform. When you have finished, close the database.

Creating a Form with a Subform to Display Information

It might be convenient to display the one-to-many relationship between items associated with the information about each insurance company.

Locate the Home Inventory8 database that you used in the previous project and rename it `Home Inventory9`.

Create a new form that uses all the fields from the Insurance Company table and the appropriate fields from the Items table. Use the subform option to display the items.

Add the Date to the Form Header.

Adjust the widths of the columns in Form view (assuming the subform is a spreadsheet) so that all of the fields are visible.

Use both navigation bars to scroll through both forms. When you are finished, close the database and exit Access.

PinPoint Assessment

PinPoint Training

You have completed the project and the associated lessons, as well as the "Checking Your Skills" and "Applying Your Skills" sections. Now use the PinPoint software Evaluation mode to assess your comprehension of the specific exam tasks you have just learned. You can also use the PinPoint Trainer mode and the SHOW ME tutorials to practice these specific exam tasks.

Project 13

Thirteen

Special Purpose Reports and Advanced Report Features

Specialized Report Wizards and Features Produce Information You Need

In this project you will learn the following objectives and their associated Microsoft Exam required activities.

Objectives	Required Activities
➤ Create Labels for Mailings	Create a Report
➤ Create Labels for Folders	Create a Report
➤ Create Calculated Fields in a Report	Calculate Fields Make a Calculation on a Report Use Expressions in Calculated Controls
➤ Create Reports That Group Data	Group Data in a Report
➤ Add Calculated Fields to Group Headers and Footers	Calculate Fields Customize Headers and Footers Sort Data in a Report Label a Report

Why Would I Do This?

If you expect to send mailings to employees, group members, customers, or anyone else in your database, you can produce mailing labels with a special type of report in Access. This type of report prints several fields together and has preformatted layouts that match commercially available adhesive labels.

You may also want to produce labels for folders. This can be done using the same type of report. In this section, you learn to select different fields and label sizes.

In many cases, you want to show information in a report that is derived from other fields in the table or query. You learn how to perform calculations based on existing fields to produce additional columns in your reports.

A report can be made easier to read by grouping data and introducing visual breaks between the groups. You learn how to group and subgroup your data.

Another reason to group data is to determine subtotals. In this project, you learn how to add subtotals and totals to report headers and footers.

Lesson 1: Creating Labels for Mailings

Reports are used to list many records. A mailing label report lists the records in a format that is traditionally used for addressing letters.

In this lesson, you create a report to produce labels that can be attached to envelopes or brochures for mailings. A report Label Wizard helps you design your report. Creating labels, even using the Label Wizard, is a process that involves many steps.

To Create a Mailing Label Report

1. **Copy the Proj1301 file from the Project-13 folder on the CD, and paste it into your own directory on your disk. Rename the copy `Hardware Inventory3`.**

2. **Launch Access 97 and open the `Hardware Inventory3` database.**

   The Database window should now be open to the Tables area. If it is not, click the Tables tab.

3. **In the Hardware Inventory3 database, click the `Vendors` table to select it, then click Open.**

   Notice that this table contains data that is necessary to contact the vendor by mail or by phone (see Figure 13.1).

Figure 13.1
The Vendors table includes vendor addresses and phone numbers.

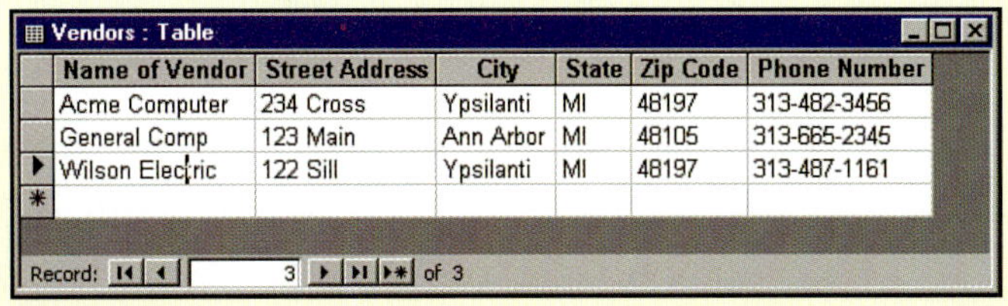
Vendors : Table

Name of Vendor	Street Address	City	State	Zip Code	Phone Number
Acme Computer	234 Cross	Ypsilanti	MI	48197	313-482-3456
General Comp	123 Main	Ann Arbor	MI	48105	313-665-2345
Wilson Electric	122 Sill	Ypsilanti	MI	48197	313-487-1161

Record: 3 of 3

4 **Close the Vendors table. Click the Reports tab and then click the New button.**

The New Report dialog box is displayed.

5 **Click the drop-down button to reveal a list of the tables and queries that are available in this database (see Figure 13.2). Click Vendors in the list to select the Vendors table.**

Figure 13.2
The New Report dialog box shows a list of tables and queries you can base your report on.

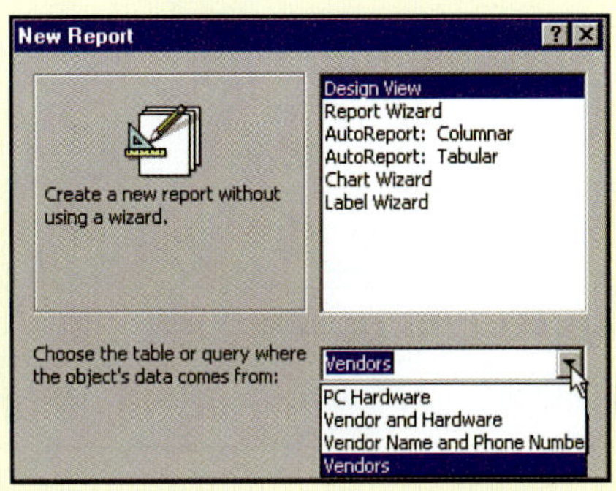

6 **Select Label Wizard from the list of available reports and wizards, then click OK.**

The first Label Wizard dialog box is displayed after a short delay (see Figure 13.3).

7 **In the Label Type area, select Sheet Feed (if necessary).**

The list of available label types displayed depends on whether you have selected Sheet Feed or Continuous.

8 **Click the label size with Avery number 5160.**

This is a form that prints three labels across a single 8 1/2-inch form. Print these labels on ordinary paper for the purposes of this exercise.

9 **Click Next.**

The second Label Wizard dialog box is displayed (see Figure 13.4).

10 **Change the font size to 12 and the font name to Arial, if necessary.**

Arial is a *Sans serif* style font that is appropriate for titles or labels.

Serif
A fine, horizontal line finishing off the main strokes of a letter, as at the top and bottom of the letter M.

Sans serif
A typeface without serifs.

continues

To Create a Mailing Label Report (continued)

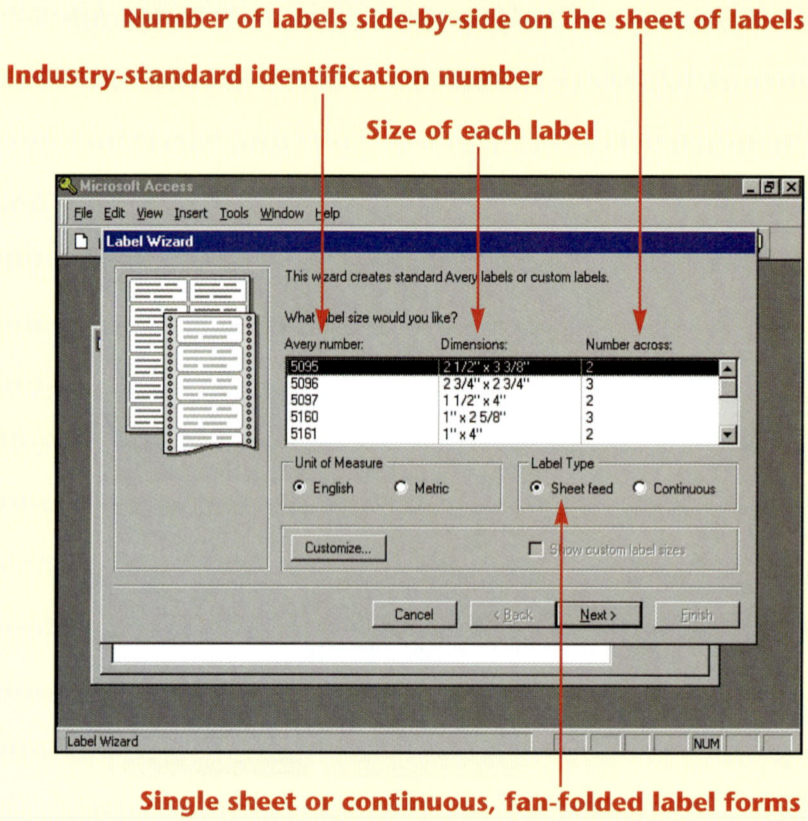

Figure 13.3
Select the label size in the first Label Wizard dialog box.

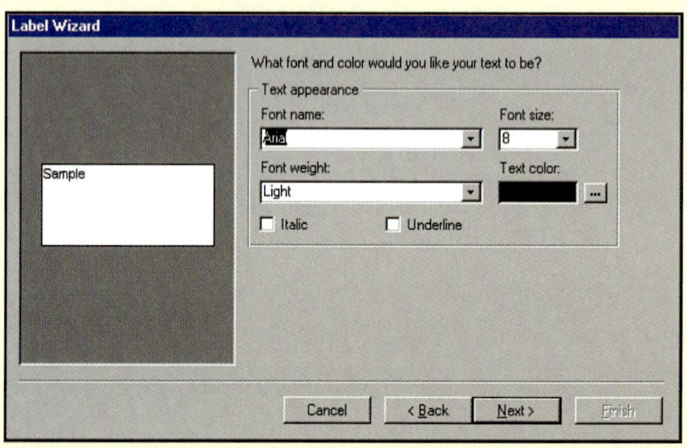

Figure 13.4
In the second Label Wizard dialog box, choose the text font and color.

11 Click Next to accept the settings for the font style and size.

The third Label Wizard dialog box is displayed (see Figure 13.5). This dialog box enables you to construct your labels using existing fields and enter other items you would like to include.

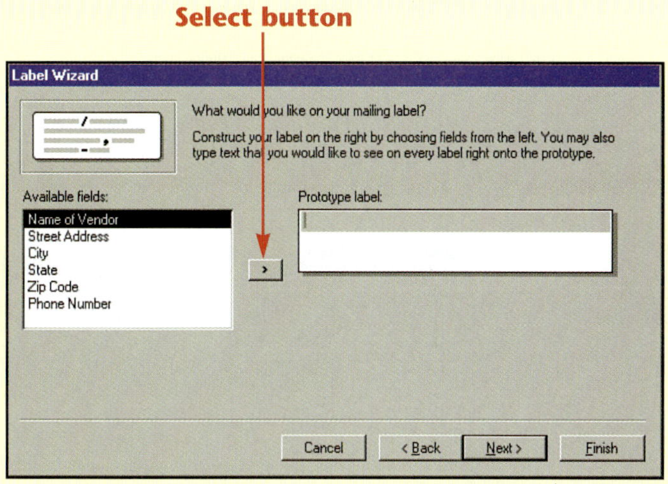

Figure 13.5
Choose what you want to include on the label in the third Label Wizard dialog box.

12 **Click the Name of Vendor field to select it, if necessary, then click the Select button to add this field to the Prototype label. Press Enter to move to the next line of the label.**

13 **Click the Street Address field, if necessary, to select it, then click the Select button to add this field to the label.**

14 **Press Enter to move to the next line of the label.**

If you make a mistake creating the label, you can edit the sample label in the Prototype label box as if it were a normal document.

15 **Click the City field to select it, if necessary, then click the Select button to add it to the label. Type a comma and a space from the keyboard.**

16 **Add the State field to the same line of the label. Type in two more spaces from the keyboard.**

17 **Add the Zip code field to the label.**

You have now set up your mailing label. Curly braces, {}, surround each field from the Vendors table (see Figure 13.6).

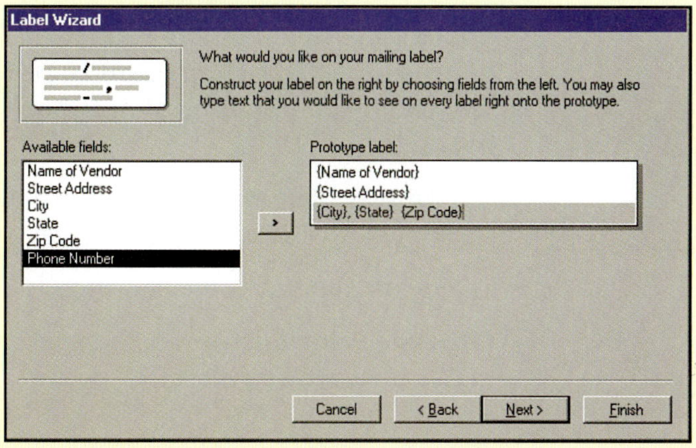

Figure 13.6
The Prototype label now includes inserted fields.

continues

To Create a Mailing Label Report (continued)

18 Click Next.

The fourth Label Wizard dialog box is displayed (see Figure 13.7). This dialog box enables you to choose the field or fields on which you want to sort.

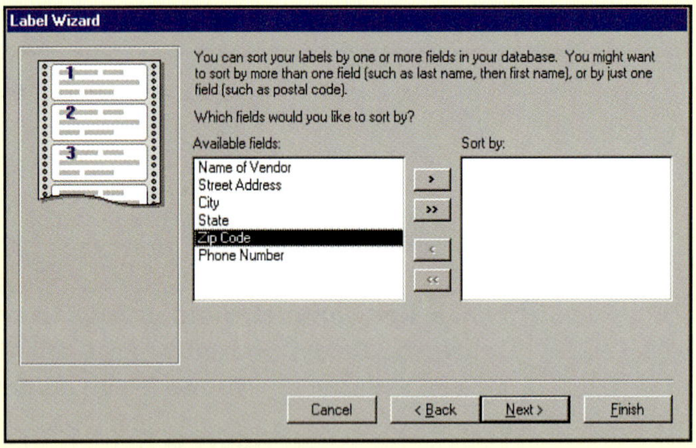

Figure 13.7
Use the fourth Label Wizard dialog box to choose the sort fields.

19 Click the Zip Code field to select it, then click the Select button to add it to the Sort By list.

Most labels are sorted by ZIP code because of postage savings for mass mailings.

If you select more than one field the program sorts the records by the first field listed. Then it sorts the records within that grouping by the next field listed. For example, if you had a table with many vendor names and had chosen to sort first by City and then by Name of Vendor, you would get a set of labels for each city. Within each city, the labels would be sorted alphabetically by the name of the vendor.

20 Click Next.

The final Label Wizard dialog box is displayed.

21 Change the name of the report to `Mailing Labels for Vendors`. Check to see that the option to preview the labels is selected and the Display Help option is not selected. Click the Finish button.

The Display Help option would have the same effect as using the Help menu to ask for help about creating reports.

The report appears in Preview mode (see Figure 13.8).

22 Click the Print button on the toolbar to print a copy of the labels on a regular sheet of paper.

Access

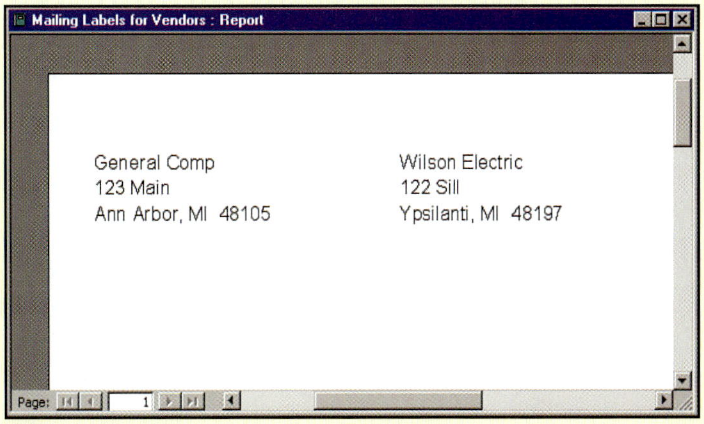

Figure 13.8
After you complete the Label Wizard, a preview of the mailing labels appears.

23 Click the Close button in the upper-right corner of the Print Preview window. Close the Report Design window, if necessary.

Keep the database open for the next lesson.

If you have problems...

Be careful not to click the Close button in the upper-right corner of the Access window. If you do, it will close the database and close Access. If this happens, reopen Access and reopen the database for the next lesson. Access saves your changes automatically when it is closed.

Inside Stuff

The many different typefaces available can be divided into two groups—those with serifs and those without serifs, or sans serifs. These horizontal lines at the end of each vertical letter stroke helped the old-time typesetters line up the letters when they set the type. Today's reading experts find that typefaces with serifs are easier for people to read when the words are arranged in long lines like this paragraph. Sans serif letters are often used for short word groups like titles or labels.

Some printers require minimum margin settings that are larger than the label settings used in this example. You may get a warning message such as "Some data may not be displayed." Proceed to print if you get such messages, and examine the printout to see if any characters have been left off.

For this project we assume you have a printer that uses separate sheets of paper rather than the continuous, folded paper that has holes in the sides for a sprocket. If you have a printer that uses continuous feed paper, you can either select a different label that is about the same size as the one indicated in the lesson or follow the directions as written and simply preview the labels without sending them to the printer. Ask your instructor for additional advice about the printing arrangement that is available with your computer.

Lesson 2: Creating Labels for Folders

Labels can also be produced for use with file folders and for equipment identification. In this lesson you will create labels suitable for use with file folders that could be used to hold warranty information for a company's personal computers.

In this lesson, you create labels for letter-size manila file folders with tabs that are about 1/2 inch high by 3 1/2 inches long. The label consists of a single line of print with the name of the processor and its inventory code number. You adjust the font size so that the letters are 1/4 inch high for better legibility.

To Create File Folder Labels

1. **In the Hardware Inventory3 database, click the Reports tab, then click New.**

   The New Report dialog box is displayed.

2. **Select PC Hardware from the drop-down list of tables and queries.**
3. **Click the Label Wizard option, and then click OK.**

   After a short delay, the first Label Wizard dialog box is displayed.

4. **In the Label Type area, click Sheet Feed, if necessary.**

   Ask your instructor for assistance if you have a continuous feed printer.

5. **Scroll down the list of labels to find the one named Index Maker 3 Tab, and click on it (see Figure 13.9).**

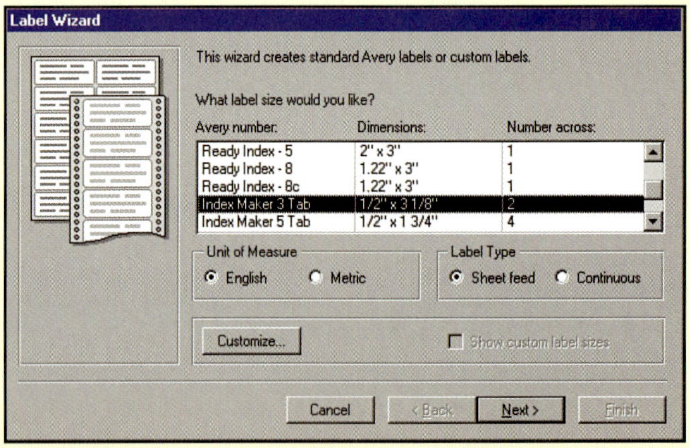

Figure 13.9
Choose the label size in the first Label Wizard dialog box.

6. **Click Next.**

   The second Label Wizard dialog box appears.

7. **Click the down-arrow button in the Font Size box and select 16.**

   This font size setting makes the letters slightly less than 1/4 inch high.

Access

8 Click the down-arrow button next to the Font Name box to reveal a list of available fonts, then scroll down to the Times New Roman font and select it (see Figure 13.10).

Compare the Times New Roman (serif) font to Arial (sans serif) to decide which font you find most readable for a label.

There are other formatting options available on the second Label Wizard dialog box, including italic, underlining, and degree of boldfacing, which is found in the Font weight box. You can even change the font color if you have a color printer available.

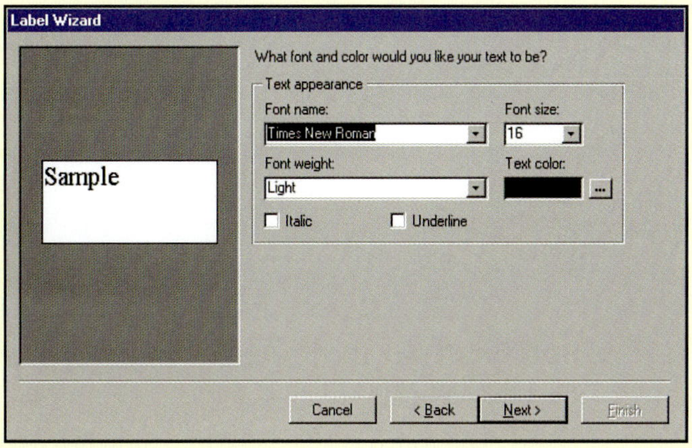

Figure 13.10
The sample label now appears in the Times New Roman font.

9 Click Next.

The third Label Wizard dialog box is displayed (see Figure 13.11).

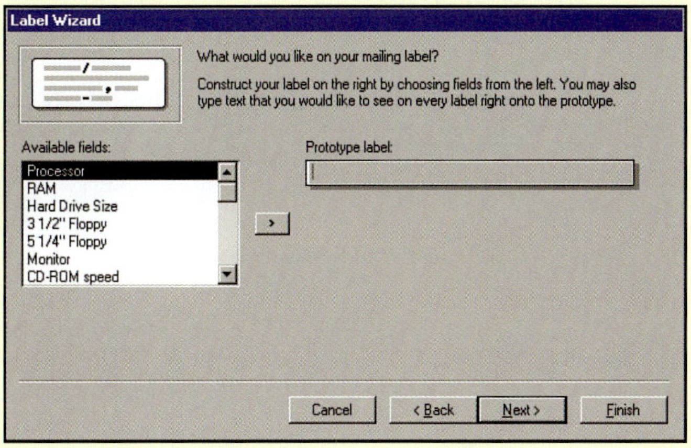

Figure 13.11
Enter the label text in the third Label Wizard dialog box.

10 Type `Processor:` in the Prototype label box and press the Spacebar once.

11 Click the Processor field name, then click the Select button to select this field for the label.

continues

To Create File Folder Labels (continued)

12 Type a comma, press the Spacebar once, then type `ID:` and press the Spacebar once again.

13 Scroll down the field list and select the Inventory Code Number field, then click the Select button to add it to the label (see Figure 13.12).

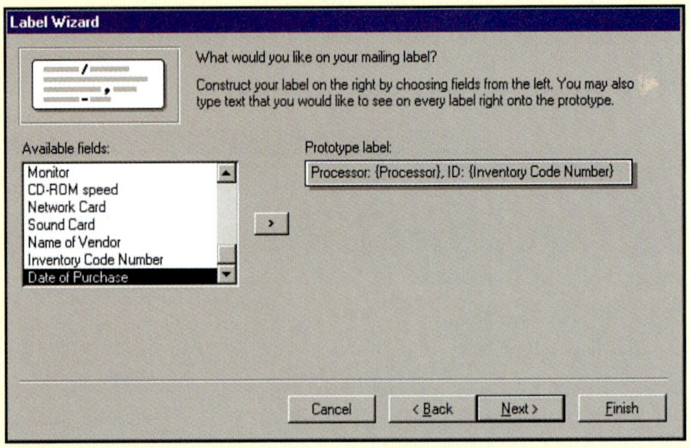

Figure 13.12
The Prototype label includes the Processor and ID fields.

14 Click Next.

The fourth Label Wizard dialog box is displayed.

15 Click the Processor field name (if necessary), then click the Select button.

This tells the program to sort on the Processor field.

16 Click Next, then change the name of the report to `Folder Labels by Processor`.

17 Click Finish to preview the labels (see Figure 13.13).

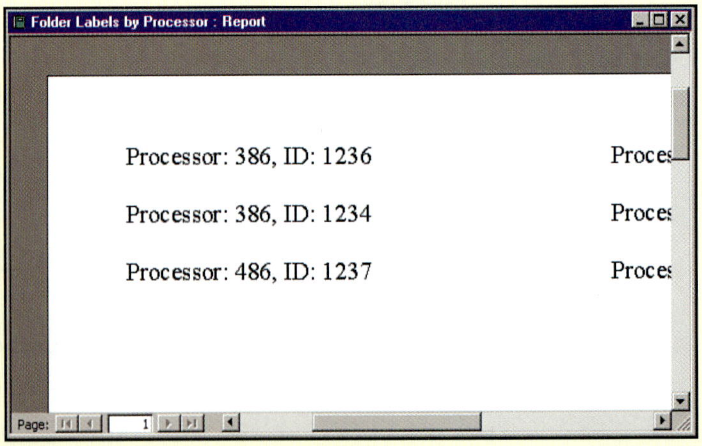

Figure 13.13
The folder labels now appear in Preview mode.

18 Print a sample of the labels on a plain sheet of paper. Click the Print button on the toolbar to print the labels.

Access

If you have problems...

Check with your instructor to be sure that your computer is set up to print this example. If the printer does not respond, do not send the same file again until you resolve the issue. Otherwise, you may ultimately wind up with multiple copies of your label page. Printer setups vary and may require special assistance from your instructor.

19. **Click the Close button in the upper-right corner of the Print Preview window.**

20. **Close the database.**

Inside Stuff

The height allowed for each line of print is measured in points. This is an old typesetter's measurement that goes back to the days of manual printing presses. There are 72 points to the inch, so 1/4 inch would be 18 points. This is the amount of space allowed for the line of print and includes enough space above and below the letters so that the top of the tallest letters do not touch the bottom of the previous lines. The height of the letters also affects their width.

Lesson 3: Creating Calculated Fields in a Report

You may want to display information calculated from data in one of your tables. In this lesson, you learn how to take data from two fields and display the result of dividing the contents of one field by those in another.

First you look at a tabular report that contains the fields you use to calculate an average pay per employee.

To Examine the Report That Will Be Modified

1. **Copy the Proj1302 file from the Project-13 folder on the CD, paste it in your own directory on your disk, and rename the copy `Service Businesses 2`.**

2. **Open the `Services Businesses 2` database.**

3. **Click the Reports tab, if necessary.**

   The Pay per Employee report should be selected.

4. **Click the Preview button.**

   A preview of the report appears.

   The `0` ZIP code in the first row is a code used by the government to indicate totals for the entire state. Since Access sorted the report in ZIP code order, this summary line appears at the top of the report.

continues

To Examine the Report That Will Be Modified (continued)

5 Move the pointer onto the report. It becomes a magnifying glass with a minus sign in it. Click once to decrease the magnification.

You are able to see the entire first page of the report. Notice that there is room on the right for an additional column (see Figure 13.14).

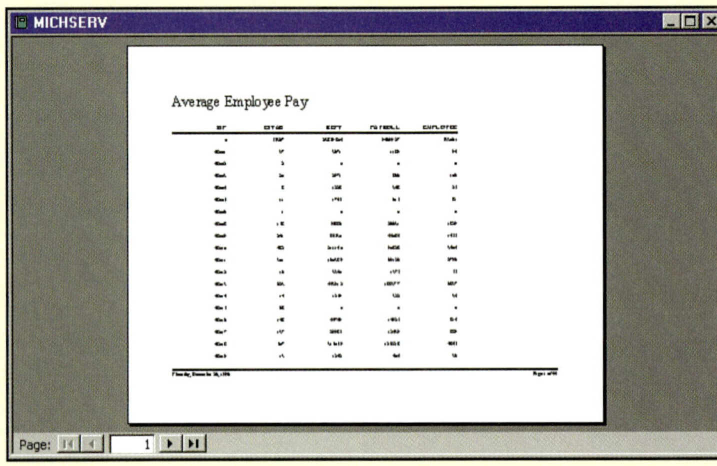

Figure 13.14
The Pay per Employee report is shown in Preview mode.

6 Click the View button on the toolbar to switch to Design view.

7 Scroll the design window to the right so you can see the right side of the report, then arrange the design window and the toolbox as shown in Figure 13.15. (Open the toolbox, if necessary.)

Keep the database open for the next procedure.

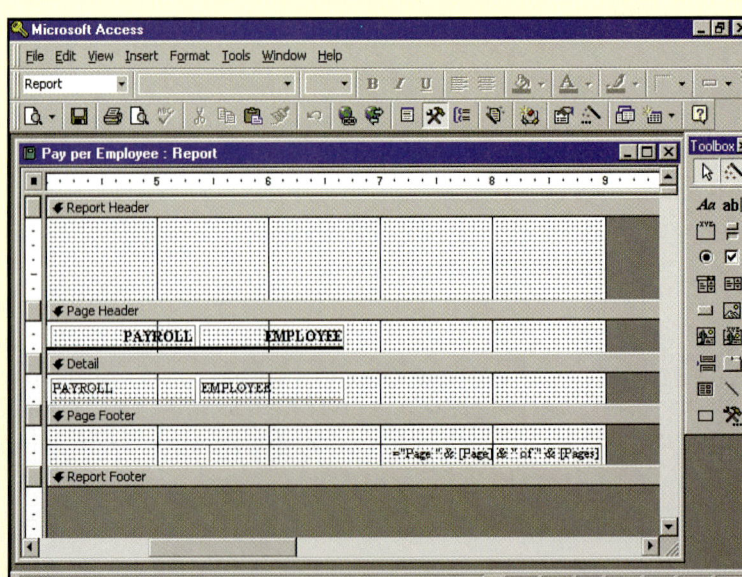

Figure 13.15
The right side of the report design and the toolbox.

You have now set up the Report window. In this next section, you add calculated fields to the report.

To Create Calculated Fields in a Report

1 Click the Text Box button in the toolbox.

2 In the Detail section of the report design, drag a text box that is approximately the same size as the other text boxes in the Detail section (see Figure 13.16).

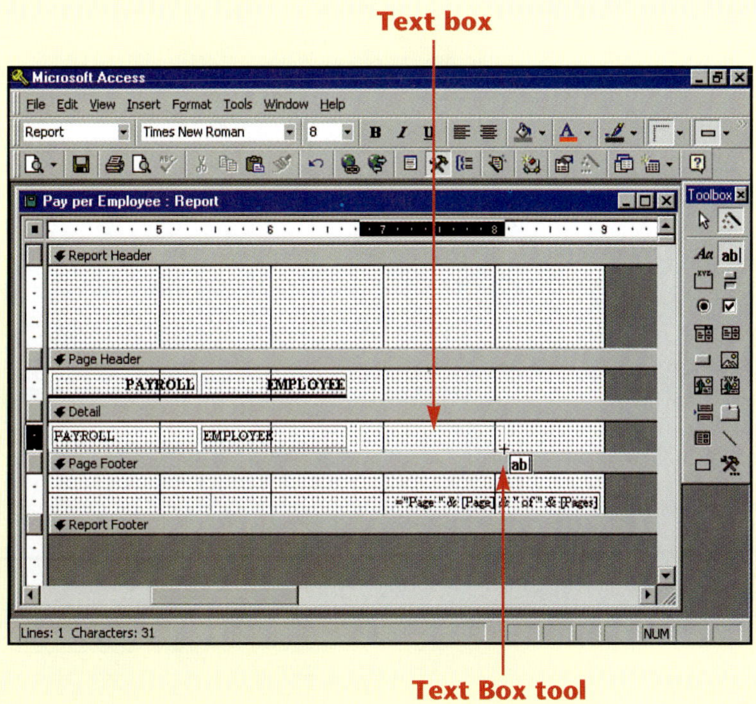

Figure 13.16
The Text Box tool enables you to add a calculated field in the Detail area of the report design.

When you release the mouse button, an Unbound (not connected to an underlying table) text box appears along with its label box (see Figure 13.17). The label will probably appear over the top of another field.

If you have problems...

When drawing a new text box, it takes some skill to get the box the size you want. You may need to turn the Snap to Grid feature off in the Format menu. If it is not the correct size, press Del and try again. If the size is okay, but the position is not where you want it, point at the text box with your mouse until the pointer turns into a hand, then click and drag the box to a position that is in line with the other boxes.

3 Click an empty part of the report design to deselect the new text box.

4 Click in the unwanted label box to select it. Press the Del key to delete the label box.

continues

To Create Calculated Fields in a Report (continued)

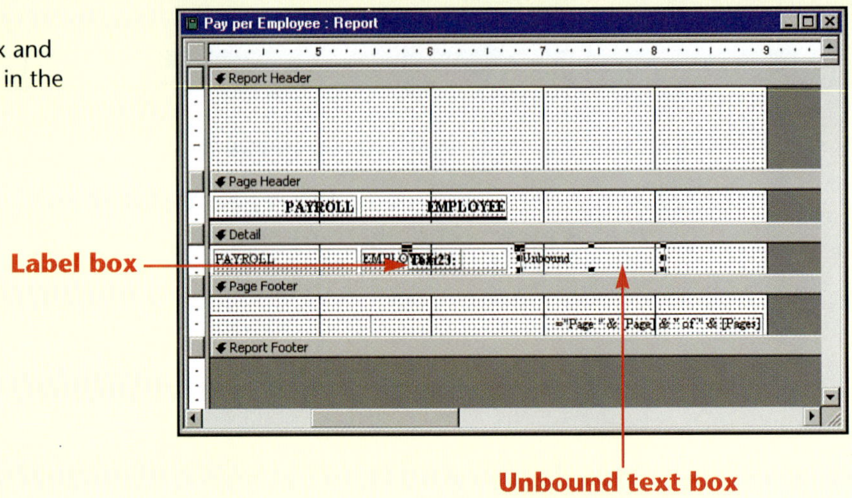

Figure 13.17
The new text box and label box appear in the report design.

5 **Click the new text box to select it.**

6 **Click the word `Unbound` to turn on the text editing mode (see Figure 13.18).**

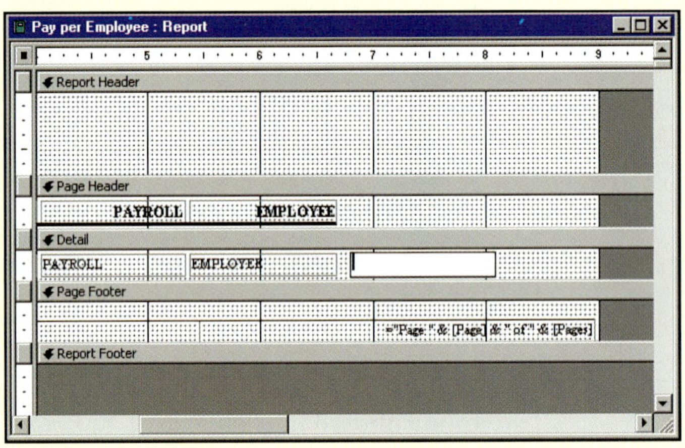

Figure 13.18
The text box is now ready for formula entry.

7 **Type in the following formula (be sure to use square brackets):**

```
=[PAYROLL]*1000/[EMPLOYEE]
```

This formula takes the contents of the PAYROLL field (the amount paid to area employees in thousands of dollars), multiplies it by 1,000, then divides by the number of employees in that ZIP code area.

The principle behind the formulas in calculated fields is the same as that of any formula. Mathematical symbols are used in the same way, but the variable names are simply the field names enclosed in square brackets.

8 Click the Print Preview button to preview the report.

Scroll the report to the right to see the results of the calculated field (see Figure 13.19).

Figure 13.19
The print preview of the report shows problems with the calculated field.

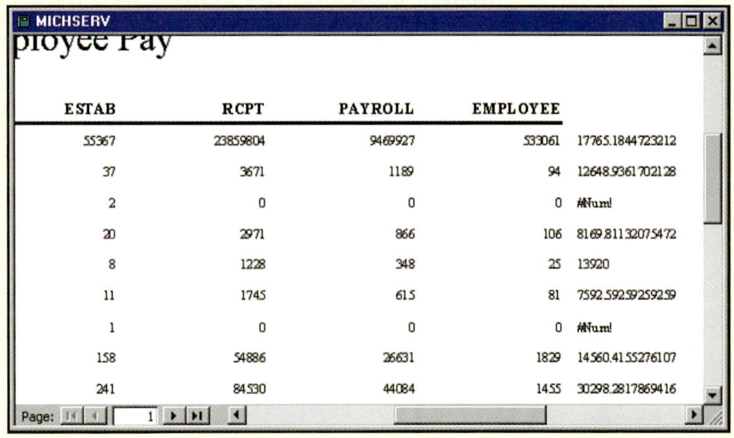

Notice that the average for the first record was approximately $17,765, but the display is showing too many decimal places. Also, there is an error message wherever the number of employees is zero. This error message is displayed when the expression divides by zero.

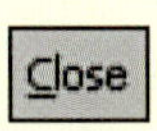

9 Click the Close button on the toolbar to close the report preview.

The Report Design window should still be open. Make sure the calculated text box is still selected.

10 Click the Properties button on the toolbar to open the Properties window, then select the Format tab.

The calculated field is still selected, even though it is off the screen. The Properties window shows the properties of the text box (see Figure 13.20).

Figure 13.20
The Properties window displays properties for the calculated field.

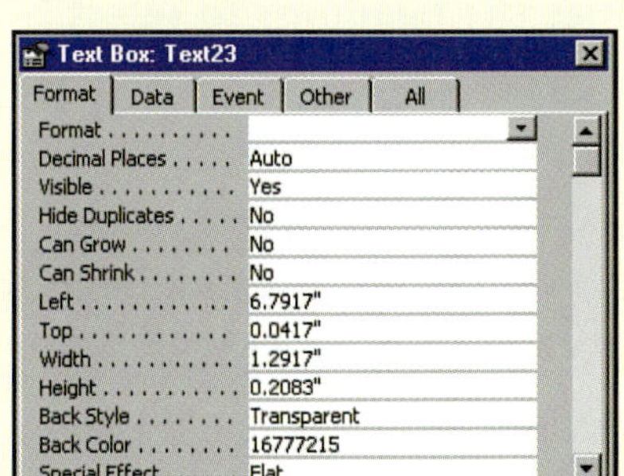

11 Click in the Format box and enter the following format:

```
$#,##0.00
```

continues

To Create Calculated Fields in a Report (continued)

This displays the number with commas inserted and two decimal places. Remember that the formats you learned in Project 9, "Making Data Entry Easier and More Accurate," Lesson 2 had three parts separated by semicolons. In this case, there are no negative numbers, and the zero values are handled in another way.

12. **Click the Data tab, and replace the formula in the Control Source box with the following:**

```
=IIF([EMPLOYEE]>0,[PAYROLL]*1000/[EMPLOYEE],"NA")
```

This formula uses an `IIF` function to test for the existence of a number of employees greater than zero. If that condition is true, it uses the same formula we used before. If it is not true, it prints the code NA for Not Applicable. (You could have entered this formula directly into the text box the same way you entered the original formula.)

13. **Close the Properties sheet.**

14. **Scroll the report design to the right, if necessary, to show the last column. Click the Label tool in the toolbox, and drag a box in the Page Header section directly above the calculated field.**

Make the box the same length as the text below it.

15. **Enter the label** `AVERAGE PAY`**, then click outside the label box to deselect it.**

16. **Click the label box to select it. Click the Right Align button on the toolbar.**

If you don't have a Right Align button, click the right mouse button and select Properties. Click the Format tab, scroll down to Text Align, then choose Right. The label appears in the heading with its text aligned right.

17. **Click the dark, horizontal line in the Report Header that underlines the headings to select it.**

You may have to expand the Page Header section to complete this step. The pointer turns into a hand and the end of the line has a handle on it (see Figure 13.21).

18. **Move the pointer to the handle at the end of the line and drag it to the right to extend it under the new heading label.**

The dark horizontal line should now extend all the way across the report.

19. **Click the Print Preview button to preview the report.**

20. **Scroll to the right to see the calculated field and its heading (see Figure 13.22).**

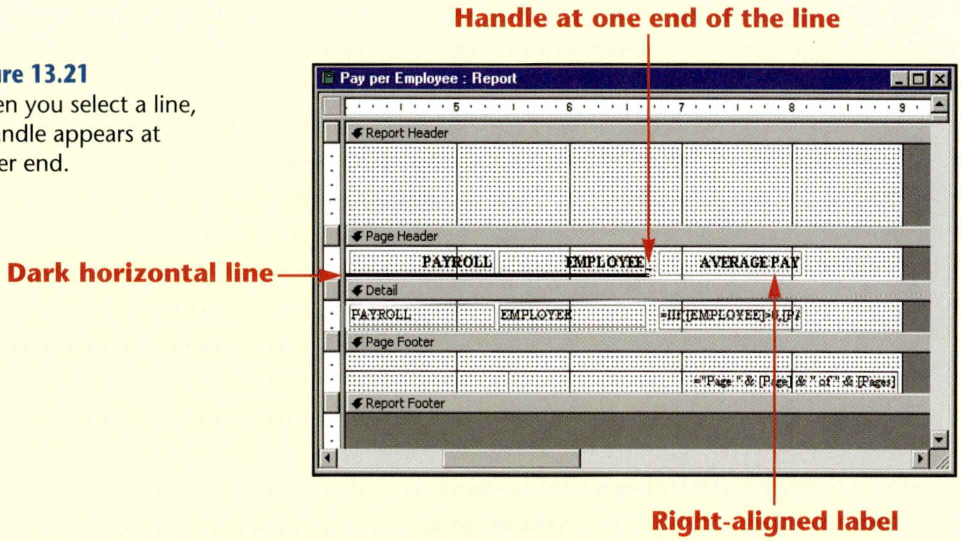

Figure 13.21
When you select a line, a handle appears at either end.

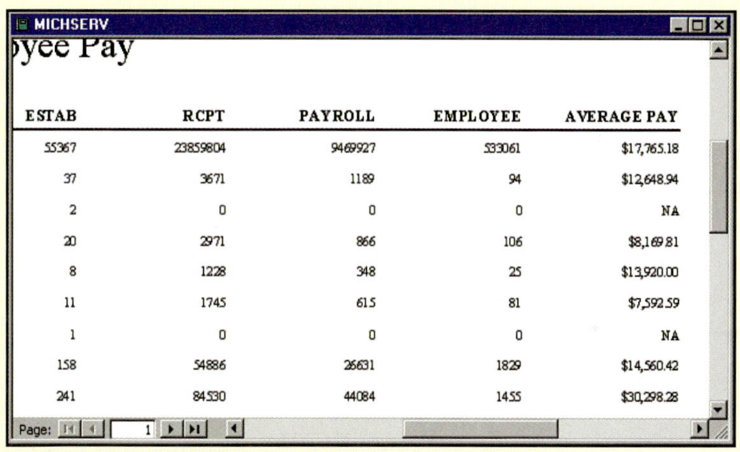

Figure 13.22
The calculated field and its heading appear in their final form on the report.

21. **In the menu bar, click File and then Print.**

    This allows you to print part of the whole report.

22. **In the Print Range area, enter 1 in the From and To boxes to print page 1, and click OK.**

    This prints page 1 of the report.

23. **Click the Close button in the upper-right corner of the Print Preview window and save the changes.**

24. **Close the database.**

Lesson 4: Creating Reports That Group Data

There are many occasions where it is important to group records for easier reading. In this lesson, you learn how to create and sort groups of records.

To Create Reports That Group Data

1 Copy the Proj1303 file from the Project-13 folder on the CD, paste it in your own directory on your disk, and rename the copy `Library10`.

2 Open the `Library10` database and click the Reports tab.

3 Click the Books Grouped by Type of Book report to select it. Click Preview to view the report (see Figure 13.23).

Scroll around the report and observe the fields it contains.

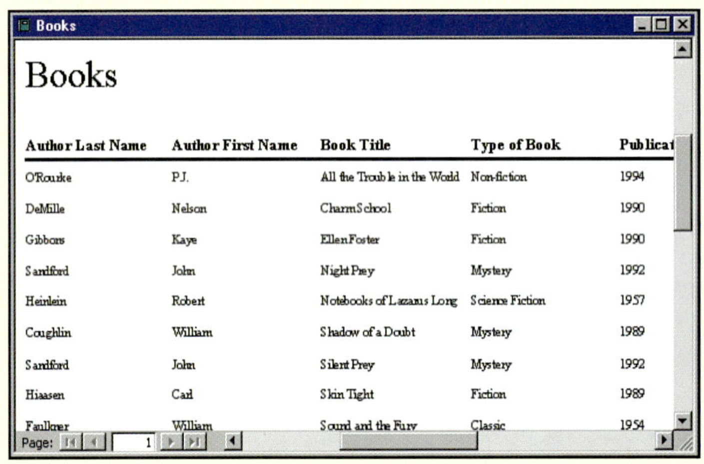

Figure 13.23
The books in the report are in no particular order.

4 Click the Close button on the toolbar.

This closes the preview and returns you to the Database window with the Reports tab chosen.

5 Select the Books Grouped by Type of Book report, then click Design.

6 Click the Sorting and Grouping button on the toolbar.

The Sorting and Grouping dialog box appears (see Figure 13.24).

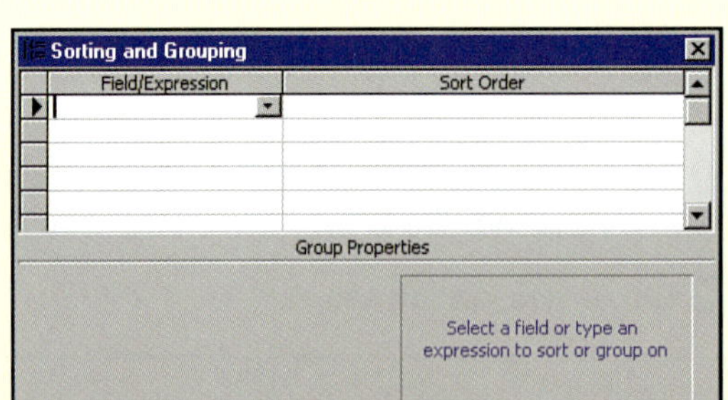

Figure 13.24
The Sorting and Grouping dialog box is used to sort data by groups.

7 Click the down arrow on the right of the Field/Expression box and select Type of Book.

The name of the field is placed in the box and the Group Properties section of the dialog box changes (see Figure 13.25).

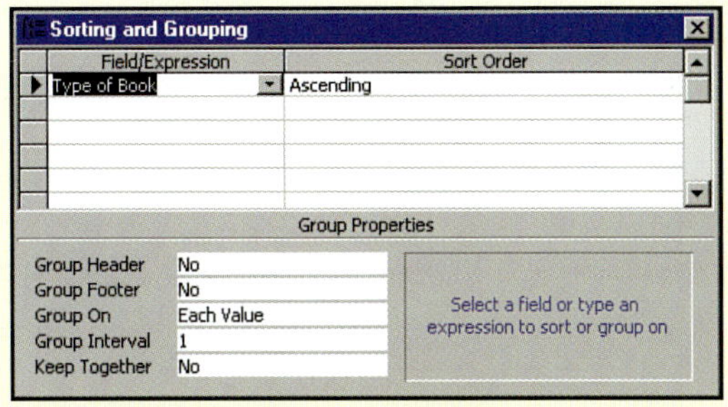

Figure 13.25
The Sorting and Grouping box is shown with a field selected.

8 **Click the Group Header box, then click the down-arrow button and change this selection to Yes.**

9 **Click the Print Preview button to preview the report (see Figure 13.26).**

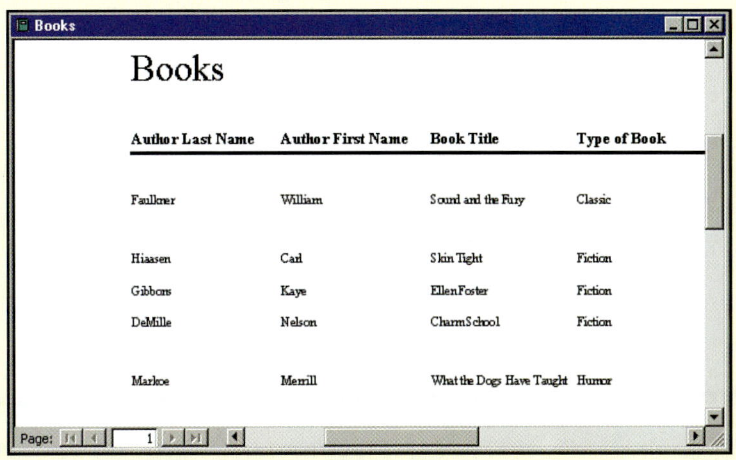

Figure 13.26
The report is grouped by type of book.

Notice that the report is sorted by the Type of Book field, and there is a space between groups. The space was created when you selected a Group Header.

10 **Click the Close button on the toolbar to return to the report Design view. Close the Sorting and Grouping dialog box.**

Notice that the report design now has a section titled Type of Book Header (see Figure 13.27).

11 **Click the Toolbox button to open the toolbox, if it is not already open.**

12 **Click the Text Box button in the toolbox, and drag a text box into the Type of Book Header section for the new header (see Figure 13.27).**

13 **Release the mouse button and a text box appears.**

It also has its own label with the word `Text` plus a number. Click an empty part of the design to deselect the text box.

continues

To Create Reports That Group Data (continued)

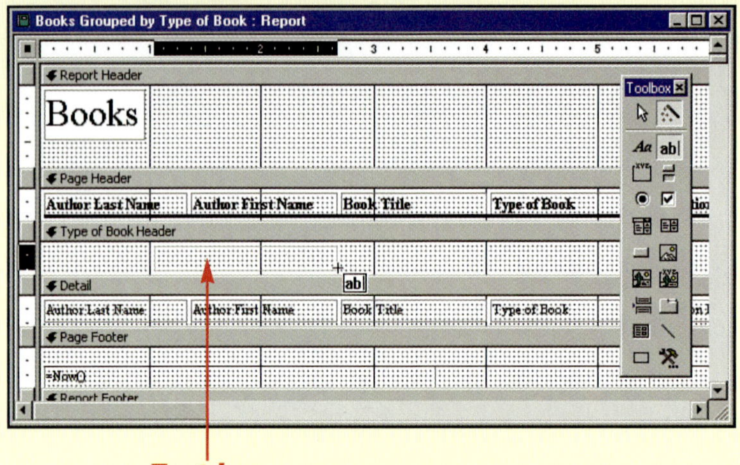

Figure 13.27
The Design view is shown with a text box drawn in the Type of Book Header section.

⑭ **Click the text box label to select it, then press the Del key to delete the label.**

The text box should remain without its label.

⑮ **Click the new text box, then click a second time to enable the Text Editing mode.**

⑯ **Type in the name of the field that is being used to group on,** `Type of Book` **(see Figure 13.28).**

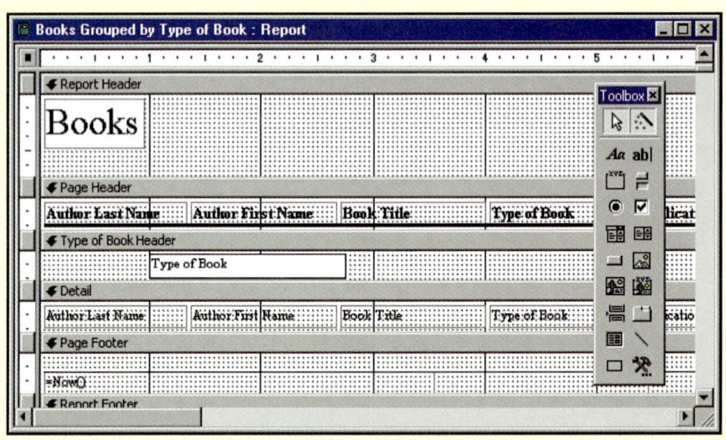

Figure 13.28
The Header text box with the Type of Book field name in it.

⑰ **Click the Print Preview button to preview the report.**

Notice that the headers are too small and not positioned correctly.

⑱ **Click the Close button on the toolbar to return to Design view.**

⑲ **Move the Type of Book text box to the left so it lines up with the left side of the report.**

20 Use a handle on the bottom of the box to enlarge the box so it is twice as high.

You can drag the bottom downward to enlarge the box, but it will not work if you try to drag the top of the box upward.

21 Use the Font Size drop-down list on the Formatting toolbar to change the font size to 16 points and click the Bold button to change the typeface to bold (see Figure 13.29).

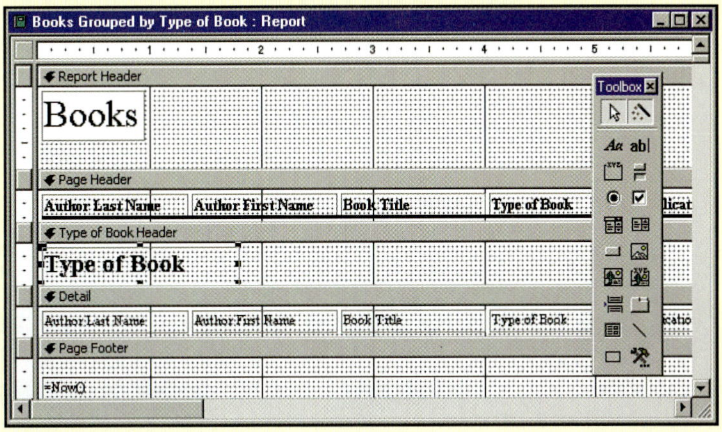

Figure 13.29
The Header text box is shown after it has been enlarged.

22 Click the Print Preview button to preview the report.

Notice that the header contains the same information as the Type of Book field (see Figure 13.30). When using headers of this type, it is often a good idea to remove the field on which the grouping is based.

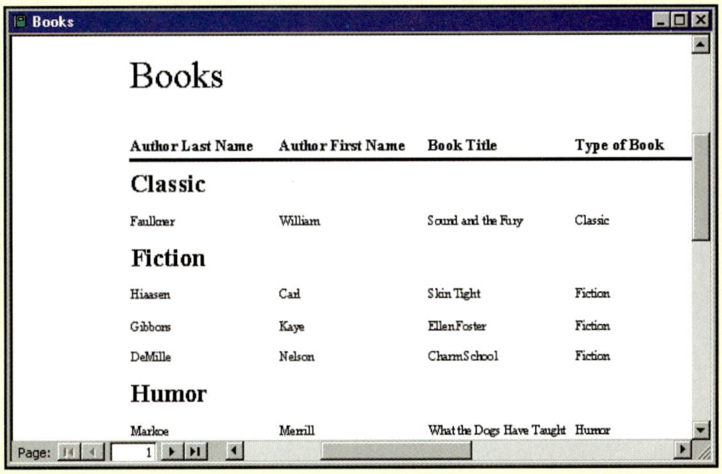

Figure 13.30
The final report is grouped on Type of Book with headers.

23 Click the Print button on the toolbar to print the report.

24 Close the Print Preview window and save the changes.

25 Close the database.

Lesson 5: Adding Calculated Fields to Group Headers and Footers

If you have a report with grouped records, it is often useful to place calculated information in a header or footer for that group. In this lesson, you learn how to add calculated fields to headers and footers.

To Customize the Header

1 Copy the Proj1304 file from the Project-13 folder on the CD, paste it in your own directory on your disk, and rename the copy `Customer Records`.

2 Open the `Customer Records` database, and click the Reports tab to reveal the existing report, Orders Grouped by Customer.

This report is based on a query (Purchases) that combines information from the Customers table and the Orders table. It has already been grouped by the customer's identification number.

3 Click Preview to look at this report (see Figure 13.31).

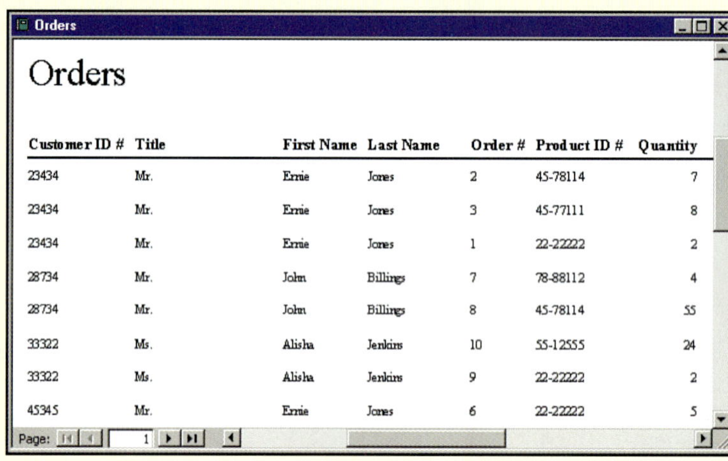
Orders

Orders

Customer ID #	Title	First Name	Last Name	Order #	Product ID #	Quantity
23434	Mr.	Ernie	Jones	2	45-78114	7
23434	Mr.	Ernie	Jones	3	45-77111	8
23434	Mr.	Ernie	Jones	1	22-22222	2
28734	Mr.	John	Billings	7	78-88112	4
28734	Mr.	John	Billings	8	45-78114	55
33322	Ms.	Alisha	Jenkins	10	55-12555	24
33322	Ms.	Alisha	Jenkins	9	22-22222	2
45345	Mr.	Ernie	Jones	6	22-22222	5

Page: 1

Figure 13.31
The Orders Grouped by Customer report shows grouping by Customer ID#.

4 Click the Close button on the toolbar to close the preview.

It is easier to recognize the grouped data if the name of the group is clearly identified in the header for that section.

5 Click Design to view the design of the Orders Grouped by Customer report (see Figure 13.32).

6 Click the Sorting and Grouping button on the toolbar.

The Sorting and Grouping dialog box is displayed.

Notice that this report has already been sorted and grouped on the Customer ID# field.

7 Move to the Group Properties section of the dialog box.

8 Change the Group Header and Group Footer properties to Yes.

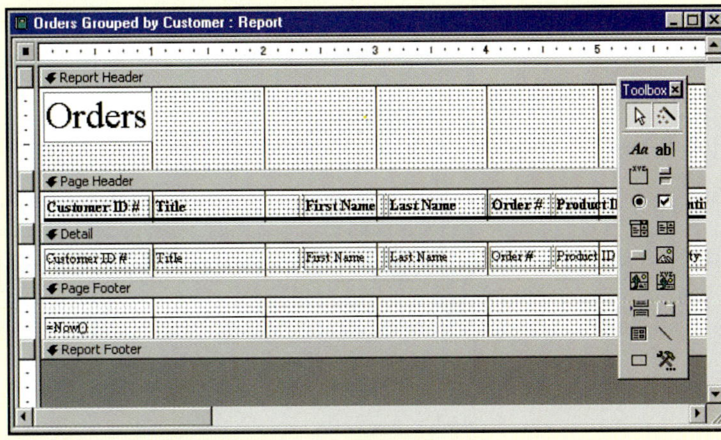

Figure 13.32
The Design view shows the layout of the Orders Grouped by Customer report.

This sets up sections for headers and footers to appear around each group in the Customer ID# field (see Figure 13.33).

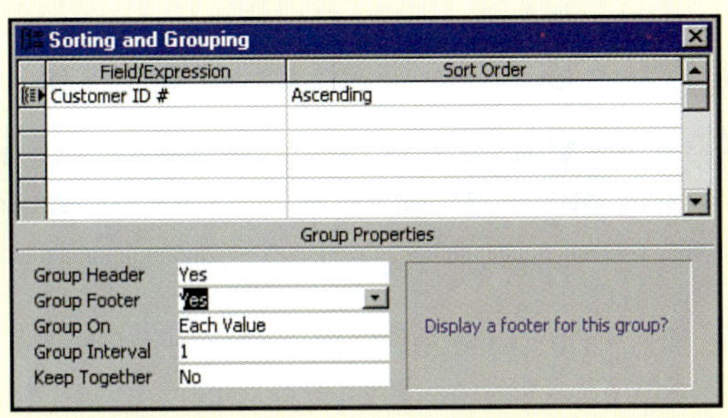

Figure 13.33
The Sorting and Grouping dialog box is displayed for this report.

9 Close the Sorting and Grouping dialog box.

The report design now has a Customer ID# header and footer (see Figure 13.34).

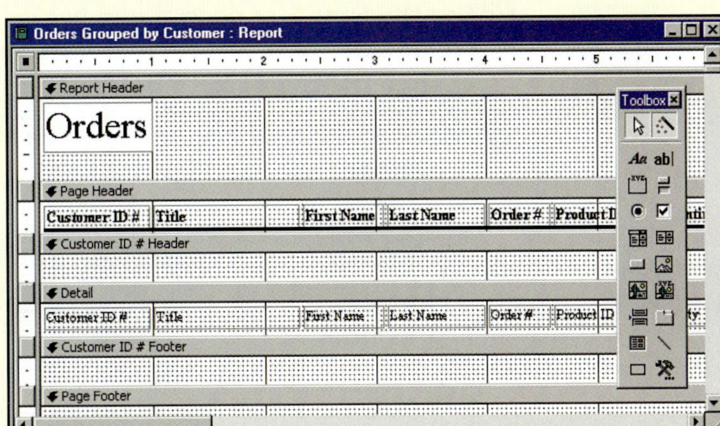

Figure 13.34
Report design showing Customer ID# header and footer.

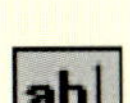

10 Click the Text Box button in the toolbox. Drag a text box in the Customer ID# header (see Figure 13.35).

continues

To Customize the Header (continued)

Figure 13.35
A text box has been added under the Customer ID# Group Header.

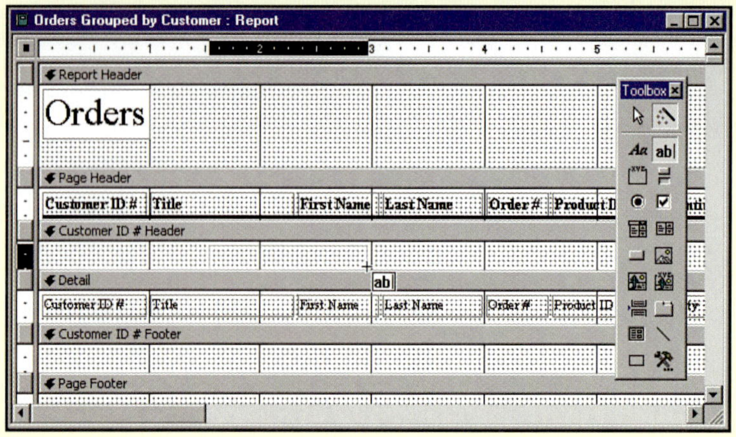

11. **Click the label box that was automatically created with the text box to select it. Delete this label.**

12. **Click the new text box to select it.**

13. **Click the new text box a second time to enable the text editing mode, then type in the following:**

```
[Last Name]+", "+[First Name]
```

The purpose of this command is to display the customer's last name, a comma and a space, and then the customer's first name. Notice that field names are always contained within square brackets, not parentheses.

14. **Click an empty area in the design to deselect the text box.**

15. **Click and drag the text box to the left side of the report.**

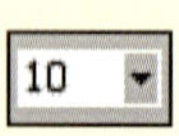

16. **Use the Font Size drop-down list on the Formatting toolbar to change the font size to 16 points and click the Bold button to change the typeface to bold.**

17. **Adjust the size of the box and the header to accommodate the larger font (see Figure 13.36).**

Figure 13.36
The font size and the text box size have been changed in the Group Header.

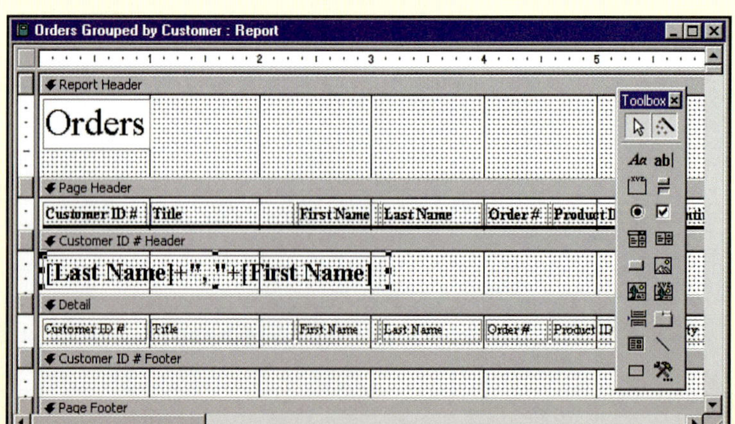

18. **Click the Print Preview button to preview the report.**

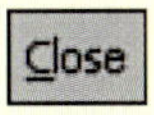

19. **Click the Close button to close the Print Preview window and return to the Design view.**

The values of a number field may be totaled or subtotaled by using a summation expression. This expression may be used in a footer. If it is used in a section footer, you see the subtotal for that section. Similarly, if it is used in a page or report footer, you see the total for the page or report respectively.

To Add an Expression to Show a Field Total

1. **In the Design view of the Orders Grouped by Customer report, scroll to the right to reveal the last three columns of the report.**

2. **Click the Text Box button in the toolbox. Drag a text box in the Customer ID# Footer section below the Item Total field.**

   Make sure the right edge of the text box is lined up with the right edge of the box above it (see Figure 13.37). This makes it easier to line up the numbers in the Detail and Footer sections.

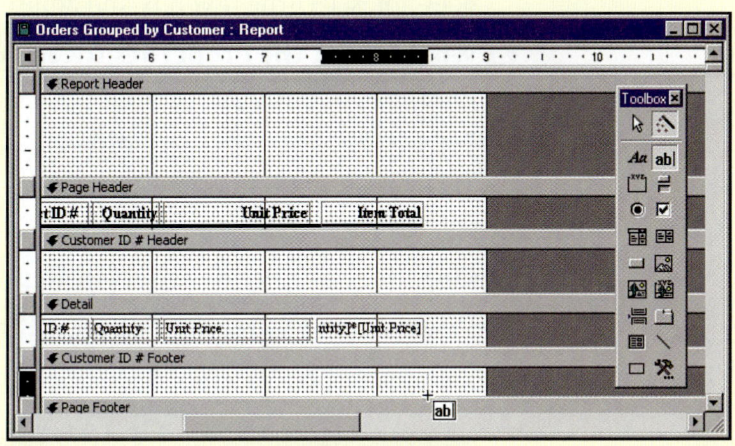

Figure 13.37
Text box drawn in the Customer ID # Footer section.

3. **Click the attached label box to select it. Click it again to turn on the text editing mode. Delete the current label and replace it with the following:**

```
Customer Total:
```

4. **Click the text box to select it. Click it a second time to enable the edit mode.**

5. **Enter the following expression:**

```
=sum([Quantity]*[Unit Price])
```

continues

To Add an Expression to Show a Field Total (continued)

Your screen should look like Figure 13.38.

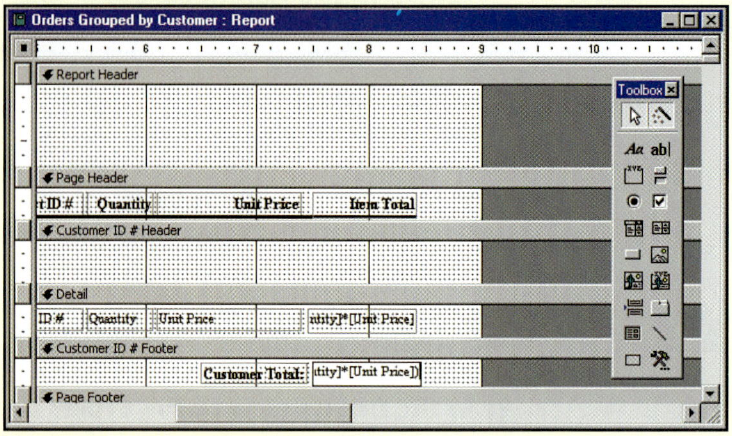

Figure 13.38
The footer is shown after an expression has been added.

6 **Click in an open area, then click on the text box again to select it. Click the Properties button, then select the Format tab, if necessary.**

7 **Scroll to the bottom and select Right in the Text Align box.**

This should line up the numbers in this field with those in the detail line above if the right edges of both boxes are lined up. If it does not, select the text box and adjust the right edge as necessary.

8 **While still in the Properties sheet, scroll up to the Format box.**

9 **Type `$#,##0.00` in the Format box.**

This matches the format of the subtotals with the numbers in the detail section.

10 **Click the Print Preview button to preview the report.**

11 **Scroll across the report to reveal the Unit Price column.**

Your report preview should look like Figure 13.39.

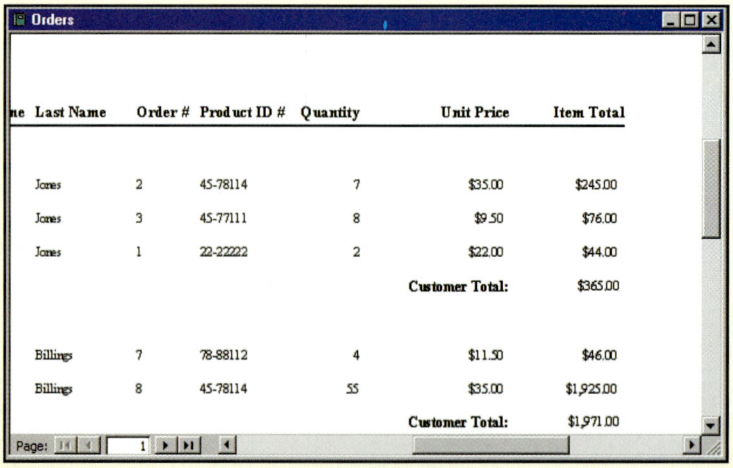

Figure 13.39
A preview of the final report shows subtotals for each customer.

12 Click the Print button on the toolbar to print the report.

13 Close the Print Preview window, close the Properties window, and then close the report and save the changes.

14 Close the database.

If you have completed your session on the computer, exit Access and shut down Windows before you turn off the computer. Otherwise, continue with the "Checking Your Skills" and "Applying Your Skills" sections in this project.

Exam Notes

Formulas and standard expressions start with the equal sign. The sum function adds all of the prices for this group. Functions like sum, average, and count are applied according to the section they are in. For example, if the sum function is in a group footer, it sums the field in that group. If the sum function is in a report footer, it sums that field for the entire report. Be careful with the square brackets and parentheses.

Project Summary

To	Do This
Create labels for mailings	Create a Mailing Labels report using the wizard. Select a standard label size, then assemble the fields for the label. Follow the directions in the wizard to sort the labels and to select font attributes.
Create labels for folders	This process is similar to creating mailing labels. You can also include spaces, commas, and your own text in each label and adjust the size and attributes of the font.
Create calculated fields in a report	Open the toolbox and click the Text Box button. Drag a box into the Detail section. Enter an expression in the box that starts with an equal sign and encloses each field name in square brackets.
Create reports that group data	Open the report in Design view. Click the Sorting and Grouping button. Select the field to group on and choose how you want the records sorted.
Add calculated fields to group headers and footers	Open the report in Design view. Click the Sorting and Grouping button. Go to the Properties section of the dialog box and select Yes for the Header and Footer options. In Design view, drag a text box into the footer or header. Add an expression like sum, average, or count to the text box.

Checking Your Skills

True/False

For each of the following statements, check *T* or *F* to indicate whether the statement is true or false.

__T __F 1. Mailing labels can have only one field per line of the label.

__T __F 2. Labels can be customized with additional text and a variety of font types and sizes.

__T __F 3. Fields that contain expressions or a combination of other fields may be used in detail, header, and footer sections of a report.

__T __F 4. When field names are used in calculated fields, they must be enclosed by curly braces, {}.

__T __F 5. To select the fields to be used for grouping, you use the Properties dialog box.

__T __F 6. If you put two fields on the same line of a label the program will automatically insert a comma and a space between them.

__T __F 7. Some reports have horizontal lines in the headers whose length needs to be adjusted if you edit the report by adding a new column to show a calculated field.

__T __F 8. If you add a text box with a calculated field in the detail section of a report, the program automatically adds a label box in the header using the name of the first field used in the calculation.

__T __F 9. The Label Wizard can be used to create labels that are specifically designed to stick onto folder tabs.

__T __F 10. The operator `IIF` may be used in a property sheet to make sure that division by zero error messages are not displayed.

Multiple Choice

Circle the letter of the correct answer for each of the following questions.

1. If a label has fields in four individual lines, what happens if some of the labels have no data in the field on the second line?
   a. The labels will be printed with an empty second line.
   b. The third and fourth lines will be automatically moved up.
   c. Those labels will not be printed.
   d. An error message warns you that you must at least enter spaces in those fields so they can be printed.

Access

2. If a report is grouped on a field named Expense, what would the report look like if the following formula were placed in a text box in the Detail section:

```
=[Expense]*.10
```

   a. Ten percent of the total of all the expenses would be displayed in the footer.

   b. Ten percent of the expense shown in each record would be printed in each record.

   c. The word "Expense" would be printed in the header of that section.

   d. Both a and b, but not c.

3. If a table contained the field Last Name and the report was grouped on that field, what effect would it have on the report if the following expression were placed in a text box in the Group Header?

```
[Last Name]
```

   a. Each record would start with the last name.

   b. Each group would begin with the last name for that group.

   c. The words "Last Name" would appear at the beginning of each group.

   d. An error message would be displayed because you forgot to start the expression with an equals sign.

4. If a currency value is calculated, it may be displayed with too many decimal places. To control the appearance of the calculated value, _____.

   a. click the Currency button on the toolbar

   b. choose Format, and Currency from the menu bar

   c. use the following form in the calculated field:

```
="$ "+[expression]
```

   d. click the Properties button and type in the format you want

5. When you create a Labels report, the Avery number _____.

   a. is used to designate industry-standard label sizes

   b. indicates the number of labels per page

   c. represents the width of the label in centimeters

   d. indicates which tray of the printer to select from

6. If you were sending a letter to the parents of each member of a children's group, the easiest way to add the phrase, To the Parents of:, to each mailing label would be _____.

   a. adding a field to the table and placing this phrase in it for each student. You could then use that field in the label

   b. ordering preprinted labels with this phrase already printed on them and then creating a custom label format to print the first line further to the right

   c. writing the phrase on each envelope by hand

   d. typing the phrase directly into the label design in the Label Wizard

7. If you use an operator like `IIF` in a calculated field, you must _____.
   a. begin the calculation with an equal sign, =
   b. place the formula within <>
   c. place the formula within {}
   d. place the formula between three asterisks

8. A Group Header or Footer _____.
   a. must contain a calculated field
   b. may contain label boxes, text boxes, and calculations
   c. will automatically contain a text box that displays the contents of the first column
   d. cannot contain the same fields as any of the boxes used in the detail section without producing an error message

9. What is wrong with the following calculated field: `=IIF([PAYROLL]<0,0,PAYROLL)`
   a. The `IF` function is misspelled.
   b. Both zeros should be enclosed by quotation marks.
   c. The field name, PAYROLL, should be within [].
   d. The field name, PAYROLL, should be within {}.

10. In order to show subtotals for each group in a grouped report, you can _____.
    a. use a calculated field with a formula in the Detail section
    b. use a calculated field with a formula in the Report Header section
    c. use a calculated field with a formula in the Page Header section
    d. use a calculated field with a formula in the Group Footer section

Completion

In the blank provided, write the correct answer for each of the following statements.

1. A fine line finishing off the main strokes of a letter, as at the top and bottom of the letter M is called a(n) _____________.
2. A typeface that does not have horizontal lines at the bottom of straight, vertical letters is called a(n) _____________ font.
3. The size of a line of type is measured in _____________.
4. If you had a field named Price and you wanted to calculate a sales tax of six percent, the expression you would place in a text box in the Detail section would be _____________.
5. If you had two fields in a report, Price and Number Sold, the expression you would place in a calculated field to multiply the Price by the Number Sold would be _____________.

6. To group the records in a report, open the report's Design view and click the ______________ button on the toolbar.

7. The report sections that are displayed in Design view when you choose to use report grouping are the ______________ and ______________.

8. To create mailing or folder labels, you create a new report using the ______________ Wizard.

9. If you use a calculated field and the result is a number with too many decimal places showing, you can change the ______________ of the text box.

10. A common standard for naming label sizes is the ______________ standard.

Matching

In the blank next to each of the following terms or phrases, write the letter of the corresponding term or phrase. (Note that some letters may be used more than once.)

a. Avery

b. Groups and Totals button

c. button with one sideways arrow that points to the right

d. Label Wizard

e. []

f. =

g. Group Header

h. Group Footer

i. text box

j. 3-Tab

_____ 1. Field names must be surrounded by these if the field name is used in a calculation

_____ 2. The standard for naming labels

_____ 3. A section of the report design that may be used to indicate the contents of a group of records

_____ 4. The toolbar button that is used to group records

_____ 5. This symbol must precede a mathematical or logical operator

_____ 6. A report section where you would be likely to place a summary calculation of the records that are shown in a group

_____ 7. A type of physical file folder that is commonly used to store papers in a file cabinet

_____ 8. The type of box that can contain a calculated field that uses field names as variables

_____ 9. Used to move the name of a field from a field list to a label design

_____ 10. Must be used to enclose field names in a calculation

Applying Your Skills

Practice

The following exercises enable you to practice the skills you have learned in this project.

Creating a Report with Records Grouped by Vendor

The database in this exercise contains a table of purchases made from various vendors. You prepare a report that groups the purchases by vendor and displays the vendor name in a Group Header. You also create a Group Footer that contains a total of the purchases from that vendor.

To create a report that shows purchases by vendor, complete the following steps:

1. Copy the database Proj1305 from the Project-13 folder on the CD and name the new file `Plumbing Purchases`.
2. Open the `Plumbing Purchases` database.
3. Create a new report based upon the Purchases table. Use the AutoReport: Tabular Wizard.
4. Close preview and open the report in Design mode.
5. Group and sort on the Vendor field.
6. Turn on the Group Header and Group Footer in the Properties section.
7. Drag the Vendor text box from the Detail section to the far-left side of the Vendor Header section.
8. Delete the Vendor field from the Page Header section. (It is not necessary to show the vendor name in each record.)
9. Shorten the line that underlines the Page Header section.
10. Change the font size so the name of the vendor will be about 1/4 inch high.
11. Adjust the size and position of the text box so it displays the larger type size. Switch back and forth between Preview and Design views to check your work. Make sure the Vendor box is wide enough to show the whole field.
12. Save the report as `Purchases`. Leave the database open for use in the next exercise.

Adding a Calculated Field to a Report

In this exercise, you create a Group Footer that contains a total of the purchases from the vendor.

To create a report that shows purchases by vendor, complete the following steps:

1. Use the Plumbing Purchases database that was used in the previous exercise. Open the report.
2. Drag a text box in the Vendor Footer below the Cost field in the Detail section.
3. Enter the calculation `=Sum([Cost])` in the text box.
4. Set the Format of the field box that contains the formula to `$#,##0.00`.

Access

5. Delete the extra label box.

6. Hold down the Shift key and click the three fields that deal with Cost (in the Header, the Detail, and the Vendor Footer sections).

7. From the menu bar select Format, Align, and Right to align the three fields. Preview the report.

   Notice the numbers in the subtotal do not line up with the numbers in the Detail section.

8. Switch back to Design view and change the format property of the calculated total from $#,##0.00 to `Currency`. These figures line up if they both use the same format.

9. Preview the report.

   Notice how the third group of records is continued on the next page without a Group Header.

10. Return to Design view. Click the Sorting and Grouping button on the toolbar. Change the Keep Together option to Whole Group.

11. Preview the report again and notice how the third group is kept together on the second page.

12. Print the report.

13. Close the report and save the changes. Close the database.

Creating Mailing Labels for a Database

In this exercise, you create a set of mailing labels that can be used for a mailing to the company's customers.

To create mailing labels based on the Customers table, complete the following steps:

1. Copy the Proj1306 file from the Project-13 folder on the CD and rename it `SBMusic11`.

2. Create a report using the Label Wizard that uses the Avery 5160 label size.

3. Arrange the fields in the label in the traditional way with the two name fields on the first line, the street address on the second line, and the City, State, and ZIP fields on the third line.

4. Use a comma after the City field.

5. Save the report as `Customer Mailing Labels`.

6. Keep the database open for use in the following exercise.

Create Folder Labels for a Database

In this exercise, you create a set of labels that can be placed on file folders. The labels are based on the Suppliers table.

To create a set of labels for folders that keep supplier information, complete the following steps:

1. Use the Plumbing Purchases database that was used in the previous exercise. Create a new report using the Label Wizard.
2. Base the report on the Suppliers table.
3. Select the Index Maker 5 tab layout.
4. The first part of all the labels say `Supplier:`.
5. The next part of the label's first line contains the name of the supplier, a space, and the phone number.
6. Sort them alphabetically by company name.
7. Preview the labels to see if this layout works.

   The company name and phone number are too long. If you make the font small enough to get all this information on one line, it is too small to read.
8. Solve this problem by generating another label report. You can try using a three tab folder or putting the information on two lines. Do not allow any suppler names to wrap to the second line.
9. Name the report `Supplier Labels`.
10. Close the database.

Creating a Report Based on a Database

In this exercise, you create a report that summarizes the salaries by department.

To create a report that summarizes salaries from the Employee Information table, complete the following steps:

1. Copy the file Proj1307 from the Project-13 folder on the CD and rename it `Human Resources3`. Open the database.
2. Create a new report based on the Employee Information table using the AutoReport: Tabular option.
3. Delete all the fields in the report except the Name, Salary, Specialty, and Date Hired. Delete the corresponding headers.
4. Group the report on Department and sort on Salary. Display a Group Header and a Group Footer.
5. In the Group Header, insert a text box that displays the department names. Change the size of the font to 20 points and adjust the size of the text box to accommodate any of the available department names. Preview the report to make sure they all fit.
6. In the Group Footer, insert a text box and a calculated field that sums the salaries. Change the associated label box in the Group Footer to `Total Department Salaries`. Adjust the size and spacing.
7. Set the Keep Together option to Whole Group.

8. Preview the report.
9. Save the report as `Department Salaries`.

Challenge

The following challenges enable you to use your problem-solving skills.

Creating a Set of Mailing Labels

In this exercise, you have a database that contains a table of membership information. You create a set of mailing labels that could be used to send a monthly newsletter to the members.

To create a set of mailing labels, complete the following steps:

1. Open the `Club` database that you have been working on in previous projects.
2. Consider the font size you want to use and estimate how high of a label would be necessary to hold five lines of address (reminder: there are 72 points per inch).
3. Examine the Members table and look for the longest address or name and count the characters. Estimate how many inches long your address label would have to be.
4. Create a label report. Look at the descriptions of the Avery numbers and their dimensions. Pick a label that you think would hold the addresses.
5. Preview the report. Look for any incomplete addresses or for addresses that have wrapped to the next line of the label.
6. Print the labels.
7. The next time you are in an office supply store, find the boxes of labels that are made for computer printers and find the Avery number on the box.

Creating Mailing Labels and Summary Reports

The first report creates a set of mailing labels that can be used to send notices to viewing households. The second report lists the viewing events by household and adds up the total hours by household.

Create a mailing label that is based on the Households table. The first line does not have an individual's name in it, but instead has the phrase `To the Cable Viewer at:`. The next two lines contain the mailing information.

Once you have created the labels, check them carefully to see if all the labels fit in the space allowed. A typical error to look for is long addresses wrapping to the next line.

Name the report `Mailing to Households`.

Since this report contains fields from three tables, you first have to create a query. Create a query that has the following fields from the tables indicated in the order that is shown below:

Table	**Field**
Households	Household ID
Participants	Person ID
Participants	First Name
Participants	Last Name
Household	Address
Household	City
Household	State
Household	ZIP Code
Viewing Data	Date
Viewing Data	Channel Name
Viewing Data	Beginning Time
Viewing Data	Ending Time

Switch to Datasheet view to make sure the query works. Save it as `Complete Viewing History`.

Next, create a report that is based on this query using the AutoReport: Tabular option. This automatic feature assumes that you want to group the data on the first two fields because they are both primary key fields in their respective tables.

Switch to the Design view of the report and do the following to clean up the appearance:

1. Use the View menu and turn off the Page Header/Footer.
2. Delete the Household ID field from the Household ID Header and move the Address field to line up at the left. Resize the fields to increase their size so that they are large enough to display their contents. Hold the Shift key and select all the fields in the header. Use the Format, Align, and Top menu options to line them up. Switch to Report view to check the sizes.
3. Delete the Person ID field and move the other two name fields to the left end of the detail section. Move the other fields in the Detail section to the left and adjust their size as needed. Leave room at the right for a new field. The two name fields have a border around them that should be removed so they look the same as the other fields in the row. Select one of the other fields in the row and use the Format Painter button to copy its format to the first and last name fields. Align the fields.
4. Click the Sorting and Grouping button on the toolbar and delete the grouping on the Personal ID. The Person ID section of the report disappears. Click the Household ID expression. Turn on the Group Footer

and set the Keep Together option to Whole Group. Add a second Field to sort on. Click the next available box and click the list arrow. Select Person ID.

5. Open the toolbox, if necessary. Drag a text box to the right of the Ending Time box. Enter the following formula in the text box:

   ```
   =([Ending Time]-[Beginning Time])*24
   ```

   Delete the label box that was created with the text box.

6. Drag a text box in the Household ID footer and enter the following formula:

   ```
   =sum([Ending Time]-[Beginning Time])*24
   ```

   Change the label box to read `Total Hours:`.

   (Both formulas are multiplied by 24 because the time calculations produces results in fractions of a day, and you want to add up the total hours.)

   Adjust the alignment of the three boxes.

7. Open the Properties sheet. Set the following properties for both text boxes:

   Format: Fixed
   Decimal Places: 0

8. Save the report as `Hours Viewed by Household`.

Creating a Set of Labels

You decide that you would like some nice looking labels for the file folders that you have for each location. In this exercise, you create a set of such labels.

Locate the Vending10 database that you worked on in the previous project and rename it `Vending11`.

Use folders that have five tabs across the top. Create a set of labels based on the Locations table that display the name of the site.

Sort the labels alphabetically.

Use the largest size type that fits on the label and still shows all the names without cutting any of them off or wrapping to the next line.

Suggestion: To do this quickly, locate the longest name in the table. Switch back and forth between Report view and Design view to see if the name fits. While in Design view, select the text box and change the font size on the toolbar. Switch to the Report Preview to see the results.

Name the report `Location Labels`.

Creating Mailing Labels and Grouped by Summary Reports

In this exercise, you create a set of mailing labels that can be used to send out advertising to the customers and a report that shows the rental activity grouped by video.

Locate the Video Store9 database and rename it `Video Store10`.

Create a set of mailing labels based on the appropriate fields in the Customer table.

Check the table to see what addresses and names are the longest, then check the labels to make sure you did not cut any of them off.

Create a report using the AutoReport: Tabular option. Group on Video ID and turn on the Group Header and Group Footer.

Delete the Customer ID field. Move the Video ID field from the Detail section to the Group Header.

Add two text boxes in the Video ID footer that have formulas that sum up the Rental Fee and the Late Fee respectively. Add a label box in the footer that says `Total:`.

Format both text boxes to Currency.

Use the Align and Size options under the Format menu to get all the boxes lined up horizontally and vertically.

Save the report as `Rental Activity`.

Creating a Form with a Subform to Display Information

It is convenient to display the items grouped below the information about each insurance company.

Locate the Home Inventory9 database that you used in the previous project and rename it `Home Inventory10`.

Create a tabular AutoReport based on the Claim List query.

Delete the agent's name and the phone number.

Move the Name of Item and the Cost fields to the left. Move the headings in the Page Header as well.

Group the records on the Company Name field and turn on the Group Footer. Set the Keep Together option to Whole Group.

Add a text box to the footer that adds up the Cost field. Change the label of that box to `Total:`.

Save the report as `Value of Items by Insurance Company`.

PinPoint Assessment

PinPoint Training

You have completed the project and the associated lessons, as well as the "Checking Your Skills" and "Applying Your Skills" sections. Now use the PinPoint software Evaluation mode to assess your comprehension of the specific exam tasks you have just learned. You can also use the PinPoint Trainer mode and the SHOW ME tutorials to practice these specific exam tasks.

Project 14
Fourteen

Using Advanced Reports

Getting More Information from Your Data

In this project you will learn the following objectives and their associated Microsoft Exam required activities.

Objectives	Required Activities
Create Simple Crosstab Queries and Reports	Set Crosstab Queries
Create Crosstab Queries with Conditions and Total Columns	Build Summary Queries Set Crosstab Queries Calculate Fields
Review Linked Tables Simultaneously Using Forms	Show Related Records on a Form and Subforms Identify Appropriate Use for Subforms Merge Two Tables into a Form
Customizing a Report by Inserting Subreports Using the Subform/Subreport Wizard	Add Custom Pages
Create Reports Using the Chart Wizard	Present Information in a Chart

Why Would I Do This?

The best database is of little use unless its data can be communicated and turned into information. A crosstab query and its report are very useful in analyzing data. You learn how to produce a table that counts, averages, or sums the data by groupings that you choose.

If you are using tables that are joined, it is very useful to view both tables at the same time. You learn how to do this using subreports. Subforms can also be used as a reporting tool to convey related information on a per account basis. You learn a new method for creating subforms in this project. The best way to communicate some types of data is to represent the data as a chart. You learn how to create a chart using the Chart Wizard, and how to edit the chart in Microsoft Graph.

Lesson 1: Creating Crosstab Queries and Reports

A crosstab query produces a dynaset where the contents of one field provide the column headings and the contents of another field are used as row headings. The cells of the query are calculated based on the fields that match the values of both the row and column fields.

In this example, you learn how to create a crosstab query based on two tables that show customer information and orders placed by those customers for various types of cleaning supplies. The crosstab query calculates the total quantity of each item sold to each customer.

To Create a Crosstab Query Based on Two Tables

1. **Make a copy of the Proj1401 database file from the Project-14 folder on the CD and name the copy `Orders`. Return to Access and open the `Orders` database.**

   The Database window should now be open to the Tables area (see Figure 14.1).

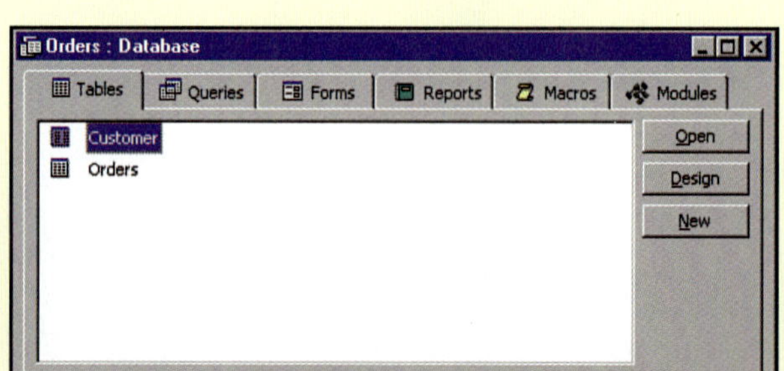

Figure 14.1 The Database window displays the Tables area of the Orders database.

2. **Click the Queries tab, then click the New button.**

   The New Query dialog box is displayed.

3 Click Design View, then click OK.

The Show Table dialog box appears (see Figure 14.2).

Figure 14.2
The Show Table dialog box is displayed.

4 Click the Customer table name and click Add.

The Customer table is added to the Query design window.

5 Click the Orders table name and click Add.

6 Click Close on the Show Table dialog box.

The Show Table dialog box closes and the Query design window shows the Customer and Orders tables (see Figure 14.3).

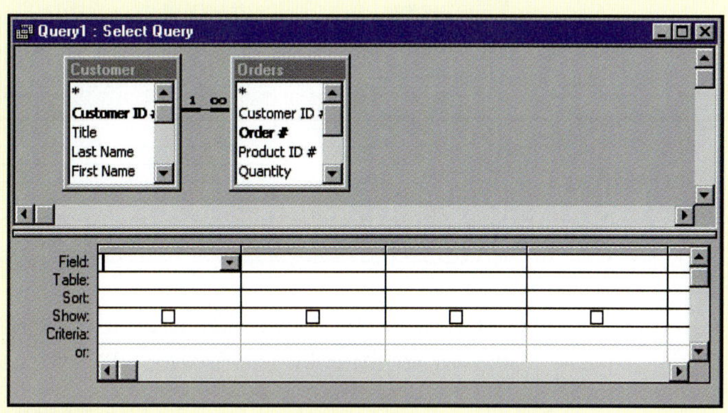

Figure 14.3
The Query design window shows that the Customer and Orders tables have been added.

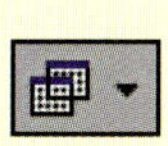

7 Click the Query Type button.

A menu of query types are displayed (see Figure 14.4).

8 Click the Crosstab Query option.

Notice that the design grid now has two new rows named Crosstab and Total (see Figure 14.5).

9 Scroll down the list of fields in the Customer table to the Company name. Drag this field name to the first column of the query table.

The first column shows the Company field and fills in the next two boxes with the table name and the default setting of Group By in the Total box.

continues

To Create a Crosstab Query Based on Two Tables (continued)

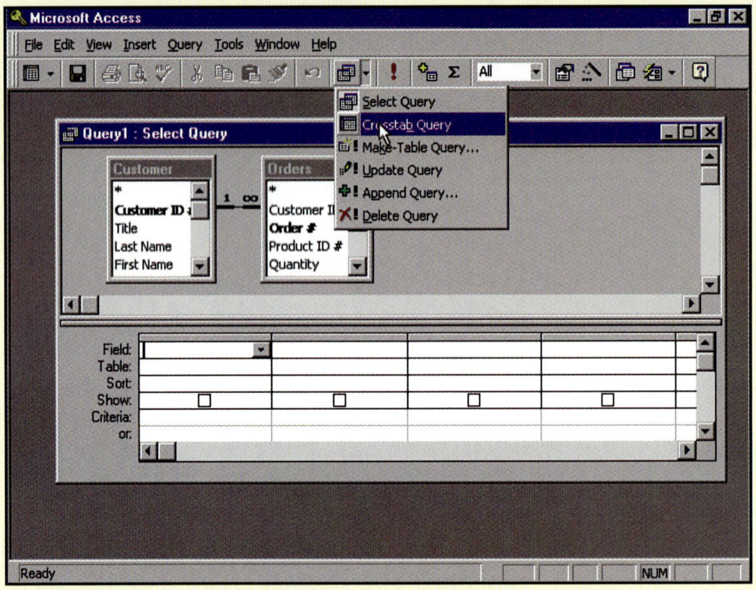

Figure 14.4
The Query Type menu displays the various query options.

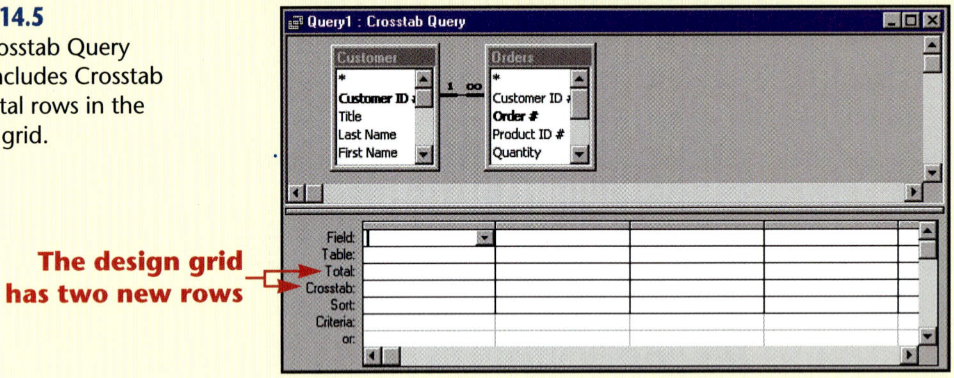

Figure 14.5
The Crosstab Query table includes Crosstab and Total rows in the design grid.

The company names are used as row headings on the left side of the Crosstab table that is produced.

10 Click the Crosstab box in the Company column, then click the down arrow at the right side of the box to reveal a menu of choices.

A menu of options for the Crosstab box appears (see Figure 14.6).

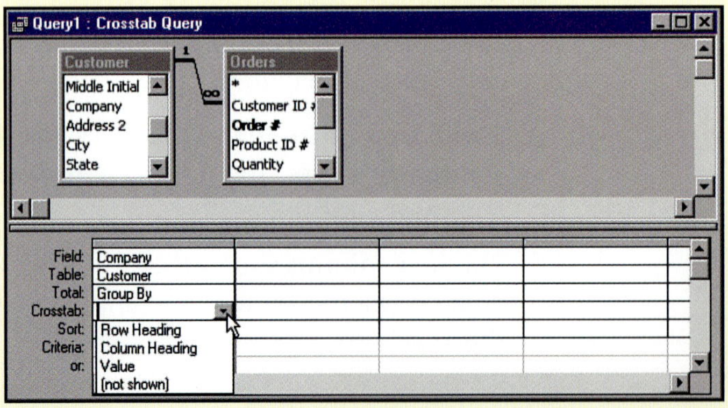

Figure 14.6
The options for the Crosstab box in the Company column.

Access

11 Click the Row Heading option.

12 Scroll down the list of fields in the Orders table. Drag the Product Description field into the second column.

The name of each type of product is used as the column headings in the resulting Crosstab table.

13 Click the Crosstab box in the Product Description column and the down arrow in that box. Select Column Heading from the list of options.

14 Drag the Quantity field from the Orders table into the third column.

You want to know the quantity of each type of product sold to each customer and display it in the cells of the resulting Crosstab table.

15 Click the Crosstab box in the Quantity column and click the down arrow in that box. Select Value from the list of options.

This specifies that the program will calculate a numeric result to be placed in the table. The Total box must be changed from Group By to a mathematical operation.

16 Click the Total box in the Quantity column, then click the down arrow to reveal a menu of mathematical operations.

A drop-down menu is displayed (see Figure 14.7).

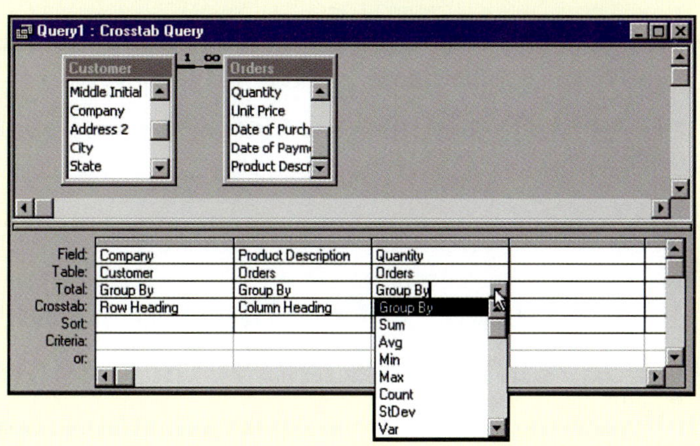

Figure 14.7
The Total drop-down menu displays several mathematical operators.

17 Click the Sum option.

This adds up the quantity sold for each product to each customer. Check to see if your settings in the three columns match those in Figure 14.8.

18 Click the View button to view the resulting Crosstab Query table.

The Crosstab Query table is displayed (see Figure 14.9).

continues

To Create a Crosstab Query Based on Two Tables (continued)

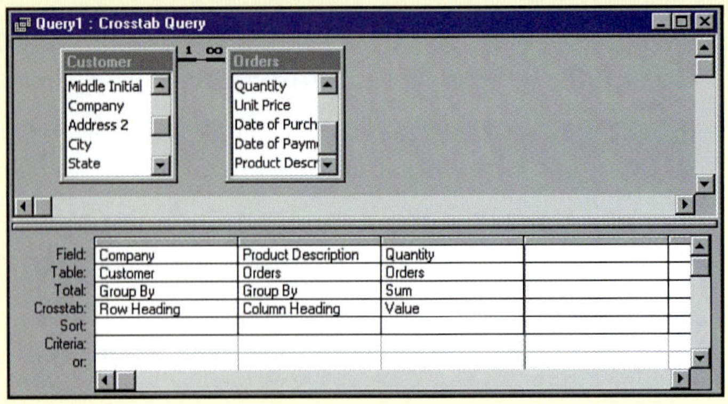

Figure 14.8
The Crosstab Query design window displays the necessary settings.

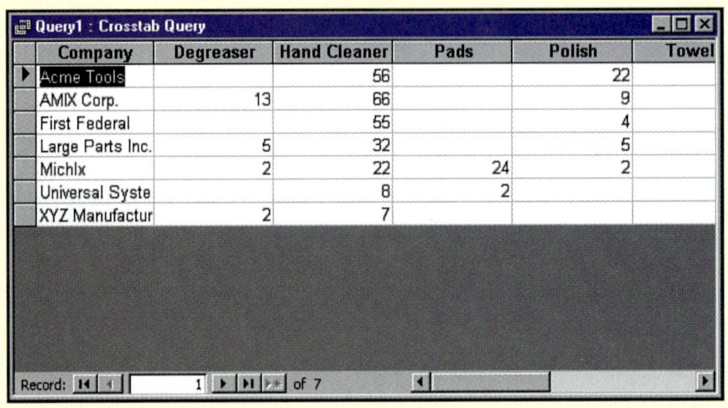

Figure 14.9
The Crosstab Query table shows the quantity of each product sold for each customer.

19 Click the Save button on the toolbar and save the query with the name `Products Sold by Customer`**.**

20 Click the View button to return to Design view.

Leave the Design view open for the next lesson.

Lesson 2: Creating Crosstab Queries with Conditions and Total Columns

It is possible to use criteria to limit the crosstab query calculations. You can also include additional columns of summary data.

In this lesson, you learn how to limit the orders in the crosstab query to those sold between two given dates. You also learn how to add a column to the table to calculate the total bill for each customer.

To Use Criteria Based Upon Another Field in a Crosstab Query

1 In the Design view of the Crosstab Query in the Orders database, drag the Date of Purchase field from the Orders table to the fourth column of the query table.

2 Click the Total box in Date of Purchase column, then click the down arrow to reveal the menu of choices. Scroll down and click Expression.

The Total box in the fourth column contains the word `Expression`.

3 Enter the following expression in the Criteria box for the Date of Purchase column:

```
Between 1/1/96 and 1/31/96
```

If you press the Enter key or click another cell, the program adds # signs on either side of the dates (see Figure 14.10). (The fourth column in the figure has been widened to show the expression. It is not necessary for you to do so.)

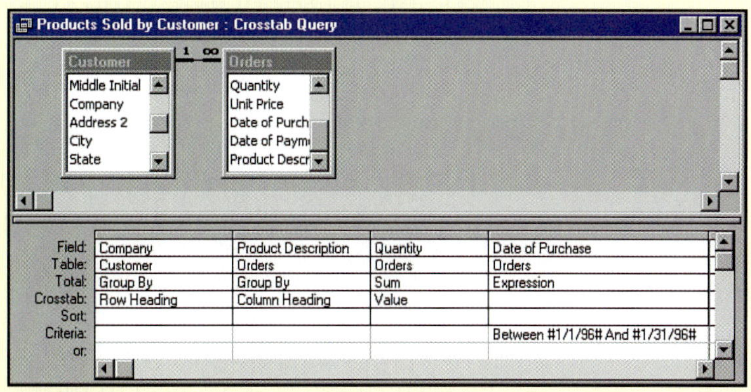

Figure 14.10
A criteria expression has been added to the Date of Purchase field.

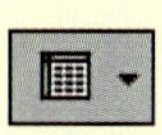

4 Click the View button to view the Crosstab Query datasheet.

The table only includes those purchases made in January 1996 (see Figure 14.11).

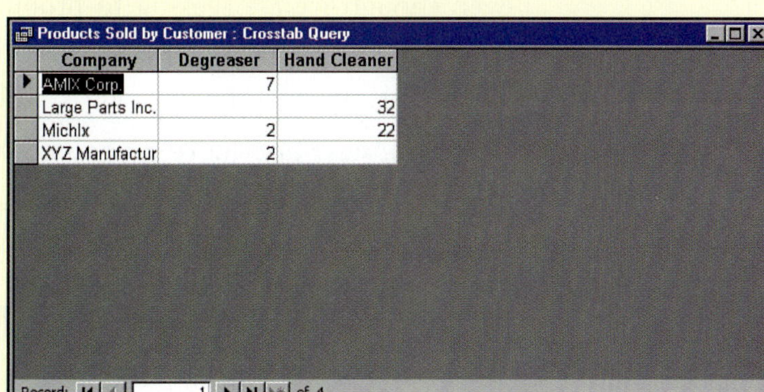

Figure 14.11
The Crosstab Query table shows purchases made in January 1996.

5 Click the View button to return to Design view.

Leave Design view open for use in the next section.

Exam Notes

The `Between` expression is inclusive; that is, purchases made on the beginning and end dates are included in the table.

In the next section of the lesson, you delete the Date of Purchase criteria and add a column to display the total cost to the customer for each type of purchase.

To Include a Column of Totals in a Crosstab Query

1 Click the narrow column selector bar at the top of the Date of Purchase column to select the column.

The Date of Purchase column is highlighted.

2 Press the Del key to delete this column from the crosstab query design.

The column is deleted, you now have only three columns in your query.

3 Enter the following expression in the fourth Field box:

```
Total Cost: [Quantity]*[Unit Price]
```

The words to the left of the colon are used as the label for the new column. The expression to the right of the colon multiplies the contents of the Quantity and Unit Price fields for each type of purchase for each customer. Each field in the expression must be enclosed by its own set of brackets. The mathematical symbol (in this case, *) is outside of square brackets.

4 Click the Crosstab box in the new column. Click the down arrow, then click Row Heading.

Even though we are seeking to produce a column of totals, these totals are considered by the program to be row headings.

Notice that the Total box has the default entry Group By.

5 Click the View button to go to the Datasheet view.

The crosstab query will display the cost for each purchase by customer with a separate row for each purchase (see Figure 14.12).

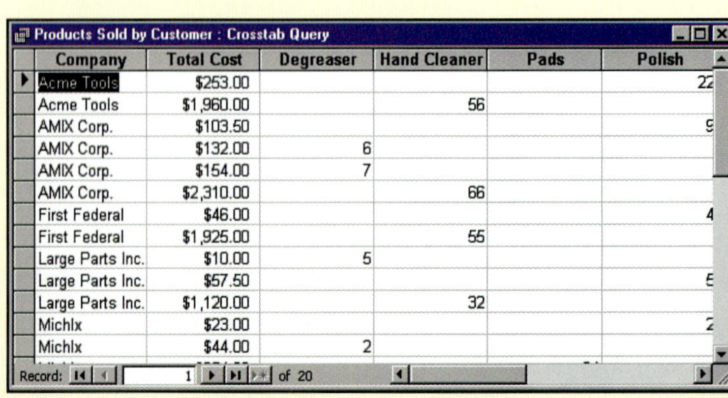
Products Sold by Customer : Crosstab Query

Company	Total Cost	Degreaser	Hand Cleaner	Pads	Polish
Acme Tools	$253.00				22
Acme Tools	$1,960.00		56		
AMIX Corp.	$103.50				9
AMIX Corp.	$132.00	6			
AMIX Corp.	$154.00	7			
AMIX Corp.	$2,310.00		66		
First Federal	$46.00				4
First Federal	$1,925.00		55		
Large Parts Inc.	$10.00	5			
Large Parts Inc.	$57.50				5
Large Parts Inc.	$1,120.00		32		
Michlx	$23.00				2
Michlx	$44.00	2			

Record: 1 of 20

Figure 14.12 The crosstab query shows the cost for each purchase by customer with a separate row for each purchase.

6 Click the View button to return to the Design view.

7 Click the Total box in the Total Cost column that was added in step 3, then click the down arrow to display the menu of choices. Click Sum.

This creates a sum to show the total cost of all purchases for each customer.

8 Click the View button to view the Crosstab Query datasheet.

The Total Cost expression column now shows a total for each customer for each product. These totals are considered to be row headers (see Figure 14.13).

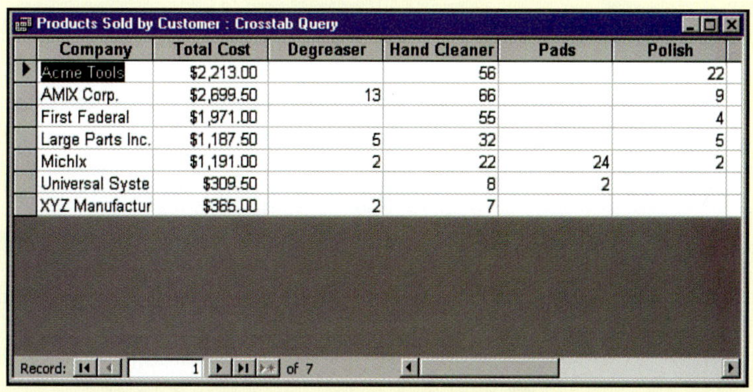

Company	Total Cost	Degreaser	Hand Cleaner	Pads	Polish
Acme Tools	$2,213.00		56		22
AMIX Corp.	$2,699.50	13	66		9
First Federal	$1,971.00		55		4
Large Parts Inc.	$1,187.50	5	32		5
Michlx	$1,191.00	2	22	24	2
Universal Syste	$309.50		8	2	
XYZ Manufactur	$365.00	2	7		

Figure 14.13
The crosstab query displays the total cost for each customer.

9 Click the Save button on the toolbar to save the query design.

10 Close the query and leave the database open for use in the next lesson.

Exam Notes

Crosstab queries can be confusing if you jump into the design of one without a clear objective in mind. Decide ahead of time which field should be used as a row header or column header. Determine which field should be used to calculate the value in each cell and what mathematical expression to use.

The Crosstab Query Wizard creates simple crosstab queries for you. You must have at least one choice for row, column, and value fields. You have an option of adding a totals column. If you want to use a calculated expression, you can use the wizard to create most of the query then modify the design according to the directions in the latter section in this lesson.

Lesson 3: Reviewing Linked Tables Simultaneously Using Forms and Subforms

It is often useful to be able to review the data in linked tables simultaneously. Using the form/subform approach, you can create an individualized statement that shows all of the orders placed by one customer on a single form. This provides a reporting tool that could be used to communicate with customers, or it could be used by sales representatives to track sales by customer.

Subform
A form placed within another (main) form, showing data from another table related to the selected record from the main form.

In Project 12, "Using Advanced Form Features," you learned how to create a form/subform using the Form Wizard. You then added a record to the main part of the form and to the *subform*. In this lesson, you take an existing form and add another existing form to it in the Design view of the form. This process is different from the one you learned in Project 12. You also see how to modify the new form so you could print a copy of it as a report of a customer's orders. You place a form based on a customer orders table (the subform) within another form based on a table of general customer information.

To Review Two Tables Simultaneously Using a Form and a Subform

1 In the Orders database, click the Forms tab, click the Customer Information form, then click the Design button.

The Customer Information form opens in Design view.

The first step in adding a subform to an existing form is to open the form that is based on the table that has the primary key field. This is the main part of the form. In this case, the Customer table contains the primary key field, Customer ID #.

2 Maximize the design window.

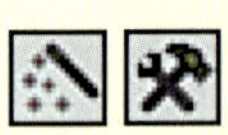

3 Click the Toolbox button on the toolbar if the toolbox is not already displayed on the screen.

Make sure the Control Wizards button is selected on the toolbox.

4 Click the Subform/Subreport button on the toolbox. Draw a rectangle that fits in the lower portion of the currently open form.

When you draw the rectangle, it appears as a thin line. This marks the boundary of the subform (see Figure 14.14).

When you release the mouse button, the Subform/Subreport Wizard is activated. After a short delay the first Subform/Subreport Wizard dialog box appears.

If you have problems...

The Subform/Subreport feature may not be installed on your computer. It is not installed if the "Typical" option was used when Office 97 was installed. If you are working on your own computer, you can run the Setup program on your Office 97 master disc and add the advanced wizards.

5 Click the Forms option. Click the down arrow to show a menu of available forms, then select Orders.

You can use the wizard to create a subform or use an existing form (see Figure 14.15).

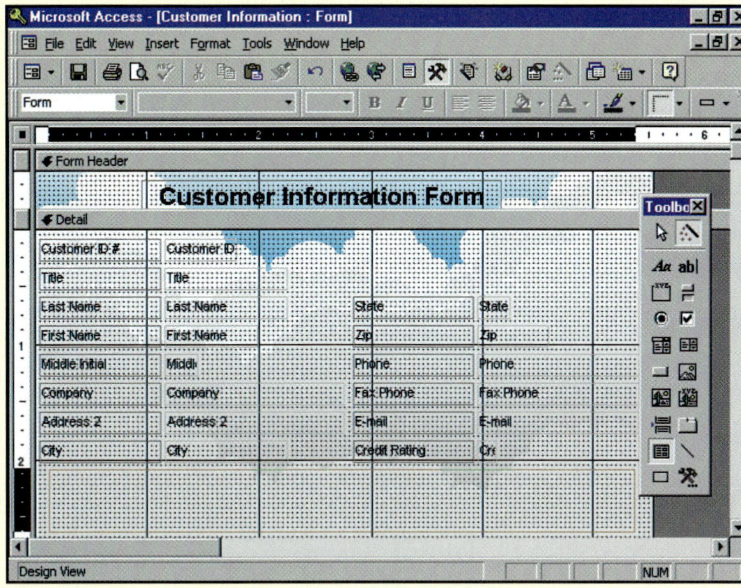

Figure 14.14
The Customer Information form displays the designated area for the subform.

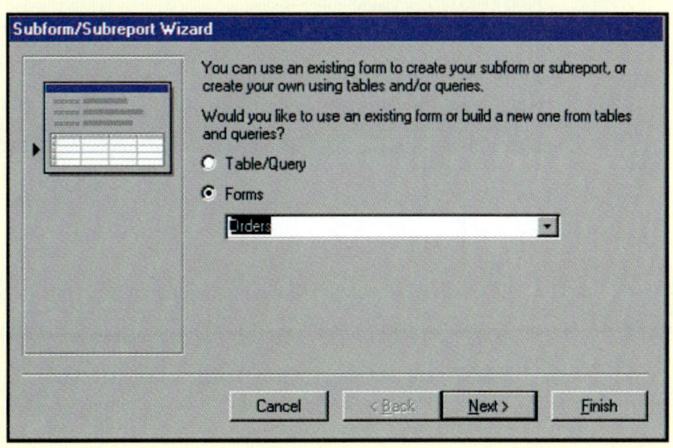

Figure 14.15
The second Subform/Subreport Wizard dialog box asks for a source.

6 Click Next.

The next Subform/Subreport Wizard dialog box is displayed. It identifies the field that links the two tables and gives you the option of linking the two forms using that field or leaving the two forms unlinked.

7 Click the option named `Show orders for each record in Customer using Customer ID #`. Make sure the Choose from a list option is selected, then click Next.

The next wizard dialog box asks for a form name.

8 Click the Finish button to accept the default name, `Orders`.

The wizard finishes the design and returns you to the design of the Customer Information form.

9 Click the View button to switch to Form view.

continues

To Review Two Tables Simultaneously Using a Form and a Subform (continued)

The Customer Information form is shown with the subform Orders embedded in it. The subform used in this example is a tabular form (see Figure 14.16).

Figure 14.16
The Customer Information form is shown with the Orders form embedded in it.

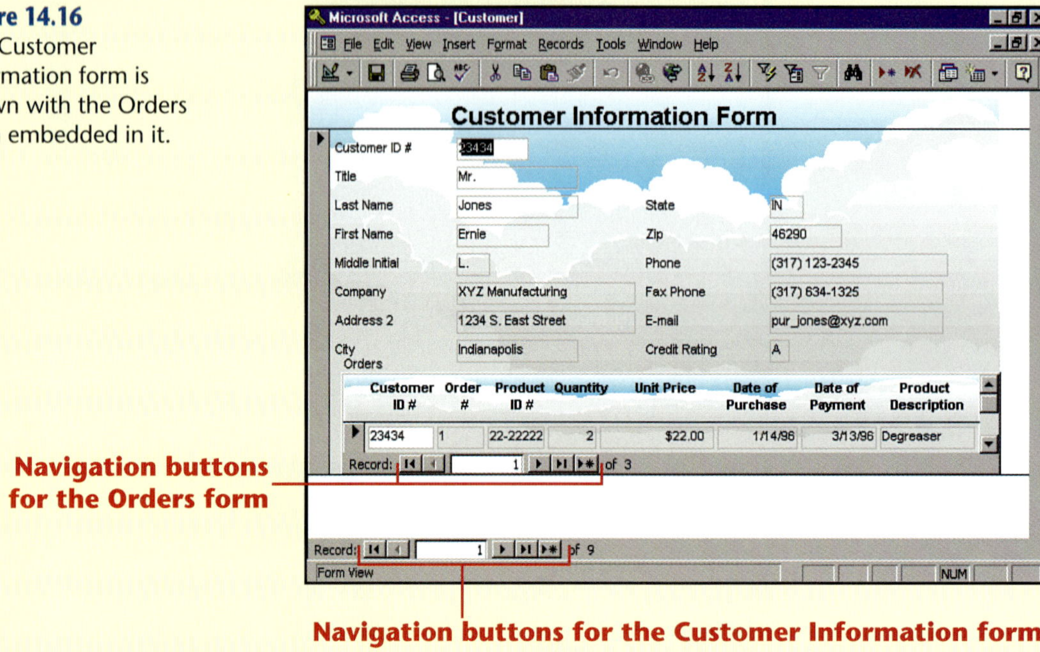

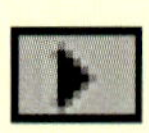

10 Click the Next Record navigation button for the Orders form to navigate through the records that match the currently displayed customer in the Customer Information form.

Notice that the Orders form only shows the records that match the customer in the Customer Information form.

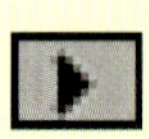

11 Click the Next Record navigation button at the bottom of the screen to look at the information for the next customer.

Notice that the available orders change when you change customer names.

This design still needs a few refinements. The area for the subform is too small to show more than one record at a time.

12 Click the View button to return to Design view.

13 Scroll down to show the bottom part of the form. Click in the gray area at the bottom of the screen to deselect the subform.

The form footer and subform area are moved to the middle of the screen, and the subform is no longer selected (see Figure 14.17).

Notice that the Orders subform has a title box that was automatically created when you inserted the subform. It is unnecessary in this example, and it may overlap the label of the City field depending on where you drew the box.

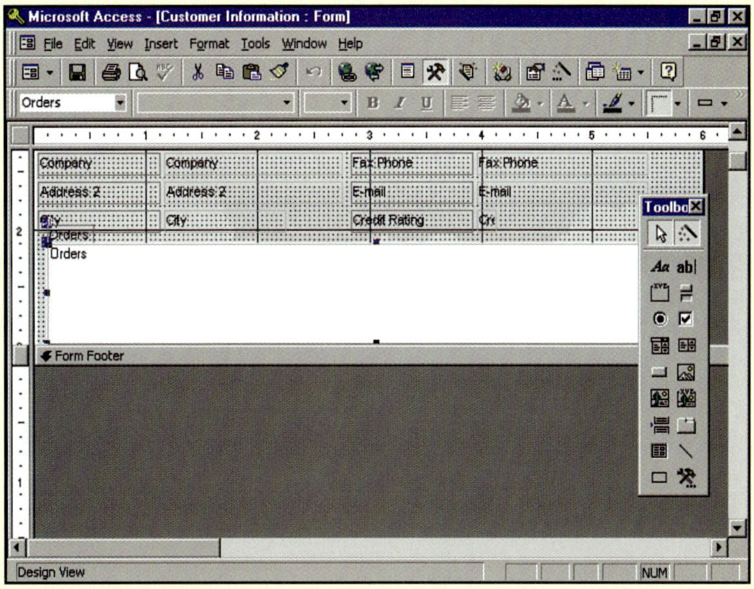

Figure 14.17
The bottom portion of the Customer Information form displays a blank area where the subform will go.

14 Carefully move your pointer to a portion of the Orders title that does not also include a portion of the City label. Click to select the title.

Handles appears around the Orders title (see Figure 14.18).

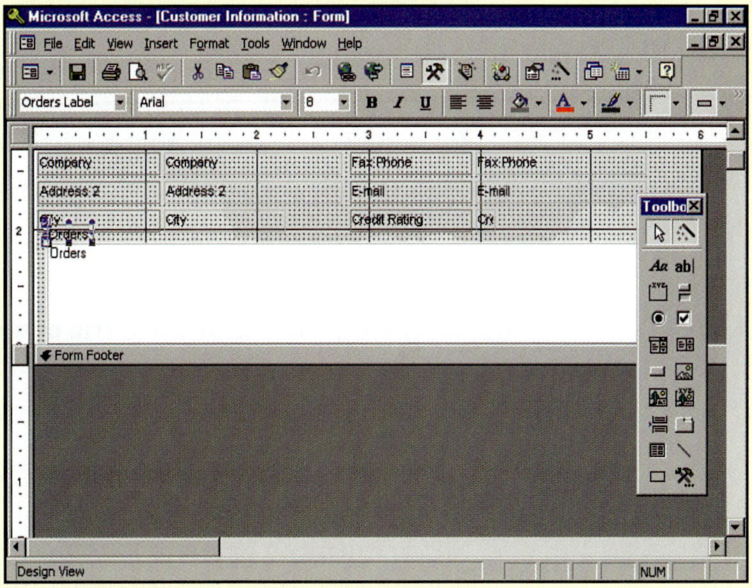

Figure 14.18
Click carefully on the Orders title to select it.

15 Press Del to delete the Orders title.

If you accidentally delete something else, use the Undo button on the toolbar. If the title completely overlaps the field above it, drag the entire Orders subform downward to eliminate the overlap, delete the title, and then move the subform back.

continues

To Review Two Tables Simultaneously Using a Form and a Subform (continued)

16. **Place the pointer on the top edge of the Form Footer bar and drag it down to increase the detail area of the form.**

    The pointer turns into a double-headed arrow. Make sure you place it at the top edge of the Form Footer bar (see Figure 14.19).

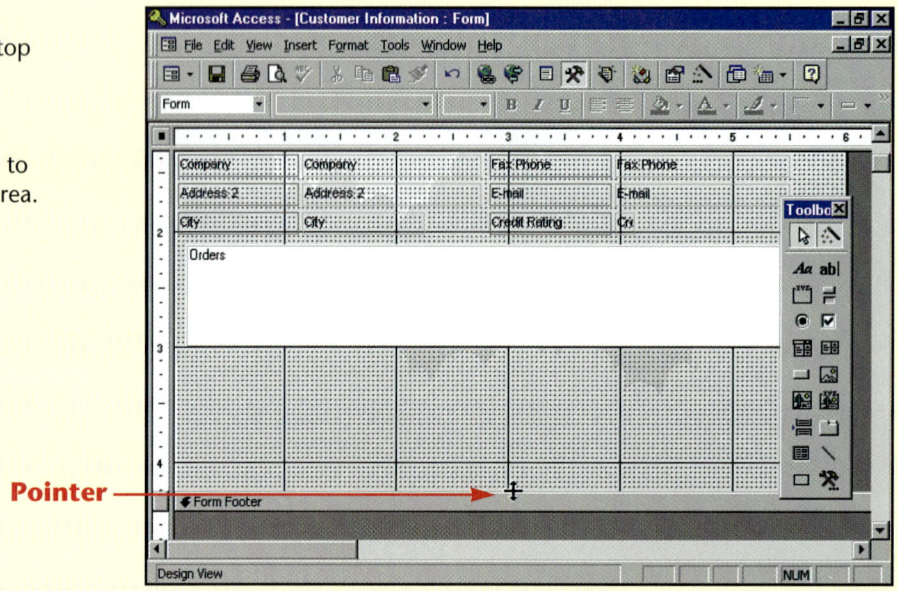

Figure 14.19
The pointer on the top edge of the Form Footer bar is shown after it has been dragged downward to increase the detail area.

17. **Click the Orders subform area to select it. Click and drag down the handle in the middle of the bottom side of the area to increase its size by about a half inch.**

18. **Click the View button on the toolbar to switch to Form view.**

    The form should show both forms and their navigation bars (see Figure 14.20).

19. **Compare your design with the one shown in Figure 14.20.**

    You probably need to adjust the size of the subform and detail area. Switch back to Design view if necessary and make those adjustments.

20. **Close the form and save the changes.**

    Notice when you return to the Forms tab in the Database window, a new subform is not created when this process is used. The procedure used in Project 12, where both forms are created from scratch, creates a separate subform.

    Leave the database open for the next lesson.

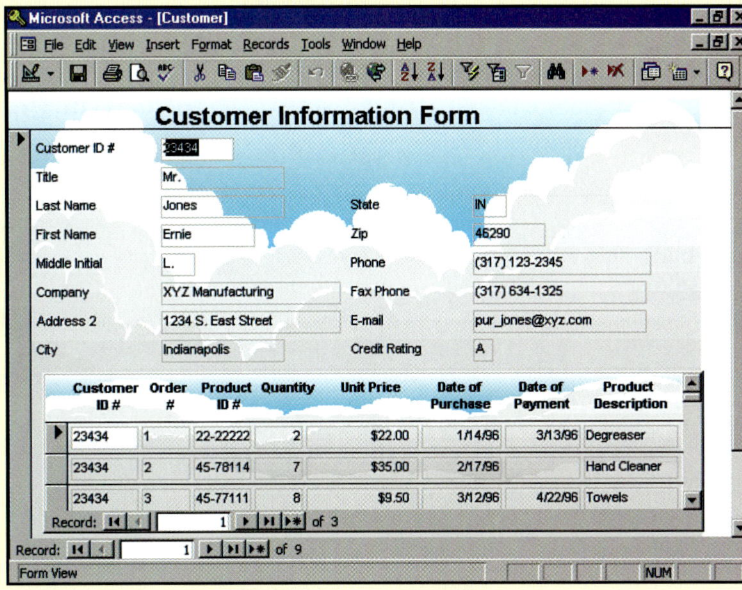

Figure 14.20
The two forms have been adjusted for size so that they both fit on one screen with both sets of navigation buttons.

Exam Notes

If you do not have the Subform/Subreport Wizard installed, you can still set up a subform. Click the Control Wizards button to turn it off, then click the Subform/Subreport button and drag a rectangular box as you did in the steps above. The box is Unbound. Click on the Unbound box with the right mouse button and select Properties from the shortcut menu. Click the Data tab, then click the drop-down arrow in the Source Object box. Select the Orders table from the list. This method may actually be faster for you than using the wizard.

Lesson 4: Customizing a Report by Inserting Subreports Using the Subform/Subreport Wizard

It is also possible to combine two reports that are based on joined tables. In this lesson, you learn how to customize a report that shows the customer information from the Customer table in columnar format by inserting a subreport with the individual orders by that customer shown in a tabular format report.

Previewing the Reports

First, you see a preview of the two reports that will be joined. These reports are already provided, for your convenience. The Customer report is based on the Customer table and was created with a columnar AutoReport then modified by rearranging the fields. The Orders report is based on the Orders table and was created with a tabular AutoReport.

To Preview the Two Reports

1 In the Orders database, click the Reports tab. Click the Customer report, then click the Preview button.

The preview of the Customer report is displayed (see Figure 14.21).

Figure 14.21
The Preview button displays the Customer report.

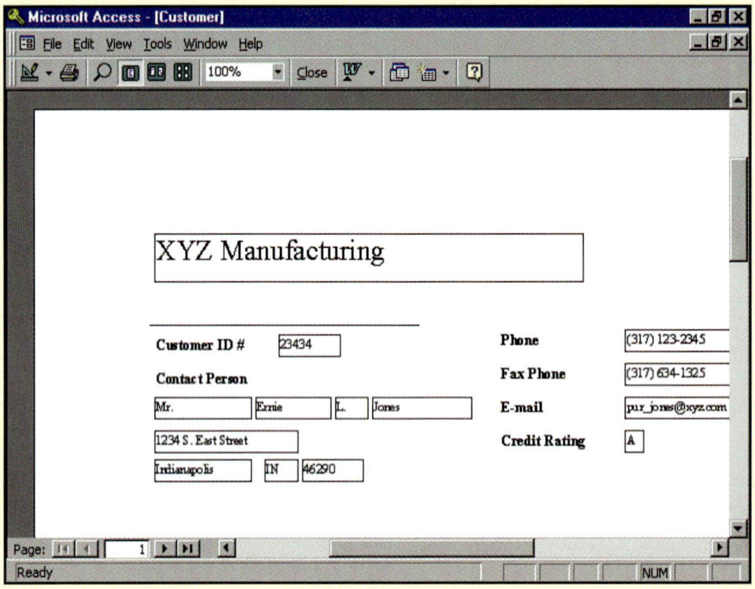

2 Maximize the Report window, if necessary. Scroll around to view the report, and use the navigation buttons to examine more than one page.

Notice there is a separate page for each customer record.

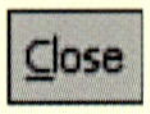

3 Click the Close button on the toolbar to close the preview.

4 Click the Orders report to select it, and click the Preview button.

The preview of the Orders report is displayed (see Figure 14.22).

5 Click the Close button on the toolbar to close the preview.

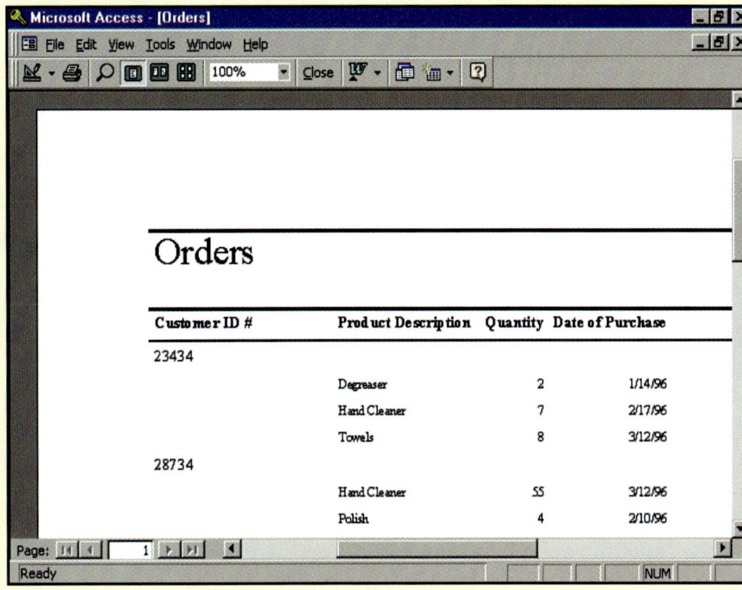

Figure 14.22
The Preview button displays the Orders report.

Combining the Reports

In the next section, you learn how to make the Orders report a subreport of the Customer report.

To Combine the Reports

1 Click the Customer report to select it, then click Design.

The Customer report opens in Design view (see Figure 14.23).

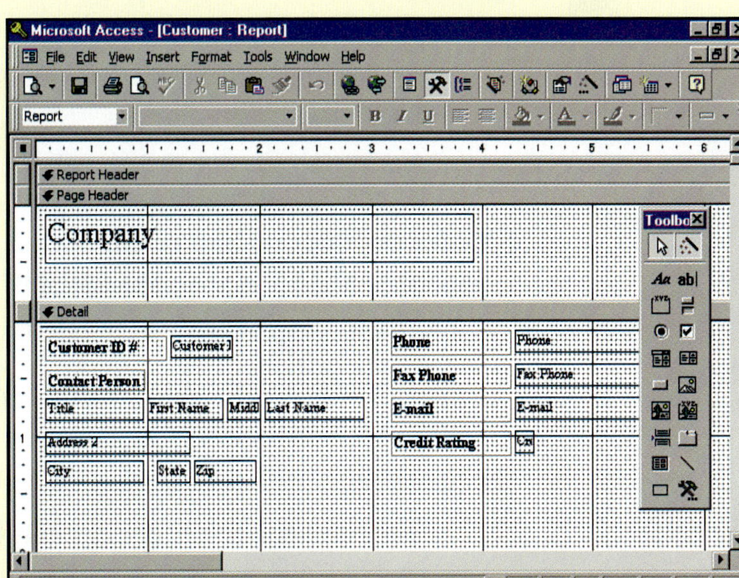

Figure 14.23
The Design view of the Customer report shows the report layout.

continues

To Combine the Reports (continued)

2 Make sure the Control Wizards button is selected on the toolbox.

The wizard helps establish the link between the two reports.

3 Maximize the Report design window, if necessary, and scroll down to show the bottom part of the report design.

The bottom portion of the Detail area (see Figure 14.24) is empty. This is where the subreport is added.

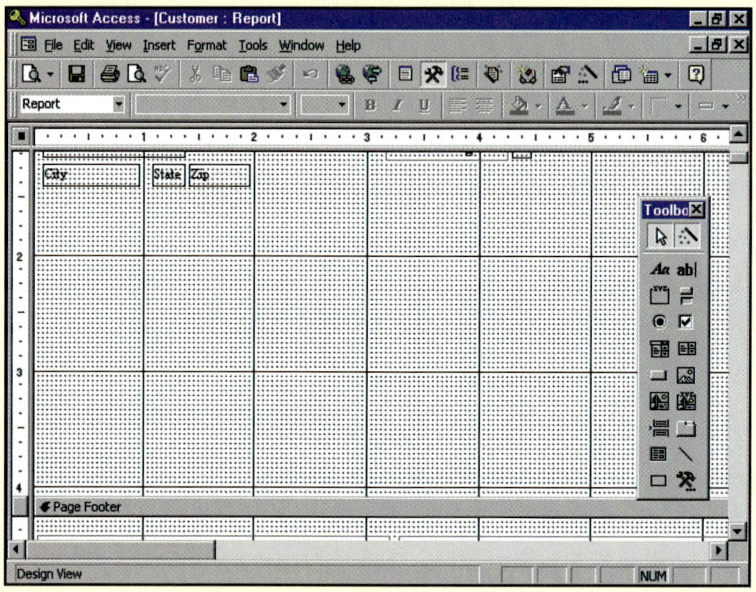

Figure 14.24
The the Customers report is empty on the bottom of the Detail section.

4 Click the Subform/Subreport button in the toolbox and draw a rectangle in the empty portion of the report design.

Draw a rectangle to indicate the location of the subform (see Figure 14.25).

When you release the mouse button, the first Subform/Subreport Wizard dialog box is displayed.

5 Click the Reports and Forms option button. Click the down arrow next to the text box and click the Orders report.

This dialog box enables you to select an existing report or to create a new report from a table or query. In this case, you choose an existing report. Make sure you choose the Orders report, not the Orders form.

6 Click Next.

The second dialog box is displayed. If the reports you have selected are based on tables that are joined in a one-to-many relationship, you see a choice that links the reports in the same way (see Figure 14.26).

Access

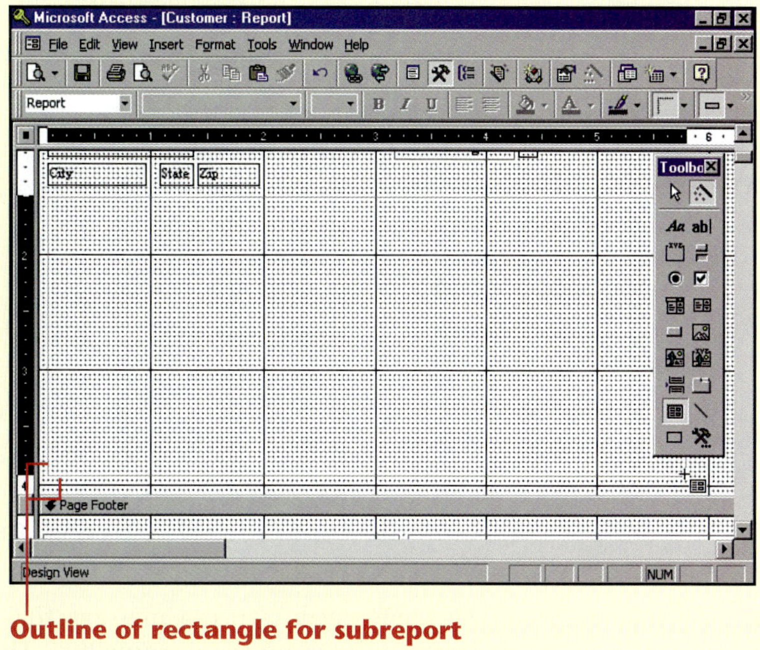

Figure 14.25
The Customer report with the area for the subreport drawn.

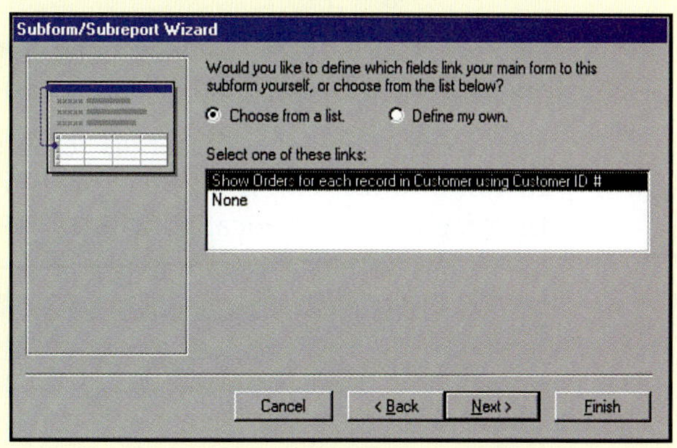

Figure 14.26
The Subform/Subreport Wizard dialog box that shows a choice that links the two reports.

7. **Click the option Choose from a list, if necessary. Select the first link, `Show Orders for each record in Customer using Customer ID #`, and then click Next.**

   The final dialog box appears that asks for a name for the subreport.

8. **Accept the default name `Orders` and click Finish.**

   The wizard places the subreport in the report design. Notice that the title of the subreport may overlap the City label and that the size of the subreport may not match the rectangle you drew.

9. **Drag the subreport down about a half-inch, if necessary, so its title does not overlap the City label.**

   The subreport should not overlap the other fields (see Figure 14.27).

continues

To Combine the Reports (continued)

Figure 14.27
The report design is adjusted to avoid overlap.

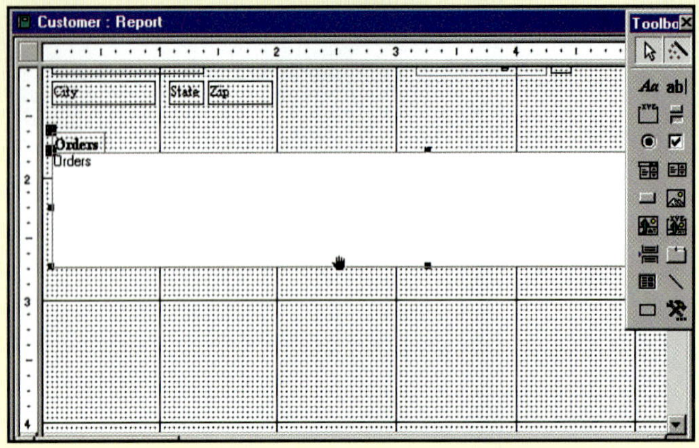

10 **Click the Print Preview button on the toolbar to preview the report.**

You may get a warning message that the report does not fit the page. Click OK on the warning box. This problem will be dealt with in following steps.

11 **Maximize the window. Scroll the window so that you can see the subreport and most of the main report.**

Notice that the list of orders is restricted to those that match the customer information above. Also, there is an extra "Orders" title the program automatically included (see Figure 14.28).

Access

Figure 14.28
A preview of the final report that shows orders for one customer.

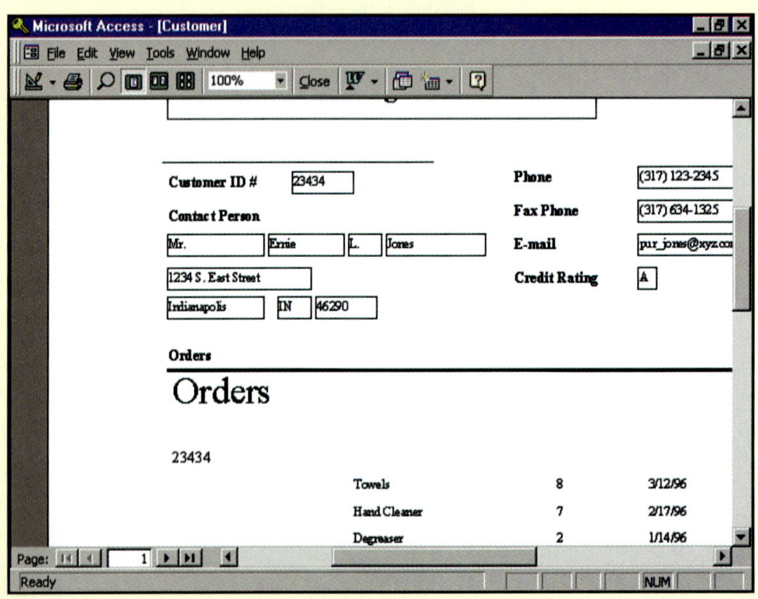

12 **Close the preview to return to Design view.**

13 **Click the Orders title above the subreport to select it and delete it.**

14. **Click the subreport to select it. Scroll to the right until you can see the right edge of the subreport control.**

15. **Place the pointer on the middle sizing handle on the right edge of the subreport and drag it until the edge of the subreport control is at the 5 1/2-inch mark on the horizontal ruler.**

    The size of the subreport is reduced so you can now decrease the width of the report.

16. **Move the pointer to the edge of the border of the report grid. When the pointer changes to a two-headed arrow, click and drag the edge of the report to the left until it is slightly to the left of the 6 1/2-inch mark on the horizontal ruler (see Figure 14.29). (The toolbox was closed in the figure.)**

    It is necessary to reduce the overall width of the report so it does not produce empty pages.

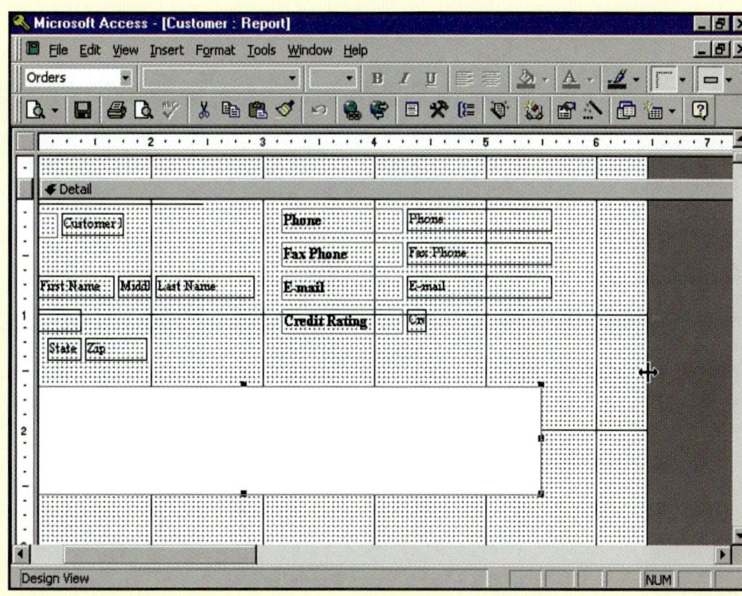

Figure 14.29
The edge of the report is adjusted to reduce the overall size of the report so empty pages are not created.

17. **Click the Print Preview button to return to the report. Click the navigation buttons to verify that each customer is on a single page and that there are no empty pages in the report.**

18. **Close the report and save the changes.**

    Leave the database open for use in the next lesson.

Lesson 5: Creating Reports Using the Chart Wizard

Some types of information are best presented using charts instead of numbers. Access has a built-in Chart Wizard that uses an application called Microsoft Graph to help you create a chart. Charts created in Access are somewhat difficult to edit, however, and the chart module has only limited charting capabilities. If you have Excel, you may find it easier to export or copy your data to a spreadsheet and create your charts there.

In this lesson, you create a chart to show the relative frequency with which products are ordered. The chart you create counts the number of orders placed by product description.

To Create Reports Using the Chart Wizard

1 In the Orders database, click on the Report tab, if necessary.

2 Click New.

The New Report dialog box appears.

3 Select the Chart Wizard. Select Orders from the drop-down list, then click OK.

The first Chart Wizard dialog box is displayed, asking which field contains the data you want to chart (see Figure 14.30).

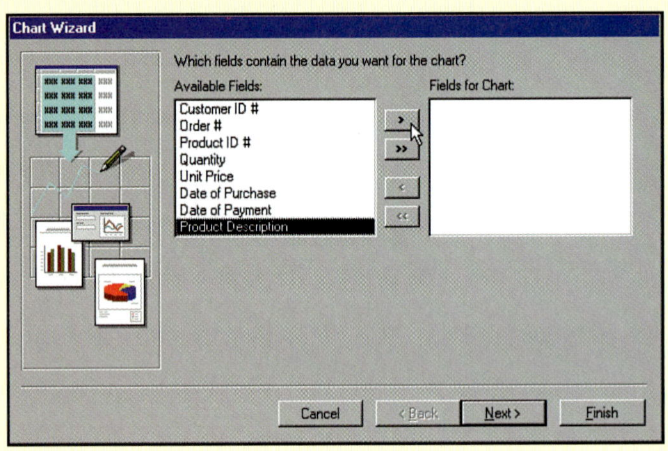

Figure 14.30
The Chart Wizard enables you to select the field to chart.

4 Select the Product Description field, then click the right-arrow button to move it to the Fields for Chart list box. Click Next.

The second Chart Wizard dialog box appears, asking what type of chart you want to use (see Figure 14.31). When you click a chart type, a description of that type appears in a box on the right-hand side of the dialog box.

5 Select the Column Chart, the first example in the first row, then click Next.

The third Chart Wizard dialog box is displayed, giving you a preview of the chart (see Figure 14.32). No changes are made in this dialog box.

Access

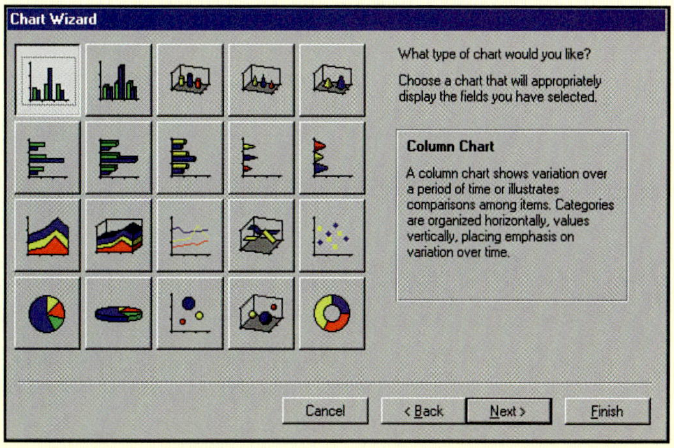

Figure 14.31
The second Chart Wizard dialog box asks you to choose a chart type.

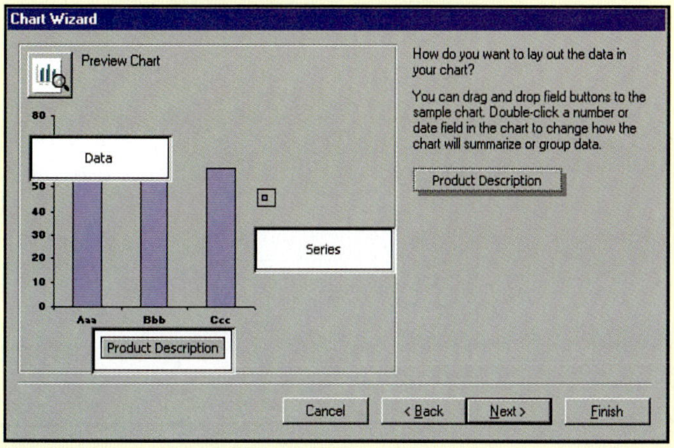

Figure 14.32
The third Chart Wizard dialog box shows a preview of the final chart.

6 Click Next.

The fourth Chart Wizard dialog box is displayed, giving you several additional options (see Figure 14.33).

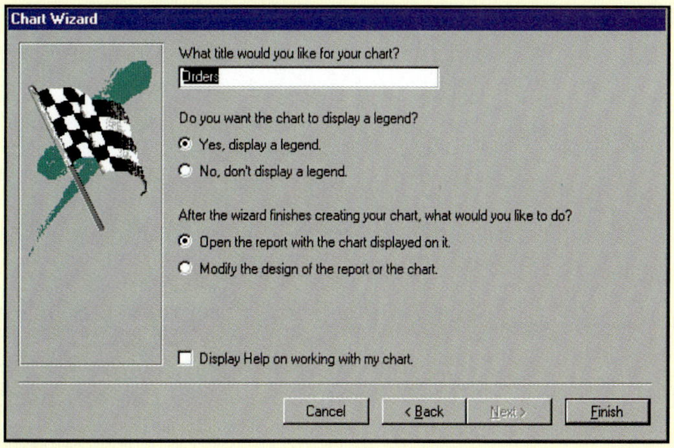

Figure 14.33
The fourth Chart Wizard dialog box includes several formatting options.

continues

To Create Reports Using the Chart Wizard (continued)

7 Change the title of the chart to `Orders for Each Product`**.**

8 Click the option button for `No, don't display a legend`**.**

Because there is only one data set in this chart, a legend is unnecessary. If you had two or more data sets, a legend would be necessary.

9 Click Finish.

The final report is shown in Preview mode. There are problems with the chart, particularly the data labels on the x-axis (see Figure 14.34). The Chart Wizard has automatically chosen to display every other label on the x-axis.

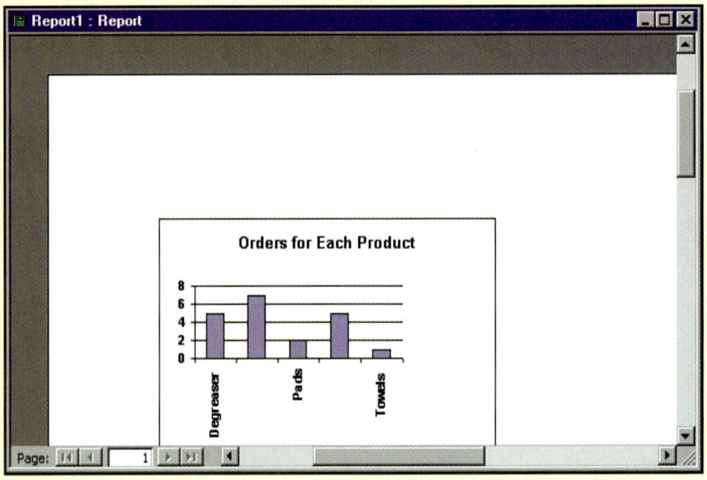

Figure 14.34
The x-axis labels only display every other label on the initial chart produced by the wizard.

10 Click the Close button in the toolbar.

You are now in the Report Design view.

11 Double-click the chart to launch Microsoft Graph.

The Microsoft Graph window appears, showing both the datasheet for the graph and the graph itself (see Figure 14.35). Notice that the graph and numbers are not those you requested. Instead, they are the default values from Microsoft Graph.

12 Maximize the Microsoft Graph window, if necessary.

13 Move the pointer to the lower-right corner of the Chart window.

The pointer turns into a two-sided arrow.

14 Click the corner of the Chart window and drag it down and to the right to increase the width and height by about 50%.

The size of the Chart window increases (see Figure 14.36).

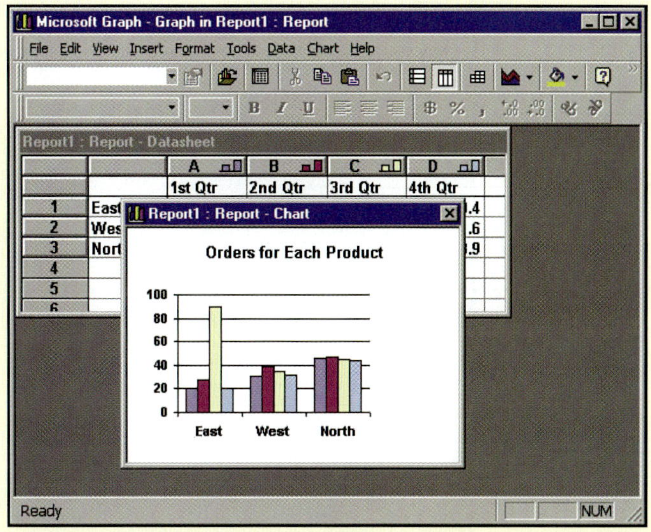

Figure 14.35
Chart editing is done in the Microsoft Graph window.

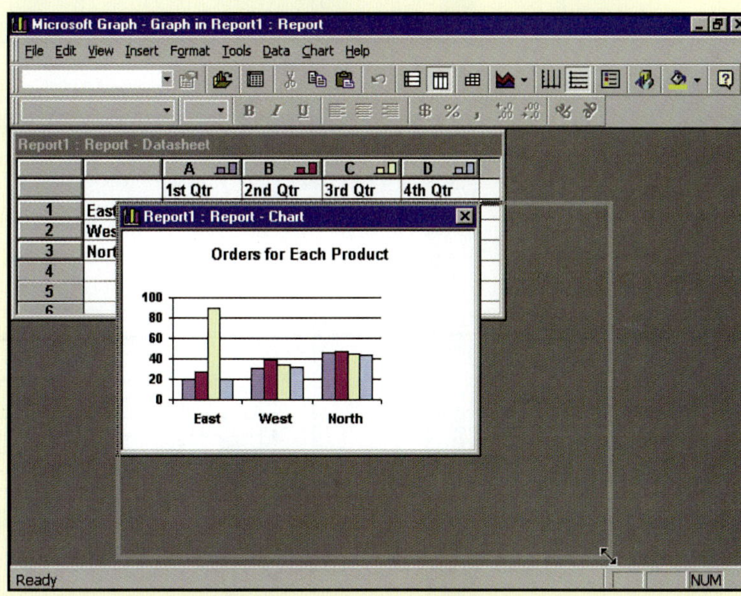

Figure 14.36
Increase the size of the Chart window to make enough room for all of the x-axis labels.

15 Choose File and Exit & Return to Report1.

The Microsoft Graph program closes, and the view returns to the Design view of the report. Notice that the chart no longer fits in the object placeholder (see Figure 14.37).

16 Click the handle on the lower-right corner of the chart and drag to the right and down until the chart is a couple of inches larger in both directions.

17 Click the Preview button.

Your chart should appear with all five data labels (see Figure 14.38). If you have cut off any of the chart, or have too much room on the right edge, adjust the size again.

continues

To Create Reports Using the Chart Wizard (continued)

Figure 14.37
Changing the size of the chart in Microsoft Graph causes problems in the Access report design.

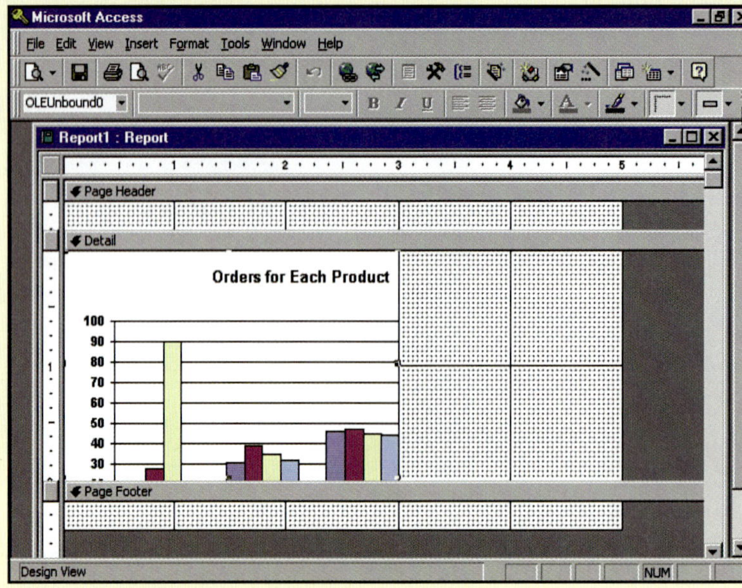

Figure 14.38
The chart displays all of the product labels after it has been resized and reformatted.

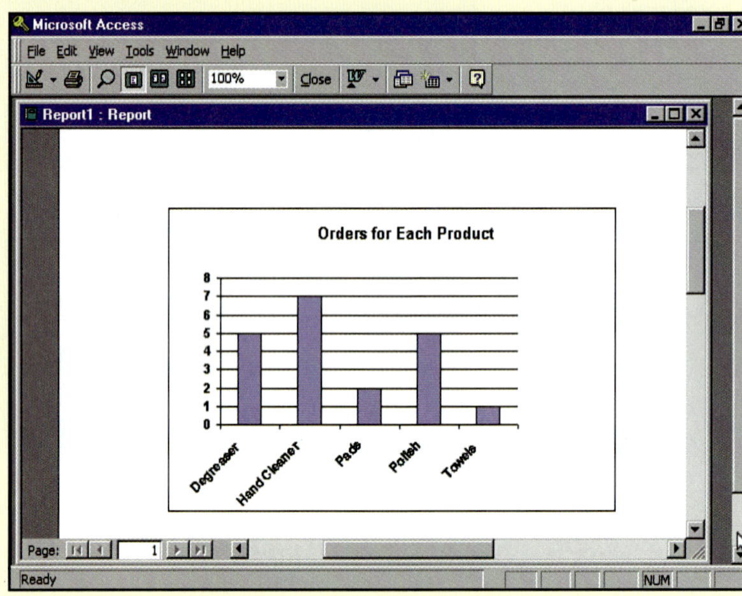

18. **Close the Preview window and close the Design view.**

19. **Save your changes, and give the new report the name `Orders for Each Product`.**

20. **Close the database.**

If you have completed your session on the computer, exit Access and shut down Windows before you turn off the computer. Otherwise, continue with the "Checking Your Skills" and "Applying Your Skills" sections in this project.

Project Summary

To	Do This
Create a simple crosstab query	Create a select query based on the desired table or tables. Use the Query Type button to change the type of query to Crosstab. Drag the necessary fields to the query design grid. Use the Crosstab box to choose which fields will be used as row header, column header, and cell value. Click the Total box in the column that will be used as the cell value and pick the type of mathematical operation desired. Click View to see the crosstab query.
Create crosstab queries with conditions	Follow the previous directions to create a crosstab query. Drag any additional fields that may be necessary for setting conditions. Change the Total box in those fields to Expression. Enter the condition(s) in the criteria box(es).
Create crosstab queries with a column of simple totals	Create a query as previously described. Drag a field to the next empty column in the query design grid. Change the contents of the Crosstab box in that column to Row Heading. Change the contents of the Total box to Sum.
Create crosstab queries with a column of calculated totals	Create a query as previously described. Enter an expression in the field box of the next empty column in the query design grid. Change the contents of the Crosstab box in that column to Row Heading. Change the contents of the Total box to Sum.
Insert subforms into forms	Open an existing form in Design view. Open the toolbox and make sure the Control Wizards button on the toolbox is selected. Click the Subform/ Subreport button on the toolbox and draw a rectangle in the Form design window where the subform will go. Select the subform from a list of existing forms, or create it using the wizard. The two forms must be based on tables that are joined one-to-many.

To	Do This
Insert subreports into reports	Open a report in Design view. Open the toolbox and make sure the Control Wizards button on the toolbox is selected. Click the Subform/Subreport button on the toolbox and draw a rectangle in the Report design window where the subreport will go. Select the subreport from a list of existing reports or create it using the wizard. The two reports must be based on tables that are joined one-to-many.
Create a report using the Chart Wizard	Create a new report. Choose a table or query, then select the Chart Wizard. Choose the chart type, then add a title and decide whether to include a legend. Alternate between the Chart Wizard and the Report Design view to adjust the final appearance of the chart.

Checking Your Skills

True/False

For each of the following statements, check *T* or *F* to indicate whether the statement is true or false.

__T __F 1. The design for a crosstab query must have at least one row header, column header, and value.

__T __F 2. In a crosstab query design, the field that has been chosen to provide the values in the cells must have its Totals box changed to "Group By."

__T __F 3. If the records in a subform are going to be linked to the records in the main form, the tables on which they are based must be joined in a one-to-many relationship.

__T __F 4. In Access, you can use the Chart Wizard to create a chart and then use Microsoft Chart to edit the chart.

__T __F 5. If you want to display data in chart form, you must export the table to Excel and use the Excel charting option.

__T __F 6. To add a restriction on a crosstab query using another field, add the field to the field box, and write the limitation in the crosstab box.

__T __F 7. The Between expression is inclusive; that is, purchases made on the beginning and end dates will be included in the table.

__T __F 8. To create a main form/subform, you use the SubForm Wizard found in the New Form dialog box.

__T __F **9.** When you edit a chart in Access, the data displayed in the Microsoft Graph program is the data that is being charted.

__T __F **10.** A crosstab query produces a dynaset where the contents of one field provide the column headings and the contents of another field are used as row headings.

Multiple Choice

Circle the letter of the correct answer for each of the following questions.

1. If a field name is used in an expression, it must be enclosed by _____.

a. []

b. ()

c. {}

d. <>

2. To add an additional set of values such as totals on the left side of a crosstab query, the Crosstab box must be set to _____.

a. Column Header

b. Row Header

c. Value

d. Expression

3. If a form and its subform are based on tables that are joined in a one-to-many relationship, _____.

a. the records shown in the subform are limited to those that match the record shown in the main form

b. they use the same navigation buttons

c. they cannot both show a record with the same key field value

d. you cannot change the contents of a field in the subform

4. To add a subreport to a report, you can _____.

a. choose from a list of existing reports

b. create a report based on a table

c. create a report based on a query

d. all of the above

5. Charts can be created in Access as a type of _____

a. report

b. macro

c. query

d. table

6. The types of charts you can create in Access include _____.

a. bar charts

b. column charts

c. pie charts

d. all of the above

7. The SubForm/Subreport Wizard found in the toolbox can be used to _____.

a. add a subreport only from an existing report

b. add a subform from an existing report

c. create both reports with subreports and forms with subforms

d. create the main part of the form

8. In a crosstab query, the data that appears in the intersection of the columns and rows is known as the _____.

a. value field

b. quantity field

c. amount field

d. count field

9. To have a total in a subform, add the calculated expression in a new field box and change the Total row to _____.

a. Group by

b. Total

c. Sum

d. Quantity

10. In a query, to create a new label for a column that will be used for a calculated field, type the label name followed by _____.

a. a semicolon

b. a colon

c. a period

d. a comma

Completion

In the blank provided, write the correct answer for each of the following statements.

1. In a crosstab query design, the Row Header setting goes in the _______________ box.

2. In a crosstab query, the Totals box must be set to _______________ to show totals in the cells of the query.

3. The subreport must be based on a table that is the _______________ (choose one or many) of a one-to-many relationship.

4. To scroll through the records in a subform, you use the _______________ buttons at the bottom of the subform.

5. In a chart, a(n) _______________ is necessary if there is more than one data set.

6. A form placed within form that shows data from another related table is known as a(n) _______________.

7. When you created a calculated field, each field name used in the calculation must be in _______________.

8. When you create a subreport using existing reports you first open the report that contains the _______________ key.

9. In a crosstab query, the field designed as _______________ in the Crosstab box creates headings along the left side of the query dynaset.

10. In a crosstab query, the field designed as _______________ in the Crosstab box creates headings along the top of the query dynaset.

Matching

In the blank next to each of the following terms or phrases, write the letter of the corresponding term or phrase. (Note that some letters may be used more than once.)

a. Row Heading
b. Column Heading
c. values
d. Sum
e. table, query, form
f. Control Wizards
g. table, query, form, report
h. Bar
i. Total
j. Microsoft Graph

_____ 1. Must be selected before the Subform/Subreport Wizard can be activated
_____ 2. Operation used to find totals
_____ 3. Type of chart that can show quantity by group
_____ 4. Appears in the top row of a crosstab query dynaset
_____ 5. Used to edit charts in Access
_____ 6. A subreport can be based any of these
_____ 7. Row used in a crosstab query
_____ 8. The cells of a crosstab query are calculated based on the fields that match the _______of both the row and column fields
_____ 9. A subform can be based on any of these
_____ 10. Determines the information that shows on the left side of a crosstab query

Applying Your Skills

Practice

The following exercises enable you to practice the skills you have learned in this project.

Creating a Crosstab Query

In the following exercise you create a crosstab query to display the total quantity purchased by item for each date. The rows consist of the product descriptions, the columns are the months of the year, and the cells contain the total of the quantity field.

To create a crosstab query, complete the following steps:

Create a crosstab query that shows the total quantity of each item purchased in each month.

1. Rename the Orders database that you used in this project `Orders2`.
2. Create a query based on the Orders table. Change its type to Crosstab.
3. Drag the Quantity, Product Description, and Data of Purchase fields to the query design grid.
4. In the Crosstab box, select Row Heading for Product description, Column Heading for Date of Purchase, and Value for Quantity.

5. Change the contents of the Total box for the Quantity field to Sum.
6. Switch to the Datasheet view to see how it worked.
7. Close and save the query. Name it `Products sold by date`.
8. Leave the database open for use in the next exercise.

Creating a Crosstab Query Using the Crosstab Query Wizard

In the following exercise, you create a crosstab query using the Crosstab Query Wizard. The wizard guides you through the process and inserts some advanced features automatically.

To create a crosstab query using the wizard, complete the following steps:

Create a crosstab query that shows the total quantity of each item purchased in each month.

1. Use the Orders2 database. Create a new query using the Crosstab Query Wizard.
2. Select the Orders table. Use the Product Description field for row headings.
3. Use the Date of Purchase for the column headings. Choose Month as the Interval.
4. Choose Quantity and Sum for the value to be displayed. Deselect the Yes, include row sums option at the left of the window.
5. Name the query `Products Sold by Month` and click Finish.
6. Examine the Datasheet view to see the results.
7. Leave the database open for use in the next exercise.

Adding a Subform to Another Form

In this exercise you create two forms using the Autoform Wizard. These forms are based on two linked tables. You then place one form inside the other as a subform.

To add a subform to another form, complete the following steps:

1. Open the `Orders2` database created in the previous exercise or copy Proj1401 from the Project-14 folder on the CD and rename it `Orders2`. Create a form based on the Orders table. Use the Autoform: Tabular Wizard.
2. Close the form and name it `Orders2`.
3. Create a form based on the Customer table. Use the Autoform: Columnar option. Save it and name it `Customers2`.
4. Open the `Customers2` form in Design view. Move some of the fields to make the two columns of fields approximately the same length.

5. Open the toolbox and make sure the Control Wizards button is selected. Click the Subform/Subreport button and draw a rectangle across the bottom of the form where the subform will go.

6. Select the Orders2 form from the list.

7. Edit the placement of the fields and the size of the subform. Make the subform large enough to view three records.

8. Switch to Datasheet view to check your work. Save the resulting form. Leave the database open for use in the next exercise.

Creating a Report with the Chart Wizard

Create a chart based on the Orders table to display the number of items ordered by product. In this case you select two fields to be charted. The text field Product description is used as the x-axis label and the Quantity field is totaled for each product.

To create a report with the Chart Wizard, complete the following steps:

1. Use the Orders2 database or copy Proj1401 from the Project-14 folder on the CD and rename it `Orders2`. Create a new report using the Chart Wizard.

2. Use the Orders table as the data source.

3. Select the product description and the quantity as the fields to be charted.

4. Use a column chart format.

5. Make the chart title `Number of Items Ordered by Product`.

6. Increase the size of the chart to approximately six inches wide and four inches high.

7. Save the report as `Items Ordered` and print a copy.

Creating a Report with a Subreport

In the following exercise, you create a report with a subreport that uses the Sound Byte Music database. The report lists the suppliers and the orders from each supplier.

To create a report that displays the supplier followed by the orders from that supplier, complete the following steps:

1. Copy the file Proj1402 from the Project-14 folder on the CD and rename it `SBMusic12`.

2. Create a new report based on the Suppliers table using the AutoReport: Columnar option. Name it `Suppliers`.

3. Create a new report based on the Orders table using the AutoReport: Tabular option. Name it `Orders`. You will combine the two reports.

4. Open the `Suppliers` report in Design view. Make room at the bottom of the details section and place a subreport there, using the Toolbox option. This is the Orders report.
5. Adjust the width of the subreport and report to less than 6 1/2 inches.
6. Preview the report. Notice that more than one supplier is included on a page. Switch back to Design view.
7. Click the Page Break button on the toolbox and drag it on the report design just below the subreport.
8. Preview the report and save it.

Challenge

The following challenges enable you to use your problem-solving skills.

Comparing a Report/Subreport to a Report Created with the Report Wizard

In this exercise, you create a report based on members with a subreport based on donations. Next, you generate a similar report using the Report Wizard. Finally, you compare the two reports.

Open the `Club` database that you have been working on in previous projects. Create a Columnar report based on the table that contains member information. Create a Tabular report based on the table that contains the donation information.

Place the Donation report in the Membership report as a subform and save the report.

Create a new report that is based on the Members table. Use the wizard to select member information from the Members table and donation information from the Donations table.

Sort the donations by date and preview the report. Switch to Design view and adjust the widths of the fields to display the numbers, if necessary.

Save the report and then compare the two reports. Finally, write a paragraph describing the strengths and weaknesses of each method of creating a report that includes fields from two tables.

Creating a Crosstab Query

Crosstab queries are ideal for analyzing research data. In this exercise, you modify the Complete Viewing History query that you created earlier to include the Sex field a calculated field that determines the difference between the starting and ending times. Then you do a crosstab query based on the Complete Viewing History query that displays the number of hours each channel is viewed by each sex.

Rename the Human Research12 database as `Human Research13`. Open the Complete Viewing History query in Design view. Drag the Sex field from the Participants table onto the design grid. Scroll the design to the next available column and enter the following in the Field box:

```
Time: ([Ending Time]-[Beginning Time])*24
```

This expression finds the difference between the two times in fractions of a day and then multiplies by 24 to turn it into hours. Change the property of the field to Fixed with one decimal place. Save the changes and close the query.

Create a crosstab query that is based on the Complete Viewing History query. The query displays the channels by name, the total time watched, and the time watched for each sex. Set up the query grid as follows:

```
Channel Name - Group by, Row Heading
Sex - Group by, Column Heading
Time - Sum, Row Heading
Time - Sum, Value
```

Set the properties of the two Time columns so that they are fixed numbers that show one decimal place. Then, preview the results and save the query as `Viewing by Sex`.

Create a Report/Subreport Based Certain Data

This report lists the location and a list of machine information for each machine.

Locate the Vending11 database that you worked on in the previous project and rename it `Vending12`. Create a columnar report based on the Locations table. Create a tabular report based on the Machines table. Make the Machines report a subreport of the Locations report. Check and adjust the width of the report, if necessary.

Creating a Crosstab Query that Summarizes Data

In this exercise, you create a crosstab query based on the Rentals and Fees query. You then create a chart report to compare the amount of rentals each title contributes to the total of the rental fees.

Locate the Video Store10 database and rename it. Create a crosstab query based on the Rentals and Fees query using the Crosstab Query Wizard. Use the Title as the row heading, the Date Rented as the column heading, and the Rental Fee as the value. Check the option that creates a totals column and group the dates by month. Name the query `Rentals and Fees Crosstab`.

Check the table to see what addresses and names are the longest, then check the labels to make sure you did not cut any of them off.

Create a pie chart based on the Rentals and Fees query. Select the Title and the Rental Fee as the two fields to be used in the chart. Name the pie chart `Rentals and Fees Pie Chart`. Edit the chart and make it about six inches wide by four inches tall. Preview the chart to see if all the titles are shown in the legend. Revise the chart's size if necessary.

Creating a Report Based on a Table and a Subreport Based on a Different Table

It would be valuable to be able to supply each insurance company with a detailed list of the items that you may wish to claim in case of a fire or disaster. In this exercise you create a report with subreport that displays all of the pertinent information about the insurance company, then list each item insured by that company.

Locate the Home Inventory10 database that you used in the previous project and rename it `Home Inventory11`. Create a columnar AutoReport based on the Insurance Companies table and name it `Insurance Companies`. Create a tabular AutoReport based on the Items table and name it `Items`.

Modify the Insurance Companies report and insert the Items report into it as a subreport. Check the width of the report and adjust it so that it is less than six and a half inches.

Insert a page break after the subreport to force a new page for each insurance company. Then, save the changes to the Insurance Companies report.

PinPoint Training

PinPoint Assessment

You have completed the project and the associated lessons, as well as the "Checking Your Skills" and "Applying Your Skills" sections. Now use the PinPoint software Evaluation mode to assess your comprehension of the specific exam tasks you have just learned. You can also use the PinPoint Trainer mode and the SHOW ME tutorials to practice these specific exam tasks.

Project 15
Fifteen

Using Access Macros

Automating Your Database for Easier Use with Macros

In this project you will learn the following objectives and their associated Microsoft Exam required activities.

Objectives	Required Activities
Create a Macro to Open a Form in the Edit Mode	
Create a Macro to Open a Form in the Add Mode	
Create a Macro to Open a Form in the Read Only Mode	
Create a Macro to Open a Report in Preview View	
Create a Macro to Close a Form	
Run a Macro from a Button on a Form	
Create Switchboard Forms	
Create a Macro to Automatically Launch the Main Switchboard Form	

Why Would I Do This?

Macros
A group of instructions that provides additional commands or functionality to a program.

Switchboard
The term Access uses for a menu of choices represented by buttons on a form. Clicking a button on a switchboard runs an associated macro to perform functions such as opening forms or printing reports.

Action
An Access-defined function that performs some process within the database, table, form, or query.

Argument
A value needed for a macro to perform its function.

One of the functions computers are best suited for is automating repetitive tasks, and *macros* are the mechanisms that enable you to perform this automation. Access macros make your database applications more productive. A few simple macros can automate mundane, repetitive procedures.

Almost any action in Access can be assisted or completely performed by a macro. You can create a form that contains buttons that activate macros. You can also create an automated menu, referred to as a *switchboard*, that enables the user to preview and print reports, review tables or query contents using forms, enter new records into tables, close open windows, or complete any other task a macro can perform by simply clicking on a button.

This chapter covers how to create a macro and how to enter *actions* and *arguments* that control the macro, as well as comments that describe the function of the macro. You learn how to work with the Macro Design window and toolbar. You also learn how to name, save, and run macros. In some of the sections, you create additional macros that are used to create a customized form to serve as a switchboard.

Access

Lesson 1: Creating a Macro to Open a Form in the Edit Mode

You create Access macros by starting with an empty Macro Design window, then adding the actions and arguments that make your macro do its work. In this lesson, you create a macro that automatically opens a form allowing you to edit the records in a table or query.

To Create a Macro to Open a Form in the Edit Mode

1. **Make a copy of Proj1501 from the Project-15 folder on the CD, and place it in your own directory on your disk. Rename the copy `Customer Records2`.**

2. **Open the `Customer Records2` database, and select the Macros tab.**

3. **Click the New button.**

   The Macro dialog box is displayed.

4. **Click the drop-down arrow in the first Action box and select OpenForm from the list of possible actions (see Figure 15.1).**

   OpenForm is a macro instruction that automatically opens the form you select in the following steps.

Figure 15.1
The Macro window drop-down box shows a list of available Actions.

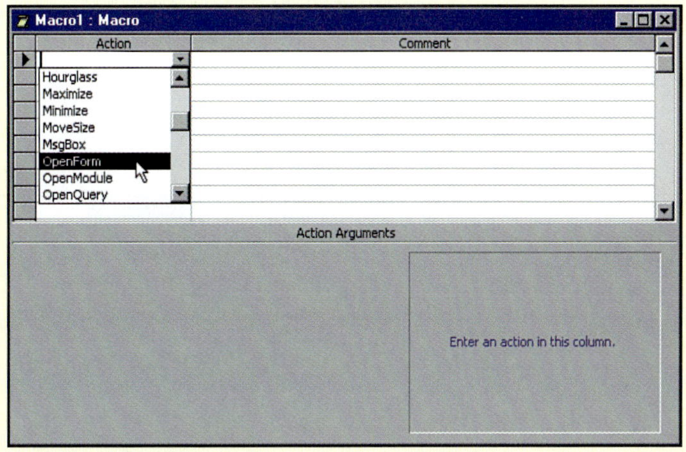

5 **Move the cursor to the Action Arguments section of the window, and click the Form Name box.**

This box is used to select the form opened by the macro. After you click the box, a drop-down arrow appears at the right side of the box.

6 **Click the drop-down arrow and select the Customer Information form (see Figure 15.2).**

The list shows all of the forms in the database.

Figure 15.2
The Form Name drop-down box lists all available forms.

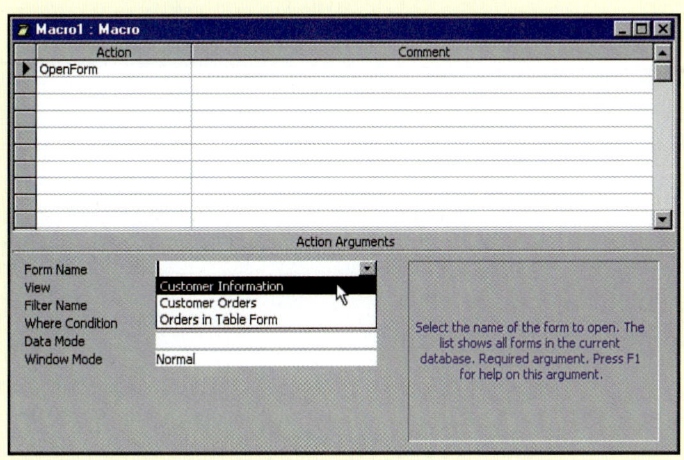

7 **Click the Data Mode box and use the drop-down menu to choose Edit.**

This enables you to edit or add records.

8 **Click the close button in the upper-right corner of the window, and save the macro with the name `Open Customer Information Form`.**

continues

To Create a Macro to Open a Form in the Edit Mode (continued)

Macro names can be used as command buttons on forms. When you name a macro, consider how its name would look on a command button on a form (see Figure 15.3).

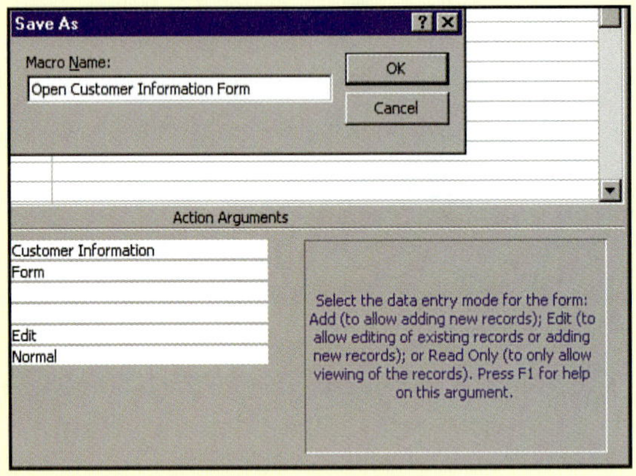

Figure 15.3
The name you give a macro can be used on a command button in a form.

9 Click the Run button to test the macro.

The Customer Information form opens automatically.

10 Close the Customer Information form.

Leave the database open for the next lesson.

Inside Stuff

A quick way to select an action in the macro window is to type the first letter of the action that is needed. The list scrolls automatically to the first action that begins with that letter, then you can click the drop-down arrow if needed, and select the specific action. For example, OpenForm is the first action under "O" and by typing an "O" in the Action box, OpenForm automatically fills in. Pressing Tab or Enter then activates the argument section of the window.

Lesson 2: Creating a Macro to Open a Form in the Add Mode

When you open a form in Edit mode, you see the data from one of the existing records filling the form. If your intent is to add a new record, you must click the new record button to move to the next available empty record. It is possible to open the form directly to the next available empty record. This option is useful when you want to create a data entry form that allows the addition of records, but not the viewing of existing records.

Access

To Create a Macro to Open a Form in the Add Mode

1. **Click the Macros tab, if necessary, and click New.**

   This opens the Macro design window.

2. **Click the drop-down arrow in the first Action box.**

   A list of possible actions is displayed.

3. **Scroll down the list and click OpenForm.**

   The Action Argument section of the window is displayed.

4. **Click in the Form Name box.**

   A drop-down arrow appears, indicating that there is a list of possible forms.

5. **Click the drop-down arrow, and then click Customer Orders.**

   The list disappears and Customer Orders appears in the Form Name box.

6. **Click the Data Mode box.**

   A drop-down arrow appears at the right of the box.

7. **Click the drop-down arrow to show the list of Data Mode options. Click Add.**

   The Data Mode is now shown as Add (see Figure 15.4).

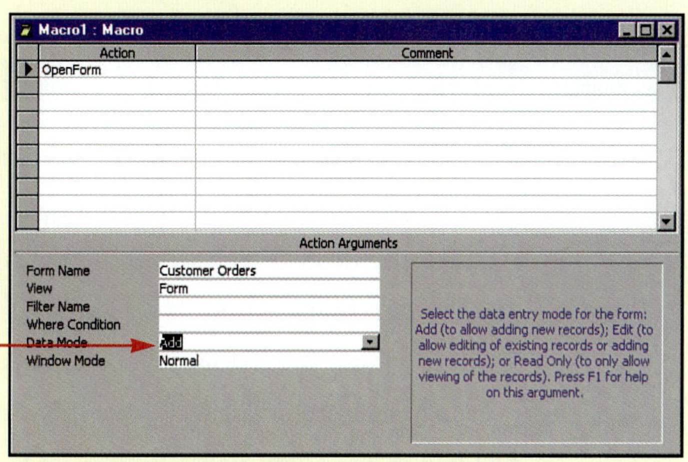

Figure 15.4
Choosing Add in the Data Mode allows you to enter a new record when the form is opened.

8. **Click the close button in the upper-right corner of the Macro dialog box.**

   You are asked if you want to save the changes to the design of Macro1.

9. **Click Yes.**

continues

To Create a Macro to Open a Form in the Add Mode (continued)

10 Type the name `Open Orders Form` in the Save As dialog box that appears.

The Database window appears with the new macro shown.

11 Click the Open Orders Form macro and click Run to test the macro.

The Customer Orders form appears, ready to receive new data.

12 Close the Customer Orders form.

Leave the database open for the next lesson.

Inside Stuff

It is always a good idea to run each macro after it has been created to make sure it works the way you intended. You can run a macro by double-clicking on the macro name.

Lesson 3: Creating a Macro to Open a Form in the Read Only Mode

In some cases, you may want to allow someone else to read the data in a table, but you do not want him to be able to change it. It is possible to open a form in the Read Only mode for this purpose.

To Create a Macro to Open a Form in the Read Only Mode

1 Click the Macros tab, if necessary, and click New.

This opens the Macro design window.

2 Click the drop-down arrow in the first Action box.

A list of possible actions is displayed.

3 Scroll down the list and click OpenForm.

The Action Argument section of the window is displayed.

4 Click in the Form Name box.

A drop-down arrow appears, indicating there is a list of possible forms.

5 Click on the drop-down arrow, and then click Orders in Table Form.

The list disappears and Orders in Table Form appears in the Form Name box.

6 Click the Data Mode box.

A drop-down arrow appears at the right of the box.

7 Click the drop-down arrow to show the list of Data Mode options. Click Read Only.

The Data Mode is now shown as Read Only (see Figure 15.5).

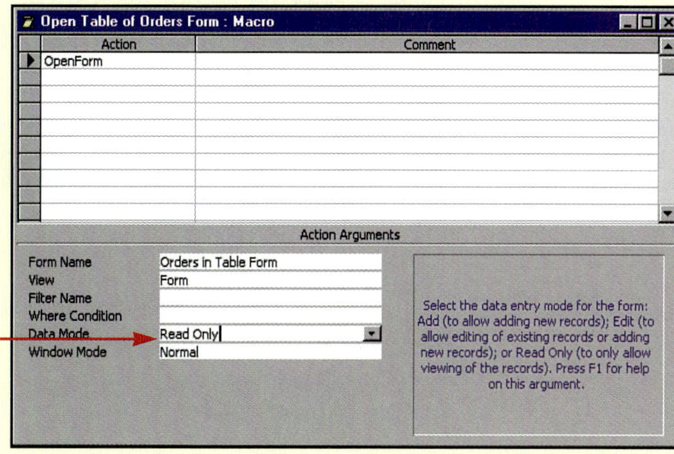

Figure 15.5
The Read Only Data Mode allows the user to look at, but not change, the data.

The Data Mode has been changed to Read Only

8 Click the close button in the upper-right corner of the Macro dialog box.

You are asked if you want to save the changes to the design of Macro1.

9 Click Yes

10 Type in the name `Open Table of Orders Form` in the Save As dialog box that appears.

The Database window appears with the new macro shown.

11 Click the Open Table of Orders Form macro and click Run.

The Table of Orders form opens in Datasheet view and in Read Only mode.

12 Try to change an existing record.

Notice that no error message is displayed; Access just does not allow any changes to be made.

13 Close the Orders form.

Leave the database open for the next lesson.

Inside Stuff

To look at a description of the actions available in a macro, or to get more information on creating macros, click the Macros tab, and then click the Office Assistant button on the toolbar. Choose `Create or modify macros`.

Lesson 4: Creating a Macro to Open a Report in Preview View

It is possible to open forms or reports in different data modes. Forms are usually opened in Edit, Add, or Read Only mode. Reports are opened in Preview view or sent directly to the printer. Since it is possible to print from the Preview view, it is a good idea to preview before you print in order to catch mistakes.

To Create a Macro to Open a Report in Preview View

1. **Click the Macros tab, if necessary, and click the New button to create a new macro.**

   The Macro1 dialog box opens.

2. **Click the Action box and its drop-down arrow. Scroll down and click the OpenReport action.**

   The OpenReport action is shown.

3. **Click the Report Name box in the Action Arguments section and then click its drop-down arrow. Select the report named Customer List by City.**

   The Report Name box now shows Customer List by City.

4. **Select Print Preview in the View box if it is not already selected.**

   The Macro window should now look like Figure 15.6.

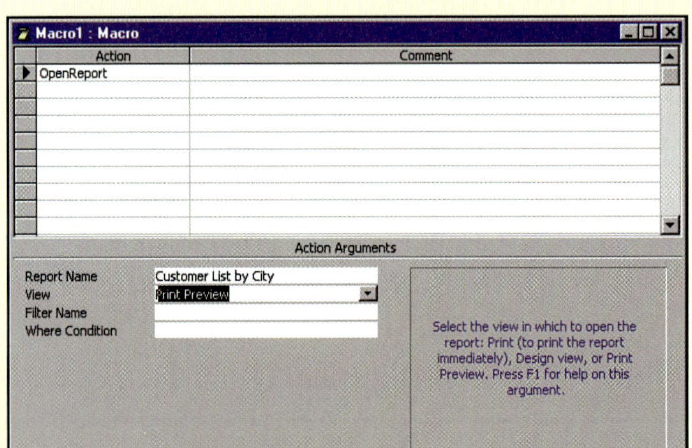

Figure 15.6
The Action Arguments are different for a report action than for a form action.

5. **Close and save the macro with the name** `Preview Customer List Report`.

6. **Follow steps 1–5 to create a macro that previews the Label for Each Receivable report. Name it** `Preview Mailing Labels for Receivables`.

7 Run each of the new macros to see how they work.

Keep the database open for the next lesson.

Lesson 5: Creating a Macro to Close a Form

It is possible for some macros to perform a generic function, such as closing a form, query, or table. The Close action closes whatever object it is attached to. This macro can be attached to a button that can be used by those who are less familiar with Access. In this lesson, you add this type of macro to the database you have been working on in the previous lessons. Later this macro is added to several forms, so it can be used to close those particular forms.

To Create a Macro to Close a Form

1 Click the Macros tab, if necessary, and click the New button to create a new macro.

2 Click the Action box and select Close from the list of actions.

Do not specify an Object Type or Object Name in the arguments section of the design window (see Figure 15.7). This action applies to whatever form happens to be open when the macro is run.

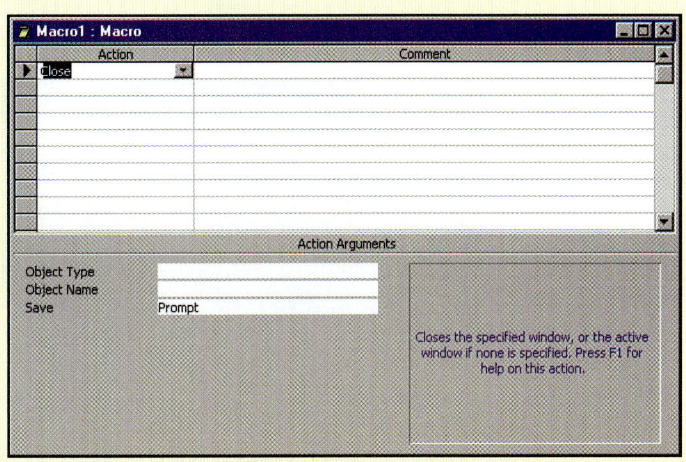

Figure 15.7
For a general action such as Close, no Object Type or Object Name needs to be selected.

3 Close and save this macro with the name `Close`.

Keep the Customer Records2 database open for the next lesson.

Lesson 6: Running a Macro from a Button on a Form

Simple macros can be run from the Database window. They are much more valuable, however, when they are attached to buttons on a form. This process creates the equivalent of a command button on a form that performs the action that has been designated by the macro. A form can contain several different types of command buttons. When you want to create command buttons that are specific to a particular form, it is better to use the Command Wizard in the Form design window toolbox. In this lesson, you add the generic close macro to several forms. This creates a command button on the form that closes the form.

To Run a Macro from a Button on a Form

1. **In the Customer Records2 database, click the Forms tab in the database window to display the existing forms.**
2. **Open the `Customer Information` form in Design view.**
3. **Open the Window menu and choose Tile Vertically to arrange the Database window and the Form design window so they do not overlap.**

   This step enables you to see both windows clearly without overlap (see Figure 15.8). It is not a necessary step in the following process, but it is faster than dragging and resizing windows to see what you are doing.

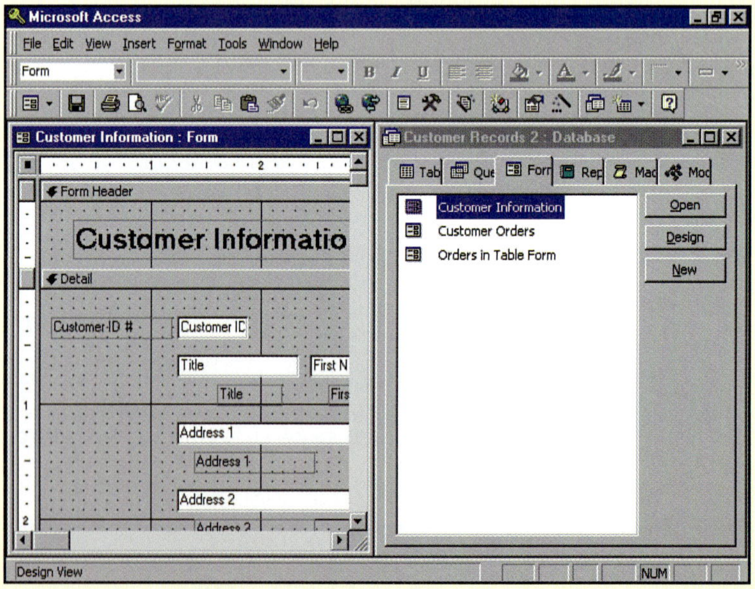

Figure 15.8 The Database and Form design windows are shown side-by-side.

4. **Close the toolbox and properties windows, if they are open.**

Access

5 **Scroll the Form design window so you can see the right side of the form.**

6 **Select the Macros tab on the Database window to show a list of available macros.**

7 **Move the pointer to the Close macro. Click and drag it to the header in the Form design window.**

A button is placed on the form when you release the mouse. It has the name of the macro on the button (see Figure 15.9).

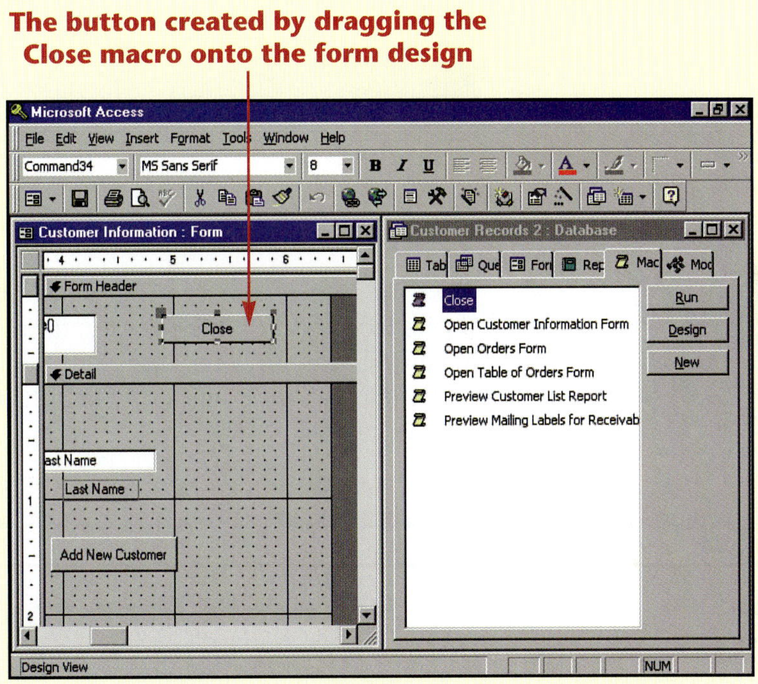

Figure 15.9
A Close command button has been added to the Design view of the Customer Information form.

8 **Close the form and save the changes.**

9 **Maximize the Database window. Click the Forms tab to display the names of available forms.**

10 **Open the `Customer Information` form by selecting it and clicking the Open button.**

Notice the new button in the form header (see Figure 15.10).

11 **Close the form by clicking the new Close button.**

12 **Follow steps 2–8 to add a Close button to the header of the Customer Orders form.**

continues

To Run a Macro from a Button on a Form (continued)

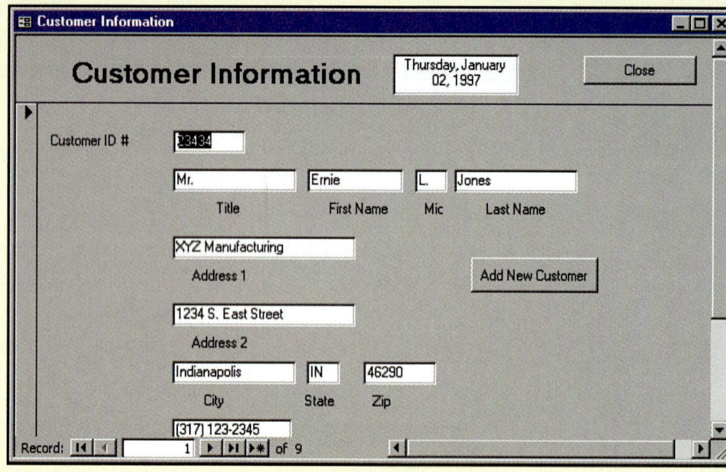

Figure 15.10
The Close command button appears on the Customer Information form.

13 Follow steps 2–8 to add a Close button to the header of the Orders in Table form.

Place the Close button to the right of the Product Description label in the form header. If necessary, decrease the length of the button. Make sure the button and the right edge of the form do not extend past the 6 1/2-inch mark or the button will not fit on the page in Portrait mode.

Keep the database open for the next lesson.

Lesson 7: Creating Switchboard Forms

It is possible to create a switchboard form that links all the parts of the database. This allows part-time workers or others who are unfamiliar with Access to enter data and produce reports easily and conveniently. Once you have created a new form, the process of creating the switchboard is broken down into three parts: creating a title, creating command buttons, and testing the switchboard.

Creating a Switchboard and Adding a Title

The first step in creating a switchboard is to build a form to hold the buttons and labels you will use to make the database easier to use.

To Create a Switchboard and Add a Title

1 In the Customer Records2 database, click the Forms tab, and then click New to create a new form.

Do not select a table or query.

2 Click Design view and click OK.

3 Open the toolbox by clicking the Toolbox button on the toolbar.

4 Click the Label button on the toolbox. Click and draw a rectangle on the form where the title goes (see Figure 15.11).

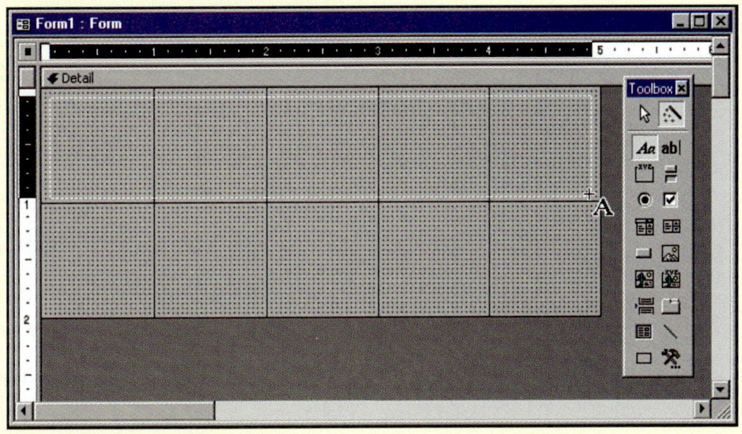

Figure 15.11
A label box has been added for the switchboard title.

5 Type in `Customer Information Management System` and press Enter.

Handles appear on the edges of the label box. You can now format the label.

6 Use the Font Size button on the toolbar to change the font size to 24.

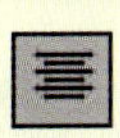

7 Use the Center button on the toolbar to center-align the text.

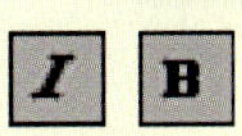

8 Use the Italic and Bold buttons to enhance the text.

9 Adjust the size of the box to fit the title, if necessary (see Figure 15.12).

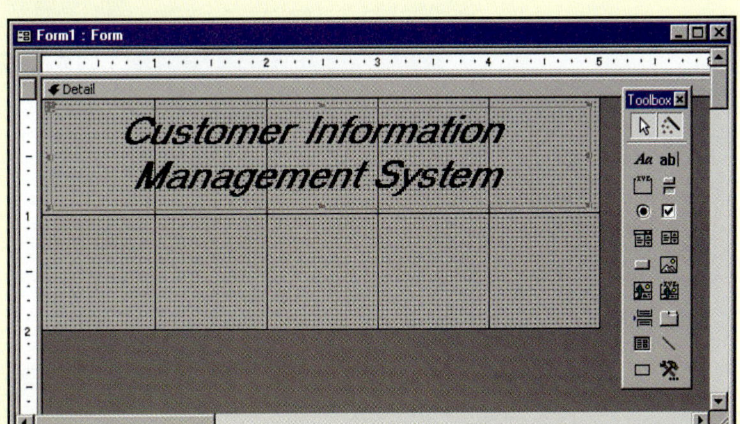

Figure 15.12
The finished title box and title.

10 Close the toolbox.

Keep the form open for the next procedure.

Creating Command Buttons

Next, you create buttons on the form to activate the macros that open the forms and reports.

To Create Command Buttons on the Switchboard Form

1. **With the new form still open in Design view, open the Window menu and choose Tile Vertically to place the Database window and the Form design window side-by-side.**
2. **Click the Macro tab in the Database window to reveal the available macros.**

   These are the macros you created earlier in this project.
3. **Click and drag the Open Customer Information Form macro from the Database window to the form.**
4. **Click and grab the middle handle on the right edge of the button, and then adjust the size so the whole macro name fits (see Figure 15.13).**

If you have problems...

If you don't place the button where you want it, you can easily move it. Deselect the button, then point to the button and click with your mouse pointer. When the pointer changes into a hand, you can drag the button to a new location. This is the same technique that is used to move text boxes around in a form.

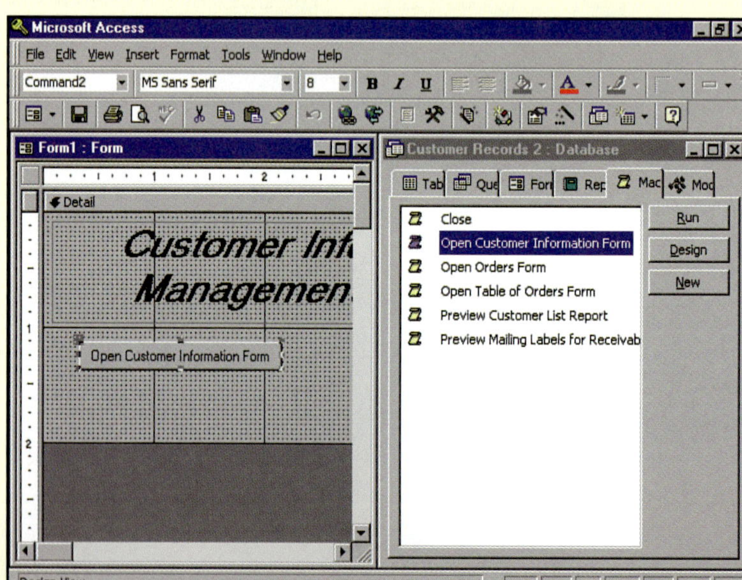

Figure 15.13
The Switchboard form is shown with a title and one button.

You can drag the macro onto a dark gray section of the form if you want. The boundary of the form automatically moves to include the new button.

5 Drag the following macros onto the form (see Figure 15.14):

Open Orders Form
Open Table of Orders Form
Preview Customer List Report
Preview Mailing Labels for Receivables
Close

6 Maximize the design window. Adjust the position and size of the buttons so their names fit on the buttons and they are arranged as shown in Figure 15.14.

To move more than one button at a time, you can select several boxes by selecting one button and then doing a Shift+click to select additional buttons. Once you have selected the buttons, you can move them as a group, or use the Format menu options to adjust size and alignment.

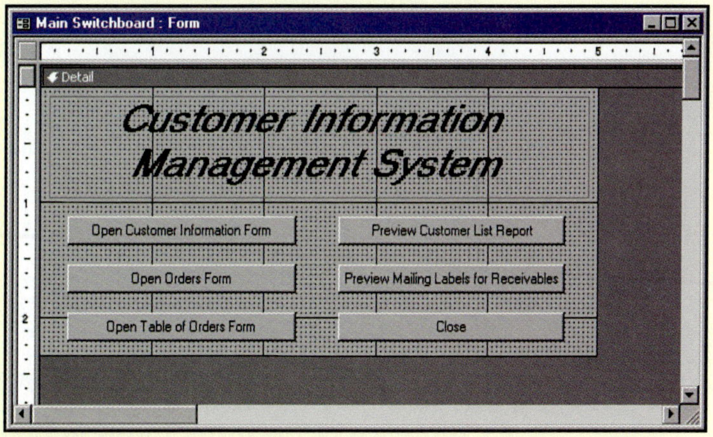

Figure 15.14
The Switchboard form is shown with all of the buttons added.

7 Select the whole form by choosing Edit, Select Form.

8 Open the Properties box. Find the Navigation Buttons property in the Format tab and change it to No.

Switchboard forms are not used to scroll through records.

9 Close and save the form with the name `Main Switchboard`.

Keep the database open for the next procedure.

Inside Stuff

A switchboard can also be created using the Switchboard Manager Wizard found under Tools, Add-Ins. This procedure is demonstrated in Lesson 4 of Project 17, "Sharing a Database with Others."

Testing the Switchboard

Next, you want to test the switchboard to see if it works.

To Test the Switchboard

1. **In the Customer Records2 database, click the Forms tab if necessary.**

2. **Click the `Main Switchboard` form, and then click Open.**

   The Main Switchboard opens (see Figure 15.15). Notice that the switchboard is not centered on your screen. You can always go back and adjust the location of the title and buttons in the Design view.

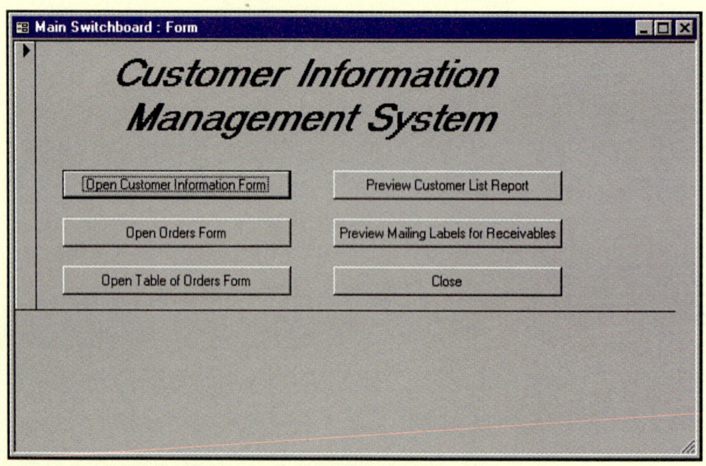

Figure 15.15
The Main Switchboard form is shown.

3. **Click the Open Customer Information Form button.**

   The Customer Information form opens.

4. **Click the Close button to close the form.**

   The program returns to the Main Switchboard.

5. **Test each of the other forms in that column of buttons.**

   Use the Close buttons you added to these forms to return to the Main Switchboard.

6. **Click the Preview Customer List Report button.**

7. **Click the Close button on the menu bar to close the report.**

   You did not add the Close button to the headers of the reports because you view the reports in Preview mode. This is not an interactive view, but an image of how the printed report will look. Use the Close button on the menu bar when previewing reports.

8. **Click the Preview Mailing Labels for Receivables button.**

   Scroll through the report to check it out.

9. **Click the Close button on the menu bar.**

10. **Click the Close button on the Main Switchboard form.**

    Keep the database open for the next lesson.

Access

Lesson 8: Creating a Macro to Automatically Launch the Main Switchboard Form

The Main Switchboard form now performs most of the functions someone would need for everyday use of the database. You could turn the maintenance of the database and production of routine reports over to a staff person who has much less training on Access. It would be convenient if the Main Switchboard form came up automatically whenever this database is opened. Fortunately, there is a special macro name that is reserved for this purpose.

To Create a Macro to Automatically Launch the Main Switchboard Form

1. **In the Customer Records2 database, click the Macros tab and click the New button.**
2. **Select the OpenForm action.**
3. **Select the form name Main Switchboard in the Action Arguments area.**
4. **Click the next Action box and select Maximize.**

   This action maximizes the Switchboard form to fill the screen (see Figure 15.16).

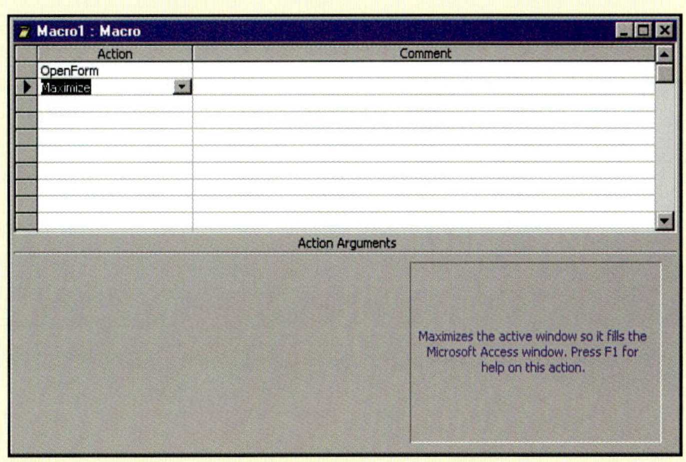

Figure 15.16
The Autoexec macro contains two actions.

5. **Close the macro and name it `Autoexec`.**

   This name means "automatically execute" and is recognized as a macro that is run whenever the database is opened.

6. **Close the database.**
7. **Open the database to test this feature.**

   The Main Switchboard should appear automatically.

continues

To Create a Macro to Automatically Launch the Main Switchboard Form (continued)

8 Close the Main Switchboard form.

This takes you back to the usual Database window.

9 Close the database.

If you have completed your session on the computer, exit Access and shut down Windows before you turn off the computer. Otherwise, continue with the "Checking Your Skills" and "Applying Your Skills" sections in this project.

Inside Stuff

You can also create a macro to close the database and Access. The action for that macro is Quit, with the Save All argument.

Project Summary

To	Do This
Create a macro to open a form	Select the Macros tab and click New. Select the action OpenForm. Select the form to be opened in the Action Arguments section. Select the mode: Edit, to edit existing records; Add, to only add new records; or Read Only, to disable add and edit capabilities. Save and close the macro. Use a name that would work as the label on a command button.
Create a macro to open a report in Preview view	Select the Macros tab and click New. Select the action OpenReport. Select the report to be opened in the Action Arguments section. Select Preview as the View argument. Save and close the macro. Use a name that would work as the label on a command button.
Create a macro to close a form	Select the Macros tab and click New. Select the action Close. Save and close the macro. Use a name that would work as the label on a command button.
Run a macro from a button on a form	Open the form in Design view. Use Window and Tile Vertically to split the window to show the opening Database window and the Form design. Click the Macros tab in the Database window. Drag the name of a macro to the Form design to create a command button. Save and close the Form design.

To	Do This
Create switchboards	Create a new form that is not based on a table. Open in Design view. Use the Labels tool in the toolbox to create a title. Drag macro names from the Database window onto the form. Save the form and close it.
Create a macro to automatically launch the Main Switchboard form	Create a macro to open the Switchboard form. Add a second action to maximize the Switchboard window. Name the macro Autoexec and save it.

Checking Your Skills

True/False

For each of the following statements, check *T* or *F* to indicate whether the statement is true or false.

__T __F **1.** Read Only mode is a macro option for reports that prevents changes when previewing the report.

__T __F **2.** A switchboard can be a form with macro buttons on it.

__T __F **3.** Actions in a macro can be chosen from a drop-down list.

__T __F **4.** If you name a macro Autorun, it will run each time the database is opened.

__T __F **5.** One way to create a command button on a form is to drag a macro from the list of macros in the Database window onto the form.

__T __F **6.** In the Action box of the Macro window, you can type the first letter of the desired action to quickly scroll to the actions that begin with that letter.

__T __F **7.** If you use the Add mode for an OpenForm macro, the form that is opened can be used to add new or edit existing records.

__T __F **8.** Each macro can perform only one action.

__T __F **9.** A generic close macro does not have to specify an object name.

__T __F **10.** A switchboard is a useful tool for a database that will be maintained by someone who does not know much about Access.

Multiple Choice

Circle the letter of the correct answer for each of the following questions.

1. An easy way to automate repetitive tasks is to use _____.
   a. a macro
   b. the drag-and-drop procedure
   c. the Automate command
   d. the Repeat button
2. A value needed for a macro to continue its action is called a(n) _____.
   a. action
   b. macro
   c. function
   d. argument
3. Which of the following Data Modes would enable the user to enter new records in a form without scrolling to the next empty record?
   a. Read Only
   b. New Record
   c. Edit
   d. Add
4. The form that is used as a switchboard _____.
   a. is always based on a select query
   b. is not directly based on any table or query
   c. must always be opened from the Database window under the Forms tab
   d. should only be used by advanced users
5. Immediately after creating a macro, you should _____.
   a. copy it to a working directory
   b. save it in a special macro directory
   c. sort the arguments alphabetically
   d. run it to test it
6. You can open a form using a macro in _____ mode.
   a. Preview
   b. Print
   c. Add
   d. All of the above
7. To make a form that is opened by a macro fill the screen, choose _____ as the second action in the macro.
   a. Expand
   b. Maximize
   c. Fill screen
   d. Optimize
8. To see the Switchboard form and the macro list at the same time, go to the Design view of the switchboard and choose _____ from the Window menu.
   a. Show Macros
   b. Cascade, then click the Macros tab
   c. Tile Vertically, then click the Macros tab
   d. Display List

9. After a macro has been created, it should be run to _____.

    a. make sure it works as intended

    b. set the macro

    c. establish a macro program

    d. clear the macro path for a new macro

10. When you name a macro, it is best to use a name that _____.

    a. is one word

    b. includes the word macro

    c. is no longer than 10 letters or spaces

    d. would make sense if it were on a button

Completion

In the blank provided, write the correct answer for each of the following statements.

1. A group of instructions that provides additional commands or functionality to a program is called a(n) ______________.
2. A value needed for any macro to continue its action is a(n) ______________.
3. The action used in a macro to close a specified window, or to close the active window if no other is specified, is the ______________ action.
4. The action that opens an existing form is the ______________ action.
5. The special macro name that is used to automatically launch the Switchboard form is ______________.
6. ______________ is the term Access uses for a menu of choices represented by buttons on a form.
7. In a macro, a function that performs some process within the database, table, form, or query is known as a(n) ______________.
8. A switchboard is created using the blank ______________ design.
9. To add a macro to a form, click on the macro and ______________ it to the Design view of the form.
10. Macros are used to help ______________ repetitive tasks in a database.

Matching

In the blank next to each of the following terms or phrases, write the letter of the corresponding term or phrase. (Note that some letters may be used more than once.)

a. Autoexec	_______	1. Found under Tools, Add-Ins
b. add	_______	2. When a macro is placed on a form, it works like this type of button
c. Switchboard Manager	_______	3. Macro command used to expand a form to the full size of the screen

d. OpenReport ______ 4. Mode used to enter new records only

e. command ______ 5. This macro cannot be placed on the Preview view of a report

f. Quit ______ 6. Most flexible mode to use on an OpenForm macro

g. edit ______ 7. Name of self-starting macro

h. Close ______ 8. This macro action can be used to print a report

i. Print Preview ______ 9. One of the action arguments in an OpenReport macro

j. Maximize ______ 10. Macro command used to close and exit Access

Applying Your Skills

Practice

The following exercises enable you to practice the skills you have learned in this project. Take a few minutes to work through these exercises now. If you are saving your files on a floppy disk, you may need to start with an empty disk to assure that you have enough room for all the files.

You can make the Hardware Inventory3 database more convenient to use by automating the common functions with macros.

Adding Close Macros to a Form

Create a Close macro and add it to both forms.

1. Copy the file Proj1502 from the Project-15 folder on the CD to your disk and rename it `Hardware Inventory3`.
2. Create a macro with the Close action. Name it `Close`.
3. Open the PC Hardware form in Design view and choose Window, Tile Vertically.
4. Drag the Close macro onto the header of the form.
5. Close the form and save the changes. Repeat this process for the Vendors form.
6. Leave the database open for use in the next exercise.

Creating Macros to Open Forms

Create two macros that open their respective forms in the Add mode so they are ready to receive new records.

1. Create a new macro that uses the OpenForm action.
2. Select PC Hardware Form from the list of form names in the Action Argument section.

3. Change the Data Mode to Add.
4. Save the Macro with the name `Add New PC Hardware`.
5. Repeat this process to create a macro to open the Vendors form in Add mode. Name it `Add New Vendor`.
6. Leave the database open for use in the next exercise.

Creating Macros to Open Two Reports in Print Preview View

Create two macros that open the folder label and mailing label reports in Preview mode.

1. Create a new macro that uses the OpenReport Action.
2. Select Folder Labels by Processor from the list of reports in the Action Arguments section.
3. Change the view to Print Preview.
4. Close the macro and name it `Preview Folder Labels`.
5. Repeat this process for the Mailing Labels for Vendors report.
6. Name the macro `Preview Mailing Labels`.

Creating a Form to Be Used as a Switchboard

Create a form that is not based on a table or query. Add a label box to it to serve as a title and then drag the macros onto it to create a series of buttons. Create one more macro that opens the form automatically whenever the database is opened.

1. Open a new form and drag a label box across the top of the blank form.
2. Enter the following text to be used as a title:

    ```
    Hardware Inventory System
    ```

3. Format the title so that it is 24 points in size, centered, bold, and italicized.
4. Tile the Form and the Database windows.
5. Drag the macros you created in the previous exercises onto the form and arrange them into rows and columns.
6. Select the entire form and change one of its properties so that it does not display navigation buttons.
7. Save and close the Switchboard form. Name it `Switchboard`.
8. Create a macro to open the Switchboard form and maximize it. Save the macro as `Autoexec`.
9. Run the Autoexec macro and test the new switchboard.

Automating a Database Using Macros

Make the Human Resources database more convenient to use by automating the common functions with macros.

To create a set of macros that open and close the forms and reports, follow these steps:

1. Copy the file Proj1503 from the Project-15 folder on the CD to your disk and rename it `Human Resources4`.
2. Create a macro with the Close action. Name it `Close`.
3. Drag the Close macro onto the design of the Employees form to the right of the text box that contains the expression `=time()`.
4. Create a macro to open the Employees form in the Edit data mode. Name the macro `Edit Employee Records`.
5. Create a macro to open the Employees form in the Add data mode. Name the macro `Add a New Employee`.
6. Create two macros to preview the two reports. Name one of them `Preview Employee Information` and the other `Preview Mailing Labels`.
7. Create a Switchboard form that has the title `Human Resources System` and has command buttons for each of the macros.
8. Select the form and use the Properties sheet to turn off the navigation buttons.
9. Save and close the Switchboard form. Name it `Switchboard`.
10. Create a macro to open the Switchboard form. Add a second action to Maximize. Save the macro as `Autoexec`.
11. Run the Autoexec macro and test the new switchboard.

Challenge

The following challenges enable you to use your problem-solving skills.

Creating a Switchboard to Manage a Database

In this exercise, you create a switchboard that uses macros to open forms and preview reports. You also create a macro to open the switchboard whenever the database is opened.

Open the `Club` database that you have been working on in previous projects. Create a macro to open the Member Information form that includes the Donations subform. Open the form in Read Only mode and name it `Review Member Donations`. Create another macro to open the same form in Add mode and name it `Record New Donations`.

Create a macro that opens the List of Members report in Print Preview mode. Name it `Preview List of Members`. Create another macro that opens the report displaying members with a subreport of their donations in Print Preview mode. Name it `Preview Members and Donations Report`.

Create a macro to close whatever form is open at the time. Name it `Close`. Drag the Close macro onto the design of the form mentioned above.

Create a form that has a title and buttons that run each of the five macros created previously. Turn off the navigation buttons. Save it as `Switchboard`. Create a macro to open the Switchboard form automatically whenever the database is opened. Close the database and reopen it. Check each button to see that it works.

Creating a Switchboard to Manage the Forms and Reports

A user of this database needs to add new viewing data and new view information as well as preview and print reports. In this exercise, you create macros and a switchboard that allow someone else who is unfamiliar with Access to perform these functions.

Rename the Customer Research12 database as `Customer Research13`. Create a macro to open the Participants form that includes the Viewing Data subform. Open the form in Edit mode and name it `Viewer Activity`. Create a macro to open the Survey Participants form in Add mode and name it `Add New Participants`. Create a macro that opens the Hours Viewed by Household report in Print Preview mode. Name it `Preview Hours Viewed by Household`. Create a macro that opens the Mailing to Households report in Print Preview mode. Name it `Preview Mailing to Households Report`.

Create a macro to close whatever form is open at the time. Name it `Close`. Drag the Close macro onto the design of the forms mentioned above. Create a form that has a title and buttons that run each of the macros created above. Turn off the navigation buttons. Save it as `Switchboard`. Create a macro to open the Switchboard form automatically whenever the database is opened. Close the database and reopen it. Check each button to see that it works.

Creating a Switchboard to Manage the Forms and Reports of a Database

A user of this database needs to add new machine and supplier data as well as preview and print reports. In this exercise, you create macros and a switchboard that allow someone else who is unfamiliar with Access to perform these functions.

Locate the Vending12 database that you worked on in the previous project and rename it `Vending13`. Create a macro to open the Suppliers form that includes the Machines subform. Open the form in Edit mode and name it `Suppliers and Machines`. Create a macro that opens the Locations report in Print Preview mode. Name it `Preview Locations Report`.

Create a macro to close whatever form is open at the time. Name it `Close`. Drag the Close macro onto the design of the form mentioned above. Create a form that has a title and buttons that run each of the macros created above. Turn off the navigation buttons. Save it as `Switchboard`. Create a macro to open the Switchboard form automatically whenever the database is opened. Close the database and reopen it. Check each button to see that it works.

Creating a Switchboard to Manage the Forms and Reports in the Video Store Database

A user of this database needs to add new data and view existing records as well as preview and print reports. In this exercise, you create macros and a switchboard that allow someone else who is unfamiliar with Access to perform these functions.

Locate the Video Store11 database and rename it `Video Store12`. Create a macro to open the Customer form that includes the Rental Activity subform. Open the form in Edit mode and name it `Customers and their Rentals`. Create a macro that opens the Inventory Listing report in Print Preview mode. Name it `Preview Inventory Report`. Create a macro that opens the Rental Activity report in Print Preview mode. Name it `Preview Rental Activity Report`. Create a macro that opens the Inventory Listing report in Print Preview mode. Name it `Preview Chart of Rentals`.

Create a macro to close whatever form is open at the time. Name it `Close`. Drag the Close macro onto the header of the design of the form mentioned earlier. Create a form that has a title and buttons that run each of the macros previously created. Turn off the navigation buttons. Save it as `Switchboard`. Create a macro to open the Switchboard form automatically and maximize it whenever the database is opened. Close the database and reopen it. Check each button to see that it works.

Creating a Switchboard to Manage the Forms and Reports in the Home Inventory Database

A user of this database needs to add new data and view existing records as well as preview and print reports. In this exercise, you create macros and a switchboard that allow someone else who is unfamiliar with Access to perform these functions.

Locate the Home Inventory11 database that you used in the previous project and rename it `Home Inventory12`. Create a macro to open the Add Inventory Item form. Open the form in Add mode and name it `Add Inventory Item`. Create a macro to open the Company Data form. Open the form in Edit mode and name it `Edit Company Data`. Create a macro to open the Insurance Company form that includes the Items subform. Open the form in Read Only mode and name it `Review Insured Items`. Create a macro that opens the List by Value report in Print Preview mode. Name it `Preview List of Items`.

Create a macro to close whatever form is open at the time. Name it `Close`. Drag the Close macro onto the header of the design of the forms mentioned earlier. Create a form that has a title and buttons that run each of the macros previously created. Turn off the navigation buttons. Save it as `Switchboard`. Create a macro to open the Switchboard form automatically and maximize it whenever the database is opened. Close the database and reopen it. Check each button to see that it works.

PinPoint Assessment

You have completed the project and the associated lessons, as well as the "Checking Your Skills" and "Applying Your Skills" sections. Now use the PinPoint software Evaluation mode to assess your comprehension of the specific exam tasks you have just learned. You can also use the PinPoint Trainer mode and the SHOW ME tutorials to practice these specific exam tasks.

Project 16
Sixteen

Filtering Data Using Parameters and Form Filters

Use Queries, Filters, and Dialog Boxes to Add Database Flexibility

In this project you will learn the following objectives and their associated Microsoft Exam required activities.

Objectives	Required Activities
➤ Use Parameters as Criteria in a Query	
➤ Use Parameters in Calculations in a Query	Calculate Fields Use Expressions in Calculated Controls
➤ Select Records in a Form Using the Filter by Selection Feature	Add Filters (Selection and Form) Remove Filters
➤ Select Records in a Form Using the Filter by Form Feature	Add Filters (Selection and Form)

Why Would I Do This?

Parameter
An entry that can be used as a filter or an argument in a formula.

Filter by Selection
A searching feature that enables you to select the desired value in a field and then finds all of the other records that match that value.

Filter by Form
A searching feature that enables you to type the desired value(s) into one or more fields on a blank form and then finds all of the other records that match those values.

Information is entered into databases so that it can be retrieved at a future time for a variety of purposes. You will seldom need to look at all of the records at any one time. In Project 4, "Querying Your Database," you learned how to set up queries to filter the data. There are also quick methods, using both queries and forms, to view the desired subset of data (dynaset) that you need to see.

In this project, you learn how to modify queries so they are more flexible. A *parameter* query asks you for input whenever the query is used, and uses your input as the criteria for the query. In this way, you can use the same query structure repeatedly without having to open up the design of the query and make changes.

You also learn how to use two of the most powerful data-searching features of Access—*Filter by Selection* and *Filter by Form*. The Filter by Selection feature enables you to scroll through a form and select the desired entry in a field. When you click on the Filter by Selection button, all records that match the entry in the field are displayed. The Filter by Form feature gives you a blank copy of the form and enables you to type in desired field entries in one or more field at a time.

Lesson 1: Using Parameters as Criteria in a Query

The database used in this lesson contains a table of information about the customers of an industrial cleaning supplies distributor. In this lesson, you add a parameter to the City criteria to enable the user to pick a different city each time he or she wants a list of customers.

To Use Parameters as Criteria

1 Make a copy of the student data file Proj1601 from the Project-16 folder on the CD, place it in your own directory on your disk, then rename the copy `Customer Records3`.

2 Open the `Customer Records3` database.

The database window should now be open to the Tables area (see Figure 16.1).

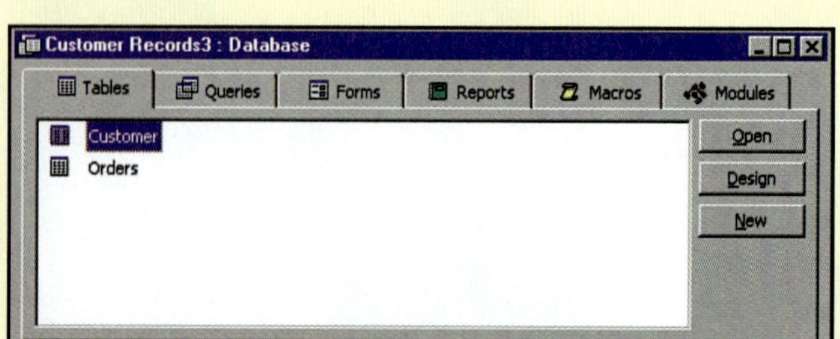

Figure 16.1
The database window displays the Tables area of the Customer Records3 database.

3 Click the Queries tab.

The names of the existing queries are displayed (see Figure 16.2).

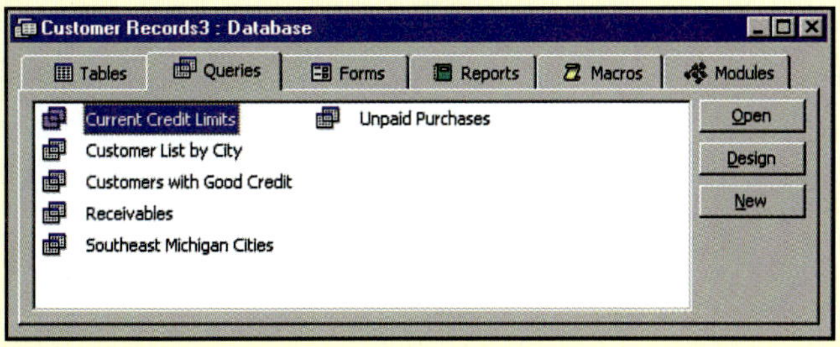

Figure 16.2
The Database window displays the Queries area of the Customer Records3 database.

4 Click the Customer List by City query and click the Design button.

The design of the Customer List by City query is displayed (see Figure 16.3).

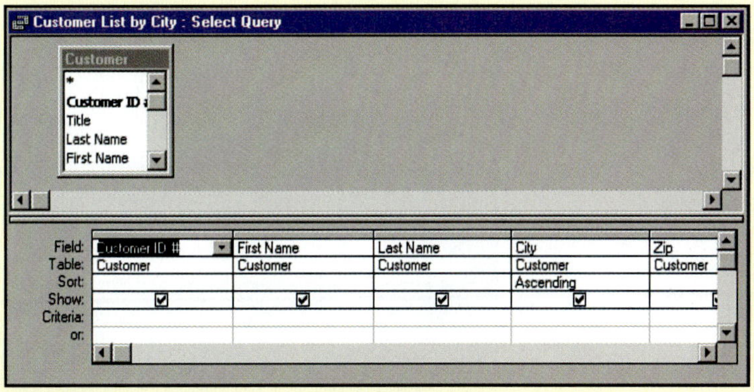

Figure 16.3
The design of the Customer List by City query is displayed.

5 Click the criteria box in the City column and enter the following:

```
[Enter the name of the city below:]
```

See Figure 16.4. (The column has been widened in the figure shown. You might only see part of the prompt.)

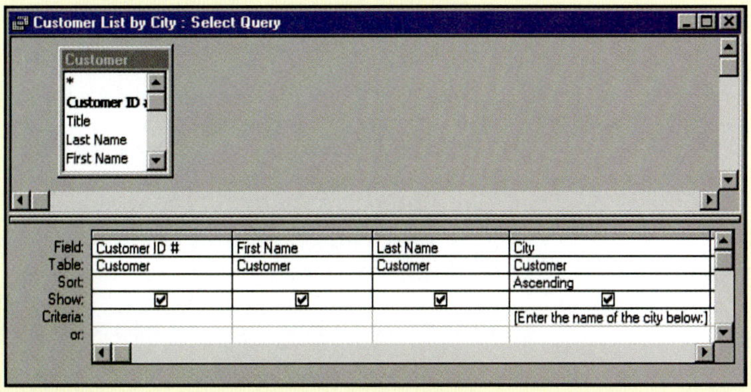

Figure 16.4
The prompt for the criteria is placed within brackets in the criteria box.

continues

To Use Parameters as Criteria (continued)

In this case, you did not enter an actual city name or the name of a field. The message you enter inside the square brackets is displayed as a message.

6 Click the View button to switch to Datasheet view.

The Enter Parameter Value dialog box appears and displays the message you entered within square brackets in the criteria box (see Figure 16.5).

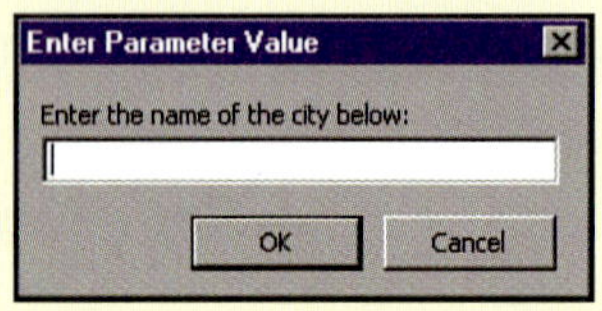

Figure 16.5 The Enter Parameter Value dialog box appears with the message you entered in the criteria box.

7 Enter the following city name in the text box:

`Ann Arbor`

Click OK. The list of customers in Ann Arbor appears in the Datasheet view (see Figure 16.6).

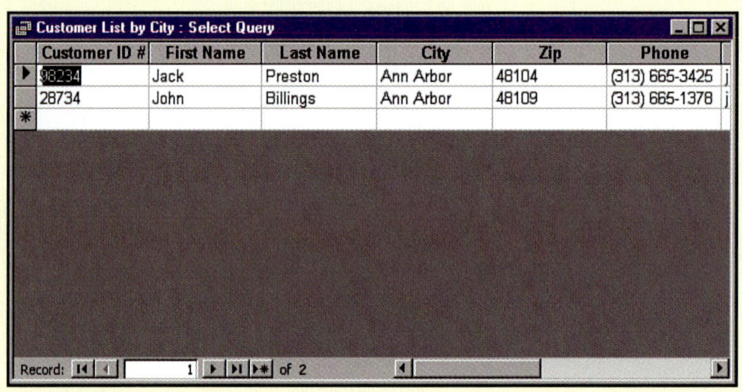

Figure 16.6 The Datasheet view of the query only shows the cities that match the parameter value you entered.

8 Close the query and save the changes.

If you open this query or use it as the basis of a report or form, the same Parameter Value dialog box appears and the report or form is limited to those records that match the criteria entered.

9 Click the Reports tab to see the available reports.

10 Click the Customer List by City report, then click Preview.

The Enter Parameter Value dialog box appears, displaying the message that you entered in the query, since this report is based on the Customer List by City query.

11 Enter the following city name in the text box:

`Ypsilanti`

Click OK. The report opens in Preview mode, displaying records for those customers in Ypsilanti (see Figure 16.7).

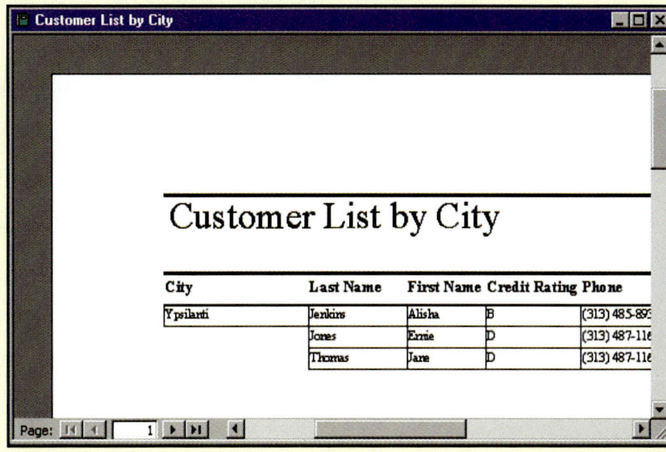

Figure 16.7
The Customer List by City report is limited to those records that match the parameter.

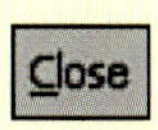

⓬ **Click the Close button on the toolbar to close the Print Preview window.**

Leave the database open for use in the next lesson.

Lesson 2: Using Parameters in Calculations in a Query

Parameters may be used in place of field names in calculated fields as well as criteria boxes. In this lesson, you use a table of customer information that includes a field for credit limit. You can print a report showing current credit limits and also raise or lower these limits each time you print the report.

In this lesson, you learn to use a parameter in an expression in a calculated field.

To Use Parameters in Calculations

❶ **In the Customer Records3 database, click the Queries tab and click Current Credit Limits to select it.**

❷ **Click Design.**

The design of the Current Credit Limits query is displayed (see Figure 16.8).

continues

Access

To Use Parameters in Calculations (continued)

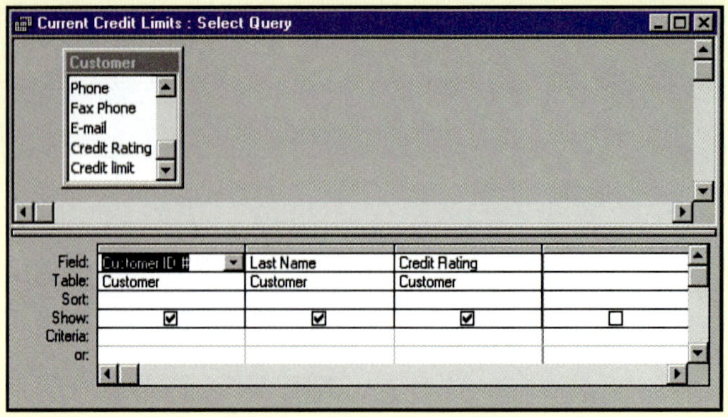

Figure 16.8 The design of the Current Credit Limits query is displayed.

3 **Click the Field box in the next empty column. Enter the following expression:**

```
Current Credit Limit:[Credit limit]*[Enter adjustment factor:]
```

The term, Current Credit Limit, is the name of the new column in the query. The expression to the right of the colon will take the value in the Credit limit field and multiply by whatever the user enters in the Parameter Values dialog box. The column has been widened to show the entire entry (see Figure 16.9).

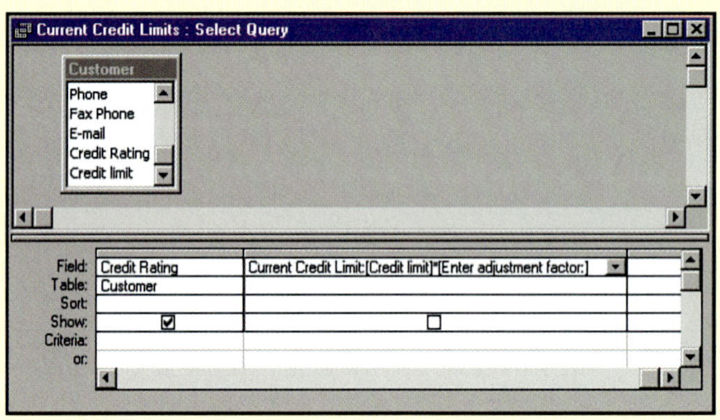

Figure 16.9 The query design shows the parameter expression entered in the Field box.

If the words inside the brackets match a field name, the program will use the current contents of that field. If they do not match an existing field, the program will assume you want to enter a value from a Parameter Value dialog box.

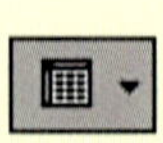

4 **Click the View button to switch to Datasheet view.**

The Enter Parameter Value dialog box appears (see Figure 16.10).

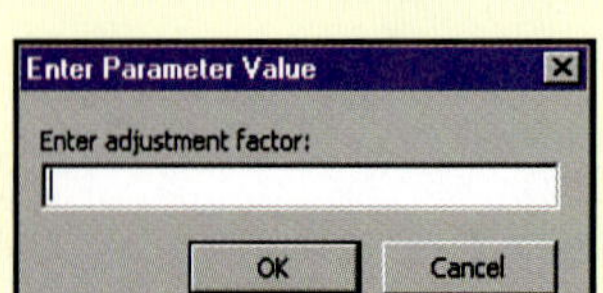

Figure 16.10 The Enter Parameter Value dialog box showing the parameter message.

5 Increase all of the current credit limits by 20%. Enter `1.2` in the dialog box and click OK.

The query is displayed in Datasheet view with the new values for the Current Credit Limit (see Figure 16.11).

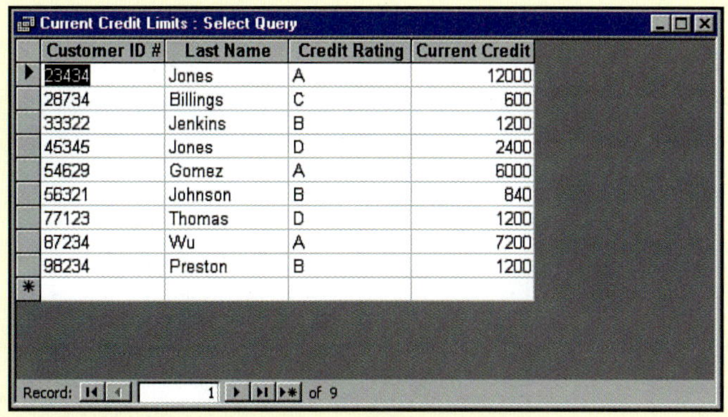

Customer ID #	Last Name	Credit Rating	Current Credit
23434	Jones	A	12000
28734	Billings	C	600
33322	Jenkins	B	1200
45345	Jones	D	2400
54629	Gomez	A	6000
56321	Johnson	B	840
77123	Thomas	D	1200
87234	Wu	A	7200
98234	Preston	B	1200

Figure 16.11
The query displaying the adjusted credit limits.

Any report or form based on this query will also display the Enter Parameter Value dialog box and enable you to adjust the credit limits displayed.

6 Close the query and save the changes.

Leave the database open for use in the next lesson.

Exam Notes

It is easy to produce expressions that are too long to fit within the small field box in the query design grid. To see the whole expression in a window of its own, right-click the expression in the field box and choose Zoom from the shortcut menu.

Lesson 3: Selecting Records in a Form Using the Filter by Selection Feature

The filters that you created in the previous lessons in this project may be used with forms or reports. Forms, tables, and queries may be filtered by the user either by using the filter buttons on the toolbar or by clicking the right mouse button while pointing at a particular field.

In this lesson, you learn how to filter the records shown in a form by selecting one field in the form and specifying the criterion to be used for a filter.

Using Filter by Example

It is possible to select an example from an existing record and use it as criteria.

To Filter the Records of a Database by Selecting an Example Value from a Form

1 In the Customer Records3 database, click the Forms tab. Open the `Customer Information` form.

The Customer Information form is displayed (see Figure 16.12). Notice that there are nine records that can be viewed with this form.

Figure 16.12
The Customer Information form prior to filtering.

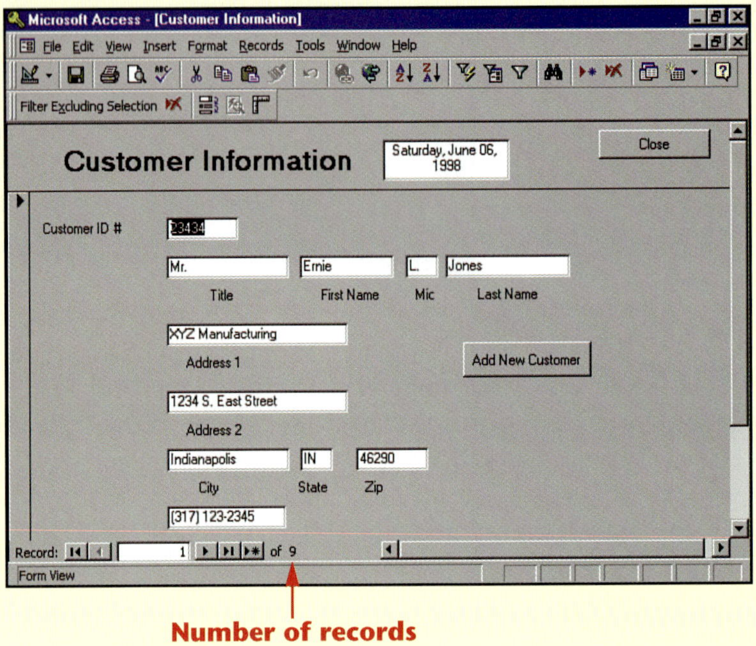

2 Click the Next Record navigation button twice to display a customer with an address in the city of Ypsilanti.

3 Click the City field once to place the cursor in the field.

The entire name of the city does not need to be selected—the cursor just needs to be somewhere in the field.

4 Click the Filter by Selection button on the toolbar.

A filter is automatically created that restricts the records shown to those that match the contents of the selected field. The FLTR mode button on the status bar indicates that a filter is in use. A note is shown next to the navigation buttons, indicating that the records shown using the navigation buttons are those that match a filter (see Figure 16.13).

5 Click the navigation buttons to scroll through the records to verify that the filter is working.

Access

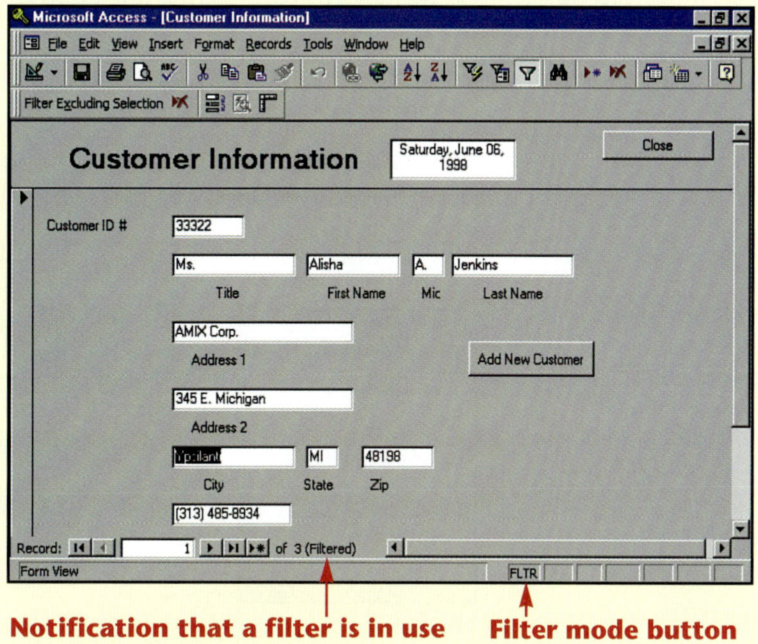

Figure 16.13
The Customer Information filtered for customers from the city of Ypsilanti.

6 Click the Remove Filter button on the toolbar to disable the filter.

The filter is not deleted and may be applied again. The database stores the most recently used filter for future use even if the database is closed and reopened.

Keep the form open for the next procedure.

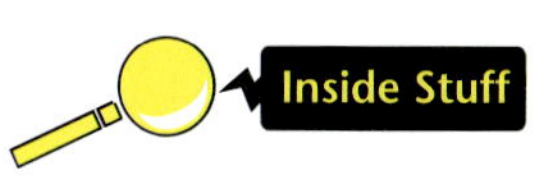

To permanently remove a filter, a new empty filter condition needs to be created and applied to the form or query. Until this is done, the last filter that was created will be reapplied every time you click the Apply Filter button.

There are several options for defining filtering criteria. You may enter a specific word that must be matched, you may use logical expressions such as between and like, or you may exclude matches. These options are available when you click the field with the right mouse button to activate the shortcut menu.

Using Exclusion by Example

It is also possible to display all the records that do not match an example that you select.

To Create a Filter to Exclude Records that Match a Field

1 Click the Next Record navigation button until you locate a customer from the city of Ypsilanti, if necessary.

2 Move the pointer to the City field (showing Ypsilanti). Click the right mouse button.

A menu appears with several filtering options (see Figure 16.14).

Figure 16.14
A menu of Filter by Selection options is revealed by pointing at a field and clicking with the right mouse button.

3 Click the Filter Excluding Selection option.

This will exclude the three records that have Ypsilanti city addresses.

4 Use the navigation buttons to scroll through the records to confirm that the filter works.

5 Click the Remove Filter button to disable the filter.

Leave the form open for use in the next section.

Matching a Range of Values

You can use the shortcut menu to create a filter based on a logical comparison. The same logical comparisons that are used in the criteria field of a query design can be used here. In this section you filter the records to show the ZIP codes for the area of Michigan that includes the cities of Ann Arbor and Ypsilanti. All the ZIP codes in this area are between 48100 and 48200.

To Create a Filter to Match a Range of Values

1 Move the pointer to the Zip field and click the right mouse button.

The menu appears with a box named Filter For that can be used for entering a logical comparison or exact matches (see Figure 16.15).

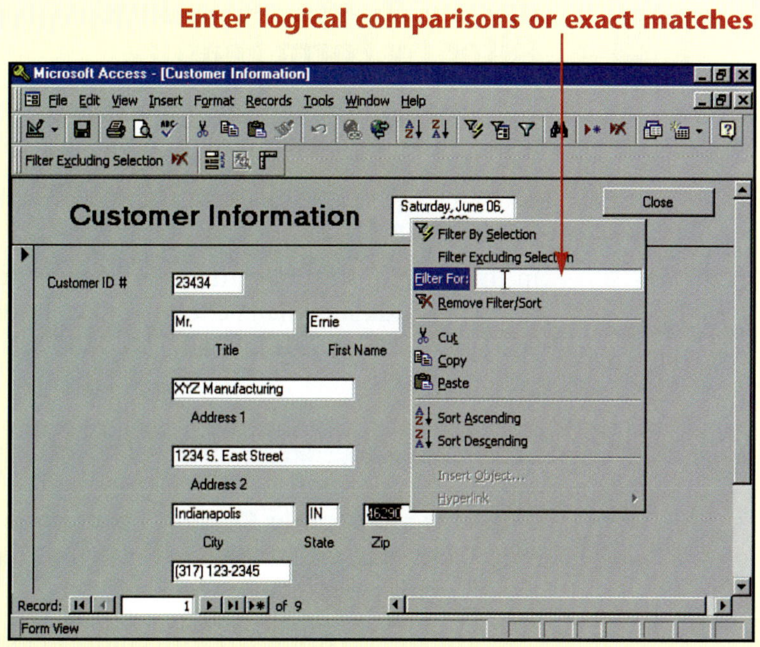

Figure 16.15
Pointing at a field and clicking the right mouse button reveals a menu that enables you to enter comparisons or values to be matched.

2 **Click in the Filter For box and type in the following to filter for ZIP codes between 48100 and 48200:**

```
Between 48100 and 48200
```

See Figure 16.16.

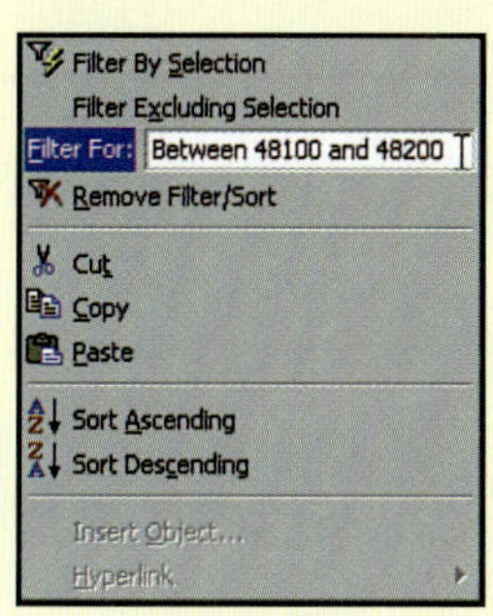

Figure 16.16
The Between function may be used as a filter.

3 **Press Enter to activate the filter. Use the navigation buttons to confirm that the records shown have been restricted to those with ZIP codes between 48100 and 48200.**

In this example, there are five records that match the filter.

4 **Click the Remove Filter button on the toolbar to disable the filter.**

This button toggles the filter on and off, but does not actually remove the filter from memory. The filter remains available until it is replaced by another or the conditions are deleted in the Form View described in the next lesson.

Leave the form open for use in the next lesson.

Lesson 4: Selecting Records in a Form Using the Filter by Form Feature

You may want to filter the records using criteria that affect more than one field. In that case, you would use the Filter by Form button on the toolbar.

Creating a Filter by Filling in a Form

In this procedure you learn how to use criteria in more than one field to filter the records shown. The following example is used to identify the female customers (Mrs. or Ms.) who live in Michigan.

To Use Filter Criteria in More Than One Field

1 In the Customer Records3 database, make sure that the Customer Information form window is open. Click the Filter by Form button on the toolbar.

The form is displayed with empty fields (see Figure 16.17).

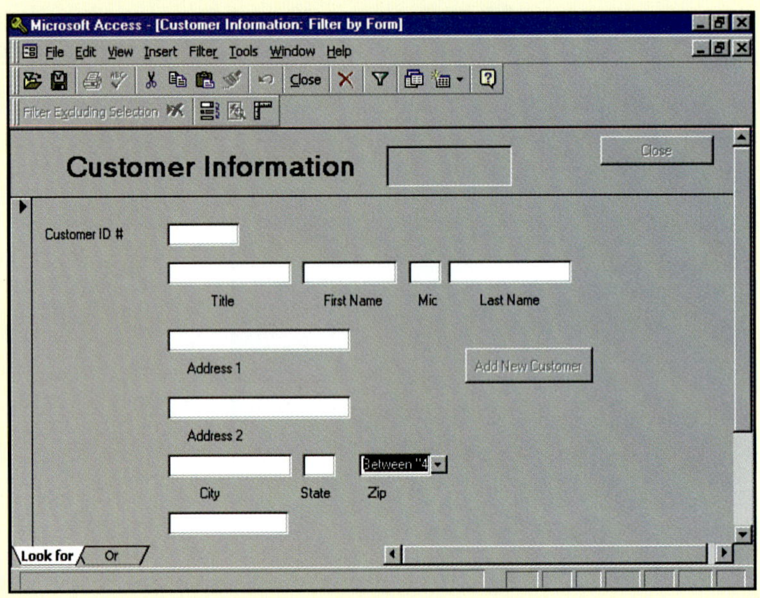

Figure 16.17
The form may be used to enter multiple filtering criteria.

Notice that the condition from the previous lesson is displayed in the Zip field and that it is already selected.

2 Press the Del key to remove the previous filter criteria.

3 Click the Title field box.

A list arrow appears at the right side of the box.

4 Click the list arrow to reveal all of the current values for this field.

The titles used in this table were Mr., Mrs., and Ms. (see Figure 16.18).

Access

Figure 16.18
The current contents of the field may be selected from a list to be used for matching criteria.

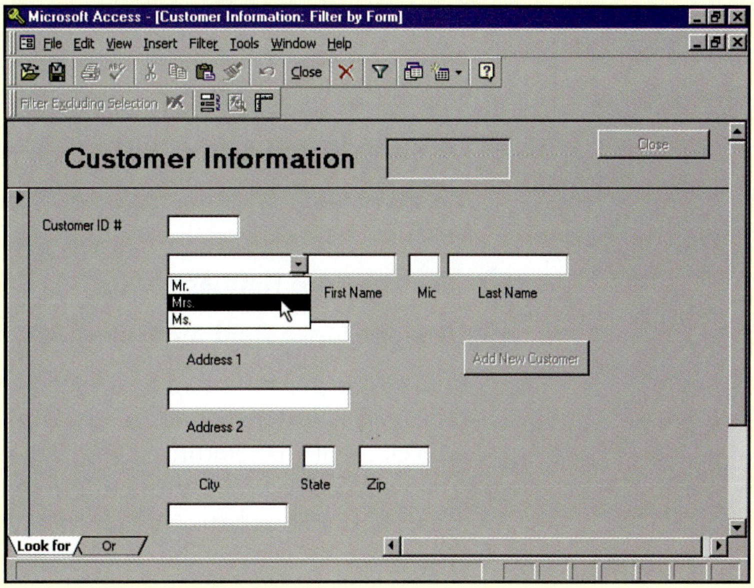

5 **Select Mrs. from the list.**

The selection is placed in the field box and enclosed by quotation marks. This filter limits the results to people with a title of Mrs.

6 **Click the State field box. Select MI from the list.**

The form should now have two criteria, one for Title and another for State (see Figure 16.19). This second condition further limits the results of the filter to only those people in Michigan with the title of Mrs.

Figure 16.19
Values or expressions may be entered into more than one field to be used as a filter.

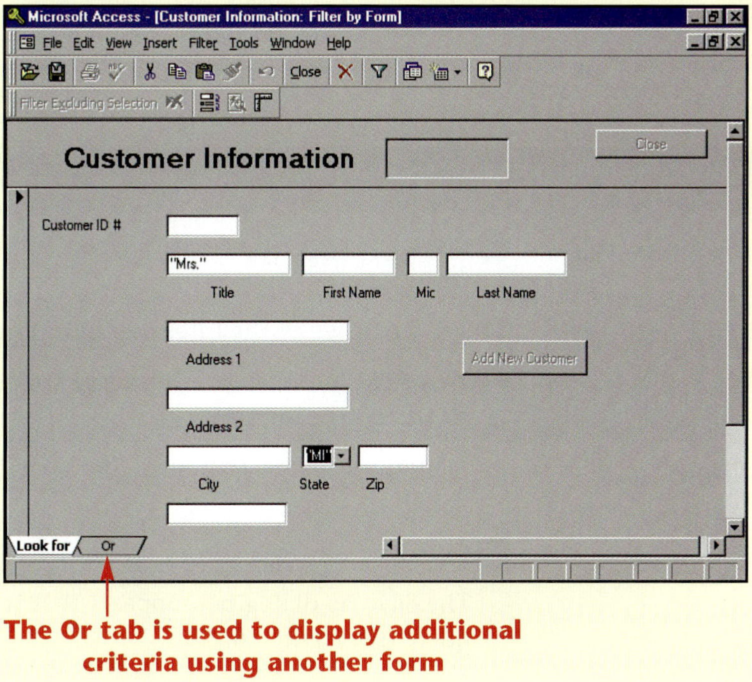

continues

To Use Filter Criteria in More Than One Field (continued)

These two criteria are both required to find matching records. This type of logical condition is called AND.

7. **Click the Or tab at the bottom of the form.**

   Another empty form is displayed where additional criteria may be specified.

8. **Click the Title field and select Ms. from the list.**

9. **Click the State field and select MI from the list.**

   Notice that the state had to be specified again. The records that are displayed must match all of the conditions specified on the first form or all of the conditions on the second form. The two forms are used with the logical Or function to match records. The Or function expands the search to include people in Michigan with the title Mrs. or Ms.

10. **Click the Apply Filter button on the toolbar.**

    There should be two customer records that match these criteria.

    Keep the form open for the next procedure.

The form filter feature is not available for reports; however, it is possible to design an appropriate filter using the form and then save it as a query. A report can be created that is based upon the query that would contain the same records as displayed using the form filter.

Saving the Filter as a Query

In this part of the lesson, you learn how to save the filter design as a query.

To Save the Form Filter Criteria as a Query

1. **Click the Filter by Form button to reveal the design of the filter.**

   The first page of the filter design is displayed.

2. **Move the pointer to an empty space on the form and click the right mouse button.**

   A menu appears that has the Save As Query option (see Figure 16.20).

3. **Click the Save As Query option.**

   The Save As dialog box appears that is used to assign a name to the query (see Figure 16.21).

Figure 16.20
The filter may be saved as a query using a menu that is displayed when you click the right mouse button on an empty area of the filter design.

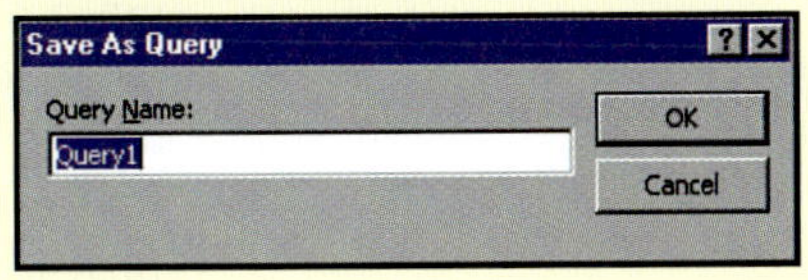

Figure 16.21
The filter may be saved as a query.

4 Enter `Women in Michigan` as the name of the query and click OK.

This action creates a new query that can be used as the basis for a report.

5 Click the Close button on the toolbar.

This closes the Filter by Form design.

6 Close the Customer Information form.

7 Click the Queries tab of the database to display the available queries.

Women in Michigan is now one of the queries in the database (see Figure 16.22).

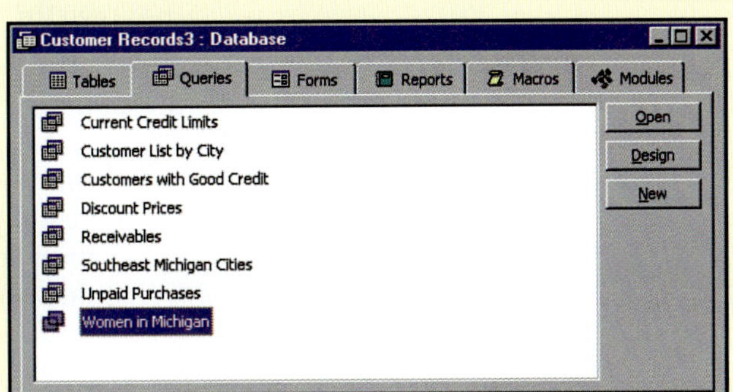

Figure 16.22
The filter has been saved as one of the queries.

8 Close the database.

If you have completed your session on the computer, exit Access and shut down Windows before you turn off the computer. Otherwise, continue with the "Checking Your Skills" and "Applying Your Skills" sections in this project.

Project Summary

To	Do This
Use parameters as criteria in a query	Place a message that will prompt the user in the criteria box in the query design grid. Enclose the message within square brackets. Whenever the query is run, a dialog box appears displaying your message as the prompt and a box where the user may enter a value. The query will operate as if you had entered that value in the criteria box.
Use parameters in calculations in a query	If a calculation is used in a criteria box or if a new field is created as a calculated field, you can replace a field name with a prompt message. If the query is run, a dialog box appears with your message as the prompt and a box where the user can enter a value. The query will operate as if you had entered that value in the calculation box.
Filter a form by selecting the contents of a field	Open a form and find a record that has a value that you want to use as a filtering criteria for one of the fields. Click the value to place the cursor in that field box. Click the Filter by Selection button on the toolbar.
Remove a filter	Click the Remove Filter button on the toolbar.
Create a filter to exclude records	Find an example of a record that contains the value that you want to use as the criteria for excluding records. Point at the value and click the right mouse button. Choose Filter Excluding Selection.
Create a filter range	Point at the field that will be used to define a range. Click the right mouse button. Enter the logical expression in the Filter For box in the menu that appears. Other logical expressions may be used as well.
Filter by filling in a form	Click the Filter by Form button on the toolbar. Enter the values to be matched in the empty form. The values entered in one form will be used with a logical AND function. Additional forms can be used to specify additional criteria by clicking the Or tab. These criteria will be used with those on the first form with the logical Or function.

Access

To	Do This
Save a form filter	Click the Filter by Form button, if necessary, as a query to display the filter design form. Point at an empty space on the form and click the right mouse button. Select Save As Query from the menu that appears.

Checking Your Skills

True/False

For each of the following statements, check *T* or *F* to indicate whether the statement is true or false.

__T __F 1. If you enclose a phrase inside square brackets in a query design, the program prompts you to enter a value to be used in place of the phrase unless the word or phrase in the brackets is a field name.

__T __F 2. In the query design, a parameter is enclosed in parentheses.

__T __F 3. Using parameters enables user input to restrict the output of a report.

__T __F 4. There are three filter buttons that can be used with tables, queries, or forms.

__T __F 5. If you click the Remove Filter button, the filter is erased and you have to create it again if you need it in the future.

__T __F 6. If you base a report or form on a parameter query, the report or form is limited to those records that match the criteria entered in the Parameter Value dialog box.

__T __F 7. In the design of a query, if the words inside square brackets match a field name, the program will use the current contents of that field.

__T __F 8. To use the Zoom box for writing a long expression, right-click the expression in the field box and choose Zoom from the shortcut menu.

__T __F 9. If a database is closed and reopened, the most recently used filter no longer is available for use.

__T __F 10. Different logical comparisons are used in the criteria field of a query design than are used with filters.

Multiple Choice

Circle the letter of the correct answer for each of the following questions.

1. Which of the following is used to enclose a parameter?
   a. ( )
   b. { }
   c. < >
   d. [ ]

2. Which of the following expressions correctly uses a parameter to prompt the user for input? (Assume that Company and Product are field names.)
   a. (Enter the Company Name)
   b. [Enter the Product Name]
   c. [Company]
   d. [Product]

3. The filter buttons that are used are in Access are _____.
   a. Apply Filter, Create Filter, Remove Filter
   b. Filter by Selection, Filter by Form, Filter by Design
   c. Apply/Remove Filter, Filter by Selection, Filter by Form
   d. Create Filter, Delete Filter

4. If you had a database of books that had been loaned out from a library and wanted to create a form-based filter that showed all the books by a certain popular author that had been loaned out during a particular month, you would _____.
   a. place the cursor in the Author field and use Filter by Selection
   b. place the cursor in the Date field and use Filter by Selection
   c. scroll through the records using the navigation buttons and place a bookmark in each record that met the criteria
   d. use the Filter by Form button and put the author's name in the Author field and a logical criteria such as, Between 1/1/97 and 1/31/97, in the Date field

5. Operators that can be used with a filter include _____.
   a. comparison operators
   b. matching operators
   c. excluding operators
   d. all of the above

6. When you click the Remove Filter button, the filter is _____.
   a. deleted
   b. permanently removed; it would have to be recreated
   c. inactivated, but still available to be re-applied until another filter is created
   d. removed but saved as a permanent filter that can be re-applied at anytime by right clicking on the Apply Filter button

7. To permanently remove a filter, _____.

   a. create a new empty filter and apply it to the form or query

   b. press the Del key on the keyboard

   c. right-click on the filter and click Delete from the shortcut menu

   d. click the Remove Filter button

8. To use a filter with a report, you need to _____.

   a. save the filter as a query

   b. click the File, Save Filter command and give the filter a name

   c. save the filter with the form and use the form as a basis for the report

   d. click the Save Filter button

9. An advantage of using a parameter query is _____.

   a. users can control the output of the query by entering a value in the Parameter Value dialog box

   b. you can use the same query structure repeatedly without having to open up the design of the query and make changes

   c. a form or report can be based on a parameter query

   d. all of the above

10. In a query, if the text entered inside square brackets is not a field name, the program _____.

    a. gives you an error message and tells you it cannot locate the field

    b. uses the text as the heading for a column

    c. assumes you want to enter a value from a Parameter Value dialog box

    d. ignores the text that has been entered

Completion

In the blank provided, write the correct answer for each of the following statements.

1. If you want to save a filter for future use with other objects, you should save it as a(n) _____________.

2. To further restrict data with a filter use the logical _____________ operator.

3. Write an example of a prompt to be used in a parameter query. Enclose your prompt in the correct symbols: _____________.

4. If you want to expand a search to include more variables, use the logical _____________ operator.

5. To search for a range of data you can use the _____________ operator.

6. To create a parameter message that allows the user to restrict the data, you write the parameter message on the ______________ line in the Design view of a query.

7. To create a parameter that allows the user to calculate a new value when a query is run, write the calculated expression on the ______________ line in the Design view of a query.

8. If you need to use the logical Or condition it is best to use the Filter by ______________ method.

9. The dialog box that appears that prompts a user to enter criteria is called the ______________.

10. ______________ is the mode button on the status bar that indicates a filter is applied.

Matching

In the blank next to each of the following terms or phrases, write the letter of the corresponding term or phrase. (Note that some letters may be used more than once.)

a. Filter by Form
b. Zoom
c. >
d. Or
e. Between...And
f. Filter by Selection
g. Remove/Apply Filter
h. AND
i. Save as query
j. parameter

______ 1. Example of a comparison operator that can be used with a filter

______ 2. A logical condition that further limits data

______ 3. A logical condition that expands restrictions on data

______ 4. A searching feature that enables you to select the desired value in a field and then finds all of the other records that match that value

______ 5. A searching feature that enables you to type the desired value(s) into one or more fields on a blank form and then finds all of the other records that match those values

______ 6. Box that enables you to see a long expression written in a query design

______ 7. Example of a toggle button

______ 8. An entry that can be used as a filter or an argument in a formula

______ 9. Command used to permanently save a filter

______ 10. Example of a comparison operator

Applying Your Skills

Practice

The following exercises enable you to practice the skills you have learned in this project. Take a few minutes to work through these exercises now. If you are saving your files on a floppy disk, you may need to start with an empty disk to ensure that you have enough room for all the files.

Using Parameters as Criteria in a Query

Create a parameter query that enables the user to limit the type of books shown based upon what they select.

To use parameters as criteria in a query, complete the following steps:

1. Copy the file Proj1602 from the Project-16 folder on the CD and rename it `Library11`.
2. Open the `Library11` database and open the query `Mysteries` in the Design mode.
3. In the Type of Book column, replace the `Mystery` criteria with the following:

   ```
   [Enter the type of book:]
   ```

4. Click the View button to look at Datasheet view. When the Enter Parameter Value dialog box appears, type any one of the following and click OK.

   `Mystery, Fiction, Classic, Non-Fiction, Science Fiction, or Humor`

5. Return to Design view. Add the conditional word `Like` to the criteria. The new criteria should be

   ```
   Like [Enter the type of book:]
   ```

6. Switch to Datasheet view. Enter an asterisk to see all of the titles. Asterisks can be used to replace parts of fields you are trying to match when you use the Like operator; for example, Mys* would find any book type starting with the letters *Mys*.
7. Leave the database open for use in the next exercise.

Creating a Filter Based on a Form

In this exercise, you open a form that shows the books that have been borrowed from a library and filter for those that were borrowed in 1997.

To create a filter using a form, complete the following steps:

1. Use the Library11 database from the previous exercise or copy the Proj1602 database from the Project-16 folder on the CD and rename it `Library11`.
2. Open the form `Books on Loan`.
3. Point at the Borrow Date field and click the right mouse button.
4. Enter the following condition in the Filter For box:

   ```
   Between 1/1/97 and 12/31/97
   ```

5. Use the navigation buttons to scroll through the three records that show descriptions of the books borrowed in 1997.
6. Click on the Remove Filter button to disable the filter.
7. Close the form and the database.

Using Parameters in Calculations in a Query

Create a query that has a calculated field that enables the user to enter a parameter to be used in the calculation.

To use parameters in calculations in a query, complete the following steps:

1. Use the Customer Records3 database that you used in the project or open the file Proj1601 from the Project-16 folder on the CD and rename it `Customer Records3`.
2. Open the `Discount` database and open the query `Discount Prices` in the Design mode.
3. Scroll to the right to display the last two columns. Right-click on the expression in the Sale Price column and choose Zoom from the shortcut menu.

   In the Sale Price column, a formula has been used to subtract 0.2 from 1 and then multiply by the Unit Price. This is one way to calculate a discount of 20%.
4. Edit the Sale Price formula so that the discount factor (0.2) is replaced by a parameter. The resulting formula should look like the following example:

   ```
   Sale Price: (1-[Enter the discount factor:])*[Unit Price]
   ```

   Click OK to close the Zoom window.
5. Click the View button to change to Datasheet view. When prompted by the message that was entered in the formula, enter a decimal number between zero and one.
6. Examine the resulting datasheet to determine if the discount was used correctly to determine the new sale price and the resulting Amount Due.
7. Close the query and save the changes. Close the database.

Replace Single-Purpose Queries with a Parameter Query

In the following exercise, you delete a query that displayed record companies from California and modify a query that displayed record companies from New York into a parameter query that is more flexible.

To delete a query, complete the following steps:

1. Copy the file Proj1603 from the Project-16 folder on the CD and rename it `SBMusic13`.

2. Click the Queries tab and select the California query.
3. Press the Del key.
4. Click Yes to confirm the deletion.

To change the New York query into a parameter query, complete the following steps:

1. Open the `New York` query in Design view.
2. Select NY in the criteria box in the State field and delete it.
3. Enter the following in the criteria box for the State field:

   `[Enter State (two letters):]`

4. Click the View button to switch to Datasheet view. Type `NY`. The records displayed are limited to those companies in New York.
5. Click the View button twice to switch to Design view and then back to Datasheet view. This time, enter `CA`. This query replaces both the previous queries and also works for any other state as well.
6. Save the changes to this query and close it.
7. Right-click on the New York query and select Rename from the shortcut menu. Change the name to `Record Companies from One State`.
8. Leave the database open for use in the next exercise.

Modify a Query to Display Orders Placed Between Two Dates

In the following exercise, you add a parameter to the criteria of the Order Date field in the Orders and Supplier Contacts query so that the dynaset is limited to orders placed between two dates.

To create a parameter query using the Between function to select orders placed between two dates, complete the following steps:

1. Use the SBMusic13 database from the previous exercise or copy the file Proj1603 from the Project-16 folder on the CD and rename it `SBMusic13`.
2. Click the Queries tab and select the `Orders and Supplier Contacts` query. Open it in Design view.
3. Enter the following in the criteria box for the Order Date field:

   `Between [Beginning Date:] And [Ending Date:]`

4. Click the Save button to save the change and click the View button to switch to Datasheet view.

   You can use this feature to pick any pair of dates in the table. For example, if you wanted to compare recent sales to a similar period in the past, you can bring up records from several years ago or from recent months.

5. Enter 6/15/95 as the Beginning Date and 7/15/95 as the Ending Date.

   Notice that one of the dates is 7/15/95. The Between function includes the two dates used as the beginning and ending dates.

6. Close the query and close the database.

Challenge

The following challenges enable you to use your problem-solving skills. Take time to work through these exercises now.

Using a Form Filter

In this exercise, you create a form filter to limit the donations displayed to those over a given amount.

Open the Club database that you worked on in the previous Project. Choose the form that is used to review member donations. Use the form filter to place a condition in the Donations field similar to the following example that limits the records displayed:

```
>50
```

Activate the filter and scroll through the list of donors. If you find no matches, try a lower number. Close the form and the database.

Selecting Items to Be Included in a Report Based on a Database and Filtered Form

Some reports are based on queries. If you add parameters to the query, they also show up whenever you run the report.

Rename the Customer Research14 database that you worked on in the previous project as Customer Research15. Open the database and close the Switchboard form. Open the Complete Viewing History query in Design view. Enter the following parameter in the criteria box of the Channel Name field:

```
Like "*"+[Channel:]+"*"
```

This criteria shows any channel whose names contain your entry. Save the change and click the View button. Test the query by entering part of a channel name. Run the Hours Viewed by Household report. Since this report uses the Complete Viewing History query, you see the same dialog box and have an opportunity to enter a channel name. The report includes only those channels who meet the criteria.

Open the Participants form and click the Form Filter button. Enter the following criteria in the Birthdate field:

```
>1/1/1988
```

Apply the filter and scroll through the records. Change the filter so that will shows only those people who were born between 1/1/1979 and 1/1/1985. Then, close the form and close the database.

Adding a Parameter

This query is currently limited to displaying the 6 Head Candy machine records only. Replace the criteria in this query's Machine Type column so that it allows the user to select the machine type each time the query is run.

Refer to the method used in Challenge exercise #2 earlier and write criteria that displays machine types correctly even if you only enter part of the name.

Using the Form Filter to Display Records in a Database

In this exercise, you create a form filter to show those records where the value in the Late Fee field is greater than zero.

Locate the Video Store12 database and rename it `Video Store13`. Open the `Customer` form and place a condition in the Late Fee field that restricts the display to those records that have a value greater than zero.

Open the `Rentals and Fees` query in Design view. Use the following expression in the criteria box of the Date Rented column:

```
Between [Enter Beginning Date:] and [Enter Ending Date:]
```

Run the query and select dates that display only some of the records such as 6/15/98 to 6/22/98. Open the `Switchboard` form and select the Preview Chart of Rentals report. Since this report is based in the Rentals and Fees query, you see the same dialog boxes. Enter the dates shown above. Note that the chart is redrawn based on the records included in the query.

Using a Form Filter to View Items in a Database

Most insurance companies do not pay for claims less than a certain amount that you select. In this exercise you use the form filter to limit the records shown to those that have cost values greater than the amount you select.

Locate the Home Inventory12 database that you used in the previous project and rename it `Home Inventory13`. Open the `Insurance Companies` form and click the Form Filter button. Enter `>500` in the Cost field and apply the filter. Scroll through the records to confirm that the filter is working. Then, close the form and the database.

PinPoint Assessment

You have completed the project and the associated lessons, as well as the "Checking Your Skills" and "Applying Your Skills" sections. Now use the PinPoint software Evaluation mode to assess your comprehension of the specific exam tasks you have just learned. You can also use the PinPoint Trainer mode and the SHOW ME tutorials to practice these specific exam tasks.

Project 17
Seventeen

Sharing a Database with Others

Protecting Your Database with Passwords and Adding Switchboards

In this project you will learn the following objectives and their associated Microsoft Exam required activities.

Objectives

Required Activities

- Assign a Password to Your Database
- Change or Remove a Database Password
- Encrypt a Database
- Create a Switchboard Using the Switchboard Manager Add-In
- Set Startup Parameters
- Set Access Defaults

Why Would I Do This?

Many features of Access are designed to allow users to share data and gain access to data used by others. Problems can arise from sharing data with others, however. Someone may make changes to the tables, forms, reports, or queries you have created, or he or she may enter data into the tables in a non-standard format. In some cases, your database may contain sensitive information that is not for general distribution, or proprietary information that is valuable to the company. In this lesson, you learn some techniques that provide protection from accidental changes. You also learn useful safeguards to protect your database from intentional damage or theft.

Many people need to use databases who do not have the need or the time to learn how to use Access. It is possible to customize a database so that these users are guided through the functions they need to use. This can be done by setting startup and default parameters that lead these users to custom menus that open forms with customized toolbars.

Lesson 1: Assigning a Password to Your Database

Adding security to your database is like putting a new lock on a door. It provides a measure of protection from some intruders, but it also has several drawbacks:

- It slows you down every time you want to pass through the door.
- Other people who need to pass through the door must take up your time by asking you for the key.
- If you give a duplicate key to someone, you do not always know what he or she has done with it.
- There are people who have master keys to that type of lock.
- There are people who understand how the lock works and know how to pick it.
- If you lose the only key, it can be very inconvenient.

In spite of these disadvantages, most of us still use locks on our doors. You may also want to add a measure of security to your database.

In this lesson, you learn how to require a password to open a database.

To Assign a Password to Your Database

1 Make a copy of the data file Proj1701 from the Project-17 folder on the CD, place it in your own directory on your disk, then rename the copy `Prices`.

2 Launch Access 97.

Close the dialog box that displays previously used files.

3 Click the Open Database button.

The Open dialog box appears. Use the navigation buttons in this window to locate the folder you are using for your files.

4 Click the `Prices` database to select it and click the Exclusive check box.

This prevents any other users from accessing the database while you are making this change. It is required for the following procedure even if you are not using Access in a network environment. (see Figure 17.1).

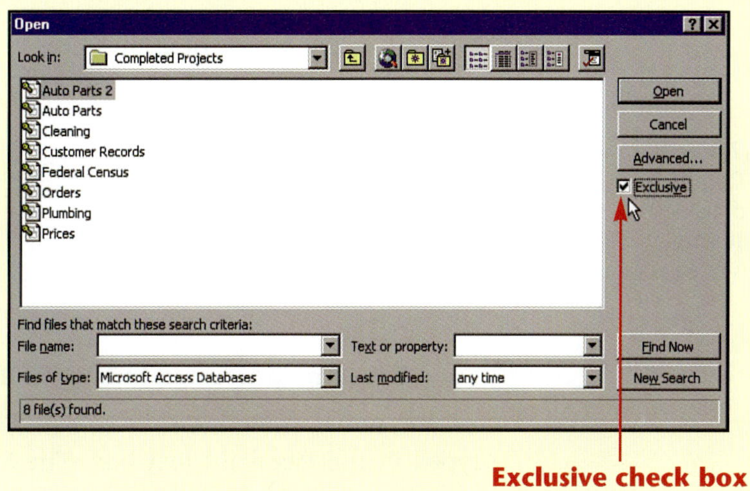

Figure 17.1
Use the Open dialog box to open the Prices database for exclusive use.

5 Click Open.

This action opens the Prices database for your exclusive use. The Prices database is displayed (see Figure 17.2).

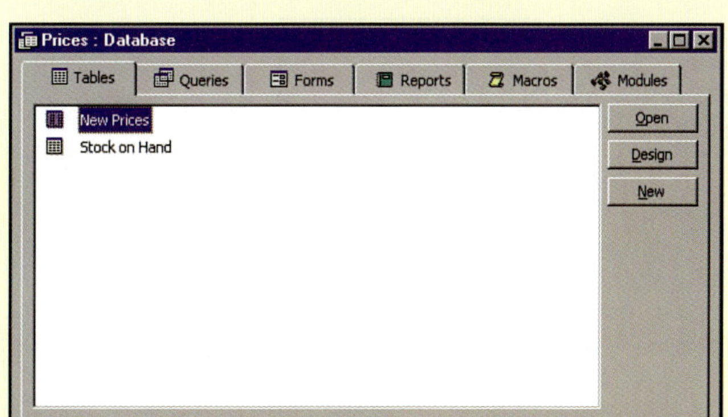

Figure 17.2
The Prices database is shown with the Database window open.

continues

To Assign a Password to Your Database (continued)

6 Choose Tools, Security from the menu, then select Set Database Password.

The Set Database Password dialog box is displayed (see Figure 17.3)

Figure 17.3
The Set Database Password dialog box enables you to set a new password.

7 Type the following password in the Password box:

```
ABCabc!
```

The letters are represented by asterisks (see Figure 17.4). If you are not sure what you typed, press ←Backspace and try again carefully.

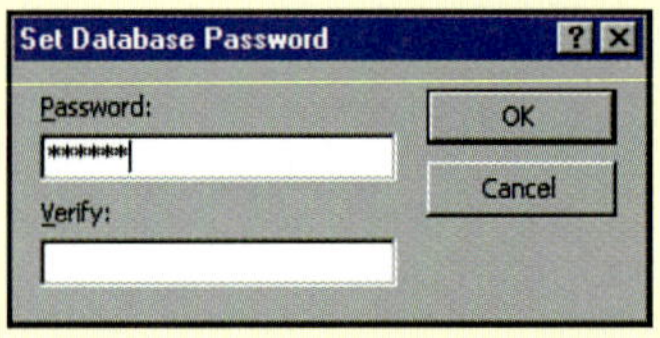

Figure 17.4
The Set Database Password dialog box is shown after the password has been entered.

8 Type the same password in the Verify box. Click OK.

Be sure to use the same case (uppercase and/or lowercase) that you typed in the Password text box. The Set Database Password dialog box closes and the Database window reappears.

9 Close the database, then open it again.

You do not have to select the Exclusive option this time. The Password Required dialog box appears (see Figure 17.5).

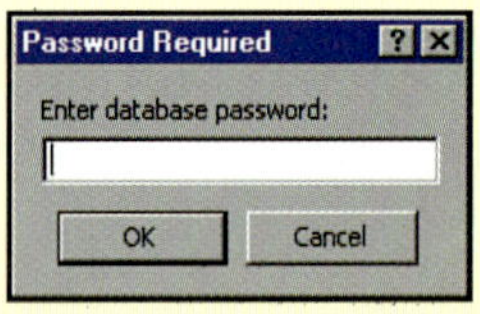

Figure 17.5
The Password Required dialog box is shown before the password has been entered.

10 Carefully type the password you entered in step 8 and click OK.

The database opens if you correctly matched the password. If you did not match the password exactly, including the proper upper- and lowercase characters, you see a warning box telling you that the password you entered was not valid. Return to the Password Required dialog box to try again.

11 Close the database.

Inside Stuff

Passwords in Access can be very simple and short or complex and up to 14 characters in length. To get the best security out of your password, do not use a date or a word that would be listed in a dictionary. Do not use passwords others might be able to guess, such as a family member's name, your Social Security number, or a commonly used phone number. Make the password at least six characters long and include a character that is not a letter. If you do want to use an easily recalled word or date, insert an extra symbol. In the example in this lesson, the password included an exclamation mark for this purpose.

Lesson 2: Changing or Removing a Database Password

Once you have added a password to your database, you may need to change or remove it.

In this lesson, you learn how to change or remove the database password.

To Change or Remove a Database Password

1. **Click the Open Database button, and open the Prices database in Exclusive mode.**

   The Password Required dialog box is displayed.

2. **Enter the password you created in Lesson 1, step 8, then click OK.**

3. **Choose Tools, Security from the menu bar, then choose Unset Database Password.**

   The Unset Database Password dialog box is displayed (see Figure 17.6).

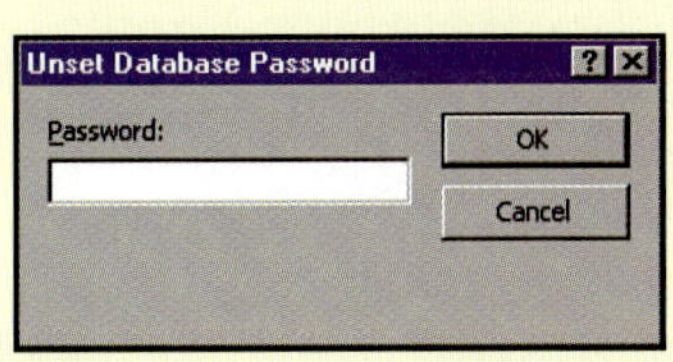

Figure 17.6 The Unset Database Password dialog box is used to remove a password.

4. **Type the original password you created in Lesson 1.**

   `ABCabc!`

5. **Click OK.**

   The password has been removed. The database can now be opened without a password.

   If you want to change the password, follow the above procedure, then choose Tools, Security, Set Database Password, and type a new password.

continues

To Change or Remove a Database Password (continued)

6 Close the database.

Leave Access open for use in the following lesson.

Lesson 3: Encrypting a Database

Encryption
Data scrambled and stored in coded form that is not easily read by someone who does not have the code.

Even though the database program is protected by a password, it is possible to view the data in a table by opening the database with a word processing program. Most of the screen of the word processing program would be filled with unrecognizable characters, but some of the data in the tables would still be readable (see Figure 17.7).

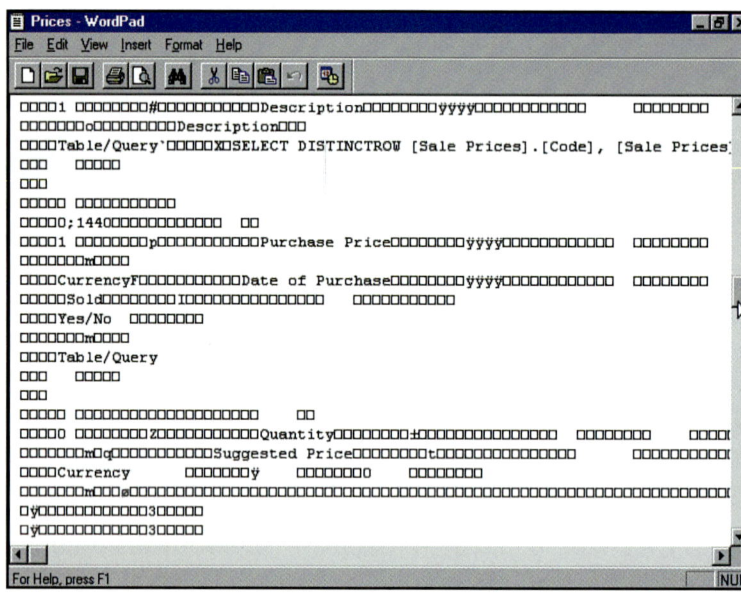

Figure 17.7
The Prices database (with a password) as displayed by the WordPad program.

In this lesson, you learn how to save the database in an encrypted mode that will prevent someone from reading the data with a text editor, such as a word processing program.

To Store a Database in Encrypted Form

1 In Access, without a database open, choose Tools, Security from the menu bar, then choose Encrypt/Decrypt Database.

2 Use the navigation buttons to locate the folder that contains the Prices database, if necessary (see Figure 17.8).

3 Click the Prices database, then click OK.

The Encrypt Database As dialog box is displayed.

Figure 17.8
The Encrypt/Decrypt Database dialog box is used to locate the database you want to encrypt.

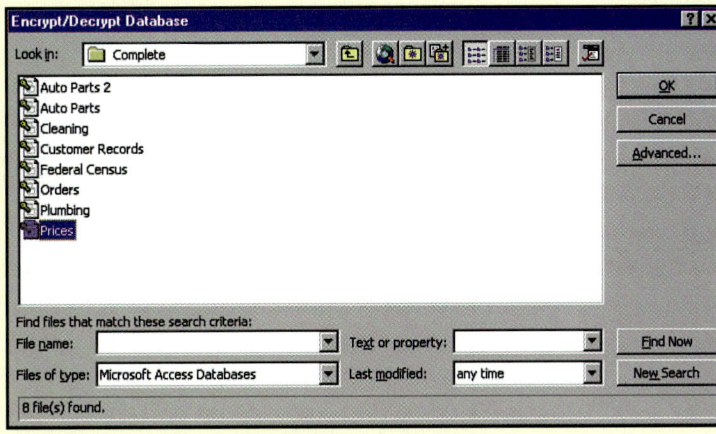

4 In the File Name text box, enter the following name to be used for the new database:

```
Prices-Encrypted
```

The dialog box should appear as shown in Figure 17.9.

Figure 17.9
The Encrypt Database As dialog window is displayed with the new name.

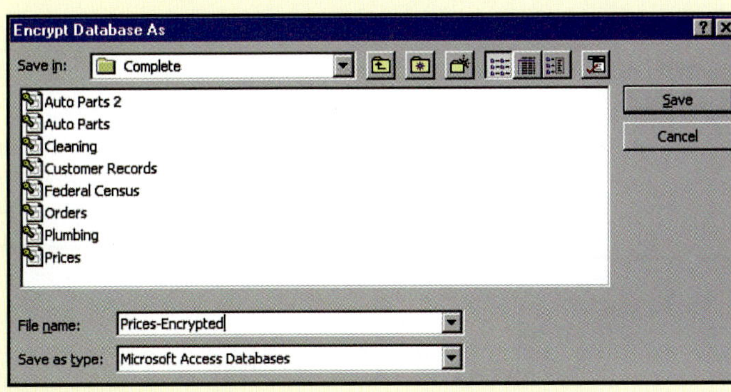

5 Click the Save button.

The data is now encrypted so that the text cannot be read. Figure 17.10 displays the database as it would now appear if it were opened using a word processor such as WordPad.

Leave the Access open for the next lesson.

You can now use the encrypted database instead of the original. The original can be deleted after you have tested the encrypted version.

continues

To Store a Database in Encrypted Form (continued)

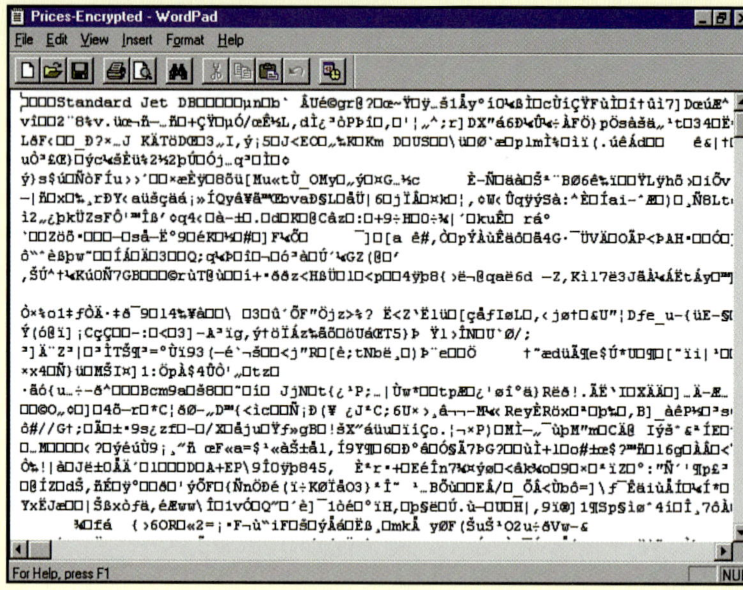

Figure 17.10
The Prices-Encrypted database viewed by WordPad.

Inside Stuff

The security measures mentioned in these lessons are useful in providing a first line of defense. Access provides a more sophisticated level of security that is particularly useful in a network environment. It is called user-level security. To find out more about security, use the Help menu and search for help on the word Security. Make copies of any databases that are important. You could lock yourself out!

Lesson 4: Creating a Switchboard

It is also useful to create a switchboard to guide someone else through a set of common tasks, such as entering data and producing standard reports. You created one in Project 15, "Using Access Macros," by creating macros and dragging them to an empty form.

In this lesson, you learn how to create a switchboard using the Switchboard Manager. The sample database you use already includes tables, forms, and reports that can be used in a switchboard.

To Create a Switchboard

1. **Make a copy of the data file Proj1702 from the Project-17 folder on the CD, place it in your own directory on your disk, then rename the copy `Customer-Switchboard`.**

2. **Open the `Customer-Switchboard` database.**

3 Choose Tools, Add-ins from the menu bar, then choose Switchboard Manager.

Since there is no switchboard to manage yet, a dialog box asks if you would like to create one (see Figure 17.11).

Figure 17.11
This dialog box appears if a switchboard does not already exist.

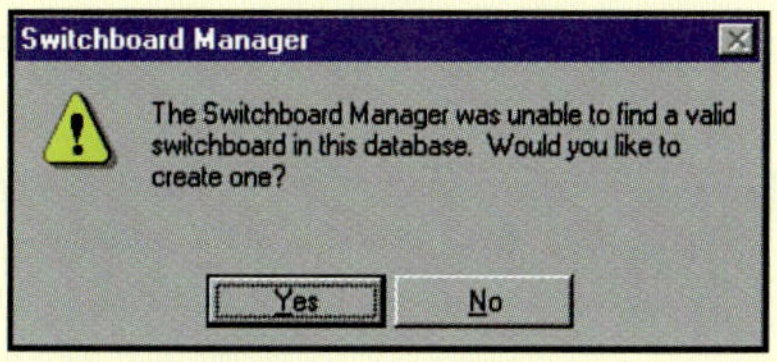

4 Choose Yes.

After a brief delay, another Switchboard Manager dialog box appears that displays the default switchboard (see Figure 17.12).

Figure 17.12
This Switchboard Manager dialog box displays the default switchboard option.

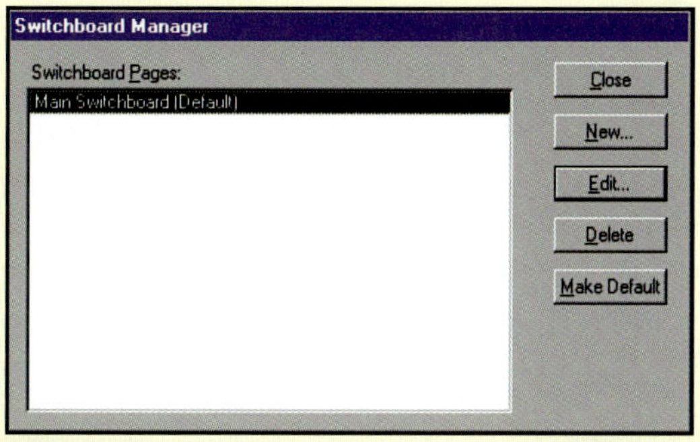

It is possible to link several switchboards together. In this case you only use one.

5 Click Edit.

This allows you to add action buttons to the switchboard. The Edit Switchboard Page dialog box is displayed (see Figure 17.13).

Figure 17.13
The Edit Switchboard Page dialog box can be used to add action buttons to the switchboard.

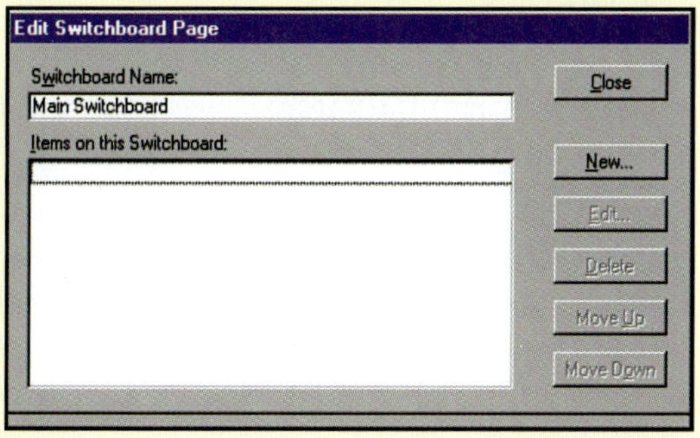

continues

To Create a Switchboard (continued)

6 Click New.

This action opens the Edit Switchboard Item dialog box (see Figure 17.14). This box contains a Text box that can be used to create a label for the action button. The Command box can be used to specify commands to do things like open forms or preview reports.

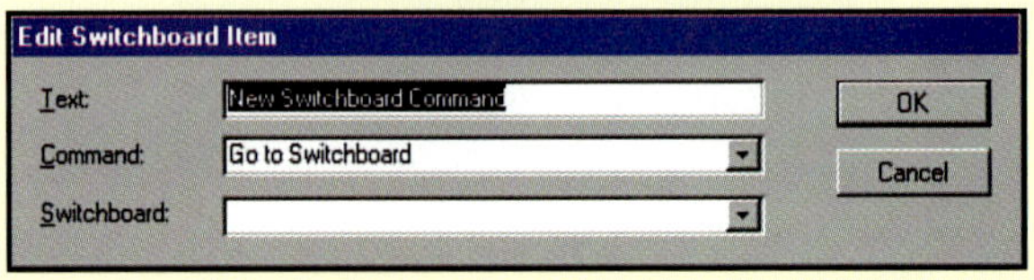

Figure 17.14
The Edit Switchboard Item dialog box is used to specify actions.

7 Change the text in the Text box to the following:

```
Add New Customers
```

8 Use the down-arrow at the right of the Command box to select the Open Form in Add Mode option.

Notice that the title of the third box changes depending on your choice in the Command box (see Figure 17.15).

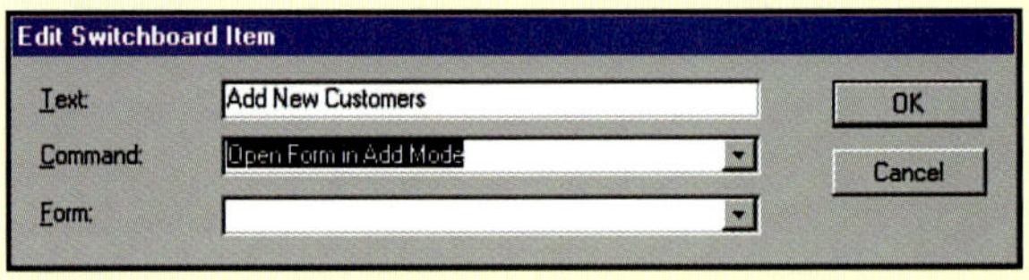

Figure 17.15
The Edit Switchboard Item dialog box changes the third choice in response to the contents of the Command box.

9 Use the down-arrow at the right of the Form box to select the Customer Information form. Click OK.

The Edit Switchboard Page dialog box reappears showing the Add New Customers item on its list of switchboard items (see Figure 17.16).

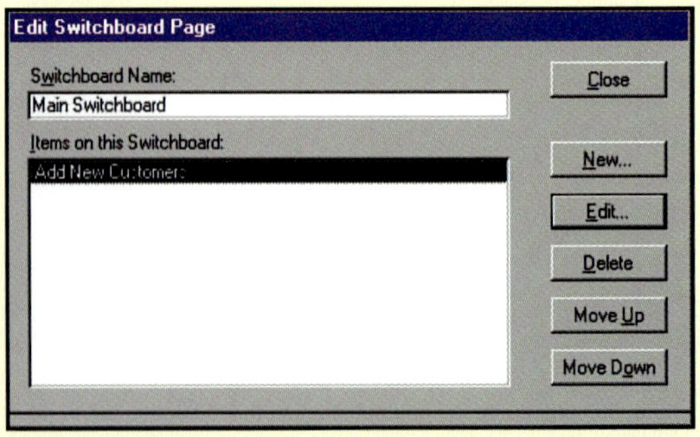

Figure 17.16
The Edit Switchboard Page dialog box displays the items that have been added to the switchboard.

Access

10 Repeat steps 6–9 to create another switchboard item to open the `Customer Orders` form in Add mode. Use the text `Add New Orders`.

The next switchboard item is defined as shown in Figure 17.17.

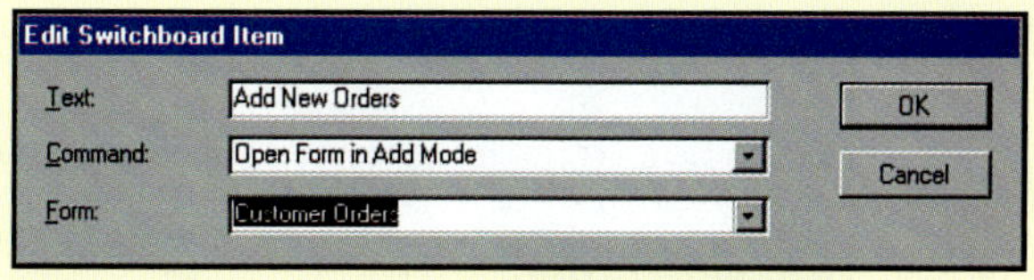

Figure 17.17 The Edit Switchboard Item dialog box defined to add the next item.

11 Repeat steps 6–9 to create the next switchboard step, except this time, select the Open Report command and pick the Orders Grouped by Customer report. Use the text `Preview the Report on Orders Grouped by Customer`.

The last item is set up to open a report (see Figure 17.18).

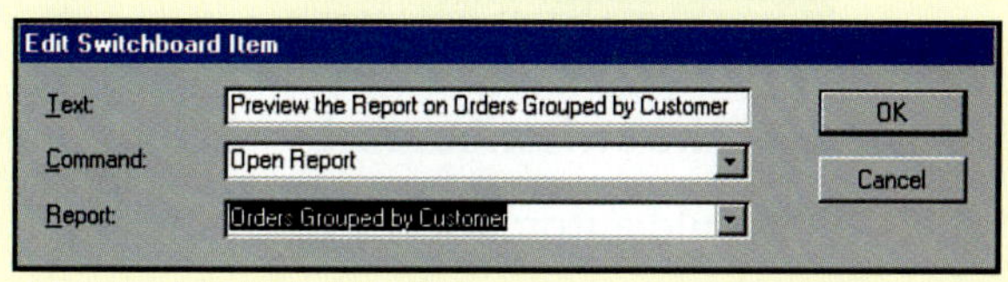

Figure 17.18 The Edit Switchboard Item dialog box set up to open a report.

12 Click OK.

The Edit Switchboard Page dialog box displays the three action items (see Figure 17.19).

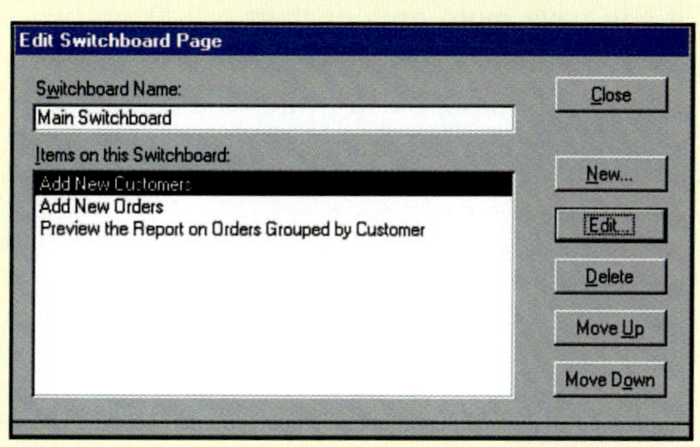

Figure 17.19 The Edit Switchboard Page dialog box displays the three action items.

13 Click Close.

The Switchboard Manager dialog box appears, displaying the single switchboard that has been created to this point.

14 Click Close.

The Switchboard Manager dialog box closes, and the Database window is displayed. The database now has an extra table named Switchboard Items and a new form named Switchboard.

continues

To Create a Switchboard (continued)

15 **Click the Forms tab to display the available forms. Click `Switchboard` to select it and then click Open.**

The new switchboard appears (see Figure 17.20).

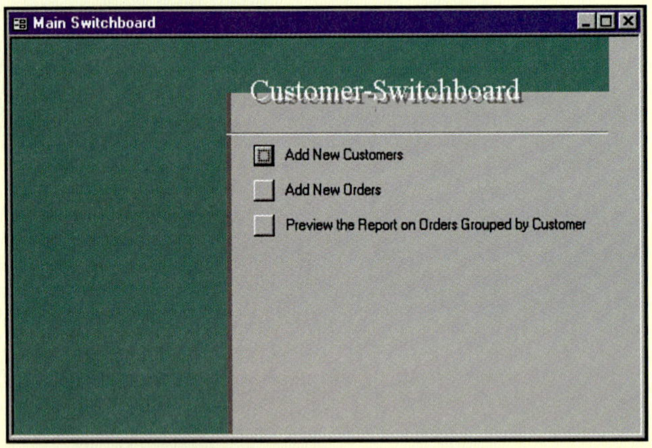

Figure 17.20
The new Switchboard form opens.

16 **Test the switchboard by clicking on one of the buttons.**

It should automatically open the appropriate form or report.

17 **Close the form or report and close the Switchboard form.**

Leave the database open for the next lesson.

If you have more options than will fit on one switchboard or you would like to have multiple levels of switchboards, one of the commands available in the Command box is Go to Switchboard. You can use this to string together several switchboards and to branch from one to another.

Lesson 5: Setting Startup Parameters

It is possible to control the way the database appears when it is opened. You can decide which toolbars are available to the user and you can open a switchboard form automatically. In this lesson, you learn a second way to open the switchboard automatically whenever the database is opened. You can also disable several features that are very useful while the database is being designed but that are not necessary while it is being used by someone else.

Access

To Set Startup Parameters

1 Open the Customer-Switchboard database, if necessary, and choose Tools, Startup from the menu.

The Startup dialog box is displayed (see Figure 17.21).

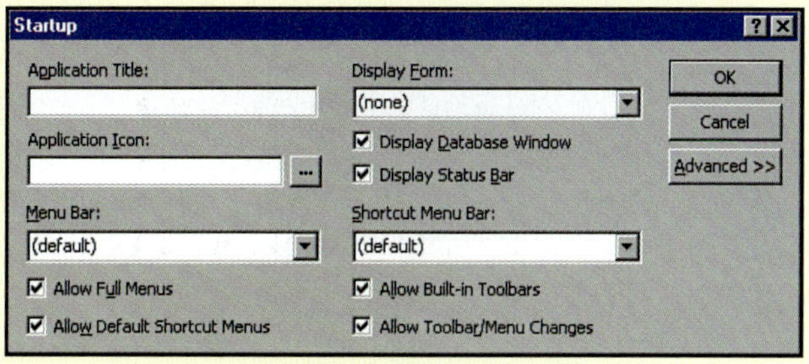

Figure 17.21
The Startup dialog box allows the designer to control the toolbars and menus to simplify them or to restrict the user's ability to change the design.

2 Click the down-arrow at the right end of the Display Form box and select Switchboard.

This causes the Switchboard form to open automatically when the database is opened.

3 Check the Display Status Bar check box to make sure it is selected.

This option could remove the status bar from the bottom of the screen to increase the available window space and simplify the screen. Leave it turned on in this example.

4 Click Allow Built-in Toolbars to deselect it.

This option removes the toolbar from the top of the screen to increase the available window space and simplify the screen.

5 Click Allow Toolbar/Menu Changes to deselect it.

This prevents a user from adding the toolbars back to the screen.

6 Click Allow Full Menus to deselect it.

This changes the menu options from a full list of editing choices to a short list of choices that are appropriate to using the database rather than designing it.

7 Click Allow Default Shortcut Menus to deselect it.

This disables the shortcut menu options that are normally available by clicking with the right mouse button.

8 Click Display Database Window to deselect it.

When you close the Switchboard form, the Database window is not available to the user, so he or she cannot get into the design of the database.

continues

To Set Startup Parameters (continued)

The Startup dialog box can also help you design your own menu bars and shortcut menus. You can also use this dialog box to create a special icon on the desktop that will run this version of the database. You do not use these options at this time.

Check to make sure that your dialog box looks like Figure 17.22.

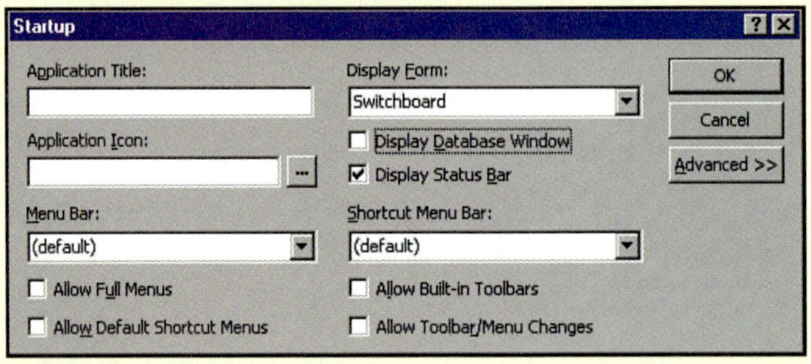

Figure 17.22
The Startup dialog box showing the new settings.

9. **Click OK to close the Startup dialog box. Close the database.**

The next time the Customer-Switchboard database is opened, the startup parameters are used and the switchboard is opened automatically.

10. **Open the `Customer-Switchboard` database again.**

The Switchboard form opens automatically. Notice that there are several differences. The menus have fewer choices, the right mouse button does not produce a shortcut menu, and the toolbar is not available (see Figure 17.23).

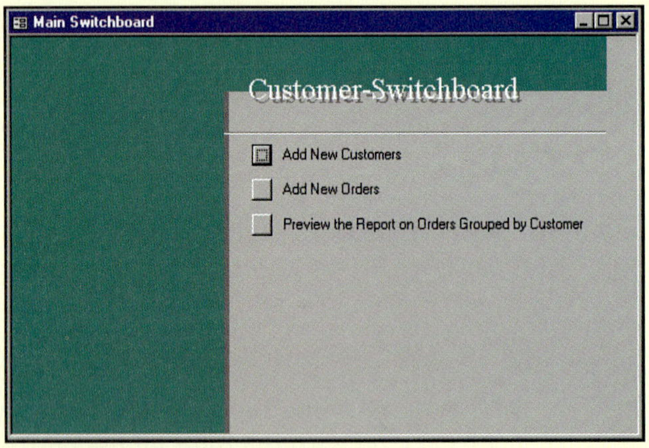

Figure 17.23
The Switchboard form can be displayed with fewer user options available on the Access menus and the toolbars are turned off.

11. **Close the Switchboard form.**

The startup settings used in the database is applied to any other database that you open until Access is closed and launched again.

12 Close Access.

When you start Access again, the normal toolbars and menus are displayed for other databases. If the Customer-Switchboard database is opened, the startup settings are reapplied.

Inside Stuff

To bypass the startup settings, hold down the Shift key when you open the database. This allows you to make changes to your database if you have turned off the menus.

Lesson 6: Setting Access Defaults

Startups control the environment of a single database, while Access defaults control the environment for any Access database that is opened from your installed copy of Access. To activate the appropriate menus, a database with menus needs to be open.

In this lesson, you learn how to change some of the Access defaults.

To Set Access Defaults

1 Launch Access and open the `Prices` database you used in Lessons 1–3.

The Prices database opens, and the menus and toolbars are visible.

2 Choose Tools, Options from the menu.

The Options dialog box is displayed (see Figure 17.24).

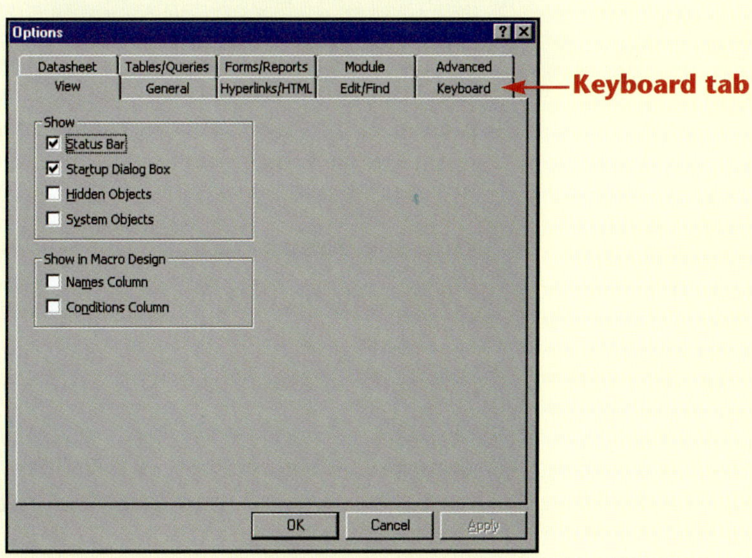

Figure 17.24
The Options dialog box can be used to set defaults for the Access program.

continues

To Set Access Defaults (continued)

3 Click the Keyboard tab on the Options dialog box.

The default settings are displayed for movement of the cursor after the ↵Enter key is pressed or when the arrow keys are used (see Figure 17.25).

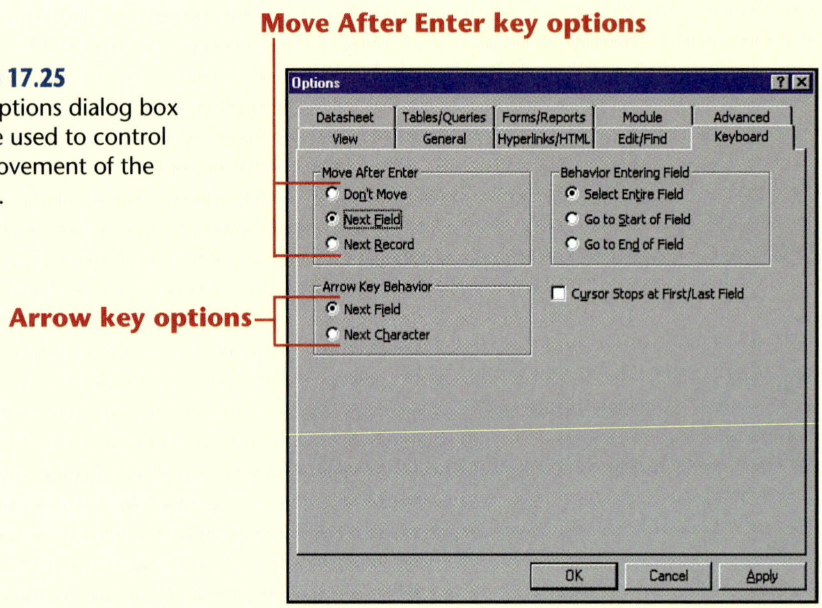

Figure 17.25
The Options dialog box can be used to control the movement of the cursor.

The default setting for movement of the cursor after the ↵Enter key is pressed is to move it to the next field to the right in the current record. If you are entering or changing the data in one field, it would be more convenient to automatically move to the next record.

4 Click on Next Record in the Move After Enter area.

5 Click the Apply button.

The cursor now moves down the column of data each time you press the ↵Enter key when you are in a table view. If you are in a form, the view pages from one record to the next and remains in the same field when you press the ↵Enter key.

6 Click the Datasheet tab.

The default options for the appearance of the datasheet are displayed (see Figure 17.26).

Changes on this form affect the appearance of any datasheet opened in Access.

7 Change the default colors to White, Gray, and Aqua for the Font, Background, and Gridlines options, respectively. Click the Vertical Default Gridlines check box to deselect it.

Your Options Datasheet dialog box should look like Figure 17.27.

Access

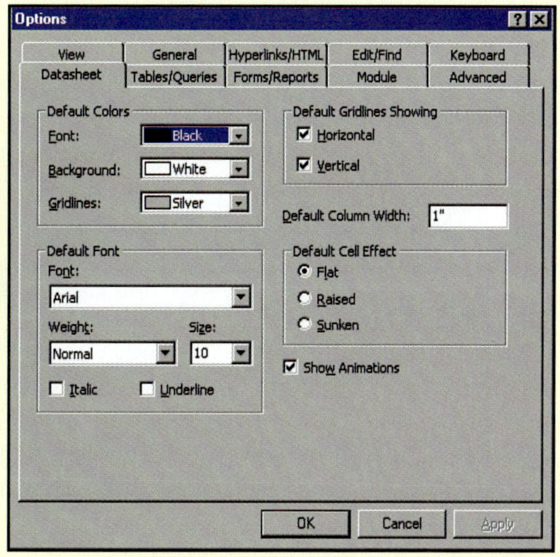

Figure 17.26
The default values for Datasheet view are displayed.

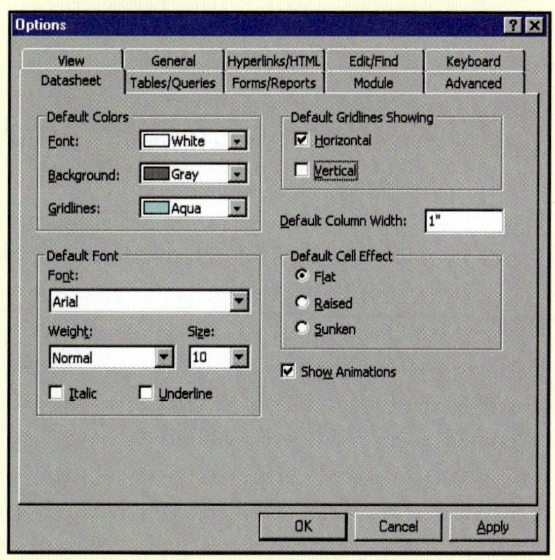

Figure 17.27
The Options Datasheet dialog box displaying the new settings.

8. **Click OK to close the Options dialog box.**

   This also applies the new settings.

9. **Open the Stock on Hand table in Datasheet view.**

   The new default colors and gridlines settings are displayed (see Figure 17.28).

10. **Press the Enter key several times.**

    Notice how the cursor moves down the column, staying in the same field, rather than across the fields.

11. **Close the table.**

continues

To Set Access Defaults (continued)

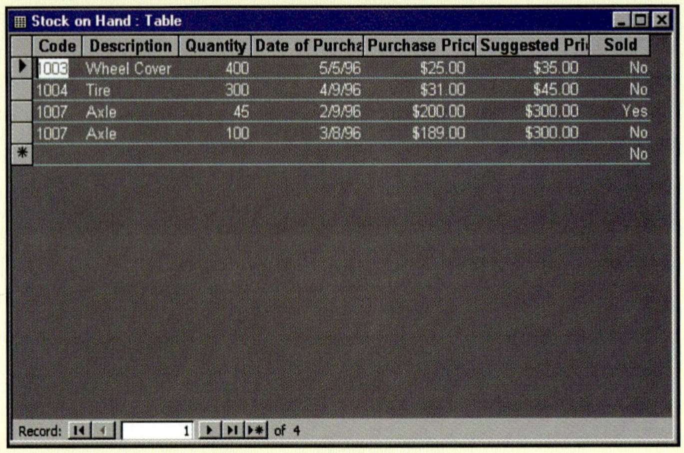

Figure 17.28
The Customer table in Datasheet view displays the new default settings.

12 Choose Tools, Options from the menu.

If you share your computer with others, it is important that you return the settings to their original values.

13 Click on the Datasheet tab. Change the default colors back to Black, White, and Silver for the Font, Background, and Gridlines options, respectively. Click the Vertical Default Gridlines check box to select it.

14 Click on the Keyboard tab. Change the Move After Enter option to Next Field.

15 Click on OK to make the changes and restore the original settings.

16 Close the table and close the database. Close Access.

If you have completed your session on the computer, exit Access and shut down Windows before you turn off the computer. Otherwise, continue with the "Checking Your Skills" and "Applying Your Skills" sections in this project.

Inside Stuff

Use caution when changing the default Access settings, because they affect all of your Access databases. If you share your computer with others in a laboratory setting, it would be discourteous to personalize the program without the consent of others who may not know how to change it back. Also, if you are using a copy of Access that is installed on a network server, the defaults affect anyone else in your workgroup who uses the program. In the previous lesson, we only changed defaults that affected appearance. You could change operational defaults that could affect the function of the program, and you may not remember the original settings. Use this feature with care!

Project Summary

To	Do This
Assign a password to a database	Open the database by choosing File, Open, and selecting the Exclusive option. Use the Tools, Security, Set Database Password command to display the Set Database Password dialog box. Enter the password. Enter the password again to verify it. Close the database.
Remove a password from a database	Open the database in Exclusive mode using the File, Open command and the Exclusive option. Enter the correct password. Choose Tools, Security, Unset Database Password from the menu. Type the current password and click OK.
Encrypt a database	Start Access, but do not open a database. Use the Tools, Security, Encrypt/Decrypt command from the menu. Select the database to be encrypted, and enter a new name for it. Click Save to encrypt and save the new version.
Create a switchboard	Select a database that already has several forms and reports. Choose Tools, Add-Ins, Switchboard Manager from the menu. Click Yes to create a new switchboard. Click Edit to add options to the main switchboard. Click New to add new action buttons. Fill in the resulting dialog box to determine the text to be shown on the switchboard, the action to be taken, and the report or form that is the object of that action. Repeat this process to add more action buttons to the switchboard. Close the dialog boxes. Go to the Forms tab and open the Switchboard form. Click the buttons to test them.
Set startup parameters	Open the database and choose Tools, Startup from the menu. Select the desired form that will be opened when the database is opened, such as the Main Switchboard. Click any other check boxes to set startup parameters like status box. Close the dialog box and the database. Open the database to test the startup parameters.

continues

To	Do This
Set Access defaults	Open the database. Choose Tools, Options from the menu. Make whatever changes are necessary from any of the numerous options. Write down original settings if you may want to reinstate them.

Checking Your Skills

True/False

For each of the following statements, check *T* or *F* to indicate whether the statement is true or false.

__T __F **1.** To add a password to a database, the first step is to open it by double-clicking on its name or icon.

__T __F **2.** To remove the password from a database, you must open it. This implies that you know what the password is.

__T __F **3.** You can only use one switchboard with a database.

__T __F **4.** Encrypting a database prevents someone from reading data in the database by using a word processing program.

__T __F **5.** Default settings are changed with no databases open because they affect all of the databases that are opened with that installation of Access.

__T __F **6.** In Access, the length of a password is unlimited.

__T __F **7.** Passwords in Access are not case sensitive.

__T __F **8.** Several switchboards can be strung together using the Switchboard Manager.

__T __F **9.** You cannot change the appearance of Access for a specific database.

__T __F **10.** You can control the movement of the cursor when you press ↵Enter by changing the default options.

Multiple Choice

Circle the letter of the correct answer for each of the following questions.

1. Startup parameters _____.

a. are set with all the databases closed

b. affect all databases opened by that installation of Access

c. are set after a database has been opened and only affect that database

d. are used to flash warning messages on the screen if there is too much traffic on the network

2. Which of the following is a parameter setting that you could disable to simplify the appearance of the screen?
   a. displaying toolbars
   b. displaying menus
   c. displaying database names
   d. displaying title bar

3. If you wanted to limit the menu choices to those that would be useful for a user but not display those choices a designer would use, you would make which of the following changes to the Startup?
   a. Deselect the Allow Built-in Toolbars option.
   b. Deselect the Allow Full Menus option.
   c. Deselect the Allow Toolbar Changes option.
   d. Deselect the Display Status Bar option.

4. A good password should have the following characteristics to make it hard to guess.
   a. It should be an easy-to-remember date.
   b. It should be an obscure word from the dictionary.
   c. It should include a symbol that is not a normal letter or number.
   d. It should be the same for all of your accounts.

5. If you have set the startup parameters so that they do not allow full menus, the Tools option does not appear. How do you change the startup parameters?
   a. Reinstall Access.
   b. Copy the data, forms, queries, and reports into a new database.
   c. Hold down Ctrl when you start Access.
   d. Close and re-open Access. Hold down the Shift key when you open the database.

6. The length of an Access password _____.
   a. can be up to 14 characters long
   b. is limited to between six and eight characters long
   c. is unlimited
   d. must be less than six characters long

7. You should use caution when changing Access default settings because _____
   a. the changes will affect all of your Access databases
   b. others may use that computer and want to use the standard default settings
   c. you could change an operational default and not remember the original settings
   d. all of the above are reasons to use caution

8. To change startup parameters, _____.

   a. choose Tools, Startup with all databases closed

   b. choose Tools, Startup with the database open

   c. choose View, Startup with all databases closed

   d. choose View, Startup with any database open

9. The label that appears next to a switchboard action button is _____.

   a. dictated by the options chosen in the Switchboard Manager

   b. selected from a drop-down list in the Edit Switchboard Item dialog box

   c. set by the designer in the Edit Switchboard Item dialog box

   d. set in the Switchboard window by typing next to the button

10. What would be your first step as a way to prevent unauthorized use of data in an Access database file?

    a. Set a password for the database file.

    b. Deselect the Allow Full Menus option.

    c. Encrypt the database.

    d. Create a switchboard.

Completion

In the blank provided, write the correct answer for each of the following statements.

1. Data scrambled and stored in coded form that is not easily read by someone who does not have the code is said to be _______________.

2. The term that Access uses for a menu of choices represented by buttons on a form is called a(n) _______________.

3. A setting that applies to all of the databases opened in Access is called a(n) _______________.

4. A setting that applies to one database and is activated when that database is opened is called a(n) _______________.

5. When you want to add or remove a password, the database must be opened in _______________ mode.

6. A(n) _______________ can be used to help restrict access to a database to only those persons who have been authorized.

7. The standard setting for an Access datasheet is for the cursor to move to _______________ when the ↵Enter key is used.

8. To prevent someone from changing database objects, you would need to create a switchboard, set it to display when the database is opened, and disable the Display _______________ option.

9. You can change the colors in a datasheet, by choosing Tools, __________, Datasheet tab, and changing the colors for Font, Background, or Gridlines.

10. The Switchboard Manager is found under Tools, __________, Switchboard Manager.

Matching

In the blank next to each of the following terms or phrases, write the letter of the corresponding term or phrase. (Note that some letters may be used more than once.)

a. Shift

b. encryption

c. Unset Database Password

d. Open Form in Add Mode

e. #123ABC

f. asterisks

g. Tools, Startup

h. Exclusive

i. Tools, Options

j. Go to Switchboard

_____ 1. Mode used to add a password to a database

_____ 2. Example of a good password

_____ 3. Command used to string several switchboards together

_____ 4. What you see when you type a password in the Set Password dialog box

_____ 5. Used to prevent someone from using an Access table in a word processing program

_____ 6. Option used in a switchboard to enable the user to add new records, but not look at existing records

_____ 7. Choose this to change the default settings

_____ 8. Used to bypass startup settings when opening a database

_____ 9. Go here to make the switchboard form open automatically when the database is opened

_____ 10. Dialog box used to remove a password from a database

Applying Your Skills

Practice

The following exercises enable you to practice the skills you have learned in this project. Take a few minutes to work through these exercises now. If you are saving your files on a floppy disk, you may need to start with an empty disk to assure that you have enough room for all the files.

Adding a Password to a Database

In the following exercise, you add a password to protect a database named Books.

To add a password to a database, complete the following steps:

1. Copy the Proj1703 file from the Project-17 folder on the CD and rename it `Library12`.
2. Open the `Library12` database in Exclusive mode.
3. Choose Tools, Security, Set Database Password from the menu.
4. Type the password `Books`.
5. Verify the password by typing it again. Make sure to capitalize the first letter as shown.
6. Close the database and reopen it. Try typing in the password as `books` to see if capitalization makes a difference. If that does not work, try `Books`.
7. Leave the database open for use in the next exercise.

Adding a Switchboard and Running It Automatically Whenever the Database Is Opened

In this exercise, you set the startup parameters of a database to open a switchboard whenever the database is opened. In this way, you create a database that a novice can use successfully without having to master the details of the Access program.

To add a switchboard and run it automatically whenever the database is opened, complete the following steps:

1. Use the Library12 database from the previous exercise or copy the Proj1703 database from the Project-17 folder on the CD and rename it `Library12`.
2. Open the `Library12` database if necessary. Choose Tools, Add-Ins, Switchboard Manager to create a switchboard.
3. Edit the existing main switchboard to add two new action buttons:
   - Add a button to open the Quick Entry form in Add mode. Use the text `Add new books`.
   - Add a button to open the Book List report. Use the text `Preview report on book status`.
4. Close the dialog boxes.
5. Open the Startup parameters dialog box from the Tools menu.
6. Choose the Switchboard form as the display form opened upon startup.
7. Close the database and reopen it. Provide the password, `Books`, if necessary. The switchboard should appear automatically.
8. Test the Switchboard form. Close the form and the database.

Removing a Password from a Database

In this exercise, you remove a password from the Books database.

To remove a password from a database, complete the following steps:

1. Copy the Proj1704 file from the Project-17 folder on the CD and rename it `Group`.
2. Open the `Group` database in Exclusive mode. Use the Password `Club`.
3. Choose Tools, Security, Unset Database Password from the menu.
4. Enter the password `Club`. Click OK.
5. Close the database and then reopen it. Confirm that the password is no longer required.
6. Close the database.

Adding a Password and Encrypting a Database

In the following exercise, you encrypt and add a password to the database that you have been keeping for the Sound Byte Music company.

To encrypt the Sound Byte Music database, complete the following steps:

1. Make sure Access is open to a blank (gray) screen. All databases should be closed.
2. Choose Tools, Security, Encrypt/Decrypt Database.
3. Locate the Proj1705 database on the Project-17 folder on the CD, select it, and click OK.
4. Select your disk or folder and enter the name `SBMusic14` in the File name box. Click the Save button.
5. Right-click on the Start button on the Windows taskbar and choose Explore. Change the View to Details.
6. Find the file Proj1705 on the Project-17 folder on the CD and notice the size of the file. Find `SBMusic14` and compare the size of the encrypted file. Determine whether the encryption process changed the size of the file.

To create a password, complete the following steps:

1. Open the `SBMusic14` database in Exclusive mode.
2. Choose Tools, Security, Set Database Password.
3. Enter the following in the Password box and then enter it again in the Verify box:

   `Music!`

4. Click OK. Close the database.

5. Open the database and provide the password.
6. Leave the database open for use in the next exercise.

Adding a Switchboard to the Sound Byte Music Database

In the following exercise you use the Switchboard add-in to create a switchboard.

To create a switchboard for the Sound Byte Music database, complete the following steps:

Create a switchboard and buttons for one form and two reports.

1. Use the SBMusic13 database from the previous exercise or copy the file Proj1705 from the Project-17 folder on the CD and rename it `SBMusic14`. Open the `SBMusic14` database.
2. Choose Tools, Add-Ins, Switchboard Manager and confirm that you want to create a new switchboard.
3. Edit the switchboard to open add a button that says

   `Add New Customers`

   Open the form in Add mode and use the Autoform.
4. Create a button that says

   `Customer Mailing Labels`

   that opens the Labels Customers report.
5. Create a button that says

   `Print List of Suppliers and Orders`

   that opens the Suppliers report.
6. Open the Switchboard form and test the buttons. Close the form and the database.

Challenge

The following challenges enable you to use your problem-solving skills. For these exercises, you open files that are similar to the ones you have been working on. You set passwords and restrict editing options, and create switchboards using the Switchboard manager. Take time to work through these exercises now.

Securing the Club Database and Adding a Switchboard

In this exercise, you add a password, a switchboard, and remove editing options.

Locate the file Proj1706 on the Project-17 folder on the CD. Make an encrypted copy of it on your disk and name it `Club with Security`. Open the

`Club with Security` database in Exclusive mode. Add a password. Use your last name as the password if you are doing this as a class exercise. Otherwise, choose a password that will not be easily guessed at by others. General guidelines for good passwords suggest that you do not use birth dates, words that exist in the dictionary, and that you mix numbers and letters. To help you remember the password, you may want to choose the first letters in a memorable phrase.

Create a switchboard that does the following:

- Opens the Member Information form in Add mode
- Opens the Member Data form in Edit mode
- Opens the List of Members report

Change the Startup options to remove the toolbars, menus, and the Database window. Set the option to start the Switchboard form automatically. Close the form and the database. Open the database and test the password, switchboard, and menu options. Close the database and close Access. Open the `Club` database that you have been working on. Compare the switchboard that you created using macros in Project 15 to the switchboard that you created in this exercise. Determine which you want to use in the future.

Securing the Customer Research Database and Adding a Switchboard

In this exercise, you add a password, a switchboard, and remove editing options.

Locate the file Proj1707 on the Project-17 folder on the CD. Make an encrypted copy of it on your disk and name it `Customer Research with Security`. Open the `Customer Research with Security` database in Exclusive mode. Add a password. Use your last name as the password if you are doing this as a class exercise. Otherwise, choose a password that will not be easily guessed at by others. General guidelines for good passwords suggest that you do not use birth dates or words that exist in the dictionary, and that you mix numbers and letters. To help you remember the password, you may want to choose the first letters in a memorable phrase.

Create a switchboard that does the following:

- Opens the Participants form in Edit mode
- Opens the Survey Participants form in Edit mode
- Opens the Hours Viewed by Household report
- Opens the Mailing to Households report

Change the Startup options to remove the toolbars, menus, and the database window. Set the option to start the Switchboard form automatically. Close the form and the database. Open the database and test the password, switchboard, and menu options. Close the Database and close Access.

Securing the Vending Database and Adding a Switchboard

In this exercise, you add a password, a switchboard, and remove editing options.

Locate the file Proj1708 on the Project-17 folder on the CD. Make an encrypted copy of it on your disk and name it `Vending with Security`. Open the `Vending with Security` database in Exclusive mode. Add a password. Use your last name as the password if you are doing this as a class exercise. Otherwise, choose a password that will not be easily guessed at by others. General guidelines for good passwords suggest that you do not use birth dates, words that exist in the dictionary, and that you mix numbers and letters. To help you remember the password, you may want to choose the first letters in a memorable phrase.

Create a switchboard that does the following:

- Opens the Suppliers form in Edit mode
- Opens the Machine Locations form in Edit mode
- Opens the Supplier Phone List report
- Opens the Machine Locations report

Change the Startup options to remove the toolbars, menus, and Database window. Set the option to start the Switchboard form automatically. Close the form and the database. Open the database and test the password, switchboard, and menu options. Close the database and close Access.

Securing the Video Store Database and Adding a Switchboard

In this exercise, you add a password, a switchboard, and remove editing options.

Locate the file Proj1709 on the Project-17 folder on the CD. Make an encrypted copy of it on your disk and name it `Video Store with Security`. Open the `Video Store with Security` database in Exclusive mode. Add a password. Use your last name as the password if you are doing this as a class exercise. Otherwise, choose a password that will not be easily guessed at by others. General guidelines for good passwords suggest that you do not use birth dates, words that exist in the dictionary, and that you mix numbers and letters. To help you remember the password, you may want to choose the first letters in a memorable phrase.

Create a switchboard that does the following:

- Opens the Customer form in Edit mode
- Opens the Inventory Listing report
- Opens the Rental Activity report
- Opens the Rentals and Fees Pie Chart report

Change the Startup options to remove the toolbars, menus, and Database window. Set the option to start the Switchboard form automatically. Close the form and the database. Open the database and test the password, switchboard, and menu options. Close the database and close Access.

Securing the Home Inventory Database and Adding a Switchboard

In this exercise, you add a password, a switchboard, and remove editing options.

Locate the file Proj1710 on the Project-17 folder on the CD. Make an encrypted copy of it on your disk and name it `Home Inventory with Security`. Open the `Home Inventory with Security` database in Exclusive mode. Add a password. Use your last name as the password if you are doing this as a class exercise. Otherwise, choose a password that will not be easily guessed at by others. General guidelines for good passwords suggest that you do not use birth dates, words that exist in the dictionary, and that you mix numbers and letters. To help you remember the password, you may want to choose the first letters in a memorable phrase.

Create a switchboard that does the following:

- Opens the Add Inventory Item form in Add mode
- Opens the Company Data form in Add mode
- Opens the Insurance Companies form in Edit mode
- Opens the Insurance Companies report

Change the Startup options to remove the toolbars, menus, and Database window. Set the option to start the Switchboard form automatically. Close the form and the database. Open the database and test the password, switchboard, and menu options. Close the database and close Access.

PinPoint Assessment

PinPoint Training

You have completed the project and the associated lessons, as well as the "Checking Your Skills" and "Applying Your Skills" sections. Now use the PinPoint software Evaluation mode to assess your comprehension of the specific exam tasks you have just learned. You can also use the PinPoint Trainer mode and the SHOW ME tutorials to practice these specific exam tasks.

Project 18

Eighteen

Using Access 97 on the Web and Linking to Other Documents

Hyperlink Techniques and HTML Documents Can Expand Database Use and Flexibility

In this project you will learn the following objectives and their associated Microsoft Exam required activities.

Objectives	Required Activities
➤ Add Hyperlinks from Forms to Word 97 Documents	Create Hyperlinks
➤ Add Hyperlinks from Forms to Excel 97 Spreadsheets	Create Hyperlinks
➤ Save Tables, Queries, Forms, or Reports as Static HTML pages	
➤ View HTML Pages on a Local Drive Using a Browser	
➤ Edit HTML Pages with Notepad	
➤ Publish Pages on the Internet	
➤ Create an Interactive Form on the Web	Build Order Forms for Internet Use

Why Would I Do This?

Internet technology is changing the way people communicate within a company. Many companies are setting up private internets called *intranets*. These intranets use the same *World Wide Web browsers* that are used on the *Internet* but are limited to company networks. For the purpose of brevity, the term "net" is used in this project to refer to either the Internet or a company intranet.

Internet
The worldwide computer communication network that is based on open standards for operating systems and communication.

Intranet
A communication network within a company that uses the same software and standards as the Internet.

World Wide Web
A graphical interface that links sites on the Internet and enables the user to easily jump from one site to another.

Web browser
A software application used to view and interact with sites on the World Wide Web. Two popular examples are Netscape Navigator and Microsoft Internet Explorer.

Hyperlinks
Hyperlinks are connections to other documents, spreadsheets, databases, or presentations on your computer or on the net.

The advantage of using the Internet or a company intranet to disseminate information is that you retain control of the data. Formerly, you would make copies of your data and distribute them to the intended users. This method has two significant drawbacks: 1) The data may become out of date, and 2) some people in the company may need the information but may not be on the distribution list.

If you publish your data on the net, others may visit the site whenever they need the information, and you can make sure the site has the current information. Similarly, you can insert *hyperlinks* from your forms, documents, spreadsheets, or presentations to sites provided by others.

Information can also be collected on the net. You can post forms that colleagues, clients, or potential clients can fill out. The information can be directly deposited into an Access database.

Access

Lesson 1: Adding Hyperlinks from Forms to Other Documents

In this lesson you use two files. The Proj1801 file is a document in Microsoft Word 97 and Proj1802 is a database in Access 97. Both are located in the Project-18 folder on the CD. You create a link from the form in Access 97 to a bookmark in a document written in Word 97.

Viewing Existing Bookmarks

A sample document is provided that already has bookmarks in it. This document contains names of vendors that are grouped by acceptability. Each group is bookmarked.

To View the Bookmarks That Already Exist in the Sample Document

1. **Make a copy of the data file Proj1801 from the Project-18 folder on the CD, place it in your own directory on your disk, then rename the copy** `Approved Vendors`**.**

2. **Open the** `Approved Vendors` **document in Microsoft Word. A list of vendors is displayed (see Figure 18.1).**

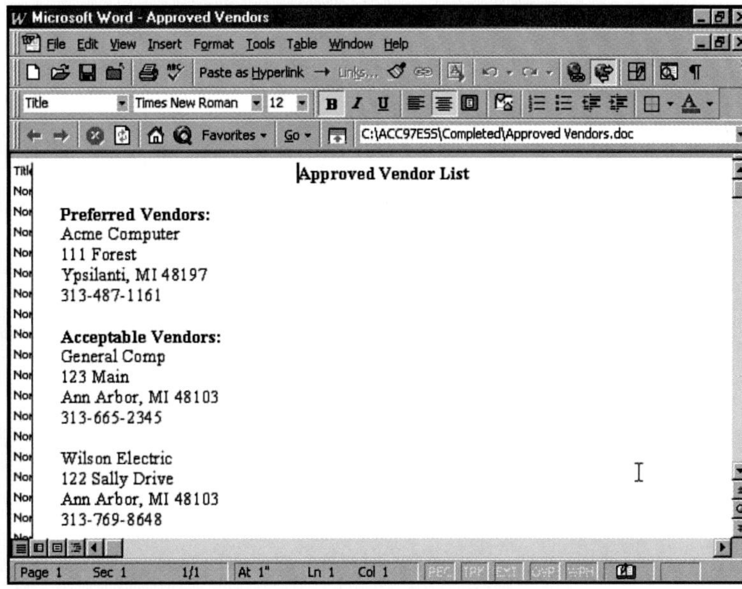

Figure 18.1
The Approved Vendors document contains a rated list of vendors.

❸ **Open the Edit menu and choose Go To.**

The Find and Replace window is displayed with the Go To tab selected (see Figure 18.2).

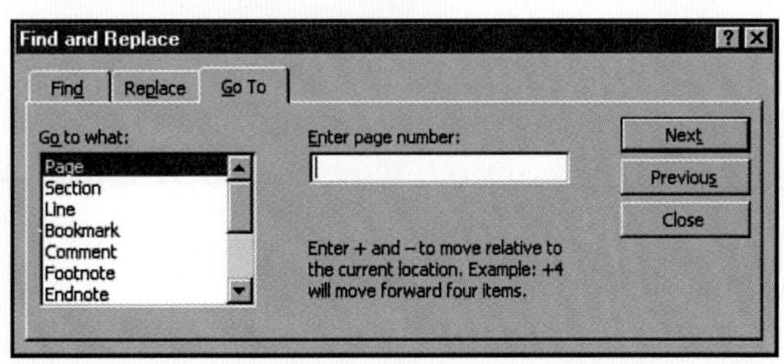

Figure 18.2
The Find and Replace dialog box with the Go To section displayed can be used to go directly to different sections of a document.

❹ **Click Bookmark in the Go to what section. Click the list arrow next to the Enter bookmark name box to reveal the three bookmarks that have been placed in this document (see Figure 18.3).**

It is possible to create a hyperlink from an Access 97 form directly to a bookmark within a Word 97 document. (Bookmarks can be added to Word 97 documents using the Insert menu and the Bookmark option.)

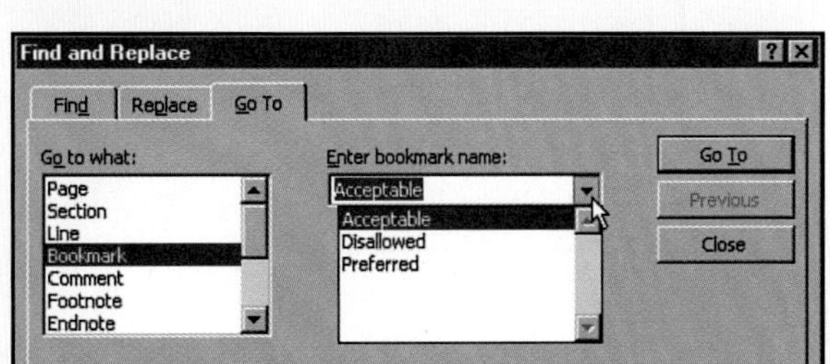

Figure 18.3
This document has three bookmarks.

continues

To View the Bookmarks That Already Exist in the Sample Document (continued)

5 Close the Find and Replace dialog box.

6 Close the document and close Word 97.

Creating a Hyperlink to a Document

Access forms can contain hyperlinks that connect the user directly to pertinent portions of documents stored on the user's local area network.

To Create a Hyperlink Between an Access 97 Form and a Word 97 Document

1 Make a copy of the data file Proj1802 from the Project-18 folder on the CD, place it in your own directory on your disk, then rename the copy `PC Purchase`.

2 Open the database.

This database illustrates the kind of data that a department may keep for tracking purchases of personal computers. The Vendors table contains a list of Vendors that can be used for corporate purchases. In this example, you assume that the Purchasing department keeps a current list of approved vendors and makes that list available to other departments as a Word 97 document. The vendor rating can change, and it is important that the user's purchase request reflect the current vendor rating. Access 97 enables you to place a hyperlink in the Vendor Information form that allows you to check the current rating from the Purchasing department document.

3 Click the Forms tab to reveal the available forms.

4 Select the Vendor Information form and click the Design button to reveal the design of the form. Maximize the window for convenient editing (see Figure 18.4).

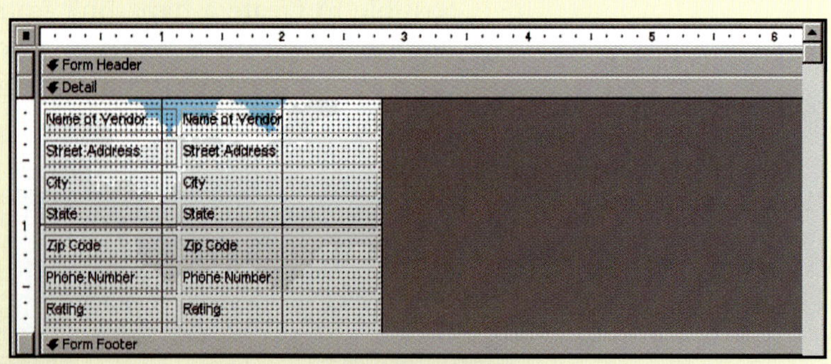

Figure 18.4
Hyperlinks may be placed in a form using Design view.

5 Click the Insert Hyperlink button on the toolbar.

The Insert Hyperlink dialog box is displayed (see Figure 18.5).

Access

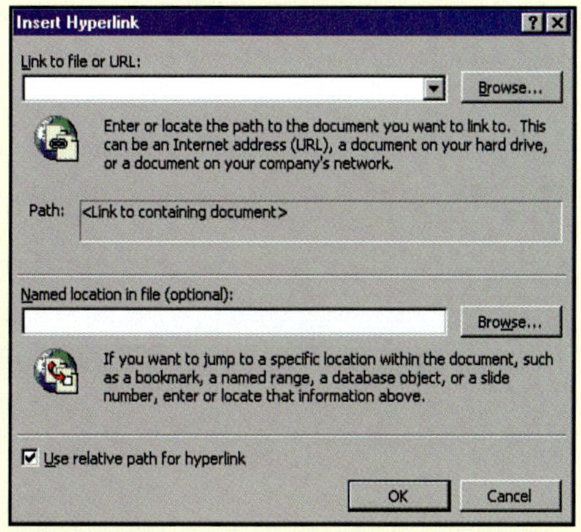

Figure 18.5
The Insert Hyperlink dialog box is used to locate and specify the file to which the hyperlink refers.

URL
An Internet address. The acronym stands for Uniform Resource Locator.

The `Link to file or URL` box can contain the address of the file. In this example, the file is on your hard drive, and the Browse button to the right of the box help you find the Approved Vendors file that you used earlier in this lesson.

6 Click the Browse button next to the `Link to file or URL` box. Use the buttons on the toolbar of this dialog box to find the Approved Vendors document used in the previous lesson.

7 Click the Approved Vendors document and click OK.

The file name and location on the hard drive are added to the dialog box (see Figure 18.6).

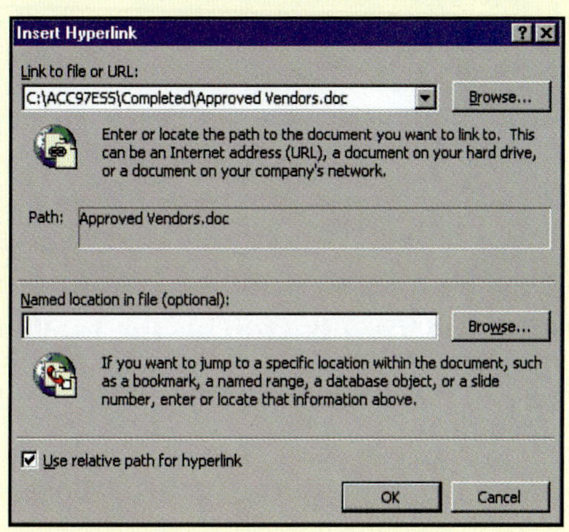

Figure 18.6
The Browse option can be used to find the file or it may be entered directly.

8 Type the name of the bookmark, `Preferred`, in the `Named location in file` box.

The Browse button next to this box only works if you are linking within the current file. To link to a bookmark or named range in a different file, as in this example, you must find out the name of the bookmark or named range using another method, such as opening the document and looking up the bookmark names as we did earlier in this lesson.

continues

To Create a Hyperlink Between an Access 97 Form and a Word 97 Document (continued)

9 Click OK.

A link is placed on the form in the upper-left corner (see Figure 18.7).

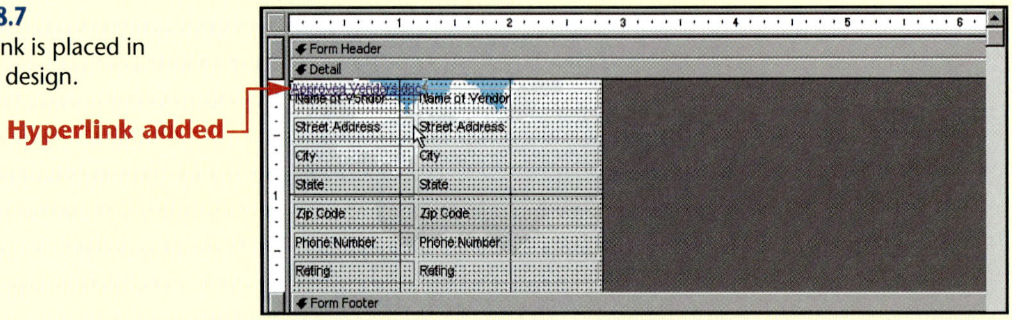

Figure 18.7
A hyperlink is placed in the form design.

10 Deselect the hyperlink, then click and drag the hyperlink to a new location to the right of the Rating field (see Figure 18.8).

You can drag the hyperlink and drop it in the gray area to the right of the current right edge of the form. The form widens to accommodate the hyperlink.

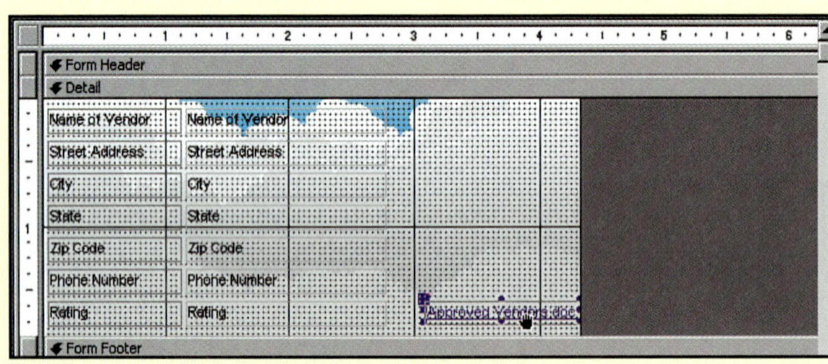

Figure 18.8
The hyperlink can be moved to another location in the form.

11 Click the View button on the toolbar to change to Form view.

The hyperlink is displayed on the form in dark blue with underlined text.

12 Move the pointer to the hyperlink on the form.

The pointer changes into a small hand. This indicates that this text represents a hyperlink (see Figure 18.9).

13 Click the hyperlink to the Approved Vendors document.

The Word 97 program is launched, if necessary, and the Approved Vendors document is opened. The cursor is placed at the bookmark, Preferred.

(In this short document, the use of bookmarks is not necessary but is included to demonstrate how they could be used in larger documents.)

Figure 18.9
The pointer turns into a small hand when pointing at a hyperlink.

Leave the document open for use in the next section.

Copying and Moving Between Linked Files

You can copy information from one file and paste it into another. You can also use navigation buttons on the toolbar to quickly jump back and forth between the files once the link is established.

To Copy Information and Move Between Linked Files

In this example, the address of the Acme Computer Company has changed, as shown in the Approved Vendors document, since the last time it was used in the database.

1. **Select and copy the new address, 111 Forest, in the Approved Vendors document.**

   (You may need to select Edit and Copy from the menu. The Cut, Copy, and Paste buttons may not be shown on the toolbar.)

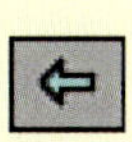

2. **Click the Back button on the Web toolbar.**

   This button returns you to the Access Form.

If you have problems...

The Web toolbar should open automatically when you use a hyperlink to move between applications. If for some reason you do not see the Web toolbar, go to View, Toolbars and click the Web option to turn on this toolbar, or click the Web toolbar button on the Standard toolbar. If the Back button does not work for some reason, you can still move between applications using the Windows taskbar.

3. **Select the old address for the Acme Computer Company and paste in the new one.**

4. **In the Rating box, type in `Preferred` (see Figure 18.10).**

continues

To Copy Information and Move Between Linked Files (continued)

Web Toolbar button

Figure 18.10
The information from the Approved Vendors document has been used to update the Vendors table.

Web toolbar

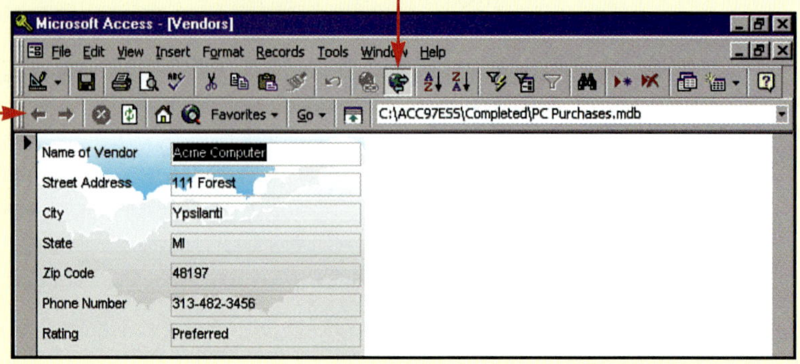

5. **Click the Forward button on the Web toolbar to return to the Approved Vendors document.**

6. **Close the document and close the Word 97 program.**

   Access should be displayed after you close the Word 97 document. If not, use the taskbar to return to Access.

7. **Close the form and save the changes.**

   Leave the database open.

Lesson 2: Adding Hyperlinks from Forms to Excel 97 Spreadsheets

Excel 97 spreadsheets have a feature called named ranges that is similar to bookmarks in Word documents. You can establish links from Access 97 Forms to Excel 97 spreadsheets and to particular named ranges within a spreadsheet.

To Link a Form and Spreadsheet

1. **Make a copy of the data file Proj1803 from the Project-18 folder on the CD, place it in your own directory on your disk, then rename the copy `Computer Budget`.**

   This Excel 97 spreadsheet represents the budget for computer purchases for three departments. It consists of a separate sheet for each of three departments—Sales, Marketing, and Engineering. Each department has a cell that represents the available funds for computer purchases. Each cell has been given a name—Sales, Marketing, and Engineering, respectively. These named ranges are similar to the bookmarks used in a Word document.

2. **Return to Access and open the `Orders` form in Design view. Maximize the window if necessary (see Figure 18.11).**

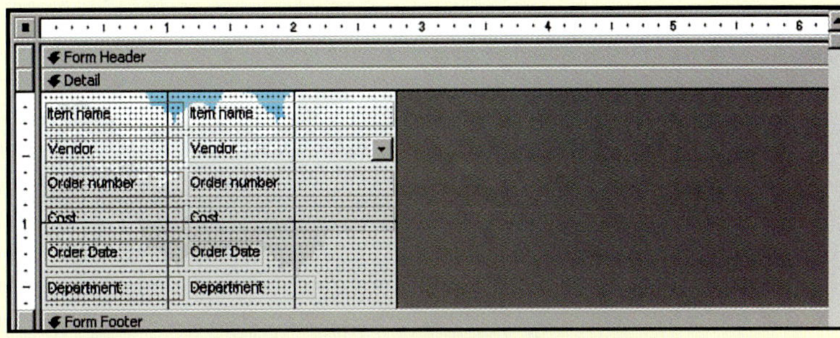

Figure 18.11
Hyperlinks to spreadsheets may be placed in a form in Design view.

This form is used to enter computer purchase requests.

3 Click the Insert Hyperlink button on the toolbar.

The Insert Hyperlink dialog box is displayed.

4 Click the Browse button and locate the folder that contains the copied and renamed file.

5 Click the Excel file Computer Budget. Click OK.

The location of the file is entered in the `Link to file or URL` box (see Figure 18.12).

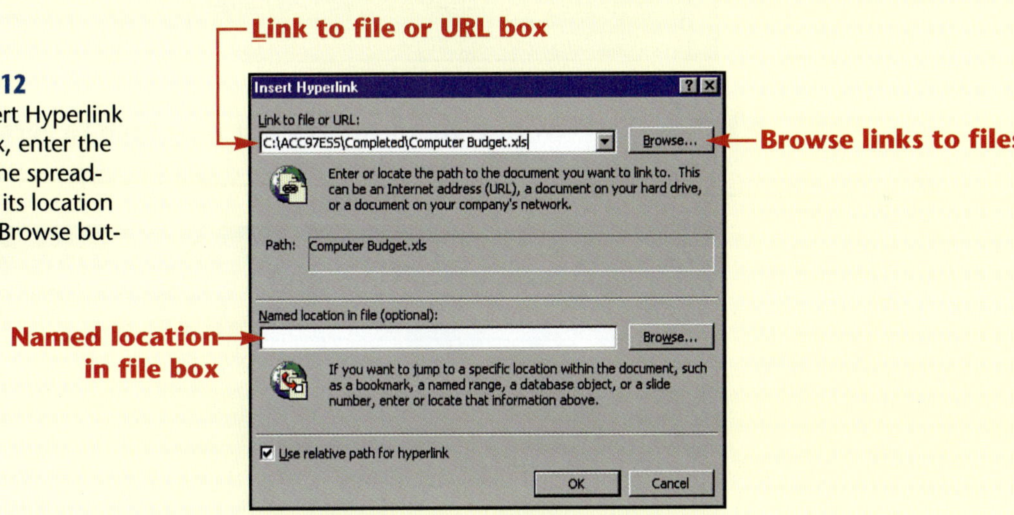

Figure 18.12
In the Insert Hyperlink dialog box, enter the name of the spreadsheet and its location using the Browse button.

6 Type the named range `Engineering` in the `Named location in file` box.

The Browse button does not work in this case because the named range is not in the same file as the source of the link.

7 Click OK to place the link in the form.

The link is placed in the form in the upper-left corner (see Figure 18.13).

continues

To Link a Form and Spreadsheet (continued)

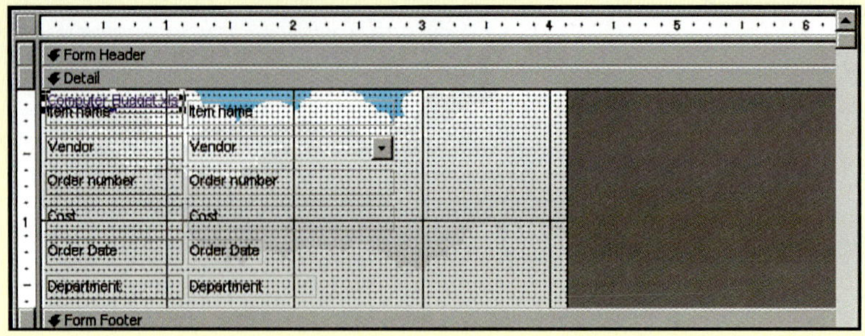

Figure 18.13
The link to the spreadsheet is placed in the form.

8 **Drag the hyperlink to a position to the right of the other cells (see Figure 18.14).**

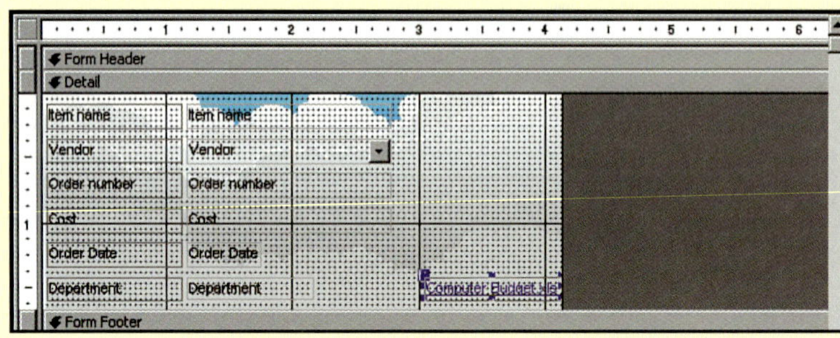

Figure 18.14
The link to the spreadsheet may be moved anywhere on the form.

9 **Click the View button on the toolbar to switch to Form view (see Figure 18.15).**

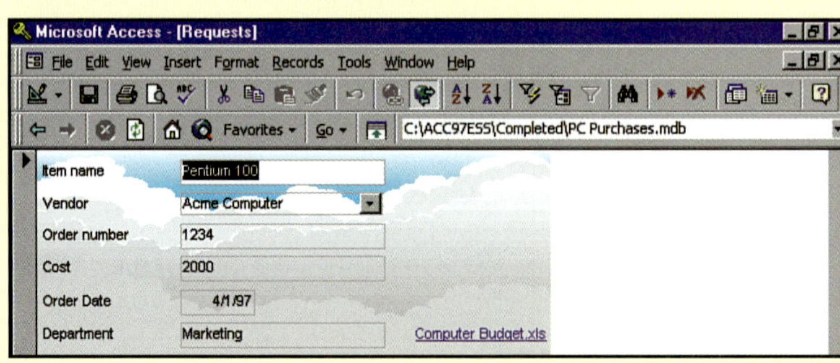

Figure 18.15
The hyperlink is displayed in the form.

10 **Click the hyperlink to move directly to the budget sheet to see if there is adequate funding for further computer purchases.**

The hyperlink launches Excel 97, opens the spreadsheet, and moves to the named range on the appropriate sheet (see Figure 18.16).

11 **Close the spreadsheet and close Excel.**

12 **Close the form and save the changes.**

Leave the database open for use in the next lesson.

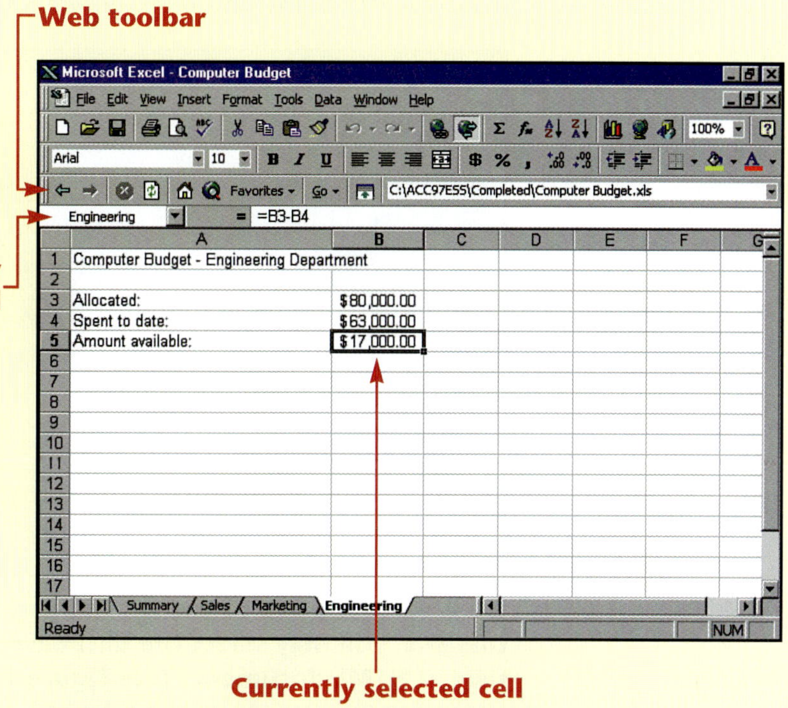

Figure 18.16
The hyperlink launches Excel and opens the sheet to the named range Engineering.

Lesson 3: Saving Tables, Queries, Forms, and Reports as Static HTML Pages

HTML
The standard programming language used for writing documents that can be viewed on the Internet by many different browsers. The acronym stands for Hypertext Markup Language.

The World Wide Web is designed to be used by a variety of different computers. They share a common way of sending documents to each other and a common way of viewing those documents. These documents are created with a special set of codes that tell the browser program how to display the text. This set of codes is called *HTML*, the Hypertext Markup Language. It is used to create a basic document that has a limited set of formatting features. Some browsers support additional features that are not common to all browsers. These browsers use additional HTML codes called extensions that handle features such as columns, tables, and animation.

In this lesson you save tables, forms, and reports as static HTML documents that may be viewed by an Internet Web browser, but that are not interactive. Use the database from the previous lesson.

To Save Your Tables, Forms, and Reports as HTML Documents

1. **The PC Purchase database should still be open with the Forms tab selected. In the File menu, choose Save as HTML.**

   This action launches the Publish to the Web Wizard (see Figure 18.17). The wizard may take a while to open.

continues

To Save Your Tables, Forms, and Reports as HTML Documents (continued)

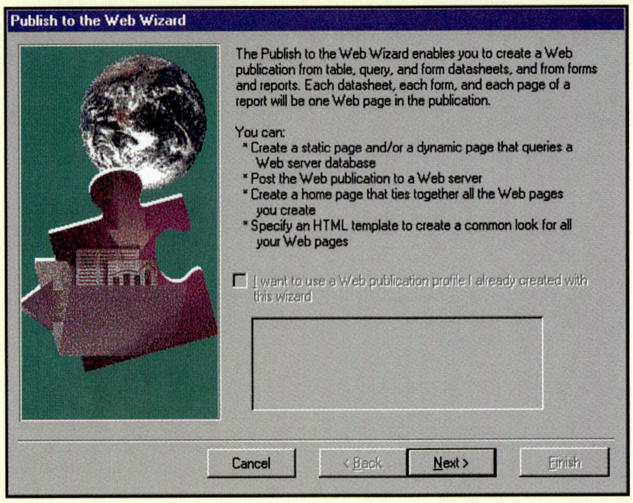

Figure 18.17
The Publish to the Web Wizard helps create HTML documents from the database.

2 Click Next to move to the next dialog box of the wizard. In this box, you may select the database objects you want to save as HTML documents (see Figure 18.18).

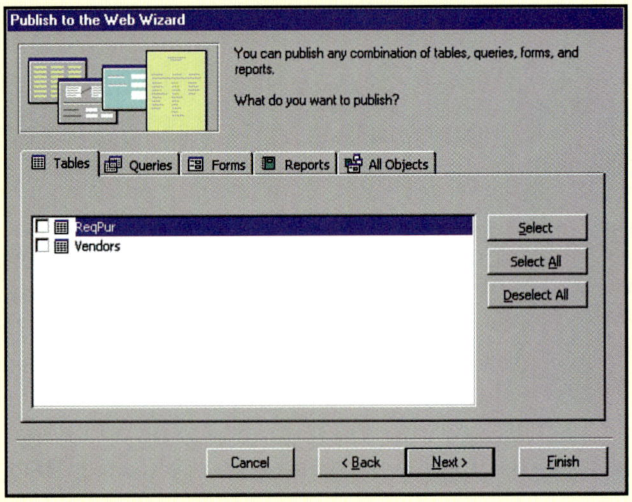

Figure 18.18
The wizard enables you to choose the tables, queries, forms, or reports you want to save as HTML.

3 Click the Tables tab, if necessary, to display the two tables in this database. Click the check box next to the ReqPur table.

For this example, choose a table, a form, and a report.

4 Click the Forms tab to display the available forms. Click the check box next to Orders.

5 Click the Reports tab to display the reports. Click the check box next to CompOr.

6 Click Next.

The next dialog box gives you the option of using one of several sample pages as templates to give your page(s) a finished look (see Figure 18.19).

Access

Figure 18.19
You may use templates to design your HTML documents.

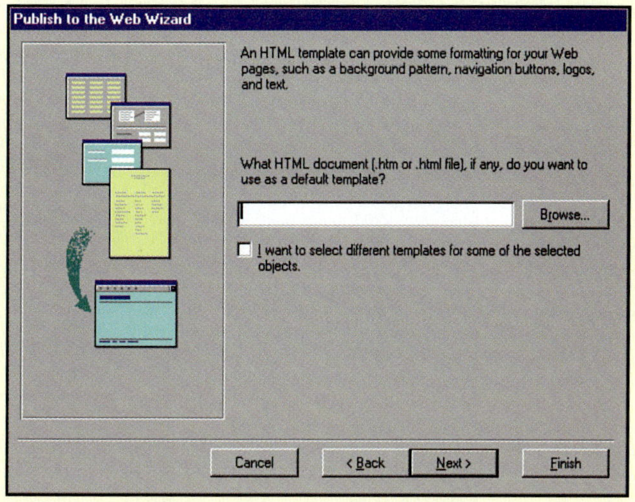

7 Click the Browse button to display the available templates.

The Select an HTML Template window opens. Click the Details button if necessary to display the templates as shown in Figure 18.20.

If you have problems...

The Select an HTML Template dialog box may not display any HTML templates. To find them, you can use the Advanced search to look for files with .htm extensions, or you can search for Sky.htm. If Microsoft Office is installed on your hard drive, the HTML files are usually found at C:\Program Files\MSOffice\Templates\ Access\.

Figure 18.20
There are several templates from which to choose.

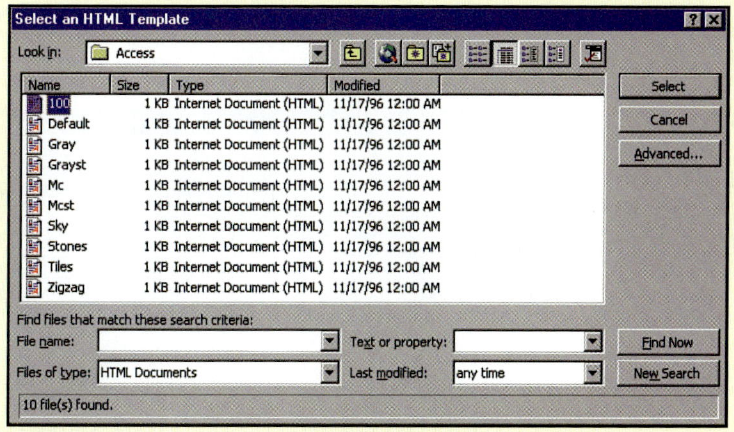

8 Click the Sky option, then click the Select button.

The template name and its path are displayed in the wizard's dialog box.

9 Click Next.

A dialog box is displayed that may be used to determine how you want to share your database (see Figure 18.21).

continues

To Save Your Tables, Forms, and Reports as HTML Documents (continued)

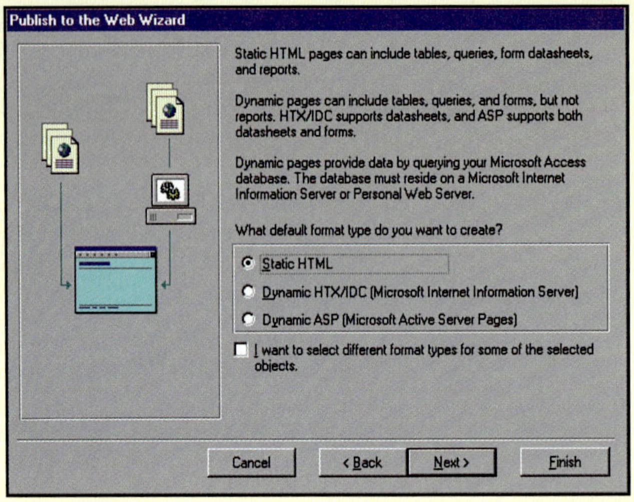

Figure 18.21
The database objects may be saved as static or dynamic objects.

The static Web pages may be transferred to a Web server that can make them available to anyone on the Web. Static pages can be viewed but not changed, whereas dynamic pages can be used to create an interactive object than can be used to update information in the database. In this lesson, you address only the use of static pages.

10 Make sure the option button next to the Static HTML selection is selected and click the Next button.

The next dialog box is displayed and gives you options for saving your HTML pages (see Figure 18.22). Change the destination for the files to the same disk location you have used for previous exercises, if necessary.

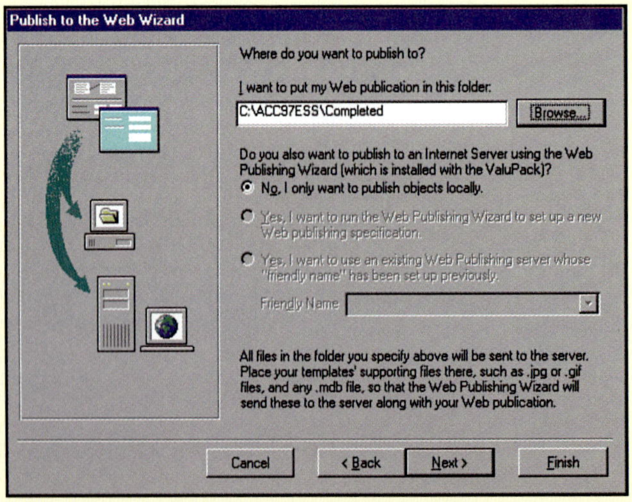

Figure 18.22
The HTML pages may be published to your disk.

11 Click Next to go to the next wizard page. Click the check box to indicate that you want to create a home page.

Access

The home page contains hyperlinks to each of the tables, queries, forms, or reports you have selected to publish. It serves as a switchboard that coordinates searching the other pages.

12. **Give the home page the name** `pcorders`**. Click Next to continue.**

13. **Click Finish. Do not select the option to save this publication profile for later use.**

    The program takes a moment to create the documents in the destination folder you previously selected. No change in the database is apparent.

14. **Close the database and close Access.**

If you have problems...

Many viewers and Internet server computers do not support filenames longer than eight characters or file extensions longer than three characters. Access saves the files with a four-letter extension, html. If you view these files directly from your disk in the next lesson with an older browser, they will not link to each other properly.

When Access saves the database objects as HTML documents, it adds a sequence number to the name of the file. For example, Form.html becomes Form_1.html. If the name of the table, query, form, or report is longer than six characters, the resulting filename will be longer than eight characters.

To avoid problems with older browsers and Internet servers, make a copy of any of the tables, queries, forms, or reports that will be saved as HTML documents to a name that is six characters or less. Save these copies as HTML documents. Once the files have been created, edit the names and change the extensions to .htm rather than .html.

Lesson 4: Viewing HTML Pages on a Local Drive Using a Browser

HTML documents are made to be viewed by a browser on the Internet. If you have a browser on your computer, you can open and view the documents created in the previous lesson, even if you are not connected to the net. There are several brands of World Wide Web browsers, but the most popular ones share the features that are used in this lesson. The examples shown use Microsoft's Internet Explorer 3.0 browser, but you should be able to adapt the following commands to most other browsers.

It is common practice to check your HTML documents on your computer before transferring them to the computer that makes them available on the Internet.

Internet servers often refer to the location of supporting files, such as background images, using relative references rather than absolute references. To conveniently check the files before you place them on an Internet server, copy all of the supporting files to the same folder.

In this lesson, you learn how to copy image files to the folder that contains your HTML document.

To Copy Image Files to the Folder That Contains the HTML Documents

1 Open the Windows Explorer and create a new folder named `Publish`.

2 In the Windows Explorer, locate the folder that contains the Access logo and the background image.

It is probably in a folder whose location is similar to the following example (see Figure 18.23):

```
C:\Program Files\Microsoft Office\Templates\Access
```

Figure 18.23
Supporting image files for the pages may be copied to the same folder as the HTML documents for convenient checking.

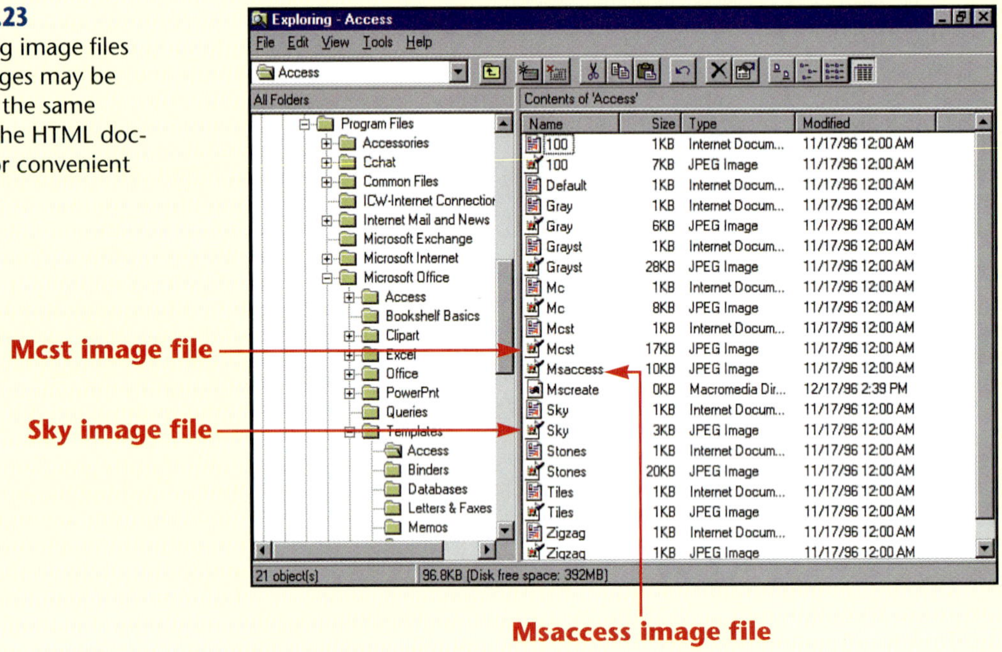

Your folder may be in a different location, or the templates may not have been installed. Check with your instructor, if necessary.

JPEG (Joint Photographic Experts Group)
A type of image format that is commonly used with Internet pages.

3 Copy the *JPEG* images `Msaccess`, `Sky`, and `Mcst` to the new Publish folder.

4 Copy the HTML documents that you created in Lesson 3 from their current location to the Publish folder.

Your Publish folder should contain the HTML documents created in the previous lesson plus the three image files (see Figure 18.24).

5 Double-click the pcorders HTML document. If you have an Internet browser identified in Windows 95, it launches automatically and opens the document.

Access

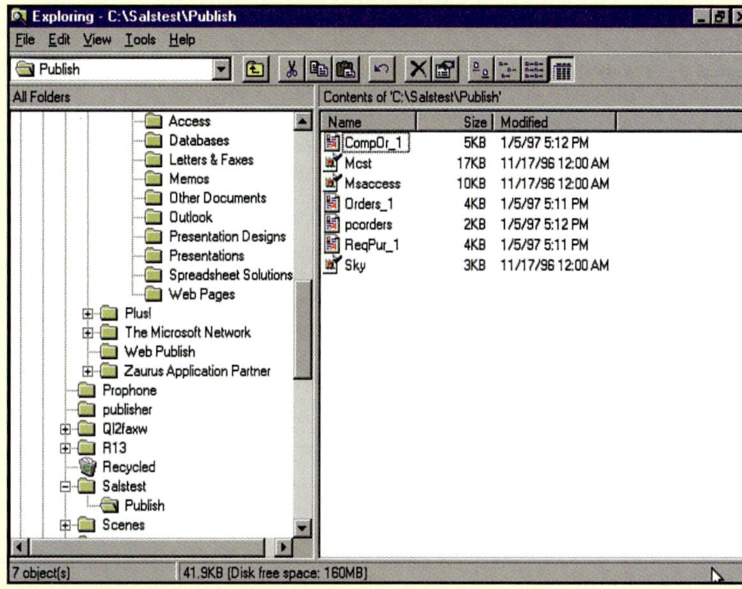

Figure 18.24
One folder showing the HTML documents and the supporting images.

Home page
An HTML document containing links to other pages. It corresponds to a switchboard form in Access.

The Internet Explorer opens the PC-Order document and displays a table showing the database objects that have been saved as HTML documents (see Figure 18.25).

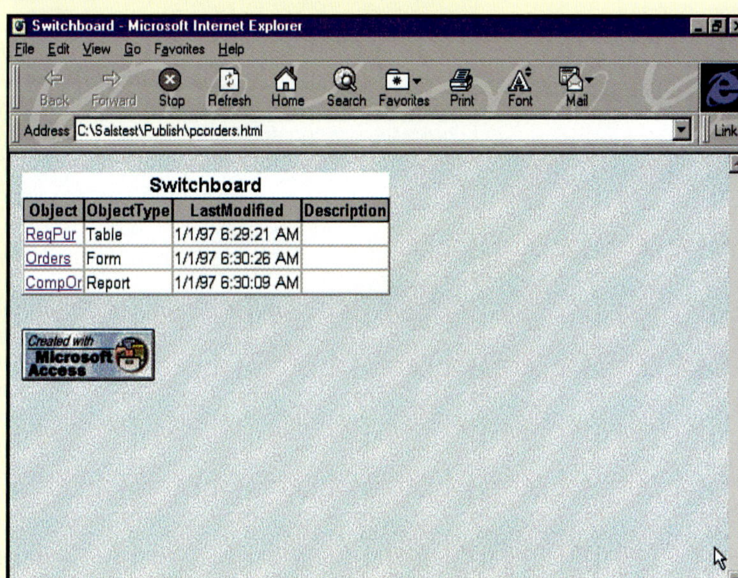

Figure 18.25
The *home page* can be used to link to the HTML documents that display the contents of the database objects.

The Sky image is used to provide the blue and white background; the Microsoft Access logo image indicates the program used to create the page.

continues

To Copy Image Files to the Folder That Contains the HTML Documents (continued)

If you have problems...

If you do not have an Internet browser identified, you may need to launch the browser first. When asked if you want to connect, choose the Cancel option. This opens the browser without connecting you to the Internet. (You do not have to connect to an Internet server for this lesson.) The examples in this lesson use Microsoft Internet Explorer.

Once the browser is open, select File and Open from the menu. Enter the name and folder that contains the home page document, pcorders.

It will resemble the following folder location: C:\ACC97ESS\Publish\pcorders.html.

If you are using another browser, such as Netscape 3.0, open the file using Netscape's menu options. Select File, then chose Open File in Browser (the menu option is called Open Page in Netscape 4.01). Use the open dialog box to find the folder that contains the pcorders HTML document and open the file.

6 Click the hyperlink that connects to the ReqPur table.

The browser opens the ReqPur HTML document (see Figure 18.26).

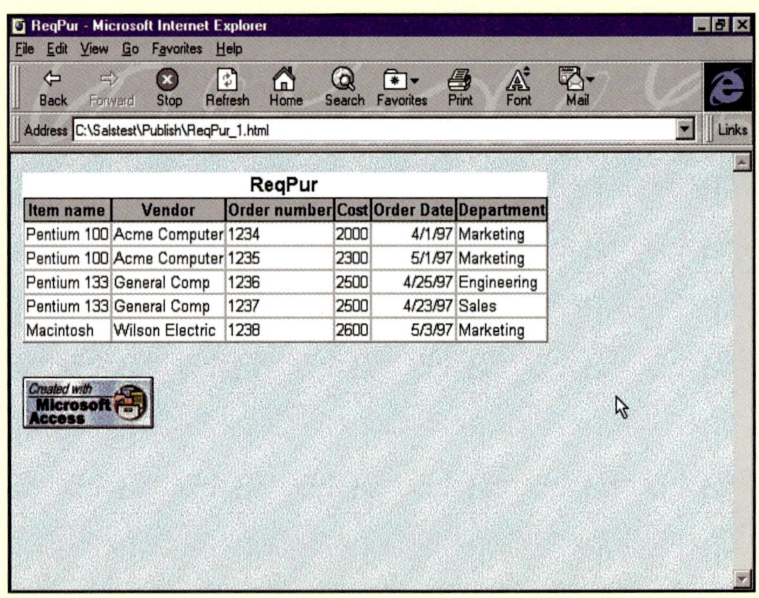

Figure 18.26
The hyperlink from the home page opens the ReqPur document.

7 Click the Back button on the toolbar to return to the home page.

Notice that the Forward button is now active on the toolbar. Documents are stored in a temporary memory queue when they are opened. The user can move backward and forward through this list of documents using the Forward and Back buttons.

8 Click on the Orders hyperlink to test it.

Notice that the HTML document is in table form, even though the Orders form was not. The default choice for forms is the tabular form (see Figure 18.27).

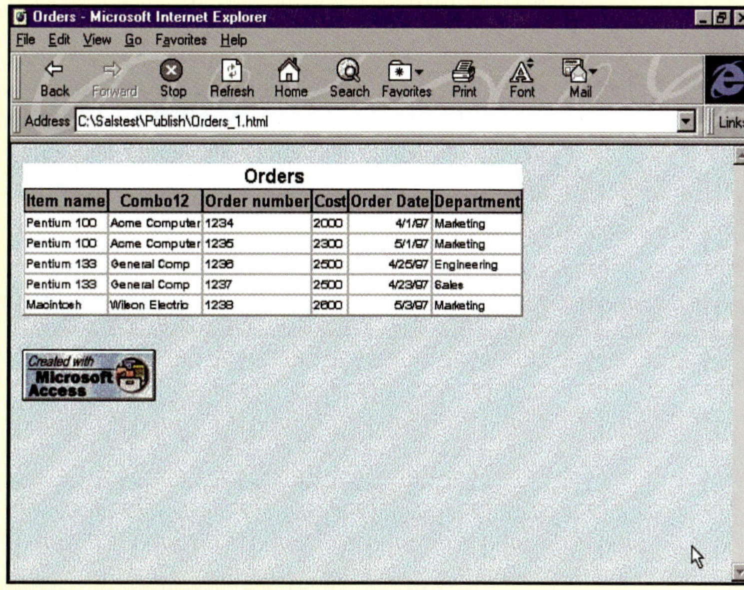

Figure 18.27
The Orders form opens as a tabular form.

❾ **Use the Back button to return to the home page.**

❿ **Click the CompOr hyperlink to open the report document (see Figure 18.28).**

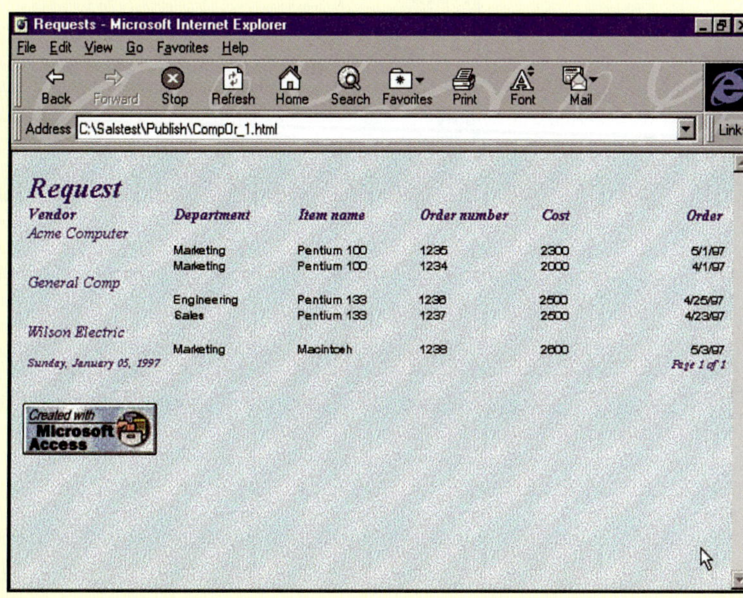

Figure 18.28
The report document is displayed.

⓫ **Click the Back button to return to the home page.**

Leave the browser open for the next lesson.

Lesson 5: Editing HTML Pages with Notepad

Hypertext Markup Language, HTML, is a standard method of describing the content of a document so that it can be displayed on a variety of computer monitors. It is beyond the scope of this text to describe the HTML language in detail, but there are some simple things that you can do that are useful.

Editing HTML Code to Delete an Image

In this procedure, you learn how to use the browser to edit the source code directly to remove the Access logo and how to change the background image.

To Remove the Access Logo from the Home Page

1 In the Internet Explorer, select View, Source from the menu.

A small word processing program, Notepad, is automatically launched to display the HTML source code for this document (see Figure 18.29).

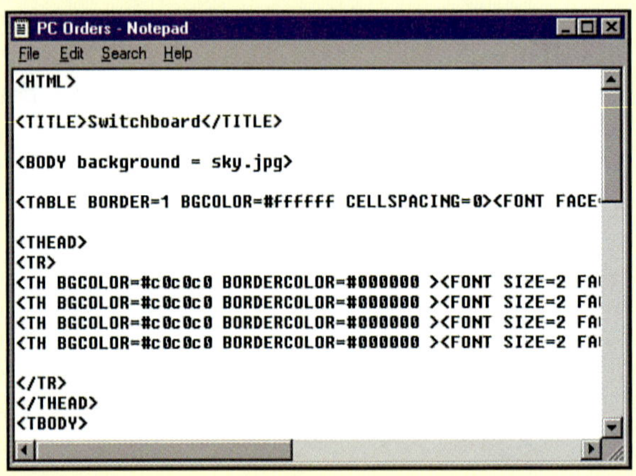

Figure 18.29 The Notepad word processor program displays the HTML source code.

2 Scroll to the bottom of the document until you see the following line:

```
<IMG SRC = "msaccess.jpg">
```

3 Select this line, and then choose Edit, Cut from the menu.

4 Close the Notepad window and save the changes.

The changes are not immediately apparent. Internet pages are downloaded from their source, then the connection is dropped. To see any changes, the page must be reloaded or refreshed.

5 Select View, Refresh from the menu of the browser.

The Msaccess image is no longer displayed.

6 Select View, Source from the menu again.

7 Scroll to the bottom of the document. Paste the previously cut line just before the last line in the document.

If you no longer have the line in the clipboard, type in the missing line as shown below:

```
<IMG SRC = "msaccess.jpg">
```

This line should be placed before the closing line, `</HTML>`.

8 Close the Notepad window and save the changes.

9 Select View and Refresh again to verify that the MSAcess logo has been added back to the switchboard.

Leave the browser open.

You have learned how to delete and add items to an HTML document. Now you edit the HTML code to change the look of the page. If you want to learn more about creating and editing HTML code, there are many books available on the topic.

Editing HTML Code to Use a New Background

You can use other images as a background by changing the reference in the HTML code and by placing the image file in the same location as the previous file.

To Change the Background Image

1 In the Internet Explorer, select View and Source from the menu.

2 Change the third line of the source code to the following:

```
<BODY background = Mcst.jpg>
```

This image was one you copied to your completed files folder in a previous lesson.

3 Close Notepad and save the changes.

4 Select View and Refresh from the menu to view the results of this change (see Figure 18.30).

5 Close the browser.

continues

To Change the Background Image (continued)

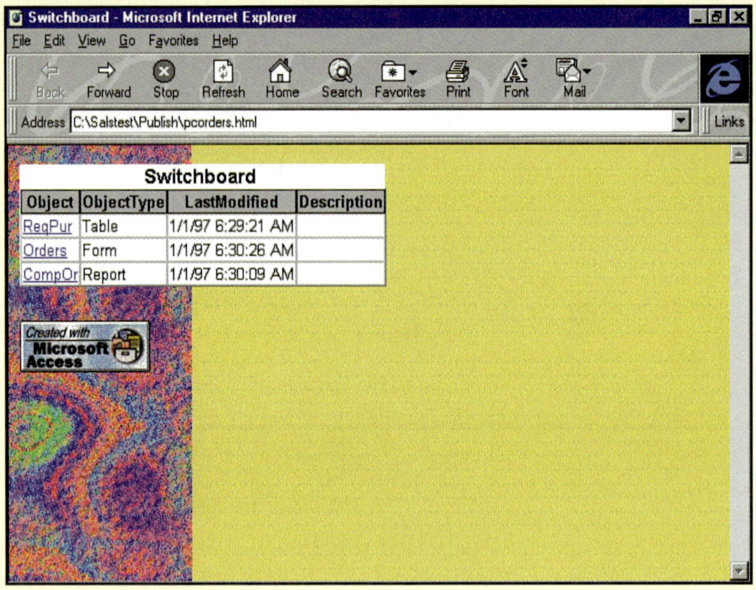

Figure 18.30
The background pattern may also be changed by editing the source code.

Inside Stuff

If you wanted to use another image, such as your own company logo, you could edit this line and replace msaccess.jpg with your own image file. The image file must be of a type that is supported by your browser. The file extension indicates the type of image file.

Lesson 6: Publishing Forms and Reports on the Internet

Client software
Client software communicates between you and the computer. Internet Explorer is a client software.

Server software
Server software handles communication between computers.

Microsoft NT
Microsoft NT is an operating system used for Local Area Networks.

UNIX
UNIX is a non-proprietary operating system language for mainframe computers. It is commonly used to run servers for Internet communication.

To publish your documents on the Internet, you need to transfer them to a computer that is running Internet *server software*. This could be a personal computer, a LAN server, or a larger mainframe computer. Some server software runs on *Microsoft NT*, but many servers run other server software such as *UNIX*. The following lesson is provided as a guide, but it is likely that you will have to adapt the instructions shown to fit the requirements of your server's software.

Copying your files to a server requires that you have:

- Permission to write files on the server's disks and the address of the folder into which you can copy your files
- A working connection to the server by *LAN* or dial-up Internet service
- A program to transfer files from a personal computer to a server

You need to check with your *Internet service provider* or your network administrator to determine your authoring privileges and the location of the file or folder into which you may store your files. These locations almost certainly differ from the following examples in this lesson. Substitute your specific information for those examples shown.

LAN
LAN stands for Local Area Network. This consists of a group of personal computers connected through a computer that coordinates their communications with each other and the outside world.

ISP
ISP stands for Internet Service Provider. An ISP can supply the connection between your home computer and the Internet.

FTP
FTP stands for File Transfer Protocol. It is a method for transferring files between computers over a network or the Internet.

There are many simple programs available at no cost to assist you in transferring your files to a server. They use a common method called *FTP*. The program used in the following lesson is Microsoft Web Publishing Wizard (WPW) version 1.0. It is a relatively small program (29 Kilobytes) and may be downloaded from Microsoft's Web page at

`http://www.microsoft.com/windows/software/webpost`

or search for Web Publish at the Microsoft home page at

`http://www.microsoft.com`

Open the text file Readme.txt, which comes with the program, for additional information about the program.

You can gain access to the Internet through one server and publish your Web pages to another server. In the example shown in this lesson, the author connects to the Microsoft Network using a dial-up modem and Microsoft's Internet Explorer. He then publishes the Web pages to a university mainframe computer named Orphan that uses the UNIX operating system.

To Publish Your Pages to a Server

1. **To launch the Web Publishing Wizard, click the Start button.**
2. **Select the Programs folder, then Accessories, then Internet Tools, and click Web Publishing Wizard.**

   The first window of the wizard is displayed.

If you have problems...

If you do not find the Web Publishing Wizard in the location described above, search for a file named Wpwiz.

3. **Click the Next button.**

   The next dialog box enables you to specify the file or folders you want to publish. By placing all of the files and images in one folder, Publish, this can be accomplished by selecting this folder.

4. **Enter the location of your Publish folder, as shown (see Figure 18.31).**

   Use the Browse Folders button if necessary to locate the folder.

5. **Click the Next button.**

   Your Web page publishing server is identified using this dialog box. The example shown in Figure 18.32 is a site used by the author.

   If the server where you have permission to publish is not shown in the Web server list, click the New button and follow the directions to identify your Web server.

continues

To Publish Your Pages to a Server (continued)

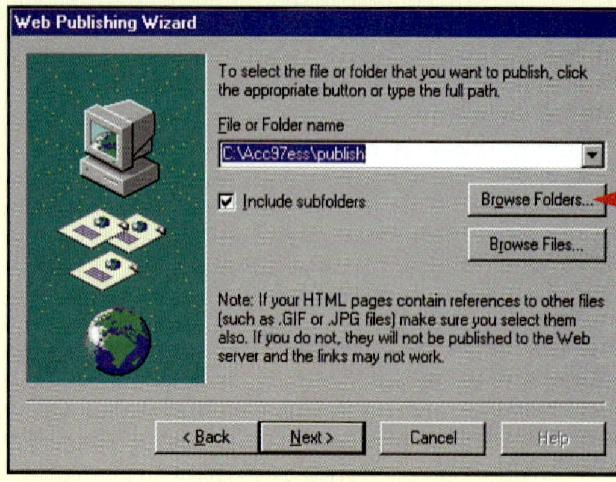

Figure 18.31 A folder can be selected and all of its contents transferred.

6 Select your publishing Web server.

You must have permission to save files on this server.

Figure 18.32 Web Publishing Wizard window showing the publishing server that can be used.

7 Click Next and then click the Finish button.

The Web Publishing Wizard is now ready to connect to the server that will host the pages through your connection service. The wizard launches a program to connect you to your server. Select the method you use to connect to the server. Your dialog box displays your current Internet connection method. The example shown in Figure 18.33 is the connection used by the author.

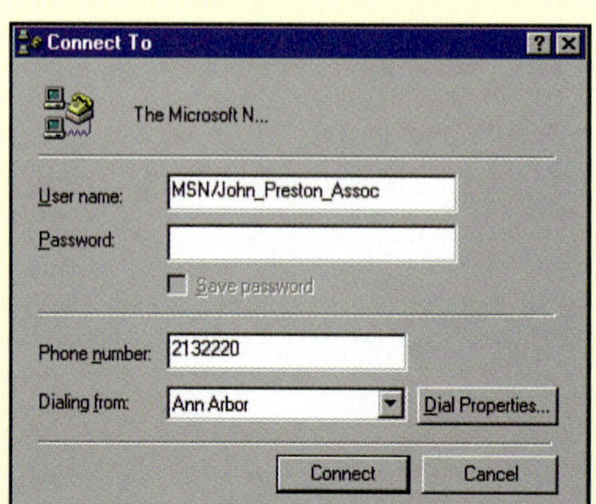

Figure 18.33 The wizard starts a connection to the Internet.

8 Enter your password and click the Connect button.

The Web Publishing Wizard connects to your Internet service provider. The wizard then connects to your Web publishing server and requests another password for this server.

9 Enter your user name and password, then click OK.

The wizard transfers your files automatically.

10 Click OK when the transfer is complete.

The Web Publishing Wizard disconnects from both servers.

11 Test your new pages. Open your browser and enter the location of your files followed by your home page name. Use the following format for the location name (see Figure 18.34):

```
http://www.yourserver.com/yourfolder/pcorders.html
```

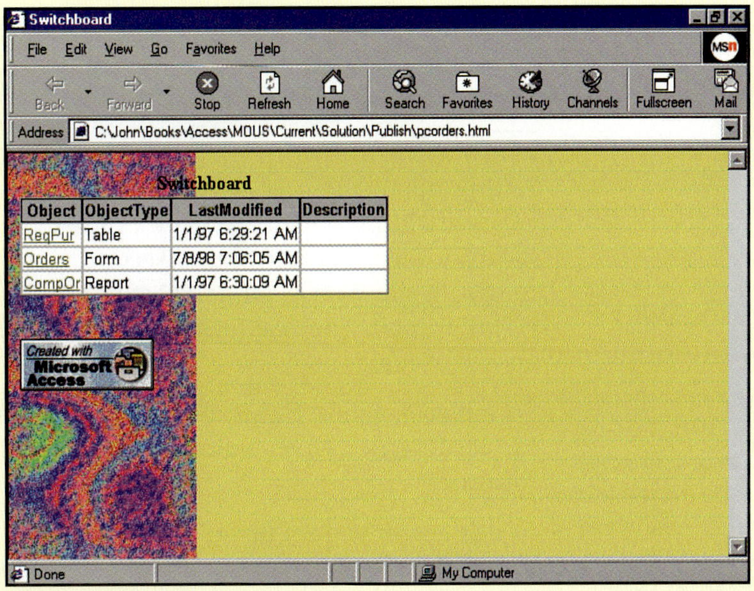

Figure 18.34
The pcorders page as viewed on the Internet using Internet Explorer 4.0.

If you have problems...

If you do not see the Microsoft Access logo on your page, it may be due to a problem with a case-sensitive Web server. Edit the source code of pcorders.html as described earlier and make sure that the name of the linked file contains the same upper- and lowercase characters as the filenames in your Publish folder. If not, edit the document to match the filenames (or edit the filenames to match the source code) and publish your folder to the Web server again.

12 Close the browser and sign off of your Internet provider, if necessary.

Inside Stuff

Many servers use an unusual character as part of the folder name. This character, "~", is called a tilde.

Your server's extension tells you what type of server it is: edu=education, com=commercial, mil=military, org=nonprofit, and gov=government.

Lesson 7: Creating an Interactive Form on the Web

The World Wide Web has great potential for businesses or other organizations that want to gather information from clients or other interested parties. Access has the capability of taking an existing form, putting it on the Web, then gathering information into one or more tables of the same database.

Exam Notes

Interactive forms on the Web is a feature that is not supported by all servers. If you are not using a server that has Microsoft NT with ActiveX support, this feature will not work. You can still learn how to create an ODBC data source and an ActiveX Server Page that will meet test requirements.

ODBC
A standard protocol for connecting to a variety of external database servers or files. The acronym stands for Open Database Connectivity.

ASP
A Web page format, used instead of HTML, that allows data entered into an online form to be entered into an Access table. The acronym stands for ActiveX Server Page.

Setting up an Internet order form is a two-step process. First, you need to create an *ODBC* (Open Database Connectivity) data source and link it to the database file you want to use. Second, you need to save the form you want to use on the Web as an *ASP* (ActiveX Server Page) file format instead of an HTML format. The ASP format allows the form to pass the data through to an Access table.

To build Dynamic HTML links to your database using ASP files, you must use an Internet server that is using Microsoft Internet Information Server software.

In this lesson you set up an ODBC data source, then save a form in ASP format. You use a database set up for a genealogical society. It contains a table that contains information about potential society volunteers and their areas of interest. It also contains a form that can be interactive if it is published on the Web to a Microsoft NT Server running Microsoft BackOffice with ActiveX support.

Creating an ODBC Data Source

In this procedure you create the files that would be used if you had the necessary connection to a suitably equipped server.

To Create an ODBC Data Source

1. **Make a copy of the data file Proj1804 from the Project-18 folder on the CD, place it in your own directory on your disk, then rename the copy `Volunteers`. Do not open the database at this time.**

Access

2 Click the Start button on the Windows taskbar. Select Settings, Control Panel from the Start menu.

3 If you are using Windows 95, Windows 98, or Windows NT Workstation 4.0, double-click the 32bit ODBC icon. If you are using Windows NT Workstation 3.51, double-click the ODBC icon.

The ODBC Data Source Administrator dialog box is displayed (see Figure 18.35).

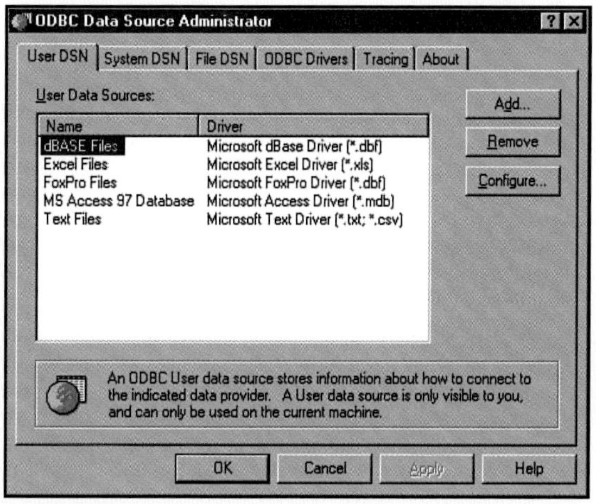

Figure 18.35
The ODBC Data Source Administrator enables you to add a driver for your Web form.

If you have problems...

If the ODBC icon does not appear in your control panel, you need to install the Microsoft SQL Server ODBC driver from the original Access installation disc.

4 Click the Add button.

The Create New Data Source dialog box is displayed.

5 Make sure to scroll down, if necessary, select the Microsoft Access Driver, and click Finish.

The ODBC Microsoft Access 97 Setup dialog box is displayed.

6 Enter `Volunteers on the Web` as the Data Source Name and `Volunteer Form` as the Description.

Your dialog box should look like Figure 18.36. Now you need to identify the database to be connected to this data source.

7 Click the Select button in the Database section. Find and select the Volunteers database from the Select Database dialog box.

8 Click the OK button to return to the ODBC Data Source Administrator.

continues

To Create an ODBC Data Source (continued)

Volunteers on the Web is now included in the list of drivers (see Figure 18.37).

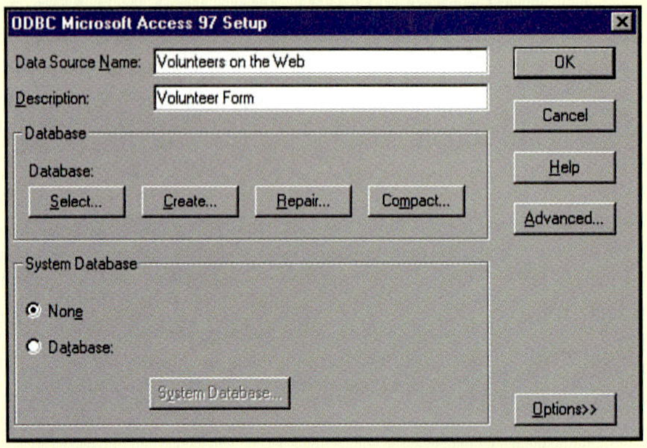

Figure 18.36
A Data Source Name and a Description have been added to the Setup dialog box.

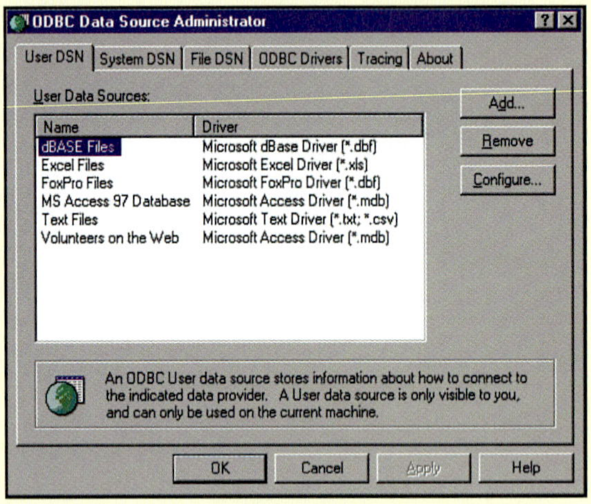

Figure 18.37
The new driver is listed in the ODBC Data Source Administrator.

9. **Click OK.**

This returns you to the Control Panel.

10. **Close the Control Panel.**

Saving a Form in ASP Format

The first part of the two-step process to put a form on the Web is complete. Now you need to save the existing form in the Volunteers database in ASP format.

To Save a Form in ASP Format

1. **Open the `Volunteers` database and click the Forms tab, if necessary. Highlight the Volunteers and their Areas of Interest form, but do not open it.**

Access

❷ **Choose File, Save As/Export from the menu. Select the To an External File or Database option and click OK.**

The Save Form dialog box is displayed.

❸ **Select a folder where you want to store this file. Select Microsoft Active Server Pages from the list of choices in the Save as type box (see Figure 18.38).**

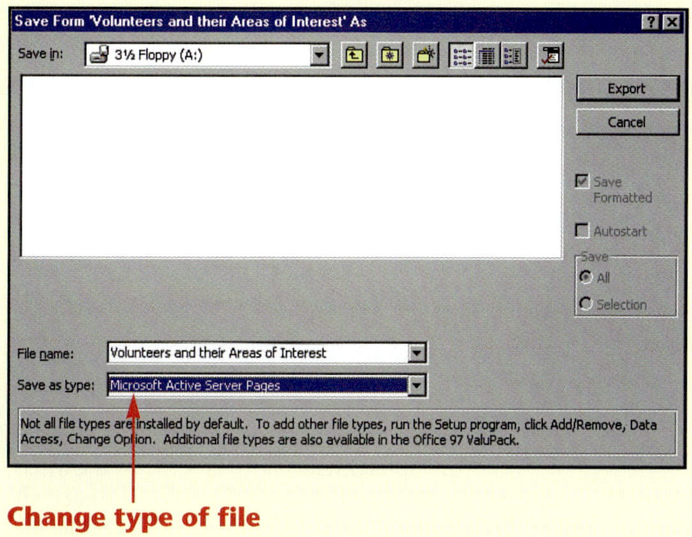

Figure 18.38
The Save Form dialog box provides several options for exporting forms.

❹ **Click Export.**

The Microsoft Active Server Pages Output Options dialog box opens.

❺ **Enter the name of the database upon which the form is based in the Data Source Name box.**

❻ **Enter the URL of your server in the Server URL box.**

This information is used to connect the form, its database, and the server with ActiveX support (see Figure 18.39).

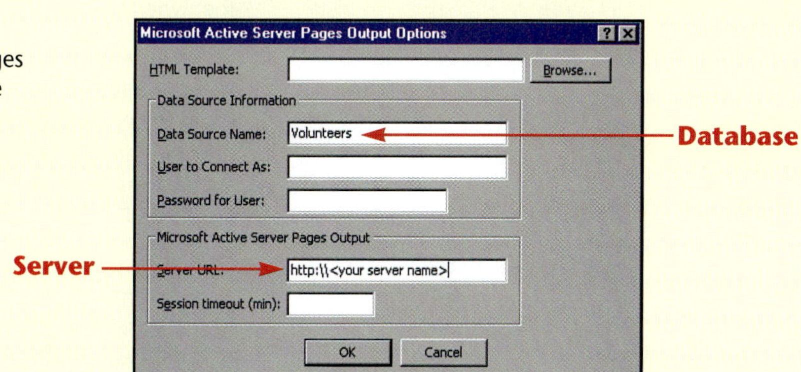

Figure 18.39
The Active Server Pages Output Options page provides information used to operate the form on the Web.

continues

To Save a Form in ASP Format (continued)

7 If you have the use of the appropriate server, use a Web browser and open the form. Otherwise, close the database.

If you have completed your session on the computer, exit Access and shut down Windows before you turn off the computer. Otherwise, continue with the "Checking Your Skills" and "Applying Your Skills" sections in this project.

Project Summary

To	Do This
Add hyperlinks from forms to Word 97 documents	Open the form in Design view. Click the Insert Hyperlink button on the toolbar. Specify the document and its folder location. Specify the particular bookmark in the document (optional).
Add hyperlinks from forms to Excel 97 spreadsheets	Open the form in Design view. Click the Insert Hyperlink button on the toolbar. Specify the name of the spreadsheet and its folder location. Specify the named range in the spreadsheet (optional).
Save tables, queries, forms, and reports as HTML pages	Choose File and Save as HTML from the menu. Select the database objects you want to place on the Internet. Choose a template. Create a home page to serve as a switchboard. Copy any supplementary images to the same folder.
View HTML pages on a local drive using a browser	Launch the browser. (Connection to the Internet is optional.) Select File and Open from the menu. Open the home page. Test the hyperlinks.
Edit HTML pages with Notepad	Select View and Source from the menu. You can edit the source HTML code directly using the Notepad window. For more powerful editing functions, click the Edit button on the toolbar to open the HTML document in Word 97.
Publish pages on the Internet	Obtain permission to publish Web pages to an Internet server. Write down the URL of the folder that will contain your pages, your user name, and password. Download a copy of Microsoft's Web Publishing Wizard. Specify the folder that contains your HTML pages and the associated images. Specify the server that will host your pages. Connect to the Internet and the wizard will transfer the files in the folder.

To	Do This
Create an ODBC data source	Click the Start button on the Windows taskbar. Open the Control Panel and click the ODBC icon. Click the Add button, choose Microsoft Access Driver, and click Finish. Enter the form name in the Data Source Name box. Click Select, locate and select the database that contains the form, and click OK.
Save a form in ASP format	Open the database and select the form. Choose File, Save As/Export, To an External File or Database, and click OK. Use the Microsoft Active Server Pages option in the Save as type box. Click Export. Enter the name of the database in the Data Source Name box and the URL of the server in the Server URL box.

Checking Your Skills

True/False

For each of the following statements, circle *T* or *F* to indicate whether the statement is true or false.

__T __F **1.** Hyperlinks can only be used to jump to other HTML pages.

__T __F **2.** You can place hyperlinks in Access 97 reports.

__T __F **3.** Static HTML pages can be viewed but are no longer linked to the database. They cannot be used to edit data in the database table.

__T __F **4.** It is possible to use a browser to check HTML files without connecting to the Internet.

__T __F **5.** You can use a word processing program like Word 97 to edit HTML documents.

__T __F **6.** Before you can create a hyperlink to a document, you must create a bookmark in that document.

__T __F **7.** You can use the Web Wizard to create HTML documents of a specific Access object.

__T __F **8.** When using the Web Wizard to save an Access object in HTML format, you have to save the object in static format.

__T __F **9.** In a browser, documents are stored in a temporary memory queue when they are opened, enabling the user to move backward and forward through this list of documents.

__T __F **10.** When a form is saved in HTML format, the default layout is tabular, even if the form was not originally created in that layout.

Multiple Choice

Circle the letter of the correct answer for each of the following questions.

1. Once a hyperlink has been used to jump from an Access form to a Word 97 document, how do you return to the Access form?
   a. Press the Page Up button on the keyboard.
   b. Use the roller button on the mouse.
   c. Press the Back button on the toolbar.
   d. Press the Forward button on the toolbar.

2. You cannot insert hyperlinks into which of the following database objects in Access 97? (Circle all that apply.)
   a. reports
   b. tables
   c. queries
   d. forms

3. Which of the following is not necessary to publish your HTML pages to the Internet?
   a. permission to save files on the server's disk
   b. a detailed knowledge of UNIX commands for saving files
   c. a connection from your computer to the server
   d. a program to transfer the files from your computer to the server

4. Which of the following best describes HTML?
   a. a code for describing a document so it can be viewed by a variety of computers
   b. an application software similar to Word or Access
   c. a type of Web browser like Netscape or Internet Explorer
   d. a Web server operating system such as Windows NT or UNIX

5. Which of the following is not a function of a Web publishing software package, such as Web Publishing Wizard?
   a. search for appropriate pages on the Internet that can provide related hyperlinks
   b. transfer files from your personal computer to the Web server
   c. establish a connection between your personal computer and the Web server
   d. reduce the size of your files to lessen the cost of storage

6. If you edit an HTML document that is currently opened on your browser, to see the effect of the changes you _____.
   a. close the editor and the changes are immediately visible
   b. must close the browser before you make any changes
   c. choose View, Refresh from the menu bar
   d. have to close the file, close the browser, then reopen the browser and reopen the file

Access

7. To publish your documents on the Internet, you need to transfer them to a computer that is running Internet server software on _____.

   a. a personal computer

   b. a LAN server

   c. a mainframe computer

   d. any of the above are acceptable

8. Setting up an Internet order form requires the following two steps:

   a. Create an ASP data source linked to the form, and save the database as an HTML file.

   b. Create an ODBC data source linked to the database file, and save the form as an ASP file.

   c. Create an HTML data source linked to the form, and save the database as an ASP file.

   d. Create an ASP data source linked to the database file, and save the form as an ODBC file.

9. An advantage of using the Internet or a company intranet to disseminate information is _____.

   a. you don't have to worry about updating the information

   b. anyone who wants to can change the information

   c. you retain control of the data

   d. there's no cost involved

10. Which of the following is not true about information that is published on a company intranet?

   a. It is updated automatically.

   b. People who need access to the information can view it when they need to.

   c. You can insert links from your forms, documents, spreadsheets, or presentations to sites provided by others.

   d. Information can be collected via the intranet.

Completion

In the blanks provided, write the correct answer for each of the following questions.

1. A communication network within a company that uses the same software and standards as the Internet is called a(n) _____________.

2. Internet Explorer and Navigator are examples of _____________.

3. Special connections between Office 97 applications and sites on the Internet are called _____________.

4. The address for a location on the Internet is known by the acronym _____________.

5. The standard programming language for writing documents that may be viewed on the Internet by many different browsers is known by the acronym _____________.

6. The graphical interface that links sites on the Internet and enables the user to easily jump from one site to another is known as the ______________.

7. JPEG is a type of ______________ format that is commonly used with Internet pages.

8. An HTML document that is similar to a switchboard form in Access is known as a(n) ______________.

9. Internet Explorer is an example of ______________ software that is used to communicate between you and the computer.

10. ______________ is a Web page format, used instead of HTML, that allows data entered into an online form to be entered into an Access table.

Matching

In the blank next to each of the following terms or phrases, write the letter of the corresponding term or phrase. (Note that some letters may be used more than once.)

a. Open Database Connectivity (ODBC)
b. HTML
c. ActiveX Server Page (ASP)
d. World Wide Web
e. Internet
f. hyperlink
g. File Transfer Protocol (FTP)
h. browser
i. edu
j. named ranges

_______ 1. Connections to other documents, spreadsheets, databases, or presentations on your computer or on the net

_______ 2. Something used in Excel that is similar to bookmarks in Word

_______ 3. Worldwide computer communication network that is based on open standards for operating systems and communication

_______ 4. Netscape Navigator

_______ 5. Used instead of HTML to create an interactive access form on the net

_______ 6. Programming language used for writing documents that may be viewed on the Internet

_______ 7. Extension that would be found on an educational server

_______ 8. A standard protocol for connecting to external database servers or files

_______ 9. A method for transferring files between computers over a network or the Internet

_______ 10. A graphical interface that links sites on the Internet and enables the user to easily jump from one site to another

Applying Your Skills

Practice

The following exercises enable you to practice the skills you have learned in this project. Take a few minutes to work through these exercises now. If you are saving your files on a floppy disk, you may need to start with an empty disk to assure that you have enough room for all the files.

Editing HTML to Change a Background Image

To do so, complete the following steps:

1. Use the Windows Explorer to copy another JPEG image file from its location on C:\Program Files\Microsoft Office\Templates\Access to your Publish folder.
2. Launch your browser. Open the CompOr_1 HTML document and edit the line that determines the background image so that it refers to the new image.
3. View the HTML document with your browser to see if the new background image was used successfully.

To check your document for use by visually handicapped users or those without graphical browsers, complete the following steps:

Some visually handicapped users have partial sight and rely upon large, clear typefaces. Others rely upon special voice synthesizers that convert text into audio. Designing your pages so they are easy to read and contain text alternatives to graphical options is good design for everyone, but it is very important for those who cannot use graphical interfaces well.

1. Open the `CompOr_1` HTML document that was created in Lesson 3 and look for the following:
   - Are there any graphical objects used as hyperlinks? Is a text-based hyperlink provided as an alternative?
   - Is the typeface large enough to be easily read?
2. Open the `PC Purchase` database and edit the design of the original CompOr report.
3. Increase the font size from 8 points to 12 points so it is easier to read.
4. Adjust the field widths as necessary.
5. Save the report again as an HTML document.
6. View the report with a browser.

Saving a Report That Is Longer Than One Page

In the following exercise, you save a report from the Library database as two HTML pages.

To save a multipage report as HTML, complete the following steps:

1. Copy the Proj1805 file from the Project-18 folder on the CD and rename it `Library13`.

2. Open the `Library13` database and select the Books Grouped by Type of Book report, but do not open it.
3. Use File, Save As HTML.
4. Use the wizard to publish the report as a static HTML page. The wizard creates two HTML pages.
5. Close the database.
6. Open the first page in your browser.
7. Scroll to the bottom of the page. Use the hyperlink buttons that were automatically added to the page by the wizard to go to the second page.
8. Use the Back button on your browser's toolbar to go back to page one of the report. Leave the page and browser open for use in the next exercise.

Changing the Background of the Library Report by Editing the HTML Code

In this exercise, edit the HTML code of the report to add a background.

To add a background image to a report, complete the following steps:

1. Use Windows' Start button or taskbar to open the Windows Explorer or My Computer program. Go to the folder on your computer that contains the Access images and copy an image file.
2. Paste the image in the same folder that contains the Books Grouped by Type of Book_1.html file.
3. Open the `Books Grouped by Type of Book_1` HTML page in your Web browser, if necessary.
4. View the HTML source code.
5. Find the line of code that contains the title. It looks like the following:

```
<TITLE>Books</TITLE>
```

6. Insert a new line after the title line. Enter a line of code similar to the following but replace stones.jpg with the name of the image file that you selected:

```
<BODY background = stones.jpg>
```

7. Save the changes to the source and close the text editor program.
8. Choose your browser's refresh option to reload the report. It should have the new background.
9. Examine your choice of backgrounds. The stones.jpg image is not a good choice because it is hard to read the left side of the report.

10. Try other images to find one that does not interfere with the readability of the report.
11. Close the browser.

Adding a HyperLink to a Word Document

In this exercise, you add a hyperlink from a form to a Word 97 document.

To add a hyperlink to a form, complete the following steps:

1. Copy the Proj1806 file from the Project-18 folder on the CD and rename it `SBMusic15`. Copy the Proj1807 file from the Project-18 folder on the CD and rename it `Customer Letter`.
2. Open the `SBMusic15` database. Use the password `Music!`.
3. Open the `AutoForm` form in Design view.
4. Insert a hyperlink to the Customer Letter document.
5. Drag the hyperlink to the lower part of the detail section of the form.
6. Click the View button to switch to Form view. Click the hyperlink to test it.
7. Click the Back button on the Web toolbar to return to the form.
8. Close the form and save the changes. Close the database.

Challenge

The following challenges enable you to use your problem-solving skills. For these exercises, you will open files that are similar to the ones you have been working on. You will set passwords and restrict editing options, and create switchboards using the Switchboard manager. Take time to work through these exercises now.

Saving a Club Report as an HTML Document and Changing the Background

In this exercise, save the List of Members report as a series of HTML pages and edit the HTML code to display a background image.

Open the `Club` database that you worked with in Project 16, "Filtering Data Using Parameters and Form Filters," that does not have the password and other security features. Select the report that lists the members. Then, save the pages as HTML. Close the database.

Use Windows Explorer or My Computer to find the pages that were created. Double-click on the first page. This should launch your browser and display the page. Edit the HTML source code to include an image as the background of the first page.

View the page in the browser. Use the hyperlink buttons at the bottom of the page to move to the second page. Notice it does not have the new background. Edit each of the other pages that were created as part of the report so that they all have the same background. Browse through the pages to make sure that they all have the new background, then close the browser.

Saving a Customer Research Database Form for Interactive Use on the Web

In this exercise you create a new form, add an ODBC driver, and save a form in ASP format.

Locate the Customer Research15 database that you used in Project 16 that does not have the security features and rename it `Customer Research16`. Select the Viewing Data table. Create a new form using the AutoForm option and save it as `Viewing Data`.

Open the ODBC Data Source Administrator from the Control Panel. Add a new data source that uses a Microsoft Access 97 driver. Use the Viewing Data form as the Data Source and Select the Customer Research16 database.

Switch back to the database if necessary. Select the Viewing Data form. Save it as a Microsoft Active Server Page. Use Windows Explorer or My Computer to verify that the file was created in your folder. Close the database.

Adding a Link to the Vending Database to Use a Shared Document

You have found that another division in your company has gone to the trouble of qualifying PC Vendors and has placed the list of approved vendors on the company network. Your vending machines are becoming more computerized all the time, and you would like to add a link from one of your forms to that document. In this exercise, you create an AutoForm based on the Repairs table and add a hyperlink to the Approved Vendors document that you used in this Project.

Locate the Vending14 database that you used in Project 16 that does not have the security features and rename it `Vending15`. Open the `Vending15` database and select the Repairs table. Use the button on the toolbar to create an AutoForm.

Switch to Design View and insert a hyperlink to the Approved Vendors document that you created in this Project. (You can also copy Proj1801 from the Project-18 folder on the CD and rename it `Approved Vendors`.) Close the form and save it as `Suppliers`. Close the database.

Securing the Video Store Database and Adding a Switchboard

You have reached an agreement with another video store in town to refer customers to each other if either of you is out of a particular title. In this exercise, prepare an interactive form to be placed on a server that would allow the other store to use the Rental Activity form to see if a video is checked out.

Locate the Video Store13 database that you used in Project 16 that does not have the security features and rename it `Video Store14`. Open the ODBC Data Source Administrator from the Control Panel. Add a new data source that uses a Microsoft Access 97 driver. Use the Rental Activity form as the Data Source and Select the Video Store14 database.

Open the `Video Store14` database. Select the Rental Activity form. Save it as a Microsoft Active Server Page. Use Windows Explorer or MY Computer to verify that the file was created in your folder. Then, close the database.

Adding a Hyperlink to the Home Inventory Database

You can use hyperlinks to jump from one object in a database to another. In this exercise, you add a hyperlink from a form to a report in the Home Inventory database.

Locate the Home Inventory13 database that you used in Project 16 that does not have the security features and rename it `Home Inventory14`. Open the `Home Inventory14` database. Find the `Add Inventory Item` form and open it in Design view. Insert a hyperlink that links to the Home Inventory14 database and the List by Value report.

Move the hyperlink to the Form Footer. Switch to Form view and test the hyperlink. Once the report is open, use the Web toolbar to move back to the form. Then, close the form and save the changes.

PinPoint Assessment

PinPoint Training

You have completed the project and the associated lessons, as well as the "Checking Your Skills" and "Applying Your Skills" sections. Now use the PinPoint software Evaluation mode to assess your comprehension of the specific exam tasks you have just learned. You can also use the PinPoint Trainer mode and the SHOW ME tutorials to practice these specific exam tasks.

appendix A

Working with Windows 95

In this appendix you will learn the basic components of the Windows 95 operating system and some skills needed to use Windows 95 efficiently.

Objectives

- Start Windows 95
- Use the Mouse
- Understand the Start Menu
- Identify the Elements of a Window
- Manipulate Windows
- Exit the Windows 95 Program

Why Would I Do This?

Graphical user interface (GUI)
A computer application that uses pictures, graphics, menus, and commands to help users communicate with their computers.

Desktop
The background of the Windows screen, on which windows, icons, and dialog boxes appear.

Icon
A picture that represents an application, a file, or a system resource.

Shortcut
Gives you quick access to frequently used objects so you don't have to look through menus each time you need to use that object.

Microsoft Windows 95 is a powerful operating environment that enables you to access the power of DOS without memorizing DOS commands and syntax. Windows 95 uses a *graphical user interface* (GUI) so that you can easily see onscreen the tools that you need to complete specific file- and program-management tasks.

This appendix, an overview of the Windows 95 environment, is designed to help you learn the basics of Windows 95.

Lesson 1: Starting Windows 95

The first thing you need to know about Windows is how to start the software. In this lesson, you learn how to start Windows; however, before you can start Windows, it must be installed on your computer. If you need to install Windows, refer to your Windows 95 manual or ask your instructor for assistance.

In most cases, Windows starts automatically when you turn on your computer. If your system is set up differently, you must start Windows from the DOS prompt (such as C:\>). Try starting the Windows program now.

Access

To Start Windows 95

Taskbar
Contains the Start button, buttons for each open window, and the current time.

Start button
A click of the Start button opens the Start menu.

1 Turn on your computer and monitor.

Most computers display technical information about the computer and the operating software installed on it.

If Windows starts, you can skip step 2. Otherwise, you will see the DOS prompt `C:\>`.

2 At the DOS prompt, type `win` and press Enter.

When you start the Windows program, a Microsoft Windows 95 banner displays for a few seconds; then the *desktop* appears (see Figure A.1).

Figure A.1
The Windows 95 desktop appears a few seconds after a Windows 95 banner.

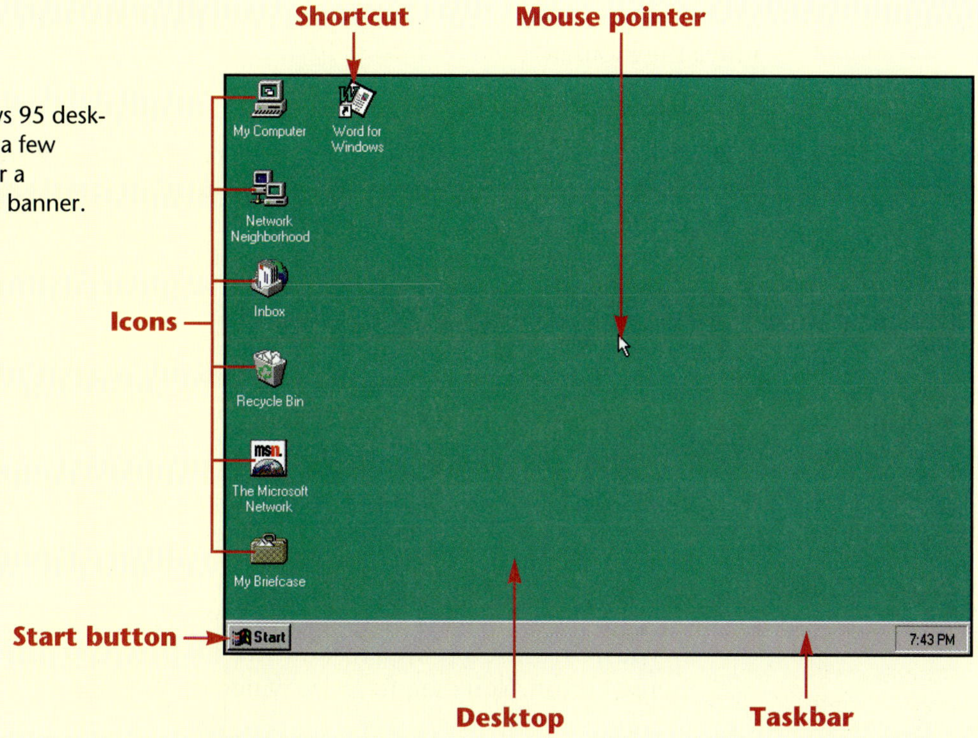

Program *icons* that were created during installation (such as My Computer, Recycle Bin, and Network Neighborhood) are displayed on the desktop. Other icons might also appear, depending on how your system is set up. *Shortcuts* to frequently used objects (such as documents, printers, and network drives) can be placed on the desktop. The *Taskbar* appears along the bottom edge of the desktop. The *Start button* appears at the left end of the Taskbar.

Mouse
A pointing device used in many programs to make choices, select data, and otherwise communicate with the computer.

Pull-down menus
Menus that cascade downward into the screen whenever you select a command from the menu bar.

Dialog box
A window that opens onscreen to provide information about the current action or to ask the user to provide additional information to complete the action.

Mouse pointer
A symbol that appears onscreen to indicate the current location of the mouse.

Lesson 2: Using the Mouse

Windows is designed to be used with a *mouse,* so it's important that you learn how to use a mouse correctly. With a little practice, using a mouse is as easy as pointing to something with your finger. You can use the mouse to select icons, to make selections from *pull-down menus* and *dialog boxes,* and to select objects that you want to move or resize.

In the Windows desktop, you can use a mouse to

- Open windows
- Close windows
- Open menus
- Choose menu commands
- Rearrange onscreen items, such as icons and windows

The position of the mouse is indicated onscreen by a *mouse pointer.* Usually, the mouse pointer is an arrow, but it sometimes changes shape depending on the current action.

Mouse pad
A pad that provides a uniform surface for the mouse to slide on.

Onscreen, the mouse pointer moves according to the movements of the mouse on your desk or on a *mouse pad*. To move the mouse pointer, simply move the mouse.

There are four basic mouse actions:

- *Click*. To point to an item, and then press and quickly release the left mouse button. You click to select an item, such as an option on a menu. To cancel a selection, click an empty area of the desktop. Unless otherwise specified, you use the left mouse button for all mouse actions.
- *Double-click*. To point to an item, and then press and release the left mouse button twice, as quickly as possible. You double-click to open or close windows and to start applications from icons.
- *Right-click*. To point to an item, and then press and release the right mouse button. This opens a context menu, which gives you a shortcut to frequently used commands. To cancel a context menu, click the left mouse button outside the menu.
- *Drag*. To point to an item, press and hold down the left mouse button as you move the pointer to another location, and then release the mouse button. You drag to resize windows, move icons, and scroll.

If you have problems...

If you double-click but nothing happens, you may not be clicking fast enough. Try again.

Lesson 3: Understanding the Start Menu

Program folders
Represented by an icon of a file folder with an application window in front of it, program folders contain shortcut icons and other program folders.

The Start button on the Taskbar gives you access to your applications, settings, recently opened documents, the Find utility, the Run command, the Help system, and the Shut Down command. Clicking the Start button opens the Start menu. Choosing the Programs option at the top of the Start menu displays the Programs submenu, which lists the *program folders* on your system. Program folders are listed first, followed by shortcuts (see Figure A.2).

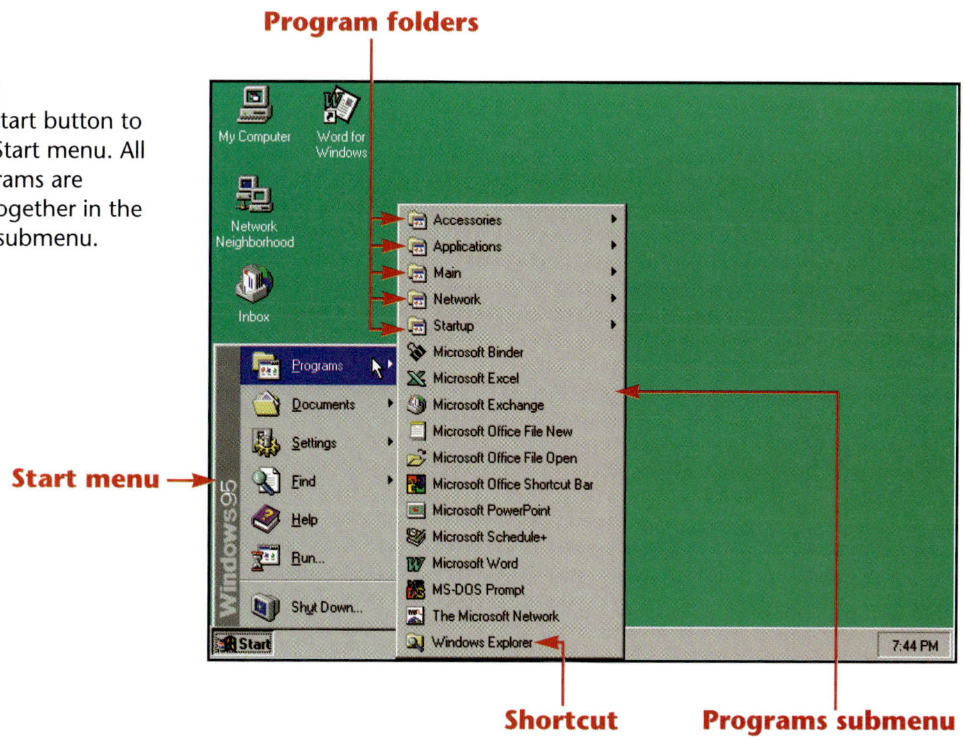

Figure A.2
Click the Start button to open the Start menu. All your programs are grouped together in the Programs submenu.

When the Start menu is open, moving the mouse pointer moves a selection bar through the menu options. When the selection bar highlights a menu command with a right-facing triangle, a submenu opens. Click the shortcut icon to start an application. If a menu command is followed by an ellipsis, clicking that command opens a dialog box.

Lesson 4: Identifying the Elements of a Window

In Windows 95, everything opens in a window. Applications, documents, and dialog boxes all open in windows. For example, double-clicking the My Computer icon opens the My Computer application into a window. Because window elements stay the same for all Windows applications, this section uses the My Computer window for illustration.

Title Bar

Across the top of each window is its title bar. A title bar contains the name of the open window, as well as three buttons to manipulate it. The Minimize button reduces the window to a button on the Taskbar. The Maximize button expands the window to fill the desktop. The Close button closes the window.

Menu Bar

The menu bar gives you access to the application's menus. Menus enable you to select options that perform functions or carry out commands (see Figure A.3). The File menu in My Computer, for example, enables you to open, save, and print files.

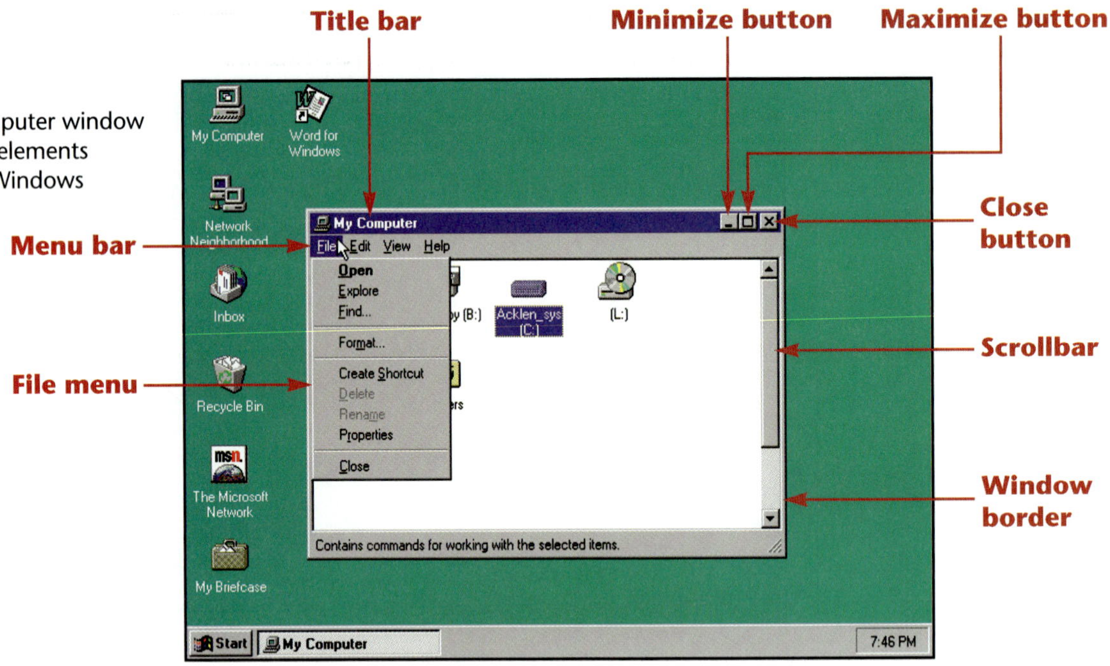

Figure A.3
The My Computer window has window elements found in all Windows applications.

Some menu options require you to enter additional information. When you select one of these options, a dialog box opens (see Figure A.4). You type the additional information, select from a list of options, or select a button. Most dialog boxes have a Cancel button, which closes the dialog box without saving the changes; an OK button, which closes the dialog box and saves the changes; and a Help button, which opens a Help window.

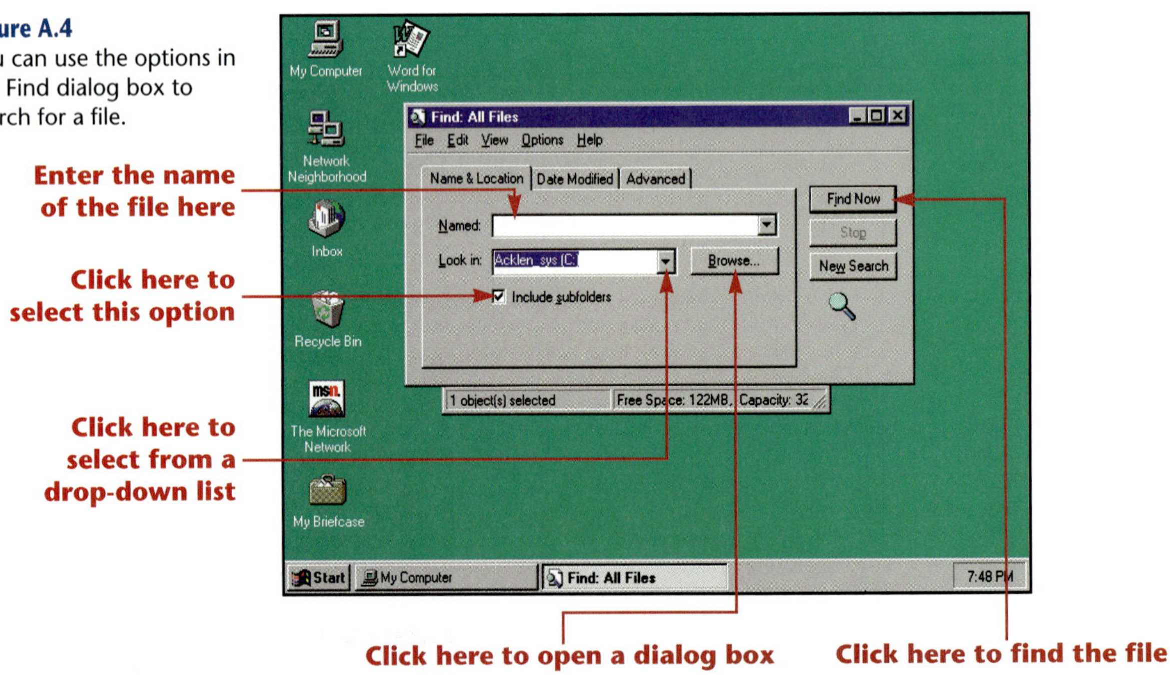

Figure A.4
You can use the options in the Find dialog box to search for a file.

Scrollbar

Scrollbars appear when you have more information in a window than is currently displayed onscreen. A horizontal scrollbar appears along the bottom of a window, and a vertical scrollbar appears along the right side of a window.

Window Border

The window border identifies the edge of the window. In most windows, it can be used to change the size of a window. The window corner is used to resize a window on two sides at the same time.

Lesson 5: Manipulating Windows

When you work with windows, you need to know how to arrange them. You can shrink the window into an icon or enlarge the window to fill the desktop. You can stack windows together or give them each an equal slice of the desktop.

Maximizing a Window

Maximize
To increase the size of a window so that it fills the entire screen.

You can *maximize* a window so that it fills the desktop. Maximizing a window gives you more space to work in. To maximize a window, click the Maximize button on the title bar.

Minimizing a Window

Minimize
To reduce a window to an icon.

When you *minimize* a window, it shrinks the window to an icon on the Taskbar. Even though you can't see the window anymore, the application stays loaded in the computer's memory. To minimize a window, click the Minimize button on the title bar.

Restoring a Window

When a window is maximized, the Maximize button changes into a Restore button. Clicking the Restore button restores the window back to the original size and position before the window was maximized.

Closing a Window

When you are finished working in a window, you can close the window by clicking the Close button. Closing an application window exits the program, removing it from memory. When you click the Close button, the window (on the desktop) and the window button (on the Taskbar) disappear.

Arranging Windows

Changing the size and position of a window enables you to see more than one application window, which makes copying and pasting data between programs much easier. You can also move a window to any location on the desktop. By moving application windows, you can arrange your work on the Windows desktop just as you arrange papers on your desk.

Use one of the following options to arrange windows:

Tile
To arrange open windows on the desktop so that they do not overlap.

Cascade
To arrange open windows on the desktop so that they overlap, with only the title bar of each window (behind the top window) displayed.

- Right-click the Taskbar and choose Tile Horizontally.
- Right-click the Taskbar and choose Tile Vertically. See Figure A.5 for an example.
- Right-click the Taskbar and choose Cascade. See Figure A.6 for an example.
- Click and drag the window's title bar to move the window around on the desktop.
- Click and drag a window border (or corner) to increase or decrease the size of the window.

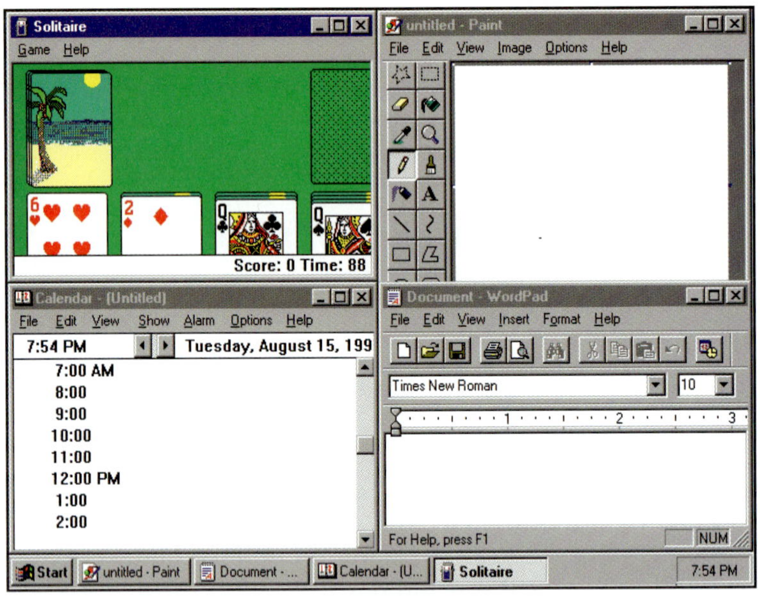

Figure A.5
The windows are tiled vertically across the desktop.

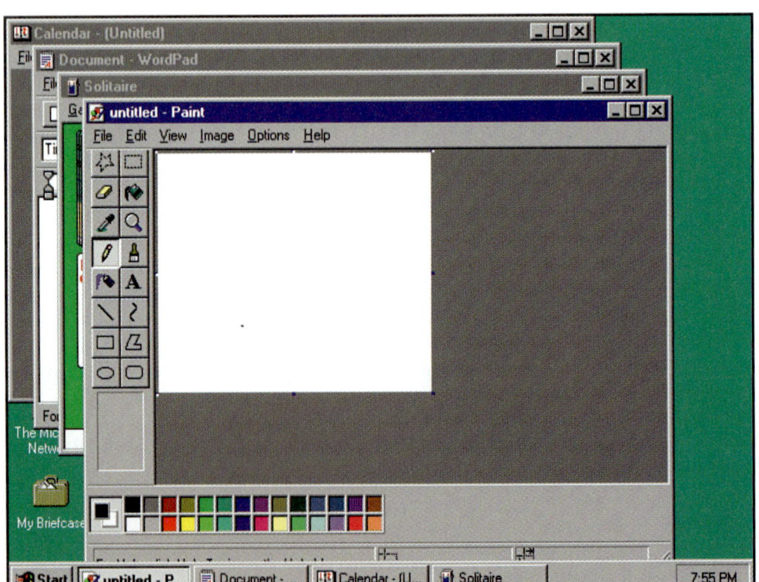

Figure A.6
The windows are cascaded on the desktop.

Access

Lesson 6: Exiting the Windows 95 Program

In Windows 95, you use the Shut Down command to exit the Windows 95 program. You should always use this command, which closes all open applications and files, before you turn off the computer. If you haven't saved your work in an application when you choose this command, you'll be prompted to save your changes before Windows shuts down.

To Exit Windows 95

1. **Click the Start button on the Taskbar.**
2. **Choose Shut Down.**
3. **Choose Shut down the computer.**
4. **Choose Yes.**

   Windows displays a message asking you to wait while the computer is shutting down. When this process is complete, a message appears telling you that you can safely turn off your computer.

appendix B

Glossary

Action An Access-defined function that performs a process within the database, table, form, or query.

Argument A value needed for a macro to perform its function.

ASCII A standard text format that all PCs can read.

ASP A Web page format, used instead of HTML, that allows data entered into an online form to be entered into an Access table. The acronym stands for ActiveX Server Page.

AutoForm A form that is created automatically by Access that includes all the fields in a table.

Client software Software that communicates between the user and the computer. Internet Explorer is a client software.

Clipboard A temporary storage area in Windows that stores copied data from which data can be pasted into documents and applications.

Column selector The area above a column in the design grid that enables the user to select the entire column.

Combo box A data entry list that looks up valid entries from a table, query, or source list.

Control Any graphical object selected from the toolbox, such as a text box, check box, or option button, that can be added to a form or report.

ControlTip A pop-up tip that can be added to a control; similar to a ScreenTip.

Criteria A test or set of conditions that limits the records included in a query. A single condition is a criterion.

Database A term used to refer to an application program, such as Access, or to a file created using that program. A database file can consist of related tables, queries, forms, reports, macros, and modules.

Datasheet view The view of the table used when entering or editing records. The field names entered appear in the first row, followed by any records entered in the table.

Default value A word, number, or date that is automatically entered in a field.

Delimiters The characters that separate fields; set off text from numbers; and separate parts of dates, times, and currencies.

Design grid Used to define the parameters of a query. Can be used to specify fields, sort order, and criteria when searching a database.

Design view The view of the table used when creating or changing fields. Columns are used for the field name, data type, and description.

Desktop The opening screen in Windows 95.

Dynaset A temporary table of data that is assembled from other tables and is not stored as a separate table. Also, a subset of records created as a result of a query.

Encryption Data scrambled and stored in coded form that is not easily read by someone who does not have the code.

Expression A predefined formula that performs some calculations. An expression in a report can be included in other Access objects, such as macros.

Expression Builder A program that helps the user create formulas for Access uses.

Field label Displays the field name.

Field separator The delimiter that separates the fields in a row of data.

Field text box A text box that holds a place for the contents of each field in the database.

Filter by Form A searching feature that enables you to type the desired value(s) into one or more fields on a blank form, then finds all of the other records that match those values.

Filter by Selection A searching feature that enables the user to select the desired value in a field, then finds all of the other records that match that value.

Find Duplicates Query Wizard A wizard that creates a query that finds records with duplicate field values in a single table or query.

Find Unmatched Query Wizard A wizard that creates a query that finds records in one table that have no related records in another table.

Fixed-width fields Fields that occupy a fixed position in the record, such as characters 5 through 12. No characters are used to separate the fields.

Folder An icon that represents a group of files.

Foreign key The corresponding field in another table that is linked to the primary key.

Form A type of object used to enter, edit, and view records. Think of a form as a fill-in-the-blanks screen.

Form headers (top of form) or form footers (bottom of form) Anything included in the section will be displayed onscreen in Form view when the form is used. Users can also add page headers and page footers, which are not visible onscreen in Form view, but appear when the form is printed.

Format The way data is displayed.

FTP File Transfer Protocol. This is a method for transferring files between computers over a network or the Internet.

Home page An HTML document containing links to other pages. It corresponds to a switchboard form in Access.

HTML The standard programming language used for writing documents that can be viewed on the Internet by many different browsers. The acronym stands for Hypertext Markup Language.

Hyperlinks Connections to other documents, spreadsheets, databases, or presentations on your computer or on the net.

Icon A pictorial representation of a program, a file, or other element.

Index A location guide built by Access for all primary key fields that helps speed up searching and sorting for that field. Indexes can also be created for other fields, as long as they are not OLE or Memo fields.

Indexed field A field for which Access builds a location guide; an index speeds up sorting or searching on a field.

Input mask A data entry structure that forces data entry into a selected format.

Internet The worldwide computer communication network that is based on open standards for operating systems and communication.

Intranet A communication network within a company that uses the same software and standards as the Internet.

ISP Internet Service Provider. An ISP can supply the connection between a home computer and the Internet.

Join The manner in which the common fields between two tables are associated.

Label Controls that are not tied to the table but are saved with the form. For example, a user may want to add a descriptive title to the form.

LAN Local Area Network. This consists of a group of personal computers connected through a computer that coordinates their communications with each other and the outside world.

List box A data entry list that looks up valid entries from a table, query, or source list, and does not allow the user to type in new data.

Macro A group of instructions that provides additional commands or functionality to a program.

Microsoft Windows NT An operating system used for local area networks.

Modules Used by power users to write and customize Access programs in the Visual Basic programming language.

Normalize Apply design rules to the tables in a database.

Null value A field with no data entered into it. It is not the same as an entry of zero.

Object A database element, such as a table, form, or report. Object can also refer to images, spreadsheets, graphs, or other items imported from other applications.

Object frame A rectangular area in a form or report that is used to display an object such as a picture.

Object Linking and Embedding (OLE) A set of standards that enables the user to insert objects, such as pictures or spreadsheets, from one document created with one application into documents created with another application.

ODBC A standard protocol for connecting to a variety of external database servers or files. The acronym stands for Open Database Connectivity.

Office Assistant An animated guide that helps the user search for help.

One-to-many A relationship that links one record in a table to many records in a different table.

Output The data that is printed or displayed that represents the answer to a request or the results of an analysis or process.

Parameter An entry that can be used as a filter or an argument in a formula.

Placeholder A character used to reserve a spot for a character in an input mask.

Primary key A field that contains a unique value for each record.

Property An attribute of a field that can be used to define characteristics of that field.

Query A question posed to the database that determines what information is retrieved.

Record selector The gray area to the left of a record in Datasheet view. Clicking in this area selects the entire record.

Relational database A database that has two or more tables that are linked together.

Relationship The connection between the two tables. This relationship connects a field in one table to a field in a second table. Relationships allow a user to draw information from more than one table at a time for forms or reports.

Reports Used to summarize and print data.

Row selector The gray area to the left of a field in Design view. Clicking a box in this area selects the entire row.

Sans serif A typeface without serifs.

ScreenTip A pop-up box that appears when the pointer stays over a button and gives a short description of that button.

Sections Subdivisions of the form or report that control what is printed and where it is printed. Record information is printed in the Detail section, for example. Text and graphics included in the Page Header section are printed at the top of the page; information included in the Page Footer section is printed at the bottom of the page.

Select query A query that lists data that meets conditions set by the user.

Selection handles Small squares that appear at the corners and on the sides of boxes and that can be used to change the size of the box.

Serif A fine, horizontal line finishing off the main strokes of a letter, as at the top and bottom of the letter M.

Server software Software that handles communication between computers.

Subform A form placed within another (main) form, showing data from another table related to the selected record from the main form.

Switchboard The term Access uses for a menu of choices represented by buttons on a form. Clicking a button on a switchboard runs an associated macro to perform functions such as opening forms or printing reports.

Tables Used to store data.

Taskbar The area at the bottom of the screen that displays the Start button and buttons for applications that are open.

UNIX A non-proprietary operating system language for mainframe computers. It is commonly used to run servers for Internet communication.

URL An Internet address. The acronym stands for Uniform Resource Locator.

Validation Rule An expression that Access uses to check the data entered into a field.

Validation Text The text that appears when data that doesn't match a Validation Rule is entered into a field.

Web browser A software application used to view and interact with sites on the World Wide Web. Two popular examples are Netscape Navigator and Microsoft Internet Explorer.

World Wide Web A graphical interface that links sites on the Internet and enables the user to easily jump from one site to another.

appendix C

Student Preparation Guide

The purpose of this appendix is to provide you with information you'll need about the certification tests—how to register, what is covered in the tests, how the tests work, and so on.

Studying for the Tests

Although you aren't required to take a training course to pass the Microsoft Office User Specialist exams, you certainly need to be sure you can successfully complete the tasks that are covered by the exams. Although a training class provides guidance, support, and practice, it may not be convenient or necessary for you.

This book provides the tutorial, review questions, and practice to help you complete your exams successfully. It can be used in a classroom situation, or you can work through the projects on your own. You don't have to work through the book from front to back, as each project stands on its own. The "Checking Your Skills" and "Applying Your Skills" sections at the end of each project give you a chance to get familiar with the tasks. The Kelly PinPoint CBT trainer located on the accompanying CD-ROM has end-of-project computer-based training and evaluation as well as a final practice examination.

Levels of Certification

There is a single designation level for Access 97:

- **Microsoft Access 97 Expert User**: Users are expected to be able to deliver presentations in a variety of media.

Microsoft also has a special Office 97 certification, the Microsoft Office Expert. To attain this level, you must be an Expert User in each of the Microsoft Office applications (Access, Excel, Word, PowerPoint, and FrontPage) and have taken the Office Integration Exam to prove you can integrate these applications.

The specific topics covered at each level are listed in the "Required Tasks" section of this appendix. In this book, these tasks are broken down into projects. At the beginning of each project is a list of tasks covered in that project and which subject area they fall under in the tests.

Expert User Required Tasks

The Expert User exam involves a list of required tasks that you may be asked to perform. The list of possible tasks is categorized by skill area.

An Expert User should be able to do the following:

- Create a database for individual use
- Create a database for small workgroup use

The skill areas covered in the exam and the required tasks for those skill areas are listed in Table C.1.

Table C.1 Expert User Skills

Skill Set	Required Activity
Create a database	Plan a database Create a table Enter data into a table Modify data in a table Enter data into a form Navigate through a table Delete data from a table
Use forms	Create a simple form Modify a form Create controls on a form Modify controls Add a record using a form Show related records on a form
Modify a database	Open a database Modify field properties Modify field layout Modify the presentation of a database
View information	Present information in a chart View information in a form View multiple records Switch between views
Organize information	Sort data on single fields Sort data on multiple fields
Locate information	Find a specific record Create a simple query Create a query with multiple criteria Add filters (selection and form) Remove filters
Refine results of a query	Add fields to a query Remove fields from a query Sort a query Join tables in a query Remove joins in a query Save a query
Analyze data	Build summary queries Calculate fields Set crosstab queries
Create subforms	Identify appropriate use for subforms Add a record with a main form Add records with subforms Merge two tables into a form
Build a relational database	Identify relationships Relate tables
Integrate information from other applications	Import data Link data Add pictures to records

continues

Table C.1 (continued)

Skill Set	Required Activity
Utilize Web capability	Create hyperlinks Build order forms for Internet use
Maintain data integrity	Identify criteria for data integrity Validate text Set required properties Set Validation Rules Set lookup fields Use expressions in calculated controls
Build a form for other users	Title a form Modify form design Improve accuracy in forms Enhance design of a form
Produce reports	Create a report Modify a report Label a report Customize headers and footers Make a calculation on a report Group data in a report Sort data in a report Add custom pages
Print	Print a report Print a form Print the result of a query

Registering for the Exams

Microsoft Office User Specialist exams are administered by Authorized Testing Centers (ATC). To find out where the nearest ATC center is, call (800) 933-4493. Contact the ATC center to find out what their test policies and schedules are, whether they accept walk-ins or must register the candidates in advance, how the exams are conducted, and what they are charging for the tests. The estimated retail price of each exam is $50.00 in the United States, but that can vary based on the center's sales policies. Payment for the tests must be paid in advance. There is no refund for missed exam appointments or failed tests.

Exams are currently available only in English, although Microsoft plans to offer the Office 97 exams in other languages as soon as the courseware in those languages becomes available.

Taking the Tests

Microsoft Office User Specialist exams are not multiple-choice or true-false tests. Instead, they are based on the types of tasks you may encounter in the everyday world. When you take the test you sit at a computer that uses

Windows® 95 or Windows NT® Workstation, work with an Access 97 database, and use the features of Access to perform the tasks outlined for you.

You can't use notes, manuals, laptops, tape recorders, or other aids during the tests. Access Help is available, but using it may cut down on the time you have available to complete the exam tasks.

Exams are one hour or less (some as short as 30 minutes). Your score is based on the number of tasks you successfully perform in the allotted time. This measures your productivity and efficiency, as well as your skill and knowledge.

Each test has a minimum score. If your score meets or exceeds that minimum, you pass the test. If not, you may take the test as many times as you need to until you pass. There is no refund if you don't pass the test.

You see your test results as soon as you complete the exam. Successful candidates receive a certificate a week or two after the testing. Test scores are confidential; only you and Microsoft see them.

To keep up to date on the Certified Microsoft Office User exams, check Microsoft's Web site:

> http://www.mous.net
>
> http://www.microsoft.com/office/train_cert/

INDEX

J - K

L

M

N